S0-BZA-937

ScottForesman

LITERATURE

AND INTEGRATED STUDIES

Annotated Teacher's Edition
Volume Two

World Literature

ScottForesman

Editorial Offices: Glenview, Illinois
Regional Offices: San Jose, California • Tucker, Georgia
Glenview, Illinois • Oakland, New Jersey • Dallas, Texas

acknowledgments

Cover (detail): *The Afterglow in Egypt* by William Holman Hunt, 1834. Southampton City Art Gallery. **449e(t)** Focus on Sports, Inc. **671c(t)** American Shakespeare Theatre/Martha Swope **671d(t)** UPI/Corbis-Bettmann

ISBN: 0-673-29463-3

1.800.554.4411
http://www.scottforesman.com

1 2 3 4 5 6 7 8 9 10 DR 03 02 01 00 99 98 97 96

ScottForesman LITERATURE AND INTEGRATED STUDIES

Middle School: Grade Six

Middle School: Grade Seven

Middle School: Grade Eight

Forms in Literature

World Literature

American Literature

English Literature

The cover features a detail of William Holman Hunt's *The Afterglow in Egypt,* which appears in full on this page. He began this study of a peasant woman during a visit to Egypt in 1854, complaining of "the difficulty of getting the model day by day and the horrible trials of dust and wind." Hunt's title refers to the period after sunset in which a brilliant light sometimes lingers in the western sky. *Southampton City Art Gallery*

ScottForesman
LITERATURE
AND INTEGRATED STUDIES

World Literature

Senior Consultants

Alan C. Purves
State University of New York at Albany

Carol Booth Olson
University of California, Irvine

Carlos E. Cortés
University of California, Riverside (Emeritus)

ScottForesman

Editorial Offices: Glenview, Illinois
Regional Offices: San Jose, California • Tucker, Georgia • Glenview, Illinois • Oakland, New Jersey • Dallas, Texas

Visit ScottForesman's Home Page at http://www.scottforesman.com

Acknowledgments

Texts

6 "Through The Tunnel" from *The Habit of Loving* by Doris Lessing. Copyright © 1955 by Doris Lessing. Originally appeared in *The New Yorker.* Copyright renewed. Reprinted by permission of HarperCollins Publishers, Inc. and Jonathan Clowes Ltd.

19 "Two Kinds" from *The Joy Luck Club* by Amy Tan. Copyright © 1989 by Amy Tan. Reprinted by permission of G. P. Putnam's Sons.

30 "The Censors" by Luisa Valenzuela. Reprinted by permission of Rosario Santos Literary Agent.

36 "The Voter" by Chinua Achebe. Reprinted by permission of the author.

45 "The Other Wife" from *The Other Woman* by Colette, translated from the French by Margaret Crosland. Copyright © 1971, 1972 by Peter Owen, Ltd. Reprinted by permission of Simon & Schuster, Inc. and Peter Owen Ltd. Publishers.

52 From *Mozart: A Life* by Maynard Solomon. Copyright © 1995 by Maynard Solomon. Reprinted by permission of HarperCollins Publishers, Inc.

66 "The Monkey's Paw" from *The Lady of the Barge* by W. W. Jacobs. Reprinted by permission of The Society of Authors.

79 "The Demon Lover" from *Collected Stories* by Elizabeth Bowen. Copyright 1946 and renewed © 1974 by Elizabeth Bowen. Reprinted by permission of Alfred A. Knopf, Inc.

87 "An Astrologer's Day" from *Malagudi Days* by R. K. Narayan. Published by Viking Press. Copyright © R. K. Narayan. Reprinted by permission of the Wallace Literary Agency, Inc.

104 "The Rain Came" by Grace A. Ogot from *Land Without Thunder.* Reprinted by permission of East African Educational Publishers Ltd.

continued on page 852

ISBN: 0-673-29448-X

1.800.554.4411
http://www.scottforesman.com

1 2 3 4 5 6 7 8 9 10 DR 03 02 01 00 99 98 97 96

Senior Consultants

Alan C. Purves

Professor of Education and Humanities, State University of New York at Albany; Director of the Center for Writing and Literacy. Dr. Purves developed the concept and philosophy of the literature lessons for the series, consulted with editors, reviewed tables of contents and lesson manuscript, wrote the Assessment Handbooks, and oversaw the development and writing of the series testing strand.

Carol Booth Olson

Director, California Writing Project, Department of Education, University of California, Irvine. Dr. Olson conceptualized and developed the integrated writing strand of the program, consulted with editors, led a team of teachers in creating literature-based Writing Workshops, and reviewed final manuscript.

Carlos E. Cortés

Professor Emeritus, History, University of California, Riverside. Dr. Cortés designed and developed the multicultural strand embedded in each unit of the series and consulted with grade-level editors to implement the concepts.

Series Consultants

Visual and Media Literacy/Speaking and Listening/Critical Thinking

Harold M. Foster. Professor of English Education and Secondary Education, The University of Akron, Akron. Dr. Foster developed and wrote the Beyond Print features for all levels of the series.

ESL and LEP Strategies

James Cummins. Professor, Modern Language Centre and Curriculum Department, Ontario Institute for Studies in Education, Toronto.

Lily Wong Fillmore. Professor, Graduate School of Education, University of California at Berkeley.

Drs. Cummins and Fillmore advised on the needs of ESL and LEP students, helped develop the Building English Proficiency model for the program, and reviewed strategies and manuscript for this strand of the program.

Fine Arts/Humanities

Neil Anstead. Coordinator of the Humanitas Program, Cleveland Humanities Magnet School, Reseda California. Mr. Anstead consulted on the fine art used in the program.

Reviewers and Contributors

Pupil and Teacher Edition

Jay Amberg, Glenbrook South High School, Glenview, Illinois **Edison Barber,** St. Anne Community High School, St. Anne, Illinois **Lois Barliant,** Albert G. Lane Technical High School, Chicago, Illinois **James Beasley,** Plant City Senior High School, Plant City, Florida **Linda Belpedio,** Oak Park/River Forest High School, Oak Park, Illinois **Richard Bruns,** Burges High School, El Paso, Texas **Kay Parks Bushman,** Ottawa High School, Ottawa, Kansas **Jesús Cardona,** John F. Kennedy High School, San Antonio, Texas **Marlene Carter,** Dorsey High School, Los Angeles, California **Patrick Cates,** Lubbock High School, Lubbock, Texas **Timothy Dohrer,** New Trier Township High School, Winnetka, Illinois **Margaret Doria,** Our Lady of Perpetual Help High School, Brooklyn, New York **Lucila Dypiangco,** Bell Senior High School, Bell, California **Judith Edminster,** Plant City High School, Plant City, Florida **Mary Alice Fite,** Columbus School for Girls, Columbus, Ohio **Montserrat Fontes,** Marshall High School, Los Angeles, California **Diane Fragos,** Turkey Creek Middle School, Plant City, Florida **Joan Greenwood,** Thornton Township High School, Harvey, Illinois **William Irvin,** Pittsfield Public Schools, Pittsfield, Massachusetts **Carleton Jordan,** Montclair High School, Montclair, New Jersey **Mark Kautz,** Chapel Hill High School, Chapel Hill, North Carolina **Elaine Kay,** Bartow High School, Bartow, Florida **Roslyn Kettering,** West Lafayette Junior/Senior High School, West Lafayette, Indiana **Kristina Kostopoulos,** Lincoln Park High School, Chicago, Illinois **Julia Lloyd,** Harwood Junior High School, Bedford, Texas **John Lord,** Ocean Township High School, Oakhurst, New Jersey **Dolores Mathews,** Bloomingdale High School, Valrico, Florida **Jim McCallum,** Milford High School, Milford, Massachusetts **Monette Mehalko,** Plant City Senior High School, Plant City, Florida **Lucia Podraza,** DuSable High School, Chicago, Illinois **Frank Pool,** Anderson High School, Austin, Texas **Alice Price,** Latin School, Chicago, Illinois **Anna J. Roseboro,** The Bishop's School, La Jolla, California **Peter Sebastian,** Granite Hills High School, El Cajon, California **Rob Slater,** East Forsyth High School, Winston Salem, North Carolina **Catherine Small,** Nicolet High School, Glendale, Wisconsin **Dennis Symkowiak,** Mundelein High School, Mundelein, Illinois **Rosetta Tetteh,** Senn High School, Chicago, Illinois **Pamela Vetters,** Harlandale High School, San Antonio, Texas **Polly Walwark,** Oak Park High School, Oak Park, Illinois **Karen Wrobleski,** San Diego High School, San Diego, California **Dru Zimmerman,** Chapel Hill High School, Chapel Hill, North Carolina

v

Multicultural Review Board

Duane BigEagle, writer and teacher, Tomales, California **Maria Campanario,** Raphael Hernandez School, Stoughton, Massachusetts **Pat Canty,** Beverly Woods Middle School, Charlotte, North Carolina **Jesús Cardona,** John F. Kennedy High School, San Antonio, Texas **Diego Davalos,** Chula Vista High School, Chula Vista, California **Sandra Dickerson,** Milwaukee Public Schools, Milwaukee, Wisconsin **Lucila Dypiangco,** Bell Senior High School, Bell, California **Marion Fleming,** Roselle Junior/Senior High School, Roselle, New York **Gloria Garcia,** Madero Middle School, Chicago, Illinois **Thelma Hernandez,** Edison Junior High School, San Antonio, Texas **Yvonne Hutchinson,** Markham Intermediate School, Los Angeles, California **Narva Jackson,** Roselle Junior/Senior High School, Roselle, New York **May Lee,** Baldwin Senior High School, Baldwin, New York **Dolores Mathews,** Bloomingdale High School, Valrico, Florida **Jack Matsumoto,** Edison Regional Gifted Center, Chicago, Illinois **James Masao Mitsui,** Hazen High School, Renton, Washington **Ed Ramirez,** Wang School, Derry, New Hampshire **Harolene Steele,** Hill Middle School, Winston-Salem, North Carolina **Suthinee Suktrakul,** North Cross High School, North Cross, Georgia **Jerry Tagami,** New Harbor High School, Newport Beach, California **Barbara Wheeler,** Harford County Public Schools, Bel Air, Maryland **Raymond Zamarippa,** Bowie Junior High School, Irving, Texas

English Language Development (ESL/LEP)

Kate Alvidrez, Newton High School, Newton, Iowa **Judy Bebelaar,** International Studies Academy, San Francisco, California **Rebecca Benjamin,** University of New Mexico, Albuquerque, New Mexico **Ioana Cummins,** Toronto, Ontario **Nancy Duke S. Lay,** City College of New York, New York, New York **Doti Foster,** Lubbock Independent School District, Lubbock, Texas **Bridget Hawthorne,** Oliver Hazard Perry Middle School, Providence, Rhode Island **Sandra Huezo,** Gompers Secondary School, San Diego, California **Nancy Hykel,** Harlandale High School, San Antonio, Texas **Mary Ann Jentel,** Madonna High School for Girls, Chicago, Illinois **Jose Lebron,** Julia De Burgos Middle School, Philadelphia, Pennsylvania **Mary Linnstaedter,** Nimitz High School, Houston, Texas **Mayra Menendez,** School Board of Broward County, Fort Lauderdale, Florida **Sharese Tisby,** Waukegan High School, Waukegan, Illinois **Sylvia Velazquez,** Braddock Senior High School, Miami, Florida **Greta Vollmer,** International Studies Academy, San Francisco, California **Shirley Wright,** Longview Independent School District, Longview, Texas **Suzanne Zweig,** Norwood Park School, Chicago, Illinois

Writer's Workshop Prompt Writers

Bill Burns, Sonora High School, LaHabra, California **Patricia Clark,** Century High School, Santa Ana, California **Glenn Patchell,** Irvine High School, Irvine, California **Maureen Rippee,** Woodrow Wilson High School, Long Beach, California **Julie Simpson,** Sunny Hills High School, Fullerton, California

Student Model Writers

Julia Besterfeldt Susan Biebel Chelsea Brown Lisa Cason Elizabeth Ratliff Sheila Chalegua Brandi Cleaver Christian DeVos Lynn DeWitt William Eckmann Maggie Gorecki David Hardy Melanie Jetter Louis Kholodovsky Charly Kittay Michael J Kurcz Samantha Anne La'o Courtney Ann Lambke William McKelphin Karen Miramontes Hollie Nygaard Chinyera Osuji Adam Peterson Elizabeth Ratliff Jeremy A. Redburn Kimyona Roberts Brendon Rose Morgan Russell-Dempsey Rebecca Ryan Mark Sarna Melissa Villalon C. M. Wiggins

Student Active Reading Panel

Nina Grigsby Isaac Saposnik Mika Uehara

Contents

Unit 1 Meeting the Challenge

Part One: Pushing Toward the Top

Part Two: Trying to Beat the Odds

▶ EXPLORING A THEME THROUGH SEVERAL GENRES

Part Three: Dealing with Consequences

viii

Unit 2 Making Judgments

ix

▶ EXPLORING A THEME THROUGH SEVERAL GENRES

Part Two: Beneath the Surface

x

Unit 3 Answering the Call

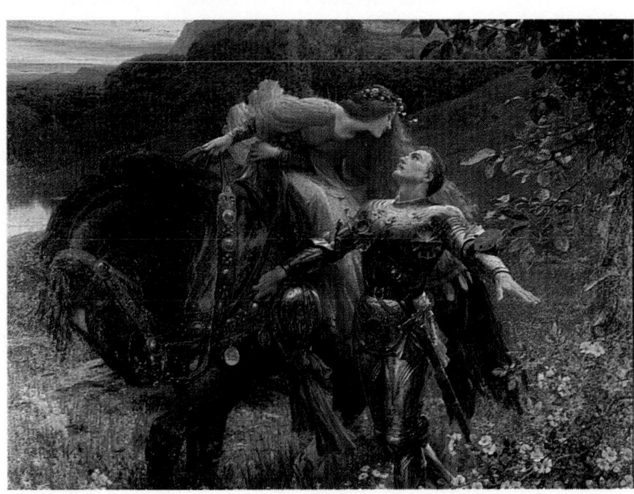

xi

▶ EXPLORING A THEME THROUGH SEVERAL GENRES

Part Two: Many Kinds of Heroes

xii

Unit 4 What Really Matters?

Part One: Worth Fighting For?

xiii

EXPLORING A THEME THROUGH SEVERAL GENRES

Part Two: Something of Value

xiv

Unit 5 A Place in the World

xv

Part Two: Reflections

EXPLORING A THEME THROUGH SEVERAL GENRES

Part Three: Culture Crossroads

xvii

Unit 6 Power Plays

Glossaries, Handbooks, and Indexes

Genre Overview

Short Stories

Poetry

xix

Plays

Nonfiction

Legends

Feature Overview

Genre Overviews

Interdisciplinary Studies

Reading Mini-Lessons

Writing Workshops

Beyond Print

xxi

Part One: Worth Fighting For?

Planning Unit 4: What Really Matters?

Literature	Integrated Language Arts			
	Literary	Writing/Grammar, Usage and Mechanics	Reading, Thinking, Listening, Speaking	Vocabulary/Spelling
from Kaffir Boy *by Mark Mathabane* Autobiography *(challenging)* p. 456	Characterization Style, setting Metaphor and simile Point of view and autobiography	Character sketch Report Book review Forming and hyphenating compound words	Connect Compare and contrast Evaluate Relate literature to personal experience	Word pairs Connotation and denotation
Living Well. Living Good. *by Maya Angelou* Autobiography *(easy)* p. 469	Irony Characterization Connotative language Frame stories and autobiography	Summarize Job description Listing sheet Using commas in a series	Recognize the use of persuasion	
from An American Childhood *by Annie Dillard* Autobiography *(average)* p. 475	Suspense Repetition Point of view Characterization	Paragraph Summary Using the dash	Draw conclusions	
By Any Other Name *by Santha Rama Rau* Autobiography *(average)* p. 481	Stereotypes Symbolism Autobiography and tone Irony Characterization Imagery	Narrative paragraph Character sketch Diary entry Using subject and object pronouns	Compare and contrast Draw conclusions	Synonyms Understand analogies

Meeting Individual Needs

Multi-modal Activities	Mini-Lessons
Motivational speech Chalk talk Exploring key statements Analyzing prepositional phrases Making cultural connections Exploring social issues Analyzing culture	Forming and hyphenating compound words Connotation and denotation Characterization Interpretive reading
Collage Recording Making personal connections	Using commas in a series
Map Film chat Monologue Exploring word choices	Using the dash
Improvisation Research Analyzing consequences and options Exploring motivation	Using subject and object pronouns Understanding analogies

Interdisciplinary Studies
What's in a Name?

Format	Content Area	Highlights	Skill
Poem: **The Naming of Cats** *by T. S. Eliot*	Multicultural	This selection portrays the importance of names.	Reciting nonsense verse
Collage: **Names Around the World**	Multicultural	This selection discusses various ways a name can effect an individual.	Researching your name

Writing Workshop

Mode	Writing Format	Writing Focus	Proofreading Skills
Narrative writing	An autobiographical incident	Writing in the active voice Review the characters	Using apostrophes correctly

Program Support Materials

For Every Selection

Unit Resource Book
Graphic Organizer
Study Guide
Vocabulary Worksheet
Grammar Worksheet
Spelling, Speaking and Listening, or Literary Language Worksheet
Alternate Check Test
Vocabulary Test
Selection Test

For Every Writing Workshop

Unit Resource Book
Prewriting Worksheet
Revising Strategy Worksheet
Editing Strategy Worksheet
Presentation Worksheet
Writing Rubric
Transparency Collection
Fine Art Transparency
Student Writing Model Transparencies

For Every Interdisciplinary Study

Unit Resource Book
Study Guide
Mini-Lesson Skill Worksheet

Assessment

Unit Resource Book
TE Check Tests
Alternate Check Test (blackline master)
Vocabulary Test (blackline master)
Selection Test (blackline master)
Test Generator Software
Assessment Handbook

Part Two: Something of Value

Planning Unit 4: What Really Matters?

Literature	Integrated Language Arts: Literary	Writing/Grammar, Usage and Mechanics	Reading, Thinking, Listening, Speaking	Vocabulary/Spelling
One Perfect Rose *by Dorothy Parker* Poem *(easy)* p. 503 **Daybreak in Alabama** *by Langston Hughes* Poem *(easy)* p. 504 **The Flying Cat** *by Naomi Shihab Nye* Poem *(average)* p. 506	Tone Understand cultural context	Sketch Write an article on traveling with pets Regular and irregular verbs	Find the main idea	Solve riddles Connotation
Tuesday Siesta *by Gabriel García Márquez* Short Story *(average)* p. 510	Mood Characterization Imagery Flashback	Paragraph Write a story summary Describe a dream Using *that* and *which*	Infer Recognize values	Etymology
from The Pillow Book *by Sei Shōnagon* Memoir *(average)* p. 518 **Porsche** *by Bailey White* Essay *(easy)* p. 520	Images Tone	Write a paragraph using vivid images Random notes Make a "has-been" list Sentence fragments	Draw conclusions	Word relationships
Nobel Acceptance Speech *by Albert Camus* Speech *(challenging)* p. 525 **Nobel Acceptance Speech** *by Elie Wiesel* Speech *(challenging)* p. 528	Style Symbolism	Essay Character sketch Fax Colons	Literal and figurative language Identify author's purpose	Opposites Using dictionaries for word meanings

Meeting Individual Needs

Multi-modal Activities	Mini-Lessons
Musical interpretation Poetry reading Designing a bumper sticker Exploring imagery	Connotation Regular and irregular verbs
Fact sheet Travel agent memo Trial Vocabulary notebooks: Homonyms Analyzing comprehension	Using *that* and *which* Etymology
Comedy workshops Making a pillow book Time capsule Linking literature and history Contrasting selections	Sentence fragments
Making an award Oral report Interviewing a holocaust survivor Vocabulary aids Exploring key concepts	Using dictionaries for word meanings Colons

Interdisciplinary Studies
Power and Horsepower

Format	Content Area	Highlights	Skill
Article: **Big Wheels: Cars as Status Symbols**	Pop Culture	This selection discusses the car culture and the car as a status symbol.	Analyzing photographs Informal outlining Word processing tips

Writing Workshop

Mode	Writing Format	Writing Focus	Proofreading Skills
Expository writing	A multimedia presentation	Using the appropriate tone Try a quick write	Avoiding run-on sentences

Program Support Materials

For Every Selection

Unit Resource Book
Graphic Organizer
Study Guide
Vocabulary Worksheet
Grammar Worksheet
Spelling, Speaking and Listening, or Literary Language Worksheet
Alternate Check Test
Vocabulary Test
Selection Test

For Every Writing Workshop

Unit Resource Book
Prewriting Worksheet
Revising Strategy Worksheet
Editing Strategy Worksheet
Presentation Worksheet
Writing Rubric
Transparency Collection
Fine Art Transparency
Student Writing Model Transparencies

For Every Interdisciplinary Study

Unit Resource Book
Study Guide
Mini-Lesson Skill Worksheet

Assessment

Unit Resource Book
TE Check Tests
Alternate Check Test (blackline master)
Vocabulary Test (blackline master)
Selection Test (blackline master)
Test Generator Software
Assessment Handbook

Media and Technology

Part One Selections

Kaffir Boy

Audiotape Students will enjoy an audio edition of *Kaffir Boy*, available through Dove Audio, 1988.

Community Resources In a part of *Kaffir Boy* not included here, Mathabane tells of meeting American tennis player Arthur Ashe at a tennis tournament in South Africa. Ashe became his hero "because he was the first free black man" Mathabane had ever seen. Students might use the resources of their local library to find out more about Ashe, whose autobiography appeared shortly before his death in 1993.

Living Well, Living Good

Audiotape *Maya Angelou*, Recorded Books, is a biography of the author's life.

Videotape Students will enjoy the video *I Know Why the Caged Bird Sings,* 100 minutes, Knowledge Unlimited, 1979, starring Diahann Carrol and Ruby Dee.

Home Connection Students might like to discuss with family members what "living well" means in their family and try to answer such questions as the following: Is "living well" shared laughter and "a love of life," as Angelou says? What are the most important things in our family? Who in the family is responsible for making family life full of joy?

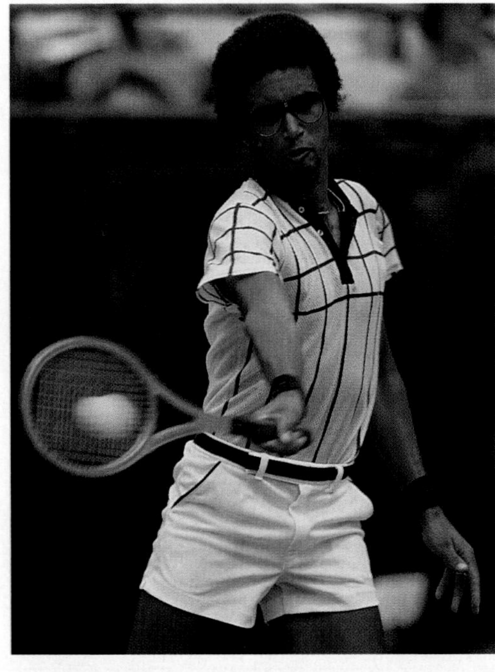

from An American Childhood

Audiotape An interview with the author, *Annie Dillard Interview,* 47 minutes, is offered by American Audio Prose Library. Consider listening to Dillard reading from *An American Childhood*, 29 minutes,

Home Connection Everyone has memories of a time when he or she committed some small act or played a prank that turned out to have larger consequences. Students might ask older family members to recall their own childhood escapades. The class might try classifying these stories of childhood adventure. Do they involve adults? friends? punishment? fear? laughter? city life? life in another country?

By Any Other Name

Videotape *A Sari Tale*, 15 minutes, TVOntario Video, 1992, is about an Indian girl's struggle with cultural identity.

Community Resources Some people have occupations that seem to reflect their names, and others have made a hobby of collecting these names that, strangely, seem to affect job choice. Would you believe a writer named Prose? a swimming coach named Drinkwater? a farmer named Corn? Students might enjoy keeping a list of people whose names seem to reflect their work. Newspapers, magazines, and various types of directories are good sources.

Connections to
Custom Literature Database

For Part One "Worth Fighting For" Selections with Lessons

- *Brown* v. *Board of Education of Topeka*
- "A 'Cub' Pilot's Experience" from *Life on the Mississippi* by Mark Twain

Additional theme-based selections can be accessed on the ScottForesman database.

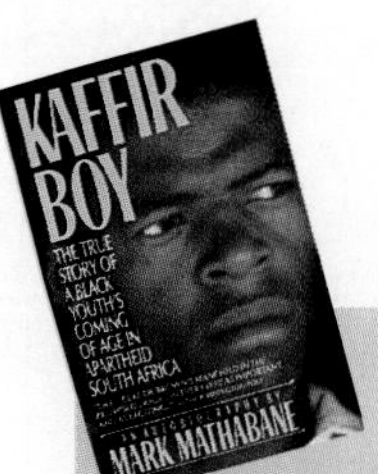

Listen to a Book

Mark Mathabane's *Kaffir Boy* is available on audiotape, in an edition by Dove Audio.

Part Two Selections

One Perfect Rose/Daybreak in Alabama/The Flying Cat

Audiotape The author reads a short story and her poetry in *An Informal Hour* with Dorothy Parker, Spoken Arts. Students can listen to many styles of love poems in *A Celebration of Love,* Poet Tree, 1995.

Videotape *A Quip with Yip & Friends*, 45 minutes, The Heritage Poetry Series, Library Video Company, 1990, features Jack Lemmon and Fred Gwynne performing the work of Dorothy Parker and others.

Audiotape Ruby Dee and Ossie Davis read selected poems in *The Poetry of Langston Hughes*, Caedmon. Also consider *Langston Hughes Reads and Talks About His Poems,* Spoken Arts.

Videotape Students will enjoy *Thank You,* Ma'am, 12 minutes, BFA Films, 1976, based on the short story by Hughes.

Audiotape Students may enjoy more cat poems in *Old Possum's Book of Practical Cats,* from the poetry of T. S. Eliot, read by Sir John Gielgud and others, available from Caedmon/Harper.

Community Resources Students might like to hold a poetry, or prose and poetry, reading to which the community is invited. Students could read their own work or the work of a favorite writer. The reading might be organized around a theme or topic, perhaps in connection with a holiday or on the theme 'Something of Value."

Tuesday Siesta

Videotape The author talks about his work in *Tales Beyond Solitude,* 60 minutes, Home Vision, 1989. *Gabriel Garcia Marquez Collection,* 166 minutes, is a 2-volume set in Spanish with English subtitles from Library Video Company, 1988.

Community Resources Students have probably guessed the origin of the name of the country where Márquez was born (it was named for Christopher Columbus). They might like to research origins of the name of their own town, county, township (if any), and state. They might also investigate the origins of street names.

from The Pillow Book/Porsche

Videotape *The Electronic Tribe*, 58 minutes, Coronet/MTI, 1988, contrasts Japan's traditional values with its advanced technological economy.

Home Connection People often think about what item they would rescue in case of fire, flood, or other disaster. Students might plan a dinner-table conversation centered around the topic of what one thing each family member would save first if they had to and why that item has value for that member of the family.

Nobel Acceptance Speeches

Audiotape Students will enjoy *Albert Camus Reading from His Novels & Essays*, from Caedmon/Harper Audio. *Elie Wiesel Reading from his Works*, Spoken Arts, explores the unbelievable horrors of the concentration camps.

Videotape *Facing Hate*, 60 minutes, PBS Home Video, is a discussion between Bill Moyers and Elie Wiesel. *Sorrow: The Nazi Legacy*, 33 minutes, Ergo Media, 1994, is an award-winning video documenting the journey of six teens to Auschwitz in search of understanding.

Home Connection What kinds of awards would students give to family members? Who would get a prize for peace? literature? chemistry? medicine? economics? Students could write a one-to-three line speech, and design a medal for each category before sharing their selections with the class and/or presenting the awards at home.

Connections to
Custom Literature Database

For Part Two "Something of Value" Selections with Lessons

- "Cargoes" and "Sea-Fever" by John Masefield
- "A Dissertation upon Roast Pig" by Charles Lamb

Additional theme-based selections can be accessed on the ScottForesman database.

Connections to
AuthorWorks

Information about the life and times of Langston Hughes, Elie Wiesel, and Albert Camus is available on ScottForesman's AuthorWorks CD-ROM.

Unit 4

What Really Matters?

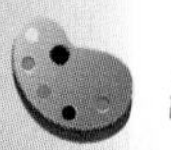

Art Study

The title of this painting by Chinese American artist Tsing-Fang Chen is *Human Achievement.*

Question Identify the subjects with which the author chose to exemplify the glories of human achievement. *(Possible responses: Albert Einstein's theory of relativity; man's exploration of the moon; the teachings of Confucius; the writings of William Shakespeare; Japanese Noh theater; Western classical music; modern dance; science and technology; mathematics and astronomy; the Egyptian system of hieroglyphics; architecture)*

Question How does the artist's use of color and shape affect the presentation of her subject matter? *(Possible responses: The bright cheerful array of colors emphasizes the celebratory mood created by the collage-style interposition of her subjects. The simple shapes, for example, the rainbow, the wheels, and the pyramid, balance the weight of the detailed depictions elsewhere in the piece.)*

UNIT 4

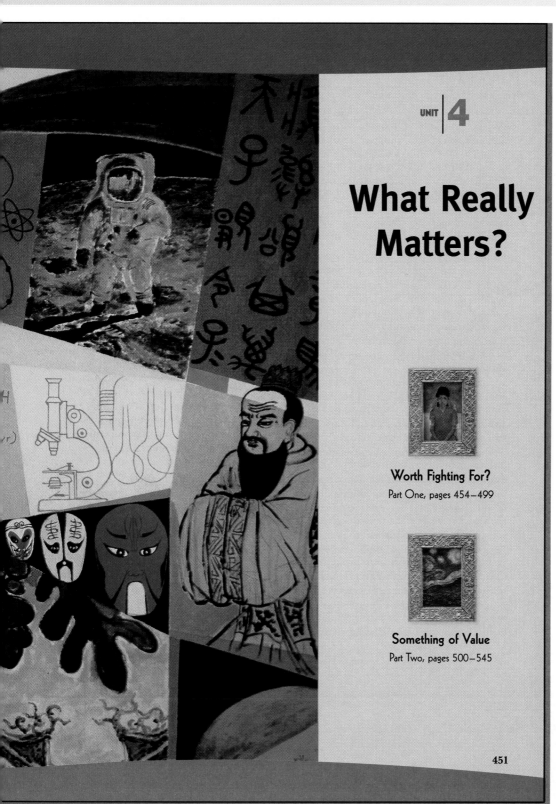

What Really Matters?

Worth Fighting For?
Part One, pages 454–499

Something of Value
Part Two, pages 500–545

451

THEMATIC CONNECTIONS

An individual's values can vary and change according to age, class, nationality, religious background, surrounding political conditions, and natural environment.

Part One
Worth Fighting For?

The narrators in Part One recount their childhood encounters with the sphere of adult values, and describe the necessary compromises between rebellion, acceptance, and change.

Ideas to Explore

- How does education play an important role in a young person's formation of values?
- How do the values of an individual change as he or she grows older?

Part Two
Something of Value

Although the selections in Part Two reflect the differences in individual values, they emphasize the importance of intangible human virtues that cannot be bought or sold.

Ideas to Explore

- How does communication play a part in understanding value judgments?
- How do the interactions between characters reflect their personal values?
- How might social and political circumstances influence an individual's values?

The portrait of the young woman is from Mexico. *Starry Night* is by Vincent Van Gogh.

Unit 4: What Really Matters?

Genre Overview: Nonfiction

EXPLORING CONCEPTS

- Forms of nonfiction writing, which describe real people or events, include biography, autobiography, essays, and speeches.
- Biography is the story of a real person's life written by another person. Autobiography is the story of a real person's life, written by the person who lived it.
- Although both biography and autobiography attempt to give an honest narrative account of the past, the "absolute" truth is necessarily compromised by the writer's subjectivity, the limitations of memory, and the conventions of good storytelling.
- Although the key literary elements in autobiography are the same as those in fiction, certain elements take on new dimensions because the writer and the main character are the same person.
- In an essay or a speech, the writer briefly expounds upon his or her knowledge of a specific topic, usually basing the body of the piece on a main idea or opinion.

Genre Overview

Reading

Nonfiction is prose literature that deals with real people and events rather than imaginary ones. A broad literary genre, nonfiction includes almost any kind of literature that does not involve fictional characters and events. Types of nonfiction you will encounter in Unit Four are autobiographies, essays, and speeches. Other forms of nonfiction include biographies, letters, and diaries.

Biography and Autobiography

A biography, an account of a person's life written by someone else, presents a third-person point of view. Biographers should give a complete picture without unfairly eliminating or slanting important information to suit their own purposes. Readers must be willing to question and, if necessary, investigate the author's use of facts.

The group of selections that follow are autobiographies, the story of a writer's own life. As you read these selections, you will enter into each person's special world and meet the people who have shared that world. By the time you have finished the autobiography, you may feel that there is a bit of your own story in this writer's life. If you have ever thrown a snowball at a car, disagreed with a parent, had a bad day at school, or fondly recalled a relative, you will find something of yourself in the selections that follow.

The most authentic autobiographies and biographies are truthful, presenting the world and the featured subject honestly without trying to glamorize or distort things. Yet even the most truthful nonfiction works resort to imagination and memory, taking license in portraying details and capturing the spirit of things rather than presenting absolute fact. For example, the dialogue in *Kaffir Boy* is recollected rather than quoted exactly. Likewise, autobiographers shape and focus their materials, highlighting interesting parts and omitting dull or unimportant details.

As you read the nonfiction selections that follow, look for the same things you find in fiction—characterization, theme, plot, and setting. It would be hard to find more memorable characters than Maya Angelou's Aunt Tee or Mark Mathabane's granny. The importance of using education as a tool in combating prejudice is a dominant theme in *Kaffir Boy*, while *An American Childhood* emphasizes the value of pursuing a goal wholeheartedly. Even though these are excerpts, they contain plot elements, including a climax and some kind of resolution. Setting is a crucial factor in all these excerpts; just try to trade the settings of Mathabane's and Dillard's stories to see how these works would fall apart without their respective settings. Especially noteworthy in this type of nonfiction is point of view. Although

Nonfiction

autobiography and biography are based on fact, the writer seldom presents these facts in a completely objective manner. So as you read, keep in mind that these writers necessarily emphasize things that they consider important and color events and people according to their own perspectives.

Watch also for tone—the writer's attitude toward a subject. Annie Dillard's light attitude—"I got in trouble throwing snowballs, and have seldom been happier since"—which is perfect for her selection, would be inappropriate in Santha Rama Rau's account.

Tips for Reading Biography and Autobiography

- Look for the same things you find in fiction—characterization, theme, plot, setting, tone, and point of view.
- Consider how the writer's personal feelings may affect his or her treatment of people and interpretation of events.
- Ask yourself why the author has focused on particular incidents. What do these incidents reveal?

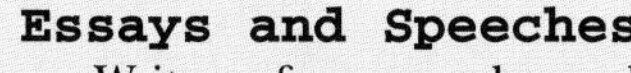

Essays and Speeches

Writers of essays and speeches explore topics and express their opinions. They may be less concerned with telling a story than with presenting their ideas. Both essays and speeches are usually brief, reflecting the writers' attitudes and knowledge. You can usually find a main idea in these works. Subject matter is virtually unlimited, and tone can range from humorous and light to serious. Both Wiesel and Camus adopt a serious tone in their Nobel speeches.

Tips for Reading Essays and Speeches

- Locate and identify the main idea.
- Find details that support the main idea—facts, arguments, and examples.
- Try to differentiate between fact and opinion.
- Draw upon your own knowledge and experience in evaluating the writer's ideas and conclusion.

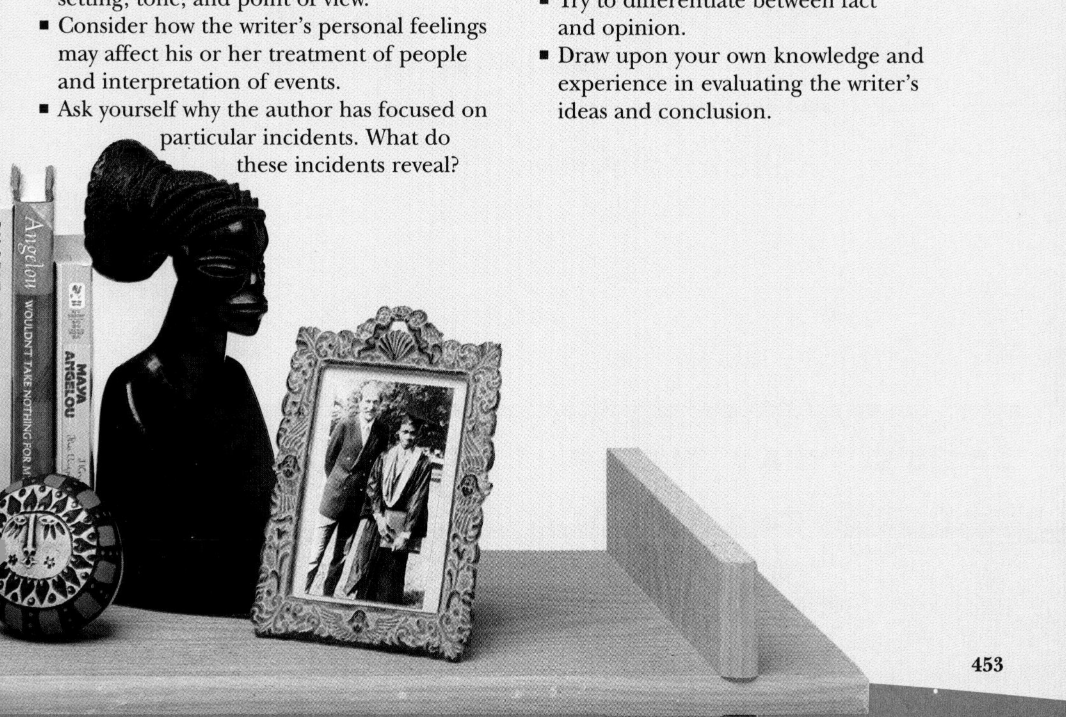

Visual Literacy Ask students to look closely at the book titles and photographs on the bookshelf.

Question What can you infer about the person who owns these books and photographs? *(Possible response: The person likes books by authors of different cultures, especially African Americans.)*

MATERIALS OF INTEREST

Books

- *Turning Memories into Memoirs* by Denis Ledoux (Soleil Press, 1993)
- *Writing Personal Essays: How to Shape Your Life Experiences for the Page* by Sheila Bender (Writer's Digest Books, 1995)

Multimedia

Cry, the Beloved Country (movie)

Preview

Worth Fighting For?

FOR ALL STUDENTS

Have students make a list of the five things that they find most important in their lives, and then compare these lists with those of their classmates.

To further explore the theme, use the transparency referred to below.

Transparency Collection
Fine Art Writing Prompt 8

For At-Risk Students

Remind students that conflict shapes the plot in a work of drama or fiction. Have students write a review of a movie in which the main character fights against someone or something. Questions to consider:

- Why is the main character fighting?
- Was their goal worth fighting for?

For Students Who Need Challenge

Have students research and report historical pacifists and their strategies of nonviolent resistance. You might suggest the following topics.

- The Quakers or Society of Friends
- Mahatma Gandhi
- Martin Luther King, Jr.

MULTICULTURAL CONNECTION

Have students work in pairs to imagine a conflict that might arise between one of the following:

- an elderly woman and her teenage grandson
- a rock-and-roll guitarist and a classical violinist

Encourage students take turns acting out the struggle. Discuss the role of communication in resolving or exacerbating the conflict.

Part One

Worth Fighting For?

What would you stand up for, speak out for, or physically protect? In defending rights and redressing wrongs, you have to determine what is worth fighting for. Pick your battles and hope for the kind of successes that some of the characters in these selections achieve.

Multicultural Connection **Communication** may be complicated when diverse factors such as age, language, culture, and social class present obstacles. In the following selections, what challenges and misunderstandings are a result of miscommunication? How do characters meet such challenges?

IDEAS THAT WORK

First-Person Point of View

What strikes me most about these selections is the strong first-person voices that resonate throughout. An examination of these voices would provide an ideal prompt for journal or other first-person student writing.

The cluster title is a fine focus for discussion. What is being fought for? What makes something worth fighting for? These value-oriented issues are great for making connections with other literature, media, world news, etc.

Each selection focuses on a pivotal moment in the speaker's life. Students should be able to relate those issues to some of their own personal pivotal life moments.

There are strong interfamilial and intergenerational issues that students can zero in on, looking at the speaker operating within specific familial and cultural settings. This examination might make for interesting comparison and contrast writing.

Kristina S. Kostopoul
Chicago, Illin

Before Reading

from Kaffir Boy

by Mark Mathabane South Africa

Mark Mathabane
born 1960

The grandmother of Mark Mathabane (ma′thä bän) gardened for the Smiths, a white family. When Mark was eleven, Clyde, the Smith's son, said to him, "My teachers tell us that Kaffirs can't read, speak, or write English like white people because they have smaller brains, which are already full of tribal things." An angry Mathabane resolved to excel in school and to teach himself English—a language blacks were not then allowed to learn—from comic books. Mathabane became a top tennis player and earned an athletic scholarship to an American college. He now lives in the United States where he is a noted writer and lecturer.

Building Background

Separate and Unequal As a young boy, Mark Mathabane encountered the word *Kaffir,* an Arabic word meaning "infidel" and used in South Africa as a derogatory term to refer to blacks. Its use was symbolic of the many indignities of *apartheid* (ə part′hāt), an Afrikaans word for "separateness" that refers to the government policy of legalized racism. Blacks were restricted to tribal reserves and allowed to work in cities only if they had identification cards. Since Mathabane's parents had emigrated illegally, they were ready prey for police raids, jail, or deportation. His father, Jackson, in fact, was imprisoned repeatedly. Through the efforts of Nelson Mandela, then head of the African National Congress, and F. W. de Klerk, then South Africa's president, apartheid was abolished in the 1990s. In 1994, Nelson Mandela succeeded de Klerk in the first multiracial election in South Africa's history.

Nelson Mandela and F. W. de Klerk

Literary Focus

Characterization As you read this excerpt from the autobiography, *Kaffir Boy,* note Mathabane's **characterization** of his mother and father. What techniques does he use to bring these two people to life? Note other memorable characters in this selection.

Writer's Notebook

School Choice Recall an early experience in school—perhaps your first day. Write several words that describe someone who made this day memorable for you.

Before Reading

Building Background

Ask students if they can think of parallels to apartheid in American history.

- The Indian Reservation system uprooted Native American tribes and relocated them into desolate areas.
- Until the Civil Rights Movement of the 1960s, segregation by race was a legal institution in parts of the U.S.

Literary Focus

Mathabane reveals the personalities of his **characters** through physical description, speech, actions, relationships between characters, and narrative commentary.

Writer's Notebook

Encourage immigrant students to describe their first day of school in the United States. What are some differences between schools in their native countries and those here?

More About Mark Mathabane

- Mathabane was actively involved in the Soweto student protests of 1976, in which hundreds of black South African students were killed by the police.
- Mathabane grew up in a ghetto called Alexandra, ten miles north of Johannesburg, a city that black South Africans call *Egoli*, or City of Gold.

SUPPORT MATERIALS OVERVIEW

Unit 4 Resource Book
- Graphic Organizer, p. 1
- Study Guide, p. 2
- Vocabulary, p. 3
- Grammar, p. 4
- Alternate Check Test, p. 5
- Vocabulary Test, p. 6
- Selection Test, pp. 7–8

Building English Proficiency
- Literature Summaries
- Activities, p. 200

Reading, Writing & Grammar SkillBook
- Grammar, Usage, and Mechanics, pp. 11–12, 250–252
- Reading, pp. 65–66, 93–94

The World of Work
- Child Advocate, p. 15
- Create a Brochure, p. 16

Technology
- Audiotape 11, Side A
- Personal Journal Software
- Custom Literature Database: For another account of a school experience, see "Stolen Day" by Sherwood Anderson on the database.
- Test Generator Software

During Reading

Selection Objectives

- to understand what certain characters value and consider worth fighting for
- to explore the techniques and function of characterization
- to learn how to recognize, form, and hyphenate compound words

Unit 4 Resource Book
Graphic Organizer, p. 1
Study Guide, p. 2

Theme Link

A black South African boy who is growing up beneath the oppression of apartheid learns from his mother's perseverance that his future is "Worth Fighting For."

Vocabulary Preview

austere, stern in manner or appearance
belligerent, fond of fights
cubicle, a very small room or compartment
peruse, read, especially thoroughly and carefully
pretext, a false reason concealing the real reason; misleading excuse

Students can add the words and definitions to their Writer's Notebooks.

Responses to Caption Question
Possible response: a decent house, enough food, access to a quality education, peace

Visual Literacy Point out that characterization, setting, and mood can function as effectively in visual works as in literary works. Have students note details such as the boy's expression, the graffiti, and the debris.

Question What do you think "Cry! The Beloved Country" means? *(Possible response: Mourn the effects of apartheid.)*

Kaffir Boy

MARK MATHABANE

EDUCATION WILL OPEN DOORS WHERE NONE SEEM TO EXIST.

When my mother began dropping hints that I would soon be going to school, I vowed never to go because school was a waste of time. She laughed and said, "We'll see. You don't know what you're talking about." My philosophy on school was that of a gang of ten-, eleven- and twelve-year-olds whom I so revered that their every word seemed that of an oracle.

These boys had long left their homes and were now living in various neighborhood junkyards, making it on their own. They slept in

SELECTION SUMMARY

Kaffir Boy

When his mother forces him to enroll in a tribal school, the narrator fights for what he perceives as his freedom. After meeting the school's principal and witnessing the humiliation and violence that his mother is willing to suffer to give him an education, the narrator reevaluates his position. He weighs the tragic mistakes of the past, which have twisted his own father, against the possibility of a better future. Finally, he decides to attend the school. Although this decision places him in opposition to his father, the narrator has gained a new courage to fight the oppression of apartheid.

For summaries in other languages, see the ***Building English Proficiency*** *book.*

An apprehensive boy looks out from a backdrop of graffiti in this photograph of a Soweto ghetto by David C. Turnley. *Cry, the Beloved Country* is the title of a well-known novel about South Africa by Alan Paton. What do you think a boy like the one pictured might hope for in a "beloved country"?

abandoned cars, smoked glue and benzene, ate pilchards[1] and brown bread, sneaked into the white world to caddy and, if unsuccessful, came back to the township to steal beer and soda bottles from shebeens,[2] or goods from the Indian traders on First Avenue. Their lifestyle was exciting, adventurous and full of surprises; and I was attracted to it. My mother told me that they were no-gooders, that they would amount to nothing, that I should not associate with them, but I paid no heed. What does she know? I used to tell myself. One thing she did not know was that the gang's way of life had captivated me wholly, particularly their philosophy on school: they hated it and considered an education a waste of time.

They, like myself, had grown up in an environment where the value of an education was never emphasized, where the first thing a child learned was not how to read and write and spell, but how to fight and steal and rebel; where the money to send children to school was grossly lacking, for survival was first priority. I kept my membership in the gang, knowing that for as long as I was under its influence, I would never go to school. 1

One day my mother woke me up at four in the morning.

"Are they here? I didn't hear any noises," I asked in the usual way.

"No," my mother said. "I want you to get into that washtub over there."

"What!" I balked, upon hearing the word *washtub*. I feared taking baths like one feared the plague. Throughout seven years of hectic living the number of baths I had taken could be counted on one hand with several fingers missing. I simply had no natural inclination for water; cleanliness was a trait I still had to acquire. Besides, we had only one bathtub in the house, and it constantly sprung a leak.

"I said get into that tub!" My mother shook a finger in my face. 2

Reluctantly, I obeyed, yet wondered why all of a sudden I had to take a bath. My mother, armed with a scropbrush and a piece of Lifebuoy soap, purged[3] me of years and years of grime till I ached and bled. As I howled, feeling pain shoot through my limbs as the thistles

1. **pilchard** (pil′chərd), *n.* small oily fish, such as a sardine.
2. **shebeen** (shi bēn′), *n.* an unlicensed establishment selling beer and soda.
3. **purge** (pėrj), *v.* make clean.

1 Literary Element
Style

Ask a volunteer to read this paragraph aloud, while other students note patterns of repetition.

Questions

- Why do you think Mathabane mentions what the environment lacks, rather than what it has? *(Possible response: to emphasize a lifestyle of deprivation)*
- What effects does the use of repetition and accumulated clauses and details achieve? (*Possible responses: There is a dramatic buildup of evidence that this is a growing problem; to establish the theme of a need for education)*

2 Literary Focus
Characterization

Question How do the narrator's mother's actions and words characterize her? (*Possible response: The mother's acts and words serve to establish her as a firm, determined woman who is used to being obeyed.)*

BUILDING ENGLISH PROFICIENCY

ESL LEP ELD SAE LD

Exploring Key Statements

In the first two paragraphs of this excerpt, the young Mathabane twice refers to schooling as "a waste of time." Use the following activity to help students see how this statement shapes the selection.

Activity Idea Explain that most students wonder about the value of education from time to time.

- Have students suggest some benefits of an education as well as some frustrating factors that can make school seem like "a waste of time." They can diagram their ideas on a Pro-Con Chart like the one pictured here.
- Have students weigh the pros and cons from the diagram.

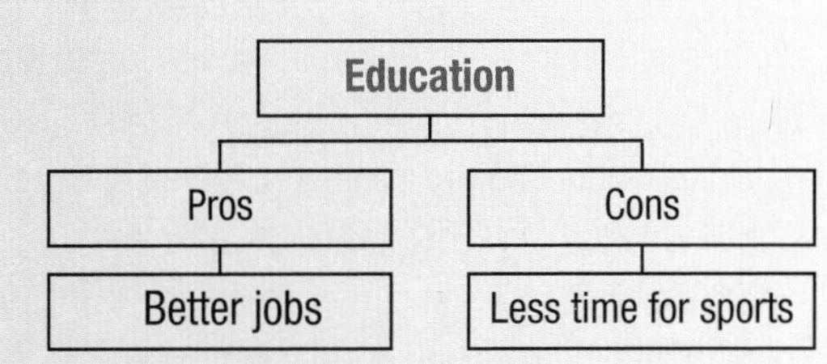

Building English Proficiency *Activities, p. 200*

3 Literary Element
Setting

Remind students that police raids were common events in the lives of black families under apartheid.

Question What does this moment of suspense reveal about the setting of the story? *(Possible response: The environment is marked with constant tension and fear.)*

4 Literary Element
Metaphor and Simile

You might point to the use of figurative language in the sentences.

- Ask students to discuss the impact of the series of similes.
- Explain that embalming is the method used to preserve a corpse from decay by the application of ointments and resins. Ask: How is the narrator "embalmed"?

5 Reading/Thinking Skills
Connect

Remind students that a matriarch is a mother with authority over her immediate family or a larger family group.

Question What does the women's method of discipline reveal about the environment? *(Possible responses: They rope the narrator as if he were an animal or a prisoner—an act that mirrors indignities they suffer from white South Africans.)*

3 of the brush encountered stubborn callouses, there was a loud knock at the door.

Instantly my mother leaped away from the tub and headed, on tiptoe, toward the bedroom. Fear seized me as I, too, thought of the police. I sat frozen in the bathtub, not knowing what to do.

"Open up, Mujaji [my mother's maiden name]," Granny's voice came shrilling through the door. "It's me."

My mother heaved a sigh of relief; her tense limbs relaxed. She turned and headed to the kitchen door, unlatched it and in came Granny and Aunt Bushy.

"You scared me half to death," my mother said to Granny. "I had forgotten all about your coming."

"Are you ready?" Granny asked my mother.

"Yes—just about," my mother said, beckoning me to get out of the washtub.

She handed me a piece of cloth to dry myself. As I dried myself, questions raced through my mind: What's going on? What's Granny doing at our house this ungodly hour of the morning? And why did she ask my mother, "Are you ready?" While I stood debating, my mother went into the bedroom and came out with a stained white shirt and a pair of faded black shorts.

"Here," she said, handing me the togs, "put these on."

"Why?" I asked.

"Put them on I said!"

I put the shirt on; it was grossly loose-fitting. It reached all the way down to my ankles. Then I saw the reason why: it was my father's shirt!

"But this is Papa's shirt," I complained. "It don't fit me."

"Put it on," my mother insisted. "I'll make it fit."

"The pants don't fit me either," I said. "Whose are they anyway?"

"Put them on," my mother said. "I'll make them fit."

Moments later I had the garments on; I looked ridiculous. My mother started working on the pants and shirt to make them fit. She folded the shirt in so many intricate ways and stashed it inside the pants, they too having been folded several times at the waist. She then choked the pants at the waist with a piece of sisal rope to hold them up. She then lavishly smeared my face, arms and legs with a mixture of pig's fat and vaseline. "This will insulate you from the cold," she said. My skin gleamed like the morning star and I felt as hot as the center of the sun and I smelled God knows like what. After embalming me, she headed to the bedroom. 4

"Where are we going, Gran'ma?" I said, hoping that she would tell me what my mother refused to tell me. I still had no idea I was about to be taken to school.

"Didn't your mother tell you?" Granny said with a smile. "You're going to start school."

"What!" I gasped, leaping from the chair where I was sitting as if it were made of hot lead. "I am not going to school!" I blurted out and raced toward the kitchen door.

My mother had just reappeared from the bedroom and guessing what I was up to, she yelled, "Someone get the door!"

Aunt Bushy immediately barred the door. I turned and headed for the window. As I leaped for the windowsill, my mother lunged at me and brought me down. I tussled, "Let go of me! I don't want to go to school! Let me go!" but my mother held fast onto me.

"It's no use now," she said, grinning triumphantly as she pinned me down. Turning her head in Granny's direction, she shouted, "Granny! Get a rope quickly!"

Granny grabbed a piece of rope nearby and came to my mother's aid. I bit and clawed every hand that grabbed me, and howled protestations against going to school; however, I was no match for the two determined matriarchs. In a jiffy they had me bound, hands and feet. 5

"What's the matter with him?" Granny, bewildered, asked my mother. "Why did he suddenly

MINI-LESSON: GRAMMAR
Forming and Hyphenating Compound Words

Teach Point to the compound words in the first paragraph.

"My philosophy on school was that of a gang of *ten-, eleven-,* and *twelve-year olds* whom I so revered that their every word seemed that of an oracle."

Review that words composed of more than one word are called compound words. Hyphens are used in some compounds to join the original words into a new word with its own meaning.

Activity Idea Have students decide whether or not the following compound words from this selection should be hyphenated. They can check their answers by referring to the page number in parentheses.

junk + yard (456 bottom)
life + style (457 top)
no + gooder (457 top)
wash + tub (457 middle)
half + naked (459 top)
thumb + sucking (459 top)

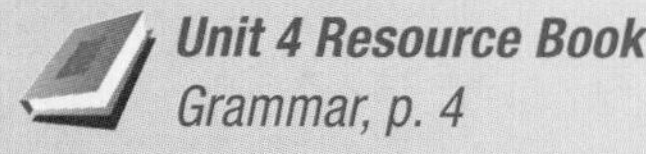

Unit 4 Resource Book
Grammar, p. 4

turn into an imp when I told him you're taking him to school?"

"You shouldn't have told him that he's being taken to school," my mother said. "He doesn't want to go there. That's why I requested you come today, to help me take him there. Those boys in the streets have been a bad influence on him."

As the two matriarchs hauled me through the door, they told Aunt Bushy not to go to school but stay behind and mind the house and the children.

The sun was beginning to rise from beyond the veld when Granny and my mother dragged me to school. The streets were beginning to fill with their everyday traffic: old men and women, wizened, bent and ragged, were beginning their rambling; workless men and women were beginning to assemble in their
6 usual coteries and head for shebeens in the backyards where they discussed how they escaped the morning pass raids[4] and contemplated the conditions of life amidst intense beer drinking and vacant, uneasy laughter; young boys and girls, some as young as myself, were beginning their aimless wanderings along the narrow, dusty streets in search of food, carrying bawling infants piggyback.

7 **CONNECT: How is life among the city poor in South Africa both alike and different from that in the United States?**

8 As we went along some of the streets, boys and girls who shared the same fears about school as I were making their feelings known in a variety of ways. They were howling their protests and trying to escape. A few managed to break loose and make a mad dash for freedom, only to be recaptured in no time, admonished[5] or whipped, or both, and ordered to march again.

As we made a turn into Sixteenth Avenue, the street leading to the tribal school I was being taken to, a short, chubby black woman came along from the opposite direction. She had a scuttle overflowing with coal on her *doek*-covered (cloth-covered) head. An infant, bawling deafeningly, was loosely swathed[6] with a piece of sheepskin onto her back. Following closely behind the woman, and picking up pieces of coal as they fell from the scuttle and placing them in a small plastic bag, was a half-naked, pot-bellied and thumb-sucking boy of about four. The woman stopped abreast. For some reason we stopped too.

"I wish I had done the same to my oldest son," the strange woman said in a regretful voice, gazing at me. I was confounded by her stopping and offering her unsolicited opinion.

"I wish I had done that to my oldest son," she repeated, and suddenly burst into tears; amidst sobs, she continued, "before . . . the street claimed him . . . and . . . turned him into a *tsotsi.*"[7]

Granny and my mother offered consolatory remarks to the strange woman.

"But it's too late now," the strange woman continued, tears now streaming freely down her puffy cheeks. She made no attempt to dry them. "It's too late now," she said for the second time, "he's beyond any help. I can't help him even if I want to. *Uswile* [He is dead]."

"How did he die?" my mother asked in a sympathetic voice.

"He shunned school and, instead, grew up to live by the knife. And the same knife he lived by ended his life. That's why whenever I see a boy-child refuse to go to school, I stop and tell the story of my dear little *mbitsini* [heartbreak]."

Having said that, the strange woman left as mysteriously as she had arrived.

"Did you hear what that woman said!" my

---

4. **pass raid,** a raid, often pre-dawn, by South African police or soldiers checking whether the inhabitants of a house have an official government pass allowing them to be there.
5. **admonish** (ad mon′ish), *v.* scold gently.
6. **swathe** (swoᴛʜ), *v.* wrap up closely or fully.
7. **tsotsi** (tsō′tsē), *n.* thug, mugger, or gangster, usually armed with a weapon such as a knife.

6 Literary Element
Setting and Characterization

Question What does the detailed description of the activities in the street tell the reader about Johannes and his family? *(Possible response: that they live in a very poor, urban neighborhood)*

7 Active Reading
Connect

- Similarities: Unemployment rates are high; boys and girls roam the streets in gangs; drug abuse and alcoholism are common; housing is below acceptable standards; hunger is a critical problem.
- Differences: In the U.S. there is a national welfare system that provides financial assistance to the urban poor; police are required to show probable cause before they raid dwellings or arrest people; Pass Laws do not exist.

8 Geographical Note
Alexandra

- In the years since the author's childhood, most of this town, Alexandra, has been destroyed to make room for white expansion.
- Under apartheid, black townships were off-limits to most white South Africans by order of the law. As a result, most whites never saw the inhumane conditions in which their black countrymen had to live.

BUILDING ENGLISH PROFICIENCY

ESL
LEP
ELD
SAE
LD

Analyzing Prepositional Phrases

You can use this selection to provide a grammar refresher about prepositional phrases.

Teach Invite two volunteers to come to the front of the class. Motion them to sit down, and offer each a book. Shake hands with them and motion them back to their seats. Then ask classmates to describe what they have just seen. On the board, note prepositional phrases they use, underlining the prepositions. Help students recognize that prepositions such as *on, beside, with,* and *to* show relationships between nouns or pronouns and other words in a sentence.

Activity Idea Have students copy into their notebooks the sentence that begins, "As we made a turn into Sixteenth Avenue. . . ."(page 459, bottom of column 1) Have a volunteer read the sentence aloud, stressing the prepositions (*into, to, from).*

9 Reading/Thinking Skills
Compare and Contrast

Questions How does the physical appearance of the principal and his assistant compare to the condition of their working environment? What does this contradiction imply about the tribal school? *(Possible response: They are dressed in flashy clothes but their tiny, dirty office is next to the toilets and is buzzing with flies. The school is a superficial operation with little substance.)*

10 Literary Focus
Characterization

Granny's commentary serves to further characterize the narrator.

Question How well does Granny seem to know her grandson? *(Possible response: Quite well; the narrator stated earlier that he idolizes the gang members who steal and take drugs.)*

11 Historical Note
Pass Laws

Under apartheid, black South Africans were not considered legal citizens. By the 1950s the Pass Laws required all non-whites to carry a booklet that contained pertinent personal records, a photograph, and fingerprints. They needed official papers to work, to walk up the street—even to stay at home with their families.

mother screamed into my ears. "Do you want the same to happen to you?"

I dropped my eyes. I was confused.

"Poor woman," Granny said ruefully.[8] "She must have truly loved her son."

Finally, we reached the school and I was ushered into the principal's office, a tiny cubicle[9] facing a row of privies and a patch of yellowed grass.

9 "So this is the rascal we'd been talking about," the principal, a tall, wiry man, foppishly dressed in a black pinstriped suit, said to my mother as we entered. His austere,[10] shiny face, inscrutable and imposing, reminded me of my father. He was sitting behind a brown table upon which stood piles of dust and cobweb-covered books and papers. In one upper pocket of his jacket was arrayed a variety of pens and pencils; in the other nestled a lily-white handkerchief whose presence was more decorative than utilitarian. Alongside him stood a disproportionately portly black woman, fashionably dressed in a black skirt and a white blouse. She had but one pen, and this she held in her hand. The room was hot and stuffy and buzzing with flies.

Once they get out into the streets, they become wild.

"Yes, Principal," my mother answered, "this is he."

"I see he's living up to his notoriety," remarked the principal, noticing that I had been bound. "Did he give you too much trouble?"

"Trouble, Principal," my mother sighed. "He was like an imp."

10 "He's just like the rest of them, Principal," Granny sighed. "Once they get out into the streets, they become wild. They take to the many vices of the streets like an infant takes to its mother's milk. They begin to think that there's no other life but the one shown them by the *tsotsis.* They come to hate school and forget about the future."

"Well," the principal said. "We'll soon remedy all that. Untie him."

"He'll run away," my mother cried.

"I don't think he's that foolish to attempt that with all of us here."

"He *is* that foolish, Principal," my mother said as she and Granny began untying me. "He's tried it before. Getting him here was an ordeal in itself."

The principal rose from his seat, took two steps to the door and closed it. As the door swung closed, I spotted a row of canes of different lengths and thicknesses hanging behind it. The principal, seeing me staring at the canes, grinned and said, in a manner suggesting that he had wanted me to see them, "As long as you behave, I won't have to use any of those on you."

Use those canes on me? I gasped. I stared at my mother—she smiled; at Granny—she smiled too. That made me abandon any inkling of escaping.

"So they finally gave you the birth certificate and the papers," the principal addressed my mother as he returned to his chair. 11

"Yes, Principal," my mother said, "they finally did. But what a battle it was. It took me nearly a year to get all them papers together." She took out of her handbag a neatly wrapped package and handed it to the principal. "They've been running us around for so long that there were times when I thought he would never attend school, Principal," she said.

"That's pretty much standard procedure, Mrs. Mathabane," the principal said, unwrapping the package. "But you now have the papers and that's what's important."

"As long as we have the papers," he continued, minutely perusing[11] the contents of the

---

8. **ruefully** (rü′fə lē), *adv.* sorrowfully.
9. **cubicle** (kyü′bə kəl), *n.* a very small room or compartment.
10. **austere** (ô stir′), *adj.* stern in manner or appearance.
11. **peruse** (pə rüz′), *v.* read, especially thoroughly and carefully.

MINI-LESSON: VOCABULARY
Connotation and Denotation

Teach Explain that Mathabane often uses the *connotation* of a word—its personal associations rather than its strict dictionary meaning—to intensify his writing.

Activity Ideas

- Write the word *education* on the board. Have a volunteer read aloud the paragraph about education that begins on the last line of page 464. Invite students to make a connotations web for this word, using associated words from the paragraph.

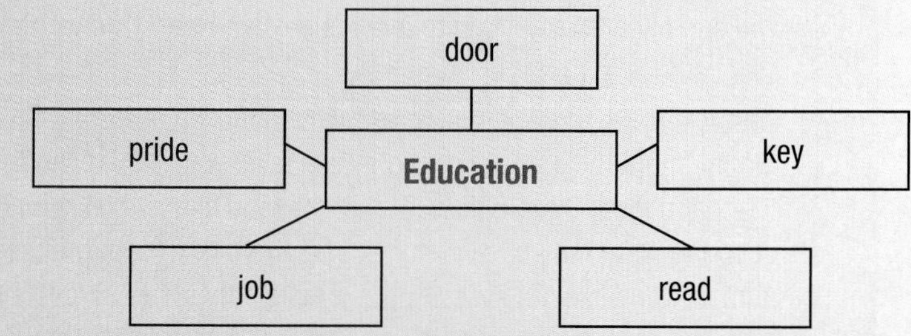

- Invite students to make a connotation web of their own associations for other words in this selection, such as *school, Granny, gang, home,* or *key.*

package, "we won't be breaking the law in admitting your son to this school, for we'll be in full compliance with the requirements set by the authorities in Pretoria."[12]

"Sometimes I don't understand the laws from Pitori," Granny said. "They did the same to me with my Piet and Bushy. Why, Principal, should our children not be allowed to learn because of some piece of paper?"

"The piece of paper you're referring to, Mrs. Mabaso [Granny's maiden name]," the principal said to Granny, "is as important to our children as a pass is to us adults. We all hate passes; therefore, it's only natural we should hate the
12 regulations our children are subjected to. But as we have to live with passes, so our children have to live with the regulations, Mrs. Mabaso. I hope you understand, that is the law of the country. We would have admitted your grandson a long time ago, as you well know, had it not been for the papers. I hope you understand."

"I understand, Principal," Granny said, "but I don't understand," she added paradoxically.

One of the papers caught the principal's eye and he turned to my mother and asked, "Is your husband a Shangaan, Mrs. Mathabane?"

"No, he's not, Principal," my mother said. "Is there anything wrong? He's Venda and I'm Shangaan."

The principal reflected for a moment or so and then said, concernedly, "No, there's nothing seriously wrong. Nothing that we can't take care of. You see, Mrs. Mathabane, technically, the fact that your child's father is a Venda makes him ineligible to attend this
13 tribal school because it is only for children whose parents are of the Shangaan tribe. May I ask what language the children speak at home?"

"Both languages," my mother said worriedly, "Venda and Shangaan. Is there anything wrong?"

The principal coughed, clearing his throat, then said, "I mean which language do they speak more?"

"It depends, Principal," my mother said, swallowing hard. "When their father is around,
he wants them to speak only Venda. And when 14
he's not, they speak Shangaan. And when they are out at play, they speak Zulu and Sisotho."

"Well," the principal said, heaving a sigh of relief. "In that case, I think an exception can be made. The reason for such an exception is that there's currently no school for Vendas in Alexandra. And should the authorities come asking why we took in your son, we can tell them that. Anyway, your child is half-half."

Everyone broke into a nervous laugh, except me. I was bewildered by the whole thing. I looked at my mother, and she seemed greatly relieved as she watched the principal register me; a broad smile broke across her face. It was as if some enormously heavy burden had finally been lifted from her shoulders and her conscience.

"Bring him back two weeks from today," the principal said as he saw us to the door. "There're so many children registering today that classes won't begin until two weeks hence. Also, the school needs repair and cleaning up after the holidays. If he refuses to come, simply notify us, and we'll send a couple of big boys to come fetch him, and he'll be very sorry if it ever comes to that."

As we left the principal's office and headed home, my mind was still against going to school. I was thinking of running away from home and joining my friends in the junkyard.

I didn't want to go to school for three reasons: I was reluctant to surrender my freedom and independence over to what I heard every school-going child call "tyrannous discipline." I had heard many bad things about life in tribal school—from daily beatings by teachers and mistresses who worked you like a mule to long school hours—and the sight of those canes in the prin-

12. **Pretoria** (pri tôr′ē ə), *n.* capital of South Africa; also called Pitori.

12 Historical Note
Pass Law Protests

In 1960, Zulu Chieftain Albert Luthuli, the leader of the African National Congress, publicly burned his pass. Although arrested, he won the Nobel Peace Prize that year for his leadership of the nonviolent resistance movement.

13 Reading/Thinking Skills
Evaluate

Question Why do you think the government segregated the black schools and neighborhoods according to tribe? *(Possible response: to keep the black population divided and unable to unite in protest against the government)*

14 Multicultural Note
Multilingual Families

Discuss the range of languages that these children spoke every day: *Venda, Shangaan, Zulu,* and *Sisotho.* Ask bilingual students to share how their days are divided between languages.

Child Advocate

For real-life experiences of a child advocate, use—

The World of Work
pp. 15–16

BUILDING ENGLISH PROFICIENCY

Making Cultural Connections

Invite students to compare and contrast Mathabane's school, as revealed in this excerpt, to schools in the United States and perhaps other parts of the world.

Activity Ideas

- Ask students to record their findings in a three-column chart—one column for the South Africa of *Kaffir Boy,* one for the United States today, and one for examples from other countries.
- Have them list facts such as who goes to school, how many days per week and months per year school is in session, how much an education costs, what subjects are studied, how many years the average student attends, and so on.
- Ask students to interview their parents or someone who has been educated in another country to complete the answers to the items above.

15 Reader's Response
Making Personal Connections

The narrator says that the thought of his mother's struggles is a more convincing argument for school than the thought of being dead in the streets.

Question Do you identify with his reasoning? Why or why not? *(Some students may say no, because he should value his life over his mother's feelings.)*

EDITORIAL NOTE The three ellipses in column two indicate these deletions: *you bastard, whore,* and *calling them whores and bitches and so on.*

16 Literary Elements
Point of View and Autobiography

Remind students that although this is a true story, the author writes from memory and through an adult's perspective, not that of a young boy.

17 Reading/Thinking Skills
Relate Literature to Personal Experience

Question Do you find the narrator's reaction to his father believable? *(Some students may say a boy this young would not have the nerve to oppose a drunken, angry father; others will say that he is emboldened by love for his mother.)*

cipal's office gave ample credence[13] to rumors that school was nothing but a torture chamber. And there was my allegiance to the gang.

15 But the thought of the strange woman's lamentations over her dead son presented a somewhat strong case for going to school: I didn't want to end up dead in the streets. A more compelling argument for going to school, however, was the vivid recollection of all that humiliation and pain my mother had gone through to get me the papers and the birth certificate so I could enroll in school. What should I do? I was torn between two worlds.

But later that evening something happened to force me to go to school.

I was returning home from playing soccer when a neighbor accosted[14] me by the gate and told me that there had been a bloody fight at my home.

"Your mother and father have been at it again," the neighbor, a woman, said.

"And your mother left."

I was stunned.

"Was she hurt badly?"

"A little bit," the woman said. "But she'll be all right. We took her to your grandma's place."

I became hot with anger.

"Is anyone in the house?" I stammered, trying to control my rage.

"Yes, your father is. But I don't think you should go near the house. He's raving mad. He's armed with a meat cleaver. He's chased out your brother and sisters, also. And some of the neighbors who tried to intervene he's threatened to carve them to pieces. I have never seen him this mad before."

I brushed aside the woman's warnings and went. Shattered windows convinced me that there had indeed been a skirmish of some sort. Several pieces of broken bricks, evidently broken after being thrown at the door, were lying about the door. I tried opening the door; it was locked from the inside. I knocked. No one answered. I knocked again. Still no one answered, until, as I turned to leave:

"Who's out there?" my father's voice came growling from inside.

"It's me, Johannes," I said.

"Go away . . . !" he bellowed. "I don't want you or that . . . mother of yours setting foot in this house. Go away before I come out there and kill you!"

"Let me in!" I cried. "Dammit, let me in! I want my things!"

"What things? Go away, you black swine!"

I went to the broken window and screamed obscenities at my father, daring him to come out, hoping that if he as much as ever stuck his black face out, I would pelt him with the half-a-loaf brick in my hand. He didn't come out. He continued launching a tirade of obscenities at my mother and her mother. . . . He was drunk, but I wondered where he had gotten the money to buy beer because it was still the middle of the week and he was dead broke. He had lost his entire wage for the past week in dice and had had to borrow bus fare. 16

"I'll kill you someday for all you're doing to my mother," I threatened him, overwhelmed with rage. Several nosey neighbors were beginning to congregate by open windows and doors. Not wanting to make a spectacle of myself, which was something many of our neighbors seemed to always expect from our family, I backtracked away from the door and vanished into the dark street. I ran, without stopping, all the way to the other end of the township where Granny lived. There I found my mother, her face swollen and bruised and her eyes puffed up to the point where she could scarcely see. 17

"What happened, Mama?" I asked, fighting to hold back the tears at the sight of her disfigured face.

"Nothing, child, nothing," she mumbled

13. **credence** (krēd′ns), *n.* belief.
14. **accost** (ə kôst′), *v.* approach and speak to first; address.

MINI-LESSON: LITERARY FOCUS
Characterization

In the introduction to *Kaffir Boy*, Mathabane states, "They turned my father—by repeatedly arresting him and denying him the right to earn a living in a way that gave him dignity—into such a bitter man, that . . . he hurt those he loved the most." Have students find examples from this excerpt that further illustrate the father's character.

Activity Idea Students can draw a Character Chart for the narrator's father, listing words that describe him.

Father
abusive
anti-education
tribal
domineering

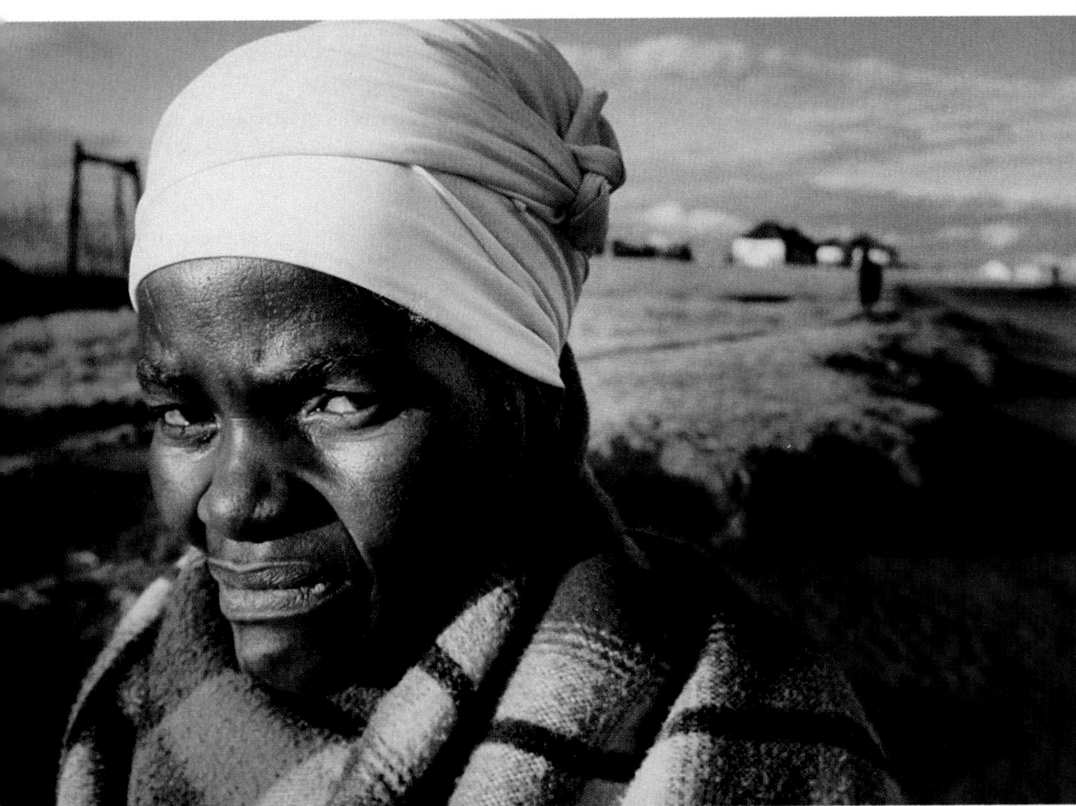

This woman's tribal homeland has become "independent," depriving its residents of South African citizenship. What advice might she give the boy photographed on page 456?

almost apologetically, between swollen lips. "Your papa simply lost his temper, that's all."

"But why did he beat you up like this, Mama?" Tears came down my face. "He's never beaten you like this before."

18 My mother appeared reluctant to answer me. She looked searchingly at Granny, who was pounding millet with pestle and mortar[15] and mixing it with sorghum and nuts for an African delicacy. Granny said, "Tell him, child, tell him. He's got a right to know. Anyway, he's the cause of it all."

"Your father and I fought because I took you to school this morning," my mother began. "He had told me not to, and when I told him that I had, he became very upset. He was drunk. We started arguing, and one thing led to another."

"Why doesn't he want me to go to school?"

"He says he doesn't have money to waste paying for you to get what he calls a useless white man's education," my mother replied. "But I told him that if he won't pay for your schooling, I

15. **millet . . . mortar.** A mortar is a bowl in which substances such as the cereal grain millet can be pounded or crushed by a pestle, a small, clublike tool.

Art Study

Response to Caption Question
Possible responses: She might tell him to stay in school and educate himself so that he can fight the white man's injustices with his mind, or use his education to help him escape from Soweto.

Background Under apartheid, most of the black African majority was relocated into crowded "native independencies," which covered less than 20 percent of South Africa's available land. By claiming that the remaining tribal homelands were also native "independencies," the Afrikaners established the black natives as "foreign migrants" with none of the rights of citizens.

Visual Literacy This image demonstrates the power of a realistic photograph to suggest the deep inner life of its subject.

Question What feelings does this woman's face convey? *(Possible responses: sadness, distrust, anger, exhaustion, resignation, strength)*

18 Literary Focus
Characterization

Questions Compare and contrast the attitudes of the mother and the grandmother as they respond to the narrator's questions. *(Possible response: The mother is apologetic and protective, the grandmother is unsparing of the boy's feelings.)*

BUILDING ENGLISH PROFICIENCY

ESL
LEP
ELD
SAE
LD

Exploring Social Issues

As Mathabane's story reaches its climax, several difficult social issues arise. Use one or more of the following activities to help students grasp those issues.

Activity Ideas

- It is clear that Mathabane's mother is an abused wife. Lead a discussion about options that are available to battered women in your community.
- Mathabane's father has a drinking problem. Invite students to share (orally or through art or another medium) what they know of the dangers of alcoholism and how alcoholism can be treated.
- Invite a social worker to team-teach with you, providing a professional perspective on these problems.

19 Reader's Response

Making Personal Connections

Questions

- Does this statement shock you? *(Possible response: Many students will be sensitive to such an extreme remark. Others may not notice its political implications.)*
- How do you think it would feel to be someone else's property? *(Possible response: Students will probably answer that it would be frustrating and even degrading.)*

20 Multicultural Note

Bride Price

Point out that in many cultures, the exchange of money and possessions has traditionally functioned as a motivating factor in the selection of marriage partners. The narrator's mother would have to pay his father the amount of the original lobola to gain freedom, but her father has already spent the entire sum.

21 Active Reading

Clarify

Possible responses Aspects include the act of "selling" women as marriage partners regardless of their wishes; the notion that wives have to obey their husbands' orders; discouragement of children attending school.

would try and look for a job and pay, but he didn't want to hear that, also. 'There are better things for you to work for,' he said. 'Besides, I don't want you to work. How would I look to other men if you, a woman I owned, were to start working?' When I asked him why shouldn't I take you to school, seeing that you were now of age, he replied that he doesn't believe in schools. I told him that school would keep you off the streets and out of trouble, but still he was belligerent."[16]

19

"Is that why he beat you up?"

"Yes, he said I disobeyed his orders."

20 "He's right, child," Granny interjected. "He paid *lobola* [bride price] for you. And your father ate it all up before he left me."

To which my mother replied, "But I desperately want to leave this beast of a man. But with his *lobola* gone I can't do it. That worthless thing you call your husband shouldn't have sold Jackson's scrawny cattle and left you penniless."

"Don't talk like that about your father, child," Granny said. "Despite all, he's still your father, you know. Anyway, he asked for *lobola* only because he had to get back what he spent raising you. And you know it would have been taboo for him to let you or any of your sisters go without asking for *lobola.*"

"You and Papa seemed to forget that my sisters and I have minds of our own," my mother said. "We didn't need you to tell us whom to marry, and why, and how. If it hadn't been for your interference, I could have married that schoolteacher."

Granny did not reply; she knew well not to. When it came to the act of "selling" women as marriage partners, my mother was vehemently opposed to it. Not only was she opposed to this one aspect of tribal culture, but to others as well, particularly those involving relations between men and women and the upbringing of children. But my mother's sharply differing opinion was an exception rather than the rule among tribal women. Most times, many tribal women questioned her sanity in daring to question well-established mores. But my mother did not seem to care; she would always scoff at her opponents and call them fools in letting their husbands enslave them completely.

CLARIFY: What aspects of tribal culture does Johannes's mother oppose? Why? 21

Though I disliked school, largely because I knew nothing about what actually went on there, and the little I knew had painted a dreadful picture, the fact that a father would not want his son to go to school, especially a father who didn't go to school, seemed hard to understand.

"Why do you want me to go to school, Mama?" I asked, hoping that she might, somehow, clear up some of the confusion that was building in my mind.

"I want you to have a future, child," my mother said. "And, contrary to what your father says, school is the only means to a future. I don't want you growing up to be like your father."

The latter statement hit me like a bolt of lightning. It just about shattered every defense mechanism and every pretext[17] I had against going to school.

"Your father didn't go to school," she continued, dabbing her puffed eyes to reduce the swelling with a piece of cloth dipped in warm water, "that's why he's doing some of the bad things he's doing. Things like drinking, gambling and neglecting his family. He didn't learn how to read and write; therefore, he can't find a decent job. Lack of any education has narrowly focused his life. He sees nothing beyond himself. He still thinks in the old, tribal way, and still believes that things should be as they were back in the old days when he was growing up as a tribal boy in Louis Trichardt. Though he's my husband, and your father, he doesn't see any of that."

"Why didn't he go to school, Mama?"

"He refused to go to school because his

16. belligerent (bə lij′ər ənt), *adj.* fond of fights.
17. pretext (prē′tekst), *n.* a false reason concealing the real reason; misleading excuse.

MINI-LESSON: SPEAKING AND LISTENING

Interpretive Reading

Explain that the dialogue between Granny and the narrator's mother on page 464 offers excellent opportunities for oral interpretation.

Activity Ideas

- Have two volunteers rehearse these parts and present them to the class as readers' theater.
- After the presentation, ask what words students would use to describe the tone of each character.

father led him to believe that an education was a tool through which white people were going to take things away from him, like they did black people in the old days. And that a white man's education was worthless insofar as black people were concerned because it prepared them for jobs they can't have. But I know it isn't totally so, child, because times have changed somewhat. Though our lot isn't any better today, an education will get you a decent job. If you can read or write you'll be better off than those of us who can't. Take my situation: I can't find a job because I don't have papers, and I can't get papers because white people mainly want to register people who can read and write. But I want things to be different for you, child. For you and your brother and sisters. I want you to go to school, because I believe that an education is the key you need to open up a new world and a new life for yourself, a world and life different from that of either your father's or mine. It is the only key that can do that, and only those who seek it earnestly and perseveringly will get anywhere in the white man's world. Education will open doors where none seem to exist. It'll make people talk to you, listen to you and help you; people who otherwise wouldn't bother. It will make you soar, like a bird lifting up into the endless blue sky, and leave poverty, hunger and suffering behind. It'll teach you to learn to embrace what's good and shun what's bad and evil. Above all, it'll make you a somebody in this world. It'll make you grow up to be a good and proud person. That's why I want you to go to school, child, so that education can do all that, and more, for you."

22 **SUMMARIZE: State the theme of the preceding paragraph in a sentence.**

A long, awkward silence followed, during which I reflected upon the significance of my mother's lengthy speech. I looked at my mother; she looked at me.

Finally, I asked, "How come you know so much about school, Mama? You didn't go to school, did you?"

"No, child," my mother replied. "Just like your father, I never went to school." For the second time that evening, a mere statement of fact had a thunderous impact on me. All the confusion I had about school seemed to leave my mind, like darkness giving way to light. And what had previously been a dark, yawning void in my mind was suddenly transformed into a beacon of light that began to grow larger and larger, until it had swallowed up, blotted out, all the blackness. That beacon of light seemed to reveal things and facts, which, though they must have always existed in me, I hadn't been aware of up until now.

"But unlike your father," my mother went on, "I've always wanted to go to school, but couldn't because my father, under the sway of tribal traditions, thought it unnecessary to educate females. That's why I so much want you to go, child, for if you do, I know that someday I too would come to go, old as I would be then. Promise me, therefore, that no matter what, you'll go back to school. And I, in turn, promise that I'll do everything in my power to keep you there."

With tears streaming down my cheeks and falling upon my mother's bosom, I promised her that I would go to school "forever." That night, at seven and a half years of my life, the battlelines in the family were drawn. My mother on the one side, illiterate but determined to have me drink, for better or for worse, from the well of knowledge. On the other side, my father, he too illiterate, yet determined to have me drink from the well of ignorance. Scarcely aware of the magnitude of the decision I was making or, rather, the decision which was being emotionally thrusted upon me, I chose to fight on my mother's side, and thus my destiny was forever altered. 23

22 Active Reading
Summarize

Possible response The values, skills, and self-esteem gained through education can empower a young black South African to overcome the limitations of an oppressive racist society.

23 Literary Focus
Characterization

Explain that a dynamic character changes during the course of the story's action, while a static character stays the same.

Questions Why is the narrator a dynamic character? Would you say the narrator's father is static or dynamic? *(Possible responses: The narrator is dynamic because he has changed his attitude toward attending school as a result of the events of the story. The father is static in that he undergoes no change.)*

Check Test

1. Who knocks on the door when the narrator is taking a bath? *(his grandmother)*

2. Where are the narrator's mother and grandmother taking him? *(to tribal school)*

3. Why is the strange woman in the street crying? *(because her son died as a gangster in the streets instead of attending school)*

4. Why does the narrator's father beat his mother? *(because he doesn't want her to send the narrator to school)*

5. What does the narrator decide at the end of the story? *(that he does want to go to school)*

Unit 4 Resource Book
Alternate Check Test, p. 5

BUILDING ENGLISH PROFICIENCY

Analyzing Culture

Activity Ideas

- Help students make a culture chart of details revealed in Mathabane's autobiography and in the background information provided on page 455.

Africa in the 1960s
lobola (bride price) apartheid (government sanctioned racism) Kaffir (derogatory term for blacks)

- Have students use their charts as a basis for a presentation to another class about life in South Africa during the 1960s.
- Use outside resources, such as the Introduction that appears in the novel *Kaffir Boy*, to expand this information.

After Reading

MAKING CONNECTIONS

1. Possible responses: Do you still hate your father? Did your mother ever get to go to school?

2. Possible responses: Yes, because people's education can affect their future jobs, friends, and environment.

3. Possible responses: the boy's wild and angry innocence; the mother's and Granny's grim determination

4. Possible responses: the pig's lard used to keep him warm; the washtub; the starving children in the streets; the fly-ridden school office

5. Possible response: It serves as a warning about the future that awaits the narrator if he stays out of school.

6. Possible responses: The mother is fighting for her son's education; the boy is fighting to stay on the streets with his gang; the father is fighting to assert his control over his family.

7. Possible response: because the white man's school system was invested in maintaining racial inequality

8. Possible response: Some students may say yes, because they learned about the obstacles Mathabane overcame to get an education, which most American citizens consider an inalienable right.

9. Possible responses: They are afraid of the differences between the races, and need to separate themselves to feel safe. The best response is to ignore them and realize that they are motivated by fear and ignorance.

After Reading

Making Connections

Shaping Your Response

1. Write down questions that you would like to ask the adult Mark Mathabane.
2. At the end of the selection, Johannes observes "and thus my destiny was forever altered." Do you think that decisions about schooling are important enough to alter a person's destiny? Explain.
3. Which qualities of the characters in Mathabane's autobiography do you think the photographs that accompany this selection capture?

Analyzing the Autobiography

4. What details in this account indicate the conditions of poverty in this South African **setting?**
5. What is the significance of the encounter with the strange woman?
6. The **theme** of this group of selections is "Worth Fighting For?" In *Kaffir Boy,* who are the fighters, and what is each fighting for?
7. Why might people in Mathabane's culture have opposed getting a formal education? Before answering, you may want to reread the paragraph that begins at the bottom of page 464 ("He refused to go to school . . .").

Extending the Ideas

8. Judging from this excerpt and from information supplied on page 455, would you recommend Mathabane's autobiography to another teenager? Explain.
9. Words such as *Kaffir* reflect prejudice and lack of **communication** among cultural groups. Why do you think people use derogatory racial terms? What do you think is the best way to react to the use of such terms?

Literary Focus: Characterization

Mathabane's **characterization** of the strange woman encountered on the street is conveyed in a number of ways.

- What does the woman look like?
- Which of the woman's actions do you think reveals the most about her?
- Which of the woman's statements do you find the most memorable?

LITERARY FOCUS: CHARACTERIZATION

Possible responses

- She is short and chubby. She has a cloth and a scuttle of coal on her head, and a baby strapped onto her back.
- The fact that she stopped to tell the narrator about her son shows that she is committed to letting others learn from her tragedy.
- Students may answer, *"Uswile* [He is dead]."

Vocabulary Study

Study the relationship of each pair of words in capital letters; then write the letter of another pair that has the same relationship.

austere
belligerent
cubicle
peruse
pretext

1. BELLIGERENT : PEACEFUL :: **a.** tiny : small **b.** sad : happy **c.** troubled : upset **d.** thrifty : sale
2. CUBICLE : SMALL :: **a.** theater : crowded **b.** classroom : school **c.** mansion : large **d.** auditorium : empty
3. AUSTERE : STERN :: **a.** fudge : candy **b.** delicious : tasteless **c.** sly : crafty **d.** nervous : calm
4. PRETEXT : EXCUSE :: **a.** pale : rosy **b.** friend : rival **c.** money : credit **d.** objective : goal
5. PERUSE : BOOK :: **a.** strum : guitar **b.** cover : wrap **c.** iron : fold **d.** expire : license

Expressing Your Ideas

Writing Choices

Writer's Notebook Update Mathabane characterizes people through their appearance, actions, and words. Use these three techniques to expand the descriptive words in your notebook into a character sketch of the person who made a school day memorable.

Mr. Mathabane's Neighborhood In this selection, Mathabane provides glimpses of the ghetto in which he lived. Now that apartheid has been abolished, the new government has hired you, a city planner, to make suggestions to improve this area. Write a description of the area and some suggestions for improvement. Organize your **report** under three headings: housing, vacant lots, and streets. You might illustrate your ideas with sketches or diagrams.

The Limits of Tyrants The following quotation by Frederick Douglass appears as a preface to *Kaffir Boy:* "The limits of tyrants are prescribed by the endurance of those whom they oppress." In a paragraph that could be used in a **book review,** explain what these words mean and how they are illustrated in Mathabane's work.

Other Options

Listen Up Write and deliver a brief **motivational speech** that Mark Mathabane might give to a youth group summarizing why he decided to attend and succeed at school.

After 1994 With a team, research what has happened in South Africa since Nelson Mandela was elected president in 1994. Present your findings in the form of a **chalk talk** or display, using visuals such as graphs, charts, and photographs.

VOCABULARY STUDY

1. b
2. c
3. c
4. d
5. a

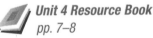

Unit 4 Resource Book
Vocabulary, p. 3
Vocabulary Test, p. 6

WRITING CHOICES

Writer's Notebook Update

For an interesting exercise in point of view, have students imagine that they have switched places with the person they just described and rewrite the exercise using themselves as the focus character.

Mr. Mathabane's Neighborhood

Suggest that students do research at the school library to learn more about the housing and zoning conditions in South African ghettos.

The Limits of Tyrants

You might suggest that students organize a main idea map around the quote to help them brainstorm supporting details.

Selection Test

Unit 4 Resource Book
pp. 7–8

OTHER OPTIONS

Listen Up

Remind students that Mathabane's intimate perspective would probably give an emotional and passionate tone to the delivery of the speech. They may wish to use loaded words or other propaganda techniques.

Before Reading

Building Background

Ask students why the number of workers in service jobs is increasing while the number producing goods is decreasing. *(Machines have displaced many people in production of goods.)*

Poll students about whether they would prefer a service job or a goods-producing job.

Literary Focus

Encourage students to recall situations from books, TV, or movies that illustrate **irony.** Have them classify their examples as either *verbal, dramatic,* or *situational irony.*

Writer's Notebook

Students might summarize their stories aloud for the class.

More About Maya Angelou

In 1962 Angelou moved to Ghana as part of a movement to unite Africans and African descendants. Martin Luther King, Jr., appointed Angelou as Northern Coordinator for the Southern Christian Leadership Conference. Other works include:

- *Gather Together in My Name*, (1974)
- *Wouldn't Take Nothing for My Journey Now*, (1993).

Before Reading

Living Well. Living Good.

by Maya Angelou USA

Maya Angelou
born 1928

She was three years old and on a train. On her wrist was a tag stating that she was Marguerite Johnson, traveling with her four-year-old brother to Stamps, Arkansas, from Long Beach, California, c/o Mrs. Annie Henderson, her grandmother. Before she was fifty, she would be known as Maya Angelou (mä′yä än′-jə lō) and have more than half a dozen successful careers: professional dancer, poet, screenwriter and director, singer, composer, civil rights worker, and college professor. Her greatest achievement may be five volumes of autobiography, from *I Know Why the Caged Bird Sings* (1970) to *Wouldn't Take Nothing for My Journey Now* (1993).

Building Background

Our Strength They are all about us, and their numbers are rapidly increasing. They cure us, they teach us, they file our letters. They fix our broken windows and our broken hearts. They buy stocks, sell shoes, cook meals, clean houses, babysit children, defend us in court, and make us attractive. They are the millions of Americans who, like the aunt Maya Angelou describes, earn their living by offering services, not by making goods. As Aunt Tee's story implies, they are America's strength and future.

Service-producing industries will continue to account for virtually all job growth.

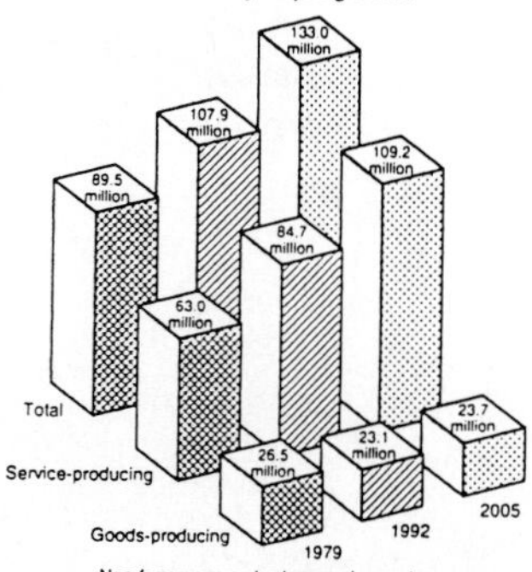

Source: Bureau of Labor Statistics

Literary Focus

Irony Each of the three kinds of **irony** involves a contradiction between what appears to be and what actually is. If someone whom you've made angry says sarcastically, "Have a nice day," that's *verbal irony*. In *situational irony,* something happens that is the opposite of what you would expect to happen, as when a wealthy person goes bankrupt. In *dramatic irony,* you as reader or audience know something that the fictional characters do not. As you read the following selection, decide which of these kinds of irony is emphasized.

Writer's Notebook

Storytellers In this selection, Maya Angelou recalls the stories related by an elderly relative. Think of a story told by a relative or an old friend of your family. In your notebook, write down several key words or phrases that you could use to summarize this story.

SUPPORT MATERIALS OVERVIEW

Unit 4 Resource Book
- Graphic Organizer, p. 9
- Study Guide, p. 10
- Vocabulary, p. 11
- Grammar, p. 12
- Alternate Check Test, p. 13
- Vocabulary Test, p. 14
- Selection Test, pp. 15–16

Building English Proficiency
- Literature Summaries
- Activities, p. 201

Reading, Writing & Grammar SkillBook
- Grammar, Usage, and Mechanics, pp. 261–266

Technology
- Audiotape 11, Side B
- Personal Journal Software
- Custom Literature Database: For an interesting comparison, see "Christmas on the Plantation" by Solomon Northup on the database.
- Test Generator Software

Living Well. Living Good.

MAYA ANGELOU

Aunt Tee was a Los Angeles member of our extended family. She was seventy-nine when I met her, sinewy, strong, and the color of old lemons. She wore her coarse, straight hair, which was slightly streaked with gray, in a long braided rope across the top of her head. With her high cheekbones, old gold skin, and almond eyes, she looked more like an Indian chief than an old black woman. (Aunt Tee described herself and any favored member of her race as Negroes.

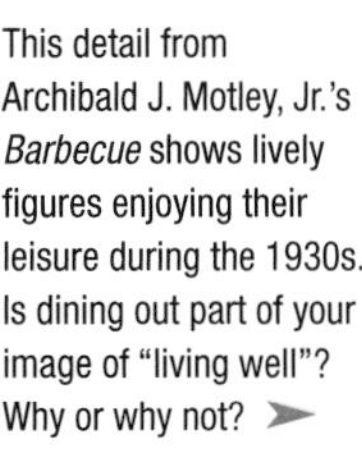

This detail from Archibald J. Motley, Jr.'s *Barbecue* shows lively figures enjoying their leisure during the 1930s. Is dining out part of your image of "living well"? Why or why not? ➤

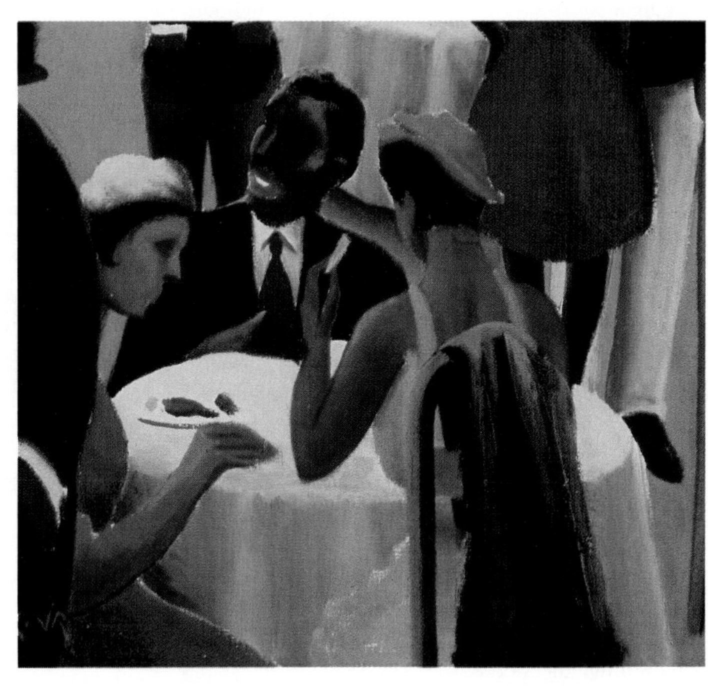

During Reading

Selection Objectives

- to examine the values that people defend in everyday battles
- to recognize and appreciate irony
- to punctuate a series using commas

Unit 4 Resource Book
Graphic Organizer, p. 9
Study Guide, p.10

Theme Link

The theme "Worth Fighting For" is shown in this housekeeper's ironic tale of sharing her riches with her wealthy employers.

Vocabulary Preview

commodious, having plenty of room
convivial, sociable
incur, bring on oneself
meticulous, extremely or excessively careful about small details
revelry, boisterous merrymaking or festivity

Students can add the words and definitions to their Writer's Notebooks.

Art Study

Responses to Caption Question
Allow for a broad range of opinions and experiences of "living well."

Visual Literacy Painter J. Motley, Jr. (1891–1981), was one of the first major artists to celebrate the diversity, dignity, and energy of his fellow urban African Americans.

Question What contributes to the festive mood of this painting? *(Possible responses: the exaggerated smiles, the dancing poses of the waiters, the string of lights, the glowing back-ground, and the animated gestures of the figures)*

SELECTION SUMMARY

Living Well. Living Good.

The narrator introduces Aunt Tee as a retired housekeeper who took great pride in her career accomplishments. She then relates one of Aunt Tee's stories about her wealthy employers who owned a luxurious mansion in Bel Air. Their lives, however, were so devoid of joy that they spent every Saturday evening getting vicarious pleasure by watching Aunt Tee and her friends enjoy themselves at their weekly card party. The narrator closes the story by pointing to its inherent lesson: The true value of life stems from the joy and acceptance with which it is lived, not from material success.

*For summaries in other languages, see the **Building English Proficiency** book.*

1 Literary Element
Characterization

Question What conclusions about Aunt Tee's personality can you draw from the descriptions of her appearance and her apartment? *(Possible response: She is strong, proud, dignified, self-sufficient, and meticulous.)*

2 Literary Focus
Verbal Irony

Question Do you think Aunt Tee actually stayed young while her employers grew old? Explain. *(Possible responses: not literally—she grew older but lived an active, full life)*

3 Literary Element
Connotative Language

Make sure students understand the connotations of the following phrases:

- social maven: literally means "social expert," a person with a busy social life
- keeping company: connotes that Aunt Tee and the chauffeur were a romantic couple

4 Literary Focus
Irony of Situation

Question Why do you think they pull Aunt Tee outside? *(It first appears they will scold her for the noisy party.)*

Black was saved for those who had incurred[1] her disapproval.)

1 She had retired and lived alone in a dead, neat ground-floor apartment. Wax flowers and china figurines sat on elaborately embroidered and heavily starched doilies. Sofas and chairs were tautly upholstered. The only thing at ease in Aunt Tee's apartment was Aunt Tee.

I used to visit her often and perch on her uncomfortable sofa just to hear her stories. She was proud that after working thirty years as a maid, she spent the next thirty years as a live-in housekeeper, carrying the keys to rich houses and keeping meticulous[2] accounts.

"Living in lets the white folks know Negroes are as neat and clean as they are, sometimes more so. And it gives the Negro maid a chance to see white folks ain't no smarter than Negroes. Just luckier. Sometimes."

Aunt Tee told me that once she was housekeeper for a couple in Bel Air, California,[3] lived with them in a fourteen-room ranch house. There was a day maid who cleaned, and a gardener who daily tended the lush gardens. Aunt Tee oversaw the workers. When she had begun the job, she had cooked and served a light breakfast, a good lunch, and a full three- or four-course dinner to her employers and their guests. Aunt Tee said she watched them grow older and leaner. After a few years they stopped entertaining and ate dinner hardly seeing each other at the table. Finally, they sat in a dry silence as they ate evening meals of soft scram-
2 bled eggs, melba toast, and weak tea. Aunt Tee said she saw them growing old but didn't see herself aging at all.

3 She became the social maven. She started "keeping company" (her phrase) with a chauffeur down the street. Her best friend and her friend's husband worked in service[4] only a few blocks away.

On Saturdays Aunt Tee would cook a pot of pigs' feet, a pot of greens, fry chicken, make potato salad, and bake a banana pudding. Then, that evening, her friends—the chauffeur, the other housekeeper, and her husband—would come to Aunt Tee's commodious[5] live-in quarters. There the four would eat and drink, play records and dance. As the evening wore on, they would settle down to a serious game of bid whist.[6]

Naturally, during this revelry[7] jokes were told, fingers snapped, feet were patted, and there was a great deal of laughter.

Aunt Tee said that what occurred during every Saturday party startled her and her friends the first time it happened. They had been playing cards, and Aunt Tee, who had just won the bid, held a handful of trumps. She felt a cool breeze on her back and sat upright and turned around. Her employers had cracked her door open and beckoned to her. Aunt Tee, a little peeved, laid down her cards and went to the door. The couple backed away and asked her to come into the hall, and there they both spoke and won Aunt 4
Tee's sympathy forever.

"Theresa, we don't mean to disturb you . . ." the man whispered, "but you all seem to be having such a good time. . . ."

The woman added, "We hear you and your friends laughing every Saturday night, and we'd just like to watch you. We don't want to bother you. We'll be quiet and just watch."

The man said, "If you'll just leave your door ajar, your friends don't need to know. We'll never make a sound." Aunt Tee said she saw no harm in agreeing, and she talked it over with

1. **incur** (in kėr′), *v.* bring on oneself.
2. **meticulous** (mə tik′yə ləs), *adj.* extremely or excessively careful about small details.
3. **Bel Air, California,** a wealthy section of Los Angeles.
4. **worked in service,** in the occupation or employment of a servant.
5. **commodious** (kə mō′dē əs), *adj.* having plenty of room.
6. **bid whist,** a card game somewhat like bridge.
7. **revelry** (rev′əl rē), *n.* boisterous merrymaking or festivity.

MINI-LESSON: GRAMMAR
Using Commas in a Series

Teach Have students examine the following sentence in order to analyze the use of commas to separate items in a series.

"On Saturdays Aunt Tee would cook a pot of pigs' feet, . . . fry chicken, make potato salad, and bake a banana pudding."

Question What are the commas separating in this example? *(a list of things Aunt Tee cooked)*

Activity Idea Dictate the following sentences, having students insert commas where needed:

- ". . . they ate evening meals of soft scrambled eggs, melba toast, and weak tea."
- "With her high cheekbones, old gold skin, and almond eyes, she looked more like an Indian chief than an old black woman."

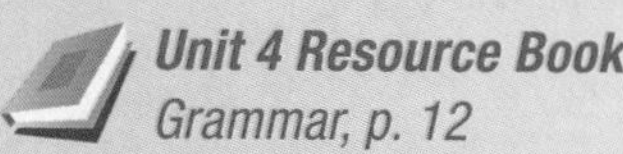
Unit 4 Resource Book
Grammar, p. 12

her company. They said it was OK with them, but it was sad that the employers owned the gracious house, the swimming pool, three cars, and numberless palm trees, but had no joy. Aunt Tee told me that laughter and relaxation had left the
5 house; she agreed it was sad.

We don't want to bother you. We'll be quiet and just watch.

That story has stayed with me for nearly thirty years, and when a tale remains fresh in my mind, it almost always contains a lesson which will benefit me.

My dears, I draw the picture of the wealthy couple standing in a darkened hallway, peering into a lighted room where black servants were lifting their voices in merriment and comradery, and I realize that living well is an art which can be developed. Of course, you will need the basic talents to build upon: They are a love of life and ability to take great pleasure from small offerings, an assurance that the world owes you nothing and that every gift is exactly that, a gift. That people who may differ from you in political
6 stance, sexual persuasion, and racial inheritance can be founts of fun, and if you are lucky, they can become even convivial[8] comrades.

Living life as art requires a readiness to forgive. I do not mean that you should suffer fools
7 gladly, but rather remember your own shortcomings, and when you encounter another with flaws, don't be eager to righteously seal yourself away from the offender forever. Take a few breaths and imagine yourself having just committed the action which has set you at odds.

Because of the routines we follow, we often forget that life is an ongoing adventure. We leave our homes for work, acting and even believing that we will reach our destinations with no unusual event startling us out of our set expectations. The truth is we know nothing, not where our cars will fail or when our buses will stall, whether our places of employment will be there when we arrive, or whether, in fact, we ourselves will arrive whole and alive at the end of our journeys. Life is pure adventure, and the sooner we realize that, the quicker we will be able to treat life as art: to bring all our energies to each encounter, to remain flexible enough to notice and admit when what we expected to happen did not happen. We need to remember that we are created creative and can invent new scenarios as frequently as they are needed.

Life seems to love the liver of it. Money and power can liberate only if they are used to do so. They can imprison and inhibit more finally than barred windows and iron chains.

8. convivial (kən viv′ē əl), *adj.* sociable.

5 Literary Element
Frame Stories and Autobiography

Explain that Angelou is telling a story about her visits to her aunt; within that frame is the story of her aunt's unhappy employers.

6 Reading/Thinking Skills
Recognize the Use of Persuasion

Question Based on what you know about Maya Angelou, why might she try to persuade the reader on this point? *(As an African American civil rights activist, she is committed to eliminating prejudices and fear.)*

7 Reader's Response
Making Personal Connections

Explain that this story is a parable because it teaches a moral lesson.

Question Do you share the narrator's belief in forgiveness and tolerance? Explain. *(Students may agree that forgiveness and tolerance towards others is an ideal. Other students may answer no, because you have to defend yourself against the folly of others.)*

Check Test

1. Where does Aunt Tee live? *(Los Angeles)*
2. What does Aunt Tee do for a living? *(She is a maid and a housekeeper.)*
3. When does Aunt Tee relax with her friends? *(Saturday nights)*
4. Why do her employers pull Aunt Tee into the hall? *(They ask to watch her and her friends enjoy themselves.)*
5. Angelou recalls Aunt Tee's story after how many years? *(30)*

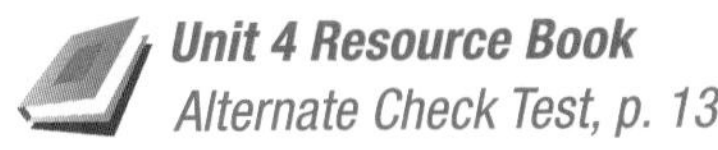
Unit 4 Resource Book
Alternate Check Test, p. 13

BUILDING ENGLISH PROFICIENCY

ESL LEP ELD SAE LD

Making Personal Connections

Angelou uses descriptions of Aunt Tee and events in her life to present her aunt's view of happiness. Invite students to explore their own views of happiness by creating a details web that illustrates what makes them happy. Allow for optional, voluntary sharing.

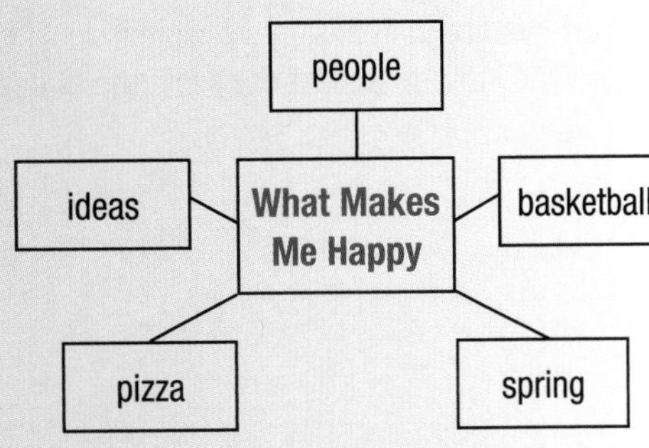

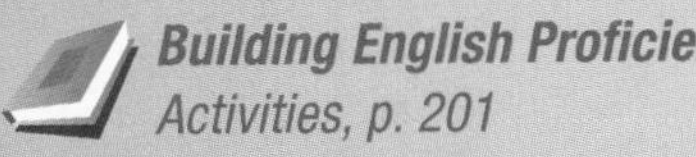
Building English Proficiency
Activities, p. 201

After Reading

MAKING CONNECTIONS

1. Possible response: "Money can't buy happiness."

2. Most students will probably choose Aunt Tee, because she enjoys life and has friends. However, some students may choose wealth over happiness.

3. Possible response: because she proved that she could manage rich white people's affairs as well if not better than they could

4. Possible response: Aunt Tee's apartment is small, neat, quaint, and uncomfortable; the Bel Air ranch house is huge, lavish, impersonal, and uncomfortable.

5. Some students may find the tone instructive or even preachy. Others will consider it friendly, personal, and concerned: the phrase *"My dears"* draws the reader in as a friend, and the "lesson" seems an effort to improve the reader's way of life without preaching any concrete dogma.

6. Possible response: Yes, because Aunt Tee is considerate and open to their request. They are comfortable enough to state their wishes clearly.

7. Possible response: By gaining enough material success to enjoy a comfortable lifestyle while filling one's days with noble actions and loving thoughts, it is possible to love both well and good.

8. Students are probably familiar with public figures from the fields of sports and entertainment who were critically unhappy despite their wealth and power. Students may also provide examples of wealthy people who are fulfilled and use their money for worthwhile purposes.

After Reading

Making Connections

Shaping Your Response

1. Aunt Tee's favorite **proverb** belongs in a frame like the one above. With a partner, decide what this proverb might be.
2. Whose child would you rather be—Aunt Tee's or the wealthy couple's? Why?
3. Why do you think Aunt Tee is so proud of having been a live-in housekeeper?

Analyzing the Autobiography

4. Compare these two **settings**: Aunt Tee's apartment and the Bel Air house.
5. Do you find the **tone** of this selection friendly, preachy, or something else? Explain your choice.
6. Do you think that despite their cultural differences, the old couple and Aunt Tee **communicate** effectively? Why or why not?

Extending the Ideas

7. How is it possible to live both well and good?
8. Angelou ends by stating that "Money and power . . . can imprison and inhibit more finally than barred windows and iron chains." What examples can you think of to prove or disprove this statement?

Literary Focus: Irony

What **ironic** comment is the painter making about youth and beauty? Like this picture, the selection "Living Well. Living Good." presents an ironic situation that appears to be one thing but in reality is another. What **situational irony** is Maya Angelou revealing?

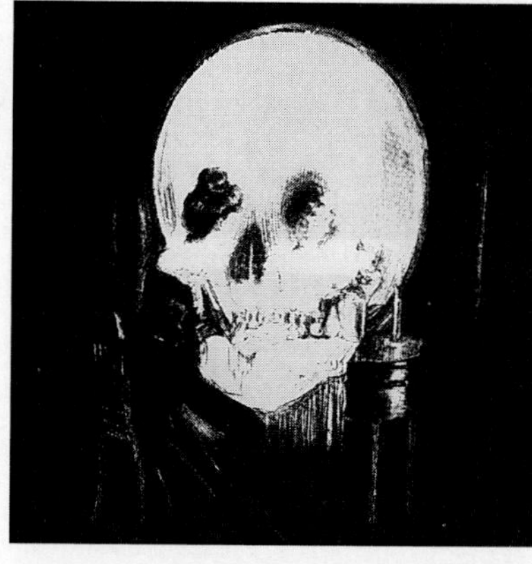

LITERARY FOCUS: IRONY

- The painting illustrates that beauty and youth are short-lived by juxtaposing the woman looking in her vanity mirror against the backdrop of death.
- Situational irony in the selection can be explained as follows: The wealthy employers have bought every possible luxury to give them pleasure. However, they envy the simple pleasure that Aunt Tee and her friends get from playing cards in her modest quarters.

Vocabulary Study

On your paper, write the letter of the most appropriate answer to each item.

commodious
convivial
incur
meticulous
revelry

1. Which of the following would most likely be *commodious*?
   a. trees **b.** food **c.** automobiles **d.** snow
2. In which job would it be most important to be *convivial?*
   a. accountant **b.** research scientist **c.** restaurant host **d.** coal miner
3. You could be said to *incur* all of the following, with the exception of which item?
   a. anger **b.** debt **c.** disapproval **d.** bad weather
4. If you are *meticulous,* you are ____.
   a. careless **b.** awkward **c.** very careful **d.** humorous
5. In which setting would you most likely find *revelry?*
   a. a funeral parlor **b.** a wedding reception **c.** a factory **d.** a library

Expressing Your Ideas

Writing Choices

Writer's Notebook Update Before reading this selection, you wrote down key words or phrases from a story told by a relative or friend. Now, summarize that story in a paragraph.

Passing the Torch Aunt Tee has decided to retire. Write the **job description** she would leave for her successor.

Dream House Aunt Tee describes her Bel Air employers' house as being a fourteen-room ranch house. Imagine that you are a real-estate agent charged with listing the house for sale. Write a **listing sheet** describing some of the rooms and emphasizing any features that would appeal to a prospective buyer.

Other Options

Good Times and Bad Working in groups of two or three, find news stories from either television or newspapers that illustrate Angelou's belief that life is an "ongoing adventure." Make a **collage** of the headlines of these stories. If the story comes from television, make up your own headline.

Blues in the Night Divide into groups, one for each of the following decades: the '20s, '30s, '40s, and '50s. Find a **recording** of a popular song or two from that decade, one that Aunt Tee might have danced to. Play it in class, and ask classmates whether or not they think that music like this could be popular today.

VOCABULARY STUDY

1. c
2. c
3. d
4. c
5. b

Unit 4 Resource Book
Vocabulary, p. 11
Vocabulary Test, p.14

WRITING CHOICES

Writer's Notebook Update

Would you say that the story you summarized contained a lesson? Following Angelou's model, write a brief commentary about what you learned from your elder's story.

Passing the Torch

Explain that a job description succinctly outlines all of the duties and responsibilities involved in a work position.

Dream House

Encourage students to creatively elaborate on the details provided about the house and its neighborhood. Remind them to include their estimated asking price!

Selection Test

Unit 4 Resource Book
pp. 15–16

OTHER OPTIONS

Good Times and Bad

Have students compare the number of positive headlines to the number of negative headlines. Discuss the media's strategy for choosing which "ongoing adventures" to report to the public.

Blues in the Night

Encourage students to solicit the participation of their relatives and family friends to complete this project. Have them include international recordings in this survey if possible.

Before Reading

Building Background

- Encourage students who agree with Dillard's observation to share examples of writers who seem to follow this mold (the Brontë sisters, Emily Dickinson, C. S. Lewis). Students may offer names of writers who don't fit this stereotype.
- Students may answer that as we grow older, we grow more reserved, less spontaneous.

Literary Focus

Point out that **suspense** is more effective when the writer has cultivated the reader's emotional connection to the characters involved in the conflict.

Writer's Notebook

Explain to students that after reading the selection, they will be asked to write briefly of the actions or descriptions that influenced their rating for each category.

More About Annie Dillard

Since Dillard claimed that she could not listen unless she was drawing, one of her high school teachers let her set up an easel and paint during class.

Other works by the author include:

- *Teach a Stone to Talk* (essays), (1982)
- *The Living,* (1992)

Before Reading

from An American Childhood

by Annie Dillard USA

Annie Dillard
born 1945

"I grew up in Pittsburgh in the 1950s, in a house full of comedians, reading books," says Annie Dillard. A voracious reader and keen observer of nature, Dillard wrote, "The visible world turned me curious to books; the books propelled me reeling back to the world." In 1975, she published *Pilgrim at Tinker Creek,* a work which combines her "penchant for quirky facts" with meditations on both the natural and the spiritual worlds. The book won a Pulitzer prize, a rare achievement for a first work. Other works include her autobiography, *An American Childhood,* from which the following excerpt is taken.

Building Background

Life Sentences In her book, *A Writing Life,* Annie Dillard muses about writers and the importance of childhood:

> It should surprise no one that the life of the writer—such as it is—is colorless to the point of sensory deprivation. Many writers do little else but sit in small rooms recalling the real world. This explains why so many books describe the author's childhood. A writer's childhood may well have been the occasion of his only firsthand experience.

Do you agree with Dillard's observation that childhood may be the "only firsthand experience"? What about growing older might make life's experiences seem less direct?

Literary Focus

Suspense In both fiction and nonfiction, the element of **suspense** impels us to read on. Will the detective find the murderer? Will the avalanche trap the skier? Will the good guys defeat the bad ones? In this selection from her autobiography, Dillard leads both readers and an unidentified man on a merry chase, using suspense to build interest.

Writer's Notebook

Is She a Ten? The incident Dillard describes occurred when she was seven. As you read the selection, rate qualities the young Dillard possesses on a scale of 1 (lowest) to 10 (highest).

Quality	Rating
Sheer Nerve	
Physical Endurance	
Imagination	
Sense of Fairness	

SUPPORT MATERIALS OVERVIEW

Unit 4 Resource Book
- Graphic Organizer, p. 17
- Study Guide, p.18
- Vocabulary, p. 19
- Grammar, p. 20
- Alternate Check Test, p. 21
- Vocabulary Test, p. 22
- Selection Test, pp. 23–24

Building English Proficiency
- Literature Summaries
- Activities, p. 202

Reading, Writing & Grammar SkillBook
- Grammar, Usage, and Mechanics, pp. 271–272

Technology
- Audiotape 11, Side B
- Personal Journal Software
- Custom Literature Database: For an interesting comparison of childhood experiences, see "Amy's Valley of Humiliation" by Louisa May Alcott on the database.
- Test Generator Software

An American Childhood

Annie Dillard

Some boys taught me to play football. This was fine sport. You thought up a new strategy for every play and whispered it to the others. You went out for a pass, fooling everyone. Best, you got to throw yourself mightily at someone's running legs. Either you brought him down or you hit the ground flat out on your chin, with your arms empty before you. It was all or nothing. If you hesitated in fear, you would miss and get hurt: You would take a hard fall while the kid got away, or you would get kicked in the face while the kid got away. But if you flung yourself wholeheartedly at the back of his knees—if you gathered and joined body and soul and pointed them diving fearlessly—then you likely wouldn't get hurt, and you'd stop the ball. Your fate, and your team's score, depended on your concentration and courage. Nothing girls did could compare with it.

Boys welcomed me at baseball, too, for I had, through enthusiastic practice, what was weirdly known as a boy's arm. In winter, in the snow, there was neither baseball nor football, so the boys and I threw snow-

This photograph captures some of the excitement of a snowball fight. What qualities of nature might be conveyed by the looming shadow of a tree and pieces of snow spraying on impact?

During Reading

Selection Objectives

- to explore the rewards and the hazards of a fair fight
- to analyze and experience the power of suspense
- to understand and practice the use of the dash
- to examine the conventions of autobiography

Unit 4 Resource Book
Graphic Organizer, p. 17
Study Guide, p. 18

Theme Link

A thrilling chase convinces a young girl that if a goal is worth fighting for, the passion of pursuit can be as important as the results of the battle.

Vocabulary Preview

embark, set out
impel, cause to move forward
improvise, make up on the spur of the moment
labyrinth, a confusing, complicated passage or arrangement
perfunctorily, mechanically, indifferently
redundant, not needed, extra
translucent, letting light through without being transparent

Students can add the words and definitions to their Writer's Notebooks.

SELECTION SUMMARY

An American Childhood

The narrator recalls her childhood as a tomboy, and goes on to describe an incident that occurred while she was throwing snowballs at cars with some neighborhood boys. An angry driver jumps from his car and chases the surprised children. The children split up, and the narrator and another boy become the sole objects of the man's pursuit. After a fierce chase, he finally captures them and punishes them with an anti-climactic lecture. The narrator concludes with an imaginative commentary on the glories of this unlikely battle.

*For summaries in other languages, see the **Building English Proficiency** book.*

Responses to Caption Question The tree's shadow suggests the mystery power, and strength of nature. The spray of snow conveys its mutability and beauty.

1 Reading/Thinking Skills
Draw Conclusions

Question Do you think the narrator's parents approved of Billy Paul and Mackie Kean? *(No. They come from a poorer area and are street smart.)*

2 Literary Element
Repetition

Question How does the author use repetition to convey the effort in making an iceball? *(The repetition of the word* perfect *conveys the level of concentration and enthusiasm a child can invest in creating an iceball.)*

3 Literary Focus
Foreshadowing and Suspense

The driver is so intent upon catching the children that he doesn't take precautions to secure his car.

Questions What does this clue suggest about the nature of the children's opponent? *(He is quick-tempered, agile, and impulsive. He is serious, possibly dangerous, and not to be shaken off easily.)*

4 Literary Element
Point of View

Point out that though the story is told through a youngster's eyes, the attitudes are those of an adult.

balls at passing cars. I got in trouble throwing snowballs, and have seldom been happier since.

On one weekday morning after Christmas, six inches of new snow had just fallen. We were standing up to our boot tops in snow on a front yard on trafficked Reynolds Street, waiting for cars. The cars traveled Reynolds Street slowly and evenly; they were targets all but wrapped in red ribbons, cream puffs. We couldn't miss.

I was seven; the boys were eight, nine, and ten. The oldest two Fahey boys were there—Mikey and Peter—polite blond boys who lived near me on Lloyd Street, and who already had four brothers and sisters. My parents approved Mikey and Peter Fahey. Chickie McBride was
1 there, a tough kid, and Billy Paul and Mackie Kean too, from across Reynolds, where the boys grew up dark and furious, grew up skinny, knowing, and skilled. We had all drifted from our houses that morning looking for action, and had found it here on Reynolds Street.

It was cloudy but cold. The cars' tires laid behind them on the snowy street a complex trail of beige chunks like crenellated[1] castle walls. I had stepped on some earlier; they squeaked. We could have wished for more traffic. When a car came, we all popped it one. In the intervals between cars we reverted to the natural solitude of children.

I started making an iceball—a perfect iceball, from perfectly white snow, perfectly spher-
2 ical, and squeezed perfectly translucent[2] so no snow remained all the way through. (The Fahey boys and I considered it unfair actually to throw an iceball at somebody, but it had been known to happen.)

I had just embarked[3] on the iceball project when we heard tire chains come clanking from afar. A black Buick was moving toward us down the street. We all spread out, banged together some regular snowballs, took aim, and, when the Buick drew nigh, fired.

A soft snowball hit the driver's windshield right before the driver's face. It made a smashed star with a hump in the middle.

Often, of course, we hit our target, but this time, the only time in all of life, the car pulled over and stopped. Its wide black door opened; 3
a man got out of it, running. He didn't even close the car door.

He ran after us, and we ran away from him, up the snowy Reynolds sidewalk. At the corner, I looked back; incredibly, he was still after us. He was in city clothes: a suit and tie, street shoes. Any normal adult would have quit, having sprung us into flight and made his point. This man was 4
gaining on us. He was a thin man, all action. All of a sudden, we were running for our lives.

Wordless, we split up. We were on our turf; we could lose ourselves in the neighborhood backyards, everyone for himself. I paused and considered. Everyone had vanished except Mikey Fahey, who was just rounding the corner of a yellow brick house. Poor Mikey, I trailed him. The driver of the Buick sensibly picked the two of us to follow. The man apparently had all day.

He chased Mikey and me around the yellow house and up a backyard path we knew by heart: under a low tree, up a bank, through a hedge, down some snowy steps, and across the grocery store's delivery driveway. We smashed through a gap in another hedge, entered a scruffy backyard and ran around its back porch and tight between houses to Edgerton Avenue; we ran across Edgerton to an alley and up our own sliding woodpile to the Halls' front yard; he kept coming. We ran up Lloyd Street and wound through mazy backyards toward the steep hilltop at Willard and Lang.

He chased us silently, block after block. He chased us silently over picket fences, through thorny hedges, between houses, around

1. **crenellated** (kren′l āt əd), *adj.* having squared-off notches at the top.
2. **translucent** (tran slü′snt), *adj.* letting light through without being transparent.
3. **embark** (em bärk′), *v.* set out.

MINI-LESSON: GRAMMAR
Using the Dash

Teach Explain that the dash can be used to indicate a brief explanation; for example, on page 475: "But if you flung yourself wholeheartedly at the back of his knees—if you gathered and joined body and soul and pointed them diving fearlessly—then you wouldn't likely get hurt. . . ."

The dash can also prepare for a list, a restatement, an elaboration, or an abrupt shift in thought, as on page 476: "I started making an iceball—a perfect iceball, from perfectly white snow. . . ."

Activity Idea Have students write a simple sentence (with no dashes) about an event they remember from childhood. Then have them insert a dash and add a phrase that elaborates on a word or idea. Have them compare and contrast the two sentences to understand the power of the dash.

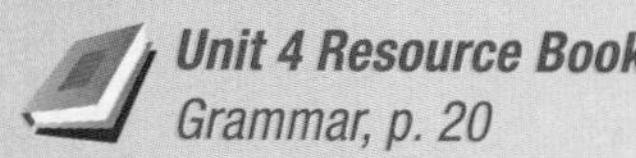
Unit 4 Resource Book
Grammar, p. 20

garbage cans, and across streets. Every time I glanced back, choking for breath, I expected he would have quit. He must have been as breathless as we were. His jacket strained over his body. It was an immense discovery, pounding into my hot head with every sliding, joyous step, that this ordinary adult evidently knew what I thought
5 only children who trained at football knew: that you have to fling yourself at what you're doing, you have to point yourself, forget yourself, aim, dive.

Mikey and I had nowhere to go, in our own neighborhood or out of it, but away from this man who was chasing us. He impelled[4] us forward; we compelled him to follow our route. The air was cold; every breath tore my throat. We kept running, block after block; we kept improvising,[5] backyard after backyard, running a frantic course and choosing it simultaneously, failing always to find small places or hard places to slow him down, and discovering always, exhilarated, dismayed, that only bare speed could save us—for he would never give up, this man—and we were losing speed.

He chased us through the backyard labyrinths[6] of ten blocks before he caught us by our jackets. He caught us and we all stopped.

We three stood staggering, half-blinded, coughing, in an obscure hilltop backyard: a man in his twenties, a boy, a girl. He had released our jackets, our pursuer, our captor, our hero: He knew we weren't going anywhere. We all played by the rules. Mikey and I unzipped our jackets. I pulled off my sopping mittens. Our tracks multiplied in the backyard's new snow. We had been breaking new snow all morning. We didn't look at each other. I was cherishing my excitement. The man's lower pants legs were wet; his cuffs were full of snow, and there was a prow of snow beneath them on his shoes and socks. Some trees bordered the little flat backyard, some
6 messy winter trees. There was no one around: a clearing in a grove, and we the only players.

It was a long time before he could speak. I had some difficulty at first recalling why we were there. My lips felt swollen; I couldn't see out of the sides of my eyes; I kept coughing.

"You stupid kids," he began perfunctorily.[7]

We listened perfunctorily indeed, if we listened at all, for the chewing out was redundant,[8] a mere formality, and beside the point. The point was that he had chased us passionately without giving up, and so he had caught us. Now he came down to earth. I wanted the glory to last forever. 7

But how could the glory have lasted forever? We could have run through every backyard in North America until we got to Panama. But when he trapped us at the lip of the Panama Canal, what precisely could he have done to prolong the drama of the chase and cap its glory? I brooded about this for the next few years. He could only have fried Mikey Fahey and me in boiling oil, say, or dismembered us piecemeal, or staked us to anthills. None of which I really wanted, and none of which any adult was likely to do, even in the spirit of fun. He could only chew us out there in the Panamanian jungle, after months or years of exalting pursuit. He could only begin, "You stupid kids," and continue in his ordinary Pittsburgh accent with his normal righteous anger and the usual common sense.

If in that snowy backyard the driver of the black Buick had cut off our heads, Mikey's and mine, I could have died happy, for nothing has required so much of me since as being chased all over Pittsburgh in the middle of winter—running terrified, exhausted—by this sainted, skinny, furious red-headed man who wished to have a word with us. I don't know how he found his way back to his car.

---

4. impel (im pel′), *v.* cause to move forward.
5. improvise (im′prə vīz), *v.* make up on the spur of the moment.
6. labyrinth (lab′ə rinth′), *n.* a confusing, complicated passage or arrangement.
7. perfunctorily (pər fungk′tər ə lē), *adv.* mechanically; indifferently.
8. redundant (ri dun′dənt), *adj.* not needed; extra.

5 Reader's Response
Making Personal Connections

Questions

- What does the narrator consider to be the secret to success? *(to throw yourself fearlessly at your goal without hesitation)*
- Could this be a useful strategy in your life? *(Encourage students to be creative as they consider challenges they have faced.)*

6 Literary Focus
Setting and Suspense

Question How does the setting contribute to the rising suspense? *(The three stand alone in an empty clearing, exposed and isolated.)*

7 Literary Element
Characterization

Questions

- How does the narrator view the driver after the chase? *(She is disappointed that after his fantastic chase he is just an ordinary man who scolds them.)*
- What does this reaction reveal about the narrator? *(She has a vivid imagination and a taste for adventure.)*

Check Test

1. What sport is described in the first paragraph? *(football)*
2. Where does the snowball hit the man's car? *(the windshield on the driver's side)*
3. What is the driver wearing?*(a business suit)*
4. Who is the narrator with when she is caught? *(Mikey Fahey)*
5. What does the man do to the children when he catches them? *(He lectures them.)*

Unit 4 Resource Book
Alternate Check Test, p. 21

BUILDING ENGLISH PROFICIENCY

Exploring Word Choices

At the end of the first column on page 476, the narrator introduces her antagonist as *the driver.* Invite students to explore other names for this character.

Activity Ideas

- Have partners or small groups work through the rest of this account, jotting down other names and descriptions for this man. (Examples: *a thin man, all action; a man in his twenties; our pursuer, our captor, our hero)*
- Discuss how the different word choices express the narrator's admiration for him.
- Invite students to supply their own labels for this man.

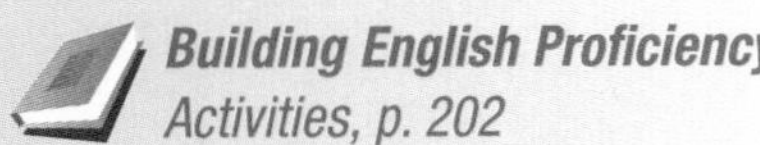

Building English Proficiency
Activities, p. 202

After Reading

MAKING CONNECTIONS

1. Possible response: because it feels thrilling and dangerous. Some students may answer that in their cultural context this kind of mischief would never occur.

2. Possible responses: Some students may answer that they would be upset about the man's extreme reaction. Others may say they would punish their child for throwing snowballs at cars.

3. Students who feel his reaction was justified may point out that the snowball temporarily blocked his vision of the road, or that this was a serious man committed to settling a score. Others may feel that his zeal was overly dramatic for the situation.

4. The cars were easy targets and provided a "delicious" diversion for the children.

5. Possible responses: "beige chunks like crenellated castle walls;" "dismembered us piecemeal, or staked us to anthills."

6. The fact that she plays with boys, loves football, and throws snowballs at cars tells the reader that she is a an independent, tough tomboy.

7. Possible responses: It shows that her fantasy of the ultimate chase scene involves outlandish and barbarous consequences.

8. Some students may account for his change by citing Dillard's observation about adulthood in Building Background, page 474. He now wears a suit and owns a car. He probably feels that the children were threatening his safety and/or his property.

9. Possible responses: Goals should be pursued wholeheartedly. Sometimes the passion of pursuit is more important and exciting than the actual attainment of a goal.

After Reading

Making Connections

Shaping Your Response

1. Why do you think some children throw snowballs at cars?
2. As the girl's parent, what would be your response to this incident? Why?
3. Do you think the skinny man was overreacting, or was he justified in his passionate chase? Explain.

Analyzing the Autobiography

4. In the third paragraph, cars are described as "targets all but wrapped in red ribbons, cream puffs." What do these **metaphors** suggest?
5. Mention some interesting or unexpected **images** that Dillard uses.
6. How does her choice of activities and playmates help **characterize** the narrator?
7. In the last two paragraphs, how does **hyperbole**, or exaggeration, emphasize Dillard's delight in the chase?

Extending the Ideas

8. The driver, "a young man in his twenties," might have been a snowball thrower himself as a child. How would you account for his change of behavior and attitude?
9. What **theme** or lesson about life do you think this incident illustrates?

Literary Focus: Suspense

Dillard uses the following techniques to create suspense:

- *exaggeration:* "He could have fried Mikey Fahey and me in boiling oil."
- *powerful imagery:* ". . . every breath tore my throat."
- *repetition:* "We kept running, block after block. . . ."
- *accumulated details:* "He chased us silently over picket fences, through thorny hedges, between houses, around garbage cans, and across streets."

Find another example of each of these techniques in the selection.

LITERARY FOCUS: SUSPENSE

Possible responses:

- "All of a sudden, we were running for our lives."
- "His jacket strained over his body."
- "We kept improvising, backyard after backyard."
- "He chased Mikey and me around the yellow house and up a backyard path we knew by heart: under a low tree, up a bank, through a hedge, down some snowy steps, and across the grocery store's delivery driveway."

Vocabulary Study

On your paper, write the word that best completes each sentence. You will not use all of the words.

embark
impel
improvise
labyrinth
perfunctorily
redundant
translucent

1. The narrator and her friends could easily ____ games on a snowy day.
2. Although they made ____ iceballs, they threw only soft snowballs at cars.
3. Why did the driver ____ on a chase, even though he wasn't dressed for it?
4. Mikey and the girl led the driver through a ____ of streets, alleys, and yards.
5. Once he caught them, the driver scolded them ____.

Expressing Your Ideas

Writing Choices

Writer's Notebook Update In your notebook, you rated some of the narrator's qualities. Add any other traits that you think characterize her. Then, focusing on these qualities, write a paragraph discussing whether or not she is someone you'd like for a kid sister.

Cliffhanger Hollywood once made short serials to be shown at Saturday matinees. Each episode ended suspensefully, with the hero or heroine in a tight spot—tied to the railroad tracks or hanging from a cliff. Write a **summary** of a scene in which a protagonist is in a dangerous situation. Use some of the techniques that Dillard uses to create suspense, as well as a few vocabulary words.

Other Options

Ditch 'Im Draw a **map** of the chase scene based on details of the story, or make a model of the neighborhood and point out where events occurred.

Zoom In Many movies include a memorable chase scene. With a partner, screen one such movie that would make appropriate viewing for the class. Get your teacher's permission to show at least the chase scene in class and afterward to describe in a **film chat** how techniques such as special effects, music, and camera shots are used to create suspense.

Speak One's Piece Once the driver catches Mikey and the narrator, he begins to talk to them. He starts, "You stupid kids. . . ." What do you think he says next? Be the driver and without swearing finish his angry **monologue**, acting it out for the class.

VOCABULARY STUDY

1. improvise
2. translucent
3. embark
4. labyrinth
5. perfunctorily

Unit 4 Resource Book
Vocabulary, p. 19
Vocabulary Test, p. 22

Writing Choices

Writer's Notebook Update

Have students cite examples from the story to support the qualities that they ascribe to the narrator. Make sure they understand they are required to make judgments about desirable qualities in a sibling.

Cliffhanger

You might suggest that students draw a Details Web with suspense techniques to organize their writing tools. They might also use some of Dillard's stylistic devices, such as accumulative details and spatial juxtapositions.

Selection Test

Unit 4 Resource Book
pp. 23–24

OTHER OPTIONS

Zoom In

Have students take notes on the chase scenes in order to compare and contrast the style and technique of the various directors. Have students decide which scene is the most effective, supporting the decision with formal evidence.

Speak One's Piece

Acting Hints: Remind students that the driver is as exhausted as the children at this point. The monologue should reflect that he is out of breath and weary.

Before Reading

Building Background

Share information about the British East India Company. Chartered in 1600, its merchants exploited India's cheap labor and natural resources, overpowering rulers of the fragmented Indian aristocracy. Though Britain's infiltration was gradual, India officially lost its sovereignty in the Indian War of 1857.

Literary Focus

Explain that the term **stereotype** comes from a French word for a solid printing block cast from a mold. Discuss connections between the printing device and the literary term. Invite students to make a chart of stereotypes from TV.

TV Stereotypes
wild, rebellious teenager hard-boiled detective rich playgirl

Writer's Notebook

Encourage students to include at least one character in their account, and to mention a distinctive trait that establishes his or her individuality.

More About Rama Rau

In 1939, when the outbreak of World War II prevented Rama Rau from continuing school in England, she returned to India, meeting leaders such as Nehru and Gandhi.

Before Reading

By Any Other Name

by Santha Rama Rau India

Santha Rama Rau
born 1923

At the age of six, Santha Rama Rau (sän′thä rä′mä rou) left India when her father, a diplomat, was sent to England. When she returned to India ten years later, the first thing her grandmother said to her was, "My dear child, where in India will we find a husband tall enough for you?" At Wellesley College in Massachusetts, Rama Rau began writing *Home to India* (1945), a book about her rediscovery of India. Rama Rau's works, which range from novels, biographies, short stories, travel books, and autobiography to a cookbook, present the dual perspective of someone equally at home in the East and the West.

Building Background

Expanding Empire The first English people to settle in India were traders interested in exporting spices and silk. As the picture suggests, local princes initially welcomed the English, along with the wealth and military power they represented. By 1860, however, England controlled India and made it a colony, part of the British Empire. The English established a judicial system and built factories, railroads, and—as the following selection indicates—schools.

Literary Focus

Stereotypes Broad generalized ideas about people and situations are called **stereotypes.** Real people are rarely one-dimensional or stereotypical. All blondes are not dizzy; all librarians are not prim; all used-car salesmen are not dishonest. As you read "By Any Other Name," be on the alert for stereotypes.

Writer's Notebook

First Impressions In your notebook, list one pleasant and one unpleasant association you have with school. Add some vivid images and details to describe each association.

SUPPORT MATERIALS OVERVIEW

Unit 4 Resource Book
- Graphic Organizer, p. 25
- Study Guide, p. 26
- Vocabulary, p. 27
- Grammar, p. 28
- Alternate Check Test, p. 29
- Vocabulary Test, p. 30
- Selection Test, pp. 31–32

Building English Proficiency
- Literature Summaries
- Activities, p. 203

Reading, Writing & Grammar SkillBook
- Grammar, Usage, and Mechanics, pp. 183–184

Technology
- Audiotape 12, Side A
- Personal Journal Software
- Custom Literature Database: For another autobiographical account of school experiences see "My Struggle for an Education" by Booker T. Washington on the database.
- Test Generator Software

By Any Other Name

Santha Rama Rau

This title comes from Shakespeare's tragedy, Romeo and Juliet. *When Juliet learns that Romeo is a Montague and, thus, an enemy of her family, she cries: "What's in a name? That which we call a rose by any other name would smell as sweet."*

At the Anglo-Indian[1] day school in Zorinabad[2] to which my sister and I were sent when she was eight and I was five and a half, they changed our names. On the first day of school, a hot, windless morning of a north Indian September, we stood in the headmistress's study and she said, "Now you're the *new* girls. What are your names?"

My sister answered for us. "I am Premila, and she"—nodding in my direction—"is Santha."

1 The headmistress had been in India, I suppose, fifteen years or so, but she still smiled her helpless inability to cope with Indian names. Her rimless half-glasses glittered, and the precarious[3] bun on the top of her head trembled as she shook her head. "Oh, my dears, those are much too hard for me. Suppose we give you pretty English names. Wouldn't that be more jolly? Let's see, now—Pamela for you, I think." She shrugged in a baffled way at my sister. "That's as close as I can get. And for *you*," she said to me, "how about Cynthia? Isn't that nice?"

My sister was always less easily intimidated[4] than I was, and while she kept a stubborn silence, I said, "Thank you," in a very tiny voice.

We had been sent to that school because my father, among his responsibilities as an officer of the civil service, had a tour of duty to perform in the villages around that steamy little provincial town, where he had his headquarters at that time. He used to make his shorter inspection tours on horseback, and a week before, in the stale heat of a typically postmonsoon[5] day, we had waved goodby to him and a little procession—an assistant, a secretary, two bearers, and the man to look after the bedding rolls and luggage. They rode away through our large garden, still bright green from the rains, and we turned back into the twilight of the house and the sound of fans whispering in every room.

Up to then, my mother had refused to send Premila to school in the British-run establishments of that time, because, she used to say, "you can bury a dog's tail for seven years and it still comes out curly, and you can take a Britisher away from his home for a lifetime and he still remains insular." The examinations and degrees from entirely Indian schools were not, in those days, considered valid. In my case, the question had never come up, and probably never would have come up if Mother's extraordinary good health had not broken down. For the first time in my life, she was not able to continue the lessons she had been giving us every

---

1. **Anglo-Indian,** relating to people either of English birth who live in India, or of mixed English and Indian parentage.
2. **Zorinabad,** a city in northern India.
3. precarious (pri ker′ē əs), *adj.* not safe or secure; uncertain.
4. intimidate (in tim′ə dāt), *v.* frighten.
5. **postmonsoon,** a dry spell. From April to October, a seasonal wind called a monsoon brings rain to southern Asia.

During Reading

Selection Objectives

- to analyze a child's encounter with prejudice and ignorance at school
- to identify the negative influence of stereotypes
- to practice using subject and object pronouns
- to examine the historical and political impact of autobiography

Unit 4 Resource Book
Graphic Organizer, p. 25
Study Guide, p. 26

Theme Link

This autobiographical account of two young Indian sisters' reactions to overt racial prejudice at their new school explores the theme "Worth Fighting For."

Vocabulary Preview

intimidate, frighten
peevishness, irritability; crossness
precarious, not safe or secure; uncertain
tepid, lukewarm
wizened, dried up; withered

Students can add the words and definitions to their Writer's Notebooks.

1 Literary Focus
Stereotypes

- Point out that since belief in racial stereotypes often stems from fear and ignorance, exposure to the cultural traditions and individual humanity of the targeted racial group can dispel prejudice.
- The teacher's refusal to learn Indian names conveys her resistance to appreciating the Indian children's culture and individuality.

SELECTION SUMMARY

By Any Other Name

Santha, a young Indian girl, and her eight-year-old sister, Premila, have recently moved to a provincial town in Northern India. On their first day at a British school, the headmistress changes their names to their approximate British versions: Pamela and Cynthia. Unscathed by the continuing racial conflicts that she encounters at school, Santha happily pursues her childish pleasures. Premila, however, angered when a teacher says that Indians cheat, takes Santha and leaves school. Their mother supports Premila's act of protest. Although Santha is aware of the racial incident, she pretends that "it had all happened to a girl called Cynthia.

For summaries in other languages, see the ***Building English Proficiency*** *book.*

2 Multicultural Note

Hindi and Krishna

- Hindi, a dialect spoken in Northern India, is related to Sanskrit, the ancient language in which sacred texts of Hinduism were written.
- According to tradition, Lord Krishna was the last earthly incarnation of Vishnu, a major Hindu deity. Many Hindus believe that he lived in India over 5,000 years ago as a cowherd who played a rustic flute. In India, tales of Lord Krishna's childhood are still enjoyed in many forms, including songs and folk tales.

3 Reading/Thinking Skills

Compare and Contrast

Question What does the contrast between the traditional Indian veranda and the British adaptation imply about the relationship between the two cultures? *(Possible response: It shows that the British have willfully imposed inappropriate traditions, developed in distant England, onto the Indian culture, whose own traditions work more effectively in this climate.)*

4 Literary Element

Symbolism

Point out that the British have recreated the structure of a British school in a vastly foreign terrain. The lizard might symbolize the survival of the indigenous world the British have tried to displace.

2 morning. So our Hindi books were put away, the stories of the Lord Krishna[6] as a little boy were left in midair, and we were sent to the Anglo-Indian school.

The first day of school is still, when I think of it, a remarkable one. At that age, if one's name is changed, one develops a curious form of dual personality. I remember having a certain detached and disbelieving concern in the actions of "Cynthia," but certainly no responsibility. Accordingly, I followed the thin, erect back of the headmistress down the veranda to my classroom feeling, at most, a passing interest in what was going to happen to me in this strange, new atmosphere of School.

3 The building was Indian in design, with wide verandas opening onto a central courtyard, but Indian verandas are usually whitewashed, with stone floors. These, in the tradition of British schools, were painted dark brown and had matting on the floors. It gave a feeling of extra intensity to the heat.

I suppose there were about a dozen Indian children in the school—which contained perhaps forty children in all—and four of them were in my class. They were all sitting at the back of the room, and I went to join them. I sat next to a small, solemn girl who didn't smile at me. She had long, glossy-black braids and wore a cotton dress, but she still kept on her Indian jewelry—a gold chain around her neck, thin gold bracelets, and tiny ruby studs in her ears. Like most Indian children, she had a rim of black kohl[7] around her eyes. The cotton dress should have looked strange, but all I could think of was that I should ask my mother if I couldn't wear a dress to school, too, instead of my Indian clothes.

I can't remember too much about the proceedings in class that day, except for the beginning. The teacher pointed to me and asked me to stand up. "Now, dear, tell the class your name."

I said nothing.

"Come along," she said, frowning slightly. "What's your name, dear?"

"I don't know," I said finally.

The English children in the front of the class—there were about eight or ten of them—giggled and twisted around in their chairs to look at me. I sat down quickly and opened my eyes very wide, hoping in that way to dry them off. The little girl with the braids put out her hand and very lightly touched my arm. She still didn't smile.

Most of that morning I was rather bored. I looked briefly at the children's drawings pinned to the wall, and then concentrated on a lizard clinging to the ledge of the 4
high, barred window behind the teacher's head. Occasionally it would shoot out its long yellow tongue for a fly, and then it would rest, with its eyes closed and its belly palpitating, as though it were swallowing several times quickly. The lessons were mostly concerned with reading and writing and simple numbers—things that my mother had already taught me—and I paid very little attention. The teacher wrote on the easel blackboard words like *bat* and *cat,* which seemed babyish to me; only *apple* was new and incomprehensible.

When it was time for the lunch recess, I followed the girl with the braids out onto the veranda. There the children from the other classes were assembled. I saw Premila at once and ran over to her, as she had charge of our lunchbox. The children were all opening packages and sitting down to eat sandwiches. Premila and I were the only ones who had Indian food—thin wheat chapatties,[8] some vegetable curry, and a bottle of buttermilk. Premila thrust half of it into my hand and whispered fiercely that I should go and sit with my class, because that was what the others seemed to be doing.

6. **Lord Krishna,** one of the most widely worshiped of the Hindu gods.
7. **kohl** (kōl), *n.* a metallic powder used to darken the eyelids and lashes.
8. **chapatty** (chə pä′tē), *n.* thin griddle cake of unleavened bread, eaten in northern India.

MINI-LESSON: GRAMMAR

Using Subject and Object Pronouns

Teach Explain that when a pronoun is the subject of a verb, it must be in the *nominative* case. When a pronoun is the object of a verb, it must be in the *objective* case.

Have students analyze the italicized pronouns in the following sentences:

They were all sitting at the back of the room, and *I* went to join *them.*
I sat next to a small, solemn girl who didn't smile at *me.*

Questions

- Which pronouns function as subjects? *(They, I)*
- Which pronouns function as objects? *(them, me)*

Activity Ideas

- Have students write sentences using the following pronouns: *I, he, she, we, they, me, him, her, us, them.*
- Have them identify the case of each pronoun after they have written the sentence.

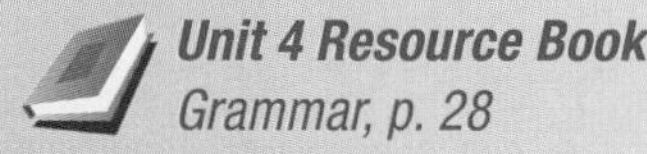

Unit 4 Resource Book
Grammar, p. 28

These Indian girls might be on their way to school. Explain how this photograph compares to the mental image you have of the sisters from descriptions in the story.

The enormous black eyes of the little Indian girl from my class looked at my food longingly, so I offered her some. But she only shook her head and plowed her way solemnly through her sandwiches.

5 I was very sleepy after lunch, because at home we always took a siesta. It was usually a pleasant time of day, with the bedroom darkened against the harsh afternoon sun, the drifting off into sleep with the sound of Mother's voice reading a story in one's mind, and, finally, the shrill, fussy voice of the ayah[9] waking one for tea.

6 At school, we rested for a short time on low, folding cots on the veranda, and then we were expected to play games. During the hot part of the afternoon we played indoors, and after the shadows had begun to lengthen and the slight breeze of the evening had come up we moved outside to the wide courtyard.

I had never really grasped the system of competitive games. At home, whenever we played tag or guessing games, I was always allowed to "win"—"because," Mother used to tell Premila, "she is the youngest, and we have to allow for that." I had often heard her say it, and it seemed quite reasonable to me, but the result was that I had no clear idea of what "winning" meant.

When we played twos-and-threes that afternoon at school, in accordance with my training, I let one of the small English boys catch me, but was naturally rather puzzled when the other children did not return the courtesy. I ran about

9. **ayah** (ä′yə), *n.* a native maid or nurse in India.

Art Study

Responses to Caption Question
Students may focus on the girls' facial expressions, which suggest a shy determination. Point out that one girl wears an ornate sari and jewelry in the Indian tradition. Their gestures convey a closeness similar to the protective alliance between Santha and Premila. Their age difference appears appropriate.

5 Literary Element
Autobiography and Tone

Questions

- How would you describe the author's tone? *(Possible responses: longing, reminiscent)*
- What does the tone reveal about the author's feelings towards her mother and nurse? *(She loves them very much and cherishes these memories.)*

6 Geographical Note
India's Heat

India is as famous for its intense heat as England is for its fog and drizzle. During this period, British officers often moved their households to cooler "hill stations," usually between March and November. Indians are better adapted to the sun's burning heat, partially due to their natural skin pigmentation. They defend themselves with customs such as the siesta, a nap taken in the hottest part of the day.

BUILDING ENGLISH PROFICIENCY

ESL LEP ELD SAE LD

Analyzing Consequences and Options

Help students understand the result of the girls' behavior as they try to adapt to school. Encourage them to use a graphic organizer like the one shown to record challenges that the sisters face, their response, the significance of that response, and other possible responses.

Building English Proficiency
Activities, p. 203

Problem	Teacher says Indians cheat.
What Premila does	She takes Santha home.
Results	Mother agrees they won't go to that school.
Other options	Mother could meet with school officials.

7 Literary Element
Irony

Questions

- What is ironic about this statement? *(Possible response: Her instinct to let others win was actually a kind and generous approach to playing.)*
- How might the narrator have learned "the spirit of the thing?" *(Possible response: from repeated exposure to Western games, which stress the value of a competitive spirit)*

8 Literary Element
Characterization

Questions

- What is Premila's real motivation for requesting sandwiches instead of Indian food? *(Possible response: She wants to fit in with the other students.)*
- What does her false presentation reveal about her character? *(Possible response: She tries to appear secure and confident but is actually self-conscious and vulnerable.)*

9 Reading/Thinking Skills
Draw Conclusions

Questions To which social class does Santha's family belong? *(upper class)* What details support your conclusion? *(Possible responses: They have servants: a cook, an ayah; their father is a diplomat; they own a car.)*

for what seemed like hours without ever catching anyone, until it was time for school to close. 7 Much later I learned that my attitude was called "not being a good sport," and I stopped allowing myself to be caught, but it was not for years that I really learned the spirit of the thing.

When I saw our car come up to the school gate, I broke away from my classmates and rushed toward it yelling, "Ayah! Ayah!" It seemed like an eternity since I had seen her that morning—a wizened,[10] affectionate figure in her white cotton sari, giving me dozens of urgent and useless instructions on how to be a good girl at school. Premila followed more sedately, and she told me on the way home never to do that again in front of the other children.

When we got home we went straight to Mother's high, white room to have tea with her, and I immediately climbed onto the bed and bounced gently up and down on the springs. Mother asked how we had liked our first day in school. I was so pleased to be home and to have left that peculiar Cynthia behind that I had nothing whatever to say about school, except to ask what *apple* meant. But Premila told Mother about the classes, and added that in her class they had weekly tests to see if they had learned their lessons well.

I asked, "What's a test?"

Premila said, "You're too small to have them. You won't have them in your class for donkey's years." She had learned the expression that day and was using it for the first time. We all laughed enormously at her wit. 8 She also told Mother, in an aside, that we should take sandwiches to school the next day. Not, she said, that *she* minded. But they would be simpler for me to handle.

. . . friendship with the English or Anglo-Indian children was out of the question.

That whole lovely evening I didn't think about school at all. I sprinted barefoot across the lawns with my favorite playmate, the cook's son, to the stream at the end of the garden. We quarreled in our usual way, waded in the tepid[11] water under the lime trees, and waited for the night to bring out the smell of the jasmine. I listened with fascination to his stories of ghosts and demons, until I was too frightened to cross the garden alone in the semi-darkness. The ayah found me, shouted at the cook's son, scolded me, hurried me in to supper—it was an entirely usual, wonderful evening. 9

It was a week later, the day of Premila's first test, that our lives changed rather abruptly. I was sitting at the back of my class, in my usual inattentive way, only half listening to the teacher. I had started a rather guarded friendship with the girl with the braids, whose name turned out to be Nalini (Nancy, in school). The three other Indian children were already fast friends. Even at that age it was apparent to all of us that friendship with the English or Anglo-Indian children was out of the question. Occasionally, during the class, my new friend and I would draw pictures and show them to each other secretly.

The door opened sharply and Premila marched in. At first, the teacher smiled at her in a kindly and encouraging way and said, "Now, you're little Cynthia's sister?"

Premila didn't even look at her. She stood with her feet planted firmly apart and her shoulders rigid, and addressed herself directly to me. "Get up," she said. "We're going home."

I didn't know what had happened, but I was aware that it was a crisis of some sort. I rose obediently and started to walk toward my sister.

10. wizened (wiz′nd), *adj.* dried up; withered.
11. tepid (tep′id), *adj.* lukewarm.

MINI-LESSON: VOCABULARY
Understanding Analogies

Teach Learning how to recognize and understand the connections between word meanings can lead to a deeper understanding of unfamiliar vocabulary.

Apply Explain the concept of word analogies to students, using synonyms and antonyms. For example:

love : hate :: hot : cold

speak : talk :: peaceful : calm

Activity Ideas

- Divide the class into teams. Have each team think of an analogy for each of the following words: *intimidate, peevishness, precarious, tepid, wizened.*
- Have the teams quiz each other with their analogies, leaving the focus words blank.

  For example: __?__ : warm :: chilly : cold

  (Response: tepid)

"Bring your pencils and your notebook," she said.

I went back for them, and together we left the room. The teacher started to say something just as Premila closed the door, but we didn't wait to hear what it was.

In complete silence we left the school grounds and started to walk home. Then I asked Premila what the matter was. All she would say was "We're going home for good."

10 It was a very tiring walk for a child of five and a half, and I dragged along behind Premila with my pencils growing sticky in my hand. I can still remember looking at the dusty hedges, and the tangles of thorns in the ditches by the side of the road, smelling the faint fragrance from the eucalyptus trees and wondering whether we would ever reach home. Occasionally a horse-drawn tonga[12] passed us, and the women, in their pink or green silks, stared at Premila and me trudging along on the side of the road. A few coolies[13] and a line of women carrying baskets of vegetables on their heads smiled at us. But it was nearing the hottest time of day, and the road was almost deserted. I walked more and more slowly, and shouted to Premila, from time to time, "Wait for me!" with increasing peevishness.[14] She spoke to me only once, and that was to tell me to carry my notebook on my head, because of the sun.

When we got to our house the ayah was just taking a tray of lunch into Mother's room. She immediately started a long, worried questioning about what are you children doing back here at this hour of the day.

Mother looked very startled and very concerned, and asked Premila what had happened.

Premila said, "We had our test today, and She made me and the other Indians sit at the back of the room, with a desk between each one."

Mother said, "Why was that, darling?"

"She said it was because Indians cheat," Premila added. "So I don't think we should go back to that school." 11

Mother looked very distant, and was silent a long time. At last she said, "Of course not, darling." She sounded displeased.

We all shared the curry she was having for lunch, and afterward I was sent off to the beautifully familiar bedroom for my siesta. I could hear Mother and Premila talking through the open door.

Mother said, "Do you suppose she understood all that?"

Premila said, "I shouldn't think so. She's a baby."

Mother said, "Well, I hope it won't bother her."

Of course, they were both wrong. I understood it perfectly, and I remember it all very clearly. But I put it happily away, because it had all happened to a girl called Cynthia, and I never was really particularly interested in her.

---

12. **tonga** (ton′gə), *n.* a horse-drawn vehicle with two wheels, commonly used in India.
13. **cooly** (kü′lē), *n.* an unskilled, native laborer in China, India, and elsewhere.
14. **peevishness** (pē′vish nəs), *n.* irritability; crossness.

10 Literary Element
Imagery

Have students notice the strong appeal to the senses in this paragraph.

11 Literary Focus
Stereotypes

Questions

- Do you think the teacher has actually experienced this to be true? *(Probably not. Judging from her past words and behavior, we can assume she is simply repeating a racist generalization.)*
- Why does her position make this broad assumption even more damaging? *(Possible response: She is negatively influencing the minds of children, who are especially impressionable and vulnerable.)*
- What is ironic about this British stereotype of the Indian people? *(Possible response: Historically, it was the British who cheated the Indians out of their sovereign rights.)*

Check Test

1. Why have the two girls never attended a school before? *(Their mother has been teaching them at home.)*

2. What name does the teacher give Santha? *(Cynthia)*

3. Why does Santha sit in the back of the classroom? *(She sees that the other Indian children are sitting there.)*

4. Who is Santha's favorite playmate? *(the cook's son)*

5. Why does Premila leave school? *(Her teacher says that "Indians cheat.")*

Unit 4 Resource Book
Alternate Check Test, p. 29

BUILDING ENGLISH PROFICIENCY

ESL LEP ELD SAE LD

Exploring Motivation

Help students understand how an eight-year-old girl could leave school so boldly, taking her younger sister with her.

Activity Ideas

- Have students list the reasons why they believe Premila chose that response. Urge them to support their ideas with details from the story.
- Ask students to describe what they would have done in Premila's situation. Discuss why those actions would or would not have been likely choices for Premila.

After Reading

MAKING CONNECTIONS

1. Most students will probably say yes, because the narrator states that she understood it perfectly. However, some students may note that young children are usually blind to boundaries of color and social class themselves.

2. Most students will probably answer yes; because it would be too damaging for her to remain in a school that discriminated against her.

3. Some students may say they would have immediately gone to the school and berated the teacher.

4. Possible responses: If they attend a British school, their certificates and degrees will be valid, and they may receive a solid Western education. However, they will be treated like second-class citizens and their cultural backgrounds will be disparaged.

5. Possible response: because the headmistress's renaming her "Cynthia" has confused her

6. The quote suggests people's names do not necessarily reflect who they are. However, the family, culture, and history associated with a person's name do prove to be a crucial factor, not only in *Romeo and Juliet*, but also in this story.

7. Both. The external conflict involves two children experiencing racism in their new school. The internal conflict occurs within Premila as she struggles both to be accepted at school and to stand up to racism.

8. Most students will probably say yes. However, they may note that this strategy deprives the sisters of this particular path of education. Examples of peaceful protests include the resistance movements led by Martin Luther King, Jr., and Mahatma Gandhi.

9. Similarities: Both face obstacles in attaining an education due to their racial heritage. Differences: Santha is wealthy, sheltered, and happy. Mathabane is poor, tough, and angry.

After Reading

Making Connections

Shaping Your Response

1. Do you think that it's possible for someone like Santha, who is not yet six years old, to understand prejudice? Why or why not?

2. In your opinion, was Premila's walking out of the school justified? Why or why not?

3. What would you have done if you had been the girls' mother?

Analyzing the Autobiography

4. What **inferences** can you make about the advantages to the sisters of attending a British-run school? the disadvantages?

5. Why do you think Santha tells the teacher she does not know her name?

6. Review the note about the title on page 481. Then explain how this **allusion** relates to this story.

7. Does this selection illustrate internal or external **conflict**—or both? Explain.

Extending the Ideas

8. Do you consider peaceful protest such as Premila's walking out of school an effective way to **communicate** opposition to prejudice? Explain. What historical examples can you find of peaceful protest?

9. In a Venn diagram, compare similarities and differences of the early school experiences of Mark Mathabane and Santha Rama Rau as described in their autobiographical excerpts.

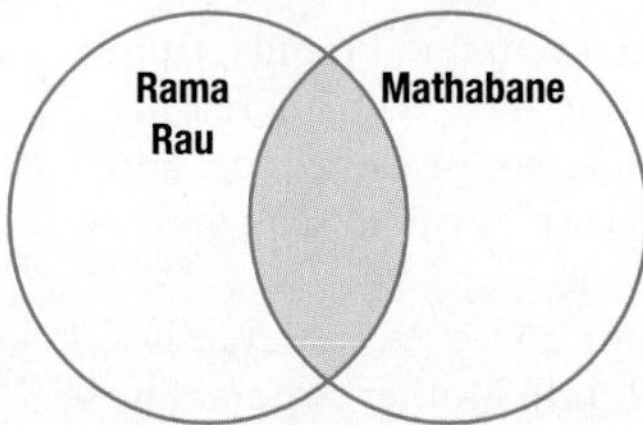

Literary Focus: Stereotype

In "By Any Other Name," the English officials at the school regard the Indian students as **stereotypes**.

- What general conclusion do the English teachers draw about Indian students?
- How might the teacher's refusal to call Indian students by their given names be stereotypical?

LITERARY FOCUS: STEREOTYPE

Possible responses

- Indians are inferior. They should be Anglicized, starting with their names, and they should be isolated from other students.
- Teachers find these names "hard" to say and remember. They are unwilling to acknowledge the culture and identities of their Indian students, and they assume that Anglo names, customs, and manners are the norm.

Vocabulary Study

Match each numbered word with the letter of its synonym. Then pantomime two of these words for the class.

intimidate
peevishness
precarious
tepid
wizened

1. precarious
2. intimidate
3. wizened
4. tepid
5. peevishness

a. irritability
b. uncertain
c. frighten
d. withered
e. lukewarm

Expressing Your Ideas

Writing Choices

Writer's Notebook Update Review your notes about a pleasant and an unpleasant association with school. Did Rama Rau's account give you any additional ideas? For example, with time and distance, does it seem like it all happened to someone else? Write about one of your associations in a narrative paragraph.

What a Character! In "By Any Other Name," you have seen Santha and Premila in their relationships with each other at school, at home, with their mother, and with their nurse. Jot down notes about these relationships and use them as the basis for a **character sketch** of either sister.

Private Life When Premila explains why she and Santha have returned home, their mother is described as *concerned, worried, startled, distant, silent,* and *displeased*. Imagine you are Mother. Write a **diary entry** that explains your feelings.

Other Options

May I Have a Word? Santha's mother will have to talk with the headmistress. What do you think she will say? With a partner, work out an **improvisation** that takes place between the two women. Be prepared to act out the scene in class.

A Dressing Down What would the clothes that Santha wore to school have looked like? If she had a brother, what would he be wearing? **Research** the kind of clothes that upper-class Indian children might have worn in the 1920s. Find pictures or make drawings of those clothes.

VOCABULARY STUDY

1. b
2. c
3. d
4. e
5. a

Unit 4 Resource Book
Vocabulary, p. 27
Vocabulary Test, p. 30

WRITING CHOICES

Writer's Notebook Update

Suggest that students identify an internal or external conflict to add structure to their narrative paragraph.

What a Character!

Suggest that students organize a Character Traits Web around the sister that they choose to characterize.

Private Life

Remind students to recall the important details that influence the mother's point of view; for example, she is controlled, yet angry at the injustice her children have experienced.

Selection Test

Unit 4 Resource Book
pp. 31–32

Transparency Collection
Fine Art Writing Prompt 8

THER OPTIONS

ay I Have a Word?

ggest that students prepare the scene by cussing the defining traits of each character. mind them that they can communicate conflict ough body language as well as words.

A Dressing Down

You might extend the project by having students compare and contrast the clothes of upper-class Indian children in the 1920s with the clothes of upper-class Indian children in the 1990s.

Interdisciplinary Study

Theme Link

There is a connection between a person's inner self and the name by which he or she is known. Ask students to examine how names and labels can function as weapons in a conflict involving prejudice.

Curricular Connection: Multicultural

You can use the information in this Interdisciplinary Study to explore the different ways that various cultures approach naming children and to examine how names relate people to themselves as well as to the world around them.

Additional Background

T. S. Eliot, a seminal modernist poet and critic, was known to be a great lover of cats. He originally wrote *Old Possum's Book of Practical Cats* for his young cousins and godchildren. Possum was, ironically, one of Eliot's nicknames.

Terms to Know

quorum, a select group
ineffable, incapable of being expressed

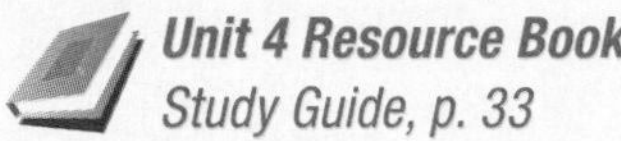
Unit 4 Resource Book
Study Guide, p. 33

INTERDISCIPLINARY STUDY

Worth Fighting For?

What's in a Name?

Multicultural Connection
Names have tremendous power, as revealed in the selection by Santha Rama Rau. Have you ever thought about how your name might affect you? about the person you could be with an entirely different name?

THE NAMING OF CATS

T. S. ELIOT

The Naming of Cats is a difficult matter,
It isn't just one of your holiday games;
You may think at first I'm as mad as a hatter
When I tell you, a cat must have three different names.
First of all, there's the name that the family use daily,
Such as Peter, Augustus, Alonzo or James,
Such as Victor or Jonathan, George or Bill Bailey—
All of them sensible everyday names.
There are fancier names if you think they sound sweeter,
Some for the gentlemen, some for the dames:
Such as Plato, Admetus, Electra, Demeter—
But all of them sensible everyday names.
But I tell you, a cat needs a name that's particular,
A name that's peculiar, and more dignified,
Else how can he keep up his tail perpendicular,
Or spread out his whiskers, or cherish his pride?
Of names of this kind, I can give you a quorum,
Such as Munkustrap, Quaxo, or Coricopat,
Such as Bombalurina, or else Jellylorum—
Names that never belong to more than one cat.
But above and beyond there's still one name left over,
And that is the name that you never will guess;
The name that no human research can discover—
But THE CAT HIMSELF KNOWS, and will never confess.
When you notice a cat in profound meditation,
The reason, I tell you, is always the same:
His mind is engaged in a rapt contemplation
Of the thought, of the thought, of the thought of his name:
His ineffable effable
Effanineffable
Deep and inscrutable singular Name.

MINI-LESSON: SPEAKING AND LISTENING

Reciting Nonsense Verse

Teach Explain that this poem's nonsensical qualities—the made-up words, the rhythm, the heavy end rhyme, and the farfetched subject matter—require that its readers adapt a particular tone of voice.

Apply Have students take turns reading sections of the poem aloud. Encourage each reader to adapt a serious and scholarly tone, even when the words make no sense and the verse seems absurd. Explain that the contrast between the odd subject matter and diction and the reader's straight face and serious tone create elements of irony, surprise, and humor.

Activity Ideas

- Have students bring in other examples of nonsense verse to read aloud to the class.
- Have students listen to a recording of the Andrew Lloyd Webber musical *CATS* and take notes on the tone of the performance.

Unit 4 Resource Book
Study Skill Activity, p. 34

Edward Gorey, *The Naming of Cats (detail)*, 1982, from the artist's illustrations for *Old Possum's Book of Practical Cats*

Art Study

Edward Gorey, an American author and illustrator, was born in Chicago in 1925. He is well-known for his unique style, which combines a gloomy mood with a sly sense of humor. His drawings usually depict eccentric characters in Victorian settings. Not only does he illustrate books by other authors, but he also writes and illustrates his own stories and poems.

Visual Literacy You might point out that *Nomines Felarem* means "Names of Cats" in Latin.

Question What details give this drawing an ironic tone? *(Possible responses: the pretentious book title, the scale of the book and of the cat; the position of the cat)*

BUILDING ENGLISH PROFICIENCY

Making Real-Life Connections

Names such as *Alonzo, Electra,* and *Jellylorum* seem quite unusual for pets—but are they really? Use the following activity to engage student interest.

1. Have students give the names of real pets (in their own family or in others' families). You might start with names for cats, go on to names for dogs, and conclude with names for more exotic pets.

2. Review Eliot's classification of known names for cats: "the name that the family use daily" and "a name that's peculiar and more dignified." Ask students to classify the names that they have suggested.

3. Remind students of what Eliot says about a cat's "secret" name. Invite students to suggest what pets with the known names given might have as their "secret" names.

MULTICULTURAL NOTE

Names have been passed among languages for centuries. As a result, you can find variations of the same name in many languages. For example: John (English), is a variation of Ian (Scottish), Evan (Welsh), Sean (Irish), Hans (German), Jean (French), Juan (Spanish), and Ivan (Russian). These versions all stem from the same root, the Hebrew name *Johanen*.

Historical Note

The Puritans were members of an extreme Christian sect that based its reformative doctrines on direct religious experience, piously diligent moral conduct, and simple church services. These names reflect the strict and dogmatic nature of their code for personal godliness. Puritan ethics have greatly influenced the formation of American values, particularly in the Northeast, where early Puritan settlers founded the Massachusetts colony.

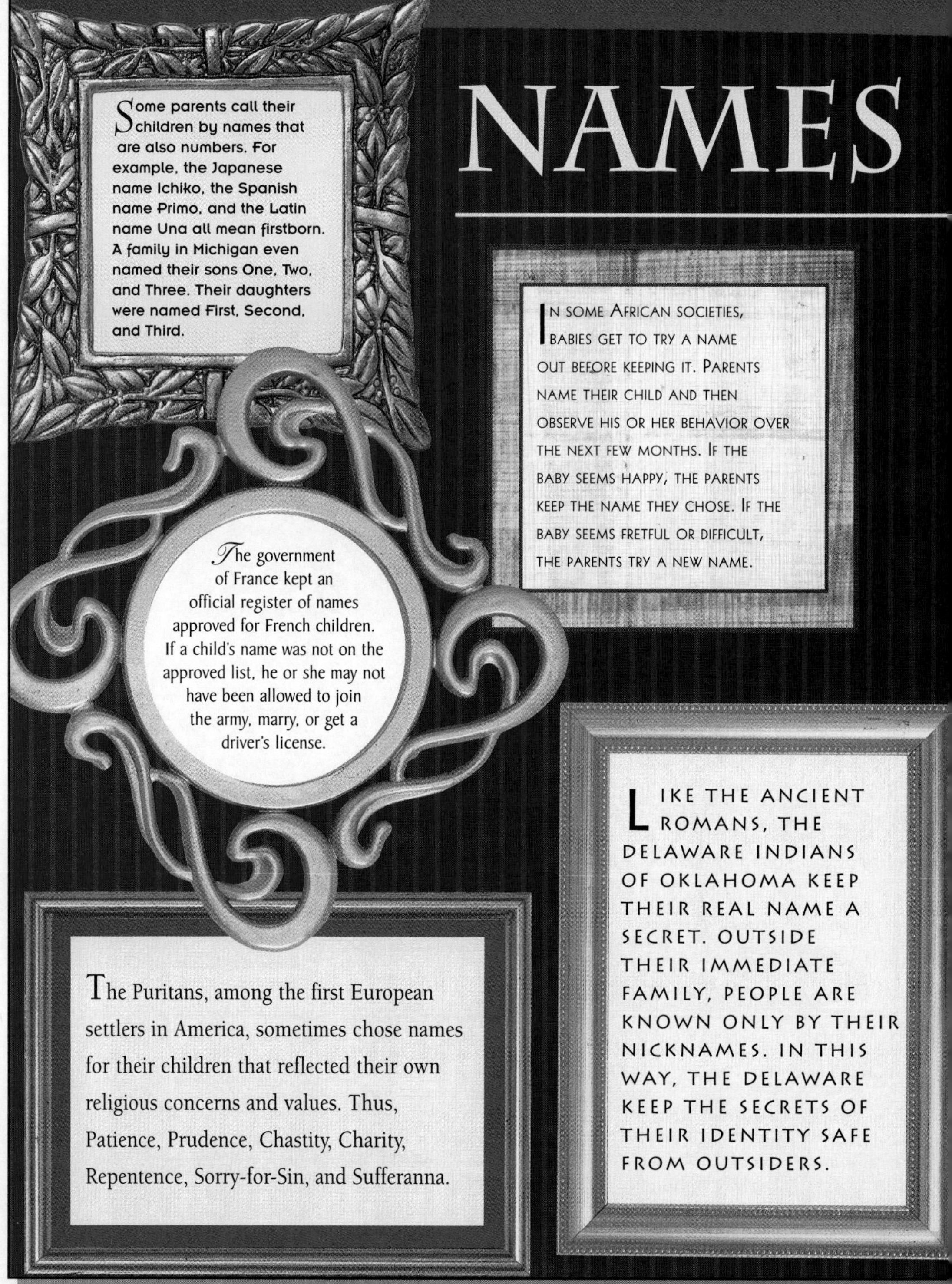

NAMES
Some parents call their children by names that are also numbers. For example, the Japanese name Ichiko, the Spanish name Primo, and the Latin name Una all mean firstborn. A family in Michigan even named their sons One, Two, and Three. Their daughters were named First, Second, and Third.
In some African societies, babies get to try a name out before keeping it. Parents name their child and then observe his or her behavior over the next few months. If the baby seems happy, the parents keep the name they chose. If the baby seems fretful or difficult, the parents try a new name.
The government of France kept an official register of names approved for French children. If a child's name was not on the approved list, he or she may not have been allowed to join the army, marry, or get a driver's license.
Like the ancient Romans, the Delaware Indians of Oklahoma keep their real name a secret. Outside their immediate family, people are known only by their nicknames. In this way, the Delaware keep the secrets of their identity safe from outsiders.
The Puritans, among the first European settlers in America, sometimes chose names for their children that reflected their own religious concerns and values. Thus, Patience, Prudence, Chastity, Charity, Repentence, Sorry-for-Sin, and Sufferanna.

MINI-LESSON: STUDY SKILLS

Researching Your Name

Teach Students who are interested in finding out the origin of their name can combine information from a variety of sources. One important source is family members. Books are another.

Apply Encourage students to first talk with family members about why a particular name was chosen and its meaning. Students can then consult reference books in the library to find out the meaning, of a name, its historical significance, and also how common it is.

Activity Idea Students can use their research to complete the Interdisciplinary Activity idea described in the Teacher's Notes on page 491. Encourage students work in small groups to compile a list of factors that are important in choosing a name based on the research they've done on their individual monikers.

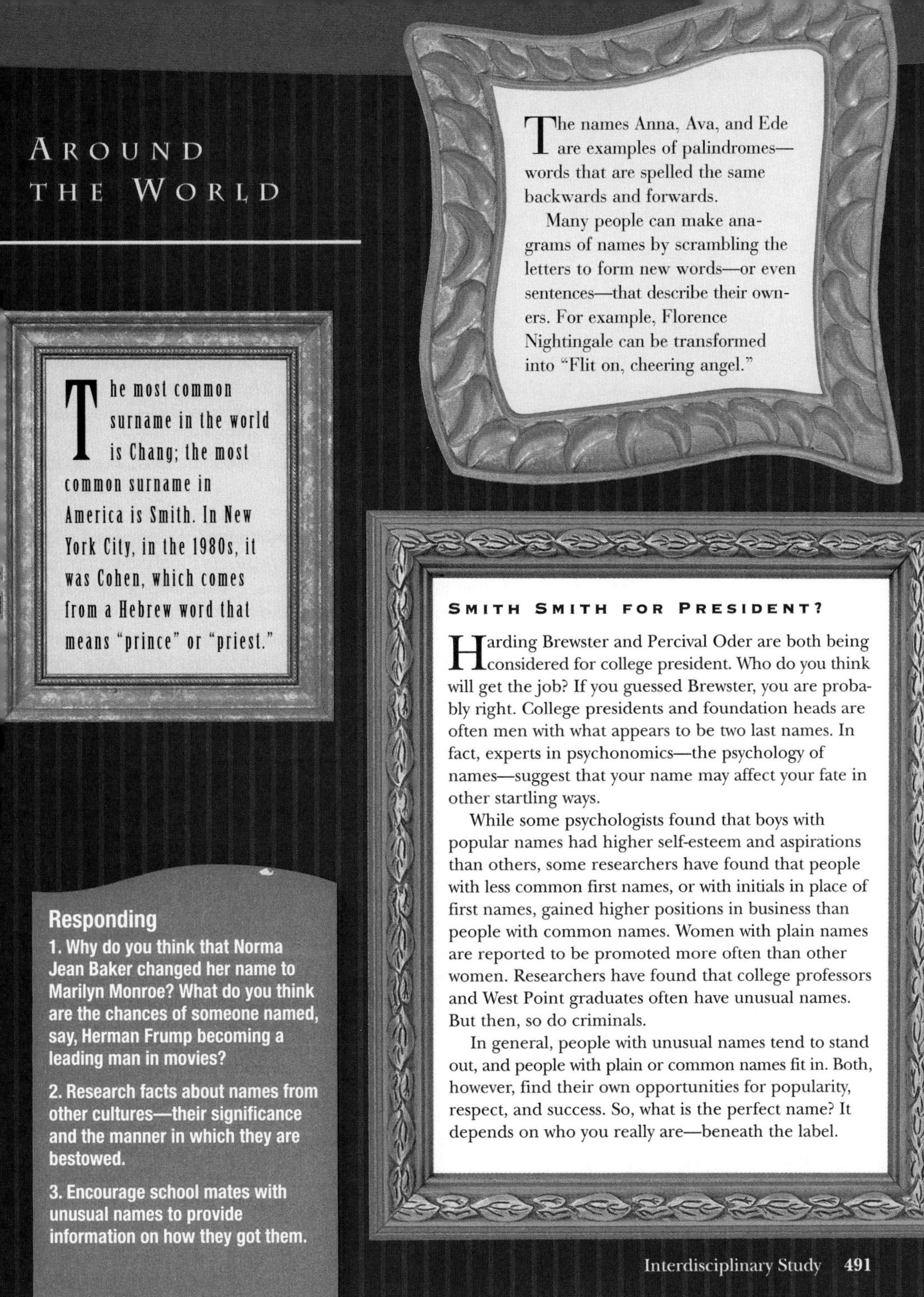

AROUND THE WORLD

The names Anna, Ava, and Ede are examples of palindromes—words that are spelled the same backwards and forwards.

Many people can make anagrams of names by scrambling the letters to form new words—or even sentences—that describe their owners. For example, Florence Nightingale can be transformed into "Flit on, cheering angel."

The most common surname in the world is Chang; the most common surname in America is Smith. In New York City, in the 1980s, it was Cohen, which comes from a Hebrew word that means "prince" or "priest."

SMITH SMITH FOR PRESIDENT?

Harding Brewster and Percival Oder are both being considered for college president. Who do you think will get the job? If you guessed Brewster, you are probably right. College presidents and foundation heads are often men with what appears to be two last names. In fact, experts in psychonomics—the psychology of names—suggest that your name may affect your fate in other startling ways.

While some psychologists found that boys with popular names had higher self-esteem and aspirations than others, some researchers have found that people with less common first names, or with initials in place of first names, gained higher positions in business than people with common names. Women with plain names are reported to be promoted more often than other women. Researchers have found that college professors and West Point graduates often have unusual names. But then, so do criminals.

In general, people with unusual names tend to stand out, and people with plain or common names fit in. Both, however, find their own opportunities for popularity, respect, and success. So, what is the perfect name? It depends on who you really are—beneath the label.

Responding

1. Why do you think that Norma Jean Baker changed her name to Marilyn Monroe? What do you think are the chances of someone named, say, Herman Frump becoming a leading man in movies?
2. Research facts about names from other cultures—their significance and the manner in which they are bestowed.
3. Encourage school mates with unusual names to provide information on how they got them.

Interdisciplinary Study 491

Responding

1. Possible Response Because "Marilyn Monroe" sounds glamorous and rolls off the tongue. "Norma Jean Baker" evokes a small town country girl. Herman Frump might be successful as a supporting actor, but would probably never have top billing.

2. Possible Response Categories to consider are naming patterns, the relationship between first names and last names, roots of given names, and roots of surnames.

3. Possible Response Remind students that names from other cultures may be very common to those cultures and are not unusual.

Research Topics

- the influence of the Bible on modern names
- registration practices at Ellis Island in the nineteenth century
- T. S. Eliot, Edward Lear, and English nonsense verse

Interdisciplinary Activity Ideas

- Students can create a Name Book. Each student should prepare one page that explains the roots of his or her full name.
- Students can write their own version of "Old Possum's Book of Cats." Encourage them to write brief, rhyming poems modeled after T. S. Eliot's piece. They might write about a family pet, or they can create an imaginary pet to eulogize.

BUILDING ENGLISH PROFICIENCY

ESL LEP ELD SAE LD

Making Cultural Connections

Use one or more of the following activities to help students focus upon the importance of names.

Activity Ideas

- Explain that last names have histories. *Johnson,* for example, means "son of John"; *Chandler* means "candle-maker." Encourage volunteers who know the meaning of their last names (or their first names) to share that information.
- One of the notes on page 491 gives examples of common names in different parts of the world. Ask: How "common" or "rare" is your name? How do you feel about that name?
- Play a recording of the Jim Croce song "I've Got a Name"; then invite personal interpretations. These may be oral or written; they could include art, music, or drama. Together, plan a format for sharing interpretations.

Reading Mini-Lesson

Teaching Objectives

- to differentiate between connotation and denotation
- to understand the effects of connotation within the names of characters and people

Introduce

Explain that a word's effect on a reader depends on the feelings, images, and ideas that the reader associates with it. Lead the students in a word association game: call out a word and have students write down the first five words that come to mind. Compare responses.

Follow Up

Have students pay attention to how advertising uses word connotations to name and promote products. Students might bring in magazine or newspaper advertisements that capitalize on positive word connotations.

Activity Options

Activity 1 Brainstorm words that you associate with each category before beginning.

Activity 2 Remember that the name of the product can have powerful connotations as well!

Activity 3 Trade words with another student and complete a second web. Compare your responses.

Reading Mini-Lesson

Connotation and Denotation

Close your eyes and think for a moment about the word *home*. What things do you associate with this word? In one dictionary, a definition of *home* is "place where a person or family lives," but if you're like most people, the word *home* evokes a series of other images—perhaps love, sisters, noise, food smells, or lots of shoes at the front door.

The dictionary definitions of a word are its *denotations.* The special meanings and associations that go beyond dictionary definitions are a word's *connotations.* Connotations come from people's individual or group experiences. For example, to different students, *breakfast* might be a roll on the run, a nourishing sit-down ritual, a school cafeteria meal, or memories of Grandma's blueberry muffins. Understanding denotation and connotation is important for getting the most from what you read.

Names, too, can have different connotations. In the article, "Smith, Smith for President?" (page 491), the author mentions the names Harding Brewster and Percival Oder. Which of these names would you consider more desirable for a male? What connotations do the names *Percival* and *Oder* have for you? How might these connotations negatively influence Percival Oder's chances for success?

Some authors give characters connotative names that reflect personality or physical traits. Readers of novels by Charles Dickens are familiar with the Murdstones, Mr. Bumble, Alfred Jingle, and the Gradgrinds. Public figures such as movie stars and wrestlers sometimes choose their names with an eye toward connotations.

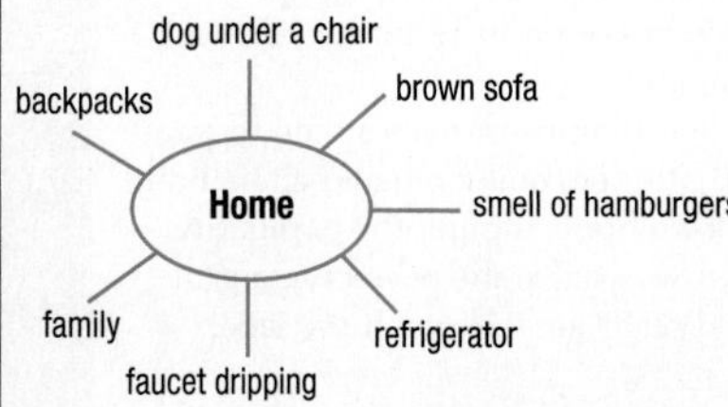

Activity Options

1. Make a list of names that you think would be suitable for: a computer whiz, a sports fanatic, a studious person, an actor, a talkative person, and a miser.
2. Create an ad for a car, clothes, vacation, drink, or cosmetic. Use words with highly connotative associations suitable to the product. Consider words such as *luxury, elite, distinctive, power, rugged, soothing,* and *breathtaking.*
3. Think of a word that has many connotations for you. Then make a web like the example at the left.

CONTENT AREA READING

Recognizing Connotations

The ability to recognize connotations within names of characters and places can give a reader important clues into an author's tone. Although sometimes an author utilizes the power of connotation in a subtle manner, other authors, for example Charles Dickens and the Russian playwright Anton Chekhov, deliberately choose obvious names to suit the personality or social position of their characters. Attention to connotation can thus tip the reader off to clues about characterization and plot. A reader who can confidently infer the connotations not only of titles and names, but of language throughout the narrative, will be able to enjoy the hidden richness of effective writing.

- Point out to students that many words have connotations and the special meaning that a word has to the author may not be the same meaning that it has for the reader.
- Tell students to note comparisons of fictional characters and real people to celebrities and historical figures as they read. For example: The statement, "Terrence may be another Michael Jordan." connotes that Terrence has basketball skills that rival the famous athlete.

Writing Workshop

Standing Tall

Assignment In this part of the unit you've read about individuals and groups who stand up for something they believe in. Now write about a time in your life when you did the same.

WRITER'S BLUEPRINT

Product	An autobiographical incident
Purpose	To tell about a time you stood up for something you believed in
Audience	People who want to know more about you
Specs	As the writer of a successful paper, you should:

- ❑ Describe a memorable incident from your life when you decided to stand up for something you believed in.
- ❑ Tell what happened in chronological order, from start to finish, using the first-person ("I") point of view.
- ❑ Explain how you felt about what happened and what made the incident memorable for you.
- ❑ Finish by telling whether you succeeded in standing up for what you believed in and whether you'd behave the same way today, and why.
- ❑ Write in the active voice. Use dialogue where appropriate.
- ❑ Follow the rules of grammar, usage, spelling, and mechanics. Take care to use apostrophes correctly.

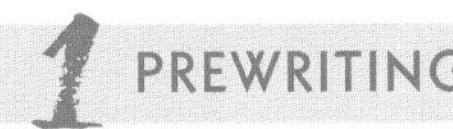

STEP 1 PREWRITING

Review characters in the literature. Create a chart like the one on the next page, showing how the characters in the selections you have read stood up for something they believed in.

Writing Workshop

WRITER'S BLUEPRINT

Specs

The Specs in the Writer's Blueprint address these writing and thinking skills:

- recognizing values
- organizing information in chronological order
- writing a narrative
- writing dialogue
- writing in the active voice
- reflecting on prior life experiences
- using apostrophes correctly

These Specs serve as your lesson objectives, and they form the basis for the **Assessment Criteria Specs** for a superior paper, which appear on the final TE page for this lesson. You might want to read through the Assessment Criteria Specs with students when you begin the lesson.

Linking Literature to Writing

Discuss with students reasons why it is important to share stories about people who act according to their principles. Encourage students to share their own stories for these same reasons.

STEP 1 PREWRITING

Review characters in the literature

Before students work independently, discuss as a class some of the quotes that most vividly illustrate a character's ethos.

WRITING WORKSHOP OVERVIEW

Product
Narrative writing: An autobiographical incident

Prewriting
Review characters in the literature—Choose an incident from your life—Describe the incident—Try a quickwrite—Plan your essay—Ask a partner
Unit 4 Resource Book
Prewriting Worksheets pp. 35–36

Drafting
Before you draft—As you draft
Transparency Collection
Student Models for Writing Workshop 15, 16

Revising
Ask a partner—Strategy: Writing in the Active Voice
Unit 4 Resource Book
Revising Worksheet p. 37

Editing
Ask a partner—Strategy: Using Apostrophes Correctly
Unit 4 Resource Book
Grammar Worksheet p. 38
Grammar Check Test p. 39

Presenting
Cover Sheet—Read Aloud—Dramatize—Someone Else

Looking Back
Self-evaluate—Reflect—For Your Working Portfolio
Unit 4 Resource Book
Assessment Worksheet p. 40
Transparency Collection
Fine Art Writing Prompt 8

Choose an incident from your life

For additional support, see the worksheet referenced below.

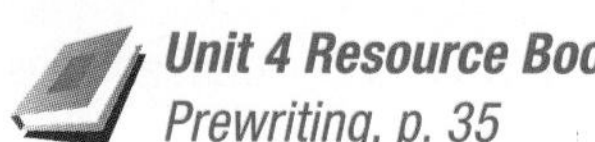

Unit 4 Resource Book
Prewriting, p. 35

Describe the incident

Encourage students to probe for more information with questions and comments as they listen to their peers' stories.

Try a quickwrite

Start students writing with the following prompt: "At this moment I knew I had to take control of the situation. . . . "

Plan your essay

For students who want to exercise the Or . . . option, have them first look up models of time lines in history texts and reference books. For additional support, see the worksheet referenced below.

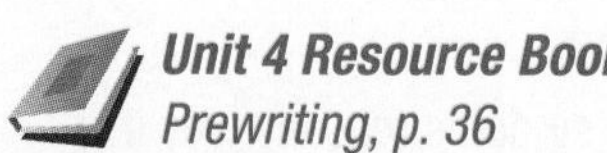

Unit 4 Resource Book
Prewriting, p. 36

Connections to **Writer's Notebook**

For selection-related prompts, refer to Writer's Notebook.

Connections to **Writer's Resource**

For additional writing prompts, refer to Writer's Resource.

Title and Character's Name	What Character Did and Why	Supporting Quote	What Character Stood Up For
"By Any Other Name" Premila	Premila, taking her little sister with her, left school because the teacher said that all Indians cheat.	"She said it was because Indians cheat," Premila added. "So I don't think we should go back to that school."	Dignity of her heritage; self-respect

OR . . . In groups of four, have the group members each select one of the main characters and, acting as those characters, explain how they stood up for themselves. Take notes on the results.

Choose an incident from your life. Recall incidents you have experienced, arguments you have had, or actions you have taken to support a strong personal belief. Look back at your literature chart for ideas. Make sure that for each incident on your list you can identify what it was you stood up for. Then select the incident you'll write about.

Describe the incident to a partner. Be sure to include details that explain what happened, and to describe how you stood up for yourself.

OR . . . Tape-record your description and listen to it when you make your writing plan.

Try a quickwrite. Write for five minutes about what made the incident so memorable for you. The point of a quickwrite is to write down your ideas as fast as they come to you, so don't worry about developing full sentences or paragraphs right now. Check your quickwrite to make sure this really is the incident you'll want to write about.

Plan your essay. Look back at your prewriting activities as you develop your writing plan. Organize your notes into a an informal outline like the one shown here.

Introduction
Time and place
Why I was there

Body
What happened first
How I felt about it
Lines of dialogue I might use
What happened next
How I felt about it
Lines of dialogue I might use
and so on

Conclusion
How well did I succeed in standing up for my beliefs?
Would I behave the same way today?
Why?

OR . . . Make a time line that shows your incident broken into individual events, from start to finish. Along the line, list each event and make notes about what happened and how you felt about it.

MINI-LESSON: PREWRITING

Review the characters

Teach This activity focuses on the first Or . . . option at the top of the page. Explain the concept of improvising to students. Tell them that with a good idea of who a character is, inside and out, you can put yourself in that character's place and make up your own dialogue.

Activity Idea Have students break into groups. Have each student choose a character and make quick notes on what he/she knows of that character in terms of outer appearance, mannerisms, and speech; and the inner qualities of character and personality. Then have students follow the first Or . . . option.

Apply Have students input what they've learned into a chart like the one at the top of the page.

Ask a partner to review your plan.

✔ Have I written in first-person point of view?

✔ Have I narrated events in chronological order, from first to last?

✔ Have I explained why this incident was so memorable for me?

✔ Have I followed the Specs in the Writer's Blueprint?

Use any helpful comments from your partner to revise your plan.

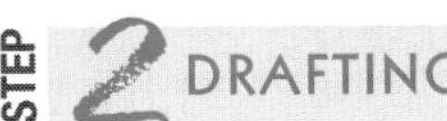

STEP 2 DRAFTING

Before you write, look at your prewriting notes and writing plan and reread the Writer's Blueprint.

As you draft, concentrate on putting the ideas from your writing plan on paper; worry about spelling and punctuation mistakes later. Here are some drafting tips.

- Begin your paper with dialogue that creates an air of suspense: "You don't really believe that, do you?"
- Sustain the suspense. Let your readers discover what happened, as you did, as the incident unfolded.
- Write in the active voice. (See the Revising Strategy in Step 3 of this lesson.)

STEP 3 REVISING

Ask a partner to comment on your draft before you revise it. Exchange papers and respond to these statements:

✔ What you took a stand on was _____.

✔ This incident was memorable to you because _____.

✔ I could/could not follow the sequence of events because _____.

✔ This incident made you feel _____. I can tell because _____.

✔ You did/did not succeed in standing up for what you believe in because you say _____.

STEP 2 DRAFTING

Ask a partner (Peer assessment)

Have students be sure to look at papers in terms of the second point on the checklist, chronological order, to be sure the narrative is coherent.

As you draft

Have students experiment with story beginnings by generating a list of five or more interesting pieces of dialogue that might hook the reader immediately. Have them ask peers which of their openers is the most intriguing.

The Student Models

The **transparencies** referenced below are authentic student models. Review them with students before they draft. These questions will help.

1. Is model 15 written in chronological order? How can you tell?

2. Look at sentence 3 in paragraph 3 of model 16. Rewrite it in the active voice. Does it seem better that way?

3. Look over paragraph 3 of model 16 for apostrophe usage.

Transparency Collection
Student Models for Writing Workshop 15, 16

STEP 3 REVISING

Ask a partner (Peer assessment)

If the reader cannot fill in all the blanks, the writer should look for reasons why.

BUILDING ENGLISH PROFICIENCY

Writing Effective Dialogue

Students are encouraged to use dialogue in their autobiographical incidents. Offer these suggestions.

Activity Ideas

- If students have difficulty creating realistic dialogue, have them speak their part into a tape recorder and play it back before they write.
- Have volunteers read the dialogue from their drafts aloud. Ask: Is too much small talk included? Does the dialogue sound realistic? How does it help create suspense?

Revising Strategy: Writing in the Active Voice

Encourage students to note the parts of the paper that work as well as the parts that need revising. For additional support, see the mini-lesson at the bottom of this page and the worksheet referenced below.

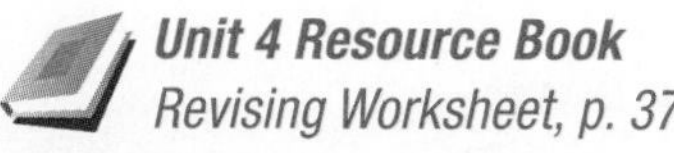

Unit 4 Resource Book
Revising Worksheet, p. 37

Connections to **Writer's Resource**

Refer to the Grammar, Usage, and Mechanics Handbook on Writer's Resource.

Revising Strategy

Writing in the Active Voice

In the **active voice,** the subject does something: *We planted the new tree* that afternoon. *Mrs. Gordon thanked us*.

In the **passive voice**, something is done to the subject: *The new tree was planted* by us that afternoon. *We were thanked* by Mrs. Gordon.

Which pair of sentences sounds more natural? Most writing, especially narrative writing, is in the active voice because the active voice sounds more natural and direct. Here are more examples:

Passive The wallet was picked up by me from where it had fallen on the sidewalk.

Active I picked up the wallet from where it had fallen on the sidewalk.

Passive It was returned by me to its rightful owner.

Active I returned it to its rightful owner.

Check your narrative to see that it moves along in the active voice. When you find sentences that sound awkward, it may be because they're in the passive voice and need to made active, as in the student model that follows.

Coach Paustion worked with me during the off season as well as during the season. *He noticed* My intense desire to excel ~~was noticed by him~~ and he went above and beyond the call of duty to help me. *My teammates* ~~I was~~ sometimes made fun of *me* ~~by my teammates~~ and teased *me* about my size. However, thanks to the guidance of Coach Paustion, I had the confidence to stand up to them and show them I could make an important contribution to the team.

MINI-LESSON: WRITING STYLE

Writing in the Active Voice

Teach Go over with students the difference between passive and active voice, using the Revising Strategy feature. Then perform an action, such as picking up a book, and ask volunteers to express this action in the passive voice (A book is picked up by ____) and the active voice (____ picks up a book.)

Activity Idea Have students break into groups and carry through the activity you just modeled, with students taking turns. After a few turns, have students discuss briefly why the passive voice is generally less natural than the active.

Apply Encourage students to read their papers looking for passive sentences that read awkwardly and revising them by putting them into the active voice.

STEP 4 EDITING

Ask a partner to review your revised draft before you edit. When you edit, look for errors in grammar, usage, spelling, and mechanics. Look over each sentence to make sure you've used apostrophes correctly.

Editing Strategy

Using Apostrophes Correctly

Use apostrophes to form the possessives of nouns.

1. Add **'s** to form the possessive of most singular nouns (Alice**'s** courage, one class**'s** desks)
2. Add only an apostrophe to form the possessive of plural nouns ending in **s** (five whales' spouts, the kites' long tails).
3. Add **'s** to form the possessive of plural nouns that do not end in **s** (the children**'s** room, two deer**'s** tracks).

Use apostrophes to form contractions, showing where letters have been omitted.

do not = don't let us = let's there is = there's it is = it's

But do not use apostrophes to form plurals (four desks, two pairs of jeans).

Notice how this writer corrected mistakes with the use of apostrophes.

> Practice was always hard for me. The teams goal was supposed to be to work together, but it sometime's seemed like it was every player for himself. I made good block's, but that would only make the player I blocked angry, even though we were teammate's. It wasnt long and I was thinking about quitting.

STUDENT MODEL

FOR REFERENCE
See the Language and Grammar Handbook at the back of the book for more information on using apostrophes correctly.

STEP 4 EDITING

Ask a partner (Peer assessment)

Have students read the paper once through while looking only for errors with apostrophes.

Editing Strategy: Using Apostrophes Correctly

Remind students that mistakenly using apostrophes to form plurals is a common error in student writing, and that if they use a word processor, they should search for apostrophes, using the Find function, to make sure they've been used correctly. For additional support, see the mini-lesson at the bottom of this page and the worksheets referenced below.

Unit 4 Resource Book
Grammar Worksheet, p. 38
Grammar Check Test, p. 39

Connections to **Writer's Resource**

Refer to the Grammar, Usage, and Mechanics Handbook on Writer's Resource.

MINI-LESSON: GRAMMAR

Using Apostrophes Correctly

Remind students of the rules for the uses of apostrophes. Display the following paragraph. For each sentence, have students choose the correct word in parentheses and tell why they chose it.

(Your, You're) going to love New Orleans. (It's, Its) one of my favorite (cities, city's) to visit, just for the architecture alone. The (cities, city's) history is fascinating and the French (Quarters, Quarter's) night life is almost legendary. Of course, (theres, there's) plenty of excellent food to try, including my (favorites, favorite's), gumbo and fried catfish.

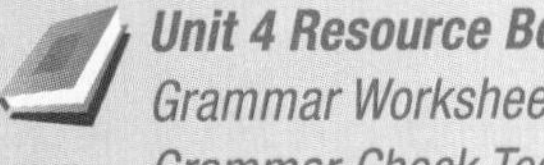

Unit 4 Resource Book
Grammar Worksheet, p. 38
Grammar Check Test, p. 39

STEP 5 PRESENTING

Cover Sheet

Students working with word processors might have a graphics program that would help here.

Read Aloud

After students share their stories, return to the discussion prompted by the "Linking Literature to Writing" section at the beginning of this lesson.

Dramatize

Students might want to consult a speech or drama teacher or media specialist here.

Someone Else

This might lead to a discussion on different points of view.

STEP 6 LOOKING BACK

Self-evaluate

The *Assessment Criteria Specs* at the bottom of this page are for a superior paper. You might want to post these in the classroom. Students can then evaluate themselves based on these criteria. For a complete scoring rubric, use the *Assessment Worksheet* referenced below.

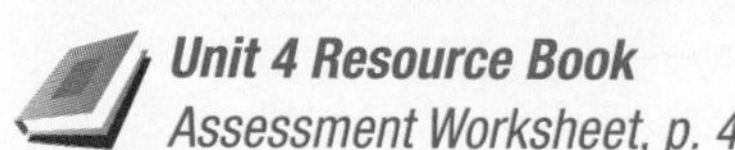

Reflect

As students review their earlier drafts, encourage them to reflect on the progress they have made.

To further explore the theme, use the Fine Art Transparency referenced below.

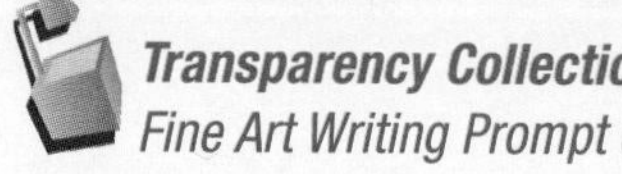

Consider these ideas for presenting your essay.

- Make a cover sheet with graphics to enhance your paper. Illustrate your topic by drawing a time line to picture the events.
- Read your papers aloud in a small student group. In a discussion, compare and contrast the different strategies people took in standing up for something they believed in. Which strategies seemed to work best?
- Dramatize your narrative. Turn it into a stage, radio, or video production. You might work with classmates to put your productions together into a program of autobiographical performances.
- Read your narrative to someone else who was involved in the incident and ask for their comments. How does their memory of things differ from yours?

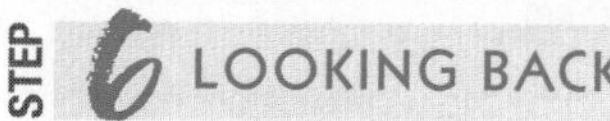

Self-evaluate. Look back at the Writer's Blueprint and give your paper a score for each item, from 6 (superior) to 1 (inadequate).

Reflect. Think about what you've learned from writing this paper as you write answers to these questions.

✔ Is there something that you believe in that you could or should stand up for now? How might you go about addressing this issue?

✔ Compare drafts. What kinds of mistakes did you catch at the editing stage? How did you do in terms of grammar, usage, mechanics, and spelling? Assess your strengths and weaknesses.

For Your Working Portfolio Add your narrative and reflection responses to your working portfolio.

ASSESSMENT CRITERIA SPECS

6 Superior The writer of a 6 paper impressively meets these criteria:

- Narrates a specific, memorable incident from the writer's life in which the writer stood up for something he/she believed in.
- Writes in first-person point of view throughout.
- Carefully guides the reader through the narrative by presenting events in time order, from start to finish.
- Gives the reader a clear idea of how the writer felt about what happened and what made the incident memorable.
- Finishes by telling whether the writer succeeded in standing up for what he or she believed in.
- Writes in the active voice, and uses dialogue correctly.
- Makes few, if any, mistakes in grammar, usage, mechanics, or spelling. Uses apostrophes correctly.

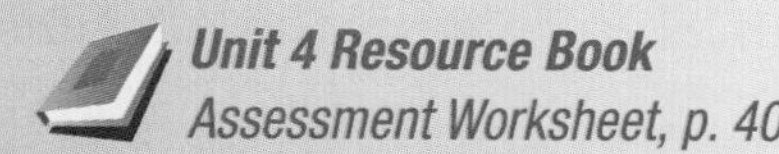

Beyond Print

Visualizing

Writers use many strategies to help readers visualize a scene. Some writers accompany their text with maps, photos, or diagrams, but most of them rely on descriptive details. It's up to you to do the visualizing. Here are some tactics to help you do that—and to remember what you read. To form a mental picture of a scene, consider these points.

Location In the excerpt from *Kaffir Boy,* Mark Mathabane describes a school principal's office. Notice the arrangement of people and things.

"He was sitting behind a brown table upon which stood piles of dust and cobweb-covered books and papers. In one upper pocket of his jacket was arrayed a variety of pens and pencils; in the other nestled a lily-white handkerchief whose presence was more decorative than utilitarian. Alongside him stood a disproportionately portly black woman. . . ."

Motion In the excerpt from *An American Childhood,* Annie Dillard describes being chased. She uses several prepositions to help readers visualize the escaping children.

"He chased Mikey and me **around** the yellow house and **up** a backyard path we knew by heart: **under** a low tree, **up** a bank, **through** a hedge, **down** some snowy steps, and **across** the grocery store's delivery driveway."

Appearances (sizes, shapes, colors, and textures) In "By Any Other Name," Santha Rama Rau describes a classmate, largely through the use of adjectives.

"She had long, glossy-black braids and wore a cotton dress, but she still kept on her Indian jewelry—a gold chain around her neck, thin gold bracelets, and tiny ruby studs in her ears."

Activity Options

1. Review "By Any Other Name," and find other passages that mention size, shape, color, or texture.
2. Look back at your own writing to find parts that you could rewrite using one or more of the strategies that help readers visualize.

Beyond Print

Teaching Objectives

- to sharpen visualization skills
- to examine literary techniques that encourage and support visualization

Curricular Connection: Visual Skills

You can use the material in this article to help students appreciate the power of literature to create a strong visual experience.

Introduce

Point out that many popular forms of entertainment—television, movies, video games—produce their effect through direct visual presentation. Encourage students to experiment with visual appreciation skills by wearing a blindfold while watching a favorite television show. Discuss how much of the action they understood without visual information. Discuss whether students think an author could affect a reader without appealing to his or her visual imagination.

Activity Options

Activity 1 Before students return to the text, suggest that they close their eyes and picture the most memorable scenes from the story. They may find that the scenes that have stayed in their memory contain the most visually descriptive imagery.

Activity 2 Discuss the combination of memory and imagination that contribute to effective writing. You might discuss the definition of *imagination*, which stems from the Latin verb *imaginari:* "to form an image in one's mind."

ANOTHER APPROACH

"I Spy"

Have students divide into groups. Each group will visually dissect a scene from one of the selections, making a list of the objects that they "see" in that scene. For example, in the scene from "An American Childhood" described on page 499, the list would include: a yellow house, a low tree, a hedge, and a grocery store driveway. The students in one group should try to guess which scene the other group is describing, based on the visual clues.

Preview

Something of Value

FOR ALL STUDENTS

Students can weight the values on their lists and show the results in a pie-chart.

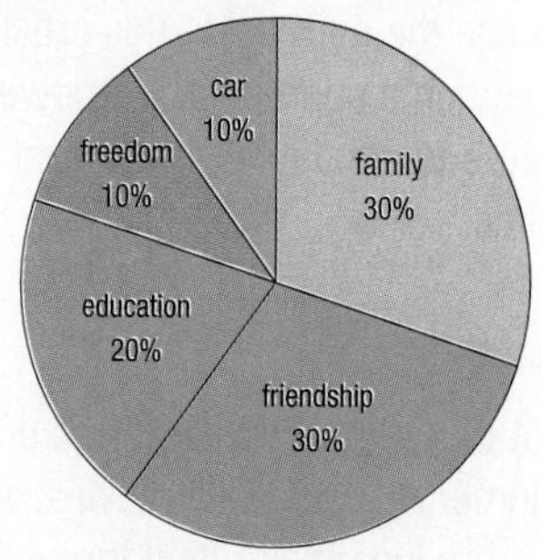

To further explore the theme, use the transparency referred to below.

Transparency Collection
Fine Art Writing Prompt 9

For At-Risk Students

Invite students to name values held by people they know, characters in movies, or heroic figures of any era. List their responses on the board.

Question How do or did these people demonstrate their values—through actions, words, or in some other way?

For Students Who Need Challenge

Challenge students to answer the question "Do values change over time?" by reviewing previous selections and analyzing what people in different eras valued.

MULTICULTURAL CONNECTION

To show how perspective influences decision making, have students work in small groups. Assign each student a different role for the following scenario: A student group must decide how a $100 donation to the school should be spent. One of the students is an athlete, another is in an overcrowded classroom, and so on.

Part Two

Something of Value

A flower? a pet? a sunrise? a car? a beautiful object? freedom? What things do you hold dear? Make a mental list and then compare your "treasures" with those in the following selections.

Multicultural Connection **Perspective** involves seeing people, things, and events from diverse viewpoints. These viewpoints—shaped by history, heritage, culture, and experiences—cause people to place different values on things. As you read these selections, determine to what extent the backgrounds and experiences of the authors determine what they value.

Literature

IDEAS THAT WORK

Tolerate or Oppose?

"One man's garbage is another's treasure" might be a definition of perspective. So how do we judge whether a value is a value or a personal whim? Just how much do we honor and give space to other people's values?

Motivate by getting students to make lists like Sei Shōnagon's. Share these to see if they can show understanding and at the same time build up a tolerance of differences in tastes and styles. As another approach, mention the dead man in "Tuesday Siesta," who was loved as a son and reviled as a thief; and ask how they themselves are valued from different perspectives. You might also challenge students to conduct an imaginary debate with torturers and argue that their values should have no place if life, liberty, and justice are threatened.

May Lee
San Francisco, California

Before Reading

One Perfect Rose by Dorothy Parker USA
Daybreak in Alabama by Langston Hughes USA
The Flying Cat by Naomi Shihab Nye USA

Building Background

True Value The poems you are about to read describe different things that have value for the poets. Fill out a chart like the one below to describe something that has value in your life.

____________ **has great value in my life.**
I value it because
____
______________________________________.
Qualities I associate with it are
______________________________________.
Other things that are important to me are
______________________________________.

Literary Focus

Tone The attitude of an author toward a subject and toward the reader is called **tone**. Try to determine the authors' attitudes toward their subjects in the following poems.

Writer's Notebook

Get the Picture? As you read each of the poem titles—"One Perfect Rose," "The Flying Cat," and "Daybreak in Alabama"—what images pop into your mind? Quickly sketch one of these images in your notebook. Then as you read the poem, jot down details that would help you add to or change your illustration.

Before Reading

Building Background

If most students are willing to share their completed charts, you might tally answers to see if there is any general consensus about the kinds of things the class values. List both material and nonmaterial items, and arrive at criteria for determining their value. Results might be shown in this way:

Items Valued	Criteria
happiness	well-being
money	power
intelligence	academic success

Literary Focus

Caution students not to confuse **tone,** which is the author's attitude toward a subject or characters, with mood, which is the atmosphere or feeling of a piece of writing.

Writer's Notebook

Suggest students first think about the literal meaning of the titles and then speculate on figurative meanings.

Connections to **AuthorWorks**

Langston Hughes is a featured author in the AuthorWorks CD-ROM series.

SUPPORT MATERIALS OVERVIEW

Unit 4 Resource Book
- Graphic Organizer, p. 41
- Study Guide, p. 42
- Vocabulary, p. 43
- Grammar, p. 44
- Alternate Check Test, p. 45
- Vocabulary Test, p. 46
- Selection Test, pp. 47–48

Building English Proficiency
- Literature Summaries
- Activities, p. 204

Reading, Writing & Grammar SkillBook
- Reading, pp. 41–44
- Grammar, Usage, and Mechanics, pp. 181–182, 185–186, 201–204

Technology
- Audiotape 12, Side A
- Personal Journal Software
- Custom Literature Database: For another poem that explores valued things, see "The Day Is Done" by Henry Wadsworth Longfellow on the database.
- Test Generator Software

More About the Poets

Dorothy Parker was born Dorothy Rothschild in 1893. She married Edwin Pond Parker II in 1913. "I married him," she said, "to change my name." The marriage didn't last, but the name stuck. Parker died in 1967, leaving her estate, including copyrights, to Dr. Martin Luther King, Jr. Works by Parker include:

- *Complete Stories*, Penguin, (1995)
- *The Portable Dorothy Parker*, Viking, (1973)

Langston Hughes grew to prominence as a poet and member of the Harlem Renaissance in the 1920s. He traveled across the country giving public readings of his poetry. But he always returned to Harlem, where he helped young writers who sought his advice. Works by Hughes include:

- *The Dream Keeper and Other Poems*, Knopf, (1932)
- *One-Way Ticket*, Knopf, (1949)

Naomi Shihab Nye has said, "For me the primary source of poetry has always been local life, random characters met on the streets, our own ancestry sifting down to us through small essential daily tasks." Her works include:

- *Hugging the Jukebox*, Dutton, (1982)
- *Yellow Glove*, Breitenbush, (1986)

Dorothy Parker
1893–1967

When told that solemn U.S. President Calvin Coolidge had died, Dorothy Parker asked, "How could they tell?" Such biting wit typifies Parker's verse and stories, which have delighted readers for many years. While working as a critic in New York in the 1920s, she was a member of the Algonquin Round Table, a witty and influential group of literary figures. The titles of some of Parker's books of poetry suggest the wry humor that she favored: *Enough Rope, Death and Taxes,* and *Not So Deep as a Well*. She later went to Hollywood where she worked as a screenwriter. She also taught English at Los Angeles State College, where she claimed, "The students read things and then they fight. It's called discussion."

Langston Hughes
1902–1967

Like his poems, Langston Hughes's novels, short stories, plays, and translations have given voice to the concerns and the changing roles of African Americans. When he was in second grade, he observed that "books began to happen to me, and I began to believe in nothing but books and the wonderful world in books." His poetry career was launched when his eighth-grade class in Lincoln, Illinois, voted him the Class Poet. "My classmates, knowing that a poem had to have rhythm, elected me unanimously—thinking, no doubt, that I had some, being a Negro." Hughes believed that "humor is a weapon . . . of no mean value against one's foes."

Naomi Shihab Nye
born 1952

Having published her first poem at age seven, Naomi Shihab Nye has long been a "quiet observer of the human condition." Her parents—a Palestinian father and an American mother—and the experiences she faced while living in the Middle East and San Antonio, Texas, during her high school years have contributed to Nye's multicultural perspective. In addition to writing several books of poetry, including *Different Ways to Pray* and *Hugging the Jukebox,* Nye, now living in Texas, has been a writer in residence, a teacher, a songwriter, and a world-wide traveler who promotes international goodwill through the arts.

One Perfect Rose

Dorothy Parker

A single flow'r he sent me, since we met.
All tenderly his messenger he chose;
Deep-hearted, pure, with scented dew still wet—
One perfect rose.

I knew the language of the floweret;
"My fragile leaves," it said, "his heart enclose."
Love long has taken for his amulet[1]
One perfect rose.

Why is it no one ever sent me yet
One perfect limousine, do you suppose?
Ah no, it's always just my luck to get
One perfect rose.

1. amulet (am′yə lit), *n.* a small object worn as a magic charm against evil, disease, or bad luck.

During Reading

Selection Objectives

- to explore various ideas on what is valuable and important
- to identify author's tone
- to identify regular and irregular forms of verbs
- to recognize connotations

Unit 4 Resource Book
Graphic Organizer, p. 41
Study Guide, p. 42

Theme Link

Each poem tells about something of value: a perfect rose as opposed to a perfect limousine; a musical composition about daybreak in Alabama; and a cat, who must travel by plane.

Vocabulary Preview

amulet, a small object worn as a magic charm against evil, disease, or bad luck

poppy, a bright red flower

pressurized, having the atmospheric pressure inside the (cabin of an aircraft) kept at a normal level in spite of the altitude

droll, odd and amusing

statistic, a numerical fact about people, the weather, business conditions, and so on to show their significance

Students can add words and definitions to their Writer's Notebooks.

1 Literary Focus
Irony

This poem illustrates irony. The effect is achieved by offering the romantic symbolism of a rose at the beginning, to lead readers to believe that this is a poem about love. The ending, however, favors material possessions (a limousine) over love.

SELECTION SUMMARY

One Perfect Rose, Daybreak in Alabama, The Flying Cat

One Perfect Rose In this poem the speaker tells of a single perfect rose she receives as a sign of her lover's affection. She wonders, though, why no one has ever sent her a perfect limousine.

Daybreak in Alabama The speaker says that, when he becomes a composer, he will write a song about daybreak in Alabama. He'll describe the beautiful, natural scene of people of all colors getting along together.

The Flying Cat The speaker imagines terrible tragedies that occur as she travels by plane with her cat, who rides in the baggage compartment. While hugging her cat before departure, she observes its trustfulness and its obliviousness to impending danger.

*For summaries in other languages, see the **Building English Proficiency** book.*

2 Writing Style
Clarification

You might point out words such as *gonna* and *purtiest. The* poet uses these words to make the narrator appear as an average, common person: someone who isn't an artist, but would like to be.

3 Reading/Thinking Skills
Find the Main Idea

Question What is the main idea of "Daybreak in Alabama"? *(Possible response: The narrator wants to write music that inspires people of all races to get along.)*

4 Literary Element
Understand Cultural Context

Question What physical details suggest an Alabama setting? *(swamp mist, tall tall trees, pine needles, red clay)* How does Hughes use color to reinforce his meaning? *(He suggests various skin colors—"red clay," "red necks," "poppy colored faces," "brown arms," "white hands," "yellow hands"—and mixes them by omitting punctuation—"Of black and white black white black people"—to imply harmony between people and integration.)*

Daybreak in Alabama

Langston Hughes

2 When I get to be a composer
I'm gonna write me some music about
Daybreak in Alabama
And I'm gonna put the purtiest songs in it
Rising out of the ground like a swamp mist
And falling out of heaven like soft dew.
I'm gonna put some tall tall trees in it
And the scent of pine needles
And the smell of red clay after rain
And long red necks
And poppy[1] colored faces
And big brown arms
3 And the field daisy eyes
Of black and white black white black people
And I'm gonna put white hands
And black hands and brown and yellow hands
And red clay earth hands in it
Touching everybody with kind fingers
And touching each other natural as dew
In that dawn of music when I
Get to be a composer
4 And write about daybreak
In Alabama.

1. poppy (pop′ē), *n.* a bright red.

Painted during the Depression by artist Aaron Douglass, *Song of the Towers* was one of a series of four large murals depicting significant episodes in African American history. What does this panel, which shows a jazz musician atop the cog of a machine gear, seem to be saying about the relationship between music and other aspects of modern life? ➤

MINI-LESSON: VOCABULARY
Connotation

Teach Write this line from the poem on the board:

"And falling out of heaven like a soft dew."

Below it, write this line:

"And dropping out of the sky like precipitation."

Questions

- Do the two lines mean the same thing? *(Literally, the two lines mean almost the same thing.)*
- Do the two lines create the same feeling, mood, and understanding? Why or why not? *(No. Although the changed words mean the same thing, they have different connotations—different feelings and ideas are associated with the words.)* Discuss the shades of meaning that words have—for example *heaven* versus *sky; dew* versus *precipitation.*

Activity Ideas

- Read lines from the poem, substituting words with the same denotative meaning for those in the poem. Have students discuss how the meaning and feeling of the poem changes.
- Have students experiment with connotation by rewriting lines from a poem or story they've written.

Art Study

Responses to Caption Question
Possible responses: Spiritual things like beauty and music are superior to the mechanical things in life. Music, especially jazz music, coexists and is responsive to the modern machine age.

Aaron Douglas (1899–1979) was a leading member of the Harlem Renaissance of the 1920s and 1930s and possibly its best-known visual artist. His style, which reflects deep influences of African sculpture, Cubism, and Modernism, is associated with the art of the Harlem Renaissance.

Visual Literacy Although there is much going on in this painting, it gives an impression of simplicity and order. The effect is achieved in several ways: the range of colors is limited; the figure and objects are drawn in silhouette, which strips them of detail; the shapes are simply drawn; there is little depth.

Question Examine the bull's-eye outline in the picture. Why might the artist have included the instrument and the Statue of Liberty at the center? *(Possible responses: perhaps to suggest that music and democracy are central to freedom and personal expression; to identify the musical roots of the Harlem Renaissance in New York.)*

BUILDING ENGLISH PROFICIENCY

Exploring Imagery

"Daybreak in Alabama" paints a picture of nature and people that Hughes knew well. Encourage students to explore the poem, image by image. You might have a volunteer read the poem aloud, supplying appropriate background music.

1. Have students volunteer the sights, sounds, and smells that come to them as they read. Point out that the language is simple but very specific.

2. Direct students' attention to the way in which Hughes changes the focus from the land to the people (line 10). Ask: Why do you think the people seem to grow right out of the land?

3. Ask students to record in their notebooks specific details that they observe in their own neighborhood.

4. Students who are gifted at drawing may want to add sketches to their notebooks.

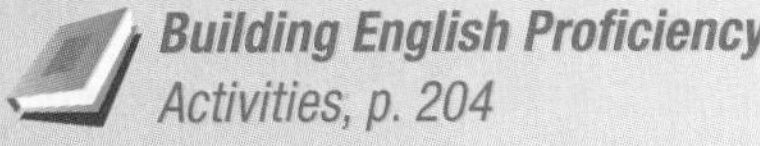

Building English Proficiency
Activities, p. 204

5 Literary Focus
Tone

Questions

- What is the tone of this poem? *(humorous, anxious)*
- What clues can you find to the tone? *(Possible responses:* Humor*: elaborate fantasies of waving fish-heads; the cat growing propellers and spinning out of sight; the cat exploding.* Anxious*: the series of questions; the impersonal, droll answers; the imagined disasters of the footlocker falling and the cat freezing.)*

Art Study

Question Do you consider this art in keeping with the theme and tone of the poem? Why or why not? *(Possible response: The tone seems humorous, and the image provides a visual pun about someone having a cat on his or her mind.)*

Check Test

1. In "One Perfect Rose," why has someone sent the speaker a rose? *(to show his love for her)*

2. What does the speaker wish that she had been sent instead of a perfect rose? *(a perfect limousine)*

3. In "Daybreak in Alabama," what does the speaker want to be? *(a composer)*

4. In "The Flying Cat," how does the cat fly? *(by airplane)*

5. From whom does the speaker get droll, impersonal answers? *(from someone on the phone connected with the airlines)*

Unit 4 Resource Book
Alternate Check Test, p. 45

The Flying Cat

Naomi Shihab Nye

Never, in all your career of worrying, did you imagine
what worries could occur concerning the flying cat.
You are traveling to a distant city.
The cat must travel in a small box with holes.

Will the baggage compartment be pressurized?[1]
Will a soldier's footlocker fall on the cat during take-off?
Will the cat freeze?

You ask these questions one by one, in different voices
over the phone. Sometimes you get an answer,
sometimes a click.
Now it's affecting everything you do.
At dinner you feel nauseous, like you're swallowing
at twenty thousand feet.
In dreams you wave fish-heads, but the cat has grown propellers,
the cat is spinning out of sight!

Will he faint when the plane lands?
Is the baggage compartment soundproofed?
Will the cat go deaf?

"Ma'am, if the cabin weren't pressurized, your cat would explode."
And spoken in a droll[2] impersonal tone, as if
the explosion of cats were another statistic![3]

Hugging the cat before departure, you realize again
the private language of pain. He purrs. He trusts you.
5 He knows little of planets or satellites,
black holes in space or the weightless rise of fear.

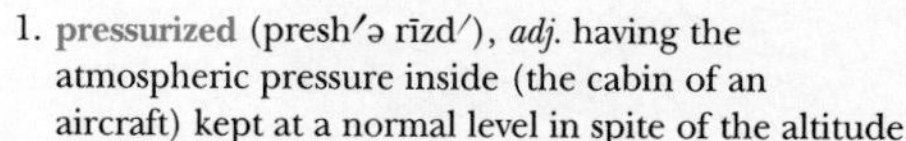

1. **pressurized** (presh′ə rīzd′), *adj.* having the atmospheric pressure inside (the cabin of an aircraft) kept at a normal level in spite of the altitude.
2. **droll** (drōl), *adj.* odd and amusing.
3. **statistic** (stə tis′tik), *n.* a numerical fact about people, the weather, business conditions, and so on in order to show their significance.

MINI-LESSON: GRAMMAR

Regular and Irregular Verbs

Teach Write these verbs from the poem on the board: *imagine, fall*

Explain that the first verb is regular, the second is irregular. The past and past participle forms of regular verbs are formed by adding *-d* or *-ed* to the present tense. Past and past participles of irregular verbs are *not* formed by adding *-d* or *-ed.*

Activity Idea Have students complete the chart.

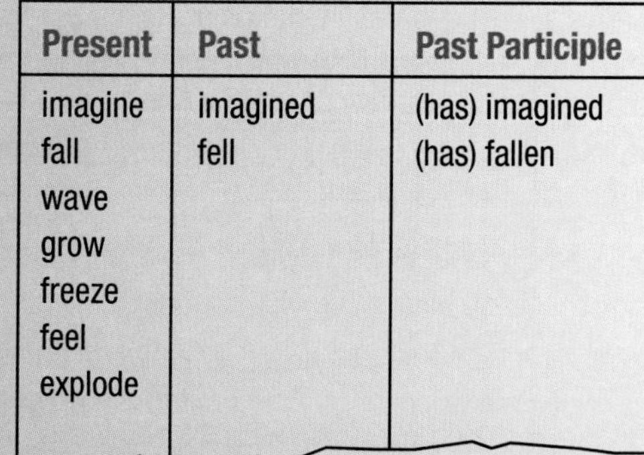

Present	Past	Past Participle
imagine	imagined	(has) imagined
fall	fell	(has) fallen
wave		
grow		
freeze		
feel		
explode		

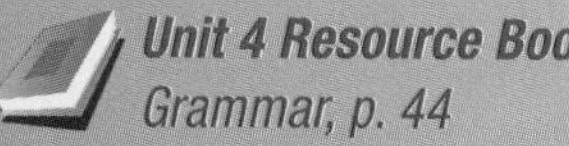

Unit 4 Resource Book
Grammar, p. 44

After Reading

Making Connections

Shaping Your Response

1. Explain which of the things these poets value comes closest to what you consider "Something of Value."
2. In your notebook, list several phrases or images from the poems that you find most memorable.

Analyzing the Poems

3. Judging from the author biographies and the poems included here, which poet do you think would make the best interviewee on a late-night talk show? Why?
4. What examples do you find of **hyperbole**, or exaggeration, in "The Flying Cat"?
5. Each of the three stanzas in "One Perfect Rose" ends with the words *one perfect rose.* Briefly explain how you think the speaker would vary her delivery each time she repeats the phrase.
6. Find **images** in "Daybreak in Alabama" that appeal to the senses of smell, sight, and touch.
7. Hughes jumbles together many images, uses the word *and* frequently, and rarely uses punctuation to slow a reader down. How does this style suit his **theme**?
8. Compare the **styles** of two of these poets. Note things such as **word choice, rhyme** and **rhythm**, **tone**, and **images**.

Extending the Ideas

9. The speaker in "Daybreak in Alabama" plans to make a musical statement about people of all colors getting along in the world. What songs do you know that make statements about cultural diversity and harmony? Check with your teacher to see if you could play them for the class and discuss their messages.
10. In which of these poems do you feel the author's cultural background contributes significantly to his or her **perspective** on what is valuable? Describe this perspective.

Literary Focus: Tone

Almost every element in a poem can reveal the author's attitude, or **tone**, including diction, or word choice; imagery; syntax, or arrangement of words in sentences; and rhythm.

- From the box below choose one or more words to describe the tone in each poem. Add your own words, if necessary.

angry	idealistic	cynical	pleasing	frustrated
romantic	hopeful	sarcastic	humorous	worried

LITERARY FOCUS: TONE

Emphasize that tone is the author's attitude toward a subject. Readers must infer tone from the way authors treat their readers and their characters and subjects. As an example, ask a student to speak the following sentence, first with concern, then with determination.

"The cat will not explode."

Possible responses: "One Perfect Rose"—*cynical, sarcastic, humorous;* "Daybreak in Alabama"—*romantic, idealistic, hopeful;* "The Flying Cat"—*humorous, frustrated, worried*

Ask students to discuss their choices.

After Reading

MAKING CONNECTIONS

1. Students should identify the things they value most and give reasons.

2. Students should be able to explain what they find memorable about the phrases or images.

3. Possible response: Parker, because her wit and humor would make her interesting

4. Possible responses: feeling like you're swallowing at twenty-thousand feet; a cat exploding; the cat's awareness of planets, satellites, black holes

5. Possible responses: end of first stanza—calmly as if stating a fact; end of second stanza—romantically; end of final stanza—sarcastically

6. Smell—scent of pine needles, smell of red clay after rain; sight—songs rising out of the ground like a swamp mist, dew falling from heaven, tall tall trees, long red necks, poppy colored faces, big brown arms, field daisy eyes, black and white people, black, brown, yellow, red clay earth hands; touch—hands touching, kind fingers

7. Words and images flow smoothly like music and mix naturally like people of all colors should.

8. Possible responses: Parker uses rhyme, regular rhythm, and simple images; Nye's poem is unrhymed, the rhythm is like that of normal speech, and the images are elaborate. Parker's word choices are formal, poetic; Nye's are informal, colloquial. Parker's tone is cynical; Nye's is humorous.

9. If you do not play the music, ask students to summarize some of the lyrics.

10. Possible response: Langston Hughes's poem reflects his perspective as an African American who has witnessed racial injustice.

VOCABULARY STUDY

1. pressurized
2. droll
3. amulet
4. statistic
5. poppy

Unit 4 Resource Book
Vocabulary, p. 43
Vocabulary Test, p. 46

WRITING CHOICES

Writer's Notebook Update

Invite students to share their "before" sketches and tell how the title did or did not lead them to an accurate sketch of the image as it was developed in the poem.

Pet Worries

Suggest students begin by listing concerns of pet owners who take their pets with them and the concerns of owners who leave their pets at home. Encourage them to brainstorm solutions to these problems before beginning to write.

Selection Test

Unit 4 Resource Book
pp. 47–48

Vocabulary Study

Solve the riddles by writing on your paper a vocabulary word for each numbered item.

amulet
droll
poppy
pressurized
statistic

1. This can describe an aircraft's interior or the inside of a cast-iron cooker.
2. This refers to something odd or amusing.
3. Some people believe this can fend off evil or disease.
4. This is a numerical fact about things or people to show their significance.
5. This is a flower or a vibrant color.

Expressing Your Ideas

Writing Choices

Writer's Notebook Update How well does your original sketch suit the actual poem? Look back at the notes you jotted down as you read the poem, and decide how the sketch should be changed. If you like the sketch as is, add a few more details.

Pet Worries "Should I put Poopsie in the pet motel while I'm away, or should she come with me?" Many travelers have worried about what to do with pets when vacations or work call them away from home. Imagine you are a writer for an airlines travel magazine. Write an **article** describing pet owners' concerns about their pets that travel with them or remain at home and offering possible solutions to owners' problems.

Other Options

The Scent of Music How can a song smell like pine needles and red clay? Read "Daybreak in Alabama" again and work with a partner to decide what kind of music might suit this poem. Then bring a recording or, if possible, produce your own **musical interpretation** of this song for the class.

Getting It Down Pat Many poems, like songs, lend themselves to memorization because they have a regular rhythm. Choose one of the poems you have just read or any poem of your choice, and memorize it for a **poetry reading** to be performed for a group of classmates. Try to capture the tone of the poem in your voice.

Bumper Wisdom What are the most memorable bumper stickers you have seen? Why are they memorable? With a partner, brainstorm ideas for a **bumper sticker** about something you value. Quickwrite thoughts about these ideas. Then express them as bumper stickers.

OTHER OPTIONS

Getting It Down Pat

As students practice, encourage them to use tape recorders or video recorders. The recordings will help them analyze and polish their speaking style and the tone they use.

Bumper Wisdom

Encourage students to brainstorm a list of bumper stickers they've seen in order to stimulate their own creativity. Suggest students think about ways their bumper stickers can protect, promote, or inform people about the things they value.

Before Reading

Tuesday Siesta

by Gabriel García Márquez Colombia

Gabriel García Márquez
born 1928

Gabriel García Márquez (gäv′rē el′ gär sē′ə mär′kez) was born in a coastal town in Colombia that resembles the magical town of Macondo, where he sets much of his fiction. He was raised in part by grandparents whose myths, legends, and world full of ghosts and "fantastic terrors" served as inspiration for his richly imaginative writing. His best-known novel, *One Hundred Years of Solitude,* which has sold over eleven million copies and been translated into more than thirty languages, illustrates magic realism, a style that blends incredible events with realistic details. In 1982, he was awarded the Nobel Prize for literature.

Building Background

The sweltering setting of "Tuesday Siesta" is an unnamed, rural town in Colombia—perhaps Aracataca, where García Márquez was born.

Fact Sheet Colombia	
Location	northwest corner of South America
Capital	Bogotá
Land area	440,000 square miles—about the size of Texas and California together
Language	Spanish
Climate	coastlands: tropical; highlands: moderate
Currency	1 peso = 100 centavos
Religion	about 98% Roman Catholic
Farm exports	coffee, bananas, sugar cane, tobacco
Minerals	emeralds, platinum, gold, iron, petroleum
Livestock	cattle

Literary Focus

Mood The title, "Tuesday Siesta," is the first clue to the story's **mood**, its overall atmosphere or prevailing feeling. What atmosphere do you associate with the word *siesta?* Throughout the story, phrases like "oppressive sun" and "floating in the heat" help establish the mood.

Writer's Notebook

The Little Things in Life "Tuesday Siesta" begins with a description of a poor woman and her daughter as they travel on a train. Although these people have no material goods, you will note during the course of the story that they value nonmaterial things. During your reading, list things that are meaningful in the mother's and daughter's lives. Be prepared to make some inferences.

Before Reading

Building Background

Refer to the map of Colombia on page 395. Students can add to the fact sheet on Colombia. (*per capita income, political climate, famous Colombians, etc.)*

Literary Focus

Students should recognize that the word *siesta* suggests a slow, sleepy mood and that details about the sun and heat suggest oppressiveness.

Writer's Notebook

Question What nonmaterial things do you value? *(Answers will vary: Guide a discussion of the kinds of nonmaterial things students value and why they value them.)* Students might keep these things in mind as they look for items valued by characters in the story.

More About Gabriel García Márquez

García Márquez says, "I began my career as a journalist in Colombia, and a reporter is something I've never stopped being. When I'm not working on fiction, I'm running around the world, practicing my craft as a reporter." Other works include:

- *Leaf Storm and Other Stories,* Harper, (1972)
- *Collected Stories,* Harper, (1984)
- *Love in the Time of Cholera,* Knopf, (1988)

SUPPORT MATERIALS OVERVIEW

Unit 4 Resource Book
- Graphic Organizer, p. 46
- Study Guide, p. 50
- Vocabulary, p. 51
- Grammar, p. 52
- Alternate Check Test, p. 53
- Vocabulary Test, p. 54
- Selection Test, pp. 55–56

Building English Proficiency
- Literature Summaries
- Activities, p. 205

Reading, Writing & Grammar SkillBook
- Vocabulary, pp. 9–10, 13–14
- Reading, pp. 38–40
- Grammar, Usage, and Mechanics, pp. 157–160

The World of Work
- Bereavement Counselor, p. 17
- Write a Classified Ad, p. 18

Technology
- Personal Journal Software
- Custom Literature Database: For another story about honoring the dead, see "Miss Tempy's Watchers" by Sarah Orne Jewett on the database.
- Test Generator Software

During Reading

Selection Objectives

- to explore characters' values
- to identify mood
- to use *that* and *which* effectively

Unit 4 Resource Book
Graphic Organizer, p. 49
Study Guide, p. 50

Theme Link

The mother and her daughter are very poor, but they do have "Something of Value"—their ethical standards and family attachments.

Vocabulary Preview

interminable, seemingly endless
serenity, quiet; calmness
oppressive, hard to bear
permeated, spread throughout; filled with
spinster, an unmarried woman
scrutinize, examine closely
rummage, search in a disorderly way
galvanized, covered with a thin coating of zinc to prevent rust
inscrutable, so mysterious or obscure that one cannot make out its meaning
skeptical, doubtful

Students can add the words and definitions to their Writer's Notebooks.

Art Study

Responses to Caption Question Crosses, grave markers, and submerged figures suggest a cemetery.

Visual Literacy The flattened perspective gives everything equal value. Bright color is everywhere, even in the cemetery. Stars seem artificial and hang like ornaments.

Question What is the artist's attitude toward death? *(Possible response: It is part of the natural world, sharing importance with life and not altogether dreadful.)*

Tuesday Siesta

• Gabriel García Márquez •

In this picture of a cemetery, María de Mater O'Neill uses vivid color, flattened perspective, and varied patterns to convey the energy that exists even in death. What details can you find that indicate this is a cemetery?

SELECTION SUMMARY

Tuesday Siesta

A woman and her twelve-year-old daughter, both dressed in mourning, are traveling by train through the banana plantations on a sweltering day in August. They get off at a town just as siesta has begun and go to see the priest. The woman wants to visit the cemetery to see the grave of her son, who was shot and killed the previous week while breaking into a house. When the priest asks about her son's morality, the woman says that her son was a good man, who boxed to support his family and never stole anything that anyone needed to eat. As he gives her the key to the cemetery, the priest notices that people have gathered outside. He suggests she wait until later when it is cooler, but mother and daughter walk out into the street.

*For summaries in other languages, see the **Building English Proficiency** book.*

The train emerged from the quivering tunnel of sandy rocks, began to cross the symmetrical, interminable[1] banana plantations, and the air became humid and they couldn't feel the sea breeze anymore. A stifling blast of smoke came in the car window. On the narrow road parallel to the railway there were oxcarts loaded with green bunches of bananas. Beyond the road, in uncultivated spaces set at odd intervals there were offices with electric fans, red-brick buildings, and residences with chairs and little white tables on the terraces among dusty palm trees and rosebushes. It was eleven in the morning, and the heat had not yet begun.

"You'd better close the window," the woman said. "Your hair will get full of soot."

The girl tried to, but the shade wouldn't move because of the rust.

They were the only passengers in the lone third-class car. Since the smoke of the locomotive kept coming through the window, the girl left her seat and put down the only things they had with them: a plastic sack with some things to eat and a bouquet of flowers wrapped in newspaper. She sat on the opposite seat, away from the window, facing her mother. They were both in severe and poor mourning clothes.

The girl was twelve years old, and it was the first time she'd ever been on a train. The woman seemed too old to be her mother, because of the blue veins on her eyelids and her small, soft, and shapeless body, in a dress cut like a cassock. She was riding with her spinal column braced firmly against the back of the seat, and held a peeling patent-leather handbag in her lap with both hands. She bore the conscientious serenity[2] of someone accustomed to poverty.

By twelve the heat had begun. The train stopped for ten minutes to take on water at a station where there was no town. Outside, in the mysterious silence of the plantations, the shadows seemed clean. But the still air inside the car smelled like untanned leather. The train did not pick up speed. It stopped at two identical towns with wooden houses painted bright colors. The woman's head nodded and she sank into sleep. The girl took off her shoes. Then she went to the washroom to put the bouquet of flowers in some water.

When she came back to her seat, her mother was waiting to eat. She gave her a piece of cheese, half a cornmeal pancake, and a cookie, and took an equal portion out of the plastic sack for herself. While they ate, the train crossed an iron bridge very slowly and passed a town just like the ones before, except that in this one there was a crowd in the plaza. A band was playing a lively tune under the oppressive[3] sun. At the other side of town the plantations ended in a plain which was cracked from the drought. **1**

The woman stopped eating.

"Put on your shoes," she said.

The girl looked outside. She saw nothing but the deserted plain, where the train began to pick up speed again, but she put the last piece of cookie into the sack and quickly put on her shoes. The woman gave her a comb.

"Comb your hair," she said.

The train whistle began to blow while the girl was combing her hair. The woman dried the sweat from her neck and wiped the oil from her face with her fingers. When the girl stopped combing, the train was passing the outlying houses of a town larger but sadder than the earlier ones.

"If you feel like doing anything, do it now," said the woman. "Later, don't take a drink anywhere even if you're dying of thirst. Above all, no crying." **2**

The girl nodded her head. A dry, burning

1. interminable (in tėr′mə nə bəl), *adj.* seemingly endless.
2. serenity (sə ren′ə tē), *n.* quiet; calmness.
3. oppressive (ə pres′iv), *adj.* hard to bear.

1 Literary Focus
Mood

Questions

- What mood has the author established? *(Possible responses: sadness, dread, oppression)*
- List five words in the story thus far that contribute to this mood. *(Possible responses: interminable, heat, soot, mourning, shapeless, braced, poverty, mysterious, shadows)*

2 Literary Element
Characterization

Question What do you know about the woman and her daughter? *(Possible responses: They are poor, but try to do the best they can with their appearance. Evidently they are on their way to a funeral, because they are dressed in mourning and have brought flowers. Both are calm and self-possessed. The girl is obedient. They are proud and do not want the world to see them as weak and tearful.)*

BUILDING ENGLISH PROFICIENCY

Expanding Vocabulary Notebooks: Homonyms

Students can devote a section of their vocabulary notebooks to homonyms, starting with those in this story. List *write* and *right* on the board and explain that they are homonyms—words that are pronounced the same but have different spellings and meanings. Ask a volunteer to act out the meaning of *write* and *right* without speaking.

Activity Ideas

- Write these word pairs on the board and ask partners to define or act out each word and use it in a sentence.
  morning/mourning
  vein/vain
  plane/plain
  peace/piece
  loan/lone
- Ask groups of students to supply other homonyms. They can write these homonyms on index cards, which can be shuffled and used in a matching game.

3 Literary Element
Imagery

Questions

- What sound images has the author created? *(Possible responses: fingernail scratching on a metal grating, humming of an electric fan, creaking door, cautious voice)*
- How does this imagery help create mood? *(Possible response: It adds to the oppressiveness of the setting. The grating fingernail is a harsh, unpleasant sound. The humming fan suggests droning repetitiveness, further emphasizing the quiet and heat. The creaking door and cautious voice add suspense.)*

4 Literary Focus
Mood

Point out the details that help establish the mood in this paragraph: the old smell of flowers that permeates the room; the mother standing absent-mindedly, clutching her handbag; no noise but the electric fan.

Question How do these details and images make you feel? *(Possible responses: oppressed, sad, uneasy)*

THE WOMAN SCRATCHED THE METAL GRATING ON THE DOOR WITH HER FINGERNAIL. . . .

wind came in the window, together with the locomotive's whistle and the clatter of the old cars. The woman folded the plastic bag with the rest of the food and put it in the handbag. For a moment a complete picture of the town, on that bright August Tuesday, shone in the window. The girl wrapped the flowers in the soaking-wet newspapers, moved a little farther away from the window and stared at her mother. She received a pleasant expression in return. The train began to whistle and slowed down. A moment later it stopped.

There was no one at the station. On the other side of the street, on the sidewalk shaded by the almond trees, only the pool hall was open. The town was floating in the heat. The woman and the girl got off the train and crossed the abandoned station—the tiles split apart by the grass growing up between—and over to the shady side of the street.

It was almost two. At that hour, weighted down by drowsiness, the town was taking a siesta. The stores, the town offices, the public school were closed at eleven, and didn't reopen until a little before four, when the train went back. Only the hotel across from the station, with its bar and pool hall, and the telegraph office at one side of the plaza stayed open. The houses, most of them built on the banana company's model, had their doors locked from inside and their blinds drawn. In some of them it was so hot that the residents ate lunch in the patio. Others leaned a chair against the wall, in the shade of the almond trees, and took their siesta right out in the street.

3 Keeping to the protective shade of the almond trees, the woman and the girl entered the town without disturbing the siesta. They went directly to the parish house. The woman scratched the metal grating on the door with her fingernail, waiting a moment, and scratched again. An electric fan was humming inside. They did not hear the steps. They hardly heard the slight creaking of a door, and immediately a cautious voice, right next to the metal grating: "Who is it?" The woman tried to see through the grating.

"I need the priest," she said.

"He's sleeping now."

"It's an emergency," the woman insisted.

Her voice showed a calm determination.

The door was opened a little way, noiselessly, and a plump, older woman appeared, with very pale skin and hair the color of iron. Her eyes seemed too small behind her thick eyeglasses.

"Come in," she said, and opened the door all the way.

They entered a room permeated[4] with an old smell of flowers. The woman of the house led them to a wooden bench and signaled them to sit down. The girl did so, but her mother remained standing, absent-mindedly, with both hands clutching the handbag. No noise could be heard above the electric fan. 4

The woman of the house reappeared at the door at the far end of the room. "He says you should come back after three," she said in a very low voice. "He just lay down five minutes ago."

"The train leaves at three-thirty," said the woman.

It was a brief and self-assured reply, but her voice remained pleasant, full of undertones. The woman of the house smiled for the first time.

"All right," she said.

When the far door closed again, the woman sat down next to her daughter. The narrow waiting room was poor, neat, and clean. On the other side of the wooden railing which divided the room, there was a worktable, a plain one

4. permeated (pėr′mē āt əd), *adj.* spread throughout; filled with.

MINI-LESSON: GRAMMAR
Using That and Which

Teach Write these sentences on the board.

It was her son that had been shot.

The woman shot him with a pistol which had not been used in years.

Discuss the use of the relative pronouns *that* and *which.* Point out that the pronoun *that* can be used to refer to either a person or a thing. *Which* can be used to refer to a thing but never to a person.

Activity Ideas

- Ask students to make up sentences about the people and things in the story, using the pronouns *that* and *which* correctly.
- Have students review a piece of their writing and check for the correct use of *that* and *which.*

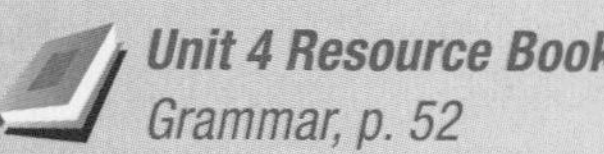
Unit 4 Resource Book
Grammar, p. 52

with an oilcloth cover, and on top of the table a primitive typewriter next to a vase of flowers. The parish records were beyond. You could see that it was an office kept in order by a spinster.[5]

The far door opened and this time the priest appeared, cleaning his glasses with a handkerchief. Only when he put them on was it evident that he was the brother of the woman who had opened the door.

"How can I help you?" he asked.

"The keys to the cemetery," said the woman.

The girl was seated with the flowers in her lap and her feet crossed under the bench. The priest looked at her, then looked at the woman, and then through the wire mesh of the window at the bright, cloudless sky.

"In this heat," he said. "You could have waited until the sun went down."

The woman moved her head silently. The priest crossed to the other side of the railing, took out of the cabinet a notebook covered in oilcloth, a wooden penholder, and an inkwell, and sat down at the table. There was more than enough hair on his hands to account for what was missing on his head.

"Which grave are you going to visit?" he asked.

"Carlos Centeno's," said the woman.

"Who?"

"Carlos Centeno," the woman repeated.

The priest still did not understand.

"He's the thief who was killed here last week," said the woman in the same tone of voice. "I am his mother."

The priest scrutinized[6] her. She stared at him
5 with quiet self-control, and the Father blushed. He lowered his head and began to write. As he filled the page, he asked the woman to identify herself, and she replied unhesitatingly, with precise details, as if she were reading them. The Father began to sweat. The girl unhooked the buckle of her left shoe, slipped her heel out of it, and rested it on the bench rail. She did the same with the right one.

It had all started the Monday of the previous 6
week, at three in the morning, a few blocks from there. Rebecca, a lonely widow who lived in a house full of odds and ends, heard above the sound of the drizzling rain someone trying to force the front door from outside. She got up, rummaged[7] around in her closet for an ancient revolver that no one had fired since the days of Colonel Aureliano Buendía,[8] and went into the living room without turning on the lights. Orienting herself not so much by the noise at the lock as by a terror developed in her by twenty-eight years of loneliness, she fixed in her imagination not only the spot where the door was but also the exact height of the lock. She clutched the weapon with both hands, closed her eyes, and squeezed the trigger. It was the first time in her life that she had fired a gun. Immediately after the explosion, she could hear nothing except the murmur of the drizzle on the galvanized[9] roof. Then she heard a little metallic bump on the cement porch, and a very low voice, pleasant but terribly exhausted: "Ah, Mother." The man they found dead in front of the house in the morning, his nose blown to bits, wore a flannel shirt with colored stripes, everyday pants with a rope for a belt, and was barefoot. No one in town knew him.

"So his name was Carlos Centeno," murmured the Father when he finished writing.

"Centeno Ayala,"[10] said the woman. "He was my only boy."

The priest went back to the cabinet. Two big rusty keys hung on the inside of the door; the girl imagined, as her mother had when she was

---

5. spinster (spin′stər), *n.* an unmarried woman, especially an older woman.
6. scrutinize (skrüt′n īz), *v.* examine closely.
7. rummage (rum′ij), *v.* search in a disorderly way.
8. **Aureliano Buendía** (ou′rā lyä′nō bwän dē′ä).
9. galvanized (gal′və nīzd), *adj.* covered with a thin coating of zinc to prevent rust.
10. **Centeno Ayala** (cen tē′nō ä yä′lä). In Spanish-speaking countries, a person's first name and surname are 7
customarily followed by his or her mother's maiden name. Thus, the young man's full name was Carlos Centeno Ayala.

5 Reading/Thinking Skills
Infer

Questions

- Why does the priest blush? *(The woman's stare and quiet self-control make him self-conscious and aware of the rudeness of his open scrutiny.)*
- How is the woman able to remain so quiet and self-controlled? *(Possible response: She is not embarrassed to be the mother of Carlos Centeno.)*

6 Literary Element
Flashback

This passage breaks the story's chronological sequence as the narrator gives important information about the son's death.

Question How might this information be introduced if the point of view were first person rather than third person? *(Possible response: The priest might relate it.)*

7 Multicultural Note
Names

Expand on footnote 10: In contemporary usage, especially in the United States, the final surname is often dropped. In this passage, the woman makes a point of giving both names, perhaps to reinforce her pride in her son by calling attention to the surname Ayala that she contributed.

BUILDING ENGLISH PROFICIENCY

ESL
LEP
ELD
SAE
LD

Analyzing Comprehension

You can use "Tuesday Siesta" to try an experiment in reading comprehension.

1. Ask small groups of students to review the story and note the passage that makes the least sense to them and the passage that makes the most sense (that is, the passage that is clearest and easiest to understand).

2. Have the groups work through the most difficult passages, rewriting them in their own words.

3. As a class, discuss the reasons that particular passages are easy or difficult to grasp (for example, vocabulary, sentence structure, concepts). Invite students to offer their strategies for dealing with comprehension problems.

8 Reading/Thinking Skills
Recognize Values

The woman's statement that she told her son "never to steal anything that anyone needed to eat," implies that morality is sometimes determined by circumstances.

Questions

- Are there occasions when acts such as stealing, lying, or disobeying are permissible? *(Encourage students to think through the issue from moral, personal, and societal points of view and to cite specific situations.)*
- What selections from this book or from other reading you have done illustrate examples of characters acting against laws or authority but according to their own consciences? *(Possible responses: Antigone, "The Rain Came," Red Azalea)*

The World of Work
Bereavement Counselor

For real-life experiences of a bereavement counselor, use—

The World of Work
pp. 17–18

Check Test

1. What method of transportation do the woman and her daughter use? *(train)*

2. Why are the woman and her daughter traveling to the town? *(to visit the cemetery where their son and brother is buried)*

3. Why do they go to the priest? *(to get the key to the cemetery)*

4. How did the woman's son die? *(He was shot while trying to break into someone's home.)*

5. Why did the son box on Saturday nights? *(to earn money to support his family)*

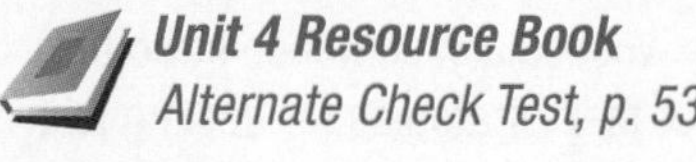

---

a girl and as the priest himself must have imagined at some time, that they were Saint Peter's keys. He took them down, put them on the open notebook on the railing, and pointed with his forefinger to a place on the page he had just written, looking at the woman.

"Sign here."

The woman scribbled her name, holding the handbag under her arm. The girl picked up the flowers, came to the railing shuffling her feet, and watched her mother attentively.

The priest sighed.

"Didn't you ever try to get him on the right track?"

The woman answered when she finished signing.

"He was a very good man."

The priest looked first at the woman and then at the girl, and realized with a kind of pious amazement that they were not about
8 to cry. The woman continued in the same tone:

"I told him never to steal anything that anyone needed to eat, and he minded me. On the other hand, before, when he used to box, he used to spend three days in bed, exhausted from being punched."

"All his teeth had to be pulled out," interrupted the girl.

"That's right," the woman agreed. "Every mouthful I ate those days tasted of the beatings my son got on Saturday nights."

"God's will is inscrutable,"[11] said the Father.

But he said it without much conviction, partly because experience had made him a little skeptical[12] and partly because of the heat. He suggested that they cover their heads to guard against sunstroke. Yawning, and now almost completely asleep, he gave them instructions about how to find Carlos Centeno's grave. When they came back, they didn't have to knock. They should put the key under the door; and in the same place, if they could, they should put an offering for the Church. The woman listened to his directions with great attention, but thanked him without smiling.

The Father had noticed that there was someone looking inside, his nose pressed against the metal grating, even before he opened the door to the street. Outside was a group of children. When the door was opened wide, the children scattered. Ordinarily, at that hour there was no one in the street. Now there were not only children. There were groups of people under the almond trees. The Father scanned the street swimming in the heat and then he understood. Softly, he closed the door again.

"Wait a moment," he said without looking at the woman.

His sister appeared at the far door with a black jacket over her nightshirt and her hair down over her shoulders. She looked silently at the Father.

"What was it?" he asked.

"The people have noticed," murmured his sister.

"You'd better go out by the door to the patio," said the Father.

"It's the same there," said his sister. "Everybody is at the windows."

The woman seemed not to have understood until then. She tried to look into the street through the metal grating. Then she took the bouquet of flowers from the girl and began to move toward the door. The girl followed her.

"Wait until the sun goes down," said the Father.

"You'll melt," said his sister, motionless at the back of the room. "Wait and I'll lend you a parasol."

"Thank you," replied the woman. "We're all right this way."

She took the girl by the hand and went into the street.

11. **inscrutable** (in skrü′tə bəl), *adj.* so mysterious or obscure that one cannot make out its meaning.
12. **skeptical** (skep′tə kəl), *adj.* doubtful.

MINI-LESSON: VOCABULARY
Etymology

Discuss the use of etymologies in figuring out and remembering the meaning of words. As an example, point out the word *inscrutable* and tell students that it comes from the Latin root *scrutari*, which means "examine" and the Latin prefix *in-*, which means "not."

Question Now that you know the meanings of the word and prefix it comes from, what do you think *inscrutable* means? *(not to be examined* or *mysterious)*

Activity Ideas

- Have students look up the following words in a dictionary to learn their etymologies: *oppressive; permeated; rummage; skeptical; spinster*
- Have students skim other selections they have read to find unfamiliar words. Ask them to compare the etymologies of these words with their dictionary definitions.

After Reading

Making Connections

Shaping Your Response

1. In your opinion, would "Tuesday Siesta" make a good episode for a television series? Why or why not?
2. What do you think happens after the woman and her daughter leave the parish house?
3. If you could control the characters' fate, how would you change the events of the story?

Analyzing the Story

4. How does the **setting** help create the **mood** of the story?
5. What do you think the description of the mother "riding with her spinal column braced firmly against the back of the seat" suggests about her **character**?
6. Explain what qualities you **infer** the mother possesses as you read about the following.
   - her warning to her daughter as they get off the train;
   - her statements when the priest's housekeeper opens the door;
   - her actions at the end of the story.
7. At the **conclusion** of the story, the woman assures the priest, "We're all right this way." Do you think she will be able to maintain her dignity among the townspeople? Why or why not?

Extending the Ideas

8. What are your feelings about gun control? Does this story confirm or go against these feelings? Explain.
9. Review the things that are valued in these works by Parker, Nye, Hughes, and García Márquez. Then explain whether or not you think these people of different countries or cultures share similar **perspectives** about what is valuable.

Literary Focus: Mood

The atmosphere or general feeling the author conveys to the reader through setting, imagery, details, and descriptions is called **mood**. In "Tuesday Siesta," the use of mood helps evoke feelings of pity toward the characters and anger toward the social conditions that create such human suffering.

- Describe the mood of "Tuesday Siesta."
- Find five details, images, or phrases that help establish the mood.

After Reading

MAKING CONNECTIONS

1. Possible response: No, because there is little action.

2. Possible response: The people will follow the woman and girl to the cemetery. They might be curious and ask rude questions. The woman and girl will remain calm and unprovoked, pay their respects, and then quietly leave.

3. Remind students that although they can change events, actions must be consistent with what they know about the characters and the situation.

4. The intense heat, interminable plantations, drought-stricken plains, silence, and brooding atmosphere of the parish house all evoke the oppressive mood.

5. Her stiff back suggests she is determined and purposeful.

6. Possible responses: The woman's warning to her daughter suggests she is strong and in control. Her statements to the housekeeper suggest that she is determined. Her actions at the end of the story suggest that she is fearless.

7. Possible response: Yes. She is a strong woman who is loyal to her son and to his memory. She will not be harassed or embarrassed.

8. Instruct students to give reasons to support their opinions. The topic lends itself to a debate.

9. Possible response: With the exception of Parker, they seem to share similar perspectives on what is valuable, although the specific things they value differ. Each thinks nonmaterial things (love, loyalty, human relationships, relationships with animals, and so on) are most valuable.

ITERARY FOCUS: MOOD

iscuss the differences between mood and tone. emind students that tone is the author's attitude ward the subject or characters. In this story, the ne might be described as detached or objective. ood is the atmosphere created by the text that auses an emotional response in the reader. Mood d tone may be very different, as they are in uesday Siesta."

Possible responses:

- oppressive, sympathetic
- Responses may include words and phrases such as the following: *symmetrical, interminable banana plantations; the oppressive sun; town was floating in the heat; weighted down by drowsiness, the town was taking a siesta; a room permeated with an old smell of flowers*

VOCABULARY STUDY

1. f
2. j
3. e
4. h
5. c
6. g
7. b
8. i
9. d
10. a

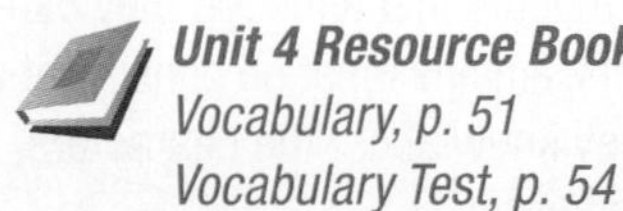

Unit 4 Resource Book
Vocabulary, p. 51
Vocabulary Test, p. 54

WRITING CHOICES

Writer's Notebook Update

Students might organize their paragraph by order of importance, beginning with the most important things.

Looking for New Ideas?

Suggest students brainstorm a list of conversations and sights. Have them choose one and write about it for three minutes before beginning their summary.

Travels with My Mother

Encourage students to review the story and imagine what is going through the girl's mind as she witnesses each episode.

Selection Test

Unit 4 Resource Book
pp. 55–56

Vocabulary Study

On your paper, match each numbered word with the letter of its definition.

galvanized
inscrutable
interminable
oppressive
permeated
rummage
scrutinize
serenity
skeptical
spinster

1. interminable	**a.** an unmarried woman
2. serenity	**b.** coated with zinc
3. oppressive	**c.** to watch closely
4. permeated	**d.** doubtful
5. scrutinize	**e.** burdensome
6. rummage	**f.** seemingly endless
7. galvanized	**g.** to search haphazardly
8. inscrutable	**h.** spread throughout
9. skeptical	**i.** not easily understood
10. spinster	**j.** calmness

Expressing Your Ideas

Writing Choices

Writer's Notebook Update Using your list of items that the mother and daughter value, write a paragraph about why they may have considered those things to be important. Support your ideas with examples from the story.

Looking for New Ideas? "Tuesday Siesta" was inspired by the author's boyhood memory of a woman and a small girl he had seen carrying an umbrella in the afternoon sun, and the comment someone made to him: "She's the mother of that thief." Think of a sight or a comment overheard—on the bus, in the cafeteria, in the street—that could inspire a story. Then write a story **summary**.

Travels with My Mother She has only one line of dialogue, but the daughter has many unspoken thoughts. Imagine what she's thinking as she returns home. Then describe a **dream** she might have about the day's events. Remember that dreams aren't always logical.

Other Options

Just the Facts, Ma'am Jot down ideas for a **fact sheet**, like the one on Colombia preceding this story, that lists at least eight facts about *your* town, area, or neighborhood. Write your fact sheet on a posterboard. Add a map of important sites.

Come to Sunny Colombia You are a travel agent investigating the possibility of conducting tours to Colombia. Research to find out if it's a place tourists would enjoy visiting. You might start with information provided in Before Reading and build from there. Then make a recommendation in a **memo** about whether or not to add Colombia to your tour sites.

Woman Shoots Night Visitor The town prosecutor has charged Rebecca with murder. Her attorney has claimed that she was merely defending herself. Hold a **trial** with a prosecution team, a defense team, and a judge. Let the class act as jury.

OTHER OPTIONS

Come to Sunny Colombia

You might suggest that students investigate articles about Colombia in travel magazines.

Woman Shoots Night Visitor

Encourage the legal teams to investigate laws regarding rights of homeowners to protect property. Have students consider whom they can call to provide testimony.

Before Reading

The Pillow Book by Sei Shōnagon Japan

Porsche by Bailey White USA

Sei Shōnagon
965–?

Sei Shōnagon (sī shō′nə gon), lady-in-waiting to an empress of Japan, recorded thoughts in a "pillow book" kept by her bedside. *The Pillow Book,* with its lively anecdotes and character sketches, is today considered one of the greatest works of Japanese literature.

Bailey White
born 1950

This first-grade teacher in Georgia is also a commentator on National Public Radio—interesting careers for someone who, as a teenager, tried "to be not noticed." "Porsche" is an excerpt from White's book, *Mama Makes Up Her Mind . . . ,* a humorous account of an eccentric Southern family.

Building Background

Sei, Meet Bailey In the selections you are about to read, two women, writing over a thousand years apart, present lively, perceptive pictures of their respective cultures. Sei Shōnagon said of her writing, "I set about filling the notebooks with odd facts, stories from the past, and all sorts of other things, often including the most trivial material." But those "trivial" accounts of court life, etiquette, and nature provide a vivid and fascinating picture of Japanese culture.

Just as Sei Shōnagon's telling images provide clues to medieval Japan, Bailey White's description of her cluttered household and 1958 Porsche may provide people living in the 30th century with important insights about our culture. Her other works, such as the collection, *Sleeping at the Starlight Motel,* include daft characters (Red the Rat Man) and details of Americana (vignettes of the one-room schoolhouse and the flashes of human nature behind the "No Fishing" sign) that will entertain and inform generations to come.

Literary Focus

Imagery Concrete details that appeal to the five senses are called **images.** A writer uses images to give readers a sense of experiencing what they are reading. *The Pillow Book* and "Porsche" are memorable for their images. As you read these selections, list several images in your notebook that you find appealing.

Images	
The Pillow Book	Porsche

Writer's Notebook

Writing Inspirations How many times have you read something and thought to yourself, "Why didn't I think of that?" or "That reminds me of the time. . . ." Well, keep that pen handy as you read the following selections. Use your notebook as a portable "pillow book" to jot down any writing ideas that pop into your head.

Before Reading

Building Background

Lead students in brainstorming a list of facts, stories, and cultural trivia that they might want to preserve in writing to give future generations a picture of life today.

Literary Focus

List the five senses on the board: *sight, sound, smell, touch,* and *taste.* Ask students to find images as they read that involve these senses.

Writer's Notebook

Urge students to write down any ideas that occur to them. They needn't stop to evaluate whether they are good topics. They can assess the material later as they look for ideas for the writing assignment on page 523.

More About Sei Shōnagon and Bailey White

Shōnagon, the author's name at court, means "Minor Counselor." Her real name may have been Nagiko.

Bailey White comes from an old-fashioned southern family like the one described in "Porsche." She and her mother share a cluttered household.

Other works by Bailey White include: *Mama Makes Up Her Mind and Other Dangers of Southern Living,* Addison-Wesley, (1993)

SUPPORT MATERIALS OVERVIEW

Unit 4 Resource Book
- Graphic Organizer, p. 57
- Study Guide, p. 58
- Vocabulary, p. 59
- Grammar, p. 60
- Alternate Check Test, p. 61
- Vocabulary Test, p. 62
- Selection Test, pp. 63–64

Building English Proficiency
- Literature Summaries
- Activities, p. 206

Reading, Writing & Grammar SkillBook
- Grammar, Usage, and Mechanics, pp. 140–141

Technology
- Audiotape 12, Side B
- Personal Journal Software
- Custom Literature Database: For a diary account that combines acute observations and humor, see "The Diary of Adam and Eve" by Mark Twain on the database.
- Test Generator Software

During Reading

Selection Objectives

- to explore what people from different eras and cultures value
- to identify images
- to recognize sentence fragments

Unit 4 Resource Book
Graphic Organizer, p. 57
Study Guide, p. 58

Theme Link

The theme "Something of Value" is reflected in these selections. Sei Shōnagon values things such as beauty, power, and pleasure. Bailey White values the accumulated clutter left by her family.

Vocabulary Preview

ritualist, person who practices or advocates observance of rites, or ceremonies
fluently, speaking or writing easily and rapidly
impiety, lack of respect
wisteria, a climbing shrub with large drooping clusters of flowers
reprimand, criticize

Students can add the words and definitions to their Writer's Notebooks.

Response to Caption Question
Appearance is important because it is pleasing to others. She is young and eager to be attractive.

Visual Literacy In the painting—a hanging scroll made of silk—the girl is looking into a pocket mirror. The piece of paper tissue in her teeth suggests that she has also been fixing her makeup. Her kimono is actually two garments, an outer transparent gauze kimono and an under kimono.

from
The Pillow Book
Sei Shōnagon

Things That Give a Pleasant Feeling

A set of well-executed pictures of women, accompanied by interesting texts.

The return journey from a festival, with a large number of escorts in attendance. The costumes of the women passengers spill out at the sides of the carriage, and, thanks to the skill of the ox-drivers, the carriages run smoothly along the road.

On a pretty sheet of white Michinoku paper someone has written a letter with a brush that would not seem capable of making such delicate strokes.

The sight of a boat as it glides downstream.

Well-blackened teeth.[1]

To throw equal numbers repeatedly in a game of dice.

Fine strands of silk that have been entwined.

A skilled Master of Divination performs a purification service[2] on a river bank.

A drink of water when one wakes up at night.

One is in a rather bored mood when a visitor arrives—a man with whom one's relations are neither too intimate nor too distant. He tells one what has been happening in society, things pleasant and disagreeable and strange; moving from one topic to another, he discusses matters both public and private—and all in so clear a fashion that there is no possibility of misunderstanding. This gives one a very pleasant feeling.

One has visited a shrine or a temple with the request that certain prayers be said on one's behalf. What a pleasure to hear the ritualist[3] or priest intone them in a better voice, and more fluently,[4] than one had expected!

This painting, done in the 1820s by Japanese artist Keisai Eisen, shows the teenage daughter of a well-to-do family fixing her hair and makeup. Based on the cultural **perspective** presented by Sei Shōnagon in her *Pillow Book,* why do you think this young woman is giving such attention to her appearance?

1. **well-blackened teeth.** In Sei Shōnagon's time, blackening the teeth was thought to help keep Japanese girls healthy and attractive.
2. **purification service,** the ritual cleansing of the body with water, performed before the beginning of any Japanese ceremony.
3. ritualist (rich′ü ə list), *n.* person who practices or advocates observance of the form or system of rites, or ceremonies.
4. fluently (flü′ənt lē), *adv.* speaking or writing easily and rapidly.

SELECTION SUMMARY

The Pillow Book and Porsche

The Pillow Book In *The Pillow Book,* the author shares observa-tions on different topics: *Pleasant things* (delicate brush strokes on pretty paper, a boat gliding downstream, well-blackened teeth); *Good-looking preachers* (so that people will listen to them); *Elegant things* (duck eggs, a rock crystal rosary, snow on wisteria); and *Things that have lost their power* (a stranded boat, a defeated sumo wrestler).

Porsche In "Porsche," the narrator explains tha her home is a place where things accumulate. He father, who could no longer stand the clutter, left in his red Porsche and was never seen again. Thirty years later, he died and left her and her mother the Porsche, which they added to their collection.

For summaries in other languages, see the ***Building English Proficiency*** *book*

A Preacher Ought to Be Good-Looking

A preacher ought to be good-looking. For, if we are properly to understand his worthy sentiments, we must keep our eyes on him while he speaks; should we look away, we may forget to listen. Accordingly an ugly preacher may well be the source of sin. . . .

But I really must stop writing this kind of thing. If I were still young enough, I might risk the consequence of putting down such impieties,[5] but at my present stage of life I should be less flippant.[6]

Some people, on hearing that a priest is particularly venerable[7] and pious, rush off to the temple where he is preaching, determined to arrive before anyone else. They, too, are liable to bring a load of sin on themselves and would do better to stay away.

Elegant Things

A white coat worn over a violet waistcoat.
Duck eggs.
Shaved ice mixed with liana syrup and put in a new silver bowl.
A rosary of rock crystal.[8]
Snow on wisteria[9] or plum blossoms. 1
A pretty child eating strawberries.

Things That Have Lost Their Power

A large boat which is high and dry in a creek at ebb-tide.

A woman who has taken off her false locks to comb the short hair that remains.

A large tree that has been blown down in a gale and lies on its side with its roots in the air. 2

The retreating figure of a *sumo* wrestler who has been defeated in a match.

A man of no importance reprimanding[10] an attendant. 3

An old man who removes his hat, uncovering his scanty topknot.

5. impiety (im pī′ə tē), *n.* lack of respect.
6. **flippant** (flip′ənt), *adj.* disrespectful or pert in speech.
7. **venerable** (ven′ər ə bəl), *adj.* worthy of reverence or respect.
8. **rock crystal,** a colorless, transparent variety of quartz, often used for jewelry.
9. wisteria (wi ster′ē ə), *n.* a climbing shrub with large drooping clusters of flowers.
10. reprimand (rep′rə mand), *v.* criticize.

1 Literary Element
Tone

Question What is the author's tone as she lists these elegant things? *(respectful, serious, philosophical)*

2 Historical Note
Sumo Wrestling

Sumo is a highly ritualized form of Japanese wrestling that gained prominence under the samurai. Its object is to throw an opponent to the ground or outside of the ring. Many sumo wrestlers weigh over 350 pounds, with large stomachs for a low center of gravity.

3 Literary Focus
Images

Question In *The Pillow Book,* which senses are used to create images? Give examples. *(Possible responses: sight and smell—snow on wisteria; taste—a drink of water; sound—a ritualist intoning prayers; touch—shaved ice)*

Literary Criticism

Murasaki Shikibu, a writer who lived around the time of Sei Shōnagon, said, "She is a gifted woman, to be sure. Yet, if one gives free rein to one's emotions even under the most inappropriate circumstances, if one has to sample each interesting thing that comes along, people are bound to regard one as frivolous.

BUILDING ENGLISH PROFICIENCY

ESL LEP ELD SAE LD

Linking Literature and History

These notes were written by a young woman living in a different time, under different circumstances. Encourage students to explore and understand the world of Sei Shōnagon.

1. Ask students to jot down details that define Sei Shōnagon's period in history (ox-drivers, for example) and any references that they don't understand (such as blackened teeth, a fashion of the time).

2. Ask students to consider the class differences of Japan at this time. Ask: Was Sei Shōnagon a typical Japanese woman? How can you tell?

3. Invite students to speculate or to do research on the role of women in Imperial Japan. Ask: How does Sei Shōnagon seem to spend her days? What are her main interests? What can you infer about the life of a lady-in-waiting?

Building English Proficiency
Activities, p. 206

4 Reader's Response
Making Personal Connections

Question Do you think getting rid of the junk would convince the father to return? Explain your answer. *(Possible response: No. The junk is probably symptomatic of an eccentric, unchanging household.)*

5 Literary Focus
Imagery

Question What images does the author create in this paragraph? *(a Model 356 Porsche speedster complete with wild-eyed driver with his hair on end; an area behind the garden cluttered with two tractors and something like a lawnmower)* Invite interested students to illustrate one image.

6 Reading/Thinking Skills
Draw Conclusions

Questions

- Why doesn't the mother get rid of some of the old, useless things she has accumulated? *(Possible responses: They are treasured momentos of family; she is a compulsive collector.)*
- Why doesn't the mother sell the Porsche? *(Possible responses: It provides an important memory; she cannot get rid of anything.)*

Bailey White

Mama and I live in one of those houses where things accumulate. Something can get laid down on a table or in the seat of a broken chair and just stay there forever. There's my great-grandmother's coat she hung on a nail before she died, and an old cousin's unfinished model of the *Flying Cloud.* There's a couple of bamboo chinaberry-seed popguns from three generations back and six bottles of Maybloom Cream beginning to turn iridescent with the tops rusted on. There's a row of Mason jars with some spooky-looking mold growing inside, left over from an old dead aunt's experiments with lethal herbs, and a drop-seat viyella union suit folded up on top of the carburetor of a Model A Ford. After a while the things begin to interlock. I really don't think we could get the ship model out in one piece even if we tried.

When I was eight years old, it got to be too much for my father. I remember the day he left for good. "I can't take it anymore!" he wailed. "I'm stagnating here! That coat!" He clutched the top of his head. I looked at my great-grandmother's coat. "That coat has been hanging there for fifty years!" And he hurled himself out of the house, jumped into his little red Porsche, and scratched off in a swirl of dust.

I missed my father. "Why don't we move the coat?" I asked my mother. "Then maybe he'll come back."

"It's not just the coat, child," she told me. I looked around. There were my great-aunt Bertie's lavender satin wedding shoes perched
4 on the seat of my Uncle Luten's unicycle, and Uncle Ralph's wall-eyed, hunchbacked, one-legged stuffed turkey on the library table. She was right. Even I could see it wasn't just the coat.

We never saw my father again, but we heard that he had driven that Porsche all the way to Hollywood, California, and made piles of money writing scripts for TV shows. Our neighbors told us they had actually seen his name on TV. We wouldn't know. We didn't have a TV set. Where would we have put it?

The years went by. Twenty years, thirty years. Then one fall my father died. His fourth wife, now his widow, called us on the phone. "He left you something," she said. "It should be there in a few days."

And a week later it arrived. It was my father's Porsche, the same one he had left us in—a 1958 Model 356 speedster, in original condition, complete with a wild-eyed driver whose hair stood straight up on end. Mama told him, "Just park it out behind the garden with those two tractors and that thing that might have been a lawnmower."

But he wouldn't do it. "Lady, you're crazy. You don't know what this is." He rubbed the car's fender with his shirttail. "You don't park a car like this out with the tractors."

We stood around and looked at it. Mama 5
sighed. Then she went over and started pulling a section of screen off the side porch. We built a ramp, and the man drove the car up onto the porch. We drained the oil and gas out of it, put it up on blocks, and replaced the screen.

Now a man who says he belongs to the Porsche Club of America calls us up almost every night hoping to buy the car. We keep telling him no, no, no. Besides, that car has been in our house almost a year now. Even if he came all the way down here, I doubt he could get to it.

6

French sculptor Arman embedded sixty automobiles in concrete to create *Long Term Parking,* a project he worked on from 1975 to 1982. What **perspective** on the automobile in modern culture do you think is expressed by this work? ➤

MINI-LESSON: GRAMMAR
Sentence Fragments

Teach Write these sentences from the story on the board.

"The years went by. Twenty years, thirty years."

Explain to students that the first sentence is a complete sentence: it has a subject *(years)* and a verb *(went).* Tell students that the second "sentence" is a sentence fragment.

Question What part of a sentence is this fragment missing? *(a verb)* Explain that people often use fragments when speaking and that sometimes writers use them to create authentic sounding, informal conversation. In formal writing, however, fragments should be avoided.

Activity Ideas

- Hold a brief conversation with a student. Challenge other students to listen carefully and jot down any fragments used.
- Ask students to review a piece of their own writing and check for fragments.

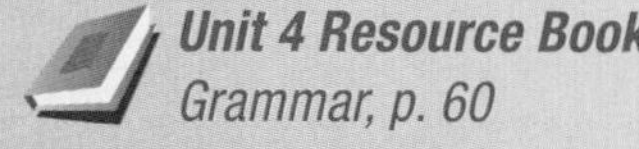
Unit 4 Resource Book
Grammar, p. 60

Art Study

Response to Caption Question Possible responses: The automobile is here to stay; it is embedded in our culture.

Visual Literacy Arman was born Armand Fernandez, but in 1957 he decided he wanted to be known by one name only and chose Armand. A printer made an error, however, and spelled the name as Arman, and so it was shortened even further. Arman was born in France but is now a U.S. citizen. His best-known art is assembled from junk.

Check Test

1. Why does the author of *The Pillow Book* say a preacher should be good-looking? *(Audiences are more likely to look at him and to pay attention to what he says.)*

2. What are two things the author says have lost their power? *(Answers should include two of the following: a boat high and dry in a creek, a woman who has removed her false hair, an uprooted tree, a defeated sumo wrestler, an unimportant man reprimanding an attendant, a hatless old man with a scanty topknot.)*

3. In "Porsche," why does the narrator say her father left? *(He couldn't stand the accumulation of things in the house.)*

4. What does the father leave his family when he dies? *(his red Porsche)*

5. What does the narrator's mother do with the car? *(She has it parked on the porch.)*

Unit 4 Resource Book
Alternate Check Test, p. 61

BUILDING ENGLISH PROFICIENCY

ESL LEP ELD SAE LD

Contrasting Selections

Students will recognize that both Bailey White and Sei Shōnagon are witty observers of their respective cultures. A close look at their writing, however, reveals many differences between the two authors. A chart such as the one shown might help students compare and contrast the lives, society, and writing styles of these women.

	Sei Shōnagon	Bailey White
Writing style	spare, dignified	humorous, informal
Tone		
Subjects		
Social class		
Cultural details		

After Reading

MAKING CONNECTIONS

1. Students will provide answers based on their experiences and attitudes and give reasons for their answers.

2. Possible response: I'd put it in storage until I get my driver's license and can afford car insurance.

3. Possible responses: Many of her observations remain relevant today; pleasure, good looks, elegance, and power are valued today, although modern writers would supply contemporary examples.

4. The question should prompt lively discussion and could lend itself to role playing. Students might analyze what makes people collectors and savers.

5. Possible responses: *The Pillow Book*—observant, worldly opinionated; "Porsche"—easygoing, amusing, patient.

6. Possible responses: First-person point of view allows immediacy; both narrators are keen observers who give firsthand accounts of what they see happening around them.

7. Possible response: The Porsche was important to the father, and he knew his ex-wife was a collector who would keep the car just as he left it.

8. Possible response: The father sees the Porsche as a symbol of freedom; Mother sees it as a memento of an experience, a time, a person; the daughter sees it as a symbol of her father, who was on the move.

9. Possible response: This refers to ship models painstakingly built in narrow-necked bottles. It's impossible to remove the ship without breaking the bottle—just as the clutter could not be removed from their house.

10. In providing answers, students should note how the differences in social class and value systems of each writer determine what is important.

After Reading

Making Connections

Shaping Your Response

1. Do you think the father in Bailey White's account had a right to leave? Why or why not?
2. What would you have done with the Porsche if it had been delivered to your house?
3. How relevant do you think Sei Shōnagon's observations are today—more than one thousand years after she wrote them?
4. List five items in your house about which a visitor might ask, "Why do you keep that thing?"

Analyzing the Selections

5. What three words would you use to describe the **narrator** of *The Pillow Book?* of "Porsche"?
6. Do you think the first-person **point of view** is more effective for these selections than third person would have been? Explain.
7. Why do you think the father sent the Porsche back to his ex-wife and daughter?
8. In your opinion, what does the Porsche **symbolize** for the father? for the mother and the narrator?
9. In the first paragraph, Bailey White says, "I really don't think we could get the ship model out in one piece even if we tried." To what is she comparing her cluttered house in this **figure of speech?**

Extending the Ideas

10. Both writers mention things they value. What cultural insights into medieval Japan and modern America do these valued items provide?

Literary Focus

Images Details that stimulate the reader's senses or imagination and bring pictures to mind are called **images**. Both Bailey White and Sei Shōnagon evoke images from the world around them.

- List four concrete details in "Things That Give a Pleasant Feeling" that bring pictures to your mind.
- To which senses does "Elegant Things" appeal?
- In "Porsche," how does Bailey White help you visualize the accumulated clutter in the house?

LITERARY FOCUS: IMAGES

Possible Responses

- Women's costumes spilling out of a carriage; a boat gliding downstream; well-blackened teeth; a violet coat
- All the senses, with the possible exception of hearing
- She provides many detailed images of the things that have accumulated.

Discuss some of the images that students identify. Suggest that students close their eyes and visualize each one, telling what they see or smell and what th image reminds them of. Guide them to understand that the power of an image is not just the details of the image but the way in which they connect to idea or memories that the reader already has.

Vocabulary Study

Study the relationship of the following pairs of words in capital letters; then choose another pair that has the same relationship.

fluently
impiety
reprimand
ritualist
wisteria

1. REPRIMAND : SCOLD :: **a.** annoy : bother **b.** listen : attention **c.** forget : remember **d.** accept : gift
2. RITUALIST : CEREMONY :: **a.** clown : laugh **b.** secretary : office **c.** athlete : trophy **d.** entertainer : performance
3. FLUENTLY : HALTINGLY :: **a.** quickly : swiftly **b.** happily : smilingly **c.** angrily : boldly **d.** gracefully : clumsily
4. SHRUB : WISTERIA :: **a.** book : magazine **b.** bacteria : antibiotic **c.** sport : basketball **d.** leaf : flower
5. IMPIETY : RESPECT :: **a.** disrespect : peace **b.** prayer : church **c.** blame : praise **d.** hatred : scorn

Expressing Your Ideas

Writing Choices

Writer's Notebook Update What kinds of writing ideas did the selections trigger? Choose one of the ideas you wrote down as you read the selections and expand it into a paragraph. Engage the reader's imagination by including vivid images.

Zuihitsu A type of occasional writings and random notes, such as *The Pillow Book,* is known in Japan as *zuihitsu.* Start your own ***zuihitsu*** of observations similar to Sei Shōnagon's. Share your work with a classmate.

Old Sneakers, Faded Celebrities Both people and things can lose their power. Reread Sei Shōnagon's "Things That Have Lost Their Power." Then write a **"has-been list"** of five people or things that were once popular, but now have little importance or value.

Other Options

Comedy Stage Like Sei Shōnagon and Bailey White, who closely observed their surroundings, stand-up comedians cast a humorous eye toward *their* world—personal experiences, public figures, news events—to find material for their routines. With a small group, conduct a **comedy workshop** in which you try out various comedic routines based on close observations of daily life.

Pillow Talk Make your own contemporary **pillow book**, based on "chapters" such as Things That I Like But Can't Afford, The Worst Things to Give Teenagers for Birthdays, Things That Represent Me, and so forth. List appropriate things under your heads and illustrate them.

Time Will Tell How will people one hundred years from now know about the things your generation treasures today? With a group, list things that could be put into a **time capsule** to inform future generations about What Really Matters to young people today.

VOCABULARY STUDY

1. a
2. d
3. d
4. c
5. c

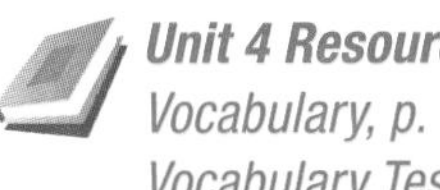

Unit 4 Resource Book
Vocabulary, p. 59
Vocabulary Test, p. 62

WRITING CHOICES

Writer's Notebook Update

Before students begin writing, suggest they list images they can use to illustrate the idea. Encourage them to think of images drawn from as many of the five senses as possible.

Zuihitsu

Suggest that students use a small notebook and keep it with them constantly for a week, jotting notes whenever an idea occurs to them.

Selection Test

Unit 4 Resource Book
pp. 63–64

THER OPTIONS

omedy Stage

ggest the following:

- eep a journal at hand for a few days to jot down otes about events observed or ideas gotten from he newspapers and television.
- Jse the workshop for experimentation with deliv- ery, gestures, facial expression, and so on. Other students should offer suggestions.

Time Will Tell

Students might organize their list by topics, such as "Things That Have Great Power" and "People Who Matter."

Before Reading

Building Background

When Alfred Nobel died in 1896, he left $9 million to fund the award. The interest is paid annually to prize winners. In 1992, each prize was worth about $1.2 million.

Literary Focus

Students can analyze these writers' **styles** by filling out a chart, noting stylistic elements as they read.

Style	Camus	Wiesel
Images		
Figurative language		
Tone		

Writer's Notebook

As they read, have students list abstract nouns that have positive connotations *(truth, liberty, commitment)* and negative connotations *(tyranny, oppression, suffering, humiliation).* These words will help define the writers' duties.

Connections to **AuthorWorks**

Albert Camus and Elie Wiesel are featured authors in the AuthorWorks CD-ROM series.

Before Reading

Nobel Acceptance Speeches by Elie Wiesel Romania/USA and Albert Camus France

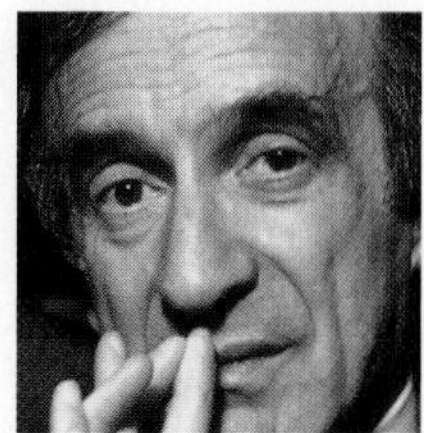

Elie Wiesel
born 1928

In 1944, when Elie Wiesel (el′ē wē zel′) was fifteen, most of his family perished in an extermination camp in Auschwitz. His account, *Night,* documents the horrors of the Holocaust. He was awarded the Nobel Prize for peace in 1986.

Albert Camus
1913–1960

Albert Camus (kä mü′) captured the moral dilemma of World War II and the postwar era in his writings. Awarded the Nobel Prize for literature in 1957, Camus responded, "What else have I done but meditate on an idea I found in the streets of my time?"

Building Background

It's a "Dynamite" Award In 1888 a French newspaper mistakenly reported the death of Alfred Nobel, Swedish inventor of dynamite. Shaken by the premature obituary and its reference to "the dynamite king," Nobel established a prize to promote international peace, as well as awards in literature, physics, chemistry, economics, and physiology or medicine. Wiesel and Camus are only two of the authors represented in this book who have been awarded the prestigious Nobel Prize. With the exception of Wiesel, who won the peace prize, all the writers listed have won the prize for literature.

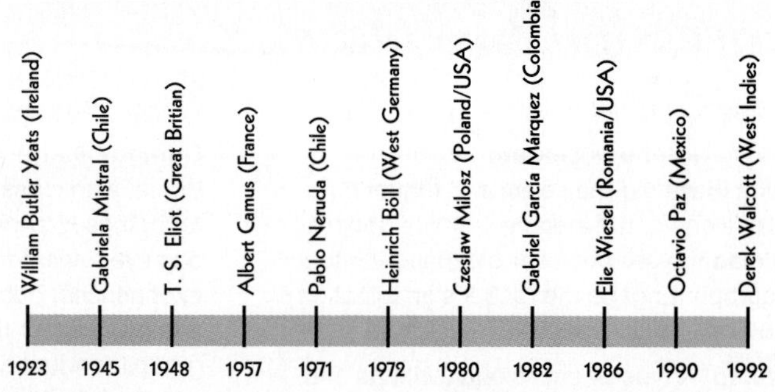

Literary Focus

Style The manner in which writers use words to fit their ideas is called **style**. A writer's style is a combination of many techniques and devices that work together to express ideas. In the following acceptance speeches, note things such as **word choice, images,** and **rhythms.**

Writer's Notebook

Mixed Emotions In his speech, Albert Camus says that he and other artists are "obliged to understand rather than to judge." As you read both speeches, jot down other phrases that explain each writer's **perspectives** and view of his duty.

SUPPORT MATERIALS OVERVIEW

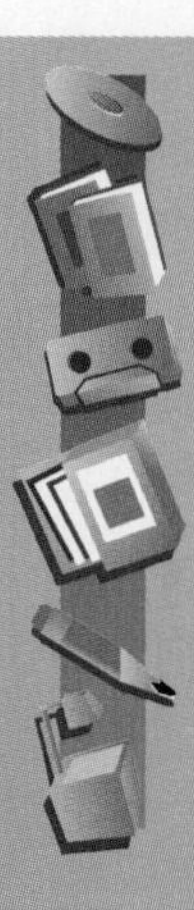

Unit 4 Resource Book
- Graphic Organizer, p. 65
- Study Guide, p. 66
- Vocabulary, p. 67
- Grammar, p. 68
- Alternate Check Test, p. 69
- Vocabulary Test, p. 70
- Selection Test, pp. 71–72

Building English Proficiency
- Literature Summaries
- Activities, p. 207

Reading, Writing & Grammar SkillBook
- Grammar, Usage, and Mechanics, pp. 267–268

Technology
- Audiotape 12, Side B, Audiotape 13, Side A
- Personal Journal Software
- Custom Literature Database: For another speech about freedom and duty, see The Gettysburg Address by Abraham Lincoln on the database.
- Test Generator Software

NOBEL ACCEPTANCE SPEECH
(1957)

ALBERT CAMUS

In receiving the distinction with which your free Academy has so generously honored me, my gratitude has been profound, particularly when I consider the extent to which this recompense[1] has surpassed my personal merits. Every man, and for stronger reasons, every artist, wants to be recognized. So do I. But I have not been able to learn of your decision without comparing its repercussions to what I really am. A man almost young, rich only in his doubts and with his work still in progress, accustomed to living in the solitude of work or in the retreats of friendship: how would he not feel a kind of panic at hearing the decree that transports him all of a sudden, alone and reduced to himself, to the center of a glaring light? And with what feelings could he accept this honor at a time when other writers in Europe, among them the very greatest, are condemned to silence, and even at a time when the country of his birth is going through unending misery?

I felt that shock and inner turmoil. In order to regain peace I have had, in short, to come to terms with a too generous fortune. And since I cannot live up to it by merely resting on my achievement, I have found nothing to support me but what has supported me through all my life, even in the most contrary circumstances: the idea that I have of my art and of the role of the writer. Let me only tell you, in a spirit of gratitude and friendship, as simply as I can, what this idea is.

For myself, I cannot live without my art. But I have never placed it above everything. If, on the other hand, I need it, it is because it cannot be separated from my fellow men, and it allows me to live, such as I am, on one level with them. It is a means of stirring the greatest number of people by offering them a privileged picture of common joys and sufferings. It obliges the artist not to keep himself apart; it subjects him to the most humble and the most universal truth. And often he who has chosen the fate of the artist because he felt himself to be different soon realizes that he can maintain neither his art nor his difference unless he admits that he is like the others. The artist forges himself to the others, midway between the beauty he cannot do without and the community he cannot tear himself away from. That is why true artists scorn nothing: they are obliged to understand rather than to judge. And if they have to take sides in this world, they can perhaps side only with that society in which, according to Nietzsche's[2] great words, not the judge but the creator will rule, whether he be a worker or an intellectual.

By the same token, the writer's role is not free from difficult duties. By definition he cannot put himself today in the service of those who make history; he is at the service of those who suffer it. Otherwise, he will be alone and deprived of his art. Not all the armies of tyranny with their millions of men will free him from his isolation, even and particularly if he falls into step with them. But the silence of an unknown prisoner, abandoned to humiliations at the other end of the world, is enough to draw the writer out of his exile, at least whenever, in the midst of the privileges of freedom, he manages not to forget that 1

1. **recompense** (rek′əm pens), *n.* reward.
2. **Nietzsche** (nē′chə), Friedrich Wilhelm, 1844–1900, German philosopher and writer.

During Reading

Selection Objectives

- to explore two Nobel writers' views of their mission
- to identify a writer's style
- to use colons correctly
- to identify a word's exact meaning in a dictionary

Unit 4 Resource Book
Graphic Organizer, p. 65
Study Guide, p. 66

Theme Link

For both Camus and Wiesel; "Something of Value" involves the writer's mission of working to expose the world's injustices.

Vocabulary Preview

homage, dutiful respect
presumptuous, acting without permission or right; bold
anguish, severe physical pain or mental suffering
traumatized, undergoing great shock
insidious, working secretly or subtly

Students can add the words and definitions to their Writer's Notebooks.

1 Literary Focus
Style

Remind students that an author's style is a combination of many qualities, including tone, point of view, and use (or little use) of figurative language.

Questions

- How would you describe Camus's tone? *(Possible responses: respectful, honored, polite)*
- What is his point of view? *(first person)*
- To what degree does he rely on figurative language and imagery? *(very little)*

SELECTION SUMMARY
Nobel Acceptance Speeches

In his acceptance speech, Albert Camus reveals his feelings of panic, shock, and humility upon receiving this honor. He acknowledges that he gains strength from his art, which connects him to humanity. He recognizes the mission of the writer in exposing injustice and reaffirms his commitment to keeping alive the hopes of those who endure persecution and misery.

Elie Wiesel accepts the award on behalf of victims of the Holocaust. Directing his words to a Jewish boy, Wiesel says the world knew about the Holocaust, but remained silent. Now he speaks out on behalf of people worldwide who suffer. Victims must know they are not alone; people must lend their voices and efforts to end injustice.

*For summaries in other languages, see the **Building English Proficiency** book.*

2 Active Reading
Clarify

Response He bears the miseries of his generation because he makes a commitment to write about the miseries endured by all people.

3 Reading/Thinking Skills
Literal and Figurative Language

Point out the phrase ". . . intelligence has debased itself to become the servant of hatred and oppression. . . ." Ask what this phrase means literally. Then explain that this is an example of figurative language, which goes beyond the literal meaning of the words. Guide students to appreciate how figurative language adds levels of meaning to writing.

4 Active Reading
Connect

Response Yes; every detail that Camus uses to describe his generation is as true or even more true today than in the 1950s.

5 Historical Note
Grand Inquisitors

"Grand inquisitors" is an allusion to the Inquisition—a religious court of the Middle Ages that tried people for religious heresy. The grand inquisitors were known for their cruelty, bigotry, and fanaticism.

silence, and to transmit it in order to make it resound by means of his art.

None of us is great enough for such a task. But in all circumstances of life, in obscurity or temporary fame, cast in the irons of tyranny or for a time free to express himself, the writer can win the heart of a living community that will justify him, on the one condition that he will accept to the limit of his abilities the two tasks that constitute the greatness of his craft: the service of truth and the service of liberty. Because his task is to unite the greatest possible number of people, his art must not compromise with lies and servitude which, wherever they rule, breed solitude. Whatever our personal weaknesses may be, the nobility of our craft will always be rooted in two commitments, difficult to maintain: the refusal to lie about what one knows and the resistance to oppression.

For more than twenty years of an insane history, hopelessly lost like all the men of my generation in the convulsions of time, I have been supported by one thing: by the hidden feeling that to write today was an honor because this activity was a commitment—and a commitment not only to write. Specifically, in view of my powers and my state of being, it was a commitment to bear, together with all those who were living through the same history, the misery and the hope we shared.

2 **CLARIFY: In what sense does the writer bear the misery of others?**

These men, who were born at the beginning of the First World War, who were twenty when Hitler came to power and the first revolutionary trials were beginning, who were then confronted as a completion of their education with the Spanish Civil War, the Second World War, the world of concentration camps, a Europe of torture and prisons—these men must today rear their sons and create their works in a world threatened by nuclear destruction. Nobody, I think, can ask them to be optimists. And I even think that we should understand—without ceasing to fight it—the error of those who in an excess of despair have asserted their right to dishonor and have rushed into the nihilism[3] of the era. But the fact remains that most of us, in my country and in Europe, have refused this nihilism and have engaged upon a quest for legitimacy. They have had to forge for themselves an art of living in times of catastrophe in order to be born a second time and to fight openly against the instinct of death at work in our history.

THEY HAVE HAD TO FORGE FOR THEMSELVES AN ART OF LIVING IN TIMES OF CATASTROPHE. . . .

Each generation doubtless feels called upon to reform the world. Mine knows that it will not reform it, but its task is perhaps even greater. It consists in preventing the world from destroying itself. Heir to a corrupt history, in which are mingled fallen revolutions, technology gone mad, dead gods, and worn-out ideologies, where mediocre powers can destroy all yet no longer know how to convince, where intelligence has debased itself to become the servant 3
of hatred and oppression, this generation starting from its own negations has had to re-establish, both within and without, a little of that which constitutes the dignity of life and death.

CONNECT: Do you think that the preceding sentence describes the present generation as well as Camus's? Explain. 4

In a world threatened by disintegration, in which our grand inquisitors run the risk of 5

3. **nihilism** (nī′ə liz′əm), entire rejection of the established beliefs in religion, morals, government, laws, and so forth.

MINI-LESSON: VOCABULARY
Use Dictionaries for Word Meaning

Teach Point out the word *forge,* which appears in large type at the top of this page. Explain that the dictionary gives several meanings for this word, including the following: (1) to shape metal by heating and then hammering; (2) to sign another's name falsely to deceive; (3) to make, shape, or form.

Tell students they can determine which of a word's meanings applies to a particular sentence by substituting each definition in the sentence.

Question Which definition applies to the use of *forge* in the text? *(definition 3)*

Activity Idea Have students look up other words on this page *(heart, quest, prison, breed, craft)* in a dictionary and tell which of the meanings apply.

Hands raised helplessly in the air, a group of Jewish women and children are herded into captivity by Nazis in the Warsaw Ghetto during World War II. What would you suggest are the feelings and **perspective** of this photographer on the Holocaust?

establishing forever the kingdom of death, it knows that it should, in an insane race against the clock, restore among the nations a peace that is not servitude, reconcile anew labor and culture, and remake with all men the Ark of the Covenant.[4] It is not certain that this generation will ever be able to accomplish this immense task, but already it is rising everywhere in the world to the double challenge of truth and liberty and, if necessary, knows how to die for it without hate. Wherever it is found, it deserves to be saluted and encouraged, particularly where it is sacrificing itself. In any event, certain of your complete approval, it is to this generation that I should like to pass on the honor that you have just given me.

6 At the same time, after having outlined the nobility of the writer's craft, I should have put him in his proper place. He has no other claims but those which he shares with his comrades in arms: vulnerable but obstinate, unjust but impassioned for justice, doing his work without shame or pride in view of everybody, not ceasing to be divided between sorrow and beauty, and devoted finally to drawing from his double existence the creations that he obstinately tries to erect in the destructive movement of history. Who after all this can expect from him complete solutions and high morals? Truth is mysterious, elusive, always to be conquered. Liberty is dangerous, as hard to live with as it is elating. We must march toward these two goals, painfully but resolutely, certain in advance of our failings on so long a road. What writer would from now on in good conscience dare set himself up as a preacher of virtue? For myself, I must state once more that I am not of this kind. I have never been able to renounce the light, the pleasure of being, and the freedom in which I grew up. But although this nostalgia explains many of my errors and my faults, it has doubtless helped me toward a better understanding of my craft. It is helping me still to support unquestioningly all those silent men who sustain the life made for them in the world only through memory of the return of brief and free happiness.

Thus reduced to what I really am, to my limits and debts as well as to my difficult creed, I feel freer, in concluding, to comment upon the extent and the generosity of the honor you have just bestowed upon me, freer also to tell you that I would receive it as an homage[5] rendered to all those who, sharing in the same fight, have not received any privilege, but have on the contrary known misery and persecution. It remains for me to thank you from the bottom of my heart and to make before you publicly, as a personal sign of my gratitude, the same and ancient promise of faithfulness which every true artist repeats to himself in silence every day.

4. **Ark of the Covenant,** literally, the chest containing the Ten Commandments. Here, Camus refers to the solemn promises made by God to human beings.
5. **homage** (hom′ij), *n.* dutiful respect.

Art Study

Response to Caption Question
The photographer, whose picture starkly reveals the horrors of the Holocaust, seems very sympathetic to the plight of the victims.

Visual Literacy The photograph is as perfectly composed as a painting. It has three points of focus: the boy at right center; the woman at left center who may be the boy's mother; and the soldier.

Question The photographer has captured the three subjects at a moment when they seem to be visually connected. How are they linked? *(The woman appears to be looking over her shoulder at the soldier; the boy seems to cringe under the barrel of the gun; the soldier is looking at the two victims, as though he has singled them out of this crowd.)*

6 Literary Focus
Style

This paragraph illustrates two characteristics of Camus's style: the antithetical statement ("vulnerable but obstinate, unjust but impassioned for justice") and the rhetorical question ("What writer would . . . set himself up as a preacher of virtue?") Have students find other examples of these two characteristics in his speech.

BUILDING ENGLISH PROFICIENCY

Vocabulary Aids

Use one or more of the following activities to help students focus on the challenging vocabulary in these speeches.

Activity Ideas

- Work with students to determine the meanings of the following words. Then have them act out or explain them: *unite, convulsions, catastrophe, technology, obstinate, persecution, gratitude, homage.*
- Discuss the meanings of the following abstract nouns with students: *commitment, tyranny, oppression, dignity, justice, anguish, humiliation, virtue.* Have groups divide these words into two lists—those with positive and those with negative connotations. Encourage them to add other abstract nouns from the speeches to their lists.

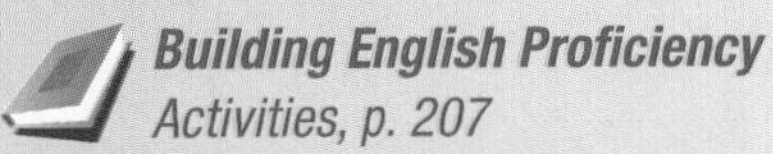

Building English Proficiency
Activities, p. 207

7 Literary Focus
Style

Point out the following elements in this paragraph that characterize Wiesel's style:

- exaggeration: "eternities ago"
- metaphors: "kingdom of night" and "fiery altar upon which the history of our people and the future of mankind were meant to be sacrificed"
- the quick rhythm produced by short clauses, sentences, and sentence fragments ("The ghetto. The deportation.")
- the repetition of words: "I remember . . . I remember"
- memorable images: "The sealed cattle car. The fiery altar . . . ."

8 Literary Criticism
Elie Wiesel

"Elie Wiesel has been . . . a witness to the range, bestiality and completeness of the destruction of European Jewry by the Germans. . . . Auschwitz informs everything he writes. . . . He is not belligerent about it, only unyielding. Nothing he can say measures up to the enormity of what he saw, what others endured. . . . He is part conscience, part quivering needle of response and part warning signal."

Thomas Lask
New York Times.

NOBEL ACCEPTANCE SPEECH
(1986)

ELIE WIESEL

It is with a profound sense of humility that I accept the honor you have chosen to bestow upon me. I know: your choice transcends me. This both frightens and pleases me.

It frightens me because I wonder: do I have the right to represent the multitudes who have perished? Do I have the right to accept this great honor on their behalf? I do not. That would be presumptuous.[1] No one may speak for the dead, no one may interpret their mutilated dreams and visions.

It pleases me because I may say that this honor belongs to all the survivors and their children, and through us, to the Jewish people with whose destiny I have always identified.

7 I remember: it happened yesterday or eternities ago. A young Jewish boy discovered the kingdom of night. I remember his bewilderment, I remember his anguish.[2] It all happened so fast. The ghetto. The deportation. The sealed cattle car. The fiery altar upon which the history of our people and the future of mankind were meant to be sacrificed.

I remember: he asked his father: "Can this be true? This is the twentieth century, not the Middle Ages. Who would allow such crimes to be committed? How could the world remain silent?"

And now the boy is turning to me: "Tell me," he asks. "What have you done with my future? What have you done with your life?"

And I tell him that I have tried. That I have tried to keep memory alive, that I have tried to fight those who would forget. Because if we forget, we are guilty, we are accomplices.

And then I explained to him how naive we were, that the world did know and remain silent. And that is why I swore never to be silent whenever and wherever human beings endure suffering and humiliation. We must always take sides. Neutrality helps the oppressor, never the victim. Silence encourages the tormentor, never the tormented.

Sometimes we must interfere. When human lives are endangered, when human dignity is in jeopardy, national borders and sensitivities become irrelevant. Wherever men or women are persecuted because of their race, religion, or political views, that place must—at that moment—become the center of the universe. 8

Of course, since I am a Jew profoundly rooted in my people's memory and tradition, my first response is to Jewish fears, Jewish needs, Jewish crises. For I belong to a traumatized[3] generation, one that experienced the abandonment and solitude of our people. It would be unnatural for me not to make Jewish priorities my own: Israel, Soviet Jewry, Jews in Arab lands.

But there are others as important to me. Apartheid[4] is, in my view, as abhorrent as anti-Semitism. To me, Andrei Sakharov's isolation is as much of a disgrace as Iosif Begun's imprisonment. As is the denial of Solidarity and its leader

1. **presumptuous** (pri zump′chü əs), *adj.* acting without permission or right; bold.
2. **anguish** (ang′gwish) *n.* severe physical pain or mental suffering.
3. **traumatized** (trô′mé tīzd), *adj.* undergoing great shock.
4. **apartheid** (ə pärt′hāt), *n.* South Africa's former governmental policy of racial segregation.

MINI-LESSON: GRAMMAR
Colons

Teach Write the following sentences on the board:

- I remember: it happened yesterday or eternities ago.
- It would be unnatural for me not to make Jewish priorities my own: Israel, Soviet Jewry, Jews in Arab lands.

Discuss the use of colons, pointing out that they can do the following:

1. Separate independent clauses when the second explains or restates the first (first example sentence)
2. Introduce a list of items (second example sentence)
3. Introduce a long quotation or formal statement

Activity Ideas

- Have students use colons in their own sentences, modeling their work on the first two examples. Remind them that the first sentence should contain two clauses, the second explaining the first; the second should introduce a list of items.
- Ask students to write sentences about the selection in which they use colons.

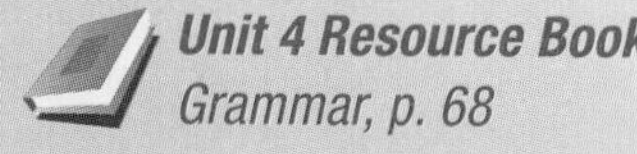
Unit 4 Resource Book
Grammar, p. 68

Lech Walesa's right to dissent. And Nelson Mandela's interminable imprisonment.[5]

There is so much injustice and suffering crying out for our attention: victims of hunger, or racism and political persecution, writers and poets, prisoners in so many lands governed by the left and by the right. Human rights are being violated in every continent. More people are oppressed than free.

And then, too, there are the Palestinians[6] to whose plight I am sensitive but whose methods I deplore. Violence and terrorism are not the answer. Something must be done about their suffering, and soon. I trust Israel, for I have faith in the Jewish people. Let Israel be given a chance, let hatred and danger be removed from her horizons, and there will be peace in and around the Holy Land.

Yes, I have faith. Faith in God and even in His creation. Without it no action would be possible. And action is the only remedy to indifference: the most insidious[7] danger of all. Isn't this the meaning of Alfred Nobel's legacy? Wasn't his fear of war a shield against war?

There is much to be done, there is much that can be done. One person—a Raoul Wallenberg, an Albert Schweitzer,[8] one person of integrity, can make a difference, a difference of life and death. As long as one dissident[9] is in prison, our freedom will not be true. As long as one child is hungry, our lives will be filled with anguish and shame.

What all these victims need above all is to know that they are not alone; that we are not forgetting them, that when their voices are stifled we shall lend them ours, that while their freedom depends on ours, the quality of our freedom depends on theirs.

This is what I say to the young Jewish boy wondering what I have done with his years. It is in his name that I speak to you and that I express to you my deepest gratitude. No one is as capable of gratitude as one who has emerged from the kingdom of night. 9

We know that every moment is a moment of grace, every hour an offering; not to share them would mean to betray them. Our lives no longer belong to us alone; they belong to all those who need us desperately.

Thank you Chairman Aarvik. Thank you, members of the Nobel Committee. Thank you, people of Norway, for declaring on this singular occasion that our survival has meaning for mankind. 10

11

5. **Andrei Sakharov's . . . imprisonment**, references to leaders who were imprisoned or in forced isolation because of their resistance to government policies and their pursuit of human rights. These dissidents have all been freed since Wiesel's speech was delivered. Walesa and Mandela have since served as presidents of Poland and South Africa, respectively.
6. **Palestinians,** people who became refugees when Israel was created as a nation in 1948 or in later shifts of Israel's boundaries.
7. **insidious** (in sid′ē əs) *adj.* working secretly or subtly.
8. **Raoul Wallenberg . . . Albert Schweitzer.** Wallenberg, a Swedish diplomat who saved many Jews from the Holocaust by intervening with the Nazis, died in a Russian prison after World War II. Schweitzer, an Alsatian physician, philosopher, and missionary, was awarded the Nobel Peace Prize in 1952.
9. **dissident** (dis′ə dənt), *n.* person who disagrees or dissents.

9 Literary Element
Symbolism

Question What is the "kingdom of night"? *(Specifically, it is the concentration camps and the Holocaust; more generally, it is the oppression, injustice, and suffering that people in many places are subjected to.)*

10 Reading/Thinking Skills
Identify Author's Purpose

Questions

- State the purpose of Wiesel's speech in your own words. *(to remind readers of the Holocaust and prevent similar atrocities form recurring)*
- What words and phrases do you find most effective in conveying Wiesel's message? *(Possible responses: "fiery altar," "Kingdom of night")*

11 The Author Speaks
Memoirs

Wiesel has said, "To write your memoirs is to draw up a balance sheet of your life . . . Am I ready for a final reckoning?" He provides such a reckoning in his memoirs, *All Rivers Run to the Sea,* Knopf, (1995).

Check Test

1. What does Camus say he cannot live without in paragraph three? *(his art)*

2. Camus says that his generation cannot reform the world, but it has a greater task. What is it? *(to prevent the world from destroying itself)*

3. What kingdom does Wiesel mention? *(the kingdom of night)*

4. Who discovers this kingdom? *(a young Jewish boy)*

5. To whom does Wiesel say the honor of the Nobel Prize rightfully belongs? *(the survivors of the Holocaust)*

Unit 4 Resource Book
Alternate Check Test, p. 69

BUILDING ENGLISH PROFICIENCY

Exploring Key Concepts

Use one or more of the following activities to help students focus on the Holocaust.

Activity Ideas

- Team-teach a lesson about the Holocaust with a social studies teacher. Together, try to clarify why Wiesel refers to the Nazi persecution of the Jews as *the kingdom of night* and the *fiery altar.*
- Involve students in a discussion of their understanding of the Holocaust. Ask: Can anything like the Holocaust happen today? What do you know about the killing fields in Cambodia? the genocide in Bosnia? How do these far-away horrors affect you, right now?
- Groups of students might benefit from viewing and reporting on movies such as *Schindler's List* or *The Killing Fields.*

After Reading

MAKING CONNECTIONS

1. Possible response: Yes. In order to prevent such horrors from recurring, people must remember what happened and help younger generations learn from the past.

2. Invite students to share their choices and explain why the images are memorable to them.

3. Possible response: Yes, because there is still injustice and suffering in the world.

4. Possible response: The young boy may be Wiesel himself as he experienced the horrors of the concentration camps. The kingdom of night is the concentration camps and the Holocaust.

5. Wiesel's tone is serious and reflective.

6. They must speak up for the oppressed who cannot speak up for themselves.

7. Camus and Wiesel both consider it the writer's responsibility to speak up for those who are oppressed, imprisoned, and suffering and who cannot speak up for themselves.

8. Possible response: Living through the Holocaust or any great tragedy would affect one's perspective throughout life. A person might be more sensitive to injustice, more aware of his or her vulnerability to oppression, and more appreciative of freedom and liberty.

9. Possible response: Yes; people such as Mother Teresa and Albert Schweitzer have made a tremendous difference. In discussion invite students to name other people who have made a difference.

After Reading

Making Connections

Shaping Your Response

1. Speaking of the Holocaust, Wiesel says, ". . . if we forget, we are guilty, we are accomplices." Do you agree? Explain.
2. What images from each speech do you find most memorable?
3. Camus says, "Each generation doubtless feels called upon to reform the world." Do you feel this observation applies to your generation? Why or why not?

Analyzing the Speeches

4. Who might you **infer** is the "young Jewish boy" mentioned in Wiesel's speech, and what is the "kingdom of night" he discovers in paragraph four?
5. How would you describe Wiesel's **tone** in this speech?
6. What does Camus consider his generation's responsibility in light of modern-day oppression?

Extending the Ideas

7. Compare Wiesel's view of the writer's mission to that of Camus.
8. Wiesel lived through the Holocaust; Camus experienced its horrors less directly. In what respects do you think experiencing the Holocaust would determine a person's **perspective** about life and values?
9. Near the end of his speech, Wiesel expresses his faith and asserts that "one person of integrity can make a difference." Do you agree? Why or why not?

Literary Focus: Style

The manner in which writers use words and sentences to fit their ideas is called **style.** Style involves choices on the part of the writer such as: from whose point of view? what tone? what mood? which words? what kind of imagery? whether or not to use figurative language?

- What do you think is the purpose of Wiesel's many **allusions** to historical figures?
- Which speech uses more **figurative language**? What are some examples of such language?
- What effect does Wiesel create by portraying things from a young boy's **point of view**?

LITERARY FOCUS: STYLE

Emphasize to students that no single element, such as point of view, tone, mood, word choices, images, or rhythm can be used to describe an author's style. Style must be inferred from these and other things.

Possible Responses

- Wiesel uses allusion to illustrate both the mistakes and the inspirations provided by history, thus providing modern readers with both warnings and models.
- Wiesel relies more heavily on figurative language Examples: "kingdom of night," "fiery altar upon which the history of our people and the future of mankind were meant to be sacrificed," "every ho an offering."
- By referring to the young boy, Wiesel suggests th he is talking about real people. He also underscores his personal experience, implying that he was the young boy who witnessed these atrocitie

Vocabulary Study

Choose the letter of the word that is most nearly the *opposite* of the italicized word.

anguish
homage
insidious
presumptuous
traumatized

1. *presumptuous* **a.** unexpected **b.** bold **c.** appropriate **d.** shy
2. *insidious* **a.** releasing **b.** questioning **c.** provoking **d.** obvious
3. *anguish* **a.** attention **b.** suffering **c.** rebellion **d.** comfort
4. *traumatized* **a.** shocked **b.** restless **c.** calm **d.** angry
5. *homage* **a.** duty **b.** disrespect **c.** celebration **d.** praise

Expressing Your Ideas

Writing Choices

Writer's Notebook Update Look back at your observations about how these Nobel Prize winners view their duties. Then use this information to explain which writers, if any, appearing in this book might share these views.

Up Close and Personal You can learn a lot about a writer who speaks from the heart, as both Wiesel and Camus do in their Nobel acceptance speeches. Refer to the notes in your notebook as you write a **character sketch** of each man based upon what you learned from his speech.

Congratulations! Image that you are a dear friend of either Wiesel or Camus, but you were unable to attend his acceptance ceremony in Stockholm. Send a **Fax** to your friend congratulating him on his well-deserved award and eloquent acceptance speech. Mention highlights of his speech.

Other Options

The Unknown Award Alfred Nobel might have planned the Nobel Prize because he wanted to be remembered as something other than the "dynamite king." For what would you want to be remembered after your death? Think of a new **award** promoting a cause that you believe in. Name the award and design a medallion, trophy, or ornament that will be distributed with it.

Find Out More In their acceptance speeches, Wiesel and Camus make allusions, or references to people, events, and ideas. Research one of these allusions—perhaps Nietzsche, Hitler, the Spanish Civil War, apartheid, or Nelson Mandela—and present an **oral report** to the class.

Bearing Witness Conduct an **interview** of someone who has survived the Holocaust. Include a question about how the experience has shaped this person's **perspectives** about what is important. You might ask for permission to record the interview and share it with the class.

VOCABULARY STUDY

1. d
2. d
3. d
4. c
5. b

Unit 4 Resource Book
Vocabulary , p. 67
Vocabulary Test, p. 70

WRITING CHOICES

Writer's Notebook Update

Suggest students review their notes and the abstract nouns they listed and then write a one- or two-sentence summary of Camus's and Wiesel's perspectives on writing to use as a reference when comparing the perspectives of other writers.

Up Close and Personal

Students might begin by listing details they learned about each man. They can use the list as they write.

Selection Test

Unit 4 Resource Book
pp. 71–72

Transparency Collection
Fine Art Writing Prompt 9

OTHER OPTIONS

Find Out More

Before they begin their research, students might write questions about the allusion. The questions will help them organize and focus their research and reports.

Bearing Witness

Have students prepare questions beforehand. Urge them to be sensitive to the feelings of the survivor, who may respond emotionally to memories of the trauma even after all these years.

Interdisciplinary Study

Theme Link

As students consider the value they place on a car, remind them that Americans as a group love their automobiles. Of course, cars seem to be a necessity in a country that is so vast. Just to go to work every day, Americans drive distances that would seem prohibitive in other countries. Other national characteristics might be discovered by examining Americans' "love affair" with cars.

Curricular Connection: Pop Culture

You can use this Interdisciplinary Study to explore with students the things that are valued as popular culture in the United States and in other countries.

Terms to Know

savvy (sav′ē), knowledge, sense, understanding slang

status symbol, anything which one acquires, often a material object, which is regarded as a sign of superior position

maharajah (mä′hə rä′jə), a former ruling prince in India

Unit 4 Resource Book
Study Guide, p. 73

INTERDISCIPLINARY STUDY

Something of Value

Power and Horsepower

Big Cars as

Pop Culture Connection

The preceding group of selections examines things people value—from peace to Porsches. These next pages explore the Car Culture and how it reflects the connection between power and horsepower.

A disastrous flop when Ford brought it out in the mid-1950s, the Edsel's most notorious feature was its grille, which reminded one observer of "an Oldsmobile sucking a lemon."

The first mass-produced American automobile, Ford's Model T, had been an open car; by contrast, closed sedans, like this 1929 Willys Whippet, offered the luxury of privacy.

The American slang term "hot rod" dates from the late 1940s, the period when the fascination of young people with fast and often vividly painted automobiles blossomed.

MINI-LESSON: VISUAL LITERACY

Analyzing Photographs

Teach Point out that photographers, like all visual artists, have a main idea that they want to communicate about their subject. To illustrate, compare the photographs of the Edsel and the hot rod. Both are frontal views, but the main idea developed for each is different. The photograph of the Edsel emphasizes the grille, the wide, horizontal stance of the car, and the sharp angles and details of the car's front end. The photograph of the hot rod emphasizes the rounded shapes and flowing paint design that streams backward. The grille, which is as large and emphatic as that of the Edsel is minimized in the photograph because that isn't the most important idea about this car.

Activity Ideas

- Have students analyze each of the other cars on these pages and identify the main idea conveyed. Then talk about how the photographer achieved the effect.
- Have students gather photographs of cars in magazines. They might collect those from articles as well as from advertisements. They can work in groups to analyze the main idea of each photograph.

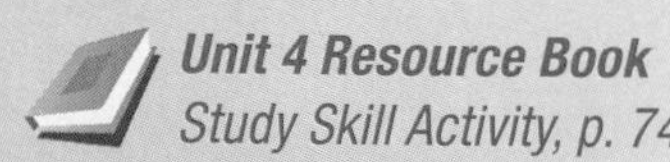

Unit 4 Resource Book
Study Skill Activity, p. 74

Wheels

STATUS SYMBOLS

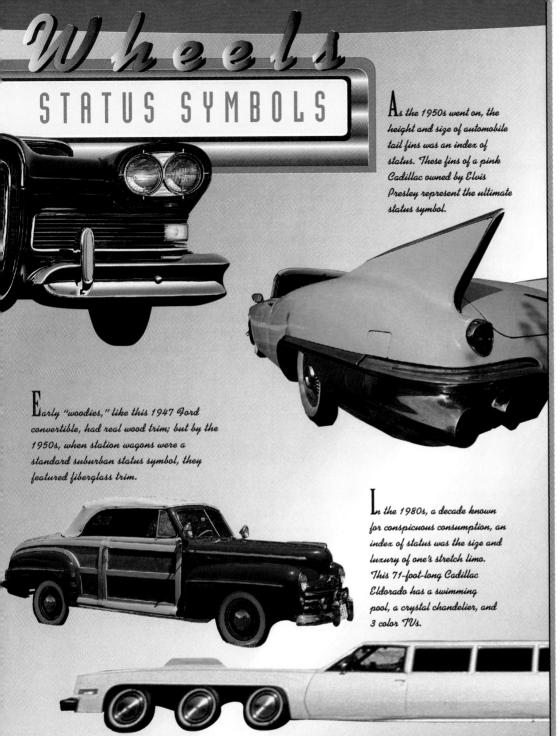

As the 1950s went on, the height and size of automobile tail fins was an index of status. These fins of a pink Cadillac owned by Elvis Presley represent the ultimate status symbol.

Early "woodies," like this 1947 Ford convertible, had real wood trim; but by the 1950s, when station wagons were a standard suburban status symbol, they featured fiberglass trim.

In the 1980s, a decade known for conspicuous consumption, an index of status was the size and luxury of one's stretch limo. This 71-foot-long Cadillac Eldorado has a swimming pool, a crystal chandelier, and 3 color TVs.

Historical Note

Ford Motor Company spent three years and $250 million in research when designing the Edsel. Even "Edsel," which was Henry Ford's son's name, was test marketed beforehand. Priced between $2,400 and $3,800, it was supposed to be the car of the future. It had a push-button automatic transmission, a V-8 engine, narrow, horizontal tail lights, and a detailed grille. It was introduced with great fanfare in August 1957, and was an instant flop. The Edsel survived for just over a year, the final car coming off the lines in November 1958. Promoted as revolutionary, the new car was ridiculed as just plain ugly.

Additional Background

David Wallace of the Ford Motor Company engaged poet Marianne Moore to suggest names for Ford's new series of cars. Ford rejected her creative, and often funny, suggestions and chose "Edsel." A close-up view of the search for the Edsel's name can be found in "Ford Motor Company Correspondence" from *A Marianne Moore Reader* by Marianne Moore, (1957).

BUILDING ENGLISH PROFICIENCY

Responding to Visual Cues

Discuss the cars shown and the idea of status. Ask students to suggest other ways to say "status symbol."

Activity Ideas

- Let students give examples of vehicles that represent status to them, describe the vehicles, and give reasons for their opinions. Then they can redesign these pages, inserting their own drawings or pictures and adding captions.
- Ask students to improvise either a skit about buying or showing off one of the cars, or do paired monologues in which one student describes how it feels to *own* one of the cars and the other describes how it feels to *be* that car.
- Invite a "classic cars" hobbyist to speak to the class about the subject (possibly coming to school in a classic car for students to see for themselves).

Historical Note

"Get a horse!" was often heard in the early years of the automobile when it was regarded as a foolish and annoying machine. While some, mainly the rich, fell in love with cars, most were slow to accept them. According to nineteenth-century British law, the speed limit was four miles per hour, and someone had to run ahead of a car with a red flag to warn people it was coming. The first person to drive a car up Broadway in New York City was fined $48,000 for frightening horses. Another U.S. law required drivers to cover their vehicles with a cloth on which a landscape was painted to fool horses. It took several years before most people considered automobiles a status symbol.

The Car Culture

"Everything in life is somewhere else, and you get there in a car!"
E. B. White

Power, mobility, speed, status! Cars have come to represent not only a means of transportation but the dreams, fantasies, and illusions of a society on-the-go. Today, due in large part to savvy marketing, competitive pricing, and a fast-paced lifestyle, the car has become essential to the American way of life.

Cars are a barometer of our history—the wars, the economics, the styles, the social climate. The market collapse of 1929 put the brakes on the era of the true luxury car, and World War II nearly halted the production of cars in general. After the war, when gasoline rationing ended and factories turned once more to building passenger cars instead of jeeps, tanks, and airplanes, there was a pent-up demand for new cars. The postwar prosperity of the 1950s and the Sputnik era of scientific advance both had their impact on car size, production, and design. (Note, for example, the rocket-like fins of Elvis Presley's car in the photo essay.) Smaller, more fuel-efficient cars came into vogue with the gas shortages of the 1970s and concerns about air pollution. Despite these adaptations, the car, as one observer put it, "reaches to the heart of the American self-image."

But the Car Culture is by no means an exclusively American phenomenon. Monarchs and politicians worldwide have equated power and horsepower. The Rolls-Royce was adopted in 1952 by Britain's Queen Elizabeth II and has been elevated to the status of the car of royalty in India, where one maharajah maintained a personal fleet of 22. VIP cars carry dignitaries and "wheeler-dealers" throughout the world, including a group of women in Togo, who are known throughout West Africa as the "Mercedes Ladies."

Cars—the ultimate monogram—serve as an extension of one's personality and a method of identification. The urge to personalize a car can have many outlets—custom paint jobs, knickknacks dangling from the rearview mirror, bumper stickers, and—the final word in personalizing—vanity license plates. And car fanciers collect anything

As concern grows about the environmental impact of fossil fuels, the future may belong to alternative vehicles, like this solar-powered General Motors Sunraycer.

MINI-LESSON: STUDY SKILLS

Informal Outlining

Teach Remind students that while doing research, they can come up with a solid working plan by making informal outlines. This method can be used to keep ideas organized, speed up note taking, and make the notes easier to use in writing. Share these tips for using informal outlines with students:

- Begin by writing a topic statement or research question.
- Organize by ideas, putting main ideas at the left margin.
- Indent details or supporting statements.
- Don't include numerals and letters.
- Don't worry about how many ideas fall under each main idea.
- Don't worry about the phrasing of notes and whether or not they are in parallel structure.

Activity Idea Have students use an informal outline to begin research for topics suggested on page 535 of this Teacher's Edition.

from hubcaps, hood ornaments, and dashboard nameplates to old cars themselves—faithfully restored and commanding astronomical prices. Even models that were originally unpopular (like the Edsel, whose grille one observer likened to an Oldsmobile sucking a lemon) are now chic.

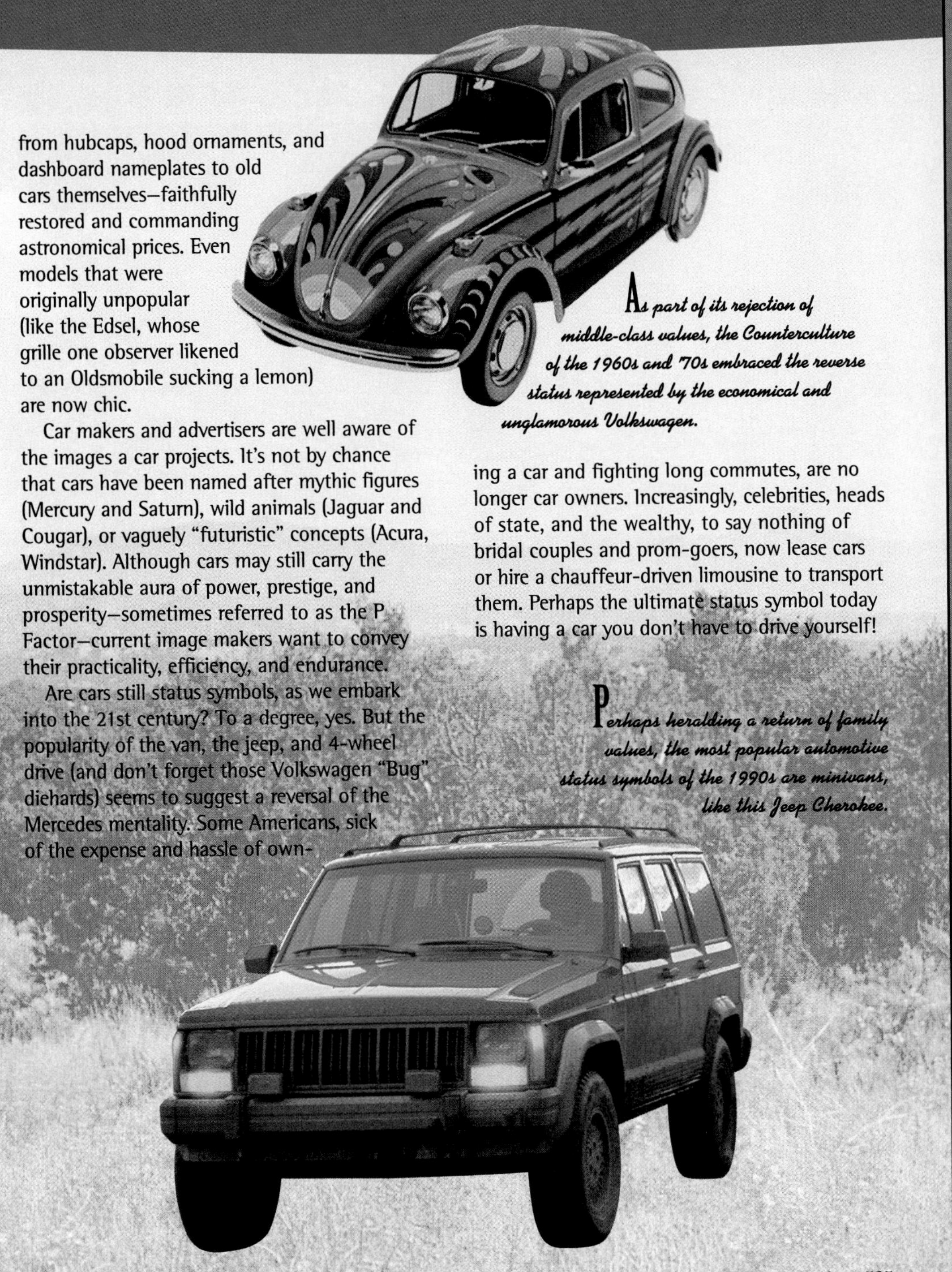

As part of its rejection of middle-class values, the Counterculture of the 1960s and '70s embraced the reverse status represented by the economical and unglamorous Volkswagen.

Car makers and advertisers are well aware of the images a car projects. It's not by chance that cars have been named after mythic figures (Mercury and Saturn), wild animals (Jaguar and Cougar), or vaguely "futuristic" concepts (Acura, Windstar). Although cars may still carry the unmistakable aura of power, prestige, and prosperity—sometimes referred to as the P Factor—current image makers want to convey their practicality, efficiency, and endurance.

Are cars still status symbols, as we embark into the 21st century? To a degree, yes. But the popularity of the van, the jeep, and 4-wheel drive (and don't forget those Volkswagen "Bug" diehards) seems to suggest a reversal of the Mercedes mentality. Some Americans, sick of the expense and hassle of owning a car and fighting long commutes, are no longer car owners. Increasingly, celebrities, heads of state, and the wealthy, to say nothing of bridal couples and prom-goers, now lease cars or hire a chauffeur-driven limousine to transport them. Perhaps the ultimate status symbol today is having a car you don't have to drive yourself!

Perhaps heralding a return of family values, the most popular automotive status symbols of the 1990s are minivans, like this Jeep Cherokee.

Historical Note

The Volkswagen Beetle was designed in 1934 by Ferdinand Porsche, the creator of the high-status Porsche sports car. The Volkswagen (which translates as "people's car") was produced as a practical car for the masses. It was introduced into the United States in 1949 but didn't catch on until the late 1950s. Its success resulted from its simplicity and reliability. Volkswagen's advertising emphasized the car's non-status. Consumers were reminded that "ugly is only skin deep" and that the Beetle was "the car nobody wanted."

MULTICULTURAL NOTE

In some crowded countries, car ownership is restricted. Space is so limited in Tokyo, that before purchasing a car, people must prove they have a parking place for it. In Singapore, taxes are set deliberately high to discourage car ownership, and persons driving into the business district during rush hours must pay a toll.

BUILDING ENGLISH PROFICIENCY

ESL LEP ELD SAE LD

Checking Comprehension

To help students understand and discuss "The Car Culture," have them complete sentences such as the following.

1. E. B. White writes that _____ are a very _____ part of life in America. *(cars, important)*

2. Companies made _____ cars when gasoline became _____ in the 1970s. *(smaller; expensive, scarce)*

3. Cars like the Rolls Royce are symbols of _____. *(power, wealth)*

4. Some of the ways in which people personalize their cars include _____. *(custom paint jobs, license plates)*

5. The purchase of _____ is a sign that people today are less interested in luxury cars. *(vans, jeeps, smaller cars)*

6. The "P Factor" means that car manufacturers want people to feel they will have _____ and _____ if they buy their cars. *(power, prestige, prosperity)*

Accept reasonable answers and encourage discussion.

Responding

1. Possible Responses Students should recognize specific techniques used by advertisers such as bandwagon and emotional appeal, as well as what is downplayed and what is emphasized in ads.

2. Possible Responses The 1929 Willys Whippet is a powerful car, as suggested by the speed waves coming off the wheels in the illustration. It looks long, huge, and strong, and the passengers appear secure and prosperous. The hot rod suggests the rebellious power and creativity of the owner in its elaborate paint. The car looks powerful with its wide stance and fast with its aerodynamic hood. The "woody" doesn't look like a powerful car, but it does look refined and expensive (alternate definitions of power and status).

Research Topics

- the history of the hot rod
- highway building in America
- hood ornaments as symbols
- early automobile advertising campaigns

Interdisciplinary Activity Idea

Have students work in groups to prepare and conduct surveys of friends, family members, and neighbors to learn what things people consider to be status symbols today. Students should assemble their surveys into a comprehensive report that can be shared with the class. The survey and report may include cars but might be expanded to include other things that people value.

The Car Culture

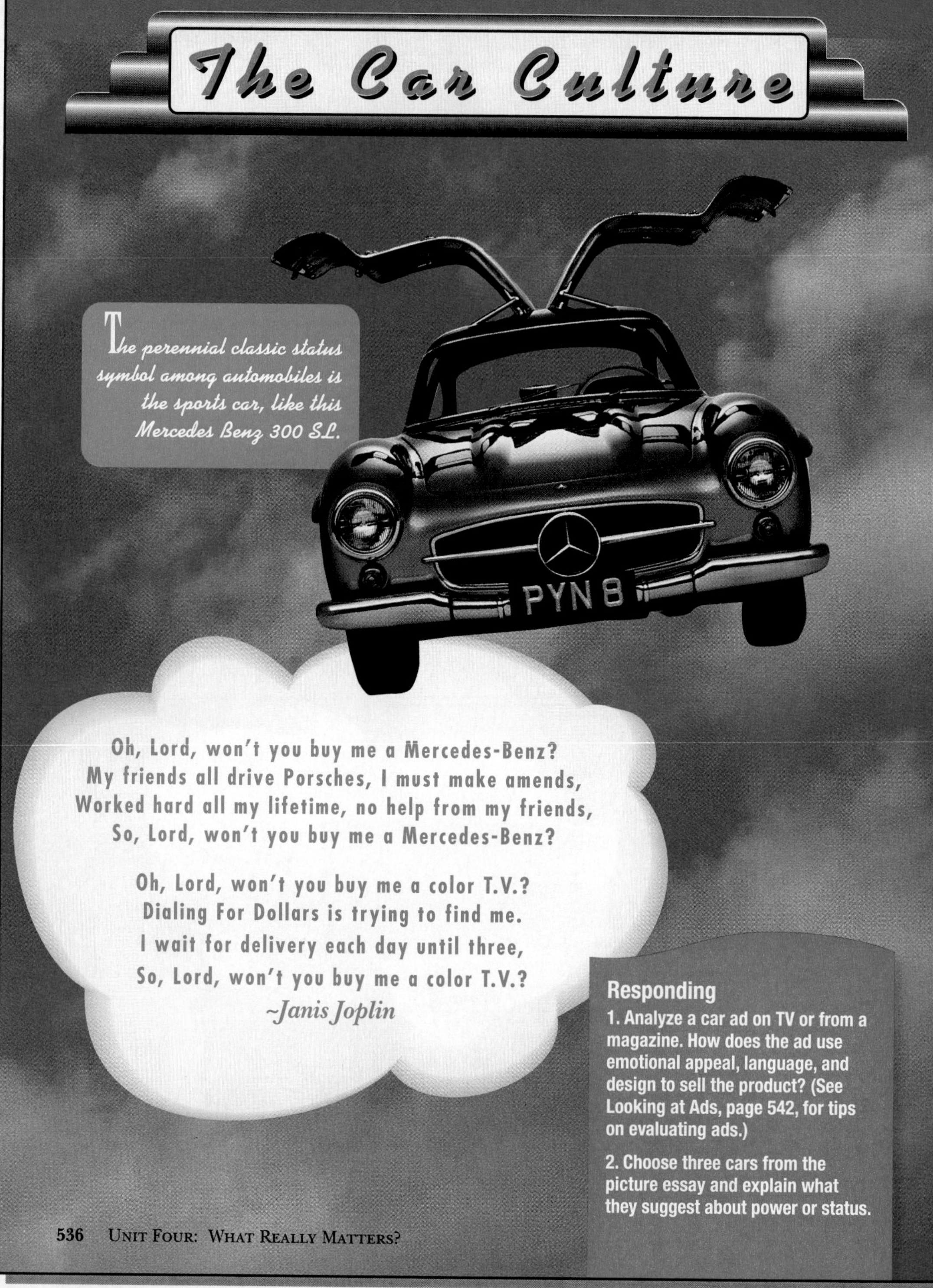

The perennial classic status symbol among automobiles is the sports car, like this Mercedes Benz 300 SL.

Oh, Lord, won't you buy me a Mercedes-Benz?
My friends all drive Porsches, I must make amends,
Worked hard all my lifetime, no help from my friends,
So, Lord, won't you buy me a Mercedes-Benz?

Oh, Lord, won't you buy me a color T.V.?
Dialing For Dollars is trying to find me.
I wait for delivery each day until three,
So, Lord, won't you buy me a color T.V.?

~Janis Joplin

Responding

1. Analyze a car ad on TV or from a magazine. How does the ad use emotional appeal, language, and design to sell the product? (See Looking at Ads, page 542, for tips on evaluating ads.)

2. Choose three cars from the picture essay and explain what they suggest about power or status.

MINI-LESSON: TECHNOLOGY

Word Processing Tips

Teach Most students don't need to be told that word processing is useful for the creation of many kinds of texts, reports, newsletters, surveys, charts, tables, and diagrams. Give them these tips about word processing:

- Save the text you are working on often.
- Make a back up copy of your text.
- Figure out a file-naming system and an organization system for filing documents so you can locate them easily.
- Be sure to use the spell check feature, but also check spelling by reading your hard copy. You often notice errors when you switch from screen to paper.

Activity Ideas

- Challenge students to learn at least one new word processing function of their program a week, such as find and replace, thesaurus, changing margins, line spacing, headers and footers, charts, and graphs.
- Challenge students to research facts about the growth, use, and popularity of automobiles and to display their information using computer-generated charts and graphs.

Writing Workshop

The Sum of My Parts

Assignment The authors of the selections in this part of the unit focus on things, great and small, that for one reason or another are of value to them. What are the things that hold value for you? Answer this question in an artful exploration.

WRITER'S BLUEPRINT

Product	A multimedia presentation
Purpose	To show people what is important to you
Audience	People who don't know you well
Specs	As the creator of a successful presentation, you should:

- ❑ Choose five or six things that are important to you and would say something about you to others. These may include objects, such as a bracelet or a basketball; places, such as your room or a lake; and living things, such as a plant or a pet.
- ❑ Present these items as part of a guided tour, an autobiographical narrative, or another method of your choice.
- ❑ Use a combination of visuals, writing, and speaking that will tell people who don't know you well why these items are important to you.
- ❑ Address your audience in a tone that's friendly and conversational, yet serious.
- ❑ When you speak, pronounce words clearly and speak loudly enough for everyone to hear.
- ❑ When you write, follow the rules of grammar, usage, spelling, and mechanics. Avoid run-on sentences.

Writing Workshop

WRITER'S BLUEPRINT

Specs

The Specs in the Writer's Blueprint address these writing and thinking skills:

- recognizing values
- organizing information
- integrating media
- using appropriate tone
- public speaking
- avoiding run-ons

These Specs serve as your lesson objectives, and they form the basis for the **Assessment Criteria Specs** for a superior paper, which appear on the final TE page for this lesson. You might want to read through the Assessment Criteria Specs with students when you begin the lesson.

Linking Literature to Writing

As you review the literature, discuss with students how character, in part, is revealed by the things each individual values. Have students consider how the various characters in the literature are revealed by the things they value.

WRITING WORKSHOP OVERVIEW

Product
Expository writing: A multimedia presentation

Prewriting
Create a chart—Discuss your ideas—Try a quickwrite—Plan your presentation
Unit 4 Resource Book
Prewriting Worksheets pp. 75–76

Drafting
Before you draft—As you draft
Transparency Collection
Student Models for Writing Workshop 17, 18

Revising
Ask a partner—Strategy: Using the Appropriate Tone
Unit 4 Resource Book
Revising Worksheet p. 77

Editing
Ask a partner—Strategy: Avoiding Run-ons
Unit 4 Resource Book
Grammar Worksheet p. 78
Grammar Check Test p. 79

Presenting
Guided Tour
Videotape

Looking Back
Self-evaluate—Reflect—For Your Working Portfolio
Unit 4 Resource Book
Assessment Worksheet p. 80
Transparency Collection
Fine Art Writing Prompt 9

STEP 1 PREWRITING

Create a chart

After students complete this activity have them share how well their perceptions matched their peers' perceptions.

Discuss your ideas

Students will need to feel "safe" before sharing personal information in this activity. Each group may want to set ground rules to ensure a sense of trust. For additional support, see the worksheet referenced below.

Unit 4 Resource Book
Prewriting Worksheet, p. 75

Try a quickwrite

Have students envision themselves at home in their room describing their most valued possessions. For more support, see the mini-lesson at the bottom of this page.

Plan your presentation

Encourage students to consider all the various options and "try them out"—that is, visualize themselves giving a tour through their favorite things, assembling them into a museum exhibit, etc. For additional support, see the worksheet referenced below.

Unit 4 Resource Book
Prewriting Worksheet, p. 76

Connections to
Writer's Notebook

For selection-related prompts, refer to Writer's Notebook.

Connections to
Writer's Resource

Refer to the Grammar, Usage, and Mechanics Handbook on Writer's Resource.

STEP 1 PREWRITING

Create a chart, like the one below, of a dozen things that you value highly. Fill in the first two columns. Then fold your paper so the second column is hidden. Exchange your chart with another group. In the third column have members of the other group note what they think the items show about you.

Item and description	What I think this item shows about me	What others think this item shows about me
stuffed unicorn; made of socks, sweet face, whimsical	I believe in imagination and fantasy.	sentimental; daydreamer; good imagination

Discuss your ideas. Meet with your group to discuss the items on your charts. Listen carefully to how others see you in relation to the items you value. Use their observations to expand your understanding of what the items mean to you.

Add relevant comments to your chart. Then answer this question: *If I were going to another country for a year, what would I take with me to introduce myself to the people I meet?* Choose a group of five or six items as the focus of your presentation.

OR . . .
Discuss your items with a partner or small group.

Try a quickwrite. Write for five minutes about why the items you have chosen are important to you, how you feel about them, and what they say about you.

Plan your presentation. Use your prewriting materials to create a plan.

First, decide on the method you'll use to organize your presentation. Here are some ideas on method:

- a tour, with you as tour guide
- a museum exhibit, with you as museum guide
- an autobiographical narrative, with you as narrator
- another method of your choice

Then decide on the order in which you'll present the items. You might:

- proceed in order of importance, from least to most important
- proceed in time order, beginning with the oldest item
- use another method of your choice

MINI-LESSON: PREWRITING

Try a Quickwrite

Teach After students produce a substantial amount of writing in their quickwrite, encourage them to "mine" their material for the best nuggets of prose. Model for the class the process of reading through rough draft writing out loud while listening for and highlighting interesting-sounding phrases or vivid images.

Activity Idea Have volunteers read through their quickwrites and jot down on the board some of these nuggets. You might want to have students do this activity in small groups.

Apply Direct students to use these nuggets when they go on to the next step in the process, "Plan your presentation."

Decide how you'll present each item visually:
- present the item itself
- show pictures of it
- show symbols, perhaps a collage, to represent it
- another method of your choice

Decide how you'll write about each item:
- a description on a note card, as you'd find in a museum
- as part of a descriptive poem
- as an anecdote—an incident or event connected with the item
- another method of your choice

Finally, make detailed notes about each item. Explain:
- why the item is important to you
- how you feel about it
- what it says about you

STEP 2 DRAFTING

Before you draft the written part of the presentation, review your prewriting materials and the Writer's Blueprint.

As you draft, concentrate on getting your ideas down on paper. The following tips may help:

- Keep your description of each item short and to the point. Don't go into long, involved explanations that get away from the main points you're trying to make about the item. Stick to telling why it's important, how you feel about it, and what it says about you.
- Use a friendly, conversational tone in your draft. See the Revising Strategy in Step 3 for ideas on establishing tone.

STEP 3 REVISING

Ask a partner for comments on your draft before you revise it.

✔ Have I written about items that are important to me?

✔ Do I go beyond a simple description and communicate what my items say about me?

✔ Is the tone of my presentation friendly and conversational, yet serious?

STEP 2 DRAFTING

As you draft

Students may want to visualize their essay as a written collage that pieces together a series of disparate images in order to create an overall picture of the writer's personality.

The Student Models

The **transparencies** referenced below are authentic student models. Review them with students before they draft. These questions will help:

1. What methods of presentation (guided tour, autobiographical narrative, and so on) did these writers use to present their things to the reader?

2. Did the writers use a friendly, conversational tone? Give examples.

3. Look over paragraph 2 of model 18 for problems with spelling and sentence structure.

Transparency Collection
Student Models for Writing Workshop 17, 18

STEP 3 REVISING

Ask a partner (Peer assessment)

Have readers point out specific places where the tone is too friendly or too serious, or appropriately balanced.

BUILDING ENGLISH PROFICIENCY

Using Prewriting Helps

Draw attention to some of the prewriting helps provided on page 538.

- For the "Discuss your ideas" activity, invite students to exchange their pared-down lists with partners. Ask partners to include in their comments what they might assume about the kind of person who would value all the items on the list.
- For the "Try a quickwrite" activity, invite students whose first language is not English to write in their first language. You also might allow students to make their presentations multilingual as well as multimedia.

Revising Strategy: Using the Appropriate Tone

Have students look over the student model and note the changes that were made. How did the changes affect the tone of the essay? Discuss other instances in which a more or less formal tone would be appropriate. For additional support, see the worksheet referenced below.

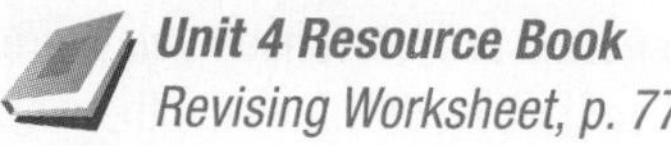

Unit 4 Resource Book
Revising Worksheet, p. 77

Connections to **Writer's Resource**

Refer to the Grammar, Usage, and Mechanics Handbook on Writer's Resource.

STEP 4 EDITING

Ask a partner (Peer assessment)

Encourage students to discuss any possible run-on sentences with their peers rather than just marking them on the paper.

Revising Strategy

Using the Appropriate Tone

For a highly personal presentation like this, you don't want to use an extremely formal tone:

> "Ladies and gentlemen, kindly allow me to present to you several items that hold much meaning. . . ."

However, you don't want to use an extremely chatty tone either:

> "Hey, guys, guess what? I cannot WAIT to show you all my cool stuff!"

Remember, you're aiming your presentation at an audience of people who don't know you well; so you'll want to aim somewhere in between the two extremes:

> "Here are some things that mean a lot to me. . . ."

Notice in the student model how the author made changes to alter the tone.

STUDENT MODEL

I ~~awakened at an unusually early hour~~ *woke up bright and early* in the *best* place ~~I favor above all others~~ *in the world*, my room. ~~Presently,~~ I opened up my eyes to see sunshine through my peach curtains. The *soft* color soothed my eyes. My troll collection was to the right of me and their smiling faces ~~affected my mood favorably~~ *made me smile*. I turned on my radio to hear ~~a~~ *my favorite* song ~~I knew~~ playing. I ~~seemed to be~~ *was* in heaven.

Ask a partner to review your revised draft before you edit. When you edit, look for errors in grammar, usage, spelling, and mechanics. Look closely for errors with run-ons.

MINI-LESSON: GRAMMAR

Avoiding Run-on Sentences

Display these run-ons and have students correct them in a variety of ways. An example of a correction follows each sentence in parentheses.

1. My bike is valuable to me as transportation it gives me a sense of freedom. (My bike is . . ., and it gives me. . . .)

2. Kareem Abdul Jabbar looks somewhat like the real Kareem Abdul Jabbar he has very long arms and legs and wears a Los Angeles Lakers' uniform with Number 33 on it. (Kareem Abdul Jabbar looks. . . . He has. . . .)

3. My uncle gave me some Star Wars figures they didn't mean much to me until I saw the Star Wars Trilogy. (My uncle . . . ; however, they didn't. . . .)

4. The ring from my grandmother had been her engagement ring my grandfather acquired the diamond by trading some of the gold he had mined. (The ring from . . . ; my grandfather. . . .)

Unit 4 Resource Book
Grammar Worksheet, p. 78
Grammar Check Test, p. 79

Editing Strategy

Avoiding Run-ons

A run-on sentence results when two or more independent clauses are run together in a sentence without a conjunction or proper punctuation:

I've had this stuffed animal since I was a baby I started collecting seashells when I was six.

Read what you've written out loud and listen for places where a natural pause should be—at the point where one thought ends and another begins. If you see you have two complete thoughts run together, make a correction:

I've had this stuffed animal since I was a baby, but I started collecting seashells when I was six.

FOR REFERENCE
More information about avoiding run-ons can be found in the Language and Grammar Handbook at the back of this book.

STEP 5 PRESENTING

- If you're giving a guided tour, make a separate note card for each item. Jot down key words and phrases and arrange the cards in order.
- Videotape your items and narrate the tape. Make background music a part of the video as well.

COMPUTER TIP
Use a computer HyperCard program to organize a HyperText presentation that includes visuals, sound, and text. See the Beyond Print article on page 447 for ideas about multimedia presentations.

STEP 6 LOOKING BACK

Self-evaluate. Look back at the Writer's Blueprint and give your presentation a score for each point, from 6 (superior) to 1 (inadequate).

Reflect. Write answers to these questions.

✔ What have you learned about combining different modes of expression (written, oral, and visual) to convey information to an audience? Were you able to make them work well together? Why or why not?

✔ What new insights have you gained about yourself as a result of doing this assignment?

For Your Working Portfolio Add your presentation material and your reflection responses to your working portfolio.

ASSESSMENT CRITERIA SPECS

Here are the criteria for a superior paper. A full six-level rubric for this paper appears on the *Assessment Worksheet* referenced below.

6 Superior The creator of a 6 paper impressively meets these criteria:

- Selects five or six items that give significant insights into the interests and character of the creator.
- Uses a method of presentation that effectively displays these items, artfully integrating visuals, writing, and speaking.
- Employs a tone that is at once friendly and serious.
- Speaks clearly and confidently.
- Makes few, if any, mistakes in grammar, usage, spelling, and mechanics. Avoids run-on sentences.

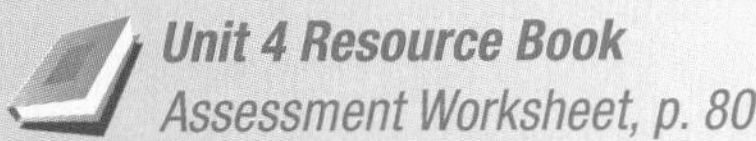

Unit 4 Resource Book
Assessment Worksheet, p. 80

Editing Strategy: Avoiding Run-ons

For additional support, see the mini-lesson at the bottom of the previous page and the worksheets referenced below.

Unit 4 Resource Book
Grammar Worksheet, p. 78
Grammar Check Test, p. 79

Connections to **Writer's Resource**

Refer to the Grammar, Usage, and Mechanics Handbook on Writer's Resource.

STEP 5 PRESENTING

Guided Tour

Have the audience circulate to the speakers stationed around the room with their displays.

Videotape

Have students consult the school's media expert.

STEP 6 LOOKING BACK

Self-evaluate

The *Assessment Criteria Specs* at the bottom of this page are for a superior paper. You might want to post these in the classroom. Students can then evaluate themselves based on these criteria. For a complete scoring rubric, use the *Assessment Worksheet* referenced below.

Unit 4 Resource Book
Assessment Worksheet, p. 80

Reflect

As students reflect on what they have learned about themselves through this project, remind them to consider what they initially wanted to portray about themselves through the items they chose.

To further explore the theme, use the Fine Art Transparency referenced below.

Transparency Collection
Fine Art Writing Prompt 9

Beyond Print

Teaching Objectives

- to understand the effect of composition and color in advertisements
- to recognize advertising techniques
- to evaluate the effectiveness of advertising

Curricular Connection: Visual Skills

Use the information in this article to help students practice the visual skills of understanding and analyzing consumer advertising.

Introduce

Let students respond to the ad on page 543 with their first impressions. Ask if this ad would have caught their attention if it was in a magazine they were browsing through.

Activity Option

When deciding on an overall rating, students might be tempted to base it on an average of the ratings for individual elements. Caution them against this approach because some elements may be more important in a particular ad.

Beyond Print

Looking at Ads

The people who make and market the products you buy or want to buy spend a lot of money on television, magazine, and newspaper advertising. Their target is *you,* and their goal is to sell. If you can become more aware of how you are being influenced through advertising, you may save some money. You will certainly be a wiser consumer.

Examine the Colt ad on the opposite page in light of the following advertising techniques.

Design

Composition What is in the background of the ad? How does this background, along with other details in the ad, serve to suggest that the car is a means to a fun getaway? Why do you think the car is headed up and forward? What purpose do the Japanese characters serve?

Color Different colors and textures create different moods. Bright and shiny colors often make things seem new, exciting, and desirable. Subdued colors create a sense of romance and well-being. Dark colors or shadows might be scary or sophisticated. Why might the car be red?

Advertising Techniques

Bandwagon *Bandwagon* appeal suggests you will be part of a popular trend if you buy a product. Note that the car is full of people going somewhere exciting. Why do you think the passengers aren't clearly shown?

Emotional Appeal Ads try to associate the product with something they assume you value. What about the image seems to imply that if you buy this product, you will be popular or happy or successful?

Language What buzz words and persuasive phrases can you find? What does "spirited" handling mean? What does the name Vista suggest?

Activity Option

Copy the chart on your paper. Rate the ad according to each design and technique factor on your chart. Use a five point scale, with five meaning the ad is highly persuasive and one meaning it is not persuasive. Then give the ad an overall rating based on its effectiveness.

Design	Advertising Techniques
Composition	Bandwagon
Color	Emotional Appeal
	Language
Overall Ad Rating	1 2 3 4 5

ANOTHER APPROACH

Broadcast Commercials

Television and radio commercials can also be analyzed using the techniques described on the page above. Remind students that a thirty-second broadcast commercial is expensive to create and to air. Everything in a commercial is carefully chosen for its impact on the listener or viewer. You might wish to record some commercials on audio or video tape to play for students. Guide them in a discussion of these points:

- design and advertising techniques
- the effect of the actor's or narrator's voice—the tone, the accent, the volume, the choice of words
- the effect of items shown on the TV commercial

Students can then rate commercials using a chart like the one above that has been adapted for radio and television commercials.

Four-wheel drive with room to 余裕.

It's the Colt Vista. The sleek new wagon with an ingenious capacity for both people and things. Designed and built by Mitsubishi in Japan.

And you'd be hard-pressed to find another wagon that offers you as much versatility.

Or fun. Or value.

With first class seating for seven passengers. And seats that fold forward and backwards to lay down more ways than those in any other small wagon.

So it'll accommodate just about any combination of family, friends and freight.

And with push-button four-wheel drive, Vista confidently moves all of the above through snow, mud and adversity on all fours. (A two-wheel drive version is also available.)

And if Vista's looks, utility and versatility aren't justification enough to consider one, wait till you drive one. The handling is precise and spirited. And its perfect size makes it perfectly easy to park and maneuver.

Colt is imported for Chrysler-Plymouth and Dodge dealers.

So try one on for size. And solve all of your transportation problems in one fell 極めて簡単.

優秀 Colt

It's all the Japanese you need to know.

Colts are built by Mitsubishi Motors Corp. and sold exclusively at Chrysler-Plymouth and Dodge dealers.

Visual Literacy Provide students with the following ways to evaluate an ad. Mention that all people use these persuasion methods, but that professional advertisers have special training and use technology to get their ideas across.

Persuaders intensify by

- repetition—slogans, logos, signs
- association—a link with something already desired
- composition—pattern and arrangement

Persuaders downplay by

- omission—deliberately covering up or concealing
- diversion—side issues, humor
- confusion—jargon, contradictions

Question How does this ad use intensifying and downplaying techniques? *(Possible responses: association and repetition of Japanese; composition to appeal to people who are interested in details; diversion through use of Japanese characters)*

BUILDING ENGLISH PROFICIENCY

ESL LEP ELD SAE LD

Exploring Persuasive Appeals

You may wish to preface this feature by having students bring in ads that they like (from a magazine or newspaper, or even on videotape); ads may be in English or another first language.

1. Invite students to explain why they like individual ads. Help them relate their comments to the concepts illustrated in the car ad.

2. Students can use their responses to create a chart that identifies elements of the ad on page 543. They should then assign pluses and minuses to the features, based on their own opinions. After they analyze the ad for themselves, have them make generalizations about how to create an effective advertisement.

What's in the Colt Ad?

Images	Color	Text	Other
+ car - people + snow	+ red - gray	+ Japanese words - too long	- price isn't mentioned

Unit Wrap-Up

MULTICULTURAL CONNECTION

Students should recognize that what matters to a person is strongly influenced by culture. The following ideas and questions will stimulate discussion about how people develop values based on their perspectives and how they communicate them.

Communication

You may wish to point out that "education" has different meanings for different people. To some, education might mean learning the traditional ways and keeping the spirit of a people alive; to others, it might mean formal sciences or a religious doctrine.

Possible Response Formal schooling will represent a different culture from that of the tribe. Eventually, the person who is learning will feel a conflict between the values of his heritage and those of represented by the schooling.

Possible Response Students should support their responses using examples from the literature. Volunteers may share experiences of when they had trouble communicating because of any these categories.

Perspective

- Everyone has a unique point of view that results from personal and cultural experiences.
- Writers express perspective in the words, actions, attitudes, and beliefs of their characters and narrators.

Possible Response Students should list ten things valued by the characters or authors of the selections and number them in an order that is meaningful to them. They should be able to explain how their personal perspective determined the order in which they numbered the ten things.

Possible Responses Some students may think it is ironic, others may say that someone who values peace or has made a contribution to humanity should be supported financially so his or her works can be continued. Students can offer reasons for the gift they would recommend in place of money.

Activities

Activity 1 Suggest that students recall discussions about values, and lists, or charts such as the one on page 500. Ask them to compare this list with the earlier statements or lists. Then they can write a summary statement about their values and perspectives.

Activity 2 Students can each take responsibility f[or] presenting one ad to the class, but they can analyze and discuss their ads as a group.

Multicultural Connections

Communication

Part One: Worth Fighting For? Cultural differences prevent effective communication between the narrator's parents in *Kaffir Boy* and between a British teacher and the young Indian students she stereotypes in "By Any Other Name."

- What threats does education pose for South Africans who, like Mathabane's father, have tribal affiliations? Explain whether or not you think that some Americans have similar fears about education.
- In each of these four autobiographical pieces, which of the following factors would you say causes miscommunication: age differences, language, culture, and social class?

Perspective

Part Two: Something of Value Perspective involves seeing people and events from a particular viewpoint. And that viewpoint, largely shaped by culture, determines what a person or a society values—from peace to pets to Porsches.

- List ten things valued by characters or authors in this unit titled What Really Matters? Arrange them in the order that *you* would value them, with the most important being number 1. Then explain what this order reveals about you and your personal perspective.
- A Nobel Prize is worth a great deal of money. Do you think it is ironic to award someone, such as Elie Wiesel or Albert Camus, who has enriched the world spiritually, with a gift that is now close to one million dollars? Suppose the prize were a gold watch, a poem, or a parade instead. From your perspective, what would the best prize be? Explain.

Activities

1. List ten things you value in order and explain what your choices reflect about you.
2. Work with a group to bring ads to class to display. Give an Ad Talk, explaining what these ads are designed to communicate and to whom (group, social class) they seem directed.

Independent and Group Projects

Art

Special Letters With a partner, explore calligraphy, the art of beautiful handwriting. Then choose five different sentences, phrases, or words from Unit 4 that reflect the theme of the unit, What Really Matters? Write this material in a calligraphic style, decorate your work with simple designs, and put on paper suitable to use as greeting cards.

Media

Commercial Values With your group, create a television commercial for an insurance company, stressing the need to insure "things of value." How will your creative team convince people that they should insure both material and nonmaterial things? Be prepared to present your commercial to the class.

Poll

Value Votes Brainstorm with classmates a list of things students consider important. Use this list to draw up a questionnaire to determine what things are most valued. Tally the results on a graph and share it with the class.

Demonstration

Display Case Your group is in charge of planning a new exhibit for the Natural History Museum. The topic you have been assigned is What Really Matters? Collect special things from your childhood as well as items that your parents, grandparents, and family friends value. (In some cases, you may have to substitute a photograph or drawing of a valued item.) Identify each item and its approximate date on a notecard. Put these items on display for the class and explain their significance.

Dialogue

A Literary Party Annie Dillard observes, ". . . you have to fling yourself at what you're doing. . . ." Imagine that five of the authors in this unit were to join Dillard at a party. In a group of six, with each student representing an author, prepare a dialogue that might follow from this statement. Base comments on what you have learned about these authors and their works.

545

UNIT 6 OPTIONS

Art

Calligraphers use special pens or brushes.

- Students might check with an art teacher who may provide suitable supplies.
- Encourage students to investigate the methods and materials used by both Asian and Western calligraphers.

Media

Students might present the commercial in one of several ways.

- as a storyboard
- as a live presentation
- as a video recording

Poll

Urge students to divide up responsibility for the poll.

- Several students might collaborate on creating the questionnaire.
- Other students might prepare the graph.

Demonstration

Remind students to use objects that symbolize important values as well as things that are interesting for their own sake.

- Urge students to include items from different generations.
- Suggest students decide on an order or design for their display.

Dialogue

Suggest that students prepare for their parts by learning more about their authors' interests, values, personality, and writing style.

Connections to **AuthorWorks**

Data for completing this project can be found on AuthorWorks CD-ROM series.

Unit Test

Unit 4 Resource Book
New Selection, pp. 81–88
Test 1, pp. 89–90
Test 2, pp. 91–96

Part One: Connections

Planning Unit 5: A Place In The World

Literature	Integrated Language Arts			
	Literary	Writing/Grammar, Usage and Mechanics	Reading, Thinking, Listening, Speaking	Vocabulary/Spelling
A New Dress *by Ruth Dallas* Poem *(average)* p. 553 **Those Winter Sundays** *by Robert Hayden* Poem *(average)* p. 554 **Tia Chucha** *by Luis J. Rodriguez* Poem *(average)* p. 556	Figurative language Tone	Chart Captions for photographs Character sketch Poem Active and passive voice	Compare and contrast	Word context
Girls Can We Educate We Dads? *by James Berry* Poem *(average)* p. 561 **If You'll Only Go to Sleep** *by Gabriela Mistral* Poem *(average)* p. 562 **Mi Prima Agueda** *by Ramón López Velarde* Poem *(average)* p. 563	Diction Dialect Imagery, tone Rhythm/rhyme Metaphor	Short essay Write a translation Lullaby Poem Idioms		Expand vocabulary using structural analysis
First Frost *by Andrei Voznesensky* Poem *(average)* p. 570 **For Anne Gregory** *by William Butler Yeats* Poem *(easy)* p. 571 **The Fist** *by Derek Walcott* Poem *(challenging)* p. 571 **The Stone** *by Wilfrid Wilson Gibson* Poem *(easy)* p. 572	Rhythm Imagery and figurative language Narrative poetry Repetition	Journal entry Editorial Using the past perfect tense	Analyze/infer Summarize	Work relationships
The Other *by Judith Ortiz Cofer* Poem *(average)* p. 579 **To Julia de Burgos** *by Julia de Burgos* Poem *(challenging)* p. 580 **We Are Many** *by Pablo Neruda* Poem *(average)* p. 582	Speaker Metaphor Tone and theme	Poem Write a review News story Using verbs with indefinite pronouns	Recognize values	Etymology

Meeting Individual Needs

Multi-modal Activities	Mini-Lessons
Cartoon Talk radio Making personal connections	Active and passive voice Word context
Oral reading Greeting card Evaluating translation Comprehending translations	Idioms Expand vocabulary using structural analysis
Diagram Mobile Image of love Reading poetry aloud Making personal connections	Using the past perfect tense Rhythm
Draw a picture Talk show Introductory speech Making personal connections	Etymology Using verbs with indefinite pronouns

Interdisciplinary Studies

It's All Family

Format	Content Area	Highlights	Skill
Article: **"Reading" a Family Portrait** *by Caroline Sloat*	History	This selection uses a portrait to determine general information about a colonial family.	Draw conclusions About/evaluate art
Photo Essay: **TV Families**	Media	This photo essay gives an overview of TV families over the past decades.	Debate

Writing Workshop

Mode	Writing Format	Writing Focus	Proofreading Skills
Narrative writing	An illustrated interview	Quoting directly and paraphrasing	Spelling homophones correctly

Program Support Materials

For Every Selection

Unit Resource Book
Graphic Organizer
Study Guide
Vocabulary Worksheet
Grammar Worksheet
Spelling, Speaking and Listening, or Literary Language Worksheet
Alternate Check Test
Vocabulary Test
Selection Test

For Every Writing Workshop

Unit Resource Book
Prewriting Worksheet
Revising Strategy Worksheet
Editing Strategy Worksheet
Presentation Worksheet
Writing Rubric
Transparency Collection
Fine Art Transparency
Student Writing Model Transparencies

For Every Interdisciplinary Study

Unit Resource Book
Study Guide
Mini-Lesson Skill Worksheet

Assessment

Unit Resource Book
TE Check Tests
Alternate Check Test (blackline master)
Vocabulary Test (blackline master)
Selection Test (blackline master)
Test Generator Software
Assessment Handbook

Part Two: Reflections

Planning Unit 5: A Place In The World

Literature	Integrated Language Arts: Literary	Writing/Grammar, Usage and Mechanics	Reading, Thinking, Listening, Speaking	Vocabulary/Spelling
Sunday Morning *by Oscar Peñaranda* Poem *(average)* p. 598 **Some Keep the Sabbath** *by Emily Dickinson* Poem *(challenging)* p. 599	Assonance Metaphor Internal rhymes	Comparison Poem Description		
Ceremony *by Leslie Marmon Silko* Poem *(average)* p. 604 **A Story** *by Czeslaw Milosz* Poem *(average)* p. 606 **The Road Not Taken** *by Robert Frost* Poem *(average)* p. 607 **from Ecclesiastes** *Bible* Poem *(average)* p. 608	Symbol Metaphor Tone Theme Repetition and opposites	Explanation Poems Advice column Origins and development of English: Biblical rhythms and parallel construction	Draw conclusions Visualize Clarify Evaluate Making personal connections	Word analogies
This Is a Photograph of Me *by Margaret Atwood* Poem *(challenging)* p. 614 **Water Picture** *by May Swenson* Poem *(average)* p. 615 **Six Haiku** *by Matsuo Bashō and Yosa Buson* Poems *(average)* p. 616	Simile Alliteration Extended metaphor Haiku form	Poem Describe objects using riddles Write a Haiku Avoiding wordiness	Make analogies Visualize	Draw a word picture

Meeting Individual Needs

Multi-modal Activities	Mini-Lessons
Monthly calendar Persuasive speech Dance Exploring key concepts	
Heritage festival Play a recording Make a booklet Sharing stories Analyzing metaphors Making personal connections	Symbol Origins and development of English: Biblical rhythms and parallel construction
Origami Creating a mural Slide show Analyzing descriptive language	Avoiding wordiness

Interdisciplinary Studies
The Eye and the Lens

Format	Content Area	Highlights	Skill
Essay: **No Headdresses or Horses** *by Wade Payton*	Career	An essay regarding photography and messages.	Express experiences in visual form
Essay: **The Cerebral Snapshot** *by Paul Theroux*	Photography	Essay discussing the differences between a photograph and written language.	Understand technology terms

Writing Workshop

Mode	Writing Format	Writing Focus	Proofreading Skills
Descriptive writing	A verbal snapshot	Showing, not telling	Avoiding careless spelling errors

Program Support Materials

For Every Selection	For Every Writing Workshop
Unit Resource Book Graphic Organizer Study Guide Vocabulary Worksheet Grammar Worksheet Spelling, Speaking and Listening, or Literary Language Worksheet Alternate Check Test Vocabulary Test Selection Test	**Unit Resource Book** Prewriting Worksheet Revising Strategy Worksheet Editing Strategy Worksheet Presentation Worksheet Writing Rubric **Transparency Collection** Fine Art Transparency Student Writing Model Transparencies

For Every Interdisciplinary Study	Assessment
Unit Resource Book Study Guide Mini-Lesson Skill Worksheet	**Unit Resource Book** TE Check Tests Alternate Check Test (blackline master) Vocabulary Test (blackline master) Selection Test (blackline master) **Test Generator Software** **Assessment Handbook**

Part Three: Culture Crossroads

Planning Unit 5: A Place In The World

Literature	Integrated Language Arts			
	Literary	Writing/Grammar, Usage and Mechanics	Reading, Thinking, Listening, Speaking	Vocabulary/Spelling
Woman from America *by Bessie Head* Essay *(easy)* p. 632	Setting	Identify stereotypes Letter of complaint Character sketch	Evaluate	Word analogy tests
Rain Music *by Longhang Nguyen* Short Story *(average)* p. 637	Conflict Point of view Mood	Essay Write two possible extended endings Using quotation marks with dialogue	Recognize values	Recognize idioms
My Father Writes to My Mother *by Assia Djebar* Autobiography *(average)* p. 644	Character Setting	Essay Media report Dialogue Interior monologue Writing compound-complex sentences		Synonyms
Legal Alien *by Pat Mora* Poem *(average)* p. 652 **For the White Poets Who Would be Indian** *by Wendy Rose* Poem *(challenging)* p. 652 **I Am Not with Those** *by Anna Akhmatova* Poem *(average)* p. 653 **Jerusalem** *by Yehuda Amichai* Poem *(average)* p. 654 **Dos Patrias/Two Countries** *by José Martí* Poem *(average)* p. 656	Allusion Metaphor Symbolism	Make a list Write a proposal Bilingual insights Using prefixes and suffixes	Evaluate Analyze Infer	Structural analysis

Meeting Individual Needs

Multi-modal Activities	Mini-Lessons
Concert Oral critique Exploring key statements	
Promotional material Interview Background music Comprehending characters	Using quotation marks with dialogue Recognize idioms
TV documentary Interview Expanding vocabulary through prefixes	Writing compound-complex sentences
Cultural crossroads chart Verbal collage Sketch/blueprint of a memorial Making personal connections Exploring symbolism	Using prefixes and suffixes Structural analysis

Interdisciplinary Studies
Culture Quilt

Format	Content Area	Highlights	Skill
Article: **It's Hard To Smile** *by K. Connie Kang*	Multicultural	This article discusses how different cultures can blend or clash.	Inflammatory speeches Newspapers on film

Writing Workshop

Mode	Writing Format	Writing Focus	Proofreading Skills
Expository writing	A personalized research report	Writing an intriguing opening Defining your topic	Works cited form

Program Support Materials

For Every Selection

Unit Resource Book
Graphic Organizer
Study Guide
Vocabulary Worksheet
Grammar Worksheet
Spelling, Speaking and Listening, or Literary Language Worksheet
Alternate Check Test
Vocabulary Test
Selection Test

For Every Writing Workshop

Unit Resource Book
Prewriting Worksheet
Revising Strategy Worksheet
Editing Strategy Worksheet
Presentation Worksheet
Writing Rubric
Transparency Collection
Fine Art Transparency
Student Writing Model Transparencies

For Every Interdisciplinary Study

Unit Resource Book
Study Guide
Mini-Lesson Skill Worksheet

Assessment

Unit Resource Book
TE Check Tests
Alternate Check Test (blackline master)
Vocabulary Test (blackline master)
Selection Test (blackline master)
Test Generator Software
Assessment Handbook

Media and Technology

Part One Selections

A New Dress/Those Winter Sundays/Tía Chucha

Videotape *Poetry Hall of Fame,* 4 60-minute videos, Monterey Home Video, 1993, is a journey through great poems throughout the ages.

Audiotape Students will enjoy stories of friendship in *Visions: Nineteen Short Stories by Outstanding Writers for Young Adults,* Listening Library. The poet reads from "The Concrete River," in *Luis Rodriguez,* 29 minutes, New Letters.

Home Connection Children often take for granted their parents' care and concern. As part of an oral history project, students might ask older adults what their parents did that they are most grateful for.

Girls Can We Educate We Dads?/If You'll Only Go to Sleep/Mi Prima Agueda

Audiotape *Poetry in Spanish: An Anthology,* Library of Congress, features poetry read by Mistral.

Filmstrip *Twentieth-Century Poetry: Spanish-American Literature and Culture,* Films for the Humanities & Sciences, includes Velarde and Mistral.

Community Resources You might invite a school counselor or psychologist to speak to the class about the friction that often occurs between teenagers and their parents or guardian, the causes of this friction, and possible ways to ease tensions between the two generations.

First Frost/For Anne Gregory/The Fist/The Stone

Audiotape The poet reads his work in *Andrei Vosnesensky,* 29 minutes, New Letters. *Poems and Memories: William Butler Yeats,* Spoken Arts, presents poems of the author and a discussion of his work. The author reads excerpts from several of his works in *Derek Walcott Reads,* 1 hour 30 minutes, Harper Audio, 1994.

Videotape *Derek Walcott: A World of Ideas,* 30 minutes, PBS Video, is an interview with the poet by Bill Moyers.

The Other/To Julia de Burgos/We Are Many

Videotape In *Birthwrite: Growing Up Hispanic,* 57 minutes, Cinema Guild, 1989, Judith Ortiz Cofer is among the writers interviewed. *The Life and Poetry of Julia de Burgos,* 28 minutes, Cinema Guild, 1981, is a docu-drama of the Puerto Rican poet. In *Pablo Neruda,* 30 minutes, The Hispanic & Latin American Heritage Video Collection, Library Video Company, 1995, a profile of the author and his work is presented. (Spanish edition available.)

Audiotape *Pablo Neruda: Selected Poems,* Spoken Arts, is read in Spanish by the author.

Part Two Selections

Sunday Morning/Some Keep the Sabbath

Audiotape Students will enjoy hearing celebrities read in *50 Poems of Emily Dickinson,* 45 minutes, Dove Audio, 1995.

Videotape Consider showing *Emily Dickinson: A Certain Slant of Light,* 40 minutes, Monterey Home Video, 1995, hosted by Julie Harris.

Connections to
Custom Literature Database

For Part One "Connections"
Selections with Lessons

- "Golden Bells" and "Remembering Golden Bells" by Po Chü-i
- "The Eve of St. Agnes" by John Keats

Additional theme-based selections can be accessed on the ScottForesman database.

Connections to
Custom Literature Database

For Part Two "Reflections"
Selections with Lessons

- "A Bride" and "Hymn to Aphrodite" by Sappho
- "Composed upon Westminster Bridge" and "It is a beauteous evening, calm and free" by William Wordsworth

Additional theme-based selections can be accessed on the ScottForesman database.

Part Three Selections

Ceremony/A Story/The Road Not Taken/from Ecclesiastes

Audiotape Leslie Silko reads from her novel, *The Almanac of the Dead,* 30 minutes, New Letters. The author reads selected poems in *Czeslaw Milosz: Fire,* 64 minutes, Watershed Tapes, 1988.

Videotape In *Robert Frost*, 10 minutes, Aims Media, 1972, students will experience an interview with the author.

Computer Software One of Frost's beloved poems is included in the videodisc, *Frost's Death of the Hired Man/Cremation of Sam McGee*, available through Britannica Films.

This Is a Photograph of Me/Water Picture/Six Haiku

Audiotape The author reads her work in *Margaret Atwood Reads*, 45 minutes, American Audio Prose Library.

Videotape *Poetry of May Swenson*, 10 minutes, Media Plus, shows the poet in her environment discussing her work. *Haiku–Short Poetry of Japan*, 28 minutes, is available from Wombat Films, 1981.

Woman from America

Videotape Students may enjoy the parallels in a story of the years author Isak Dinesen spent on a coffee plantation in Kenya in *Out of Africa*, 161 minutes, MCA/Universal Home Video, 1985, starring Meryl Streep and Robert Redford.

Community Resources Using library resources, catalogs, or, in a larger community, displays in speciality shops or museum stores, some students might like to research African sculpture and African designs in textiles. A small group could then give an illustrated talk to the class.

Rain Music

Home Connection Pollsters tell us that most Americans believe that love should be a basis for marriage, but this is not a universal belief. Some students may be willing to share other ideas about marriage in the culture from which they come.

My Father Writes to My Mother

Home Connection Muslim students may be interested in telling the class about their family customs. Students from families who have recently immigrated may also be willing to share family customs.

Legal Alien/For the White Poets Who Would Be Indian/Jerusalem/I Am Not with Those/Dos Patrias /Two Countries

Videotape *Imagining Indians,* 60 minutes, Documentary Educational Resources, 1994, filmed by Hopi filmmaker Victor Masayesva, takes a humorous approach to the relationship between Hollywood and Native Americans. Poetry and art commemorates the 1890 Wounded Knee Massacre in the award-winning *Ghost Dance*, 9 minutes, Unity Producations, 1990. *Inner Exile: The Poetry of Anna Akhmatova*, 30 minutes, Camera Three Productions, includes Irene Moore reading the poetry of Akhmatova. Interviews with Cubans born after the revolution are the focus of *Cuba Va: The Challenge of the Next Generation*, 59 minutes, Cinema Guild, 1993.

Computer Software *Jerusalem*, a CD-ROM program for Macintosh and Windows, from Simon & Schuster, 1995, is a multimedia exploration of the important city.

Audiotape Students may want to hear Marti's poetry in Spanish in *Prosa y Poesia,* 1 hour 30 minutes, Nueva Onda, 1993.

Connections to
Custom Literature Database

For Part Three "Culture Crossroads" Selections with Lessons

- "The Miracle of Purun Bhagat" by Rudyard Kipling
- Chinese Exclusion Act

Additional theme-based selections can be accessed on the ScottForesman database.

Connections to
AuthorWorks

Information about the life and times of Emily Dickinson, Robert Frost, W. B. Yeats, and Derek Walcott is available on ScottForesman's AuthorWorks CD-ROM.

Unit 5

A Place in the World

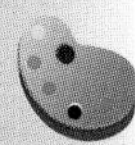

Art Study

The Fair was painted in 1906 by Russian artist Boris Kustodiev (1878–1927). His paintings celebrated the village fairs, markets, and religious festivals of Russian life. His works were often crowded with peasants and merchants.

Question How do you think the artist feels about his subjects? Why? *(Students may say he probably likes them because he has painted them as satisfied and happy. The tone of the painting is happy because of the bright colors used.)*

UNIT 5

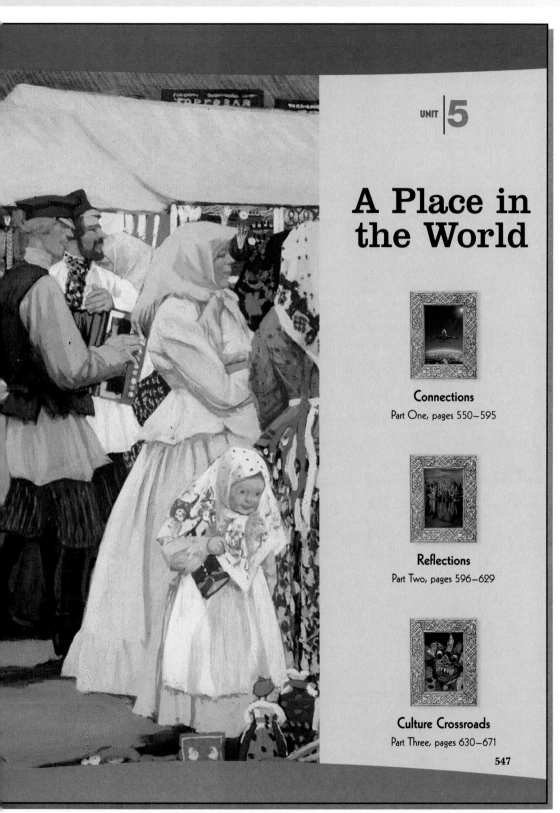

A Place in the World

Connections
Part One, pages 550–595

Reflections
Part Two, pages 596–629

Culture Crossroads
Part Three, pages 630–671

547

THEMATIC CONNECTIONS

People all over the world have a need to find where they belong in society and to ensure that their place is recognized.

Part One
Connections

Part One features poems that explore relationships or connections—to family members, romantic lovers, and the self.

Idea to Explore

How do poets communicate their stories and their emotions?

Part Two
Reflections

The poems in Part Two both reflect their writers' worlds like photographs and examine through internal reflection the cycles and choices in life.

Idea to Explore

How is a poem like a photograph?

Part Three
Culture Crossroads

The selections in Part One focuses on individuals' reactions to encounters with different cultures.

Idea to Explore

When is your reaction to a cultural difference most likely to be positive? negative?

All three images are photos. The first is a blue plane flying over the Earth. The second is fall leaves. The third is an Indonesian mask.

Genre Overview: Poetry

EXPLORING CONCEPTS

- In general, the emotional impact of a poem is as important as the story it tells or the ideas it expresses.
- The effect of poetry is based on an interplay between the literal—or what is overtly said, and the figurative—or what is implied or suggested.
- Poetry differs from prose in that it relies more on rhythm, sound devices, and imagery; may use denser and more elevated language; and is more likely to disregard or reformulate grammatical rules.
- While definitions of poetry differ greatly, many theorists would agree that a poem is an imaginative interpretation of the world around the poet.

Question How is reading poetry similar to reading prose? How is it different? *(Students may respond that sound, word choice, figurative language, and images are as important to some short stories and novels as they are to poetry, and that tips 1, 2, 3, and 5 could be equally helpful in reading those works. However, the forms of most prose works are similar—i.e., sentences joined to form paragraphs—whereas those of poems vary widely. Also, a poem is more likely to be written for a purely emotional effect than prose, which generally serves an informative or narrative purpose that is at least as important.)*

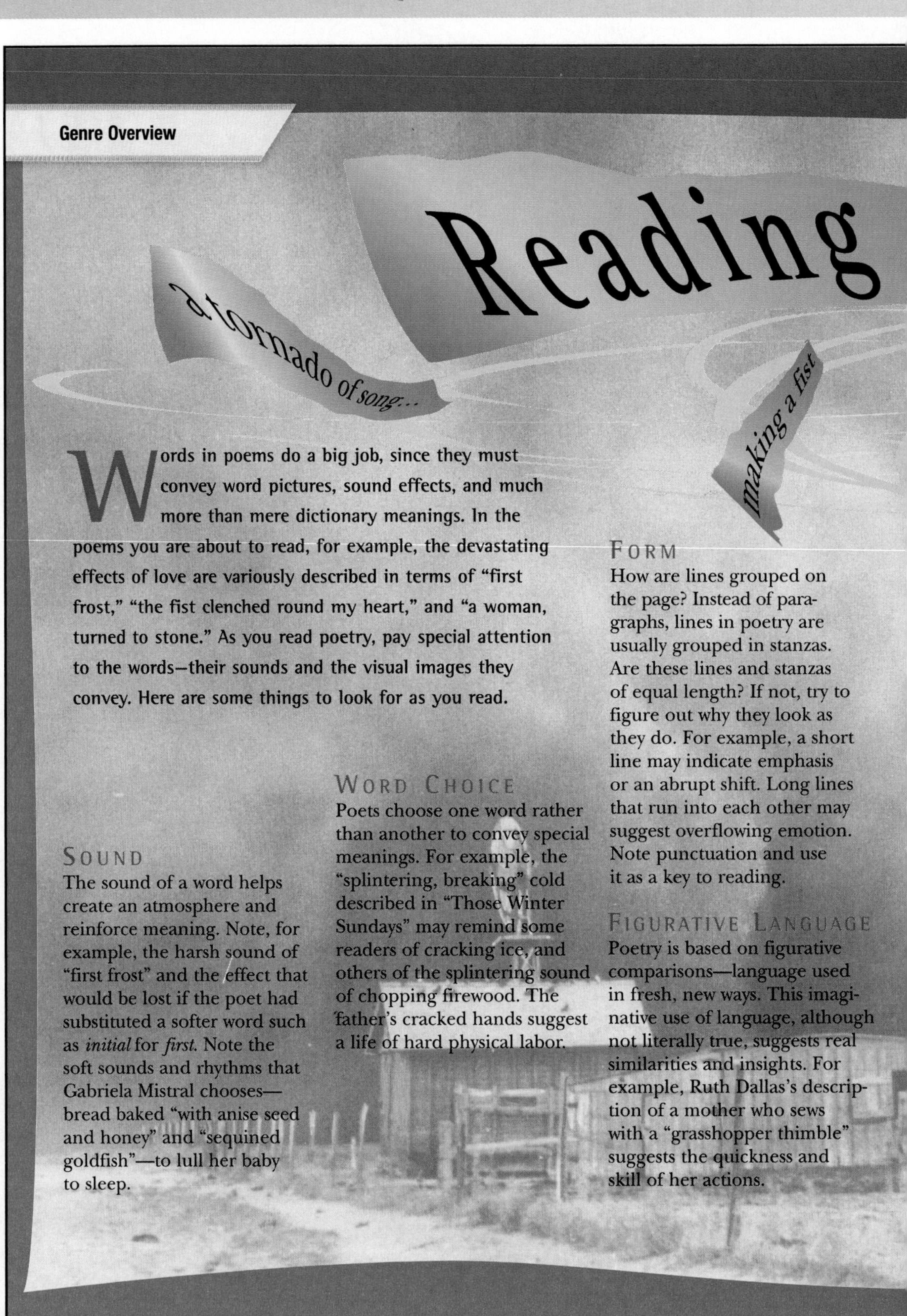

Genre Overview
Reading
a tornado of song...
making a fist
Words in poems do a big job, since they must convey word pictures, sound effects, and much more than mere dictionary meanings. In the poems you are about to read, for example, the devastating effects of love are variously described in terms of "first frost," "the fist clenched round my heart," and "a woman, turned to stone." As you read poetry, pay special attention to the words—their sounds and the visual images they convey. Here are some things to look for as you read.
SOUND
The sound of a word helps create an atmosphere and reinforce meaning. Note, for example, the harsh sound of "first frost" and the effect that would be lost if the poet had substituted a softer word such as *initial* for *first.* Note the soft sounds and rhythms that Gabriela Mistral chooses—bread baked "with anise seed and honey" and "sequined goldfish"—to lull her baby to sleep.
WORD CHOICE
Poets choose one word rather than another to convey special meanings. For example, the "splintering, breaking" cold described in "Those Winter Sundays" may remind some readers of cracking ice, and others of the splintering sound of chopping firewood. The father's cracked hands suggest a life of hard physical labor.
FORM
How are lines grouped on the page? Instead of paragraphs, lines in poetry are usually grouped in stanzas. Are these lines and stanzas of equal length? If not, try to figure out why they look as they do. For example, a short line may indicate emphasis or an abrupt shift. Long lines that run into each other may suggest overflowing emotion. Note punctuation and use it as a key to reading.
FIGURATIVE LANGUAGE
Poetry is based on figurative comparisons—language used in fresh, new ways. This imaginative use of language, although not literally true, suggests real similarities and insights. For example, Ruth Dallas's description of a mother who sews with a "grasshopper thimble" suggests the quickness and skill of her actions.

Poetry
TIPS
...a tornado of song...
...a fish in a bowl...
...what smelled of rotting fish
...splintering, breaking cold...
First frost clinging
first frost
making a fist
Two roads diverged in a wood, and I...
IMAGES
Poets rely on word pictures called *images* to help readers see, touch, feel, taste, and smell the things being described. Tía Chucha becomes an unforgettable character in Luis Rodriguez's poem from the moment she visits the family "in a tornado of song" with her perfume that smelled of rotting fish. As you read these poems, look for other images that make these characters real and memorable.
1 Read poetry aloud to enjoy the sounds and rhythms.
2 Try to get the overall meaning before zeroing in on details.
3 Visualize the images and figurative language.
4 See if the form provides any clues to the meaning.
5 Try to determine what the poet's purpose is— to entertain, to instruct, to create a mood, or something else.
549

MATERIALS OF INTEREST

Books

- *The Princeton Encyclopedia of Poetry and Poetics* edited by Alex Preminger (Princeton University Press, 1974)
- *Rose, Where Did You Get That Red?* by Kenneth Koch (Random House, 1973)
- *The Norton Anthology of Modern Poetry* edited by Richard Ellmann and Robert O'Clair, "Introduction" (W. W. Norton & Company, Inc., 1973)

Multimedia

The 1995 Grolier Multimedia Encyclopedia, "Poetry" article on CD-ROM (Grolier Incorporated, 1995)

Preview

Connections

FOR ALL STUDENTS

Ask volunteers to share what the word *family* means to them. Read together the first paragraph on page 586. Explain to students that many of the poems they will be reading in Part One illustrate the special connections between family members.

To further explore the theme, use the transparency referred to below.

Transparency Collection
Fine Art Writing Prompt 10

For At-Risk Students

- Invite students to recall movies and TV shows featuring family relations.
- Discuss similarities and differences between the colonial family on page 587 and the contemporary TV families on pages 588–589.
- Have students share what they know about colonial families and what they would like to learn.

For Students Who Need Challenge

- Ask students to make generalizations about the members of colonial families based on the facts illustrated in the photograph and discussed in the article on pages 586–587.
- Ask students to briefly research the Industrial Revolution and consider how it changed family life.
- Invite students to create plots for new TV sitcoms about family life in the year 2020.

MULTICULTURAL CONNECTION

Encourage students to discuss what they think are effective ways to communicate needs, wants, and problems to family members.

Part One

Connections

We find our own place in the world by connecting with others—through family ties and love, among other things.

Multicultural Connection **Communication** is essential in establishing connections with others and with the world at large. Communicating with a member of another generation can be a special challenge.

IDEAS THAT WORK

Getting a Jump on Poetry

Jump reading is one technique that all of my students enjoy, especially when studying poetry. First the class reads an entire poem silently. Next I read the entire poem aloud. Then individual students, without raising a hand, read a line, part of a line, or simply a single word. It is incredible how the students are able to "own" a poem with this technique. They really understand the poem, and it is really exciting to hear some of the usually reticent students join in the reading of a poem.

In addition, jump reading is excellent motivatio for writing assignments. Students can choose an line or lines from the poem to develop a writing assignment. Many of my students enjoy the poet more than any of the other units, and I feel it is because of the jump reading technique.

Dolores M. Mathew
Alrico, Florid

Before Reading

A New Dress by Ruth Dallas New Zealand

Those Winter Sundays by Robert Hayden USA

Tía Chucha by Luis J. Rodriguez USA

Building Background

Family Portraits Somewhere in your home probably sits an album of family photographs. As a child, you might have examined the pages, laughing at the funny clothes and old cars, puzzling over the identities of people who looked vaguely familiar. Poets, too, are creators of portraits, using words rather than a camera lens to create images.

Literary Focus

Figurative Language Words used outside of their literal, or usual, meanings are called **figurative language.** This type of language includes **figures of speech** such as the following**:** A **simile** is a stated comparison between two dissimilar things, using the words *like, as, appears, than,* or *seems:* "That hat looks like a bird cage." A **metaphor** is an implied comparison between two basically unlike things without a connective such as *like* or *as:* "His face was a map of suffering." **Personification** gives human qualities to nonhuman or nonliving things: "angry winds, flowers nodding their heads." **Hyperbole** is exaggeration for effect: "a street that winds on to infinity."

Restate the cartoon's caption in purely literal terms.

Writer's Notebook

Figure It Out As you read the following poems, jot down figurative language that helps you picture the people described.

"It didn't tug at my heart."

Drawing by Stan Hunt; © 1987 The New Yorker Magazine, Inc.

Before Reading

Building Background

Ask students to visualize a real or imaginary portrait of their family and then reflect on the feeling or mood that they experience. Suggest that the feeling may be the beginning of a poem.

Literary Focus

Possible response: "It didn't affect me emotionally."

Questions

- What is the figure of speech in the caption? *(tug at my heart)*
- Which type of **figurative language** is it? *(personification)*

Writer's Notebook

Encourage students to use the examples of figurative language they find in the poems as models. Ask students to choose family members or friends and write figures of speech to describe each person.

SUPPORT MATERIALS OVERVIEW

Unit 5 Resource Book
- Graphic Organizer, p. 1
- Study Guide, p. 2
- Vocabulary, p. 3
- Grammar, p. 4
- Alternate Check Test, p. 5
- Vocabulary Test, p. 6
- Selection Test, pp. 7–8

Building English Proficiency
- Literature Summaries
- Activities, p. 208

Reading, Writing & Grammar SkillBook
- Reading, pp. 53–54
- Grammar, Usage, and Mechanics, pp. 210–211

The World of Work
- Homemaker Consultant, p. 19
- Business Letter, p. 20

Technology
- Audiotape 13, Side A
- Personal Journal Software
- Custom Literature Database: For a family portrait in short story form, see "Blues Ain't No Mockin Bird" by Toni Cade Bambera on the database.
- Test Generator Software

More About the Poets

Ruth Dallas

- Ruth Dallas began her career as a child, writing for the children's page of the *Southland Daily News* in New Zealand.
- Dallas's poetry is heavily influenced by Chinese and Japanese poetry and philosophy. For her autobiography, see *Curved Horizon*, (1990).

Robert Hayden

- Much of Hayden's poetry deals with the black experience, involving historical characters such as Nat Turner, Malcolm X, and Harriet Tubman.
- Hayden once described history as "a long, tortuous, and often bloody process of becoming, of psychic evolution." Other works include *Robert Hayden: Collected Poems*, (1985).

Luis J. Rodriguez

- In addition to being a poet and journalist, Rodriguez has been a school bus driver and a carpenter; he has also worked in a lamp factory, a paper mill, and a chemical refinery.
- Rodriguez advises today's youth as follows: "I say to any young person —especially one linked to a great cause such as the fundamental progress of humanity—never give up. We all have the capabilities of great art and poetry."

Other works by the poet include:

- *Poems Across the Pavement, (*1989)
- *The Concrete River,* (1991)

Ruth Dallas
born 1919

Ruth Dallas grew up at the southernmost tip of New Zealand's South Island, which she describes as a place "where the sheer magnitude of the sky and sea seemed to dwarf human beings to insignificance." As a child who couldn't find books about New Zealand children, she vowed that when she grew up, she would write about her native country. She has published novels for children, mostly about New Zealand pioneer life, as well as many poetry collections.

Robert Hayden
1913–1980

Born in Detroit and raised by foster parents, Robert Hayden went on to write poetry that both reflected and went beyond his African American heritage to reveal his compassion for all humanity. In 1976, he was named Consultant in Poetry to the Library of Congress. In the 1930s, he did research in African American history, a recurring subject in his poems. Hayden, who taught at both Fisk University and the University of Michigan, described himself as "a poet who teaches in order to earn a living so that he can write a poem or two now and then."

Luis J. Rodriguez
born 1954

In his autobiography, *Always Running: La Vida Loca—Gang Days in L.A.*, Luis Rodriguez recounts how he escaped gang life because of a caring counselor and his own increasing love of writing. A survivor who profited from contact with the Chicano movement of the 1960s, Rodriguez now spends time working as a peace arbiter with gangs and conducting poetry workshops for the homeless. He considers the job of a writer "a heroic and necessary task." His printing company is called Tía Chucha Press, after a beloved aunt.

A New Dress

Ruth Dallas

I don't want a new dress, I said.
My mother plucked from her mouth ninety-nine pins.
I suppose there are plenty, she said, *girls of ten*
Who would be glad to have a new dress.

Snip-snip. Snip-snip. The cold scissors
Ate quickly as my white rabbit round my arm.

1 *She won't speak to me if I have a new dress!*
My feet rattled on the kitchen floor.

How can I fit you if you won't stand still?

My tears made a map of Australia
On the sofa cushion; from the hot center
My friend's eyes flashed, fierce as embers.[1]
She would not speak to me, perhaps never again.
She would paralyze me with one piercing look.

I'd rather have my friend than a new dress!

My mother wouldn't understand, my grownup mother
Whose grasshopper thimble winked at the sun
And whose laughter was made by small waves
Rearranging seashells on Australia's shore.

1. ember (em′bər), *n.* ashes in which there is still some fire.

During Reading

Selection Objectives

- to explore the theme of connections
- to identify examples of figurative language
- to understand the use of active and passive verbs

Unit 5 Resource Book
Graphic Organizer, p. 1
Study Guide, p. 2

Theme Link

Three poets make connections with their pasts by describing childhood relationships with family members.

Vocabulary Preview

ember, ashes in which there is still some fire
chronic, never stopping
austere, stern in manner or appearance; harsh
despot, ruler having unlimited power
elixir, medicine with curing powers

Students can add the words and definitions to their Writer's Notebooks.

1 Reader's Response

Making Personal Connections

Question Do you think a friend's reaction to your getting something new could be as upsetting to you as it was to the speaker in the poem? *(Possible response: Yes, because getting new things can cause jealousies; no, because I'd expect my friend to be happy for me.)*

SELECTION SUMMARY

"A New Dress," "Those Winter Sundays," "Tía Chucha"

Each of the three poems in this selection addresses a relationship between the speaker as a child and an adult family member. In "A New Dress," Ruth Dallas recalls a time when her mother could not understand her certainty that wearing a new dress would alienate a friend. In "Those Winter Sundays," Robert Hayden shows that a father's work and self-sacrifice are appreciated long after the chance is say "thank you" is gone. In "Tía Chucha," Louis J. Rodriguez describes his wild and eccentric aunt, deemed crazy by the world, but a model for him of naturalness, childlike curiosity, and freedom.

For summaries in other languages, see the ***Building English Proficiency*** *book.*

2 Literary Focus
Figurative Language

Question

- What figure of speech is "hear the cold splintering, breaking"? *(personification)*
- Why does this description fit better than, for example, "felt the cold electrifying, tingling"? *(because it shows the painfulness of the cold and it adds to the harsh environment of the setting)*
- What other images show hardship? *(Images include "ached from labor," "chronic angers," "austere . . . offices.")*

3 Literary Element
Tone

Open a discussion of the tone, or feelings the speaker displays toward his father. When students mention appreciation, love, and possibly regret, prompt them to explain how the author shows those feelings without using those words. *(appreciation: the images of cold, pain, the line "no one ever thanked him"; love: by choosing to describe the kind acts done by the father; regret: by repeating "what did I know" as a kind of wail)*

Those Winter Sundays

Robert Hayden

Sundays too my father got up early
and put his clothes on in the blueblack cold,
then with cracked hands that ached
from labor in the weekday weather made
banked fires blaze. No one ever thanked him.

2 I'd wake and hear the cold splintering, breaking.
When the rooms were warm, he'd call,
and slowly I would rise and dress,
fearing the chronic[1] angers of that house,

Speaking indifferently to him,
who had driven out the cold
3 and polished my good shoes as well.
What did I know, what did I know
of love's austere[2] and lonely offices?

1. chronic (kron′ik), *adj.* never stopping.
2. austere (ô stir′), *adj.* stern in manner or appearance; harsh.

This oil painting by Frank Joseph Dillon was completed in 1933, during the Depression. Why might the artist have painted the backs instead of the fronts of houses? Do you think the figure with the sack lives in one of the houses or is just passing by? ➤

MINI-LESSON: GRAMMAR
Active and Passive Voice

Teach Explain to students that verb choice is important when writing. One choice is using the active or passive voice. Point out that when a verb takes an object

- the verb can be in the active voice, in which the subject of the sentence acts upon someone or something

  My tears <u>made</u> a map of Australia . . . *(active voice)*
- the verb can be in the passive voice, in which the subject of the sentence receives the action

  And whose laughter <u>was made</u> by small waves *(passive voice)*

Activity Idea Explain that many writers employ the passive voice too often and that they can eliminate weak, slow-moving sentences by eliminating passive verbs. Have students experiment with statements in "A New Dress," rewriting the verbs to show both active and passive verb forms, as in this example:

Every few years Tía Chucha <u>would visit</u> the family.

Every few years the family <u>would be visited</u> by Tía Chucha.

Discuss with the class why poets might choose to use active verbs.

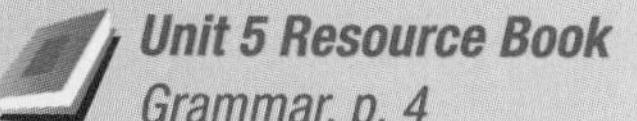

Unit 5 Resource Book
Grammar, p. 4

Art Study

Response to Caption Questions Students may say that whether the figure lives in one of the houses or not, he belongs in the setting.

Dillon's untitled painting is a realistic view of a suburban street in winter during the Depression.

Visual Literacy By painting the man with the sack in the same colors as the houses, Dillon shows a unified picture that suggests loneliness and hardship.

Question What in Dillon's painting reflects the setting or situation in "Those Winter Sundays"? *(Possible responses: Both the painting and the poem depict winter scenes; the man carrying the sack is comparable to the father in the poem—both are connected with isolation and hard labor; both are strong images of an unwelcoming house in winter; the imagery of the painting is stark and quiet like the language of the poem.)*

The World of Work

Homemaker Consultant

For consideration of family issues from a homemaker consultant's view, use—

The World of Work
pp. 19–20

BUILDING ENGLISH PROFICIENCY

ESL LEP ELD SAE LD

Making Personal Connections

Many students may have known a colorful relative or another adult, such as Tía Chucha, who made a strong impression on them as a child. Ask students to explore their memories or their impressions.

Activity Ideas

- "Tía Chucha" focuses on a visit from the speaker's aunt. Invite volunteers to talk or write about a relative's visit. Then describe what they might say or write in a "thank you" to that person.
- Some students may remember a person who frightened or embarassed them. Talk (or write privately) about how they feel about that person now that they are older.
- Students will probably encounter the following words from the poem in everyday communication. You might act out or explain them.

  unannounced
  annoying
  upheaval
  wisp

Building English Proficiency
Activities, p. 208

4 Literary Focus
Figurative Language

Point out that in Spanish, *tía* means "aunt." Discuss what might be happening in a house when an aunt arrives and opens up the family "like an overripe avocado." *(Possible responses: People might say and do things they wouldn't normally say or do; children might get rowdy; adults might argue; the house might be messy.)*

5 Reading/Thinking Skills
Compare and Contrast

Question How are the three poems in this selection similar? How are they different? *(Possible responses: All describe family members who influenced the poets; all are remembrances of childhood; all are written in the first person. The mood and tone differ. "A New Dress" has an excited mood and expresses frustration; "Those Winter Sundays" has a solemn mood and an elegiac tone; "Tía Chucha" has an excited mood and a celebratory tone.)*

Check Test

1. "A New Dress": How old is the speaker? *(ten years old)*
2. "A New Dress": What is another way of saying "my feet rattled"? *(I couldn't stand still.)*
3. "Those Winter Sundays": What kind of job did the father have? *(an outdoor job)*
4. "Tía Chucha": What "crazy" things does Tía Chucha do in the poem? *(runs out of the house naked; sings on the bus)*
5. "Tía Chucha": Which of the following does the author say Tía Chucha is like—freedom, a rabbit, austere love, a splash of water? *(freedom, a splash of water)*

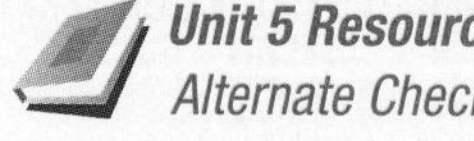

Unit 5 Resource Book
Alternate Check Test, p. 5

Tía Chucha

by Luis J. Rodriguez

Every few years
Tía Chucha would visit the family
in a tornado of song
and open us up
as if we were an overripe avocado.
She was a dumpy, black-haired
creature of upheaval,
who often came unannounced
with a bag of presents
including home-made perfumes and colognes
that smelled something like
rotting fish
on a hot day at the tuna cannery.

They said she was crazy.
Oh sure, she once ran out naked
to catch the postman
with a letter that didn't belong to us.
I mean, she had this annoying habit
of boarding city buses
and singing at the top of her voice
(one bus driver even refused to go on
until she got off).
But crazy?

To me, she was the wisp
of the wind's freedom,
a music-maker
who once tried to teach me guitar
but ended up singing
and singing,
me listening,
and her singing
until I put the instrument down
and watched the clock
click the lesson time away.

I didn't learn guitar,
but I learned something
about her craving
for the new, the unbroken
. . . so she could break it.
Periodically she banished
herself from the family
and was the better for it.

I secretly admired Tía Chucha.
She was always quick with a story,
another "*Pepito*" joke,
or a hand-written lyric
that she would produce
regardless of the occasion.

She was a despot[1]
of desire;
uncontainable
as a splash of water
on a varnished table.

I wanted to remove
the layers
of unnatural seeing
the way Tía Chucha beheld
the world, with first eyes,
like an infant
who can discern
the elixir[2]
within milk.

I wanted to be
one of the prizes

she stuffed into
her rumpled bag.

1. despot (des′pət), *n.* ruler having unlimited power.
2. elixir (i lik′sər), *n.* medicine with curing powers.

MINI-LESSON: VOCABULARY
Word Context

Teach Students can determine the meaning of a multimeaning word by considering its context in a phrase or sentence.

Activity Idea Discuss the final word *offices* in "Those Winter Sundays." Ask students to

- guess the author's intended meaning from its use in the sentence
- find four definitions of *offices* in the dictionary
- consider how each of the dictionary definitions would function in the sentence
- decide which meaning the author intended as primary and which other meaning(s) he might have wished to suggest

After Reading

Making Connections

Shaping Your Response

1. Which poetic portrait of a family member do you find most vivid? Draw this character in your notebook.
2. Which poem reminds you of a childhood incident of your own? Explain.
3. Which main character in these poems would you prefer having as a parent? Why?

Analyzing the Poems

4. What **inferences** can you make about the attitudes of the three speakers toward their family members? Cite lines to support your opinion.
5. What do you think causes the change of **tone** in the last two lines of "Those Winter Sundays"?
6. In "A New Dress," how is the phrase "my grownup mother" a clue to the **theme** of the poem?
7. What examples of surprising **images** did you find in "Tía Chucha"?
8. What phrase in each poem do you think best **characterizes** the subject? Explain your choices.

Extending the Ideas

9. Do you think that **communication** between parents and children changes once those children become teenagers? Explain.
10. Recently, newspapers and television have focused on the plight of the American family. What seems to be causing its disintegration? What remedies would you suggest?

Literary Focus: Figurative Language

Answer the following questions about **figurative language:**

- Considering the time of day mentioned, how can cold be blueblack, as described in line 2 of "Those Winter Sundays"?
- In line 17 of "A New Dress," what does the **metaphor** "grass-hopper thimble" suggest about the mother's actions?
- How does Dallas use **hyperbole** (exaggeration) and **personification** (giving human qualities to nonhuman things) to make her poem lively?
- Which figures of speech in "Tía Chucha" do you find most memorable?

After Reading

MAKING CONNECTIONS

1. Drawings might show an important characteristic or image such as impatience in the girls, the rough hands of the father, or their impression of Tía Chucha appearing at the door.

2. If responses involve family members, they should include descriptions of what the relatives were like and how students felt toward them, in general and/or as a result of the incidents described.

3. Students might choose the mother from "A New Dress" because she is a model of competent or graceful adulthood or the father from "Those Winter Sundays" because he is hardworking and caring. Most will agree that Tía Chucha would not be a good parent, even though she is exciting sometimes.

4. Possible responses: The speaker in "A New Dress" seems both frustrated by and admiring of her mother, especially in the last four lines; the speaker of "Those Winter Sundays" is admiring and grateful ("cracked hands that ached from labor;" "love's . . . lonely offices"); the speaker of "Tía Chucha" admires and is inspired by his aunt ("a wisp of the wind's freedom," "secretly admired").

5. The speaker regrets not showing his father the gratitude he now feels.

6. Possible response: It points to the contrast between a grownup and child and brings out the theme that parents are often blind to the intense struggles a child experiences.

7. Possible responses: "a tornado of song"; "she once ran out naked to catch the postman"; "she was a despot of desire."

8. Phrases should include images or descriptions of the family members which reflect the overall portraits the authors are trying to create.

9. Students may respond that as children approach adulthood, their conflicts with parents are magnified.

10. Encourage students to address communication in their answers.

LITERARY FOCUS: FIGURATIVE LANGUAGE

Review the definitions of *metaphor, simile, personification,* and *hyperbole.* Before addressing the questions, let students suggest new examples of each figure of speech.

Possible responses

- It is early morning and not yet light outside, and the author associates the cold with the color of the sky at that time of day.
- The mother moves her hands quickly while sewing, causing the thimble on her thumb to dart around like a grasshopper.
- Dallas uses hyperbole ("plucked from her mouth ninety-nine pins") to depict her mother as a woman with fearsome sewing skills, which the poet cannot escape. She uses personification (the scissors/rabbit image) to suggest that her mother's sewing tools have a life of their own, also making escape difficult.
- Students should be able to identify each figure of speech in their responses as metaphor, simile, personification, or hyperbole.

VOCABULARY STUDY

1. b
2. a
3. c
4. d
5. d

More Practice Have students brainstorm synonyms or near synonyms for each vocabulary word.

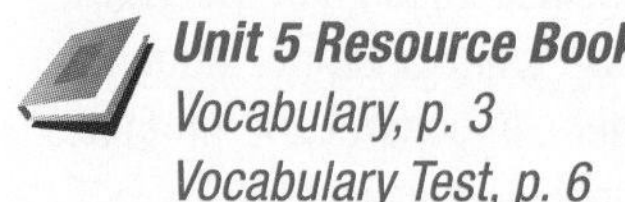

Unit 5 Resource Book
Vocabulary, p. 3
Vocabulary Test, p. 6

WRITING CHOICES

Writer's Notebook Update

Possible responses

Figure of Speech	Meaning
simile: fierce as embers	very angry
hyperbole: paralyze me	upset me greatly
metaphor: grasshopper thimble	quickly moving thimble

Family Photos

Each caption should include a family member's name and a figure of speech that describes him or her.

Example: "Cousin Ida is as silent as a dark closet."

All in the Family

You might have students read each other's sketches and define the tone, or attitude, of the writer toward his or her subject matter and audience.

Point of View

Suggest that students choose one idea and use clustering as they brainstorm related ideas and images. You might wish to provide them with poems by Emily Dickinson and Walt Whitman, available on the Custom Literature Database.

Selection Test

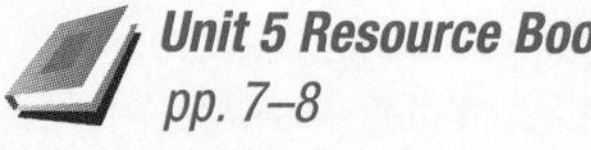

Unit 5 Resource Book
pp. 7–8

Vocabulary Study

On your paper, write the letter of the vocabulary word from the list that best completes each sentence.

austere
chronic
despot
elixir
ember

1. If you were a *despot*, your subjects would most likely react to you with ____. **a.** laughter **b.** fear **c.** sympathy **d.** joy
2. A *chronic* offender would offend ____.
   a. all the time **b.** occasionally **c.** rarely **d.** never
3. You would expect the effects of an *elixir* to be ____.
   a. painful **b.** loud **c.** beneficial **d.** destructive
4. You would most likely find an *ember* in a ____.
   a. bathroom **b.** closet **c.** car **d.** fireplace
5. If you had an *austere* appearance, strangers would most likely ____ you.
   a. smile at **b.** shout at **c.** lecture **d.** avoid

Expressing Your Ideas

Writing Choices

Writer's Notebook Update Review the figurative language you found in each poem. Make a chart that shows each figure of speech along with its meaning.

Figure of Speech	Meaning

Family Photos Look through a family photo album, noting details and characteristics of family members and settings. If you don't know some of these people personally, imagine what they would be like. Then write **captions** for several of these pictures, using figurative language.

All in the Family Every family has at least one colorful member who stands out because of his or her actions, dress, or attitudes. Write a **character sketch** of this family member showing that person's uniqueness as well as your feelings about him or her.

Point of View Respond to the ideas in one of the poems you have just read by writing your own **poem** from the point of view of one of the main characters.

Other Options

Clothes Encounters It is not uncommon for a teenager and a parent, guardian, or school official to have a difference of opinion about clothes, hair styles, or something else connected with fashion. Draw a **cartoon** that captures your differing opinions.

Talk Radio Your group will simulate a radio talk show in which listeners call in with comments on the state of the American family. One student will act as host and other group members will be the callers. Make a **recording** of the on-air comments and the host's responses, serious or humorous. Play the tape in class.

OTHER OPTIONS

Clothes Encounters

Suggest that students look at old magazines to see how fashions have changed over the past twenty years.

Talk Radio

Encourage students to do library research on the American family. They can then quote books, essays, or articles written by "experts" as part of the class radio show.

Before Reading

Girls Can We Educate We Dads? by James Berry West Indies

If You'll Only Go to Sleep by Gabriela Mistral Chile

Mi Prima Agueda by Ramón López Velarde Mexico

Building Background

Between Generations What goes on between generations? There may be a close bond, such as between mother and infant. There may be a special connection, such as between a favorite relative and a young person. Or there may be friction—for example, that between parent and child when they hold different opinions and beliefs. A lack of understanding between adults and young adults, such as that conveyed in the poem by James Berry that you are about to read, is sometimes referred to as the **"generation gap."**

Literary Focus

Diction Writers' choices of words, determined by their subject, audience, and desired effect, is called **diction.** An important element in a writer's style, diction can be described as *casual* or *formal* (bugged/vexed), *old-fashioned* or *contemporary* (steed/horse), *general* or *specific* (dog/golden retriever). When you read a poem, think about why the poet chose those particular words.

This cartoon serves as a reminder that word choice depends on the setting, the speaker, and the occasion.

"He's, like, 'To be or not to be,' and I'm, like, 'Get a life.'"

Drawing by Lorenz; © 1995 The New Yorker Magazine, Inc.

Writer's Notebook

Not To Tattoo Make a list of comments—"That's not music; that's noise!" "But everyone has pierced ears!"—that suggest some current generation gaps.

Before Reading

Building Background

Ask students to discuss movies or television shows that feature relationships between characters of different generations.

Literary Focus

To get a sense of the effect that **diction** has on the listener or reader, let students experiment with using the following forms of *home* in sentences—*digs, pad, crib* (slang); *house, home, place* (informal); *abode, domicile, residence* (formal). Then let students react to the different choices.

Writer's Notebook

Suggest that students create charts to categorize their comments. Headings might include fashion, music, social life, school, language, home, and job. This arrangement should help students structure the writing assignment in the Writer's Notebook Update, page 567.

SUPPORT MATERIALS OVERVIEW

Unit 5 Resource Book
- Graphic Organizer, p. 9
- Study Guide, p. 10
- Vocabulary, p. 11
- Grammar, p. 12
- Alternate Check Test, p. 13
- Vocabulary Test, p. 14
- Selection Test, pp. 15–16

Building English Proficiency
- Literature Summaries
- Activities, p. 209

Reading, Writing & Grammar SkillBook
- Vocabulary, pp. 13–14
- Writing, pp. 119–120
- Grammar, Usage, and Mechanics, pp. 195–196

Technology
- Audiotape 13, Side B
- Personal Journal Software
- Custom Literature Database: For another poem about generations, see "The Children's Hour" by Henry Wadsworth Longfellow on the database.
- Test Generator Software

More About the Poets

James Berry

- In his poetry collection *Lucy's Letters and Loving,* Berry describes the experience of black immigrants from the point of view of a young West Indian woman living in London.
- Berry has edited two collections of West Indian-British poetry and written two collections of short stories for children.

Other works by the poet include

- *Fractured Circles,* (1979)
- *Chain of Days,* (1985)
- *The Girls and Yanga Marshall,* (1987)

Gabriela Mistral

- Following in the footsteps of her father, who was a teacher and a minstrel, Mistral became a primary school teacher at the age of fifteen.
- Mistral may have chosen her name to refer to the archangel Gabriel and the "mistral" (a fierce wind) of southern France.
- Mistral donated the profits from her third book to Basque orphans of the Spanish Civil War.
- Mistral also wrote poetry for children and collections of fables.

She also wrote *Selected Poems of Gabriela Mistral,* translated by Langston Hughes, (1957).

James Berry
born 1925

"It's the function of writers and poets," James Berry once wrote, "to bring in the left-out side of the human family." A Jamaican living in England, Berry felt very much a part of that left-out family. He began writing while working in British schools, having noted that the school libraries had few books about children with either an African or Caribbean heritage. Berry's background is evident in his short stories and poetry, where he often uses the Creole language spoken in Jamaica to capture the character of his island's people.

Gabriela Mistral
1889–1957

Gabriela Mistral (mē sträl′) is the pen name of Lucila Godoy, who feared she might lose her teaching job if she published under her own name. After the suicide of her fiancé in 1909, she devoted herself to teaching, writing, and raising the child of her half-brother. Although she first gained renown as an educator, Mistral later became a diplomat, serving in Brazil, Mexico, Italy, and the United States. She often writes of love—physical, maternal, and spiritual. In 1945, she received the Nobel Prize for literature.

Ramón López Velarde
1888–1921

The oldest of nine children, Ramón López Velarde (bə lär′dā) published his first poetry in 1905, despite his father's strong objections to a literary career. Although he earned his law degree, he continued to write for various literary magazines. After moving to Mexico City, Velarde worked as both a government official and a professor of literature. Four days after his thirty-third birthday and just as he was beginning to be recognized for his poetry, Velarde died of pneumonia. Today he is considered the father of modern Mexican poetry.

Girls Can We Educate We Dads? [1]

James Berry

Listn the male chauvinist[1] in mi dad—
a girl walkin night street mus be bad.
He dohn sey, the world's a free place
for a girl to keep her unmolested[2] space.
Instead he sey—a girl is a girl.

He sey a girl walkin swingin hips about
call boys to look and shout.
He dohn sey, if a girl have style
she wahn to sey, look
I okay from top to foot.
Instead he sey—a girl is a girl.

Listn the male chauvinist in mi dad—
a girl too laughy-laughy look too glad-glad
jus like a girl too looky-looky roun
will get a pretty satan at her side.
He dohn sey—a girl full of go
dohn wahn stifle[3] talent comin on show.
Instead he sey—a girl is a girl.

---

1. chauvinist (shō′və nist), *n.* person excessively enthusiastic about his or her sex, race, or group.
2. unmolested (un mə lest′əd), *adj.* undisturbed.
3. stifle (stī′fəl) *v.* keep back; stop.

During Reading

Selection Objectives

- to identify and understand the literary effect of different kinds of diction
- to explore the theme of connections between different generations
- to recognize English-language idioms
- to analyze different translations of a poem

Unit 5 Resource Book
Graphic Organizer, p. 9
Study Guide, p. 10

Theme Link

Three poets show that connections between older and younger family members sometimes take the form of conflict.

Vocabulary Preview

chauvinist, person excessively enthusiastic about his or her sex, race, or group
unmolested, undisturbed
stifle, keep back, stop
odious, hateful; offensive
funereal, gloomy

Students can add the words and definitions to their Writer's Notebooks.

1 Literary Element
Dialect

Explain that dialect is a form of speech characteristic of a particular region or class. Dialect differs from standard English in pronunciation, vocabulary, and grammatical form. Discuss these examples of dialect and invite students to identify others:

- *We Dads:* the grammatically incorrect use of "we" instead of "our"
- *lisn* and *mi:* spellings corresponding to pronunciation in Jamaican dialect

SELECTION SUMMARY

"Girls Can We Educate We Dads?," "If You'll Only Go To Sleep," "Mi Prima Agueda"

The three poems in this selection are about family. The poets probe bonds and divisions between generations. A daughter, speaking in the rhythms of Jamaican dialect, objects to her father's chauvinistic opinions about women in "Girls Can We Educate We Dads?" Gabriela Mistral uses the form of a lullaby to describe how a tired parent might offer a baby beautiful things in exchange for a night of sleep. In "Mi Prima Agueda" ("My Cousin Agueda"), presented in its original Spanish by Ramón López Velarde and in translations by Cheli Durán and Willis Knapp Jones, the narrator tells of his fascination with his cousin, the embodiment to him of strange and beautiful contradictions.

*For summaries in other languages, see the **Building English Proficiency** book.*

2 Literary Element
Imagery

Question What are some vivid images in the poem? *(crimson rose, fire and cinnamon of the carnation; bread baked with anise and honey; sequined goldfish)*

Direct students to visualize those images and then judge whether the speaker in the poem would have chosen for her baby the crib shown in *Canción de cuna.*

3 Literary Element
Tone

Help students to discover the tone of gentle humor that underlies the weary, cajoling words. They might observe that the patient speaker, probably the mother, knows she is bribing and promising things to a baby who is incapable of waiting a second for any gratification.

Responses to Caption Questions

- Some students may feel the image fits with the metal of the crib; they may observe that the colors and materials differ from the pastels and warmer materials that are traditional for nurseries.
- Encourage students to debate this question, sharing their opinions about the purpose of art.

If You'll Only Go to Sleep

Gabriela Mistral

The crimson rose
Plucked yesterday,
the fire and cinnamon
of the carnation,

the bread I baked
with anise seed and honey,
and the goldfish
flaming in its bowl.

3

All these are yours,
baby born of woman,
if you'll only
go to sleep.
A rose, I say!
And a carnation!
Fruit, I say!
And honey!

And a sequined goldfish,
and still more I'll give you
if you'll only sleep
till morning.

Canción de cuna (Cradle Song) by Colombian artist Beatriz González is constructed of metal laminate and painted with enamel. Does the flat perspective make the mother-child relationship seem more personal, or less so, than other works of art on the same subject? If the crib were used for a baby, would you consider this art wasted or not?

MINI-LESSON: GRAMMAR
Idioms

Teach An idiom is a speech form or an expression of a given language that is peculiar to itself grammatically or cannot be understood from the individual meanings of its elements. Examples are

bite the dust   full of oneself
easy money   a slip of the tongue

Students should note that although dialect may also have grammatical peculiarities, dialect is found only in particular regions or among particular class groups, whereas idioms are often common to the language as a whole.

Questions

- In the last stanza of "Girls Can We Educate We Dads?" is there an idiom that you recognize? *("full of go")*
- What does "full of go" mean? (*enthusiastic, energetic)*

Mention that good writers use idioms but avoid slang. Invite volunteers to develop a list of interesting idioms by consulting the *Oxford Dictionary of Current Idiomatic Usage* and to share their findings with the class.

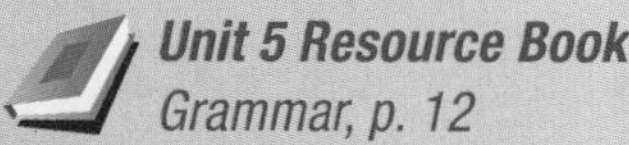

Unit 5 Resource Book
Grammar, p. 12

4

Mi Prima Agueda

A Jesús Villalpando

Ramón López Velarde

Mi madrina invitaba a mi prima Agueda
a que pasara el día con nosotros,
y mi prima llegaba
con un contradictorio
prestigio de almidón y de temible
luto ceremonioso.

Agueda aparecía, resonante
de almidón, y sus ojos
verdes y sus mejillas rubicundas
me protegían contra el pavoroso
luto. . . .
Yo era rapaz
y conocía la O por lo redondo,
y Agueda que tejía
mansa y perseverante en el sonoro
corredor, me causaba
calofríos ignotos. . . .

(Creo que hasta la debo la costumbre
heroicamente insana de hablar solo.)

A la hora de comer, en la penumbra
quieta del refectorio,
me iba embelesando un quebradizo
sonar intermitente de vajilla
y el timbre caricioso
de la voz de mi prima.
Agueda era
(luto, pupilas verdes y mejillas
rubicundas) un cesto policromo
de manzanas y uvas
5 en el ébano de un armario añoso.

The Art of Translation

The translator, no less than the original poet, must deal with words and meanings sensitively and imaginatively. A translator of poetry is in effect a poet, re-creating the poem in the new language so that it approximates (not duplicates) the effect of the original. Many elements of poetry may cause problems for a less-than-skillful translator. Consider, for example, the challenge of translating figurative language. The translation must not only be true to the meaning of the first language, but it must capture the emotions and associations of the words beyond their literal meanings.

Consider this analogy: a translator must get both the *words* (meaning) and the *tune* (spirit) right. To carry the comparison further, the translator must get the *rhythm* accurate, as well. Words must be chosen for their sound effects as well as their meanings in order to create the mood of the original. Here is a poem by Ramón López Velarde in its original Spanish, followed on the next page by two translations. Examine how the translators interpret words differently.

4 Speaking and Listening

Interpretive Reading/ Recognize Different Speaking Styles

Invite a volunteer who knows or is studying Spanish to read "Mi Prima Agueda" aloud. Encourage students to follow along in their books, listening to the rhythm of the lines and the rhyme scheme.

5 Literary Element

Rhythm/Rhyme

After reading the English translations on page 564, students can compare the versions.

Questions

- Which translation sounds more like the original poem? Why? *(Jones's translation sounds more like the original poem, because he uses rhyme and a singsong rhythm which approximates that of the original.)*
- Why do you think Durán chose not to use rhyme in her translation? *(It freed her to translate López Velarde's vocabulary and the syntax of the lines more accurately.)*

BUILDING ENGLISH PROFICIENCY

Evaluating Translation

To complement the discussion of translation in the text, ask students who speak Spanish to help the class appreciate "Mi Prima Agueda."

Activity Ideas

- Ask a Spanish-speaking student to read the poem aloud to allow everyone to appreciate the rhythm and sound of the language. (You might ask another student to read one of the translations on page 564 for contrast.)
- Have Spanish-speaking students give their impression of the poem before you examine the translations. Later, compare these with other students' impressions of one of the translations.
- Ask Spanish-speaking students to comment on the translation, perhaps pointing out where some of the phrasing was not entirely literal.

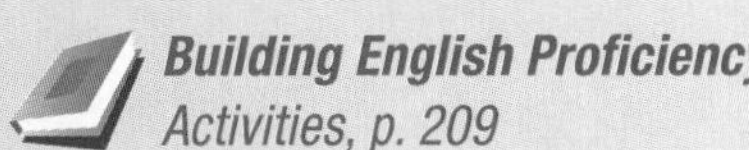
Building English Proficiency *Activities, p. 209*

6 Literary Focus
Diction

Direct students' attention to the third and fourth lines of both translations of "Mi Prima Agueda."

Questions

- How does the diction of the two translations differ? *(Durán's diction is more formal: "contradictory magic"; Jones's is more colloquial: "in a mixed-up way")*
- Compare other phrases. Does Durán continue to be formal and Jones continue to be colloquial? *(Students should use examples to support their conclusions.)*

7 Literary Element
Metaphor

Question Both translations suggest that the poet has created a metaphor at the end of the poem, comparing Agueda with a basket of apples and grapes. What do you think he means by this metaphor? *(The poet saw Agueda as a comforting presence of color and warmth in his life.)*

My Cousin Agatha

To Jesús Villalpando

translated by Cheli Durán

My godmother used to ask my cousin
Agatha
to spend the day with us,
and my cousin used to arrive
wrapped in a contradictory magic
of starch and odious[1] ritual
mourning.

Agatha entered, rustling
starch, and her green eyes
and warm red cheeks
protected me from the dreadful
black. . . .
I was only a child
who knew the O by its roundness,
and Agatha, who knitted
mildly, persistently, in the echoing
corridor,
sent little unknown shivers
up my spine.

(I think I owe her, too, my crazy
but heroic habit of talking alone.)

At dinner, in the restful twilight
of the dining room,
I was slowly bewitched by the brittle
intermittent ring of plates,
and the lilt that was like a caress
in my cousin's voice.
Agatha was
(rosy cheeks, green eyes, black mourning)
a polychrome basket of colors,
crammed with apples and grapes,
on the ebony of an old cupboard.

1. odious (ō′dē əs), *adj.* hateful; offensive.

My Cousin Agueda

translated by Willis Knapp Jones

My godmother often invited my cousin
Agueda
To come and spend the day.
My cousin used to arrive
6 Appearing in a mixed-up way,
Suggesting starch and fearful
Mourning of a funereal[1] day.

Agueda would appear rustling
With starch, and with her eyes green.
And her rosy cheeks
Protecting me against the mourning
That I'd seen.

I was a kid
And knew nothing at all,
And Agueda, who was moving
Tamely and persistently in the hall,
With her rustling brought excitement
About which I knew nothing at all.

(I even think she is responsible
For my mad habit of talking to myself.)

At the dinner hour in the quiet
Shadows of the dining room,
How delightful the fragile
Intermittent rattle of the dishes
And the affectionate tone
Of the voice of my cousin
Agueda.
7 (in her black mourning, her green eyes, and
Pink cheeks) was a many colored basket
Of apples and green grapes
On the ebony of our ancestral sideboard.

1. funereal (fyü nir′ē əl), *adj.* gloomy.

MINI-LESSON: VOCABULARY
Expand Vocabulary Using Structural Analysis

Teach Students can learn to guess the meanings of words by identifying common Latin roots, prefixes, and suffixes.

Questions

- Why did both translators of "Mi Prima Agueda" choose the word *intermittent,* meaning "stopping for a time and beginning again," in line 22? *(because López Velarde used the Spanish equivalent* intermitente *in his original poem)*
- Why would Spanish and English have a number of similar words? *(Both languages are derived in part from Latin.)*

Activity Idea Ask students to

- check a dictionary to find the simplest form of *intermittent*
- find the word's etymology
- brainstorm the connection between the etymology and the modern meaning
- list and define other words with the prefix *inter-* and the root *mit (mis)*

 This 1990 untitled work by Peruvian photographer Jeanette Ortiz Osorio is a photograph combined with a painted filter. Which English or Spanish words in the poem **communicate** the same mood as this mixed media portrait?

Art Study

Response to Caption Question
Responses may include "contradictory magic," "funereal," "shivers up my spine," "black mourning," "polychrome basket of colors."

Jeanette Ortiz Osorio says, "My photography is very intuitive. The images originate in dreams as well as in conscious experience, and vary from bright and colorful to dark, subtle forms."

Visual Literacy Some of the impact of visual art derives from deliberate contrasts put in the work to create tension.

Question What elements of Osorio's work are in contrast? *(Possible responses: the media of photography and painting; the realism of the photograph and the abstract quality of the painted lines.)*

Check Test

1. "Girls Can We Educate We Dads?": What do the speaker and her father disagree about? *(about how and when the speaker can go walking down the street)*
2. "Girls Can We Educate We Dads?": What does the speaker think her father wants to stifle? *(her talent)*
3. "If You'll Only Go to Sleep": Who is speaking? *(a parent)*
4. "Mi Prima Agueda": What color is Cousin Agueda's dress? *(black clothing)*
5. "Mi Prima Agueda": In the last line, Durán uses the phrase "an old cupboard." What is Jones's translation of this phrase? *(ancestral sideboard)*

Unit 5 Resource Book
Alternate Check Test, p. 13

BUILDING ENGLISH PROFICIENCY

Comparing Translations

After students have read both translations, help them explore the differences in word choice and tone with questions such as the following.

1. Which poem did you like best? Why?
2. Which words or phrases in either translation caught your attention? Why?
3. Was there a particular phrase that created a strong picture in your mind? In which translation did it appear?
4. Find one statement that is translated quite differently in the two versions. Which translation do you prefer, and why?

After Reading

MAKING CONNECTIONS

1. Students might make connections based on a musical piece's mood, rhythm, or ethnic origin.

2. Students should focus on the kind of connection between family members —such as "in conflict," "exasperated but loving," or "mystified and entranced."

3. Students may realize that through the treatment of the subject, a poet communicates views on universal themes and emotions.

4. The first two to four lines and the last line of each stanza represent the father's point of view. The two to three lines between represent the girl's point of view.

5. Possible responses: Girls who attract attention will get into trouble; a girl won't be respected if she doesn't act reserved and allow herself to be protected.

6. Possible response: A mood of weary tenderness is suggested by the repeated pleading "if you'll only go to sleep" and the words *crimson, fire, cinnamon, honey, goldfish,* and *sequined.*

7. Cheli Durán's translation suggests that the child is very young, since she is just learning to read and recognize letters.

8. Responses might include people not wanting to take the time to notice what is unique about a person.

9. Students might respond that both are magical and exciting to the narrator; however, while Tía Chucha's actions are overtly unconventional, Cousin Agueda dresses in black and moves "mildly" or "tamely." Her presence suggests comfort more than freedom and new ways of seeing.

10. Students may respond that reading works from other cultures helps them to recognize ways in which people are the same the world over, and to understand the differences.

After Reading

Making Connections

Shaping Your Response

1. Think of a musical piece that could accompany each poem. Explain your choices.
2. Which pair of characters in these poems bears the closest similarity to people in your own family? Explain the resemblance.
3. In your opinion, is a stubborn father, a crying baby, or an older cousin important enough to be the subject of a poem? Why or why not?

Analyzing the Poems

4. Which lines in each stanza of Berry's poem express the girl's **point of view?** Which lines express the father's viewpoint?
5. What **stereotypes** about girls appear in Berry's poem?
6. What words create the **mood** of "If You'll Only Go to Sleep"?
7. In lines 12–13 of "My Cousin Agueda," which translation do you think better suggests the speaker's age? Explain.

Extending the Ideas

8. The dad in Berry's poem is guilty of **stereotyping** girls. What current stereotypes of girls, boys, and teenagers have you noticed? How do you think they came to exist?
9. Compare Tía Chucha and Cousin Agueda.
10. Do you think that **communication** would be improved if U.S. textbooks included more works in languages other than English? Why or why not?

Literary Focus: Diction

Examine the **diction** in these three poems by discussing the following questions.

- What do you think is meant by the phrases "full of go" and "dohn wahn stifle . . . show" in lines 16–17 of Berry's poem?
- Why might Mistral mention a "crimson red" rose instead of merely a red one? the "fire and cinnamon" instead of the "smell" of a carnation?
- Which version of lines 7–11 of the three poems on pages 563–564 creates the most vivid image for you? Why?
- Imagine that Berry had chosen to write his poem in standard English. What would be gained or lost, in your opinion?

LITERARY FOCUS: DICTION

Possible responses

- "Full of go" means "energetic" or "enthusiastic." (See Mini-Lesson, page 562.) The line including "dohn wahn stifle . . ." means that girls don't want the signs of their emerging womanhood—both physical and emotional—to be suppressed.
- The words create strong images that appeal to sight and smell.
- Students may compare *"mejillas rubicundas"* (López Velarde), "warm red cheeks" (Durán), and "rosy cheeks" (Jones).
- The rhythm of the poem wouldn't reflect the speaker's personality as it does; the sense of a specific place and culture would be lost.

Vocabulary Study

For each numbered item, write on your paper a vocabulary word to complete the sentence.

chauvinist
funereal
odious
stifle
unmolested

1. The father in Berry's poem could not ____ his criticism of the girl's behavior.
2. The girl values her freedom and guards her ____ space.
3. Anyone who stereotypes either sex can be called a ____.
4. The effects of stereotyping can be ____.
5. The lively tone of Berry's poem would certainly not be described as ____.

Expressing Your Ideas

Writing Choices

Writer's Notebook Update Look over comments you made before reading these poems. What issues do these comments raise? Choose one issue that seems to be universal and discuss it in your notebook.

Say What? Write a **translation** of the Berry poem, using words that seem parallel to those Berry chooses. After reading your version aloud in class, decide what the poem has gained or lost. Alternatively, if you speak a language other than English, translate one of the poems in this unit into that language. In class, discuss the difficulties in trying to **communicate** from one language to another.

Rock-a-bye Baby The word *lullaby* comes from the words *lull*, to soothe, and *bye-bye*, sleep. Write a **lullaby** that employs the soft and liquid sounds created by the consonants *l, m, n,* and *r* and by long vowels.

In Your Own Words Write a **poem** in everyday language that expresses your ideas about communicating with someone from another generation. Your word choice could include slang and idioms.

Other Options

Who Gives a Rap? With a partner, divide the lines of the Berry poem and give an **oral reading** that captures both the rhythm of the language and the attitudes of the two voices. You might cast your reading as a rap.

Seeing Eye to Eye Make a collage of words and images to suggest that generations can communicate effectively. Cut or duplicate appropriate images from magazines, and include song lyrics, ads, bumper stickers, proverbs, and your own quotes. Arrange your material on a piece of heavy paper that could be made into a greeting card and sent to someone special you know that belongs to another generation.

VOCABULARY STUDY

1. stifle
2. unmolested
3. chauvinist
4. odious
5. funereal

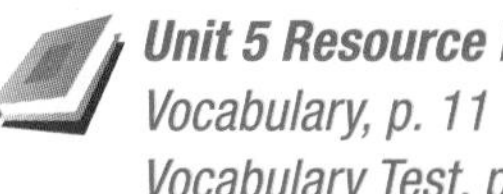

Unit 5 Resource Book
Vocabulary, p. 11
Vocabulary Test, p. 14

WRITING CHOICES

Writer's Notebook Update

Are students in agreement about which issues are at the bottom of the generation gap, or do areas of conflict differ greatly? After students write about an issue, you might poll them and discuss the results.

Say What?

To help students get started, encourage them to decide which poetic elements are most important in each poem. Then they can give priority in their translations to the more important elements.

Mention the special concerns of translators, which include receiving proper recognition for their work. For further information on literary translation, contact

Translation Committee
PEN American Center
568 Broadway, Room 401
New York, NY 10012

In Your Own Words

For creative ideas on teaching poetry to children and young adults, you might consult *Rose, Where Did You Get That Red* by Kenneth Koch, (1990).

OTHER OPTIONS

Who Gives a Rap?

Prompt students to discuss how rap artists juxtapose "high" and "low" diction and analyze the effect of this contrast.

Seeing Eye to Eye

Analyze television commercials, encouraging students to describe commercials that target different generations and commercials that focus on bridging the generation gap. You might examine such components as images, editing style, music, fashion, language, and underlying messages.

Selection Test

Unit 5 Resource Book
pp. 15–16

Before Reading

Building Background

Mention that historians say that our own age's romantic love had its roots in "courtly love," which arose in medieval times when knights wooed their ladies. Prompt students to give examples of how strong an emotion love can be. *(Possible responses: The Duke of Windsor gives up the throne to marry a commoner; a soldier jumps on a grenade to save his comrades; a mother runs into a burning house to save a child.)*

Literary Focus

To practice identifying **rhythm**, the class can practice scanning the pattern of a nursery rhyme, such as "Jack Be Nimble." Write the rhyme on the board and have students mark stressed and unstressed syllables, as shown on page 568.

Writer's Notebook

As students read the poems in the selection, encourage them to keep a t-chart of lines and phrases that indicate agreement or disagreement with the "loved and lost" quote.

Agree	Disagree
This way at least you live (Wolcott).	Only God could love you for yourself alone (Yeats).

Before Reading

First Frost by Andrei Voznesensky Russia
The Fist by Derek Walcott Trinidad
For Anne Gregory by William Butler Yeats Ireland
The Stone by Wilfrid Wilson Gibson Great Britain

Building Background

Shapes of Love As old as scraps of Egyptian poetry, as new as today's popular love songs, love fascinates, infuriates, bewilders, and, occasionally, amuses us. What aspects of love do the following quotations suggest? What other things do you associate with love?

"By heaven, I do love, and it hath taught me to rhyme, and to be melancholy." *William Shakespeare*

"Love, and a cough, cannot be hid." *George Herbert*

"Love's like the measles—all the worse when it comes late in life." *Douglas Jerrold*

"Love is much nicer to be in than an automobile accident, a tight girdle, a higher tax bracket or a holding pattern over Philadelphia." *Judith Viorst*

"Love conquers all things except poverty and toothache." *Mae West*

Literary Focus

Rhythm The term **rhythm** refers to a pattern of stressed and unstressed syllables, or beats. Regular rhythm is like the beat of a waltz or a march. "The Stone," which you are about to read, has rhythm that is generally regular. In the following lines from this poem, stressed syllables are marked ´; unstressed syllables are marked ˘.

I went to break the news to her:
And I could hear my own heart beat
With dread of what my lips might say;
But some poor fool had sped before; . . .

Writer's Notebook

Loved and Lost Quickwrite your response to the following observation: "'Tis better to have loved and lost, / Than never to have loved at all." Keep your ideas in mind as you read the following poems.

SUPPORT MATERIALS OVERVIEW

Unit 5 Resource Book
- Graphic Organizer, p. 17
- Study Guide, p. 18
- Vocabulary, p. 19
- Grammar, p. 20
- Alternate Check Test, p. 21
- Vocabulary Test, p. 22
- Selection Test, pp. 23–24

Building English Proficiency
- Literature Summaries
- Activities, p. 210

Reading, Writing & Grammar SkillBook
- Reading, pp. 49–50
- Writing, pp. 109–110
- Grammar, Usage, and Mechanics, pp. 208–209

Technology
- Audiotape 14, Side A
- Personal Journal Software
- Custom Literature Database: Among romantic love poems on the database are Shakespeare's sonnets and "Love's Apotheosis" by Paul Laurence Dunbar.
- Test Generator Software

Andrei Voznesensky

born 1933

Andrei Voznesensky (än′drā väz nə sen′skē) studied architecture in Moscow, but gave up this career after his drawings were destroyed in a fire. His poetry, which is marked by musical sounds, imaginative twists in meaning, and occasional wry humor, became known in Russia during the "thaw" of the 1960s, when Soviet writers enjoyed a period of freedom of expression. An advocate of *glasnost,* or greater openness in the former Soviet Union, Voznesensky works for continued freedom of expression in Russia today.

William Butler Yeats

1865–1939

Though he was a mediocre student, William Butler Yeats listened avidly to the Irish folk tales his sailor uncles told. Because his father was an artist, Yeats studied art, but at twenty-one he quit art school and devoted himself to writing. In the 1890s, his works were influenced by his study of Irish folklore, a study that led him to support the Irish revolt against England and to write plays for Ireland's national theater. In 1923, Yeats received the Nobel Prize for literature.

Derek Walcott

born 1930

Growing up on the West Indian island of St. Lucia, Derek Walcott was both biracial and bilingual, speaking Creole at home and English at school. A major theme in his work is "the dichotomy between black and white, subject and ruler, Caribbean and Western civilization." His complicated feelings about his mixed ancestry and allegiances are expressed in one of his poems: ". . . either I'm a nobody or a nation." Walcott's rich blend of folk and formal language, includes chants, jokes, and fables. Awarded the Nobel Prize for literature in 1992, he is considered one of the great modern masters of the English language.

Wilfrid Wilson Gibson

1878–1962

By the time he was fifty, W. W. Gibson had published more than twenty-two books of poetry. His first poems were influenced by Tennyson, especially his narrative poems about King Arthur and his knights. By 1910, however, Gibson began writing poems about the dreams, fears, and hopes of common humanity—the farmers and laborers he had known as a child.

More About the Poets

Andrei Voznesensky

- Voznesensky names Pasternak (the author of the classic Russian novel *Dr. Zhivago*) as his sole poetic influence.
- W. H. Auden once said that "every word [Voznesenky] writes, even when he is criticizing, reveals a profound love for his native land and its traditions."

William Butler Yeats

- The great love of Yeats's life was Maud Gonne, an Irish nationalist to whom he wrote poetry for three decades.
- From 1922 to 1928, Yeats was a senator for the Irish Free State.

Derek Walcott

- Walcott is an active playwright as well as a poet and has directed many of his own plays. In 1959, he founded the Trinidad Theatre Workshop.
- Walcott grew up speaking a *patois* (local dialect) of French and English.

Wilfrid Wilson Gibson

- In the 1920s and 1930s, Gibson was known as "the poet of the inarticulate poor."
- Gibson was a playwright as well as a poet.

Connections to **AuthorWorks**

Derek Walcott and William Butler Yeats are featured authors in the AuthorWorks CD-ROM series.

During Reading

Selection Objectives

- to explore the theme of connections in terms of romantic love
- to analyze meter, indicating stressed and unstressed syllables
- to recognize and use the past perfect tense

Unit 5 Resource Book
Graphic Organizer, p. 17
Study Guide, p. 18

Theme Link

Connections take the form of romantic love in these four poems.

Vocabulary Preview

abyss, bottomless or very great depth; chasm

quarry, place where stone, slate, etc., is dug, cut, or blasted out for use in building

loiter, linger idly or aimlessly

naught, nothing

marrow, the inmost or essential part

Students can add the words and definitions to their Writer's Notebooks.

Art Study

Responses to Caption Questions

- Students will probably point to the fact that the composition of the picture and Glinn's use of light, dark, and shadow evoke a mood of solemn contemplation. The expression on the girl's face fits the mood.
- Students may respond that the image of the girl is a universal one; she appears to be Caucasian, but could represent a myriad of cultures.

1 *First Frost*

Andrei Voznesensky

A girl is freezing in a telephone booth,
huddled in her flimsy coat,
her face stained by tears
and smeared with lipstick.

She breathes on her thin little fingers.
Fingers like ice. Glass beads in her ears.

She has to beat her way back alone
down the icy street.

First frost. A beginning of losses.
The first frost of telephone phrases.

It is the start of winter glittering on her cheek,
the first frost of having been hurt.

◄ Do you think the photographer, Burt Glinn, was more interested in communicating a mood or depicting a person in this photograph? Is there anything in the photo that reveals the girl's nationality, or could she be from one of several cultures?

SELECTION SUMMARY

"First Frost," "For Anne Gregory," "The Fist," "The Stone"

Each of the four poems in this selection illustrates an effect of romantic love. In "First Frost," Andrei Voznesensky describes a girl out in the cold, in a telephone booth, talking to the lover who has rejected her. In "For Anne Gregory," William Butler Yeats tells how love for a person can seem inseparable from love of his or her physical attributes—in this case, the loved one's majestic blonde hair. Derek Walcott depicts in "The Fist" how the pain of love can lead to a mad obsessic And Wilfred Wilson Gibson, in "The Stone," tells of a woman who kills herself after hearing of he lover's death at a quarry—but only after she is certain that a stone has been carved to mark his grave.

*For summaries in other languages, see the **Building English Proficiency** book*

For Anne Gregory

2

William Butler Yeats

"Never shall a young man,
Thrown into despair
By those great honey-colored
ramparts[1] at your ear,
Love you for yourself alone
And not your yellow hair."

"But I can get a hair-dye
And set such color there,
Brown, or black, or carrot,
That young men in despair
May love me for myself alone
And not my yellow hair."

"I heard an old religious man
But yesternight declare
That he had found a text to prove
That only God, my dear,
Could love you for yourself alone
And not your yellow hair."

1. **rampart** (ram′pärt), *n.* a mound of earth used to help defend a fort. Yeats uses the word to refer to coils of hair at the ears.

The Fist

3

Derek Walcott

The fist clenched round my heart
loosens a little, and I gasp
brightness; but it tightens
again. When have I ever not loved
the pain of love? But this has moved

past love to mania.[1] This has the strong
clench of the madman, this is
gripping the ledge of unreason, before
plunging howling into the abyss.[2]

Hold hard then, heart. This way at least you live.

1. **mania** (mā′nē ə), *n.* a kind of mental disorder characterized by great excitement, elation, and uncontrolled, often violent, activity.
2. abyss (ə bis′), *n.* bottomless or very great depth; chasm.

Literary Elements
Imagery and Figurative Language

Questions

- What are literal images of frost? *(the freezing girl; the icy street)*
- What figures of speech mention frost? *(Among them are "fingers like ice"; "glass beads in her ears"; "first frost of telephone phrases.")*
- Would the poem "First Frost" be stronger or weaker if Voznesensky used only figurative or only literal images of frost? *(The poem's strength lies in the parallel between the literal frost and the figurative "frost" of lost love.)*

Literary Focus
Rhythm

Questions

- What is the rhythmic structure of the poem? *(Lines have three or four stressed syllables alternating with a nearly equal number of unstressed syllables.)*
- If "For Anne Gregory" were written using the conversational rhythm of "The Fist," how would its effect on the reader change? *(Possible responses: It would seem less humorous and very serious.)*

3

Reading/Thinking Skills
Analyze/Infer

Involve the class in a discussion about whether the speaker will continue to fall in love or not.

BUILDING ENGLISH PROFICIENCY

Reading Poetry Aloud

Read the poems aloud more than once or have a student who is fluent in English read. Help students to understand key points about the poems:

- "First Frost": Explain that the setting is outdoors in winter. You may want to draw the scene on the board and let students add details.
- "For Anne Gregory": Read the poem with another reader to demonstrate the use of dialogue.
- "The Fist": Draw a heart on the board and act out how the speaker feels—his feeling of heartache, madness, and the resolution to keep on loving.
- "The Stone": The rhythm and repetition in this poem call for repeated readings. Explain that the poem is a love story. You might draw stick figures to show the initial key events in the plot, and then have volunteers draw more events as they take in the rest of the poem.

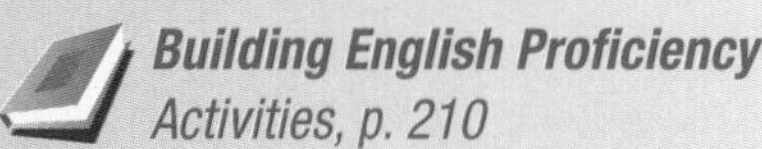

Building English Proficiency
Activities, p. 210

4 Literary Element
Narrative Poetry

At this point the poet uses flashback, a narrative technique. You may wish to involve students in a discussion of the other narrative elements in "The Stone," such as plot, characters, setting, and conflict.

5 Literary Element
Repetition

Question How does Gibson's repetition of the word *struck* affect the reader? *(The sound of the word and the image it evokes reverberate on many levels. The reader visualizes the violent action which caused the lover's death, feels the leaden sorrow of the girl, and hears, throughout the poem, the stonecutter's mallet striking on stone.)*

6 Literary Focus
Rhythm

Help students develop a sense of appropriate rhythm by discussing whether the pace of this poem is appropriate to the emotion. They may observe that the poem's steady rhythm has the quality of a prayer or incantation, complementing the subject of death.

The Stone

Wilfrid Wilson Gibson

"And will you cut a stone for him,
To set above his head?
And will you cut a stone for him—
A stone for him?" she said.

4
Three days before, a splintered rock
Had struck her lover dead—
Had struck him in the quarry[1] dead,
Where careless of the warning call,
He loitered,[2] while the shot was fired—
A lively stripling, brave and tall,
And sure of all his heart desired . . .
A flash, a shock,
A rumbling fall . . .
And, broken 'neath the broken rock,
A lifeless heap, with face of clay,
And still as any stone he lay,
With eyes that saw the end of all.

I went to break the news to her:
And I could hear my own heart beat
With dread of what my lips might say;
But some poor fool had sped before;
And, flinging wide her father's door,
Had blurted out the news to her,
Had struck her lover dead for her,
5
Had struck the girl's heart dead in her,
Had struck life, lifeless, at a word,
And dropped it at her feet:
Then hurried on his witless way,
Scarce knowing she had heard.
And when I came, she stood alone—
A woman, turned to stone:
And, though no word at all she said,
I knew that all was known.

Because her heart was dead,
She did not sigh nor moan.
6
His mother wept:
She could not weep.
Her lover slept:
She could not sleep.
Three days, three nights,
She did not stir:
Three days, three nights,
Were one to her,
Who never closed her eyes
From sunset to sunrise,
From dawn to evenfall—
Her tearless, staring eyes,
That, seeing naught,[3] saw all.

(Continued)

1. quarry (kwôr′ē), *n.* place where stone, slate, etc., is dug, cut, or blasted out for use in building.
2. loiter (loi′tər), *v.* lingered idly or aimlessly.
3. naught (nôt), *n.* nothing.

This photograph by Franz Altschuler shows the delicate effects that can be achieved by a master stonemason. What effect is achieved by having the figure gaze downward? by having patterns and a stern face in the background? ➤

MINI-LESSON: GRAMMAR
Using the Past Perfect Tense

Teach The past perfect form of a verb is used to denote that the action of the verb was completed at some definite point in the past. It is formed using the past tense of the verb *have* as in this line from "The Stone":

. . . a splintered rock
Had struck her lover dead—
Had struck him in the quarry dead

Elicit from students that the rock strikes the woman's lover three days before the woman asks the narrator to carve the stone. Point out that writers must keep their tenses consistent. When they need to switch tenses, they do so in a way that doesn't confuse the reader.

Activity Idea Students might practice using the past perfect by retelling or rewriting the story of "The Stone" in prose.

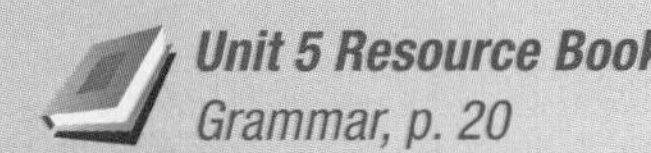

Unit 5 Resource Book
Grammar, p. 20

Art Study

Responses to Caption Questions Students may respond that the figure's downward gaze suggests refinement and classic elegance; in the background, the intricate patterns and aggressive face contrast sharply with the sensitivity, restraint, and grace of the sculpture of the woman.

Visual Literacy Mood is defined as the overall atmosphere or prevailing emotional aura of a work.

Question How is the mood of Altschuler's photograph similar to that of "The Stone"? *(Possible responses: Both are solemn, mysterious, or frightening.)*

Question What similar elements do Altschuler and Gibson use to create mood? *(Possible responses: Both works have the central image of stone, which suggests death and the passage of great amounts of time; both feature the image of a woman whose emotions are restrained, as if her heart was "dead in her.")*

BUILDING ENGLISH PROFICIENCY

ESL LEP ELD SAE LD

Making Personal Connections

Help students to find ways to make "The Stone" more accessible to modern readers.

Activity Ideas

- Ask students about modern stories of tragic young love that they may know from movies, TV, or music. Then have them imagine that a modern filmmaker is going to adapt this story for a movie. Ask: Who would be cast in the two lead roles? Who would be asked to create the soundtrack?
- Have students imagine that "The Stone" is an interactive poem. Ask them to choose a point in the poem at which they would like to step into the story and speak to the girl. Prompt students to share what they might say to her or ask her.
- Ask students to pretend that they are reporters for the evening news. Have them cover this tragic story, perhaps interviewing other students who could act as the stone carver.

7 Reading/Thinking Skills
Summarize

Encourage students to summarize the events and emotions of "The Stone."

Questions

- What matters to the woman after her lover has died? Why? *(Possible response: She wants a stone to be engraved with her lover's name, so that his grave bears a permanent record of his life.)*
- From reading the last two stanzas, what can we infer happens to the woman? *(We can infer that she dies from sorrow and is buried with her lover under the same stone.)*

Check Test

1. What is the setting of "First Frost"? *(an icy street in winter)*

2. How does the woman in "For Anne Gregory" say that she could make men love her for herself alone? *(She says that she could dye her hair.)*

3. In "The Fist," if the speaker lets go of the ledge, what will he fall into? *(an abyss)*

4. In "The Stone," how did the woman's lover die? *(He was hit by a rock while working in a stone quarry.)*

5. How many stones does the narrator of the poem cut, and for whom? *(two, one for the dead lover, and one for the grieving young woman)*

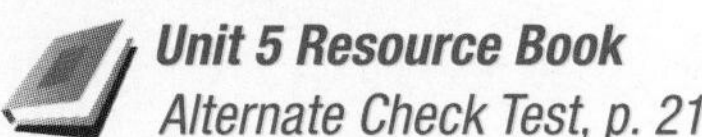

Unit 5 Resource Book
Alternate Check Test, p. 21

The fourth night when I came from work,
I found her at my door.
"And will you cut a stone for him?"
She said: and spoke no more:
But followed me, as I went in,
And sank upon a chair;
And fixed her grey eyes on my face,
With still, unseeing stare.
And, as she waited patiently,
I could not bear to feel
Those still, grey eyes that followed me,
Those eyes that plucked the heart from me,
Those eyes that sucked the breath from me
And curdled the warm blood in me,
Those eyes that cut me to the bone,
And pierced my marrow[4] like cold steel.

And so I rose, and sought a stone;
And cut it, smooth and square:
And, as I worked, she sat and watched,
Beside me, in her chair.
Night after night, by candlelight,
I cut her lover's name:
Night after night, so still and white,
And like a ghost she came;
And sat beside me, in her chair,
And watched with eyes aflame.
She eyed each stroke,
And hardly stirred:
She never spoke
A single word:
And not a sound or murmur broke
The quiet, save the mallet-stroke.

7

With still eyes ever on my hands,
With eyes that seemed to burn my hands,
My wincing, overwearied hands,
She watched, with bloodless lips apart,
And silent, indrawn breath:
And every stroke my chisel cut,
Death cut still deeper in her heart:
The two of us were chiselling,
Together, I and death.

And when at length the job was done,
And I had laid the mallet by,
As if, at last, her peace were won,
She breathed his name; and, with a sigh,
Passed slowly through the open door;
And never crossed my threshold more.

Next night I labored late, alone,
To cut her name upon the stone.

4. **marrow** (mar′ō), *n.* the inmost or essential part.

MINI-LESSON: LITERARY FOCUS

Rhythm

Point out that language has rhythm because we give words a certain stress, or accent, in pronouncing them. Elicit examples of pronunciations from students, such as *beGIN, MERcy*, and *interRUPT*.

Also mention that meter must echo sense: Poets who write solemnly of death do not want their lines to bounce along like a nursery jingle. They will use meter, in combination with other devices, to create a slow, solemn movement.

Activity Idea Point out that the most common meter is iambic, an unaccented syllable followed by an accented syllable (◡´). Have students scan a verse of "The Stone."

After Reading

Making Connections

Shaping Your Response

1. Describe how the people and situations in these poems make you feel.

Poem	Feelings

2. Do you think many people today love someone for reasons other than their "self alone"? Explain.
3. Poets write more often about lost love than about fulfilled love. Why do you think this is true?

Analyzing the Poems

4. How would you **characterize** the woman in "The Stone"?
5. In what way is Gibson's title both literal and **figurative**?
6. From the **imagery** of Walcott's poem, describe how the speaker feels.
7. How does Yeats use **hyperbole**, or exaggeration, in "For Anne Gregory" for humorous effect?
8. How would you describe the **tone** of each poem?
9. These poems include a number of **sound devices**. Find examples of repetition (both of consonant sounds and of words and phrases).

Extending the Ideas

10. With the help of your classmates, make a list of current love songs. Divide them into two groups: fulfilled, happy love and unfulfilled, painful love. Make some generalizations about the messages in current love songs.
11. Do you think that the portrayal of romantic love in the media is realistic? In answering, think about ads, TV programs, and movies that include romantic relationships.

Literary Focus: Rhythm

Rhythm refers to the pattern of stressed and unstressed syllables in a line of poetry. Poetry that lacks a regular pattern of stresses and sounds more like everyday speech is called **free verse.**

- Which of the four poems in this group have regular rhythm? Which are free verse?
- The speaker in "The Stone" is numbed by the death of her lover. The speaker of "The Fist" is "gripping the edge of unreason." Do you find the rhythm of each poem suitable to its speaker? Explain.

LITERARY FOCUS: RHYTHM

"For Anne Gregory" and "The Stone" have regular rhythms, whereas "First Frost" and "The Fist" are written in free verse.

- Students might respond that the steady rhythm is like the young woman's numb state of grief in "The Stone." On the other hand, "The Fist" has an uneven rhythm, which highlights the subject matter of mania and madness.

After Reading

MAKING CONNECTIONS

1. Possible responses

Poem	Feelings
"First Frost"	empty, chilled
"For Anne Gregory"	light, admiring
"The Fist"	longing, fear
"The Stone"	grief, heaviness

2. Students may respond that many people are attracted to purely physical or superficial qualities—at least initially.

3. Possible response: Poems often emerge out of introspection, and people are more likely to feel introspective when they are sad.

4. Possible responses: heartbroken, devoted, single-minded, silent, numb, or deadened

5. "Stone" refers both to the grave marker the narrator carves and the woman, who has figuratively been turned to stone by her loss.

6. Pain—images are the fist, clenching and gripping; insane—ledge of unreason; afraid of being lost—plunging into the abyss.

7. Exaggerations include comparing coils of hair to ramparts, stating that men are "thrown into despair" by the woman's hair, and saying only God could love the woman for herself.

8. "First Frost"—mournful; "For Anne Gregory"—teasing admiration; "The Fist"—anguish; "The Stone"—elegiac

9. You may wish to provide examples of repetition discussed on page 572, and of alliteration, such as "loosens a little" in "The Fist."

10. Generalizations may include love at first sight, all-consuming happiness, and unfulfilled love as an irremediable tragedy.

11. Students may respond that the least-realistic portrayals of love are created for commercial purposes.

VOCABULARY STUDY

1. a
2. d
3. b
4. d
5. c

More Practice

Encourage students to write their own analogies using the vocabulary words *rampart* and *mania.*

Unit 5 Resource Book
Vocabulary, p. 19
Vocabulary Test, p. 22

WRITING CHOICES

Writer's Notebook Update

Encourage students to cite a quote to support each sentence.

Bravo or Bah! Humbug!

Have students bring in local newspapers and find the editorial pages. Review with the class how the language of an editorial differs from that of a news story. Ask students to identify subjective words that express opinions and feelings.

Unit 5 Resource Book
pp. 23–24

Vocabulary Study

On your paper, next to each number write the letter of the pair of words that has the same relationship as the original pair.

abyss
loiter
marrow
naught
quarry

1. BONE : MARROW :: **a.** vein : blood **b.** speech : applause **c.** hatchet : blood **d.** frying pan : bacon
2. LOITER : LEAVE :: **a.** banana : slip **b.** laugh : giggle **c.** cup : saucer **d.** passive : active
3. QUARRY : STONE :: **a.** eagle : prey **b.** mine : ore **c.** barn : stable **d.** envelope : stamp
4. ABYSS : BOTTOMLESS DEPTH :: **a.** moon : sun **b.** mountain : valley **c.** boat : island **d.** creek : stream
5. NAUGHT : NOTHING :: **a.** never : seldom **b.** frequent: always **c.** fortunate : lucky **d.** silent : shy

Expressing Your Ideas

Writing Choices

Writer's Notebook Update Now that you have read these four poems, review your thoughts about having loved and lost. Write a sentence for each poem, explaining how you think the speaker or main character would respond to this quotation.

Bravo or Bah! Humbug! A newspaper editorial doesn't have to be about a burning issue or a national or international problem. As editor of your school newspaper, write an **editorial** about Valentine's Day, explaining whether or not it's a tradition you want to preserve.

Other Options

Love Triangle You work as an artist in an advertising agency. Your new client, the American Association of Candy Manufacturers, wants to replace the traditional Valentine heart. Make a **diagram** of the new shape of love. Beneath the diagram, write a caption explaining why this is a suitable representation.

Lovemobile Prepare a **mobile** featuring different views of love. You might include pictures, small items, cards, captions, fabric, quotations from poems you have just read—anything that represents for you a facet of love. Present your mobile to the class along with appropriate background music.

Heart to Heart Present your own image to suggest love, using a computer program, clay, origami, freehand—or anything else at your disposal.

OTHER OPTIONS

Love Triangle

Encourage students to be creative with their answers. Point out that there are many shapes that are not taught in geometry class. For example, students might draw the outline of a brain, suggesting that a person might do better to love with the head instead of the heart.

Lovemobile

Encourage students to research appropriate quotations at the library by consulting books, poems, essays, and articles on love.

Heart to Heart

Invite students to write their own poems about love. They might imitate the style or form of one of the four poems in this selection. Poems may be serious or humorous, in strict rhythm or free form.

Before Reading

The Other by Judith Ortiz Cofer USA

To Julia de Burgos by Julia de Burgos Puerto Rico

We Are Many by Pablo Neruda Chile

Building Background

Who Am I? In wood, in marble, in paint, and in words, creators of portraits attempt to establish the identity of their subjects. Often they try to capture the complexities of a person—the different personalities within. What can you guess about the girl in this picture? Keep this painting in mind when you read the following poems about identity.

Literary Focus

Speaker Each of the three poems that follow has a **speaker**, an "I" who presents information in the first person. This "I" is not necessarily the poet, but rather the imaginary voice assumed by the poet. As you read these poems, try to identify the speaker and the speaker's tone. Both are strong clues to the meaning of each poem.

Writer's Notebook

Private "I's" You can't tell a book by its cover. Nevertheless, we tend to make judgments based on people's appearances. Have you ever thought about all those exciting people living inside their plain wrappings? Quickwrite an example of someone, from literature or real life, with a misleading appearance.

Before Reading

Building Background

Fillette on Tricycle an example of cubism, shows the subject from several different positions simultaneously. Encourage students to look at the painting and notice the shifting perspective—an attempt by the artist to synthesize many aspects of the subject in a single view.

Literary Focus

Point out that the relationship of the poet to the speaker of a poem and to the speaker's tone can be compared to that of a playwright to one of his characters. Challenge students to imagine that they are writing a poem about themselves, but not using themselves as the speaker. Have them suggest speakers that they might choose.

Writer's Notebook

Lead a class discussion on dichotomy, or the division of a whole into two often contradictory parts. Have students consider how this type of contrast, or conflict, can be a powerful theme for a work of literature. Begin by eliciting examples of characters who demonstrate contrasts, such as Lancelot, the champion of the Round Table who had a love affair with Arthur's wife.

SUPPORT MATERIALS OVERVIEW

Unit 5 Resource Book
- Graphic Organizer, p. 25
- Study Guide, p. 26
- Vocabulary, p. 27
- Grammar, p. 28
- Alternate Check Test, p. 29
- Vocabulary Test, p. 30
- Selection Test, pp. 31–32

Building English Proficiency
- Literature Summaries
- Activities, p. 211
- "We Are Many" and "To Julia de Burgos" in Spanish

Reading, Writing & Grammar SkillBook
- Reading, pp. 57–58
- Grammar, Usage, and Mechanics, pp. 220–223

Technology
- Audiotape 14, Side B
- Personal Journal Software
- Custom Literature Database: For a short story probing different selves, see "The Minister's Black Veil" by Nathaniel Hawthorne on the database.
- Test Generator Software

More About the Poets

Judith Ortiz Cofer

- Ortiz Cofer says: "The 'infinite variety' and power of language interest me. I never cease to experiment with it."
- She describes her poetry as a study of the "process of change, assimilation, and transformation" from one culture to another.

Cofer is the author of *Peregrina,* (1986) and *Terms of Survival,* (1987).

Julia de Burgos

In a letter to her family in 1940, Julia de Burgos criticized her life as "a more puritan life than the most puritan of female mummies. I spend the day sewing, listening to the radio, and talking to the ladies in the *pension.* At night, I rigidly sit at a formal gathering, commenting on the ineptitude of the servants, maintaining my position of 'wife,' prejudiced and hypocritical. . . ."

Pablo Neruda

- Neruda claimed that he needed "the sound of rain on rooftops and dripping water in order to be able to write."
- Neruda, who once said, "I consider even my own name to be a falsehood, an alien element in my poetry," chose his pen name as a tribute to the Czech writer Jan Neruda.
- Neruda was the official presidential candidate of the Central Committee of the Communist Party of Chile in 1969.

Judith Ortiz Cofer

born 1952

Judith Ortiz Cofer (ôr tēz′ kō′fər) once wrote, "My family is one main topics of my poetry; the ones left behind on the island of P Rico, and the ones who came to the United States. In tracing th lives, I discover more about mine." As a Spanish speaker, Cofer greatest challenge was to master English "enough to teach it an the ultimate goal—to write poetry in it." She reached that goal b she was forty, publishing several books of poetry, a memoir title *Silent Dancing,* a play, a book of essays, and an acclaimed nove *Line of the Sun.*

Julia de Burgos

1917–1953

Like Cofer, Julia de Burgos was born in Puerto Rico, the oldest thirteen children. Her father, a farmer, often fired her imagination tales about Napoleon and Don Quixote. When the time came fo to go to school, neighbors paid her tuition. Although a fervent na alist, de Burgos left Puerto Rico and spent her final years as an in Cuba and New York.

Pablo Neruda

1904–1973

When he began publishing poetry in his teens, Ricardo Neftalí R took the pen name Pablo Neruda (pä′blō nə rü′dä). An early tea and fellow Chilean poet, Gabriela Mistral, gave him books and encouraged him to write—just as he later encouraged Julia de Burgos. Neruda became a diplomat and remained active in polit while continuing to write. His early poems tend to be political, w his later poetry looks with humor at everyday things such as soc and watermelon, which in his words, represent "the world of obj at rest." In 1971, he received the Nobel Prize for literature.

THE OTHER

JUDITH ORTIZ COFER

1

A sloe-eyed[1] dark woman shadows me.
In the morning she sings
Spanish love songs in a high
falsetto,[2] filling my shower stall
with echoes.
She is by my side
in front of the mirror as I slip
into my tailored skirt and she
into her red cotton dress.
She shakes out her black mane as I
run a comb through my closely cropped[3] cap.
Her mouth is like a red bull's eye
daring me.
Everywhere I go I must
make room for her; she crowds me
in elevators where others wonder
at all the space I need.
At night her weight tips my bed, and
it is her wild dreams that run rampant[4]
through my head exhausting me. Her heartbeats,
like dozens of spiders carrying the poison
of her restlessness,
drag their countless legs
over my bare flesh.

1. **sloe-eyed** (slō′īd), *adj.* having very dark eyes.
2. falsetto (fôl set′ō), *n.* an artificially high-pitched voice, especially in a man.
3. cropped (kropt), *adj.* cut short; clipped.
4. rampant (ram′pənt), *adj.* growing without any limits.

During Reading

Selection Objectives

- to explore the theme of connections between the outer and inner self or selves
- to identify the speaker in first-person poems
- to understand the agreement between indefinite pronouns and verbs

Unit 5 Resource Book
Graphic Organizer, p. 25
Study Guide, p. 26

Theme Link

Three poems probe the connections between a person's outer and inner selves.

Vocabulary Preview

falsetto, an artificially high-pitched voice, especially in a man
cropped, cut short; clipped
rampant, growing without any limits
essence, that which makes a thing what it is; important feature of features
frigid, cold in feeling or manner
virile, vigorous, forceful
hypocrisy, feigning to be what one is not

Students can add the words and definitions to their Writer's Notebooks.

1 Literary Focus
Speaker

Questions

- Who is the speaker in "The Other"? *(the outer self that the public sees)*
- Contrast the woman whom the world sees with the other who is inside. *(Possible response: To the outer world she wears short hair, tailored clothes, and leads an orderly life; her inner self is restless, passionate, and flamboyant.)*

SELECTION SUMMARY

"The Other," "To Julia de Burgos," "We Are Many"

The three poets in this selection confront the self that lies behind the person the world sees. In "The Other," Judith Ortiz Cofer depicts the wild, uninhibited woman who struggles to overtake her more constrained persona. Julia de Burgos describes her free inner self in "To Julia de Burgos," and bitterly criticizes the woman seen by the world as meek and hypocritical. Finally, in "We Are Many," Pablo Neruda has the speaker tell of his multiple selves—selves that are often elusive and hard to control.

For summaries in other languages, see the ***Building English Proficiency*** *book.*

2 Literary Focus
Speaker

Question Who is the speaker in "To Julia de Burgos" and whom is she addressing? *(The speaker is the self that speaks out in poetry. She addresses the self who talks in everyday language and participates in an ordinary social life.)*

3 Literary Element
Metaphor

A metaphor is a figure of speech that states or implies a comparison between two basically unlike things without using *like* or *as.*

Ask students to identify metaphors in lines 7–10 of "To Julia de Burgos." *("The frigid doll of social falsehood," "the virile sparkle of human truth," and "honey of courtly hypocrisy.")*

Question Why might a poet attack everyday social demands as false and hypocritical? *(Possible response: In public, the poet may repress her real feelings and opinions. She feels people are uncomfortable about facing the serious issues that the poet believes are the truth.)*

4 Reader's Response
Making Personal Connections

Invite students to share experiences when they have felt their social environment was false or hypocritical.

To Julia de Burgos

JULIA DE BURGOS

The word is out that I am your enemy
    that in my poetry I am giving you away.

2 They lie, Julia de Burgos. They lie, Julia de Burgos.
That voice that rises in my poems is not yours: it is my voice;
you are the covering and I the essence;[1]
and between us lies the deepest chasm.

3 You are the frigid[2] doll of social falsehood,
and I, the virile[3] sparkle of human truth.

You are honey of courtly hypocrisy,[4] not I;
I bare my heart in all my poems.

You are selfish, like your world, not I;
I gamble everything to be what I am.

You are but the grave lady, ladylike;
not I; I am life, and strength, and I am woman.

You belong to your husband, your master, not I;
I belong to no one or to everyone, because to all, to all
I give myself in pure feelings and in my thoughts.

4 You curl your hair, and paint your face, not I;
I am curled by the wind, painted by the sun.

You are lady of the house, resigned and meek,
tied to the prejudices of men, not I;
5 smelling the horizons of the justice of God.
I am Rocinante,[5] running headlong.

---

1. essence (es′ns), *n.* that which makes a thing what it is; important feature or features.
2. frigid (frij′id), *adj.* cold in feeling or manner.
3. virile (vir′əl), *adj.* vigorous, forceful.
4. hypocrisy (hi pok′rə sē), *n.* pretense.
5. **Rocinante** (rō sē nän′tä), the broken-down but spirited horse of Don Quixote (dōn kē hō′tä) in the classic Spanish novel, *Don Quixote de la Mancha,* by Miguel de Cervantes.

MINI-LESSON: VOCABULARY
Etymology

Teach Students can understand the modern meanings of words by looking up their origins and exploring the histories of words.

Activity Idea Divide students into groups. Assign one or more of the following vocabulary words to each group.

falsetto frigid
rampant virile
essence hypocrisy

Using a dictionary, groups should:

- find the simplest forms of their words
- record the etymologies of their words

Invite the class to work together to hypothesize how each word evolved from its original to its modern meaning.

Oil on copper is the medium for Frida Kahlo's 1942 work titled *Portrait of Marucha Lavin.* What things in the portrait **communicate** clues to the culture and character of the woman depicted? ➤

5 Reading/Thinking Skills
Recognize Values

Question What personal qualities can you infer that both Ortiz Cofer and de Burgos value? How can you tell? *(Possible response: Both seem to value being natural, free, and unfettered by societal conventions. Ortiz Cofer uses exciting and evocative language to describe her "Other"; de Burgos wants to be her free, natural inner self.)*

Response to Caption Question
Students may not know Kahlo's Mexican origin, but they might conclude that the woman is Mexican from the traditional Mexican blouse and the Spanish words (which mean "Drawing of Señora Marucha Lavin, Frida Kahlo painted it, 1942"). Others may draw conclusions about the subject's character from her proud bearing. Because she is surrounded with elements of nature, they may infer that she identifies more with her natural surroundings than with an indoor setting that reflects her status and era.

Visual Literacy Scientists have calculated that there are hundreds of thousands of colors. The name given to a color is its hue.

Question What hues do you see in Kahlo's painting? *(Encourage students to name particular shades.)*

BUILDING ENGLISH PROFICIENCY

ESL LEP ELD SAE

Making Personal Connections

Help students explore the idea in "The Other" that another self is hidden inside, ready to burst out. Let students draw two faces in silhouette form, one slightly smaller and almost within the first. (The drawings can be labeled "outer self" and "inner self.")

Students can talk about reasons, such as the following, that would cause them to have a "hidden" self:

- going to school in a U.S. culture and living in a different culture at home
- speaking in one language and thinking in another
- having adult responsibilities, such as a job, but not being allowed to make certain decisions

Suggest that they use lines from the poem that they identify with to help them describe their experiences. As students discuss, they can label characteristics on the drawings of the appropriate "self."

Building English Proficiency
Activities, p. 211
"We Are Many" and "To Julia de Burgos" in Spanish

Art Study

Response to Caption Question Students may respond that "We Are Many," or even more accurately, "I Am Many," would be suitable titles for the picture. Both titles refer to works that are about the many parts that comprise the whole of an individual.

Diana Ong, born in 1940, is a Chinese American artist whose multimedia work features watercolor, acrylics, etching, woodcutting, and silkscreen. She is a New Yorker whose work has been shown in more than thirty countries, as well as on book jackets throughout the world.

Visual Literacy *Theme* is defined as the underlying meaning of a work.

Question How would you express the theme shared by Ong's painting and Neruda's poem? *(Possible response: The whole of a human being is comprised of many separate parts or selves.)*

Question After reading the poem, how might the picture be redrawn to fit better with Neruda's images? *(Students might show the inner selves he values—the hero, the brave man, the intelligent man—all escaping from within him, leaving only those with the opposite qualities.)*

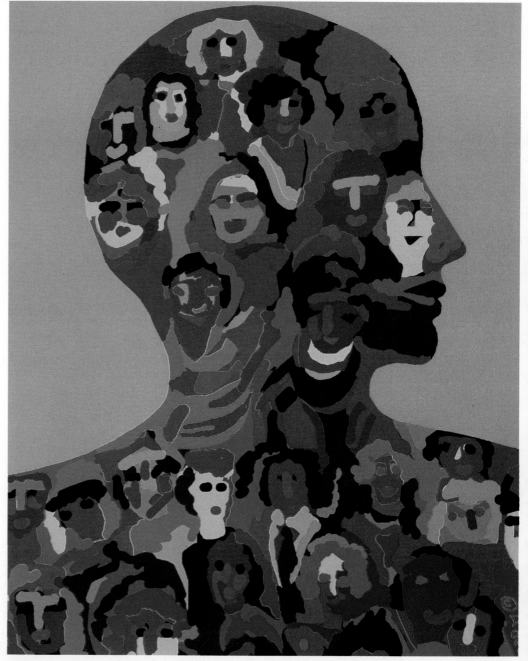

MINI-LESSON: GRAMMAR

Using Verbs with Indefinite Pronouns

Teach Indefinite pronouns do not refer to specific persons or things. In formal, written English the indefinites *any, each, either, every, neither,* and *none* are generally considered singular; *all, few, many,* and *some* are considered plural.

Activity Idea Point out the plural indefinites *many* and *all* in the first and fifth stanzas of "We Are Many." Then have students rewrite the following sentences, changing the plural indefinite pronouns to singular, and the singular indefinite ones to plural. Remind them to make the verbs agree.

We are <u>many</u>. (We are one.)

<u>All</u> the books I read are full of dazzling heroes. (One of the books I read is full of dazzling heroes.)

I can't find <u>one</u>. (I can't find many.)

You might have students create sentences with the most troublesome indefinite pronouns—*each* (which is always singular) and *none* (which varies, but is usually singular in formal writing).

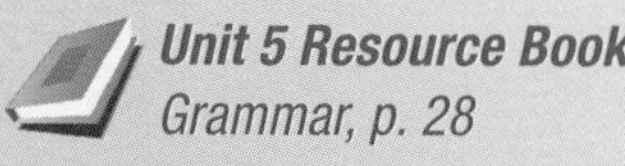

Unit 5 Resource Book
Grammar, p. 28

WE ARE MANY

PABLO NERUDA

Of the many men who I am, who we are,
I can't find a single one;
they disappear among my clothes,
they have left for another city.

When everything seems to be set
to show me off as intelligent,
the fool I always keep hidden
takes over all that I say.

At other times, I'm asleep
among distinguished people,
and when I look for my brave self,
a coward unknown to me
rushes to cover my skeleton
with a thousand fine excuses.

When a decent house catches fire,
instead of the fireman I summon,
an arsonist bursts on the scene,
and that's me. What can I do?
What can I do to distinguish myself?
How can I pull myself together?

All the books I read
are full of dazzling heroes,
always sure of themselves.
I die with envy of them:
and in films full of wind and bullets,
I goggle[1] at the cowboys,
I even admire the horses.

But when I call for a hero,
out comes my lazy old self;
so I never know who I am,
nor how many I am or will be.
I'd love to be able to touch a bell
and summon the real me,
because if I really need myself,
I mustn't disappear.

While I am writing, I am far away;
and when I come back, I've gone.

6

I would like to know if others
go through the same things that I do,
have as many selves as I have,
and see themselves similarly;
and when I have exhausted this problem,
I am going to study so hard
that when I explain myself,
I will be talking geography.

1. **goggle** (gog′əl), *v.* stare with bulging eyes.

◄ Diana Ong's work is titled *Parts Equal the Whole III.* Do you think the title of Neruda's poem would have been just as suitable for the picture? Explain.

Literary Elements
Tone and Theme

Encourage students to detect how tone is a clue to the theme. Remind them that the speaker is the tool of the poet in "We Are Many."

Questions

- How does the poet makes it easy for an ordinary person to relate to this speaker? *(He has the speaker make self-deprecating statements, use references to common experiences like cowboy movies, and make a direct appeal to the reader: "I would like to know. . . .")*
- What is the tone? *(informal, idealistic, frustrated)*
- What is the theme? *(Possible response: Everyone has difficulty living up to his or her ideals—it is the human condition.)*

Check Test

1. "The Other": Who wears a red dress? *(her inner self)*

2. "To Julia de Burgos": Who gambles everything and who is meek? *(The inner self gambles; the outer person is meek.)*

3. How does Julia de Burgos contrast her two selves' relations with men? *(One self—the outer one—is controlled by men; the other is autonomous.)*

4. Why is the speaker in "We Are Many" jealous of heroes he reads about in books? *(because they are always sure of themselves)*

5. "We Are Many": Name three of the "many selves." *(Possible responses: the fool, the intelligent one, the brave self, the fireman, the arsonist, the hero, the lazy one, the confident one)*

Unit 5 Resource Book
Alternate Check Test, p. 29

BUILDING ENGLISH PROFICIENCY

Making Personal Connections

Students may share Neruda's feelings of being many persons in one. Ask students to create a details web that explores the many people that they are. The web can include personality traits as well as roles they play in their families, at school, and among friends. Some students may want to add drawings to create a collage effect.

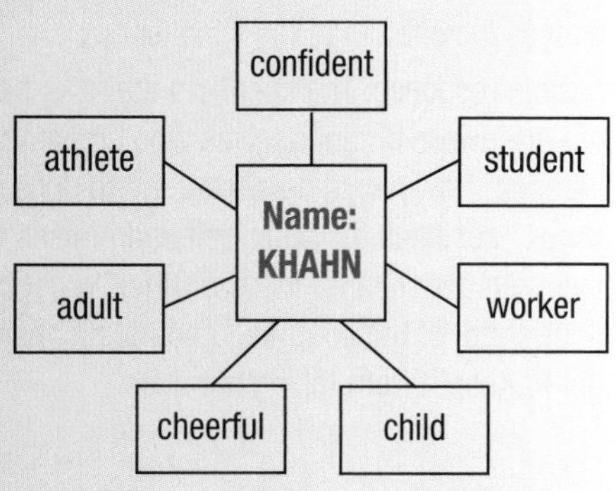

After Reading

MAKING CONNECTIONS

1. Possible responses: Most people experience conflict between their convictions and actions.

2. Possible responses: "Covering" may be physical appearance and actions the public can see; "essence" is discovered by getting to know a person's motivation.

3. Students responses should reflect what they understand about the speaker's point of view.

4. Possible response: "The Other": I am my businesslike outer self but I am pulled to be my free inner self. "To Julia de Burgos": I am my free inner self and despise my outer self. "We Are Many": I am many selves, but I will try to be only the best of them.

5. A person always experiences conflict between his or her inner and outer selves.

6. Possible response: that his true self emerges as a writer

7. Possible responses: similes in "The Other"—"mouth like a red bull's eye," "heartbeats like dozens of spiders"; metaphors in "To Julia de Burgos"—"The frigid doll of social falsehood," "honey of courtly hypocrisy," the comparison to Rocinante; metaphor in "We Are Many" —touching a bell to summon the real self

8. Students should point to different tones, such as anguish in "The Other," bitterness in "To Julia de Burgos, and idealism in "We Are Many."

9. Possible responses: Like Rocinante, she has a boundless spirit held back by a limiting shell.

10. Students may discuss why the client may allow distorted images.

11. Students should be aware that divided characters interest us because they represent our own extremes and our own potentials.

After Reading

Making Connections

Shaping Your Response

1. Do the people in these poems reveal serious personality problems, or do you think "split personalities" of this kind are typical of people in general? Explain.
2. Julia de Burgos says, ". . . you are the covering and I the essence." How would you distinguish people's covering from their essence?
3. If you could be any one of these **speakers** or alter egos, whom would you choose and why?
4. How do you think each of these three speakers would answer the question, "Who Am I?"

Analyzing the Poems

5. State a **theme** that these three poems have in common.
6. All but one of the stanzas in Neruda's poem are four to eight lines. What clues does the two-line stanza (lines 36-37) provide about the **character** of the speaker?
7. Choose three examples of **figurative language** or **imagery** from these poems that you think are effective and explain why you like them.
8. Do you find the **tone** of these poems similar? Explain.
9. How does the **allusion** to Rocinante help characterize Julia de Burgos?

Extending the Ideas

10. Many entertainment celebrities or political figures hire image makers—public relations specialists who create an image for their clients. Discuss whether public figures today have, as Neruda worries, lost the ability to "summon the real me."
11. In books, TV shows, and movies there are often characters who present a double image or a false front. Work with a group to present some of these stories to the class. Encourage the class to discuss why these posers, dreamers, and deceivers make such interesting reading and viewing.

Literary Focus: Speaker

Answer the following questions about the **speakers**—the imaginary voices the poets have chosen to "tell" the poems.

- In Cofer's poem, how does the "sloe-eyed woman" differ from the speaker?
- Is the speaker in "To Julia de Burgos" like or unlike the speaker in Cofer's poem? Explain.
- Choose five words to characterize the speaker in "We Are Many."

LITERARY FOCUS: SPEAKER

- Possible response: The sloe-eyed woman is freer and less inhibited than the speaker.
- Possible response: The speakers are alike because both are aware of inner selves who are similar in character. However, the speaker in "To Julia Burgos" despises the outer self and praises the inner self; the speaker in "The Other" recognizes the strength of the inner self and must constantly fight to keep it from taking her over.
- Students may choose such words as *complex, frustrated, self-deprecating, idealistic, forgiving,* or *determined.*

Activity Idea Challenge students to rewrite one of the poems in the selection as it would be written by either of the other two speakers. Students will need to be especially aware of tone.

Vocabulary Study

cropped
essence
falsetto
frigid
hypocrisy
rampant
virile

Write five different sentences that might be found in a fortune cookie, answering the question, "Who am I?" Use at least one of the vocabulary words in each sentence.

Expressing Your Ideas

Writing Choices

Writer's Notebook Update Review your quickwrite. Then write a brief poem with your described person acting as speaker and telling about his or her secret self.

An Arsonist Bursts on the Scene Choose one of the following lines from these poems as the title of a best-selling novel: *The Fool I Always Keep Hidden; I Goggle at the Cowboys; She Crowds Me in Elevators; The Word Is Out That I Am Your Enemy; I Will Be Talking Geography.* You have been asked to write a paragraph that praises or pans this novel. Use your imagination to write a rousing **review**!

Petite Grandma Out-muscles Burglar Sometimes people say or do things that seem "out of character." In a **news story** that might appear in the *National Wow,* describe a person who has acted or done something out of character. Conclude by trying to account for the person's behavior.

Other Options

Another Angle Look again at the picture on page 577. Draw a **picture** of yourself in a similar style that reflects different aspects of your personality.

Personality Splits The speakers of the three poems in this section are to appear on a popular television **talk show**, discussing their secret selves. What will they say? How will the audience react? What will the host or hostess say or do? As a group, present a segment from the show in class.

Getting to Know You At the first campfire of the season, you must introduce yourself to the other campers. Deliver a one- to two-minute **speech of introduction**. Use one of the following topics or one of your own. Remember, your introduction doesn't have to be serious.

- "No one would think that I. . . ."
- "An experience I wish I hadn't had is. . . ."
- "No one knows I'm good at. . . ."

VOCABULARY STUDY

Mention that whoever reads a fortune expects to find out something about his or her innermost nature, or something that will happen in the future. Encourage students to have fun with their fortunes, using as many vocabulary words in each as they are able; for example, "Your essence is virile and free," or "Hypocrisy runs rampant when ambition is not cropped."

More Practice Instruct each student to provide synonyms for five of the vocabulary words in the selection.

Unit 5 Resource Book
Vocabulary, p. 27
Vocabulary Test, p. 30

WRITING CHOICES

Writer's Notebook Update

Invite students to read their poems to the class. After each poem is read, ask the class to discuss the author's tone, or attitude toward his or her subject.

Students might also examine anthologies at the library to find other poems that feature speakers who describe their inner selves.

An Arsonist Bursts on the Scene

You might bring book reviews from newspapers and magazines to class for students to use as models. Discuss the components of a review, which include plot summary, evaluation, and a brief author biography.

Petite Grandma Out-muscles Burglar

Encourage students to use the sensationalist language of tabloids, choosing "loaded" verbs and an adjective for each noun.

OTHER OPTIONS

Personality Splits

Assign a role to each student, and encourage students to prepare for their roles. You might bring a video tape of a talk show to class; alternatively, ask students to watch one such show on television. On the day of the show, invite students to dress "in character." If equipment is available, you might video tape the performance.

Getting to Know You

To help students plan their speeches, you might encourage them to consider the following areas: school, sports, art, music, social life, home life, travel, spiritual life, fashion, and job.

Selection Test

Unit 5 Resource Book
pp. 31–32

Transparency Collection
Fine Art Writing Prompt 10

Interdisciplinary Study

Theme Link

As students explore the Interdisciplinary Study, ask them to consider how their connections with family members are similar to and different from their connections with friends.

Curricular Connection: History

You can use the information in the Interdisciplinary Study to explore with students how and why families—and also our conceptions of them—have changed over the past 150 years.

Terms to Know

colonial, pertaining to the thirteen British colonies that became the United States of America

Hitchcock chair, a side chair of the early nineteenth century—designed by L. A. Hitchcock (1795–1852)—with turned legs, a turned crest rail, and one or more slats in the back, which is painted or stenciled in colors or gold on black

satire, the use of irony, sarcasm, or ridicule to expose, denounce, or deride vice, folly, and so forth

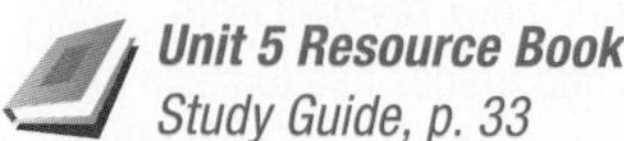
Unit 5 Resource Book
Study Guide, p. 33

Connections

It's All Family

History Connection
Many of the poems in this group explore the relationships between family members. The following pages offer a comparison between a colonial family and contemporary TV families.

"Reading" a Family Portrait

by Caroline Sloat

Joseph Lauriston Moore was eleven years old when he and his family were painted by Erastus Salisbury Field in Ware, Massachusetts, just a few miles down the road from where Old Sturbridge Village is located today. Family records have provided us with some information about the Moores, but the portrait painted a century and a half ago tells its own story in a way no written record could.

The Moore family was smaller than many in Ware at that time. In fact, the two children standing beside the mother were cousins and had only recently come to live with the family after their own mother had died in 1838. The boy, Frederick Babbit Cook (standing far left), was four years old, and the girl, Louisa Ellen, was two. Joseph's younger brother, George Francis (center, next to father), was also four. Little Louisa Ellen is wearing a white dress, but everyone else is dressed in black, perhaps in mourning over a relative's death.

Unlike the Moores' dark clothes, however, the furnishings in the portrait are bright and cheerful. The carpet design is bright red and green on a light background, and extends from wall to wall as was the fashion. The green shutters are closed. Perhaps the artist painted them that way so that he could include an additional color, or the shutters may actually have been closed to keep the summer sun from fading the carpet.

Mr. Moore is sitting casually on the fancy Hitchcock-type chair so that we can see a part of the bright stenciled decoration. The wood in both the looking glass and the square-topped work table beneath it is decorated in a fashionable style called graining.

Joseph's suit resembles the one his father is wearing. His white shirt is tied with a black neck cloth, whose ribbons are left hanging from the bow–unlike his father's bow which is tied. Young Joseph's jacket is also like his father's but cut short in a manner worn by boys of his age. Four-year-old Frederick, while old enough to handle a pocket knife to whittle

MINI-LESSON: VISUAL LITERACY

Draw Conclusions About/Evaluate Art

Teach Tell students that by paying attention to the illustrations accompanying a book or article, they can learn more about a subject than what is described in the words on the page.

Apply Direct students' attention to Caroline Sloat's careful analysis of the photograph on page 587. Encourage them to discuss the pictures on pages 588–589 in equal depth, considering the information revealed by each detail.

Activity Ideas

Tell the class to imagine that the families on pages 588–589 are real. Invite each student to write a sociological study of one of the "family portraits" in the style of Caroline Sloat. Encourage students to consider the following:

- What does each member of the family consciously communicate through his or her clothing, hairstyle, body language, and facial expression?
- What does each member of the family unconsciously reveal about the family structure of his or her decade or generation, and how?

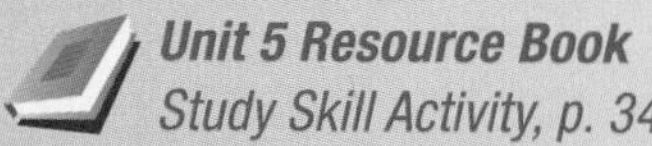
Unit 5 Resource Book
Study Skill Activity, p. 34

a stick, wears a long, loose coat called a surtout. Louisa Ellen is wearing pantalettes and a long dress.

Mrs. Almira Moore has arranged her hair elaborately for the portrait, with a tortoise shell comb stuck into a bun at the back of her head. The corkscrew curls on either side of her face, adding a touch of elegance, may well have been store bought. Needle in hand, Mrs. Moore looks as if she is so busy sewing that she could not stop even for her portrait. She probably made clothes for the entire family, including the embroidered collar she is wearing. Her choice to wear the collar and to include the sewing items tell us that she wanted the portrait to show her as an expert needlewoman.

Joseph's father belonged to the group of tradesmen and craftsmen called artisans who were beginning to set up their shops in New England town centers. He made silk hats in the winter, probably working at home, and traveled to neighboring towns as a dentist in the summer.

Like his mother, Joseph Lauriston holds an object meant to tell us something about who he is—a schoolbook he probably used in a one-room school with students ranging in age from four to nineteen, all working at different levels.

The Industrial Revolution changed Ware just as it changed many other New England towns, altering the lives of the people who lived there. But when Erastus Salisbury Field painted the Moore family portrait, he captured a history for us to enjoy.

Additional Background

- The family is one of the oldest institutions in human history.
- The "nuclear family," which exists in most societies, consists of a married man and woman and their children.
- The "extended family," prevalent in some cultures, consists of a married couple living with or near their children, their children's spouses, and their children's children.
- More than 90% of Americans still marry at least once. However, most Americans today marry later than Americans in previous generations.
- The average American family has between one and two children.

BUILDING ENGLISH PROFICIENCY

Dramatizing Information

Encourage students to bring the members of the Moore family to life through dramatics.

1. Review some of the family relationships that students have been reading about in this group. (You might have students jot down and share one thought from each selection.) Invite students to speculate about relationships between the family members.

2. Have students also speculate about some of the details in the painting. For example, ask: How does the family feel about taking care of the young cousins? Why is Joseph dressed so like his father—is he expected to become an artisan too?

3. Have volunteers improvise dialogues or monologues that might have taken place just before the portrait was painted.

Research Topics

Have students choose countries to research, addressing some or all of the following points:

- family structure
- traditions of marriage and divorce
- statistics on marriage, divorce, and number of children per marriage
- the comparison of historical family structure with families in contemporary times

Interdisciplinary Activity Ideas

- Students might create scrapbooks filled with pictures of families from different time periods and cultures. Pictures can be photocopied from library books and cut from magazines. Each "family portrait" should be labeled with a caption including place, date, source, and a relevant fact about family structure. Lead a class discussion analyzing the contents of the scrapbooks.
- Encourage students to research and create family trees—for their own families or those of people who interest them. Research might include interviewing family members or reading at the library. Arrange a time for students to present their family trees to the class, discussing any interesting facts they learned through their research.

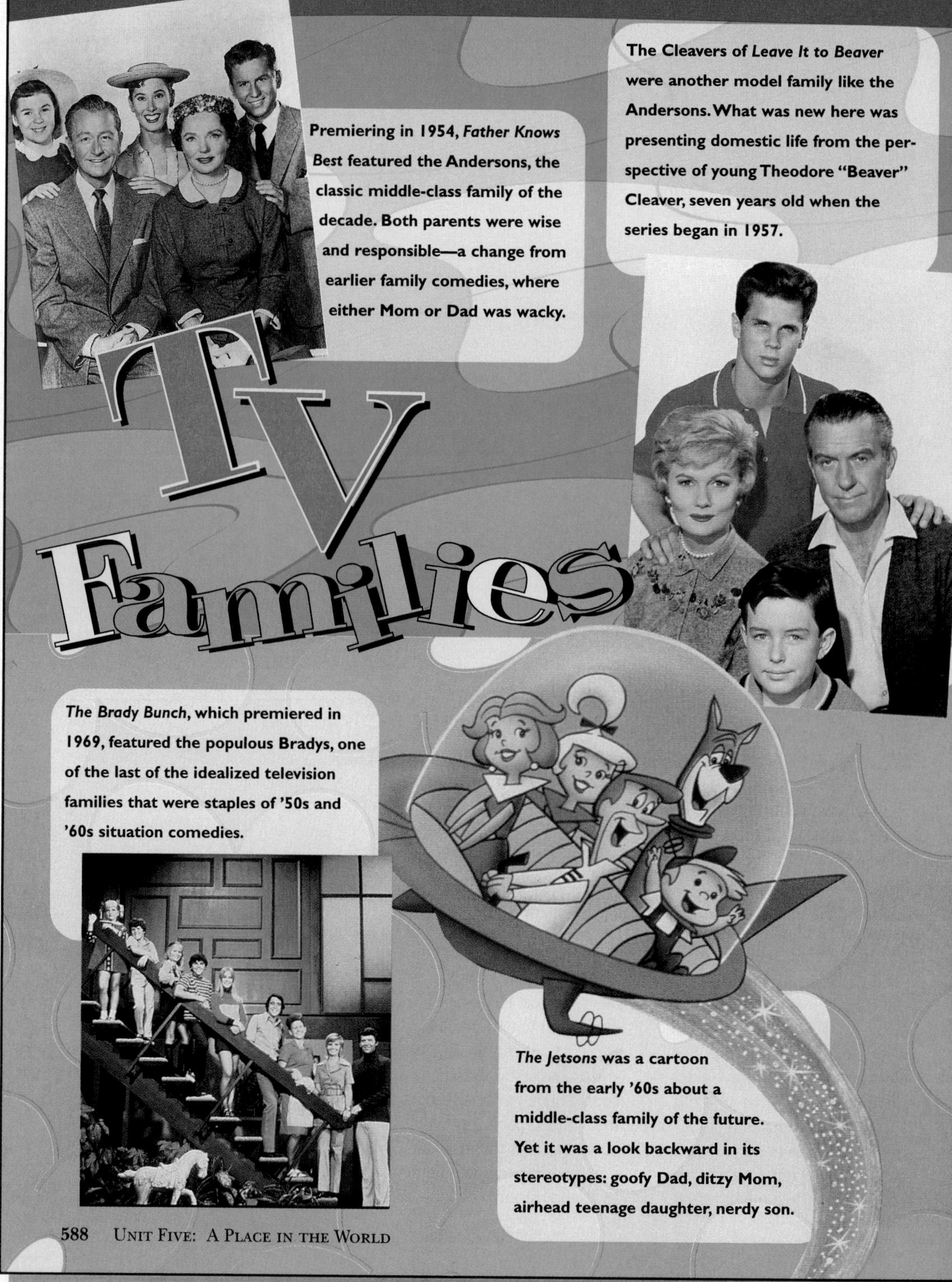

TV Families

Premiering in 1954, *Father Knows Best* featured the Andersons, the classic middle-class family of the decade. Both parents were wise and responsible—a change from earlier family comedies, where either Mom or Dad was wacky.

The Cleavers of *Leave It to Beaver* were another model family like the Andersons. What was new here was presenting domestic life from the perspective of young Theodore "Beaver" Cleaver, seven years old when the series began in 1957.

The Brady Bunch, which premiered in 1969, featured the populous Bradys, one of the last of the idealized television families that were staples of '50s and '60s situation comedies.

The Jetsons was a cartoon from the early '60s about a middle-class family of the future. Yet it was a look backward in its stereotypes: goofy Dad, ditzy Mom, airhead teenage daughter, nerdy son.

MINI-LESSON: SPEAKING AND LISTENING

Debate

Teach Remind students that every statement of opinion can be opposed by a statement to the contrary, and that facts can be produced to support most positions. Debate is a challenging and fun way to collect and present facts to support an argument.

Apply Ask students if they have watched talk shows or read articles about the "decline of the American family." Have them decide whether they agree or disagree that the American family has degenerated in recent decades.

Activity Idea Students can debate the status of the American family based on the pictures in the Interdisciplinary Study.

- Divide students into two groups based on which side of the argument they choose.
- Allow groups to brainstorm for 10–15 minutes, writing their arguments and the evidence supporting those arguments on index cards.
- Allow representatives from each side to present the argument.

Remind students that the key to their arguments will lie in *evaluating* the facts highlighted in the pictures—for example, determining whether a more relaxed family environment is positive or negative.

The Cosby Show, which premiered in 1984, introduced the Huxtables, another affluent television family. The big difference was that they were black.

Premiering in 1988, *Roseanne* broke new ground in television situation comedy by featuring a working-class family, the Connors, and a foul-mouthed Mom who was a long way from June Cleaver.

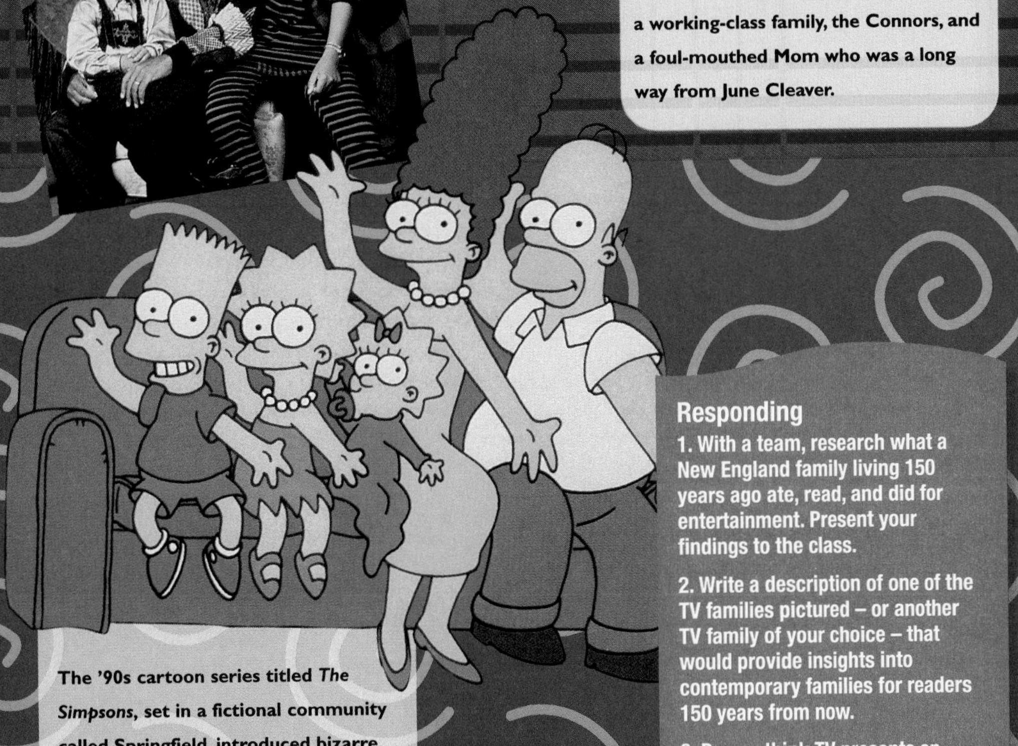

The '90s cartoon series titled *The Simpsons,* set in a fictional community called Springfield, introduced bizarre, sometimes irreverent characters and keen social satire.

Responding

1. With a team, research what a New England family living 150 years ago ate, read, and did for entertainment. Present your findings to the class.

2. Write a description of one of the TV families pictured – or another TV family of your choice – that would provide insights into contemporary families for readers 150 years from now.

3. Do you think TV presents an accurate portrayal of modern families? Why or why not?

Historical Note

One of the earliest TV family sitcoms—and one of the most successful ever—was *I Love Lucy,* which featured the real married couple Lucille Ball and Desi Arnaz. *I Love Lucy* was broadcast on CBS from 1951 to 1960.

Responding

1. Possible Response Students' research may indicate that colonial families ate and drank simple foods such as corn, squash, wild game, home-baked bread, milk. They read newspapers, almanacs, the Bible, histories of their colonies, or books on classical history. They amused themselves by visiting neighbors, playing cards, gambling, quilting, barn-raising, hunting, fishing, ice skating, playing billiards, or dancing.

2. Possible Response The photograph of the Connors *(Roseanne)* shows the typical American family of the 1990s to be relaxed and fun-loving. Family members are not glamorous. Families in the 1990s do not dress up around the home. In addition, most American families are not wealthy.

3. Possible Response The Connors are more realistic because they present families with real problems. Most TV families are still depicted in an idealized form—i.e. wealthier, more beautiful, and better dressed than the average American family.

BUILDING ENGLISH PROFICIENCY

Responding to Visual Cues

TV viewers are likely to be familiar with many details of this pictorial. Use the familiarity as a springboard to one or more of the following activities.

Activity Ideas

- Have students use their journals to respond to each family. Ask them to arrange the sitcoms in order—from 1 (most like my family) to 7 (least like my family). Allow voluntary sharing.
- Call on volunteers to share insights based upon their own viewing of these sitcoms. Ask: Do you think people watch such shows because they wish that they had such a family—or because they're glad that they don't?
- Ask students to imagine that this pictorial is part of a proposal for a TV documentary. Invite students to suggest other TV families that they would include. Have students explain their choices.

Writing Workshop

WRITER'S BLUEPRINT

Specs

The Specs in the Writer's Blueprint address these writing and thinking skills:

- developing questions
- interviewing
- recognizing values
- organizing information
- integrating text and visuals
- punctuating quotations
- spelling homophones

These Specs serve as your lesson objectives, and they form the basis for the **Assessment Criteria Specs** for a superior paper, which appear on the final TE page for this lesson. You might want to read through the Assessment Criteria Specs with students when you begin the lesson.

Linking Literature to Writing

As you review the literature, ask students to relate stories about family life that they have heard from their older relatives.

Writing Workshop

Not-So-Ancient History

Assignment You have read about family life in different countries and generations. Now work in a small group to put together a picture of life as it was lived in another time not so long ago.

WRITER'S BLUEPRINT

Product	An illustrated interview
Purpose	To show what life was like for a teenager in the recent past
Audience	Family and friends of your subject
Specs	As the creators of a successful project, your group should:

- ❑ Choose someone over fifty whom one of you knows well and who is willing to be interviewed. Interview your subject about life when he or she was a teenager, using questions you've worked out in advance.
- ❑ Gather appropriate visuals, such as photographs and home movies of your subject as a teenager, and magazine pictures, newspaper headlines, phonograph records, and movie posters from the period.
- ❑ Write a brief introduction giving a few basic facts about your subject. Then write up your interview, using the most interesting and informative parts and omitting the rest. Use a question-answer or narrative format. Make sure your readers can visualize your subject.
- ❑ Conclude by commenting on whether you would have preferred to be a teenager now or when your subject was a teenager, and why.
- ❑ Assemble your written and illustrative materials in the most effective way you can.
- ❑ Follow the rules of grammar, usage, spelling, and mechanics. Take special care to avoid spelling mistakes with homophones and to punctuate direct quotations correctly.

WRITING WORKSHOP OVERVIEW

Product
Narrative writing: An illustrated interview

Prewriting
Brainstorm a list of subjects—Do research—Plan the interview—Divide up the tasks—Interview your subject—Gather visual materials—Make an inventory of important facts
Unit 5 Resource Book
Prewriting Worksheets pp. 35–36

Drafting
Before you draft—As you draft
Transparency Collection
Student Models for Writing Workshop 19, 20

Revising
Ask another group—Strategy: Quoting Directly and Paraphrasing
Unit 5 Resource Book
Revising Worksheet p. 37

Editing
Ask another group—Strategy: Spelling Homophones Correctly
Unit 5 Resource Book
Grammar Worksheet p. 38
Grammar Check Test p. 39

Presenting
Integrate your materials

Looking Back
Self-evaluate—Reflect—For Your Working Portfolio
Unit 5 Resource Book
Assessment Worksheet p. 40
Transparency Collection
Fine Art Writing Prompt 10

STEP 1 PREWRITING

Brainstorm a list of subjects. In your group, list possible subjects for this project. The subject should be over fifty, known personally by at least one member of the group, and willing to work with you. Consider family members, neighbors, or acquaintances who like to talk about the past.

As a group, choose a person you would like to interview. Contact this person right away and be sure he or she is willing to participate.

Do research on the years when your subject was a teenager. Use newspapers and magazines from the period. Use your research to make a time line of historical events that took place during your subject's teenage years and use it to help prepare your list of questions for the interview.

Plan the interview. Working in your group, develop the questions you'll be asking when you interview your subject. Prepare questions like these:

- **General questions:** *What were teenagers like then?*
- **Specific questions**, about details of the general question: *Describe how the teenagers you went around with dressed and wore their hair.*
- **Follow-up questions** to expand on the information in the specific questions: *Did you have cliques and in-groups at your school like we have now? What were they like?*
- **Historical questions:** *Where were you when you heard that John F. Kennedy had been shot? How did you react?*

OR . . .
Ask your subject about what sorts of questions he or she would like to be asked about his or her life as a teenager.

Divide up the tasks—interviewing, gathering visuals, writing the introduction, body, and conclusion—among group members. Or you might work closely as a group on all these tasks. A successful group project needs careful planning, dedication, and cooperation from everyone.

Interview your subject. See the Beyond Print article on page 595 for information on planning and conducting a successful interview.

Gather visual materials. Locate photos or home movies of your subject that your group could borrow for the presentation. Gather pictures from magazines, movie posters, music, artifacts, and other items that present a picture of the period when your subject was a teenager.

STEP 1 PREWRITING

Brainstorm a list of subjects

Students may want to try a quickwrite about their possible subjects before they discuss them with the group.

Do research

Encourage students to look for clues to the everyday aspects of life in media such as magazines, advertisements, or movies from the time period researched.

Plan the interview

Have students brainstorm more questions than they will need before deciding on the best ones. For additional support, see the worksheet referenced below.

Unit 5 Resource Book
Prewriting Worksheet p. 35

Divide up the task

Students may follow through better if, as a group, they set their goals and responsibilities in writing. Scheduling and setting deadlines will also help students determine a time line for completion of the project. For additional support, see the worksheet referenced below.

Unit 5 Resource Book
Prewriting Worksheet p. 36

Interview your subject

Students may want to write out a "game plan" for the interview, including all of the incidentals like materials and equipment needed. Encourage students to role-play the interview to practice asking questions and taking notes.

Gather visual materials

Students may find old magazines in used bookstores.

BUILDING ENGLISH PROFICIENCY

Exploring Primary Sources

Offer one or more of the following activities to students as they become familiar with the era when their subject was a teenager.

Activity Ideas

- Ask students to go to a library to look at back issues of magazines (perhaps on microfilm) that might give them ideas about clothing and hairstyles, values, and popular entertainment.
- Have students borrow recordings of popular music from a library. Encourage them to listen to the style as well as to the lyrics.
- Suggest that students sample movies from the era on cable channels or from the audiovisual holdings of a library.

Make an inventory of important facts

First, have students look for the important facts individually, then come together as a group to discuss the highlights. A variety of perspectives may shed more light on the subject.

Connections to **Writer's Notebook**

For selection-related prompts, refer to Writer's Notebook.

Connections to **Writer's Resource**

For additional writing prompts, refer to Writer's Resource.

STEP 2 DRAFTING

As you draft

Remind students not to over-correct at this stage of the writing process. The main goal at this point should be to get the ideas flowing.

The Student Models

The **transparencies** referenced below are authentic student models. Review them with students before they draft. These questions will help:

1. In which format, question-answer or narrative, is model 19 written? model 20?

2. Which of the interviews seems more successful? Why?

3. Model 20 has no conclusion. If the writer had written one, what do you think it would be like?

Transparency Collection
Student Models for Writing Workshop 19, 20

STEP 3 REVISING

Ask another group (Peer assessment)

Have each member of the group take notes individually before discussing the responses together.

Make an inventory of important facts about your subject and about the historical period. Include where and when your subject was born, anecdotes he or she told you, personality traits, and a physical description. Include facts about what life was like when your subject was a teenager. Look back at your inventory and star the points you want to focus on when you write.

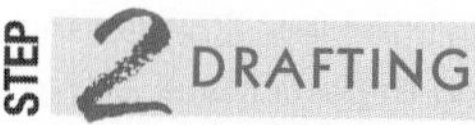

STEP 2 DRAFTING

Before you draft, decide whether you will write up the interview in **question-answer format:**

Q: Was high school all work, or was there fun too?
A: "Well, let me think. . . ."

or in **narrative format:**

Mr. Watson told us more about crewcuts. Then we asked him to tell us more about how students looked then.

"Well," he said, raising his coffee cup halfway to his mouth and pausing, "I suppose nowadays those pants with the little buckles on the back look pretty silly, but back then. . . ."

If you decide on a narrative format, read about using direct quotes and paraphrases in the Revising Strategy in Step 3 of this lesson.

As you draft, carefully pick out the best parts of the interview—the most informative and interesting—and delete the rest. You might do this as a group.

STEP 3 REVISING

Ask another group to comment on your draft before you revise it. Use this checklist as a guide.

✔ Does the introduction state enough basic facts about the subject to give the reader a good idea of who the subject is?

✔ Does the interview use direct quotes and paraphrases effectively?

MINI-LESSON: WRITING STYLE

Quoting Directly and Paraphrasing

Teach Writers have to make decisions about how to incorporate each piece of information into their interview. Have students discuss reasons to directly quote and reasons to paraphrase. Formulate some guidelines based on the discussion.

Activity Idea Have students work in pairs to write up the following excerpt from an interview. Have them double-space and write the reasons why they chose to quote or paraphrase each line or phrase.

> And what would you do on Saturdays?
>
> Oh, there was plenty to keep us busy. I don't remember me or my sisters ever complaining that much about being bored. Let's see . . . often we would take the bus downtown to the movies. Now these weren't little boxes that you sat in like a herd of cattle, but real movie houses that made you feel like you were going somewhere special. We didn't have any malls, but I'll make that trade any day. Downtown was so alive and exciting then.

Apply Have students, in their groups, go over their interviews and decide what to include in their papers and whether to quote directly or paraphrase.

Revising Strategy

Quoting Directly and Paraphrasing

A **direct quote** states the speaker's exact words:

> "No, in those days I didn't think much about styles. I was conservative, I guess you'd say."

A **paraphrase** is a summary of what was said:

> Mr. Watson said that his own clothing styles were conservative.

Paraphrase when you want to conserve space or when you want to express ideas more clearly or concisely than your subject may have stated them.

A narrative format consists of a mixture of direct quotes, paraphrases, and description:

> Mr. Watson raised a hand to his forehead. "I remember the time we sailed around the whole lake. It took us all day," he said, smiling. "Were we ever sore!" He explained that his boat had lost a vital part along the way that made steering difficult. "We zigged and zagged all over. . . ."

FOR REFERENCE
See the Language and Grammar Handbook at the back of this text for information on punctuating quotations.

Notice how this writer paraphrased part of the interview.

I asked what kinds of peer pressure Cynthia Roberts faced during her teenage years. She replied, ~~"They didn't have peer pressure back then because everyone's parents were alike. Any one of them could chastise you. If you got caught doing something you shouldn't be doing, they could yell at you and if they took you home you'd get yelled at again, so there was no peer pressure."~~ *that teenagers didn't experience peer pressure because all the parents in the neighborhood took a role in keeping them out of trouble.*

STEP 4 EDITING

Ask another group to review your revised draft before you edit. When you edit, look for errors in grammar, usage, spelling, and mechanics. Make sure you have spelled homophones correctly.

Revising Strategy: Quoting Directly and Paraphrasing

Remind students of the necessity of quoting or paraphrasing accurately in an interview article. Make sure they understand the difference between them. For additional support, see the mini-lesson at the bottom of the previous page and the worksheet referenced below.

Unit 5 Resource Book
Revising Worksheet p. 37

Connections to **Writer's Resource**

Refer to the Grammar, Usage, and Mechanics Handbook on Writer's Resource.

STEP 4 EDITING

Ask another group (Peer assessment)

Have students take turns editing the interviews so that each paper must pass through several peer reviews.

MINI-LESSON: GRAMMAR

Spelling Homophones Correctly

Remind students that homophones are troublesome because you often know how to spell them but confuse the meanings. Since homophones sound the same, and the spelling determines the meaning, it is important to know which meaning goes with which spelling. If there is a question, use a dictionary or thesaurus.

Ask students to give the meaning for each word in the following pairs of homophones, and use each word correctly in a sentence. Students may want to devise a sentence that will help them remember the meaning of each word. Use as many pairs of words as time permits.

complement, compliment	capital, capitol
affect, effect	desert, dessert
whose, who's	council, counsel
all ready, already	peace, piece
coarse, course	passed, past

Unit 5 Resource Book
Grammar Worksheet, p. 38
Grammar Check Test, p. 39

Editing Strategy: Spelling Homophones Correctly

Create a list of commonly confused homophones and their meanings. For additional support, see the mini-lesson at the bottom of the previous page and the worksheets referenced below.

Unit 5 Resource Book
Grammar Worksheet, p. 38
Grammar Check Test, p. 39

Connections to **Writer's Resource**

Refer to the Grammar, Usage, and Mechanics Handbook on Writer's Resource.

STEP 5 PRESENTING

Integrate your materials

Students may want to invite their subjects to class as honored guests for the presentations.

STEP 6 LOOKING BACK

Self-evaluate

The *Assessment Criteria Specs* at the bottom of this page are for a superior paper. You might want to post these in the classroom. Students can then evaluate themselves based on these criteria. For a complete scoring rubric, use the *Assessment Worksheet* referenced below.

Unit 5 Resource Book
Assessment Worksheet, p. 40

Reflect

Have students share their discoveries with the rest of the class.

To further explore the theme, use the Fine Art Transparency referenced below.

Transparency Collection
Fine Art Writing Prompt 10

Editing Strategy

COMPUTER TIP
A spell checker won't catch a homophone mistake, like substituting *it's* for *its*. Proofread your writing carefully for spelling, whether you have a spell checker or not.

Spelling Homophones Correctly

Homophones are words that sound alike and are spelled similarly, but do not have the same meaning. You can avoid misspelling these words in your writing by connecting their meanings with their spellings in companion sentences. For example:

it's, its: It's (it is) fun to remember my first car, a convertible. It lost its muffler on a bumpy road.

your, you're: Your question seems strange. You're the first one to ask it.

STEP 5 PRESENTING

Integrate your materials. Put the visual materials you have gathered with the introduction and interview you've written up. Arrange and rearrange your materials to get them in the order that most effectively tells your subject's story. Here are some ideas:

- If you taped the interview, play portions of it during your presentation, so the class can hear your subject's actual voice.
- Give a copy of the project to your subject.

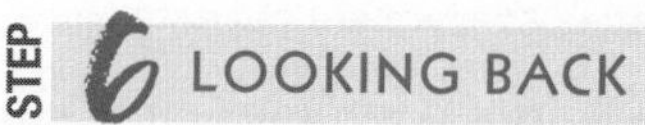

STEP 6 LOOKING BACK

Self-evaluate. Look back at the Writer's Blueprint and give your paper a score for each item, from 6 (superior) to 1 (inadequate).

Reflect. Write answers to these questions.

✔ What three things stand out to you most about the differences between being a teenager then and now?

✔ Did you learn anything surprising or memorable—either about the times or the person—from your interview?

For Your Working Portfolio Add a copy of your group's project and your reflection responses to your working portfolio.

ASSESSMENT CRITERIA SPECS

Here are the criteria for a superior paper. A full six-level rubric for this paper appears on the Assessment Worksheet referenced below.

6 Superior The writer of a 6 paper impressively meets these criteria:

- Presents the subject in a vivid, believable manner.
- Chooses details that elaborate on the subject's personality and vividly demonstrate what his or her life was like as a teenager.
- Presents an interview with the subject in an easy-to-follow format.
- Concludes by insightfully commenting on whether the writer would have liked to have been a teenager during the subject's era.
- Assembles the written and illustrative materials effectively.
- Makes few, if any, mistakes in grammar, usage, mechanics, and spelling. Punctuates quotations correctly.

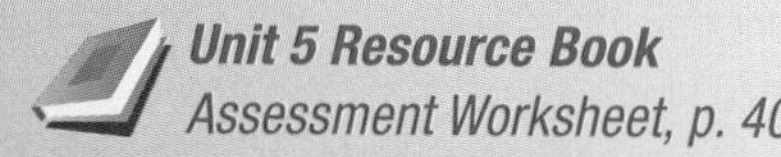

Unit 5 Resource Book
Assessment Worksheet, p. 40

Beyond Print

Conducting an Interview

Books and media are great ways to get information, but occasionally you will want to get it straight from a person! In an interview, you can choose just the right person—a recent immigrant, a Vietnam veteran, a day-care worker—and personally design your questions to get the information you need. Imagine you are interviewing an immigrant. Determine if you will need a translator. Consider asking questions like these.

1. What is unique about your background?
2. What were the most difficult adjustments you had to make?
3. What family customs and celebrations do you still observe?
4. What connections do you still maintain with your old country?

Listening Tips

You've chosen a person to interview, set up the time and place, jotted down questions, and arrived on time with a tape recorder or pencil and paper. Now what? Here are some tips for effective listening.

- **Focus your attention on what the speaker says, not on how he or she says it.** People may speak in different dialects or accents, at different rates, and at different decibels. Try to ignore the verbal habits of the speaker, and concentrate on what is being said.
- **Maintain eye contact and watch your posture.** Focus on the speaker, don't slouch, and don't fiddle with pen or paper.
- **Be patient.** Allow time for your interviewee to recall events or to find the right words. Ask another question only after you have gotten a complete answer to the previous one.

Activity Options

1. Review the interview on page 260. What are three additional questions you might ask Tamara Camp about analyzing evidence?
2. Think of someone you'd like to interview. Write four questions you would ask.

Beyond Print

Teaching Objectives

- to understand the value of the firsthand information obtained through interviews
- to prepare relevant questions for an interview
- to learn and practice effective listening techniques

Curricular Connection: Speaking/Listening Skills

Working in pairs, have each student ask his or her partner a question, listen to the answer, and repeat the answer in his or her own words.

Introduce

Discuss with students the difference between secondary sources—such as biographies, textbooks, and newspapers; and primary sources—such as autobiographies, speeches, and interviews. Elicit from students that primary sources are valuable because the information they provide has not been filtered through—and perhaps biased by—anyone else's point of view.

Activity Options

Activity 1 What exactly is a probability statement? What are some other methods of typing DNA? Does a body ever get too old to extract DNA from?

Activity 2 Encourage students to be creative in choosing their subjects. Interviewees might include historical figures from other centuries such as Joan of Arc or Abraham Lincoln, or literary characters such as Emma Bovary or Huckleberry Finn.

ANOTHER APPROACH

Seeing Is Believing: Watch an Interview

Students can learn a great deal about interviewing techniques by watching videotapes of professional interviews. If you have access to a VCR, you might tape-record a celebrity interview for classroom viewing from a television program such as *The Tonight Show* or a *Barbara Walters* special. Alternatively, you might find videotaped interviews with authors, archaeologists, scientists, and so forth, at a local library. If there is no video equipment available at school, assign students to watch an interview of their choice on TV.

Instruct students to take notes on the interviewer as they watch, focusing on the kinds of questions he or she asks and how he or she indicates that he or she is listening. Lead a class discussion in which students can present their observations.

Preview

Reflections

FOR ALL STUDENTS

Since the poetry in this section explores the concept of reflection in different ways, ask students to explain the various meanings that this word can have. Suggest that they consult a dictionary if they need help.

To further explore the theme, use the Fine Art Transparency referred to below.

Transparency Collection
Fine Art Writing Prompt 11

For At-Risk Students

Ask students to bring in photographs of interesting images from old newspapers and magazines. They can choose the most compelling ones to create a bulletin-board display entitled "Reflections."

For Students Who Need Challenge

Cameras have captured the essence of various subjects throughout this section. Have students work in groups to research how a standard camera works and draw a poster-size schematic illustrating the various parts and process.

MULTICULTURAL CONNECTION

Have students preview the illustrations that accompany the poems in this section. Ask them to choose the image that they think is the most beautiful or interesting. Remind students that their choices will be influenced by their own cultural values. As volunteers to share their reasons for their choices.

Part Two

Reflections

Finding your place in the world requires careful reflection and informed decisions about where you're going and how to get there.

Multicultural Connection **Choice** is often influenced by the cultural values of the society or smaller groups in which we live. We must learn to make informed choices that both reflect cultural insights and overcome cultural restraints.

IDEAS THAT WORK

Motivating with Personal Response

I have found that students' personal responses to poetry are far more valuable than a formalized approach. Write *REFLECTIONS* on the board. Ask the students to write in their journals their definitions of the word. After a few minutes, ask for volunteers to read their definitions. Place the definitions verbatim from five of the students on the board. Then ask the class to choose what they feel is the best definition, or use a summary of the five definitions to come up with a singular "class definition." When the definition is decided, ask students to write in their journals why it is important to reflect back on their lives. Have volunteers read their responses aloud.

James McCallum
Hopedale, Massachusetts

Before Reading

Sunday Morning by Oscar Peñaranda USA
Some Keep the Sabbath by Emily Dickinson USA

Oscar Peñaranda
born 1944

Born in the Philippines, Oscar Peñaranda (pen yə rän′də) teaches high school in California. He identifies the site of "Sunday Morning" as China Beach in San Francisco, "where they shooed the Chinese to live, in tents and shanties."

Emily Dickinson
1830–1886

"How can you print a piece of your own soul?" So said Emily Dickinson, whose brilliant unconventional, and intensely personal poems indeed revealed an unusual soul.

Building Background

Sundays and Special Days For Jews, Saturday, the Sabbath, is a holy day of rest, worship services, and special meals. Orthodox Jews do not work, travel, or carry money on the Sabbath. On Fridays, Muslims, who practice Islam, are expected to attend noon prayers at a mosque. For practicing Christians, Sunday has traditionally been a day of prayer and rest. Yet with the 7-day work week, 24-hour convenience stores, and "Sunday Special" sales, Sunday has lost some of its traditional associations. Nevertheless, certain communities still have "blue laws" that control activities such as liquor sales on Sundays. Do you think there should be legal measures to set Sundays apart from other days? Why or why not?

Literary Focus

Assonance The repetition of vowel sounds followed by different consonant sounds in stressed syllables or words is called **assonance** *(made/pale; hit/miss).* Assonance is one of several sound devices that poets use to reinforce meaning and unify ideas.

Writer's Notebook

REFLECTION
an idea or remark resulting from careful thinking

Taking a Careful Look Make a list of the places where you go to reflect. Then examine the list and write down the qualities or characteristics that draw you to those places. As you read the two poems that follow, record descriptions of the places in which the speakers like to reflect.

Before Reading

Building Background

Remind students that Sabbath is the traditional day of the week used for rest and worship. Sunday is Sabbath for most Christians. Saturday is Jewish Sabbath. Invite students from other cultures or those who have lived in other countries to share their experiences of how Sabbath is observed.

Literary Focus

Point out that **assonance**—usually in conjunction with other sound devices, such as consonance and onomatopoeia—can contribute to the overall musicality of a poem while accentuating meaning. To make students aware of sounds and language, have them sit quietly and listen to sounds and rhythms in their immediate world and try to communicate them in writing.

Writer's Notebook

Ask students to be particularly attuned to the sensory characteristics of the places they list. They might note such qualities as the comfortable solitude of a bedroom or the hypnotic rhythms they feel when riding the subway.

Connections to **AuthorWorks**

Emily Dickinson is a featured author in the AuthorWorks CD-ROM series.

SUPPORT MATERIALS OVERVIEW

Unit 5 Resource Book
- Graphic Organizer, p. 41
- Study Guide, p. 42
- Vocabulary, p. 43
- Grammar, p. 44
- Alternate Check Test, p. 45
- Vocabulary Test, p. 46
- Selection Test, pp. 47–48

Building English Proficiency
- Literature Summaries
- Activities, p. 212

Reading, Writing & Grammar SkillBook
- Vocabulary, pp. 18–19
- Reading, pp. 61–62
- Grammar, Usage, and Mechanics, pp. 256–258

Technology
- Audiotape 15, Side A
- Personal Journal Software
- Custom Literature Database: More poems by Emily Dickinson are available on the database.
- Test Generator Software

During Reading

Selection Objectives

- to compare two poems that reflect on the theme of Sabbath-keeping
- to examine the use of assonance in poetry
- to apply the conventions of capitalizing proper nouns and adjectives in writing

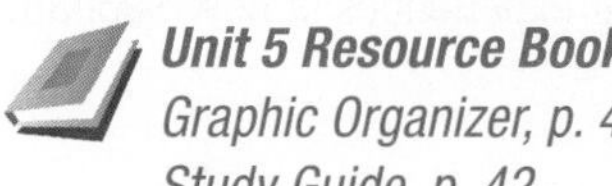

Unit 5 Resource Book
Graphic Organizer, p. 41
Study Guide, p. 42

Theme Link

Two poets describe their ways of keeping the Sabbath, the traditional day of reflection.

Vocabulary Preview

barbaric, not civilized; coarse

crag, steep, rugged rock or cliff rising above others

sexton, person who takes care of a church building

surplice, a broad-sleeved, white gown or vestment worn by members of the clergy and choir

waft, breath or puff of air, wind, scent

Students can add the words and definitions to their Writer's Notebooks.

Sunday Morning

(for my elders)

Oscar Peñaranda

Here I am again
sitting alone in my car
nostrils and mouth sucking wafts[1]
of wind rushing through open side windows
on a cliff hanging over the bay there is
music from the radio

That green monster of a gelatin sea
1 hisses white tongues of foam kneeling
to lick the shore serenading the lone
oak tree
atop the jagged crags[2] of rocks there
is music there also

they drown the chimes of distant chapel bells

come, take my hand
roll up your sleeves
and bare your chests before the naked sun

2 but

what I want to know is where
they ever got the barbaric[3] gall
to call me
an unbeliever

this is how I pray

1. waft (wäft), *n.* breath or puff of air, wind, or scent.
2. crag (krag), *n.* steep, rugged rock or cliff rising above others.
3. barbaric (bär bar′ik), *adj.* not civilized; coarse.

Would *Sunday Morning* be a good title for this photograph by Ansel Adams? Explain why it would make an appropriate title, or provide another title and tell why you think it would be better. ➤

1 Literary Element
Metaphor

Point out the elements of this extended metaphor: The sound and appearance of the sea are compared to a "green monster"; the surf is likened to hissing "tongues." The monster is "kneeling to lick the shore serenading the lone oak tree."

2 Literary Element
Internal Rhymes

Point out this internal rhyme and ask students to find other examples. *(Possible responses: take/naked; bare/where; gall/call; they/pray)*

SELECTION SUMMARY

Sunday Morning, Some Keep the Sabbath

In "Sunday Morning," the speaker describes how he spends the Sabbath. Alone, he sits in his car by a cliff overlooking a bay and enjoys the view and sound of the sea. To him, it seems like a powerful green monster that serenades the land and drowns out the sound of church bells. The speaker invites others to exult in nature's power. He defends his way of praying against those who say he is an unbeliever.

Instead of attending church services, the speaker in "Some Keep the Sabbath" prefers to stay home in her orchard listening to a bird sing. In this setting she can hear God preach a brief sermon. She feels she is always on the way to heaven.

For summaries in other languages, see the ***Building English Proficiency*** *book.*

Some Keep the Sabbath

Emily Dickinson

Some keep the Sabbath going to Church—
I keep it, staying at Home—
With a Bobolink for a Chorister—
And an Orchard, for a Dome—

Some keep the Sabbath in Surplice[1]—
I just wear my Wings—
3 And instead of tolling the Bell, for Church,
Our little Sexton[2]—sings.

God preaches, a noted Clergyman—
And the sermon is never long,
So instead of getting to Heaven, at last—
I'm going, all along.

1. surplice (sėr′plis), *n.* a broad-sleeved, white gown or vestment worn by members of the clergy and choir singers.
2. sexton (sek′stən), *n.* person who takes care of a church building.

3 Literary Focus
Assonance

Poets generally use assonance in conjunction with other sound devices to create a desired effect. Throughout this poem Dickinson masterfully mimics the summoning sound of tolling bells by combining the assonance of long and short *o* sounds with the deep alliterative resonance of *ng* and *m* sounds.

Question Where is this tolling sound most prominent in the poem? (*Possible responses: going/staying/Bobolink, which is reinforced by the Home/Dome rhyme in stanza 1; the resounding last line)*

Responses to Caption Questions
Students may agree that the majestic mountains and the church suggest reflection and "Sunday Morning."

Check Test

1. Where does the speaker of "Sunday Morning" prefer to spend his Sundays? *(in his car by the sea)*

2. How does the speaker describe those who call him an unbeliever? *(as barbaric)*

3. Where does the speaker in Emily Dickinson's poem prefer to spend the Sabbath? *(at home in her orchard)*

4. In Dickinson's poem what animal takes the place of a church choir? *(a bobolink)*

5. What "noted Clergyman" does the speaker in Dickinson's poem claim preaches directly to her? *(God)*

Unit 5 Resource Book
Alternate Check Test, p. 45

BUILDING ENGLISH PROFICIENCY

ESL
LEP
ELD
SAE
LD

Exploring Key Concepts

Draw students into the topic implied by the poems—the choice of how to spend reflective time. Encourage students to talk about their weekend activities.

Activity Ideas

- Develop students' vocabulary by beginning a web labeled *traditional.* Students can add words from the poems related to traditional Sunday activities.
- Ask students to share reflective activities they enjoy that might not be traditional. At this point you may wish to reread the poems aloud. Students can put their responses in another web labeled *nontraditional.*

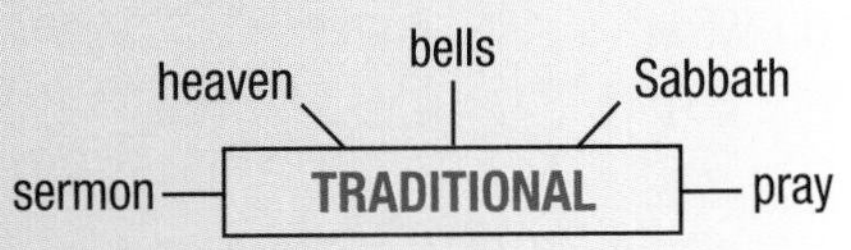

Building English Proficiency
Activities, p. 212

After Reading

MAKING CONNECTIONS

1. Students should support their choice with specific reasons based on details in the poems. Invite them to discuss the contrast between Peñaranda's appreciation of nature's raw power, shown in the image of green monster and the invitation to "bare your chest before the naked sun," and Dickinson's response to Nature's delicate beauty, shown in the images of the bobolink and the orchard.

2. Most students will probably note that both speakers choose to reflect in natural settings rather than in a church, but that they would probably seek different aspects of nature.

3. Students should support their choices with specific reasons based on details in the poems. Some might appreciate a certain form—Peñaranda's free-verse style or Dickinson's formalism.

4. Possible response: Yes. Both reflect on the way the speakers prefer to spend the Sabbath; both find God more in nature than in traditional churches.

5. Possible response: a powerful monster that nevertheless kneels to serenade the lone tree

6. Possible response: The tone changes from admiration and joyful identification with nature to anger at those who call him an unbeliever.

7. Possible response: In church, heaven is believed to be attainable only in the hereafter; the speaker finds it in the present, right in her orchard.

8. Students should address matters of rhyme, meter, and metaphor.

9. Dickinson probably meant that a successful poem thrills the mind and has a physical impact. Invite students to share examples of poetry, music, or visual art that blew off "the top of their heads."

After Reading

Making Connections

Shaping Your Response

1. With which speaker in the poems would you prefer to spend a Sunday? Why?
2. Do you think the speakers in these poems would agree on how to spend a Sunday? Why or why not?
3. Do these two works fit your idea of what a poem should be? Explain.

Analyzing the Poems

4. Do you think these poems share a common **theme**? Explain.
5. What **image**, or word picture, do you have of the sea in "Sunday Morning"?
6. How does the speaker's **tone** change in "Sunday Morning," starting in line 17?
7. How do you interpret the final two lines of Dickinson's poem?

Extending the Ideas

8. When the first volume of Dickinson's poems was published in 1890, an editor "smoothed rhymes, regularized meter, and substituted 'sensible' metaphors." If you were reprinting "Some Keep the Sabbath," which appears here in its original form, would you want to make any changes? Explain.
9. Dickinson explained that poetry had the power to make her feel "as if the top of my head were taken off." What do you think she meant? What effect do you think a good poem should have on readers?

Literary Focus: Assonance

The repetition of similar vowel sounds followed by different consonant sounds, usually in stressed syllables, is called **assonance**. Assonance differs from rhyme, in which both vowel and consonant sounds are similar. For example, *wild* and *child* are rhyming words; *mild* and *white* illustrate assonance. Like other sound devices, assonance helps create a unified effect and can reinforce meaning.

- What long vowel sound appearing in line 2 is repeated throughout the first two stanzas of "Sunday Morning"?
- How does this sound suggest the speaker's feeling of excitement and freedom?

LITERARY FOCUS: ASSONANCE

Possible responses

- long *o: alone, open, windows, over, radio, foam, lone, oak, also*
- The assonance expresses the speaker's feelings of wonder and awe—as if he were saying, "Oh, wow!"

Suggest that students set up a chart in their Writer's Notebook for recording examples of assonance and other sound devices (such as alliteration and onomatopoeia) that they encounter in the poems in this unit.

Vocabulary Study

Write the letter of the word that is *least* closely related in meaning to the first word.

barbaric
crag
sexton
surplice
waft

1. *crag* **a.** gully **b.** cliff **c.** peak
2. *waft* **a.** gale **b.** whiff **c.** puff
3. *barbaric* **a.** coarse **b.** cultured **c.** uncivilized
4. *surplice* **a.** robe **b.** undershirt **c.** vestment
5. *sexton* **a.** singer **b.** caretaker **c.** church custodian

Expressing Your Ideas

Writing Choices

Writer's Notebook Update In your notebook, compare the places where the speakers of the poems reflect with the places where you like to reflect.

Reflections of My Mind Use either of these "Sunday" poems as a model to write a **poem** about a time and place in which you reflect. Try to use assonance to help convey a mood.

Literary Self-Portrait An author once wrote to Emily Dickinson asking for her photograph. He received the following written reply: "I have no portrait, now, but am small, like the Wren, and my Hair is bold, like the Chestnut Bur, and my eyes, like the Sherry in the Glass, that the Guest leaves." Reflect on your image in a mirror. Then write a **description** of your own appearance in Dickinson's style, using some figurative language and—if you wish—unconventional capitalization.

Other Options

Daily Reflections In *The Meaning of Culture*, John Cowper Powys wrote, "Without long, lovely moments spent in day-dreams life becomes an iron-ribbed, sterile puffing machine." With a partner or a small group make up your own observations about life that will cause a reader to reflect. Then use a computer program to make a **monthly calendar** of the sayings, or copy the sayings and statements by hand onto a ready-made calendar.

Stamp of Approval The United States Postal Service issued this commemorative stamp in honor of Emily Dickinson. What poet would you like to honor with a commemorative stamp? Remember that writers of song lyrics can be considered poets too. Nominate your candidate in a **persuasive speech**—complete with a poster-size mock-up of your stamp design.

Dance a Poem Convey the mood and images of "Sunday Morning" in **dance** form. You might want to use props such as scarves, a fan, or bells to help achieve a desired effect.

VOCABULARY STUDY

1. a
2. a
3. b
4. b
5. a

Unit 5 Resource Book
Vocabulary, p. 43
Vocabulary Test, p. 46

WRITING CHOICES

Writer's Notebook Update

Students can jot ideas in a simple chart as shown.

Literary Self-Portrait

Discuss how Dickinson uses similes that refer to specific things found in her home environment—an animal, a plant, a drink. Encourage students to look to their own environments to find appropriate similes for themselves.

Place in "Sunday Mornings"	Place in "Some Keep . . ."	My place
rushing wind	peaceful orchard	loud music

Selection Test

Unit 5 Resource Book
pp. 47–48

OTHER OPTIONS

Daily Reflections

If students need help in devising a full calendar's worth of observations on life, suggest they supplement their own efforts with suitable items from *Bartlett's* or another book of quotations.

Stamp of Approval

You might want to point out to students that U.S. Postal Service regulations require that candidates for commemorative stamps be deceased.

Dance a Poem

Encourage students to work in small groups to choreograph and stage several versions of "Sunday Morning" with appropriate musical accompaniment.

Before Reading

Building Background

As students make suggestions, a student acting as recorder can organize them in the six categories—Heritage, Religion, Family and Friends, Interests and Activities, Environment, Event or Decision. The class as a whole can evaluate which categories were dominant. When the groups are done, discuss how not only major things but also minor things can make a strong impact.

Literary Focus

Symbols shown have the following meanings.

- American eagle—strength and power
- Medusa, chief of the Gorgons of Greek mythology who had the power to turn onlookers to stone—warning
- ankh (Greek)—life
- peace
- laurel wreath—victory, distinction

Writer's Notebook

To help students get started, ask them to cite memorable lines from recent popular movies, television shows, and songs.

Before Reading

Ceremony by Leslie Marmon Silko USA from Ecclesiastes Bible

A Story by Czeslaw Milosz Poland/USA

The Road Not Taken by Robert Frost USA

Building Background

And That Has Made All the Difference What has made a difference in shaping your life? Perhaps it is your heritage, your religion, your family or close friends, your interests and activities, your environment, or an event or decision. With a group, brainstorm things in your own lives and in the lives of historical figures that have determined events, shaped outcomes, and "made all the difference."

Literary Focus

Symbol Something concrete, such as an object, a person, a place, or an event, that represents something abstract, such as an idea, a quality, a concept, or a condition, is called a **symbol**. Some of the symbols pictured below have particular cultural significance. Work with a partner to add other symbols, completing a chart such as the one started here.

Symbol	Thing Represented
skull and crossbones	poison

Writer's Notebook

Life Lines When you finish watching a movie or a television show or reading an article, you may remember a certain line that has special meaning for you. The poems you are about to read deal with special things—traditions, decisions, and insights—that have made a difference. After you have read the poems, jot down what you think is the most significant line in each.

SUPPORT MATERIALS OVERVIEW

Unit 5 Resource Book
- Graphic Organizer, p. 49
- Study Guide, p. 50
- Vocabulary, p. 51
- Grammar, p. 52
- Alternate Check Test, p. 53
- Vocabulary Test, p. 54
- Selection Test, pp. 55–56

Building English Proficiency
- Literature Summaries
- Activities, p. 213

Reading, Writing & Grammar SkillBook
- Reading, pp. 59–60
- Grammar, Usage, and Mechanics, pp. 165–166

The World of Work
- Animal Control Worker, p. 21
- Inspection Report, p. 22

Technology
- Audiotape 15, Sides A and B
- Personal Journal Software
- Custom Literature Database: More works from the Bible and poems by Robert Frost are available on the database.
- Test Generator Software

Leslie Marmon Silko

born 1948

Leslie Marmon Silko's 1977 novel, *Ceremony*, which demonstrates her gift of storytelling and depicts life on an Indian reservation, helped establish her as an important Native American voice in literature. Raised in the Laguna Pueblo in New Mexico, she was introduced to a rich oral tradition at an early age. One critic has called Silko "without question . . . the most accomplished Indian writer of her generation." She is associated with the University of Albuquerque and is an assistant professor of English at the University of Arizona, Tucson. Silko observes that in order to recognize "the power of what we share, we must understand how different we are, too."

Czeslaw Milosz

born 1911

Nobel Prize laureate Czeslaw Milosz (ches′lô mē′wosh), who was born in Lithuania and raised in Poland, became a leader of the new poetry movement in Poland during the 1930s and worked for the Polish Resistance during World War II. His writings of a tragic past affirm the value of human life. One critic says "Milosz is eloquent in his call for a literature grounded in moral, as well as esthetic, values." Milosz, who now lives in the United States, tells aspiring poets to "read good poetry." He explains, "I have been taught by history, if you are completely cornered, if you have no way out except to give vent to your moral indignation, then you write poems."

Robert Frost

1874–1963

Robert Frost observed about literature: "You learn first to know what you see and to put fresh words to it," a process he termed "sights and insights." After getting married and graduating from Harvard, Frost struggled for years to get his poetry published. Discouraged, he moved with his family to England where, three days after receiving Frost's manuscript, a publisher agreed to release his work. When Frost returned to the United States, he was already famous for his fresh, original poetry. Asked to define the process of writing poetry, Frost explained that a "definition of poetry is dawn—that it's something dawning on you while you're writing it."

More About the Poets

Leslie Marmon Silko

Much of Silko's fiction and poetry explores the spiritual crisis faced by Native Americans when they must choose between contemporary materialism and tribal traditions. Silko is the author of *Laguna Woman,* (1974).

Czeslaw Milosz

A poet, critic, translator, and novelist who writes in both Polish and English, Milosz became a naturalized citizen in 1970, ten years after emigrating to the United States. He was awarded the Nobel Prize for Literature in 1980 and has been a member of the faculty at the University of California, Berkeley. Another work by the author is *The Captive Mind,* (1953).

Robert Frost

In *Frost: A Literary Life Reconsidered,* (1984), William H. Pritchard writes that Frost occasionally warned his audiences that "The Road Not Taken" is a tricky poem. Pritchard explains that it is not simply a "sincere" poem about courageously blazing a "less traveled" path through life, but also a "mischievous" one about the human tendency to justify in hindsight the impulsive decisions made in youth.

Ecclesiastes

Based on linguistic evidence, scholars date the writing of Ecclesiastes to the third century B.C. The writer identifies himself as "the son of David, king in Jerusalem," which would place the book seven centuries earlier. The title *Ecclesiastes* is a Greek translation of the Hebrew word *Qoheleth*, meaning "the Preacher," the pseudonym used by the writer.

Connections to **AuthorWorks**

Robert Frost is a featured author in the AuthorWorks CD-ROM series.

During Reading

Selection Objectives

- to examine poems that reflect on traditions, decisions, and insights that shape the course of human life
- to interpret symbols in poetry
- to understand the use of rhythm and parallel construction in English prose

Unit 5 Resource Book
Graphic Organizer, p. 49
Study Guide, p. 50

Theme Link

Poets from various cultures and historical periods reflect on the influences and events that shaped their lives.

Vocabulary Preview

abscess, pus resulting from infected tissues of the body
comprehensible, understandable
diverge, move or lie in different directions from the same point
malicious, showing ill will; spiteful
pluck, pull or tug
rend, tear or pull apart

Students can add the words and definitions to their Writer's Notebooks.

Art Study

Response to Caption Question
Students may realize that the ritual suggests that the bowls were believed to possess life themselves. Since they were placed on the heads of the dead for burial, the bowls became "dead" like the corpse.

The bowls shown are from the Mimbres (mim′brās) Valley of New Mexico and were made by the Mogollon (mō′ gə yōn′) people probably between A.D. 1000 and 1150.

These Mimbres bowls have been ceremonially "killed" by having a hole made at the base before being placed in a grave. What does this custom suggest about the role of art in Mimbres culture? ➤

SELECTION SUMMARY

Poems

Ceremony Silko's subject is traditional stories, which the speaker says have the power to ward off illness and death. The stories must be preserved against those who would destroy them for they are the very life of the people.

A Story A rampaging bear attacks Meader's cabin, and he decides to kill it. Afterwards, he discovers that its jaw had been half eaten away by an abscessed tooth. The speaker moralizes that this kind of pain also drives people to commit acts of senseless destruction.

The Road Not Taken The speaker describes how choosing one of two roads has determined the course of his life.

Ecclesiastes Through a litany of contrasting examples, the poet shows how there is a time for every human emotion and activity under heaven.

For summaries in other languages, see the ***Building English Proficiency*** *book.*

EREMONY

LESLIE MARMON SILKO

1

I will tell you something about stories,
[he said]
They aren't just entertainment.
Don't be fooled.
They are all we have, you see,
all we have to fight off
illness and death.

You don't have anything
if you don't have the stories.

Their evil is mighty
but it can't stand up to our stories.
2
So they try to destroy the stories
let the stories be confused or forgotten.
They would like that
They would be happy
Because we would be defenseless then.

He rubbed his belly.
I keep them here
[he said]
3
Here, put your hand on it
See, it is moving.
There is life here
for the people.

And in the belly of this story
the rituals and the ceremony
are still growing.

1 Multicultural Note
Shaman

Among the indigenous peoples of the American Southwest (as elsewhere), shamans, like the keeper of the stories in Silko's poem, are the repositories of tribal wisdom. The community looks to them for guidance and for overseeing religious and healing ceremonies. Ask students to identify similar personages in their own community who possess such ceremonial powers.

2 Reading/Thinking Skills
Draw Conclusions

Question Who can you infer "they" are? *(Possible responses: outsiders; institutions of the dominant outside culture)*

3 Literary Element
Metaphor

Question To what are the man's stories being compared in this passage? *(to a child in the womb; to life)*

BUILDING ENGLISH PROFICIENCY

Sharing Stories

Take this opportunity to have students share the subjects of stories that are repeated and enjoyed among their families and friends. The subjects may be their own histories in another country or in this one, traditional tales that have morals, or stories of heroes.

You may wish to have students practice telling a story to a partner and then retell it to the class.

Building English Proficiency
Activities, p. 213

4 Literary Focus
Symbol

Questions

- What are indications that the grizzly may mean more than just a hunted animal? *(The speaker begins by explaining that he will offer a moral; in line 17, he shifts from the bear to "us.")*
- What might the bear symbolize? *(Possible response: the deep pain that comes to people during life and drives them to destroy themselves or others)*

5 Literary Element
Tone

Question What is the tone of the speaker toward the grizzly? *(Possible response: pity, empathy)*

6 Literary Element
Theme

Challenge students to synthesize Milosz's use of tone and symbol and to state the moral or theme. *(Possible response: At times life can be so difficult that we are driven to do things that are unnatural.)*

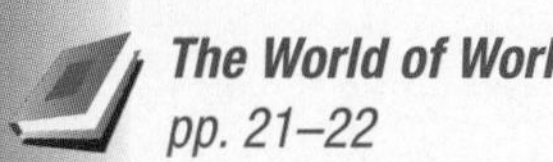

Animal Control Worker

For a look into the career of an animal control worker, use—

The World of Work
pp. 21–22

A Story

CZESLAW MILOSZ

4
Now I will tell Meader's story; I have a moral in view.
He was pestered by a grizzly so bold and malicious[1]
That he used to snatch caribou meat from the eaves of the cabin.
Not only that. He ignored men and was unafraid of fire.
One night he started battering the door
And broke the window with his paw, so they curled up
With their shotguns beside them, and waited for the dawn.
He came back in the evening, and Meader shot him at close range,
Under the left shoulder blade. Then it was jump and run,
A real storm of a run: A grizzly, Meader says,
Even when he's been hit in the heart, will keep running
Until he falls down. Later, Meader found him
By following the trail—and then he understood
5
What lay behind the bear's odd behavior:
Half of the beast's jaw was eaten away by an
abscess,[2] and caries.
6
Toothache, for years. An ache without comprehensible[3] reason,
Which often drives us to senseless action
And gives us blind courage. We have nothing to lose,
We come out of the forest, and not always with the hope
That we will be cured by some dentist from heaven.

---

1. malicious (mə lish′əs), *adj.* showing ill will; spiteful.
2. abscess (ab′ses), *n.* pus resulting from infected tissues of the body.
3. comprehensible (kom′pri hen′sə bəl), *adj.* understandable.

MINI-LESSON: LITERARY FOCUS
Symbol

Symbols are often the most difficult figures of speech for students to detect in literature.

Teach Explain that symbols belong to the same class of figures of speech as metaphors and similes. All three suggest much more than the literal, but a symbol is both literal and figurative. Also, a symbol has multiple meanings. Discuss with students how these characteristics are found in the symbol of the bear. *(The bear is an actual animal and the author uses it to convey other meanings; the bear is human suffering, destruction, self-destruction, and perhaps divine punishment.)*

Question Why would American pride be symbolized by the bald eagle? *(Possible response: because the eagle has qualities that Americans believe their country to have—strength, vision, and power)*

Activity Idea Have students review several selections they have read in this book, and list images they think have symbolic meaning. Begin by considering the symbolism of the underwater tunnel in Doris Lessing's "The Tunnel."

THE ROAD NOT TAKEN

ROBERT FROST

Two roads diverged[1] in a yellow wood,
And sorry I could not travel both
And be one traveler, long I stood
And looked down one as far as I could
To where it bent in the undergrowth;

7

Then took the other, as just as fair,
And having perhaps the better claim,
Because it was grassy and wanted wear;
Though as for that, the passing there
Had worn them really about the same,

And both that morning equally lay
In leaves no step had trodden black.
Oh! I kept the first for another day!
Yet knowing how way leads on to way,
I doubted if I should ever come back.

8

I shall be telling this with a sigh
Somewhere ages and ages hence:
Two roads diverged in a wood, and I—
I took the one less traveled by,
And that has made all the difference.

1. diverge (də vėrj′), *v.* move or lie in different directions from the same point.

7 Reading/Thinking Skills
Clarify

Point out that Frost's speaker contradicts himself in this passage, and that this contradiction undercuts the claim at the end that he took the road "less traveled by."

Questions

- According to lines 6–12, is the road the speaker took noticeably different from the one not taken? *(Though he says one has "perhaps the better claim," the roads are both "really about the same" and lay "equally" in leaves.)*
- What motivated the speaker to take one and not the other? *(Possible responses: impulse, intuition, being forced to choose)*

8 Reading/Thinking Skills
Evaluate

Question For which age reader would you say this poem would be most appropriate? Explain your response. *(Possible responses: for teenagers because they are about to make life decisions; for older persons because they may wonder about opportunities they did not take.)*

BUILDING ENGLISH PROFICIENCY

Analyzing Metaphors

"A Story" and "The Road Not Taken" both draw upon a central metaphor to express their meanings. Students can take the following steps to interpret the metaphors.

1. As students review the poems, ask them what caused the problem in each poem. *(the bear's abscessed tooth; taking the "less traveled" road)*

2. Then elicit from students that each thing is connected with a dramatic action or result—for one, pain that leads to destruction, and for the other, the events of a whole life.

3. Discuss why the sore tooth can be thought of as more than an ordinary pain, and why the road is more important than everyday roads that people travel on.

4. Prompt students to think of other things that could be symbols or metaphors.

Students may want to review this activity as they approach the Literary Focus questions on page 610.

9 Literary Elements
Repetition and Opposites

Discuss with the class these conventions of Hebrew poetry: Biblical verse did not employ meter and rhyme; instead, it relied on various rhetorical devices to create its effects. In this passage from Ecclesiastes, the repetition of "A time to . . ." gives the verse its forward drive, while the pairing of opposites creates a seesawing effect. Both devices support the theme that the positive aspects of life are balanced by negative aspects. Even the way that the writer pairs these opposites suggests something about life's pattern: its unpredictability. Sometimes the writer enumerates the positive aspect first ("A time to be born, and a time to die"); other times he puts the negative aspect first ("a time to kill, and a time to heal").

10 Reading/Thinking Skills
Making Personal Connections

Question Do you agree with the writer, that there are proper times in life for hate and war? Explain. *(Possible response: No, people should always seek to achieve the positive aspects of life, such as love and peace. Yes, sometimes hate and war are justified when they serve a greater good: hatred of racism, war to overthrow a brutal dictator.)*

ECCLESIASTES

THE BIBLE

To every thing there is a season, and a time to every purpose
under the heaven.
A time to be born, and a time to die: a time to plant, and a time
to pluck[1] up that which is planted:
A time to kill, and a time to heal: a time to break down, and a
time to build up:
A time to weep, and a time to laugh: a time to mourn, and a time
to dance:
A time to cast away stones, and a time to gather stones together:
a time to embrace, and a time to refrain from embracing:
A time to get, and a time to lose: a time to keep and a time to cast
away:
10 A time to rend,[2] and a time to sew: a time to keep silence, and a time to speak:
A time to love, and a time to hate: a time of war, and a time of peace.

1. **pluck** (pluk), *v.* pull or tug.
2. **rend** (rend), *v.* tear or pull apart.

This detail of a mandala, or symbolic circle, from a ceiling painting of an Indian palace depicts the cycle of seasons. How does this picture reinforce the message of Ecclesiastes? ➤

MINI-LESSON: GRAMMAR
Origins and Development of English: Biblical Rhythms and Parallel Construction

Teach Point out that the King James Version of the Bible was created at the command of James I of England and first published in 1611. Considered by many to be the most beautiful rendering of the Bible into English, it has had a worldwide influence on English prose writers and poets through the centuries. Its distinctive rhythms and parallel constructions (repetition of phrases or clauses having the same grammatical structures) owe much to the translators' understanding of ancient Hebrew as to their knowledge of Greek and Latin rhetorical devices.

Activity Ideas

- Have students compare the rhythms and parallelism in the excerpt from "Ecclesiastes" with those in Martin Luther King's "I Have a Dream" speech or with passages from Walt Whitman's *Song of Myself.*
- Students can write a description of a place in which they use parallel construction to heighten tension or add interest. For a model, students should read Stewart's description of the lighting in the cave in *The Hollow Hills,* page 346.

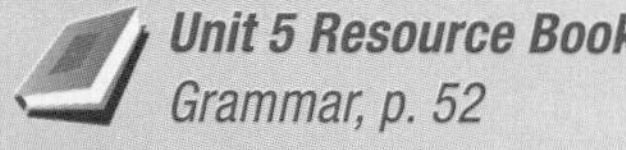

Unit 5 Resource Book
Grammar, p. 52

Art Study

Response to Caption Question The images have no starting or ending point because the seasons are continuous, just as events in life propel us forward. Students might observe that the contrasts of the positive and negative events in life are not shown.

Check Test

1. In "Ceremony" where does the man say he keeps the stories for his people? *(in his belly)*

2. In "A Story," why does Meader decide to shoot the bear? *(because he repeatedly attacks Meader's cabin)*

3. What does Meader discover was the cause of the bear's odd behavior? *(Half the bear's jaw had been eaten away by an abscess causing constant pain.)*

4. In "The Road Not Taken," what is the season? *(autumn)*

5. According to the speaker, when will he tell "with a sigh" that he took the road "less traveled by"? *("ages and ages hence")*

Unit 5 Resource Book
Alternate Check Test, p. 53

BUILDING ENGLISH PROFICIENCY

ESL LEP ELD SAE LD

Making Personal Connections

Invite students to modernize this passage from Ecclesiastes while keeping the basic truths its expresses. Encourage students to talk about or act out the opposing actions in the poem. Then have them suggest new "times to" that reflect their environment.

1. Have small groups of students use a t-chart to record pairs of opposing circumstances.

2. Allow groups to choose an order for their details and share their new poems with the class. Remind students that under "x" and "y" they should list opposite ideas, but the items don't always mean good *vs.* bad.

To every thing there is a season, and a time to every purpose under the heaven.

A TIME TO . . .

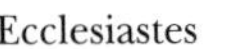

x	y
hang out with friends	be alone
travel around	settle in one place

After Reading

MAKING CONNECTIONS

1. Suggest that students bring recordings of their choices of background music to play in class.

2. Allow students ample time to prepare their tableaux. Urge them to try to capture not only a scene but also the mood of the poem.

3. Possible responses: Silko—mysterious, the spirit within stories; Milosz—tragedy and its consequences; Frost—little decisions that have lifelong effects; Ecclesiastes—songlike, life's positives and negatives

4. Possible responses: Native American folk tales, myths, legends; prayers; spells for healing

5. Possible responses: Life brings such pain that sometime people are driven to destroy themselves or others; people who do evil may be suffering themselves.

6. The bear is personified as a crazed person seeking a deliverance from life's pains.

7. Possible responses: mischievous, coy, wistful

8. Possible response: "A time" is repeated just as the seasons and cycles of life repeat endlessly.

9. Possible response: Extreme behavior may be a symptom of extreme pain. Professionals will search for an underlying cause of destructive behavior.

10. Students' responses should reflect the understanding that their choices in life are often influenced by their cultural values and background. Some students may say they want to preserve the values they grew up with, while others may decide to oppose them.

After Reading

Making Connections

Shaping Your Response

1. What music or style of music would you choose as background for an oral reading of each poem?

2. Work with classmates to pose for a tableau, or frozen picture, that captures a scene or a mood from one of the poems. Ask other classmates to guess which poem your tableau represents.

3. In your notebook, write a word or phrase to describe your thoughts about each poem.

Analyzing the Poems

4. Now that you know Leslie Silko grew up on a Pueblo Indian reservation in New Mexico, **infer** what you think the stories in "Ceremony" are about.

5. What do you think the **moral** of "A Story" is?

6. Describe the **personification** of the bear in lines 17-21 of "A Story."

7. How would you describe the **tone** of "The Road Not Taken"?

8. How does the **repetition** in the excerpt from Ecclesiastes reinforce the **theme** of the poem?

Extending the Ideas

9. What insights could the ending of "The Bear" provide for certain professionals such as counselors and social workers who work with troubled people?

10. To what degree do you think the **choices** people make are determined by their cultural values and backgrounds? In answering, focus on a major decision—marriage, career, lifestyle—and try to think through the steps you would take in making choices.

Literary Focus: Symbol

Literary **symbols**—concrete things that represent abstractions—allow readers to make associations and arrive at meaning. For example, in "A Poison Tree" by William Blake on page 288, the effects of hatred are represented by a tree that bears poison fruit.

- In your opinion, what do the diverging roads in "The Road Not Taken" symbolize?
- The passage from Ecclesiastes was made into a song titled "Turn! Turn! Turn!" What do you think the circular motion suggested by the title might symbolize about life?
- What do you think the bear's ache, which drives him to senseless action, suggests?

LITERARY FOCUS: SYMBOL

Possible responses

- two different careers or ways of life
- that the patterns of life are repeated from one generation to the next; that, even though time is linear, human life follows the circular motion of the seasons
- human desperation; spiritual despair

Vocabulary Study

Word analogy tests require you to understand the relationship between a pair of words and then to choose another pair with the same relationship. Study the relationship of the following pairs of words in capital letters; then choose another pair that has the same relationship.

abscess
comprehensible
diverge
malicious
pluck

1. COMPREHENSIBLE : UNDERSTANDABLE :: **a.** visible : hidden **b.** jolly : ridiculous **c.** reluctant : hesitant **d.** athletic : fast
2. GARDEN : PLUCK :: **a.** mall : shop **b.** chicken : feathers **c.** weed : flower **d.** kitchen : dishes
3. MALICIOUS : SPITEFUL :: **a.** big : frightening **b.** valuable : rare **c.** illiterate : ignorant **d.** happy : joyous
4. DIVERGE : MERGE :: **a.** rip : mend **b.** eat : digest **c.** cheat : swindle **d.** hide : conceal
5. INFECTION : ABSCESS :: **a.** sore : wound **b.** virus : cold **c.** brook : flow **d.** joke : smile

Expressing Your Ideas

Writing Choices

Writer's Notebook Update Take a look at the favorite lines you copied down. Then in your notebook, explain why each line stands out in your mind.

Passing the Baton Leslie Marmon Silko tells of the importance that stories play in passing on the traditions, customs, rituals, and beliefs of Native Americans. How will future generations of your family learn about their heritage? Share the importance of one of your traditions or customs in a **poem**.

Dear Gabby How do you make difficult decisions? Why not ask "Dear Gabby" in her **advice column**? Write two questions that deal with making tough choices. Then exchange questions with a partner and answer the questions as "Dear Gabby" might in her advice column.

Other Options

Pass the Torch Find out about the customs, beliefs, activities, foods, and types of clothing that have been passed in your family from generation to generation. As a class, collect information and artifacts that reveal heritage. Display this information at a **Heritage Fest** and invite other classes to view the display.

Music for All Seasons In the 1960s, musician Pete Seeger adapted the words from Ecclesiastes into a song titled "Turn! Turn! Turn!" Play a **recording** of Seeger's song for the class and pantomime the words.

Words to Live By You can spread your own "words of wisdom." What pointers about life do you want to share with a friend, classmate, or a younger brother or sister? Write at least five brief messages about life and compile them in a **booklet** entitled "Five Things That Can Make All the Difference." Illustrate your messages.

VOCABULARY STUDY

1. c (a is a synonym of b)
2. a (a is where b is performed)
3. d (a is a synonym of b)
4. a (a is an antonym of b)
5. b (a can cause b)

Unit 5 Resource Book
Vocabulary, p. 51
Vocabulary Test, p. 54

WRITING CHOICES

Passing the Baton

Help students get started by organizing a brainstorming session to come up with a list of various traditions and customs that families usually observe, such as religious holidays, special meals, and vacations. Suggest that students use "Ceremony" as a model for organizing their own poems.

Dear Gabby

You might distribute to the class an advice column from a school or commercial newspaper or magazine to use as a model.

Selection Test

Unit 5 Resource Book
pp. 55–56

OTHER OPTIONS

ass the Torch

his activity will need careful supervision. Caution udents to obtain parental consent before bringing ny valuable or irreplaceable family artifacts to class.

usic for All Seasons

ete Seeger's musical adaptation became a hit ecording by The Byrds. Students might especially njoy hearing this version.

Words to Live By

If students have difficulty devising their own maxims about life, suggest that they supplement their efforts by finding suitable quotations in *Bartlett's* or asking adults about traditional maxims that guided them.

Before Reading

Building Background

Point out that students can expand the chart to reflect other ideas. Note also that in the photo on pages 654–655, the foreground contains important details. Possible responses:

Elements of Photograph	Examples
Main focal point	Damascus Gate
Background details	boy with kite in foreground
Mood	tension
Point of view	Conflict is always present.

Literary Focus

Stress that a **simile** is a comparison between two *unlike* things. An example of a construction using *like* or *as* that is not a simile appears in Atwood's poem.

You might present the difference between these two comparisons: "The planet Venus, like Mercury, is too hot to support life" (no simile); "Venus, like a greenhouse in which a heater has been left on, is too hot to support life" (simile).

Writer's Notebook

Suggest that students think about whether they would prefer to render their detail as a photo, an oil or watercolor painting, or another visual medium.

Before Reading

This Is a Photograph of Me by Margaret Atwood Canada

Water Picture by May Swenson USA

Six Haiku by Matsuo Bashō and Yosa Buson Japan

Building Background

Snapshots The poems that follow highlight the beauty and mysteries of nature. As you read each poem, you will notice that the descriptions have a photographic quality, almost as if the writer had taken a snapshot of the scene and translated it into words.

Just as there are photographic qualities in poems, there are poetic elements in photographs. Examine the photograph on pages 654-655. Work with a partner to look at elements of the picture and describe them, filling out a chart like the one here. Save your chart for later use.

Elements of Photograph	Examples
Main focal point	
Background details	
Mood	
Point of view	

Literary Focus

Simile A figure of speech involving a direct comparison between two unlike things and using words such as *like* and *as* is called a **simile**: "Her laugh was like running water." Writers use similes to draw attention to similar qualities or feelings that two unlike people, places, or things share.

Writer's Notebook

Details Big and Small Jot down details in the following poems that would make an interesting picture. Then select one detail and illustrate it in your notebook.

SUPPORT MATERIALS OVERVIEW

Unit 5 Resource Book
- Graphic Organizer, p. 57
- Study Guide, p. 58
- Vocabulary, p. 59
- Grammar, p. 60
- Alternate Check Test, p. 61
- Vocabulary Test, p. 62
- Selection Test, pp. 63–64

Building English Proficiency
- Literature Summaries
- Activities, p. 214

Reading, Writing & Grammar SkillBook
- Vocabulary, pp. 11–12
- Reading, pp. 55–56
- Grammar, Usage, and Mechanics, pp. 246–247

Technology
- Audiotapes 15, Side B, and 16, Side A
- Personal Journal Software
- Custom Literature Database: For more w by Asian poets, see Po Chü-i, Li Po, and T Fu on the database.
- Test Generator Software

Margaret Atwood
born 1939

Margaret Atwood—known for her novels, short stories, television plays, children's books, critical works, and poetry—considers it an advantage that she did not attend a full year of school until she was in eighth grade. Born in Ottawa, Canada, she grew up in the Quebec bush as well as in Ottawa, Sault Ste. Marie, and Toronto. She was an avid reader of children's classics and comic books. When asked why she writes, she replied, "Why does the sun shine?. . . It's a human activity. I think the real question is, Why doesn't everyone?" Atwood often writes as a Canadian and a woman, creating characters searching for identity and freedom amid political and sexual oppression.

May Swenson
1919–1989

May Swenson wrote that the poetic experience is "based in a craving to get through the curtains of things as they *appear*, to things as they *are*, and then into the larger, wilder space of things as they *are becoming."* Swenson was born in Logan, Utah, and earned a degree from the University of Utah. She worked as a reporter for a Salt Lake City newspaper before going to New York City to hold a variety of jobs, including editor, reviewer, teacher, and poet-in-residence. Swenson's poems play with language, twisting words in magical ways.

Matsuo Bashō
1644–1694

Bashō, considered the greatest of all writers of haiku, was born into a family of samurai—men of the warrior class—at a time of peace and stability in Japan. At eight, he was taken into the service of a nobleman's son. By nine, he had written his first verses. Though he wrote for most of his life, he did not reach the peak of his ability until his last ten years. Some of Bashō's poems are infused with a religious mysticism, but most are simple descriptions of everyday scenes and real events.

Yosa Buson
1715–1783

Buson, considered second only to Bashō as a writer of haiku, is equally famous as a painter. An example of his work is at the left. His subject matter displays a great appreciation of the ever-changing world. Born Taniguchi Buson, he later took the name Yosa in honor of a region near Kyoto known for its scenic beauty.

More About the Authors

Margaret Atwood
In both her poetry and fiction, Atwood has demonstrated a precise eye for detail, often rendered with brutal detachment to create nightmarish effects. Other works by the author include *Bluebeard's Egg,* (1983) and *The Handmaid's Tale,* (1986).

May Swenson
Known as the "poet par excellence of sights and colors," Swenson was elected a Chancellor of the Academy of American Poets. She was awarded the Bollingen Prize, Rockefeller and Guggenheim grants, and a MacArthur Fellowship. Other works by the author include *New & Selected Things Taking Place,* (1978) and *In Other Words,* (1987).

Matsuo Bashō
This poet is credited with developing the haiku form of poetry. His poems often reflect his Zen Buddhist belief in the unity of all life. It is said that on his deathbed, he gathered his disciples around him and recited his last poem to them.

During Reading

Selection Objectives

- to appreciate photographic qualities in poetry
- to understand the figurative use of similes
- to recognize economy of expression in poetry and avoid wordiness in writing

Unit 5 Resource Book
Graphic Organizer, p. 57
Study Guide, p. 58

Theme Link

Four poets reflect on scenes from nature from unusual snapshot-like perspectives.

Vocabulary Preview

deploy, spread out in a planned or strategic position
distortion, twisting out of shape
shoal, a large number
waveringly, unsteadily
rook, a bird that resembles a crow

Students can add the words and definitions to their Writer's Notebooks.

1 Literary Focus
Simile

Ask students to explain why this comparison is not a simile.

2 Reading/Thinking Skills
Make Analogies

Question What might the speaker be making an analogy to by saying he or she has drowned? *(Possible response: to a way of life that has ended)*

3 Reading/Thinking Skills
Visualize

Invite students to draw the picture as they imagine it.

1 # This Is a Photograph of Me

Margaret Atwood

It was taken some time ago.
At first it seems to be
a smeared
print: blurred lines and grey flecks
blended with the paper;

then, as you scan
it, you see in the left-hand corner
a thing that is like a branch: part of a tree
(balsam or spruce) emerging
and, to the right, halfway up
what ought to be a gentle
slope, a small frame house.

In the background there is a lake,
and beyond that, some low hills.

2 (The photograph was taken
the day after I drowned.

I am in the lake, in the center
of the picture, just under the surface.

It is difficult to say where
precisely, or to say
how large or small I am:
the effect of water
on light is a distortion[1]

but if you look long enough,
3 eventually
you will be able to see me.)

Do you think this is an appropriate image for Atwood's poem? What details suggest that the subject is submerged in water?

1. distortion (dis tôr′shən), *n.* twisting out of shape.

SELECTION SUMMARY

Poems

This Is a Photograph of Me The speaker describes a photograph, which she or he says was taken the day after she drowned. The photograph shows a branch in one corner and a small frame house halfway up a slope that "ought to be gentle." In the background is a lake and low hills. The speaker says that the viewer will be able to see her, "just under the surface."

Water Picture The poet describes fanciful images she sees reflected in a park pond, such as buildings with chimney-legs that appear to bounce on clouds and a flag that descends like a fishhook. The inhabitants of the park appear suspended upside-down. Then a swan dips her bill into the water, causing the illusion to disappear.

Six Haiku Six haiku by two masters of the form—Bashō and Buson—capture scenes drawn from nature and daily life.

For summaries in other languages, see the ***Building English Proficiency*** *book.*

Water Picture

May Swenson

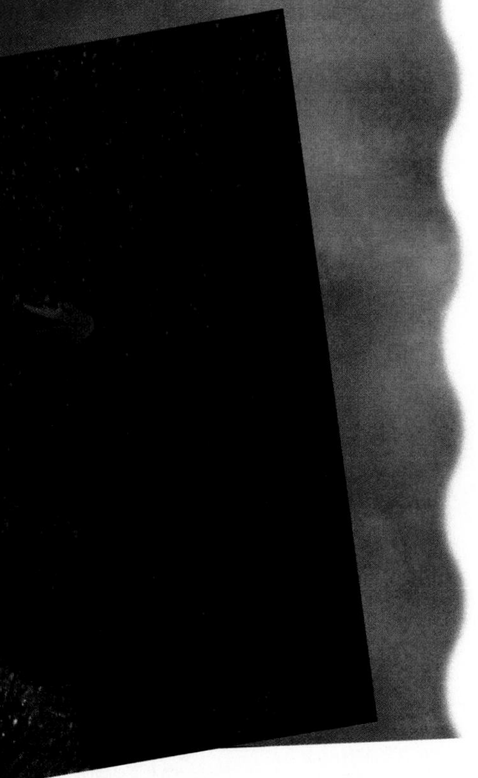

4 In the pond in the park
all things are doubled:
Long buildings hang and
wriggle gently. Chimneys
are bent legs bouncing
on clouds below. A flag
5 wags like a fishhook
down there in the sky.

The arched stone bridge
is an eye, with underlid
in the water. In its lens
dip crinkled heads with hats
that don't fall off. Dogs go by,
barking on their backs.
A baby, taken to feed the
ducks, dangles upside-down,
a pink balloon for a buoy.

Treetops deploy[1] a haze of
cherry bloom for roots,
where birds coast belly-up
in the glass bowl of a hill;
from its bottom a bunch
of peanut-munching children
is suspended by their
sneakers, waveringly.[2]

A swan, with twin necks
forming the figure three,
steers between two dimpled
towers doubled. Fondly
hissing, she kisses herself,
and all the scene is troubled:
water-windows splinter,
tree-limbs tangle, the bridge
folds like a fan.

1. **deploy** (di ploi′), *v.* spread out in a planned or strategic position.
2. **waveringly** (wā′vər ing lē), *adv.* unsteadily.

Art Study

Response to Caption Questions

Students may agree that the photo shows the face of a young woman just under the surface of the water, as in the poem. While the water is not seen, the viewer knows it is there from the sparkles of light and floating leaves on the surface.

Robert Amft is the photographer.

4 Literary Element
Alliteration

Instead of using a formal meter and rhyme scheme, Swenson uses other sound devices, especially alliteration, to create her musical tour de force. Point out the alliteration in the first line and ask students to find other examples in the poem. *(Possible responses: "bent legs bouncing/ on clouds below"; "heads with hats"; "barking on their backs"; the repeated* b*'s and* f*'s in lines 19–22; "forming the figure; folds like a fan")*

5 Literary Element
Extended Metaphor

Questions

- To what is the arched bridge compared? *(an eye)*
- How does the poet extend the basic metaphor? *(She describes the bridge/ eye as having an underlid and lens.)*

BUILDING ENGLISH PROFICIENCY

ESL LEP ELD SAE LD

Analyzing Descriptive Language

Prompt students to talk about outdoor scenes they have seen that might inspire a poem. Display this word list from the poems for students to refer to as they describe places.

Discuss the purpose of a poem students might write. Would it be to praise nature's beauty? Express fear, regret, or loss? Tell a story that has a moral? Help the class compose a series of two-line poems about the places they described. Repeat the name of the place at the beginning of each line as shown below. Encourage students to experiment with different purposes.

The mountain of Tlaxcala is a mysterious castle
The mountain of Tlaxcala guards my golden memories.

Word List	
tree	clouds
balsam	hill
spruce	branch
slope	moon
lake	petals

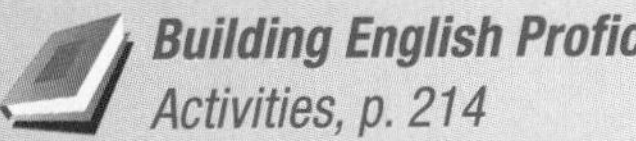

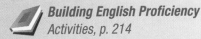

Building English Proficiency
Activities, p. 214

Art Study

Response to Caption Question
Students may be impressed by a strong sense of the lushness and brilliance of color in nature.

Hasegawa Kyüzo, who died at the age of twenty-five, executed *Cherry Blossom* under the supervision of his father, the noted painter Hasegawa Tohaku, as part of a series of sliding-door paintings for a memorial temple.

6 Literary Element
Haiku Form

Discuss with students the characteristics of the haiku form.

- Subject: A haiku distills a vivid image from nature or daily life and is set in a particular season.
- Form: A haiku traditionally has only seventeen syllables, broken into three lines of 5, 7, and 5. In English a translated haiku may have fewer syllables. Usually a haiku includes a precise shift, called a *turn*. In this haiku by Bashō, the colon marks a shift from the "close-up" of the bird to the surrounding dusk.
- Sartori: A haiku aims to capture a particular mood, a moment of enlightenment, called *satori*.

Check Test

1. In "This Is a Photograph of Me," where does the speaker say she can be found? (*under the surface of the water*)

2. What is the setting of "Water Picture"? (*a pond in the park*)

3. What causes the reflections in the pond to disappear? (*a swan "troubling" the water*)

4. What does Bashō say gives people relief from moon-viewing? (*clouds*)

5. What sound does Buson say can be heard whenever honeysuckle petals fall? (*mosquito-buzz*)

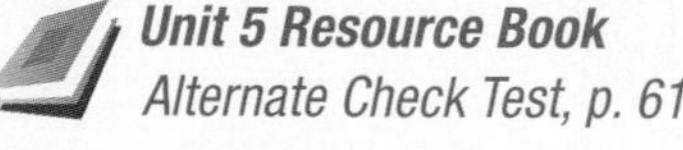

Unit 5 Resource Book
Alternate Check Test, p. 61

6 Six Haiku

▲ *Cherry Blossom*, attributed to Hasegawa Kyūzō, who lived in Japan in the 1500s, depicts a cherry tree exploding with blossoms set against glittering golden clouds. What is the main impression this painting leaves with you?

Matsuo Bashō

Spring:
A hill without a name
Veiled in morning mist.

On a bare branch
A rook[1] roosts:
Autumn dusk.

Clouds now and then
Giving men relief
From moon-viewing.

Yosa Buson

Spring rain:
In our sedan
Your soft whispers.

Mosquito-buzz
Whenever honeysuckle
Petals fall.

Sudden shower:
Grasping the grass-blades
A shoal[2] of sparrows.

1. **rook** (ru̇k), *n.* a bird that resembles the crow.
2. **shoal** (shōl), *n.* a large number.

MINI-LESSON: GRAMMAR

Avoiding Wordiness

Teach Incorporate into your discussion of the six haiku some hands-on practice in avoiding wordiness. Use this exercise as a warm-up. Copy the second stanza of "This Is a Photograph of Me" onto the chalkboard and have the class distill its images as a haiku writer might have done. For example,

Spruce branch emerging—
A small frame house halfway up
The steep, ungentle slope.

Activity Idea Distribute to the class a recent newspaper article consisting of several paragraphs. Have students edit it down by half. Then ask them to explain how they went about the task. Did they first try to shorten sentences, or did they begin by cutting out ideas?

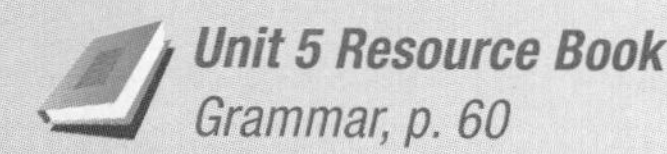

Unit 5 Resource Book
Grammar, p. 60

After Reading

Making Connections

Shaping Your Response

1. Why do you think the selections in this group are considered poems, although they lack **rhyme** and regular **rhythm**?
2. Choose a detail from one of these poems that would make an interesting photograph. Then explain whether you would "shoot" in black or white, close-up or from a distance, in sharp focus or soft focus.
3. Which poem would you want to read aloud to a younger brother or sister? Why?

Analyzing the Poems

4. From what perspective does the reader see things in "Water Picture"?
5. Explain the **image** of the swan "with twin necks forming the figure three" in Swenson's poem.
6. What causes the scene to be "troubled" in the final stanza?
7. What do you think the drowned figure might represent, or **symbolize,** in "This Is a Photograph of Me"? Refer to the end of Atwood's biography on page 613 for possible clues.
8. What season other than spring and fall is represented in these **haiku**? How can you tell?

Extending the Ideas

9. Which of these poets do you think could best describe some outdoor scenes from your neighborhood? Pick one such scene and explain how this poet might describe it.

Literary Focus: Simile

A **simile**—a comparison between two unlike things using the words *like* or *as*—adds vividness and impact to an image. Be careful not to confuse similes with metaphors, in which two things are directly compared without using *like* or *as*: "Chimneys are bent legs."

- Identify two similes in "Water Picture."
- What qualities or feelings are being compared in each simile you identified?

After Reading

MAKING CONNECTIONS

1. Students should realize that connections with the outer world and inner world are necessary to poetry. Sound devices, imagery, figures of speech, and form are poetic tools for making those connections.

2. Students should support their particular choices with precise explanation. For example, Bashō's haiku about autumn might be shot as a black-and-white close-up with a soft focus.

3. Students should support their particular choice with reasons. For example, the images in Swenson's poem would probably be more familiar and interesting to a younger child than those in Atwood's.

4. She sees things upside-down, reflected in the water.

5. The curved neck of the swan, when paired with its reflection, forms a "3."

6. When the swan dips its bill into the water, the ripples dispel the reflections.

7. The drowned figure might represent someone whose identity has been forced "beneath the surface" by oppressive circumstances in his or her life.

8. Summer: The haiku about moon-viewing is suggestive of the kind of relief people seek during summer heat. Similarly, the falling honeysuckle petals and mosquito buzz suggest early summer, and the grass blades would have to have grown sufficiently tall in order for sparrows to be able to perch among them.

9. Students might match their neighborhood—whether rural, suburban, or urban—with their impression of the poet's perspective.

ITERARY FOCUS: SIMILE

The two similes in "Water Picture" are "A flag / wags like a fishhook" and "the bridge / folds like a fan."

Possible responses: The outline of a waving flag, as reflected in the pond, is hook-shaped; the bridge, as reflected in the pond, wrinkles, or seems to fold up like delicate fan, when the swan disturbs the water.

VOCABULARY STUDY

Encourage students to be inventive. Some examples of word pictures are

- **deploy:** a peacock spreading his tail; soldiers arrayed for battle
- **distortion:** a scene or face viewed through a rain-streaked or frosted windowpane
- **shoal:** a broad bank of clouds rolling in over the horizon; a school of fish
- **waveringly:** a tightrope walker struggling to maintain his or her balance

Unit 5 Resource Book
Vocabulary, p. 59
Vocabulary Test, p. 62

WRITING CHOICES

Writer's Notebook Update

If students choose to write a haiku rather than a longer poem, encourage them to write more than one—perhaps one for each season of the year.

It's How You Look at It

To help students devise their riddles, suggest they analyze their chosen object by completing the following chart:

Object	motorcycle
Perspective	from the ground
Separate Parts	start pedal, exhaust pipe, tire treads

Selection Test

Unit 5 Resource Book
pp. 63–64

Transparency Collection
Fine Art Writing Prompt 11

Vocabulary Study

deploy
distortion
rook
shoal
waveringly

Draw a word picture to represent one of the listed words. You might capture a quality of the word or an impression the word suggests. An example has been done for *rook.*

Expressing Your Ideas

Writing Choices

Writer's Notebook Update Look at your drawing and the list of details in your notebook, as well as the items in your chart from Building Background. Let one of these activities trigger an idea for your own poem.

It's How You Look At It Both May Swenson and Margaret Atwood present things from unusual perspectives. Choose an unusual perspective of your own to describe an object in a **riddle**. To obtain a different perspective, you may want to view the object through colored glasses, in a distorted mirror, in water, or upside down. Ask a classmate to guess what you are describing.

You Too Can Haiku Haiku, a poetic form that originated in Japan, often describe nature. Some haiku consist of three lines containing seventeen syllables—five syllables in the first line, seven in the second line, and five in the third line. Others, like those on page 616, have a looser structure. Write a **haiku** describing a familiar scene from nature.

Other Options

Fantastic Folds Scenes from these poems—especially the haiku—lend themselves to **origami**, the art of paper folding. With origami paper, an instruction book, or a classmate familiar with this form of art, make a figure based on an image from these poems.

Mural, Mural on the Wall With a partner or a small group of students, create a **mural** of images from the poems in this group. You might expand on drawings from your notebooks. Post your mural on a wall or bulletin board in your classroom.

Snappy Shots With a partner choose scenes and objects in your community that you find especially picturesque or unique. Take at least ten photographic slides of these things. Make up a brief poetic caption for each slide. Then present a **slide show** to the class, reading each caption with its picture on screen.

OTHER OPTIONS

Fantastic Folds

Ask your school or local librarian to suggest books on origami that students might consult. You might also want to coordinate this activity with a member of your school's art department.

Mural, Mural on the Wall

If students choose to illustrate scenes from the haiku, suggest that they research some art books and try to imitate the style of traditional Japanese art.

Snappy Shots

Encourage students to publish their photographs in your school or community newspaper. Your school's yearbook might also be interested in using some of the more memorable images.

Reflections

The Eye and the Lens

Career Connection
A skilled photographer takes great care to compose and present images to convey particular meanings. Photographer Wade Patton has definite ideas of how he wants other people to see a building or a dog or a teepee.

No Headdresses or Horses

Wade Patton
Rapid City, South Dakota

When Wade Patton, a Native American photographer, was seven, he started taking pictures of relatives with a cheap Kodak camera and old-style flash bulbs. He bought his first real camera when he took a photography course while earning a B.A. degree in fine arts from Black Hills State University in Spearfish, South Dakota. For a year and a half after graduating, he worked as a fashion photographer. About his current work as a freelance photographer, he says, "I'm doing Native American people now. Although perhaps less glamorous than fashion photography, the photography I'm doing now is an art form."

"I start out with a general idea of what I want to do and how I want other people to see a building or a dog or a teepee. I take a picture of the object. Usually it's part of a familiar scene on the reservation. I blow it up to sixteen by twenty inches. Then I take other pictures and cut out just the parts I want and affix those to the big photograph.

"For example, the religious aspect of Native American life is dominant. It is very important. I found the steeple of a church on the reservation peering through the leaves of a tree and I took a picture and enlarged it. The steeple was shiny and silvery. I wanted to show that it was on the reservation, so I went to a powwow and took pictures, especially of men and boys dancing. The leaves and trees in front of the church were dark, but light came through them. And when I affixed the dancers on the picture of the steeple, the fringe on the dancers' clothes made them blend into the trees. It was a picture full of contrasts. You had to look hard—stare at the picture—to see the people. Being able to create a certain effect is what I find challenging about photography.

"I've done painting, but photography is more spontaneous. I try to have a deeper meaning in my work, but I have a lot of artistic energy, and I need to see the results soon. I do a lot of black and white because I think it is more real and conveys more meaning than color. There aren't so many elements to deal with. Reservation life has a contrast and starkness, which I think black and white highlights.

"My purpose in photography is to convey a point of view. I want to get away from the headdresses and the horses against the sky. I want to show real reservation life. Through montages, which combine aspects of drawing and painting with photography, I can do this. For me, photography can give the viewer an actual rendition of surroundings. A writer describes, but the reader then must imagine. Photography has more real feeling for me than words."

Responding
How do you feel about a place in school, such as the cafeteria or the gym? Brainstorm with a partner how you might photograph this place to convey your feelings. For example, what kind of light, color, and details would you choose?

Interdisciplinary Study

Theme Link

A photograph reflects life but also the photographer's intentions. Just as a poet manipulates words to createstriking images, a photographer can manipulate light and shapes to create an artistic effect.

Curricular Connection: Career

You can use the information in this interdisciplinary study to explore with students how photographers portray feelings through images.

Term to Know

montage, the art or process of making a composite picture by combining parts of different pictures

Responding

Possible Response Students should be prepared to explain how their choice of light, color, and details conveys a particular feeling about a place in school.

Unit 5 Resource Book
Study Guide p. 65

Interdisciplinary Activity Idea

Organize a trip to a photographer's studio, to an art gallery specializing in photographs, or to an art school where advanced photography is taught.

BUILDING ENGLISH PROFICIENCY

Making Personal Connections

Use one or more of the following activities to help students relate their own thoughts to those of Wade Patton.

Activity Ideas

- Ask students who enjoy taking pictures to talk about their art. Encourage them to display and explain particular photographs. Ask: How do you feel about Patton's statement that "photography has more real feeling . . . than words"?
- Point out that Patton started with simple equipment and still prefers familiar scenes. Discuss ways in which the simple and familiar have a special beauty (in art, for example, or in our choice of clothes, or in our memories).
- "My purpose in photography is to convey a point of view," Patton says. Invite students to describe how they convey their own point of view to others.

Interdisciplinary Study

Theme Link

A seasoned traveler reflects on the advantages of taking "cerebral snapshots" rather than actual photographs of his encounters around the world. After students have read the essay, ask them to summarize his main point and to explain why they agree or disagree with it.

Curricular Connection: Photography

You use the information in this interdisciplinary study to explore with students comparisons between actual photographic images and the words that describe those images.

Term to Know

lexical, having to do with vocabulary or a language's stock of words

Additional Background

A prolific novelist as well as travel writer, Paul Theroux was born in Massachusetts in 1941 and lived abroad for many years as a teacher of English in Europe, Africa, and Asia. Among his travel books are *Sailing Through China* (1984), and *The Happy Isles of Oceania: Paddling the Pacific* (1992).

INTERDISCIPLINARY STUDY

Photography Connection
The poets represented in this group offer verbal snapshots-memorable images captured in words. Following are an essay that favors the human eye over the camera lens and photographs displaying special effects achieved by a camera.

The Cerebral

by Paul Theroux

It is my good fortune that I've never owned a camera. Once, when I was in Italy, I saw about three dozen doves spill out of the eaves of an old cathedral. It was lovely, the sort of thing that makes people say if only I had a camera! I didn't have a camera with me and have spent the past two-and-a-half years trying to find the words to express that sudden deluge of white doves. This is a good exercise—especially good because I still can't express it. When I'm able to express it I'll know I've made the grade as a writer.

And recently I was driving through Kenya with a friend of mine. It was dusk, an explosion of red shot with gold, and the setting sun and the red air seemed to be pressing the acacias flat. Then we saw a giraffe! Then two, three, four—about ten of the lanky things standing still, the silhouettes of their knobby heads protruding into the red air.

I brought the car to a halt and my friend unsheathed his camera and cocked it. He snapped and snapped while I backed up. I was so busy looking at the giraffes that I zigzagged the car all over the road and finally into a shallow ditch.

The giraffes moved slowly among the trees like tired dancers. I wanted them to gallop. Once you've seen a giraffe galloping—they gallop as if they're about to come apart any second, yet somehow all their flapping limbs stay miraculously attached—you know that survival has something to do with speed, no matter how grotesque, double-bellied and gawky the beast may be.

My friend continued to fire his camera into the sunset, and pretty soon all the giraffes had either loped away or had camouflaged themselves in the trees. Both of us, rendered speechless by beauty, nodded and we continued along the road.

MINI-LESSON: VISUAL LITERACY

Express Experiences in Visual Form

Teach Paul Theroux prefers expressing his experiences through words rather than through visual forms. Indeed, his success as a popular travel writer depends on his finding "the right phrases." However, photographic images have supplemented and often been given preference over words in magazines such as *National Geographic* and *Life*.

Apply Have students reread the fourth paragraph of the essay. Ask students how they would express in purely visual terms Theroux's impression that although the giraffes' gallop is "grotesque" and "gawky" it is also a "miraculous" means of survival. *(Possible response: A film might first use slow-motion photography to capture the "flapping limbs" and then increase to real-time to demonstrate the giraffes' powerful speed.)*

Activity Idea Provide students with an opportunity to express a personal experience in visual form, such as in a painting, cartoon, photograph, or video recording. Display the student works in class.

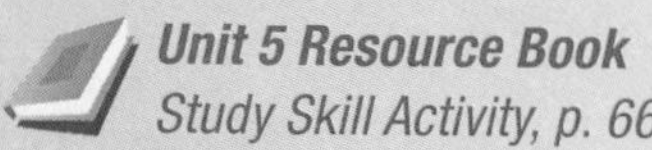

Unit 5 Resource Book
Study Skill Activity, p. 66

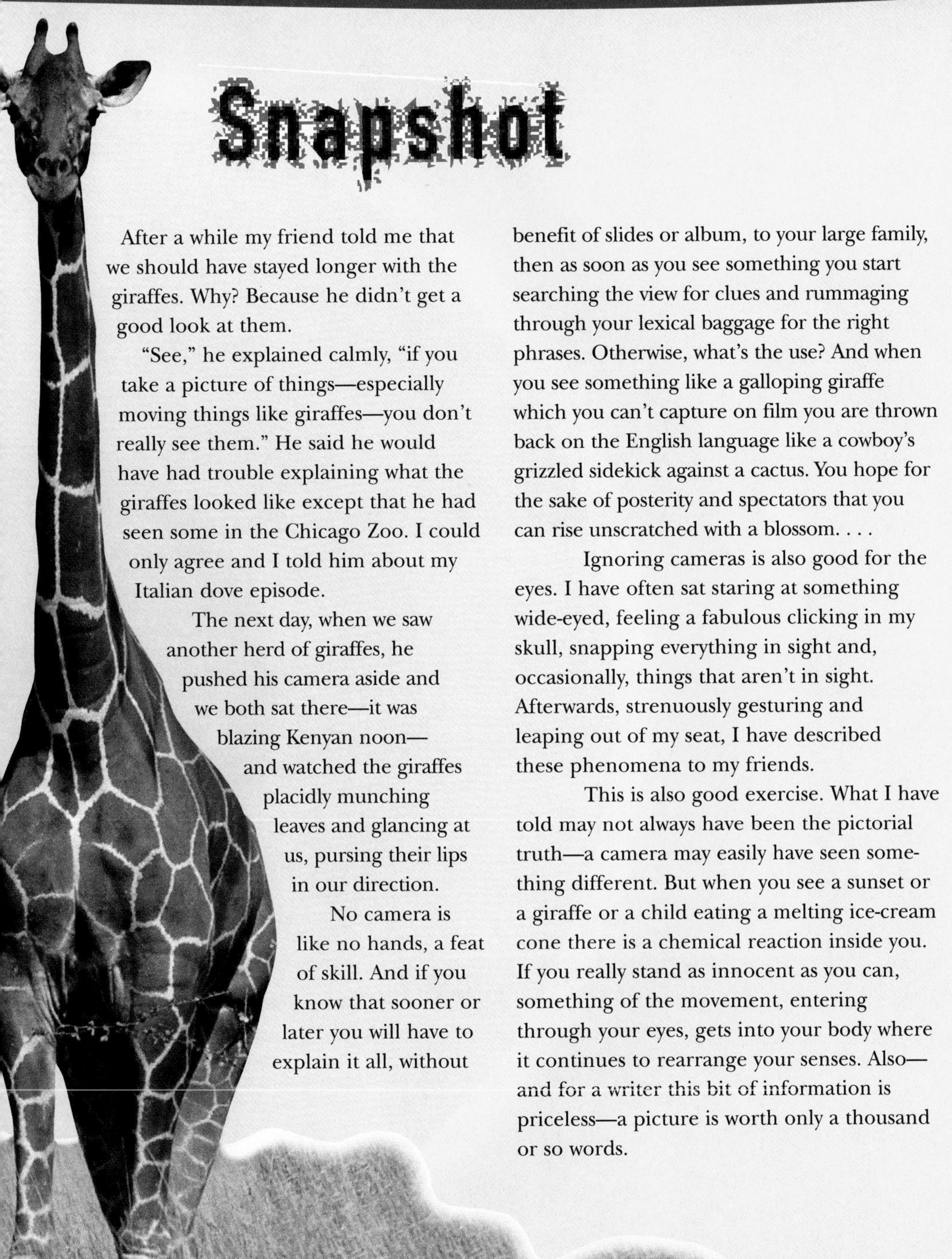

Snapshot

After a while my friend told me that we should have stayed longer with the giraffes. Why? Because he didn't get a good look at them.

"See," he explained calmly, "if you take a picture of things—especially moving things like giraffes—you don't really see them." He said he would have had trouble explaining what the giraffes looked like except that he had seen some in the Chicago Zoo. I could only agree and I told him about my Italian dove episode.

The next day, when we saw another herd of giraffes, he pushed his camera aside and we both sat there—it was blazing Kenyan noon—and watched the giraffes placidly munching leaves and glancing at us, pursing their lips in our direction.

No camera is like no hands, a feat of skill. And if you know that sooner or later you will have to explain it all, without benefit of slides or album, to your large family, then as soon as you see something you start searching the view for clues and rummaging through your lexical baggage for the right phrases. Otherwise, what's the use? And when you see something like a galloping giraffe which you can't capture on film you are thrown back on the English language like a cowboy's grizzled sidekick against a cactus. You hope for the sake of posterity and spectators that you can rise unscratched with a blossom. . . .

Ignoring cameras is also good for the eyes. I have often sat staring at something wide-eyed, feeling a fabulous clicking in my skull, snapping everything in sight and, occasionally, things that aren't in sight. Afterwards, strenuously gesturing and leaping out of my seat, I have described these phenomena to my friends.

This is also good exercise. What I have told may not always have been the pictorial truth—a camera may easily have seen something different. But when you see a sunset or a giraffe or a child eating a melting ice-cream cone there is a chemical reaction inside you. If you really stand as innocent as you can, something of the movement, entering through your eyes, gets into your body where it continues to rearrange your senses. Also—and for a writer this bit of information is priceless—a picture is worth only a thousand or so words.

Geographical Note

The East African nation of Kenya maintains several national parks and reserves for its rich array of wild animals. Many tourists visit Kenya each year to travel on safaris, in which cameras have replaced rifles.

Research Topics

- The history of photography as it relates to travel and exploration
- Travel writing as a subgenre of nonfiction
- Recent advances in photo technology
- Career opportunities for photographers

Interdisciplinary Activity Idea

Students can work in teams—consisting of both photographers and writers—to create a photo essay that captures the spirit their neighborhood, town, or city.

BUILDING ENGLISH PROFICIENCY

ESL LEP ELD SAE LD

Responding to Key Statements

Point out the statement that concludes the first paragraph—that Theroux will know that he has "made the grade as a writer" when he can capture a photographic moment in words. Invite students to complete the statement below with their own measure of success—either in writing or in another interest.

I'll know I've made the grade as a __________ when __________.

Possible responses:

writer/I can make someone feel how I felt when the event happened

skater/my mom invites a relative to my next competition

Terms to Know

magnetic resonance imaging, a diagnostic process for creating computer-generated sectional images of the body

photomicrograph, a photograph of a magnified very small object taken through a microscope

stroboscopic, produced by synchronizing short, brilliant bursts of light with multiple camera exposures of a moving object

Art Study

The images on this page are the products of various kinds of hi-tech photographic processes that are generally used by scientists to detect and study natural phenomena beyond the range of the human senses.

Question In what fields of science might these various processes be used? *(Possible responses: diagnostic medicine, physics, microbiology, microengineering, sports medicine)*

Responding

Review with students some of the kinds of "lexical baggage" that May Swenson used to convey her "verbal snapshot" in "Water Picture" on page 615.

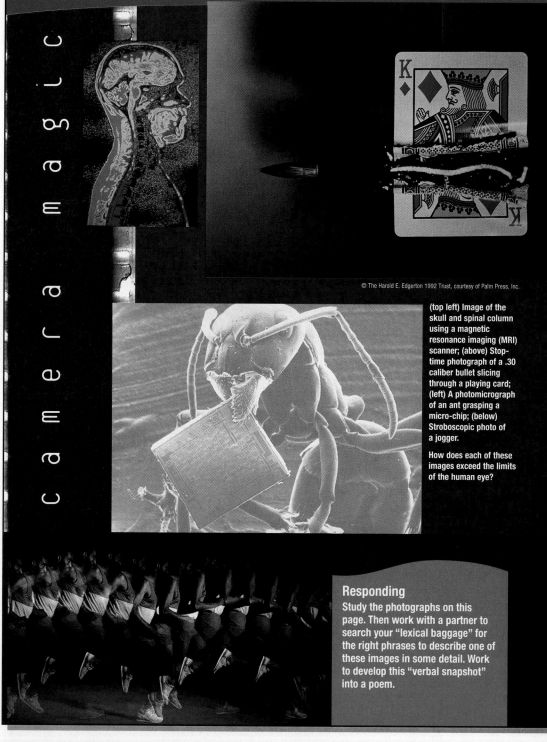

camera magic

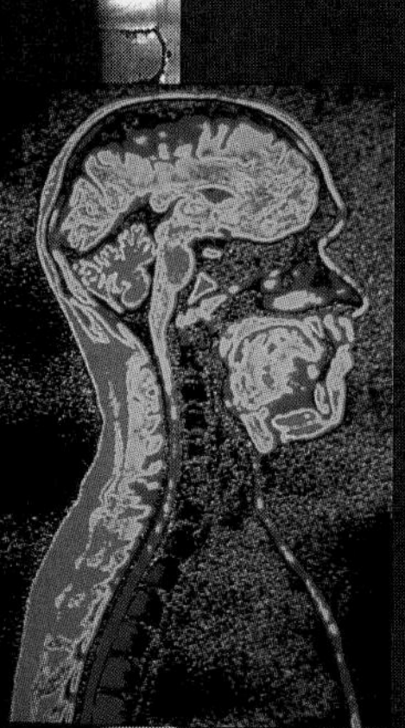

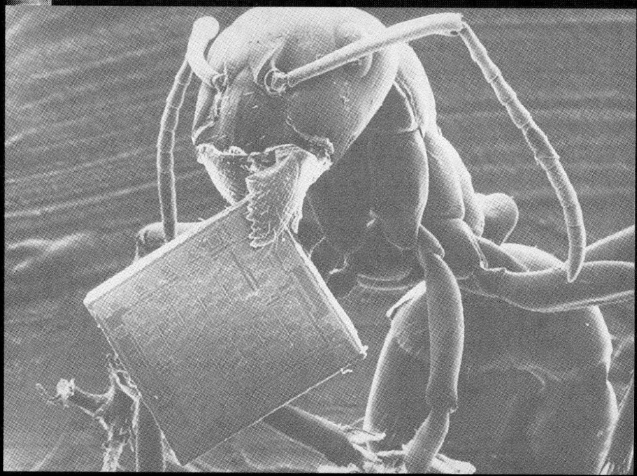

(top left) Image of the skull and spinal column using a magnetic resonance imaging (MRI) scanner; (above) Stop-time photograph of a .30 caliber bullet slicing through a playing card; (left) A photomicrograph of an ant grasping a micro-chip; (below) Stroboscopic photo of a jogger.

How does each of these images exceed the limits of the human eye?

Responding

Study the photographs on this page. Then work with a partner to search your "lexical baggage" for the right phrases to describe one of these images in some detail. Work to develop this "verbal snapshot" into a poem.

MINI-LESSON: TECHNOLOGY SKILLS

Understand Technology Terms

Teach Explain that new technology terms, such as *magnetic resonance imaging,* enter the English language every year. Make students aware that there are several ways to track down the meanings of these often baffling expressions:

- A general-audience book or article will usually define a technology term the first time it is used; in a book, consult the index to find the page where the term first appears.
- See if the book includes a glossary where the term is listed and defined.
- Consult an up-to-date unabridged dictionary or a specialized dictionary devoted the particular technology.
- If you know the term is new, try finding it in a recent encyclopedia yearbook.

Activity Idea Have students identify at least three different library reference sources that provide definitions or explanations of magnetic resonance imaging (MRI).

Reading Mini-Lesson

Compare and Contrast

Writers use comparison and contrast to show how things are alike or different. In his article, "The Cerebral Snapshot" (page 620), Paul Theroux describes an incident with a photographer in Kenya that made him aware of similarities and differences between the eyes and a camera. He makes a comparison: "I have often sat staring at something wide-eyed, feeling a fabulous clicking in my skull, snapping everything in sight and, occasionally, things that aren't in sight."

Theroux observes that eyesight combined with human perception provides the viewer a degree of insight a camera cannot provide. You could record Theroux's ideas on a comparison-contrast chart like this:

Camera	Eyesight
records images	records images
provides physical images	provides mental images
viewer relies on camera	viewer relies on own words and memories

What is being compared and contrasted in the following paragraph?

Buying a dog is a big decision. Once you're sure that you can provide adequate care, you must decide what dog is best for you. If you are on a tight budget or live in an apartment, keep in mind that large dogs, such as mastiffs and St. Bernards, require a great deal of food, space, and exercise. If you're in the market for a small dog, you might look for certain kinds of poodles, terriers, and spaniels. If size makes no difference to you, think about other considerations such as price, upkeep, temperament, and compatibility.

Activity Options

1. Make a comparison-contrast chart to record information from the paragraph on dogs.
2. Work with a group to collect the covers of different magazines. Choose two images to compare and contrast.

Reading Mini-Lesson

Teaching Objectives

- to recognize correspondences between items being compared and contrasted to improve reading and thinking skills
- to work effectively in cooperative groups

Introduce

Bring two similar products to class, such as breakfast cereals, and have students identify the aspects of the products that can be compared. List them in a chart like the following.

	Product A	Product B
Price		
Smell		
Taste		
Nutrition		
Ingredients		

Complete the chart by filling in the specific information for each aspect listed.

Follow Up

Have students work in pairs to compare two similar products that they might actually be interested in buying. Encourage them to cull information from advertisements and *Consumer Reports* to complete a chart that lists similarities and differences.

Activity Options

Activity 1 The basic comparison is between large dogs and small dogs . The chart should list the following subtopics: food, space, and exercise requirements; price; upkeep; temperament; and compatibility.

Activity 2 You might give each group of students the option of presenting their comparison-contrast in chart form, in an oral report, or as a written paragraph.

CONTENT AREA READING

Outlining

Outlining is a reading and study skill that can aid comprehension by allowing students to trace and analyze a writer's organizational strategies. This skill is especially useful in following lengthy exposition involving detailed comparisons and contrasts, as in a science or social studies textbook or in a literary analysis of two writers and their works. Outlining reveals the underlying structure of a piece of writing in a systematic way.

1. An outline usually proceeds paragraph by paragraph, noting each major idea followed by its supporting details.

Paragraph 1 main idea:
detail a:
detail b:
Paragraph 2 main idea:
detail a:
detail b:

2. Textbooks usually follow a consistent pattern of headings and subheadings that indicate the organizational breakdown of the material.

Writing Workshop

WRITER'S BLUEPRINT

Specs

The Specs in the Writer's Blueprint address these writing and thinking skills:

- visualizing
- using sensory details
- using spatial organization
- showing, not telling
- avoiding careless spelling errors

These Specs serve as your lesson objectives, and they form the basis for the **Assessment Criteria Specs** for a superior paper, which appear on the final TE page for this lesson. You might want to read through the Assessment Criteria Specs with students when you begin the lesson.

Linking Literature to Writing

Ask students to describe the most vivid pictures created by the authors in the literature.

STEP 1 PREWRITING

Examine the photographs

Have students include figurative as well as literal details.

Writing Workshop

Verbal Snapshots

Assignment The writers in this part of the unit have re-created special moments in time, freezing them in verbal snapshots. Now create your own verbal snapshot.

WRITER'S BLUEPRINT

Product	A verbal snapshot
Purpose	To re-create a memorable place through vivid description
Audience	Students in an art class
Specs	As the writer of a successful paper, you should:

- ❑ Imagine that an art teacher has asked you to prepare a verbal snapshot for her students to respond to through painting or drawing.
- ❑ Choose a place that is special for you. It could be indoors or outdoors, but it must be a place you can describe in great sensory detail. Examples: a basketball arena during a game, a place where your family took a memorable vacation, a secret hiding place you had as a child.
- ❑ Write a vivid description of this place. Guide your reader by using spatial organization.
- ❑ Show, not tell. Let the reader know why this place is memorable for you, but don't explain this directly. Let the sensory details you emphasize do the telling for you.
- ❑ Follow the rules of grammar, usage, spelling, and mechanics.

STEP 1 PREWRITING

Examine the photographs in this part as a warm-up exercise. Use the chart that follows as a guide. The example in the chart is based on the Ansel Adams photograph on page 599. Notice that the details in the second column include size, shape, location, and make-up of the items.

WRITING WORKSHOP OVERVIEW

Product
Descriptive writing: A verbal snapshot

Prewriting
Examine the photographs—Find the place—Plan your paper
Unit 5 Resource Book
Prewriting Worksheets pp. 67–68

Drafting
Before you draft—As you draft
Transparency Collection
Student Models for Writing Workshop 21, 22

Revising
Ask a partner—Strategy: Showing, Not Telling
Unit 5 Resource Book
Revising Worksheet p. 69

Editing
Ask a partner—Strategy: Avoiding Careless Spelling Errors
Unit 5 Resource Book
Grammar Worksheet p. 70
Grammar Check Test p. 71

Presenting
Art Class
Greeting Card

Looking Back
Self-evaluate—Reflect—For Your Working Portfolio
Unit 5 Resource Book
Assessment Worksheet p. 72
Transparency Collection
Fine Art Writing Prompt 11

Items	Sensory Details
mountains	tall; rising behind town; snow-covered; tall trees; majestic
buildings	steep roofs; wooden; small; part of a mining town

Find the place you want to describe. Look through family photo albums, read journal entries, take a tour of your surroundings, and talk to your family and friends to get ideas.

Plan your paper. Follow these steps.

- First, read the Beyond Print articles on visualizing (page 499) and on looking at photographs pages (628–629).
- Then draw the scene. Include as many descriptive details as possible.
- Finally, look back at your chart and drawing and make your writing plan.

Keep these ideas in mind as you make your plan:

- Take the reader on a guided tour.
- Arrange the details in spatial order, from left to right, right to left, up to down, down to up, near to far, or far to near.

OR...
Describe your scene on a tape recorder as though you were giving directions to guide your listener through unfamiliar territory.

STEP 2 DRAFTING

Before you draft, review your chart, drawing, writing plan, and any other notes. Then reread the Writer's Blueprint.

As you draft, consider these drafting tips.

- Show—don't tell—the reader why this place is memorable. (See the Revising Strategy in Step 3 of this lesson.)
- Write as though you were watching a scene in a movie, with each shot framed and edited as the camera moves from one view to the next. (See the Beyond Print article on pages 62–63.)
- Use direction words and phrases to make transitions as you move through the scene: *to the left, on the right, in front, behind, beyond, down, up, at the back, farthest, over, under,* and so on.

Find the place

Allow students time to get into groups and talk about the places that are important to them.

Plan your paper

Students might gather and organize their descriptions by creating a topic web. Encourage students to think of their papers as guided tours through the place being described. For additional support, see the worksheets referenced below.

Unit 5 Resource Book
Prewriting Worksheets pp. 67–68

Connections to
Writer's Notebook

For selection-related prompts, refer to Writer's Notebook.

Connections to
Writer's Resource

For additional writing prompts, refer to Writer's Resource.

STEP 2 DRAFTING

Before you draft

Encourage students to gather their materials before they begin to write. This will help them avoid the frustration of forgetting important pieces.

As you draft

Encourage students not to make corrections while writing the first drafts. During this time they should be creative. They can worry about correctness during the revising stage.

BUILDING ENGLISH PROFICIENCY

Being Specific

Help students practice showing instead of telling why a place is memorable by having them describe a scene of your choosing using specific verbs and describing words.

1. Present student groups with photos or postcards to write about, or show a slide to the entire class.
2. Have each group decide what atmosphere the picture suggests and which details are especially memorable.
3. Ask each group to write a few sentences that evoke the atmosphere and include the memorable details. Urge students to use active verbs, such as *peered* and *soared*, and specific adjectives, such as *elegant* and *playful.*

STEP 3 REVISING

Ask a partner (Peer assessment)

Suggest that as partners read the drafts they list the most striking images. Partners could then work together to revise the sensory details.

Revising Strategy: Showing, Not Telling

Have students look over the student model and note the changes that were made. Encourage students to discuss the impact created by the changes. For additional support, see the mini-lesson at the bottom of this page and the worksheet referenced below.

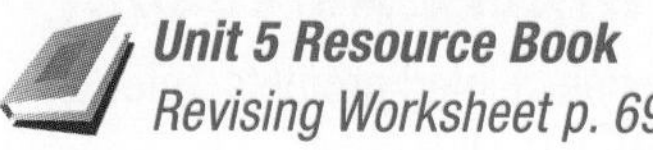

Unit 5 Resource Book
Revising Worksheet p. 69

Connections to **Writer's Resource**

Refer to the Grammar, Usage, and Mechanics Handbook on Writer's Resource.

STEP 4 EDITING

Ask a partner (Peer assessment)

Remind students that computer spell checkers do not catch all of the possible careless spelling errors.

The Student Models

The **transparencies** referenced below are authentic student models. Review them with the students before they draft. These questions will help:

1. Look at both models in terms of paragraphing. Should they be broken into more paragraphs? Why or why not?

2. Which writer did a better job of showing, not telling, why the place was memorable? How did the writer create a memorable feeling about the place?

Transparency Collection
Student Models for Writing Workshop 21, 22

STEP 3 REVISING

Ask a partner to comment on your draft before you revise it.

✔ Did I describe the place vividly with sensory details?

✔ Did I show, not tell, why this place is memorable to me?

Revising Strategy

Showing, Not Telling

Don't just tell your readers why this place is memorable. Telling is a secondhand way of doing things. Show your readers why this place is memorable to you by having them experience it the way you experienced it, in full sensory detail.

Telling The ocean waves come up to the shore near the oak tree.

Showing "That green monster of a gelatin sea / hisses white tongues of foam kneeling / to lick the shore serenading the lone / oak tree," from "Sunday Morning" by Oscar Peñaranda

Reread each paragraph to make sure that you "show" some aspect of the snapshot. If you find a paragraph that "tells" rather than "shows," revise it by rewriting from a photographer's perspective, as in the model below.

When I was twelve I went to my first football game. We arrived early on game day and had a cookout in the parking lot. Then it was time for the game. ~~When we got into the stadium it was a mess and it smelled awful. I didn't like the crowds either.~~ *Inside the stadium the floor was sticky and there was garbage everywhere. I was assaulted by the smell of cigars, and the wild crowd pushed me around like a pinball.* Luckily we soon found our seats.

STEP 4 EDITING

Ask a partner to review your revised draft before you edit. As you edit, try reading each line backwards, a word at a time, to spot careless spelling errors.

MINI-LESSON: WRITING STYLE

Showing, Not Telling

Teach Remind students that the details in their essays will enliven their memorable place. Caution them against telling things matter-of-factly. One way to create a vivid image is to answer the following questions:

What are the most important features?

What sensory details make it memorable?

What factual details are important?

What figures of speech will help the reader "see" it?

What details can I see or imagine?

Activity Have students create a word bank of sensory details. Use the following headings: Sight Words, Sound Words, Smell Words, Touch Words, Taste Words. Break the class into groups and have each group take a heading and generate words or phrases that provide sensory details. Encourage students to look in other books to find ideas.

Apply Have students reread their drafts and add more sensory details to show readers, rather than tell, about their special place.

Editing Strategy

Avoiding Careless Spelling Errors

We all make careless spelling errors—misspelling short, simple words we actually *do* know how to spell. Often, we end up writing the right letters, but in the wrong order:

Teh crowd cheered **fro** the team.

Or we write one familiar word when we mean another:

Than we moved **threw** the forest to the stream.

Or we leave out letters or add extra ones:

I didn't **rember** this place **untill** I saw an old family movie.

Because these kinds of words are so simple and so familiar, we often don't see them as we've written them. When you proofread for spelling, *look* at each word, no matter how simple or familiar.

STEP 5 PRESENTING

- Read your verbal snapshot to students in a real art class and have them draw the scene.
- Take a photograph of your memorable place and put it together with your verbal snapshot to make a greeting card to send to someone.

STEP 6 LOOKING BACK

Self-evaluate. Look back at the Writer's Blueprint and give your paper a score for each item, from 6 (superior) to 1 (inadequate).

Reflect. Think about what you have learned from writing this verbal snapshot as you write answers to these questions.

✔ How has writing this description changed the way you think of your special place?

✔ How did your writing plan work? Was it helpful? Explain what you might have done differently.

For Your Working Portfolio Add your paper and reflection responses to your working portfolio.

ASSESSMENT CRITERIA SPECS

Here are the criteria for a superior paper. A full six-level rubric for this paper appears on the *Assessment Worksheet* referenced below.

6 Superior The writer of a 6 paper impressively meets these criteria:

- Describes a scene in full sensory detail so that the reader can vividly imagine it in terms of colors, shapes, sounds, etc.
- Uses a carefully planned spatial organization to guide the reader through the scene.
- Uses sensory detail to show the reader why the scene is memorable to the writer rather than simply stating why in an explanation.
- Makes few, if any, mistakes in grammar, usage, mechanics, and spelling.

Unit 5 Resource Book
Assessment Worksheet, p. 72

Editing Strategy: Avoiding Careless Spelling Errors

Have students share mistakes they have made in their own writing. Generate a list of common mistakes to watch for. For additional support, see the worksheets referenced below.

Unit 5 Resource Book
Grammar Worksheet, p. 70
Grammar Check Test, p. 71

Connections to **Writer's Resource**

Refer to the Grammar, Usage, and Mechanics Handbook on Writer's Resource.

STEP 5 PRESENTING

Art Class

Students may tape their essays to be played for an art class.

Greeting Card

Students could easily print a box of all-occasion greeting cards using several of their papers.

STEP 6 LOOKING BACK

Self-evaluate

The *Assessment Criteria Specs* at the bottom of this page are for a superior paper. You might want to post these in the classroom. Students can then evaluate themselves based on these criteria. For a complete scoring rubric, use the *Assessment Worksheet* referenced below.

Unit 5 Resource Book
Assessment Worksheet, p. 72

Reflect

After students write about their writing plan, discuss as a class the strengths and weaknesses of using a plan for this kind of a paper as opposed to an analytical essay.

To further explore the theme, use the Fine Art Transparency referenced below.

Transparency Collection
Fine Art Writing Prompt 11

Beyond Print

Teaching Objectives

- to evaluate a photographic composition
- to respond critically to works of art

Curricular Connection: Visual Literacy

Though the questions presented in this article focus on photography, they can be adapted to give students practice in responding critically to other visual art forms as well, such as painting, sculpture, pottery and glass, and architectural design.

Introduce

Discuss the role that photography plays in modern society. Photographs document history and preserve our most cherished memories. They bring immediacy to news events and can have a profound impact on the way people shape their attitudes toward the world. When photographs aspire to art, they can define a culture or era and be as compelling as any other great work of art. Encourage students to recall some unforgettable photographic images and describe the impact that they made on them.

Beyond Print

Looking at Photographs: It's a Snap!

Looking at a photograph is much like looking at a painting or a piece of sculpture. First of all, you determine what the subject is. Then you examine details more closely and try to understand the techniques used to create the work. By this point, you are probably able to make some inferences about the photographer's purpose. Finally, you have a basis to make a judgment about this work.

Although you might think that the painter creates something from a blank canvas while a photographer can only *record* things, photographers are creators too, with a great deal of control over their subject matter. How to frame a subject? How to arrange details? What things or moods to emphasize through camera angles and techniques? How to use light and shadow? The photographer asks these and many other questions before shooting.

Here are some questions that you might ask yourself when viewing a photograph.

- What is the subject of the photograph?
- What is the photographer's vantage point? For example, the camera might be at close range, or the photograph might be an aerial shot like the one featured on the opposite page.
- Why might a photographer have chosen to shoot the image in color or in black-and-white? Do you think that the photograph on the opposite page would have been more dramatic, or less so, in color? Why?
- If a title is provided, how does it add to your understanding of the photograph?
- What do you notice about light and shadow? shapes? textures?
- Is the photographer more interested in creating a mood? portraying a person? depicting an event? capturing an emotion? something else?
- What is it about the photograph that does or does not appeal to you?

ANOTHER APPROACH

Listening to Music

Students who are visually impaired or more inclined toward music than the visual arts may prefer to work in a group and adapt the series of questions in the article to serve as a guide for exploring a serious work of music. For example, students might listen and respond critically to a recording of one of the "Four Seasons" by Antonio Vivaldi or track down a recent CD by a contemporary American composer, such as John Adams, Alvin Singleton, Michael Torke, or Ellen Taafe Zwilich. Students can them present their responses in the form of a music review.

Activity Options

1. Study this photograph by André Kertész, titled *Shadows of the Eiffel Tower,* and jot down the answers to some of the questions on the opposite page. Compare your answers to those of your classmates.
2. Apply these viewing tips to another photograph from a magazine or from this book.

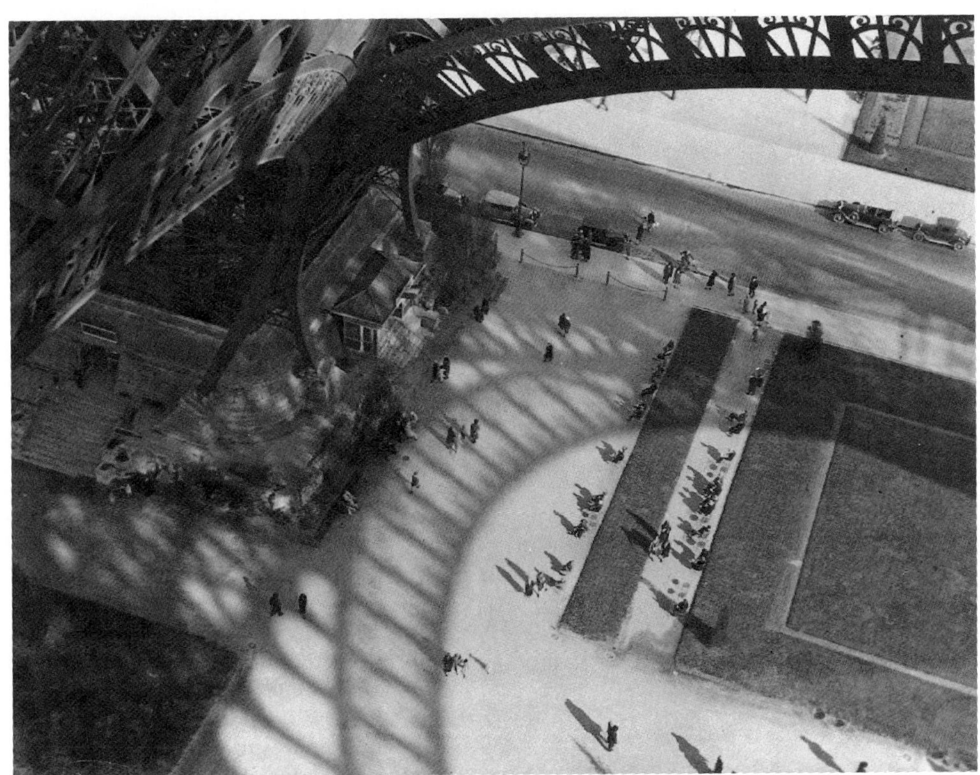

Activity Options

Activity 1 Review students' responses in class and focus on any areas of disagreement. Remind students that reactions to photographs are as subjective as reactions to other visual images.

Possible Responses to Questions on page 628:

- The subject is expressed in the title: *Shadows of the Eiffel Tower.*
- The vantage point is from above ground, from within the structure of the tower.
- Answers will vary. Students might note that the automobiles in the photograph date it to the early part of the twentieth century, before color photography was in wide use.
- The title identifies the photograph's subject.
- The shadows indicate that the photograph was taken either early or late in the day; the human figures are dwarfed by the massive arches of the tower.
- Answers will vary. The photographer seems to be concerned with capturing a monumental space made even more impressive by the light and shadows.
- Answers will vary. Students might say they are put off or intrigued by the dizzying vantage point.

Activity 2 Caution students to choose an original photograph (such as the one by Ansel Adams on page 599) and not an illustration of another work of art. You might have students present their responses in a brief essay or oral report entitled "Responding to ________."

BUILDING ENGLISH PROFICIENCY

Expanding Upon Factual Information

Use one or more of the following activities to help students grasp the information and suggestions in this feature.

Activity Ideas

- Have available a variety of newspapers and magazines, but also bring to class volumes of photographs, including works by such masters as Ansel Adams, Alfred Stieglitz, and Margaret Bourke-White. Invite students to comment on the photographs, making a distinction between photographs that merely record information and photographs that also make a statement.
- Invite students who enjoy taking photographs to bring some of their work to class. Ask them to explain what choices they made while taking each picture and why they were pleased with the result.

Preview

Culture Crossroads

FOR ALL STUDENTS

Ask students to brainstorm a list of historical examples of cultures coming face to face, such as Europeans and Asians during the Crusades, and Americans and Japanese during World War II. Talk about the results of their meetings.

To further explore the theme, use the Fine Art Transparency referred to below.

Transparency Collection
Fine Art Writing Prompt 12

For At-Risk Students

Ask students to share a time when they felt out of place. The situation might have been moving to a new neighborhood or starting a new school. Discuss how they dealt with the situation and what they'd do differently. Then have them look for connections as they read.

For Students Who Need Challenge

In 1968, author Marshall McLuhan coined the term *global village,* meaning a future civilization in which the mass media would unite and control the world with satellites, cameras, and television sets.

Question Has McLuhan's prediction materialized in the 1990s? *(Most students will probably say that satellites and cameras provide people with news as it is happening, thus shaping our perspectives of world events.*

MULTICULTURAL CONNECTION

Suggest that students begin a web of all groups to which they belong, including ethnic, racial, religious, and gender. Encourage students to expand the web as they read about interactions between cultures.

Part Three

Culture Crossroads

The world has become smaller, with cultures bumping together in amazing ways. Whether we consider such contacts collisions or opportunities for enrichment is crucial in the development of a multicultural world.

Multicultural Connection **Interactions** between people of different backgrounds require a recognition of common qualities, a respect of differences, and a willingness to arrive at understandings and compromises.

IDEAS THAT WORK

Inclusion and Exclusion

Use "Culture Crossroads" to give substance to the paradox that people develop a distinct self while all selves share much in common. Literature is where we'd like the kids to see this, but consider turning the classroom into a lab as well. Let students experience inclusion and exclusion by labeling them as members of groups. The distinctions can be arbitrary—clothing of certain color, ordinary possessions, or any common "currency" to fragment the class. Make the alienation more uncomfortable by giving certain groups preferential treatment. Now just try to keep them quiet in class or on paper after that object lesson. As an introduction or follow-up, use one of these films: *Dumbo, The Day the Earth Stood Still, Rebel Without a Cause, The Elephant Man, To Kill a Mockingbird,* or *Edward Scissorhands.*

Robert P. Slate
Greensboro, North Carolina

Before Reading

Woman from America Bessie Head South Africa

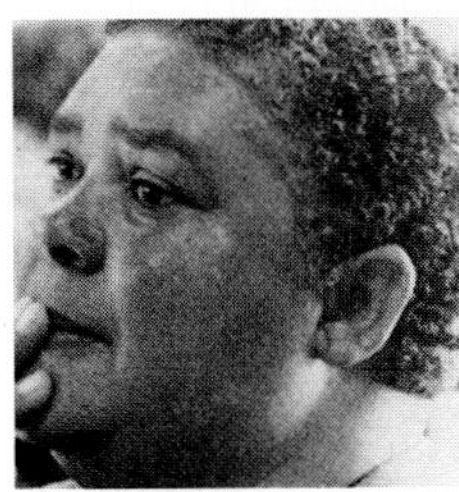

Bessie Head
1937–1986

Born of racially mixed parentage, Bessie Head was raised by foster parents. After teaching in South African primary schools, she worked as a reporter in Johannesburg and Cape Town. In an effort to flee apartheid (ə pär′tāt), she settled in Botswana, a south central African country. Ironically, she suffered discrimination as a refugee in her new land. Head writes about political and sexual oppression, exile, personal identity, and the conflict between old and new ways. Just as she was becoming recognized as a prominent literary voice, Head died of hepatitis.

Building Background

Culture Collisions Although amazing social changes have occurred recently all over the world, probably nowhere have they happened more dramatically than in Africa, with the ending of colonial rule. Villages and traditional societies have been thrust into a modern fast-paced world of technology. Since the ending of **apartheid,** South Africa's former policy of racial discrimination, in 1991, there is a new sense of power and hope, although nonwhites still face much unofficial discrimination—in education, jobs, housing, and even in social and sports activities. Given this context, the two women you are about to encounter represent two very different ways of life: the rebellious, independent newcomer versus the narrator—imbued with tribal values and fearful of authority.

Literary Focus

Setting The time and place in which a narrative occurs is called its **setting**. In this essay, Head provides information about contemporary life in a small African village. As you read, jot down details about this setting in a chart such as the one started here.

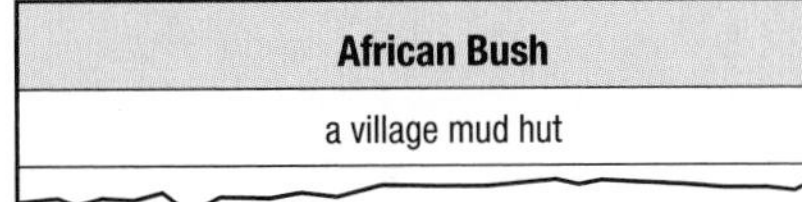

African Bush
a village mud hut

Writer's Notebook

All-American What is an American? Do Americans have certain characteristics that readily identify them? In a group, brainstorm characteristics—clothing, behavior, musical tastes, personality traits—that non-Americans might regard as particularly American. In your notebook, list these characteristics.

Before Reading

Building Background

Elicit students' understanding of racial separation. You might wish to add that apartheid was a policy under which all of South Africa's racial groups were separated from each other—black from white, black from colored, colored from Indian and black, Xhosas from Zulus, and so on. Every person was officially classified as European, Asian, Colored, or Bantu.

Literary Focus

Suggest that students pay close attention to detail, because an author will often choose to reveal the **setting** gradually through action and characterization, rather than describing it directly.

Writer's Notebook

- Encourage immigrant students to recall how they regarded Americans before they moved to the United States.
- You might ask students to brainstorm a similar list of characteristics that they attribute to Africans.

More About Bessie Head

Other works by Bessie Head include *When Rain Clouds Gather,* (1968) *and A Question of Power,* (1974).

SUPPORT MATERIALS OVERVIEW

Unit 5 Resource Book
- Graphic Organizer, p. 73
- Study Guide, p. 74
- Vocabulary, p. 75
- Grammar, p. 76
- Alternate Check Test, p. 77
- Vocabulary Test, p. 78
- Selection Test, pp. 79–80

Building English Proficiency
- Literature Summaries
- Activities, p. 215

Reading, Writing & Grammar SkillBook
- Reading, pp. 95–96
- Writing, pp. 123–125
- Grammar, Usage, and Mechanics, pp. 171–174

Technology
- Audiotape 16, Side B
- Personal Journal Software
- Custom Literature Database: For an account of a woman's travels, see *The Journal of Madam Knight* by Sarah Kemble Knight on the database.
- Test Generator Software

During Reading

Selection Objectives

- to examine the technique and function of setting
- to recognize and use singular and plural nouns
- to understand ways in which people from different countries interact

Unit 5 Resource Book
Graphic Organizer, p. 73
Study Guide, p. 74

Theme Link

When cultures cross in an African village, the results are interest and friendship.

Vocabulary Preview

cascade, fall or pour
brooding, worried
subdued, toned down
peril, danger
millet, a food grain

Students can add the words and definitions to their Writer's Notebooks.

1 Reading/Thinking Skills
Evaluate

Discuss the risks that the author would encounter if she challenged authority.

WOMAN from AMERICA

Bessie Head

This woman from America married a man of our village and left her country to come and live with him here. She descended on us like an avalanche. People are divided into two camps: those who feel a fascinated love and those who fear a new thing.

Some people keep hoping she will go away one day, but already her big strong stride has worn the pathways of the village flat. She is everywhere about because she is a woman, resolved and unshakable in herself. To make matters worse or more disturbing she comes from the west side of America, somewhere near California. I gather from her conversation that people from the West are stranger than most people.

People of the West of America must be the most oddly beautiful people in the world; at least this woman from the West is the most oddly beautiful person I have ever seen. Every cross-current of the earth seems to have stopped in her and blended into an amazing harmony. She has a big dash of Africa, a dash of Germany, some Cherokee and heaven knows what else. Her feet are big and her body is as tall and straight and strong as a mountain tree. Her neck curves up high and her thick black hair cascades[1] down her back like a wild and tormented stream. I cannot understand her eyes though, except that they are big, black, and startled like those of a wild free buck racing against the wind. Often they cloud over with a deep, intense, brooding[2] look.

It takes a great deal of courage to become friends with a woman like that. Like everyone here, I am timid and subdued.[3] Authority, everything can subdue
1 me; not because I like it that way but because authority carries the weight of an age pressing down on life. It is terrible then to associate with a person who can shout authority down. Her shouting matches with authority are the terror and sensation of the village. It has come down to this. Either the woman is unreasonable or authority is unreasonable, and everyone in his heart would like to admit that authority is unreasonable. In reality, the rule is: If authority does not like you, then you are the outcast and humanity associates with you at their peril.[4] So try always to be on the right side of authority, for the sake of peace, and please avoid the outcast. I do not say it will be like this forever. The whole world is crashing and interchanging itself and even remote bush villages in Africa are not to be left out!

It was inevitable though that this woman and I should be friends. I have an overwhelming curiosity that I cannot keep within bounds. I passed by the house for almost a month, but one cannot crash in on people. Then one day a dog they own had puppies, and my small son chased one of the puppies into the yard and I chased after him. Then one of the puppies became his and there had to be discussions about the puppy, the desert heat, and the state of the world and as a result of curiosity an avalanche of wealth has descended on my life. My small hut-house is full of short notes written in a wide sprawling hand. I have kept them all because they are a statement of human generosity and the wild carefree laugh of a woman who is as busy as women the world over about things women always entangle themselves in—a man, a home . . . Like this. . . .

"Have you an onion to spare? It's very quiet here this morning and I'm all fagged out from sweeping and cleaning

1. cascade (ka skād′), *v.* fall or pour.
2. brooding (brü′ding), *adj.* worried.
3. subdued (səb düd′), *adj.* toned down.
4. peril (per′əl), *n.* danger.

SELECTION SUMMARY

Woman from America

An African American woman arrives to set up housekeeping in an African village. The wife of a native of the village, she is assertive and independent. The villagers regard this American with admiration and fear because of her confidence and defiance of authority. At first, the narrator, a female villager, is drawn to the stranger out of curiosity, and the American enjoys talking to the village woman about housework. Eventually, thei friendship influences the narrator's views on how individuals and nations win freedom.

*For summaries in other languages, see the **Building English Proficiency** book.*

the yard, shaking blankets, cooking, fetching water, bathing children, and there's still the floor inside to sweep and dishes to wash . . . it's endless!"

Sometimes too, conversations get all tangled up and the African night creeps all about and the candles are not lit and the conversation gets more entangled, intense; and the children fall asleep on the floor dazed by it all.

She is a new kind of American or even maybe will be a new kind of African. There isn't anyone here who does not admire her. To come from a world of chicken, hamburgers, TV, escalators, and whatnot to a village mud hut and
2 a life so tough, where the most you can afford to eat is ground millet[5] and boiled meat. Sometimes you cannot afford to eat at all. Always you have to trudge miles for a bucket of water and carry it home on your head. And to do all this with loud, ringing, sprawling laughter?

Black people in America care about Africa, and she has come here on her own as an expression of that love and concern. Through her, too, one is filled with wonder for a country that breeds individuals about whom, without and within, rushes the wind of freedom. I have to make myself clear, though. She is a different person who has taken by force what America will not give black people.

The woman from America loves both Africa and America, independently. She can take what she wants from both and say, "Dammit." It is a most strenuous and difficult thing to do.

5. millet (mil′it), *n.* a food grain.

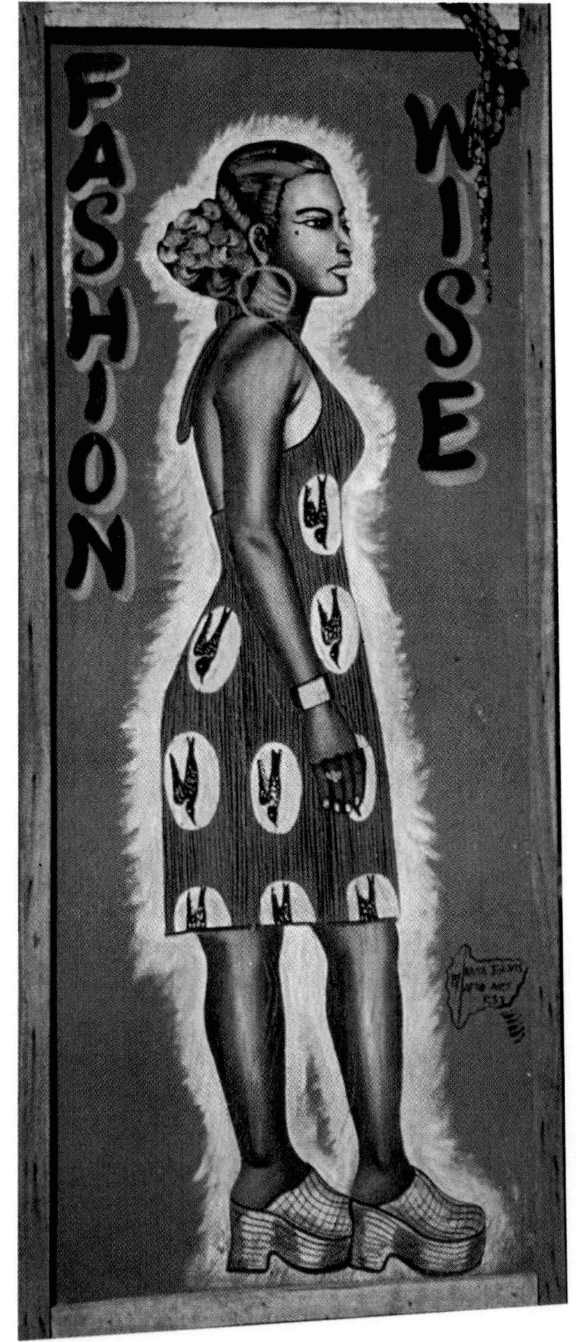

This dressmaker's sign by Nana Eln's Afro Art, photographed in Ghana in 1978, depicts clothes fashionable at the time. How is this sign alike and different from contemporary fashion ads in the United States? ➤

2 Literary Focus
Setting

Ask students to recall that setting is the time and place of a narrative. Then discuss what they believe is the author's purpose for writing "Woman from America." *(Possible responses: to describe a person of her race who is from a liberal culture; to express her views on oppression in Africa)*

Question What in this setting is essential to the story, keeping in mind the author's purpose? *(Possible responses: The description of the "tough" life and the authoritarian atmosphere are important because they contrast sharply with the American's background and actions; it is a time when Africans sense independence approaching, a good time for the author to express her views.)*

Art Study

Response to Caption Question
Students may find the medium of the hand-painted African sign less sophisticated than the glossy photographs and technical lettering of most American ads, but the content similar.

Check Test

1. Why does the American woman move to an African bush village? *(It is her husband's native home.)*

2. In which region of the United States did this American woman live? *(the West, near California)*

3. How does the narrator finally meet the American woman? *(Her son runs into the American woman's yard to play with a puppy.)*

4. How do the women get water? *(They walk miles and bring it home in a bucket.)*

5. What does the narrator feel about America? *(wonder, awe)*

Unit 5 Resource Book
Alternate Check Test, p. 77

BUILDING ENGLISH PROFICIENCY

Exploring Key Statements

The following activities can help students focus on the comment that "the whole world is crashing and interchanging itself."

Activity Ideas

- Open a discussion of whether or not they would marry a person from a different culture and move to their spouse's country.
- Let students predict what will happen to the "woman from America." Do they believe she will become a blend of two cultures, or will the unreasonable authority weaken her self-confidence?
- Some students may have loyalties both to the United States and to another country. Invite them to discuss how their own world "interchanged itself." Then they can express their individual views in writing or art.

Building English Proficiency
Activities, p. 215

After Reading

MAKING CONNECTIONS

1. Students may discuss whether or not they take for granted the freedoms the Constitution guarantees, and whether they would stand up to unreasonable authority to defend them.

2. Possible responses: Any exchange of cultural values will affect both sides. Elicit examples of changes that the characters would probably experience.

3. Possible response: The independent American and the submissive narrator cooperate for a variety of reasons—survival, curiosity, and hope for the future.

4. Possible responses: the stereotypical view of Californians as "strange" people; American women as aggressive

5. Possible response: The implications that she is "like a wild and tormented mountain stream" and "a wild free buck racing against the wind" add elements of courage and mystery to her strength and beauty.

6. Possible response: As a black American, the woman had to overcome many obstacles to achieve civil rights.

7. Possible response: The American exchanges elements of her culture with the African narrator who learns from this new perspective.

8. Students may disagree, pointing out that a person's reaction to authority would depend on the context, or that when authority oppresses the rights of those who must respect it, Head's statement applies.

9. Possible response: The United States was built on the "melting pot" philosophy, and the absence of strict immigration restrictions has encouraged diversity and freedom.

After Reading

Making Connections

Shaping Your Response

1. Do you agree with Head's observation that America ". . . breeds individuals about whom, without and within, rushes the wind of freedom"? Explain.
2. Do you think that the American will change the villagers or the villagers will change the American? Explain.
3. In what ways do the woman from America and the narrator represent **interractions** in the modern world, which "is crashing and interchanging itself"?

Analyzing the Essay

4. Do you think that there are any **stereotypes** about Americans suggested in this essay? Explain.
5. Choose a **figure of speech** in the first three paragraphs and explain how it enriches Head's portrayal of the American.
6. What do you think Head means by the following: "She is a different person who has taken by force what America will not give black people"?
7. Explain how the **interactions** in this selection illustrate the theme Culture Crossroads.

Extending the Ideas

8. Explain whether or not you agree with Head's observation, ". . . everyone in his heart would like to admit that authority is unreasonable."
9. Immigration laws and policy have been debated and revised throughout the history of the United States. Explain what restrictions, if any, you think the U.S. government should impose on immigration.

Literary Focus: Setting

Head includes a number of specific details about **setting**, the time and place in which the narrative occurs. Review details about setting in your chart. Then explain which elements you think would be difficult for an American to adjust to.

LITERARY FOCUS: SETTING

Possible responses: lack of running water; small, crude huts; lack of electronic devices; strange food; restraints on behavior

Vocabulary Study

Word analogy tests require you to understand the relationship between a pair of words and then to choose another pair with the same relationship. Analogies reflect relationships such as the following: antonyms *(impotent : powerful);* item and process *(bread : knead);* synonyms *(beg : implore).*

Number your paper from 1–5; then write the letter of the pair of words that best completes the analogy.

brooding
cascade
millet
peril
subdued

1. CASCADE : FALL :: **a.** attack : assault **b.** run : trickle **c.** remember : forget **d.** lift : drop
2. MILLET : GRIND :: **a.** carrot : orange **b.** potato : mash **c.** butter : margarine **d.** cabbage : coleslaw
3. BROODING : WORRYING :: **a.** wondering : forgetting **b.** annoying : irritating **c.** celebrating : anniversary **d.** ignoring : abusing
4. SUBDUED : EXCITED :: **a.** abused : ignored **b.** satisfied : pleased **c.** designed : colored **d.** steady : nervous
5. PERIL : SAFETY :: **a.** accident : misfortune **b.** weakness : strength **c.** adult : grown-up **d.** pour : pitcher

Expressing Your Ideas

Writing Choices

Writer's Notebook Update Reread your list of characteristics associated with Americans. In your notebook, identify why Americans are associated with these qualities. If you consider any of these characteristics stereotypical, briefly explain why they do not represent most Americans and how you think the stereotypes came about.

Go Home, Yankee! The villagers are not pleased with the new American resident. On their behalf, write a **letter of complaint** to an official in the capital about her.

The African Queen Delighted to have a friend in the village, the American writes an enthusiastic **character sketch** of the narrator in her journal. What do you think she would say?

Other Options

Musical Interlude Find recordings of African music—by Ladysmith Black Mambazo, Miriam Makeba, or another South African folk singer or group. Present a class **concert**, explaining the kinds of instruments used and/or the messages the songs contain.

Read A-Head Read one of Bessie Head's books, such as her collected essays, sketches, and stories in two books titled *Tales of Tenderness and Power* and *A Women Alone;* her collection of interviews and stories titled *Scrowe: Village of the Rain Wind;* or her short story collection titled *The Collector of Treasures.* Give the class an **oral critique** of the book.

VOCABULARY STUDY

1. a
2. b
3. b
4. d
5. b

Unit 5 Resource Book
Vocabulary, p. 75
Vocabulary Test, p. 78

WRITING CHOICES

Writer's Notebook Update

Encourage immigrant students to compare their previous impressions of Americans to what they have actually experienced.

Go Home, Yankee!

Suggest that students research the historical experiences of the South African bush tribes to better understand their fear of change.

The African Queen

Suggest that students use a t-chart to list characteristics of the two women. Remind them to write from the point of view of the American as she is described in the story.

Woman from America	Narrator
strong	curious

Selection Test

Unit 5 Resource Book
pp. 79–80

OTHER OPTIONS

Musical Interlude

If access to international recording collections is limited, encourage students to research African folk instruments and musical traditions at a center for the arts or local library.

- Encourage students to write their own folk songs about the events described in Head's essay, either applying their lyrics to a familiar melody or creating a melody of their own.

Before Reading

Building Background

- Suggest that students reflect on expectations other family members have for them. Volunteers may wish to share how such expectations are expressed—in specific terms about schooling and career or in general terms.
- Ask students if they have seen movies or plays that depict the effects of the Vietnam War on the lives of the Vietnamese people, such as *Miss Saigon.*

Literary Focus

Remind students that **conflict,** or problem, is an essential part of the plot. It leads to a climax or point at which the conflict must be resolved.

Writer's Notebook

Suggest that students use their favorite way of "getting into" a subject. They might brainstorm a list of high emotions, such as fright, anger, or resentment. After they focus on a situation, they can jot down "snapshot" details from their memory.

Before Reading

Rain Music Longhang Nguyen USA

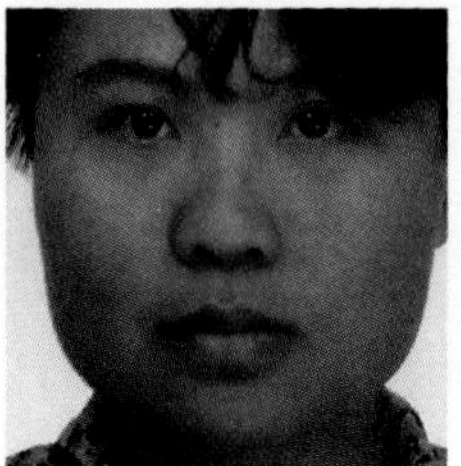

Longhang Nguyen
born 1970

Longhang Nguyen (long häng we′ən) emigrated from Vietnam to the United States in 1979. For two years her father looked after her brother and her while he attended school to reobtain his veterinary license. At the end of this time, his wife rejoined the family. Today, Nguyen lives in San Francisco where she is studying medicine. Nguyen says that "Rain Music," which you are about to read, illustrates that "love is a complex of emotions. There aren't straightforward or universal answers to its questions."

Building Background

Vietnam Until the past century, Vietnam was an agricultural society built on tradition and strong family ties, with extended families living in rural areas. In the past century, however, especially since the Vietnam War of the '60s and '70s, families were broken up by military duties and death, many people fled to cities, close family ties were severed, and people learned Western customs. Since the end of the Vietnam War (U.S. ground troops left in 1973 and South Vietnam surrendered to North Vietnam in 1975), over a million people have left the country, with the largest number moving to the U.S. Among these immigrants were Longhang Nguyen and her family. Her story, "Rain Music," will have special significance if you remember that according to Vietnamese tradition, parents choose their children's marriage partners.

Literary Focus

Conflict When cultures clash, **conflict** results. As you read "Rain Music," note both the internal conflicts within Linh and the external conflicts that involve society.

Writer's Notebook

Head Over Heart Young people are sometimes accused of acting impulsively, according to emotion rather than reason. In your notebook, record key impressions about an instance when you acted reasonably in an emotional situation.

SUPPORT MATERIALS OVERVIEW

Unit 5 Resource Book
- Graphic Organizer, p. 81
- Study Guide, p. 82
- Vocabulary, p. 83
- Grammar, p. 84
- Alternate Check Test, p. 85
- Vocabulary Test, p. 86
- Selection Test, pp. 87–88

Building English Proficiency
- Literature Summaries
- Activities, p. 216

Reading, Writing & Grammar SkillBook
- Reading, pp. 89–90
- Grammar, Usage, and Mechanics, pp. 269–272

The World of Work
- Immigration Worker, p. 23
- Flier, p. 24

Technology
- Audiotape 17, Side A
- Personal Journal Software
- Custom Literature Database: For a relate account, see "An Immigrant Goes to Scho from *The Promised Land* by Mary Antin o the database.
- Test Generator Software

Rain Music

Longhang Nguyen

Linh and I grew up penned in the same yard, so our sibling rivalry did not last very long. By third grade we had stopped physically assaulting one another and reached a permanent truce. At that time her hair was long and flowing, brushed daily by my mother as Linh closed her eyes and counted each stroke. It always felt like cool satin when I yanked it, her head jerking backward, mimicking[1] the motion of my arm. In actuality, she was very kind and I was not too violent, so we became intimate friends. I have not had any trouble from her since. 1

She is the red rose of the family and I am the green thorn. We have both decided that we are beautiful, so she tells me, but I believe she is also very beautiful outside in face and gesture. I always pout when I accuse her of being a selfish firstborn, picking, stealing the best of our parents' genes and leaving me the rejected remainder. She has wide, almond-shaped eyes like black, pearl-black reflecting pools with brown-colored flecks swirling beneath the surface, light honey-color skin and even, velvet-smooth cheeks. Her nose is just slightly upturned, her lips rosebud shaped, her chin small and delicate. Her hair still looks and feels the same now as in third grade. The vision, taken together as a whole, is breathtaking. There is something about it, a wistful,[2] dandelion, orchidlike kind of beauty that feels like notes in a chord being played separately, finger by finger, harmonizing back and forth. I marvel even now.

My mother and father have polished her until she shines. She graduated summa cum laude[3] from the College of Chemistry at Cal and double majored in Ethnic Studies. However, my parents don't count the latter. She is now a fourth-year student at UCSF[4] preparing to enter the surgical residency program next

1. mimic (mim′ik), *adj.* make fun of by imitating.
2. wistful (wist′fəl), *adj.* longing; yearning.
3. **summa cum laude** (süm′ə küm lou′də), with highest honors.
4. **UCSF,** University of California at San Francisco.

During Reading

Selection Objectives

- to recognize and examine the literary function of conflict
- to practice using quotation marks with dialogue
- to examine how a decision about whom to marry is one type of cultural crossroads

Unit 5 Resource Book
Graphic Organizer, p. 81
Study Guide, p. 82

Theme Link

A young Vietnamese American woman halts at a painful cultural crossroads to consider her next step. Should she marry a man of Vietnamese heritage or continue her involvement with an African American man?

Vocabulary Preview

mimic, make fun of by imitating
wistful, longing, yearning
preoccupation, thing that absorbs or engrosses
minutely, in small way or detailed manner
pigment, natural substance that colors skin tissue

Students can add the words and definitions to their Writer's Notebooks.

1 Reader's Response
Making Personal Connections

Open a discussion of sibling rivalry. Students can debate whether it is possible to reach a "permanent truce" or if war must break out periodically.

SELECTION SUMMARY

Rain Music

Linh, the narrator's older sister, is a beautiful and accomplished medical student who has always conscientiously met her parents' high expectations. She expects to marry a Vietnamese man who is the ideal husband, according to her family. However, she has met David, an African American writer who touches her heart with his creativity, sensitivity, and intelligence. When David kisses her, Linh is anguished, saying that the accidents of birth, such as race and heritage, will prevent them from ever having a future together. She and the narrator discuss the dilemma over a picnic in the park. Linh resolves to follow the path she had been following and marry Thanh, rather than let her feelings for David lead her into a racially mixed, financially insecure relationship. As the sisters leave the park, it begins to rain.

*For summaries in other languages, see the **Building English Proficiency** book.*

2 Reading/Thinking Skills
Recognize Values

Question What would you say are the three things Linh's parents value most? *(Possible responses: their daughter's success, maintaining their cultural heritage, Linh's happiness, their reputation in their community)*

After students have read the story, challenge them to agree on three things that Linh values most and rate them in order of importance, giving reasons for the ratings.

3 Literary Element
Point of View

Questions

- From which point of view is this story told? *(first-person point of view)*
- What is the narrator's attitude toward Linh and how does the attitude affect the reader? *(Her attitude is love and admiration based on intimate friendship; because of the narrator's attitude, the reader is sympathetic to Linh.)*

fall. My parents are bursting at the seams, gorged with devouring so much blessedness and good fortune.

2 "Will your daughter become a surgeon?" our relatives ask.

"It's possible," my father says, beaming.

"She is friends with this young man in her class. He's tall, distinguished-looking, loyal and respectful to his parents, hard-working but generous. He was even born in Vietnam! But he came over here with his family in 1975. He went to Harvard"—my mother pauses to let the relatives gasp in unison—"on a full scholarship!" she smiles modestly, then lowers her eyes.

"A possible son-in-law?" they ask.

She shrugs and sighs. "That is up to God."

Linh hasn't told my parents about David. She met him five years ago during her final year at Cal. That semester they were in three classes together: a choral class, an Afro-American literature class, and a creative writing class. They became good friends.

David is a writer. His subjects are ordinary preoccupations[5] of other writers: his mother, the father he has never seen or known, the friends of his childhood. Some of them are dead now. The others are spread out across the country. One is a construction worker in St. Louis. Another is a teacher in Baton Rouge. The third is a journalist in Washington, D.C. They write to him once in a while or call him. Linh hasn't met any of them, but she knows them all.

After David feverishly completes a story, Linh cooks him dinner. Afterward, she tucks him into bed and sits nearby in the wicker chair, legs drawn up and hugged tightly to her chest, to watch him while he sleeps. His soft, black curls rest against the white of the pillow, his closed eyelids and long lashes flutter minutely[6] while he dreams, his breath whistles through the evenness of his teeth as the cover grazes the dark honey of his skin.

They always have a good time together, and he makes her laugh in many different ways, wherever they happen to be. He always gets close to finishing her off during a tennis set, but then she cries out that he has cheated and treated her unfairly and he has to start over again. He never wins. Sometimes they sing together, his clear resonant tenor melding with her flutelike, crystalline soprano. Then they have tea.

3 I know all about David. She won't stop talking about him, but I know less about Thanh, the Vietnamese friend at UCSF. I know he's nice but that's all. She woke me up this morning at ten thirty and said, "It's a bright, beautiful, Saturday morning. Let's go and have a picnic."

"No, no," I mumbled hazily in my sleep. "Take David. Leave me alone."

"I don't want to take David. I want to spend quality time with you, my darling sister. Get up, you piece of mutton. Toast on the table in five minutes and we're leaving in half an hour."

"Oh, lord," I groaned, "I'm being punished for sins from past lives."

We arrived at the park at twelve, lugged our ample picnic hamper heavily laden with cheese, fruits, sandwiches, ice, and bottles of juice from the car, and trudged into the heart of the lightly shaded, green forest. When I opened the basket and took out the butter, she started to talk.

"David kissed me last night. . . ."

"He what?"

". . . or I kissed him. It just happened. I guess. He invited me to dinner, promised to cook a sumptuous Cajun[7] feast with Vietnamese

5. **preoccupation** (prē ok′yə pā′shən), *n.* thing that absorbs or engrosses.
6. **minutely** (mī nüt′lē), *adv.* in a small way or a detailed manner.
7. **Cajun** (kā′jən), descending from the French who came to Louisiana from Acadia in Canada.

Although Diana Ong's style is informal and her figures roughly sketched in *School Days,* she communicates precise impressions. Choose three words about school you think are suggested in this picture. What similarities and differences do you find between this and another Ong picture that appears on page 582? ➤

MINI-LESSON: GRAMMAR
Using Quotation Marks with Dialogue

Teach Have students study the quotation marks in the following paragraph. Explain that when a quotation appears within a quotation, it is enclosed within single quotation marks.

"'Rain music,' he said. 'It's for you.' After the last note on the piano had stopped to echo, he turned toward me and kissed me . . . I was raging inside, screaming in my head, 'Why can't his fingers be brown like mine, be my brown? Why is his hair curly, not straight like mine?'. . . How do I stand there and tell this man . . . that I can't be who he wants me to be?"

Activity Idea Have students use quotations within a quotation by creating dialogue based on one of the following situations:

- Linh tells her sister what Thanh said on a recent date.
- David and the sister meet at a restaurant; he tells her that Linh has told him she will not see him again.
- Thanh and Linh meet; Linh tells him about David and what she said at the picnic with her sister.

You may wish to have students work in pairs.

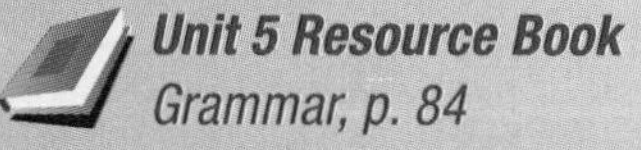

Unit 5 Resource Book
Grammar, p. 84

Responses to Caption Question Students may mention *friends, groups, color;* similarity: use of similar hues; difference: the figures which have no facial features here, as they do on page 582.

More About Diana Ong Born in New York City in 1940, Diana Ong is a Chinese American artist who experiments with mixed media. She is proficient in watercolor, acrylic, woodcut, silkscreen, etching, computer art, and ceramic art.

Visual Literacy To convey motion, an artist might use distortion of the figures and contrast of color, tone, light, and shade.

Questions Is there a feeling of motion and activity in *School Days?* What gives you this feeling? *(Possible responses: a mass of lines, especially the zigzags; distorted figures that focus on action, not personalities)*

The World of Work

Immigration Worker

For more cross-cultural experiences from the view of an immigration worker, use—

The World of Work
pp. 23–24

BUILDING ENGLISH PROFICIENCY

ESL LEP ELD SAE LD

Comparing Characters

Much of the conflict in "Rain Music" arises from the differences between the two young men in whom Linh is interested. Help students explore those differences.

1. Work with students to create a t-chart that compares Thanh and David. Have students note factual information about each man as well as their impressions of these characters.

2. Students can use their charts as they discuss the story and consider the Making Connections questions on page 641.

Thanh	David
Vietnamese	African American
medical student	aspiring writer
lives up to values of his culture	cultural values not be important

Building English Proficiency
Activities, p. 216

4 Literary Focus
Conflict

Question Linh states her inner conflict through these questions. How would you state the conflict? *(Possible response: Linh wants to love David for himself, but she feels that she could not accept him as a husband.)*

Literary Element
Mood

Point out the use of natural imagery to reinforce the mood created by dialogue.

- "The leaves rustled softly while I waited" suggests a mood of gentle, patient concern.
- "Her eyes gazing steadily at the flashing water of the stream below" captures both Linh's steady determination and the intensity of her emotions.

Multicultural Note
Karma

According to Buddhism, widely practiced in Vietnam and other Asian countries, the power that determines one's destiny within the cycle of reincarnation is *karma,* which varies according to one's purity or corruption during previous lives.

Check Test

1. What is the relationship between the narrator and the main character, Linh? *(They are sisters.)*
2. What is Linh studying to be *(a doctor)*
3. From what country did her family immigrate to the United States? *(Vietnam)*
4. Who is David?*(a close friend of Linh's from college)*
5. Who is Thanh? *(the Vietnamese man that Linh will marry)*

Unit 5 Resource Book
Alternate Check Test, p. 85

desserts. *Bánh flanc,*[8] you know. My favorite." She plucked a blade of grass from its roots and twisted it back and forth, watching a streak of feeble, yellow sun play on its linear edges. "I expected it to be a celebration. He'd just finished his first novel, not quite a love story, he says, and he wanted me to read it." She spoke more softly. "When I arrived, he had set tiny blossoms in water dishes throughout the apartment. It smelled wonderful. The food was delicious, everything so lovely, so tranquil I didn't know where to begin. After dinner he led me into the living room.

"'Rain music,' he said. 'It's for you.' After the last note on the piano had stopped to echo, he turned toward me and kissed me for a long, long time. I didn't know what I was doing. I just couldn't stop. I didn't breathe. When he let me go, I kept thinking of his hands and fingers, seeing them fly over the ivory keys like little Russian men dancing in their black fur hats and noticing how his brown was different from mine. I was raging inside, screaming in my head, 'Why can't his fingers be brown like mine, be my brown? Why is his hair curly, not straight like mine?' I saw brown pigments[9] run across my eyes, all different colored browns. Those pigments keep us apart. How do I stand there and tell this man who writes me music and whose hands burn my cheeks that I can't be who he wants me to be?"

"But he doesn't want to change you."

"No, I can't be who he thinks I am. He's a starving writer. He can't give me anything, just himself. And he doesn't even know that I'm using him. He doesn't even know." She choked on her tears, swallowed, and cried quietly, hugging her knees, until exhausted. The leaves rustled softly while I waited.

After a while she grew calm, her eyes gazing steadily at the flashing water of the stream below. "I love Thanh. I would never hurt him for anything. Throughout the four years at UCSF, he has been so patient, so kind, so dedicated to medicine for its own good, not for just its technology, even though he's brilliant and understands these details completely. He's so perfect for me, just perfect. It's like he stepped out of my story and came to life. We speak the same language and share the same past. Everything. And Mom and Dad, they've done so much for us. Now they think they've won the lottery from God for being good all their life."

"But how do you feel about Thanh? How does he make you feel?"

"He will be my lifelong friend. He'll make a wonderful father. That's what a husband should be. Our children will know the culture and customs of our homeland. They'll speak Vietnamese and English, just like us."

"And how does David make you feel?" I tugged at her gently.

She bowed her head for a long while reflecting. Then she softly murmured, "It's just not possible."

"But why? I don't understand."

The picnic basket remained quite full. Neither of us was hungry. It threatened to rain as we packed up to go home. On the drive back, we were silent. I watched the windshield wipers swing back and forth, clearing rain cascading down the front window.

8. ***bánh flanc,*** a sweet egg and milk dessert.
9. **pigment** (pig′mənt), *n.* natural substance that colors skin tissue.

MINI-LESSON: VOCABULARY
Recognize Idioms

Teach Idioms are phrases or expressions, such as "put your foot down," that cannot be understood from the ordinary meanings of the words that form them. They are called *idioms.* Idioms are listed under the most important word in the *ScottForesman Thorndike Barnhardt Dictionary.* For several idioms using a common word, have students look up *foot.* Then have them analyze the following sentence:

He always gets close to finishing her off during a tennis set, but then she cries out that he has cheated and treated her unfairly and he has to start over again.

Question Identify the idiom in the above sentence. *(finishing her off)*

Activity Ideas

- Have students substitute synonyms for the idiom as used in this context. *(Possible responses: beating her, winning)*
- Repeat the exercise. For a list of idioms, see *catch* and *part* in the dictionary.

After Reading

Making Connections

Shaping Your Response

1. Whom do you think Linh should marry? Explain.
2. If you had a friend in Linh's predicament, what would you say to her?
3. To what degree, if any, do you think parents should be able to determine their child's choice of a marriage partner?

Analyzing the Story

4. Although Linh says that "pigments" prevent her from marrying David, what other cultural factors influence her choice of a husband?
5. The narrator says of Linh, "My mother and father have polished her until she shines." What does this **figurative language** reveal about their treatment of her?
6. If Linh is the **protagonist** of this story, who or what do you think is the **antagonist**?
7. What do you think the rain of the title and of the last paragraph represents, or **symbolizes**?

Extending the Ideas

8. Does this story reinforce any **stereotypes** about Asians? about African Americans? Explain.
9. If you were choosing a husband or wife, what are the five most important characteristics you would look for?

Literary Focus: Conflict

Answer the following questions about the various **conflicts** in "Rain Music."

- What evidence can you find that David, too, may have experienced conflicts?
- What external conflicts is Linh trying to avoid?
- What conflict is implied by the observation regarding Linh's double major of Chemistry and Ethnic Studies that her parents "don't count the latter"?

After Reading

MAKING CONNECTIONS

1. Possible response: Linh feels so strongly about her heritage that she is making the right decision; her repression of her feelings may cause her difficulties later in her marriage to Thanh.

2. Possible response: Talk to Thanh to discover if he has similar conflicts; talk about your true feelings to David to discover if he can understand your true nature.

3. Possible responses: Parents should not interfere in this decision especially if the children are old enough to make the decision; everyone should seek their parents' advice, but the ones who are marrying have to make it work.

4. Possible responses: language, education, career choices, family expectations

5. Possible response: They treat her like a valuable object meant for display.

6. Possible response: the cultural ties that keep her from following her heart

7. Possible response: Rain is like Linh's natural feelings that are connected to David, symbolized in the music he composed for her; at the end, it is swept away so Linh sees her future clearly, but without David.

8. Possible response: It reinforces the stereotype that Asians are technologically oriented, and that African Americans are poor and often come from broken homes.

9. Answers will vary but should convey thoughtfulness, foresight, and some references to "Rain Music."

ITERARY FOCUS: CONFLICT

ssible responses

- He never knew his father; some of his friends have died; his other friends have moved away.
- a conflict with her parents and with her cultural community
- A conflict in values: Linh values Ethnic Studies because it helps her understand her own experiences, but her parents don't value it because it generally does not lead to a prestigious career with a high salary.

VOCABULARY STUDY

1. mimic
2. pigment
3. wistful
4. minutely
5. preoccupation

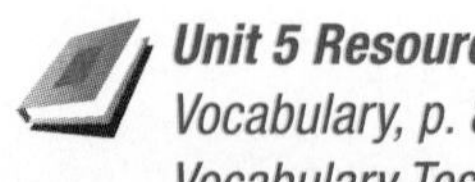

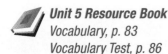

Unit 5 Resource Book
Vocabulary, p. 83
Vocabulary Test, p. 86

WRITER'S CHOICES

Writer's Notebook Update

Suggest that students identify the conflict, the climax, and the resolution to the emotional situation that they choose to describe.

Box Office Smash

Encourage students to analyze the endings of classic works that contain similar plot elements; such as "Cinderella," *West Side Story,* and *Romeo and Juliet.*

Sisters

Encourage more advanced students to write their fables in verse form. For ideas, they might refer to one of Aesop's fables, such as "The Fox and the Woodcutter" on page 287.

Selection Test

Unit 5 Resource Book
pp. 87–88

Vocabulary Study

Use context clues to help you choose the word that best completes each sentence.

mimic
minutely
pigment
preoccupation
wistful

1. Like many younger sisters, the narrator fears she cannot copy, or ____, Linh's success.
2. Linh says that ____ is what keeps her and David apart, but their differences go beyond skin color.
3. The narrator feels ____ as she yearns to be like her beautiful, talented sister.
4. Linh examines David's face ____, noting every detail as he sleeps.
5. Linh's ____ with her Vietnamese heritage will absorb her the rest of her life.

Expressing Your Ideas

Writing Choices

Writer's Notebook Update Review your impressions about a time you acted reasonably in an emotional situation. Write a paragraph explaining the situation, your response, and your feelings about it now.

Box Office Smash Imagine the story were continued. Briefly describe two possible **extended endings**. Then explain which ending you think would be more popular at the box office if the story were made into a movie.

Sisters Linh wants you, her sister, to help her decide what to do about her dilemma. Instead of giving direct advice, put your thoughts into the form of a **fable**. Like those in traditional fables, the characters should be animals; the ending should contain a moral.

Other Options

TV Newcomer It is your job to write **promotional material** for "Rain Music," which has been expanded into a weekly TV program. Name the show, design an identifying logo, and write a paragraph that captures highlights and entices prospective viewers.

Speaking Up Conduct an **interview** of someone who has emigrated from Vietnam to the U.S. since the 1970s. Beforehand, work with a group to write questions, including those about traditions, values, and family. Alternatively, you may want to invite a Vietnamese immigrant to come and speak to the class.

Your Own Rain Music With a partner, brainstorm appropriate **background music** for this story. You might consider something already on disk or CD, or you may want to write and perform your own composition. Bring this music to class and play it as background while selected passages are read aloud.

OTHER OPTIONS

TV Newcomer

Suggest that students imitate the promotional writing style and ad copy designs found in program listings for local newspapers and national magazines like *TV Guide.*

Speaking Up

Suggest that students do background research on the geography and cultural customs of Vietnam, as well as immigration and resettlement experiences common to Vietnamese Americans.

Your Own Rain Music

Students can consider the sound of rain, the emotional responses that the sound of rain inspires, and other sounds that remind them of rain.

Before Reading

My Father Writes to My Mother Assia Djebar Algeria

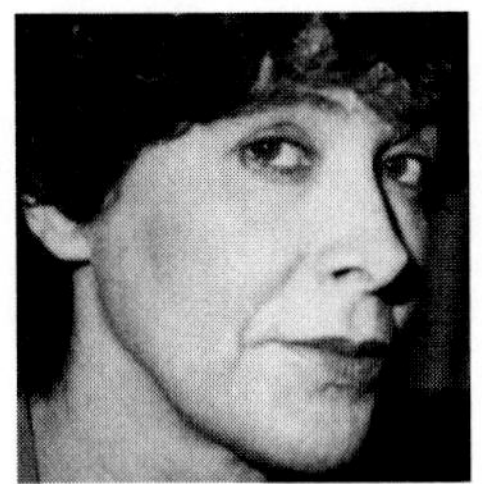

Assia Djebar
born 1936

Assia Djebar (ä sē′ə jə bär′) is both a writer and a noted film maker who uses film to reach those who cannot read, especially Islamic women, who are frequently given little or no formal education. When in her twenties, she won acclaim for her first four novels, the first of which, *The Mischief,* she wrote during the 1956 student uprising in France. Six years later, she published *Children of the New World,* an account of the Algerian war of independence from France. Her feminist leanings, along with her eloquent pleas for equality and empathy, distinguish her works. Drawing on the cultures of France and Algeria, she presents to westerners the dilemmas many Muslim women face in trying to emerge from "behind the veil."

Building Background

Words from the Koran Many Muslim customs are derived from teachings of the **Koran**, Islam's book of revelations. Below are quotations from two of its chapters, or *suras.* Think about how these standards of behavior would affect relationships between husbands and wives.

> Men have authority over women because God has made the one superior to the other, and because they spend their wealth to maintain them. Good women are obedient. ("Women")
>
> Enjoin believing women to turn their eyes away from temptation and to preserve their chastity; to cover their adornments (except such as are normally displayed); to draw their veils over their bosoms and not to reveal their finery. . . . And let them not stamp their feet when walking so as to reveal their hidden trinkets. ("Light")

Literary Focus

Character The English novelist E. M. Forster classified fictional characters as either *static* (unchanged by events) or *active* (affected by events). Using this definition, make a chart such as the one below listing at least six characters from selections in this book under the appropriate head. Then, as you read "My Father Writes to My Mother," decide whether the mother is a static or an active character.

Static	Active

Writer's Notebook

Are They Really? Quickwrite your impressions of these words from the Koran: "Good women are obedient."

Before Reading

Building Background

Invite students to consider how they feel about imposing strict limits on the roles of men and women. What, in their opinions, are the benefits and penalties of these kinds of rules for the individual and for the society as a whole?

Literary Focus

You can also display a chart with responses and let students debate how the **characters** are categorized.

Static	Active
Linh in "Rain Music"	Jerry in "Through the Tunnel"
Rufus in "The Voter"	Ulrich in "The Interlopers"
Arthur in Malory's accounts	Narrator in "Two Kinds"

Writer's Notebook

Also, you can offer this apparently contradictory quote from the Prophet Mohammed: "Men and women are as equal as two teeth on a comb."

More About Assia Djebar

Djebar, who was educated in a French boarding school, thought about becoming a writer after becoming friends with an intellectual Italian girl.

SUPPORT MATERIALS OVERVIEW

Unit 5 Resource Book
- Graphic Organizer, p. 89
- Study Guide, p. 90
- Vocabulary, p. 91
- Grammar, p. 92
- Alternate Check Test, p. 93
- Vocabulary Test, p. 94
- Selection Test, pp. 95–96

Building English Proficiency
- Selection Summaries
- Activities, p. 217

Reading, Writing & Grammar SkillBook
- Reading, pp. 97–98
- Grammar, Usage, and Mechanics, pp. 157–160

Technology
- Audiotape 17, Side B
- Personal Journal Software
- Custom Literature Database: For related literature, see readings from the Koran and the speech Ain't I a Woman? by Sojourner Truth on the database.
- Test Generator Software

During Reading

Selection Objectives

- to analyze the "culture crossroads" between Western and Muslim ways
- to analyze the development of a literary character
- to understand and practice forming compound-complex sentences

Unit 5 Resource Book
Graphic Organizer, p. 89
Study Guide, p. 90

Theme Link

A Muslim couple crosses a cultural crossroads when they allow certain Western values to influence the structure of their marriage.

Vocabulary Preview

proviso, a conditional stipulation
unequivocally, clearly
euphemism, use of a mild or indirect expression instead of a harsh, direct one
irrefutable, undeniable
taciturn, silent
imperceptible, gradual
betoken, indicate
portent, sign
brazenly, boldly
tantamount, equal, equivalent

Students can add the words and definitions to their Writer's Notebooks.

Art Study

Responses to Caption Question
Discuss the Bedouin woman's natural curiosity about the photograph. Encourage students to examine the stereotypical Western images of Muslim women and to find out facts about the culture.

Explain that the *Bedouin,* "the stateless," are nomadic Arabs who live in countries in North Africa and on the Arabian peninsula.

SELECTION SUMMARY

My Father Writes to My Mother

The narrator's mother, raised in a traditional Muslim community, has conformed to the tradition requiring her to address her husband only as *he* or *him,* never by name. By conversing with the wives of her husband's French colleagues, she learns some French and Western customs. In conversation with her women relatives, she begins to address her husband by name, causing discomfort to the others. Another custom is broken by her husband when he sends a postcard addressed to her. The relatives disapprove of this public affror to their ways. The narrator, however, observes th the mother is proud of her husband's symbolic acknowledgment of their love and believes that there may be a "possible happiness" in marriag that she had not thought existed.

For summaries in other languages, see the ***Building English Proficiency*** *book*

My Father Writes to My Mother

Assia Djebar

Whenever my mother spoke of my father, she, in common with all the women in her town, simply used the per-
1 sonal pronoun in Arabic corresponding to "him." Thus, every time she used a verb in the third person singular which didn't have a noun subject, she was naturally referring to her husband. This form of speech was characteristic of every married woman, from fifteen to sixty, with the proviso[1] that in later years, if the husband had undertaken the pilgrimage to Mecca, he could be given the title of "Hajj."[2]

Everybody, children and adults, especially girls and women, since all important conversations took place among the womenfolk, learnt very quickly to adapt to this rule whereby a husband and wife must never be referred to by name.

After she had been married a few years, my mother gradually learnt a little French. She was able to exchange a few halting words with the wives of my father's colleagues who had, for the most part, come from France and, like us, lived with their families in the little block of flats set aside for the village teachers.

I don't know exactly when my mother began to say, *"My husband* has come, *my husband* has gone out . . . I'll ask *my husband,"* etc. Although my mother did make rapid progress in the language, in spite of taking it up fairly late in life, I can still hear the evident awkwardness in her voice betrayed by her labored phraseology, her slow and deliberate enunciation at that time. Nevertheless, I can sense how much it cost her modesty to refer to my father directly in this way. 2

It was as if a floodgate had opened within

◄ A Bedouin woman examines a photograph of herself taken just moments before. Does this **interaction** between the traditional and the modern fit your ideas about Muslim women?

1. proviso (prə vī′zō), *n.* any provision or stipulation.
2. **hajj** (haj); more commonly *hajji* (haj′ē).

The Author Speaks

Rules and Muslim Conversation In an interview, Assia Djebar recalled that "the upbringing that I received from my own mother and the others around me had two absolute rules: never talk about yourself, and two, if you must, always do it anonymously—*never* use the first person pronoun."

1 Reader's Response
Making Personal Connections

Let students experiment with using only pronouns while talking about a fictitious spouse. For example, someone might ask a boy, "Will you shop for a car soon?" The boy can respond, "First I'll ask her." Or, a question for a girl might be: "Do you drive your daughter to school?" followed by "No, he drives her every day."

2 Literary Focus
Character

Questions

- Based on what you know about Muslim women, do you think it was easy for the mother to surrender her modesty? *(Possible response: No, because so much stress is placed on obedience, honor, and tradition.)*
- Why do you think she allowed this change in her customary behavior to occur? *(Possible response: She was trying to adapt to her new social circumstances.)*

BUILDING ENGLISH PROFICIENCY

Making Cultural Connections

Encourage students to apply the cultural emphasis of Djebar's story to broader experiences.

Activity Ideas

- The names for various family members are very important in this culture. Invite volunteers to tell how they have been taught to refer to parents and to older relatives. Ask: Why would affectionate nicknames for a husband or wife seem out of place in the culture of this story?
- Discuss the title of "Hajj." Then allow students to demonstrate or make drawings of various ways of showing faithfulness in other religions.
- Suggest that students teach one another proper greetings and ways to address adults in their culture or heritage. Let them talk about how they greet others in their school environment.

Building English Proficiency
Activities, p. 217

3 Active Reading

Question

Possible response Students may be curious about what consequences would befall someone who broke traditions. Also questions might arise about marriage customs, the history of Islamic patriarchy, and the present-day condition of women's rights under Islamic law.

4 Literary Element

Setting

You might explain that these patios are the private inner courtyards where women are allowed to be alone together. Also, in conservative Muslim households, the women observe the tradition of *purdah,* or confinement to the home. Errands and visits are undertaken by the males of the family.

5 Multicultural Connection

Polygyny

Explain that *harem* refers to both the wives and servants of the master of a Muslim household as well as their apartments. According to some historians, Mohammed originally institutionalized polygyny, or husbands taking multiple wives, in order to provide protection for widows and orphans whose husbands and fathers were killed in battle.

her, perhaps in her relationship with her husband. Years later, during the summers we spent in her native town, when chatting in Arabic with her sisters or cousins, my mother would refer to him quite naturally by his first name, even with a touch of superiority. What a daring innovation! Yes, quite unhesitatingly—I was going to say, unequivocally[3]—in any case, without any of the usual euphemisms[4] and verbal circumlocutions.[5] When her aunts and elderly female relations were present, she would once more use the traditional formalities, out of respect for them; such freedom of language would have appeared insolent and incongruous to the ears of the pious old ladies.

3 **QUESTION: What questions about this culture and its customs would you like to ask?**

Years went by. As my mother's ability to speak French improved, while I was still a child of no more than twelve, I came to realize an irrefutable[6] fact: namely that, in the face of all these womenfolk, my parents formed a couple. One thing was an even greater source of pride in me: when my mother referred to any of the day-to-day incidents of our village life—which in our city relatives' eyes was very backward—the tall figure of my father—my childhood hero—seemed to pop up in the midst of all these women engaged in idle chit-chat on the age-old
4 patios to which they were confined.

My father, no one except my father; none of the other women ever saw fit to refer to their menfolk, their masters who spent the day outside the house and returned home in the evening, taciturn,[7] with eyes on the ground. The nameless uncles, cousins, relatives by marriage, were for us an unidentifiable collection of individuals to all of whom their spouses alluded impartially in the masculine gender.

With the exception of my father . . . My mother, with lowered eyes, would calmly pronounce his name "Tahar"—which, I learned very early, meant "The Pure"—and even when a suspicion of a smile flickered across the other women's faces or they looked half ill at ease, half indulgent, I thought that a rare distinction lit up my mother's face. 5

These harem conversations ran their imperceptible[8] course: my ears only caught those phrases which singled my mother out above the rest. Because she always made a point of bringing my father's name into these exchanges, he became for me still purer than his given name betokened.[9]

One day something occurred which was a portent[10] that their relationship would never be the same again—a commonplace enough event in any other society, but which was unusual to say the least with us: in the course of an exceptionally long journey away from home (to a neighboring province, I think), my father wrote to my mother—yes, to my mother!

He sent her a postcard, with a short greeting written diagonally across it in his large, legible handwriting, something like "Best wishes from this distant region" or possibly, "I am having a good journey and getting to know an unfamiliar region," etc. and he signed it simply with his first name. I am sure that, at the time, he himself would not have dared add any more intimate formula above his signature, such as "I am thinking of you," or even less, "Yours affectionately." But, on the half of the card reserved for the address of the recipient, he had written "Madame" followed by his own surname, with the possible addition—but here I'm not sure—

3. unequivocally (un′i kwiv′ə kəl ē), *adv.* clearly.
4. euphemism (yü′fə miz′əm), *n.* use of a mild or indirect expression instead of a harsh, direct one.
5. **circumlocution** (sėr′kəm lō kyü′shən), *n.* the use of many words instead of a few.
6. irrefutable (i ref′yə tə bəl), *adj.* undeniable.
7. taciturn (tas′ə tėrn′), *adj.* silent.
8. imperceptible (im′pər sep′tə bəl), *adj.* gradual.
9. betoken (bi tō′kən), *v.* indicate.
10. portent (pôr′tent), *n.* sign.

MINI-LESSON: GRAMMAR

Writing Compound-Complex Sentences

My father had quite brazenly written his wife's name, in his own handwriting, on a postcard which was going to travel from one town to another, which was going to be exposed to so many masculine eyes, including eventually our village postman—a Muslim postman to boot—and, what is more, he had dared to refer to her in the Western manner as "Madame So-and-So. . . ," whereas, no local man, poor or rich, ever referred to his wife and children in any other way than the vague periphrasis: "the household." (page 647)

After students read the passage, ask:

- What do you notice about this sentence? *(It's long and involved.)*
- What effect does it have on the reader? *(It builds tension; it portrays the small act of sending a postcard as momentous.)*
- What sentence pattern is this? *(It's a compound-complex sentence, one that contains at least two independent clauses and at least one subordinate clause.)*

Activity Idea Have students underline the two independent clauses in the passage, as shown above, and write other compound-complex sentences about a minor incident they have experienced that had major consequences.

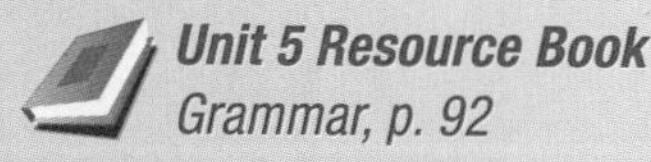
Unit 5 Resource Book
Grammar, p. 92

"and children," that is to say we three, of whom I, then about ten years old, was the eldest. . . .

The radical change in customs was apparent for all to see: my father had quite brazenly[11] written his wife's name, in his own handwriting, on a postcard which was going to travel from one town to another, which was going to be exposed to so many masculine eyes, including eventually our village postman—a Muslim postman to boot—and, what is more, he had dared to refer to her in the western manner as "Madame So-and-So . . . ," whereas, no local man, poor or rich, ever referred to his wife and children in any other way than by the vague periphrasis: "the household."

6 **CLARIFY: Why was sending the postcard considered "western" and daring?**

So, my father had "written" to my mother. When she visited her family she mentioned this postcard, in the simplest possible words and tone of voice, to be sure. She was about to describe her husband's four or five days' absence from the village, explaining the practical problems this had posed: my father having to order the provisions just before he left, so that the shopkeepers could deliver them every morning; she was going to explain how hard it was for a city woman to be isolated in a village with very young children and cut off in this way. . . . But the other women had interrupted, exclaiming, in the face of this new reality, this almost incredible detail:

"He wrote to you, *to you?*"

"He wrote his wife's name and the postman must have read it? Shame! . . ."

"He could at least have addressed the card to his son, for the principle of the thing, even if his son is only seven or eight!"

CLARIFY: What would have been the purpose of addressing the postcard to his son? 7

My mother did not reply. She was probably pleased, flattered even, but she said nothing. Perhaps she was suddenly ill at ease, or blushing from embarrassment; yes, her husband had written to her, in person! . . . The eldest child, the only one who might have been able to read the card, was her daughter: so, daughter or wife, where was the difference as far as the addressee was concerned?

"I must remind you that I've learned to read French now!" 8

This postcard was, in fact, a most daring manifestation of affection. Her modesty suffered at that very moment that she spoke of it. Yet, it came second to her pride as a wife, which was secretly flattered.

The murmured exchanges of these segregated women struck a faint chord with me, as a little girl with observing eyes. And so, for the first time, I seem to have some intuition of the possible happiness, the mystery in the union of a man and a woman.

My father had dared "to write" to my mother. Both of them referred to each other by name, which was tantamount[12] to declaring openly their love for each other, my father by writing to her, my mother by quoting my father henceforward without false shame in all her conversations.

---

11. brazenly (brā′zn lē), *adv.* boldly.
12. tantamount (tan′tə mount), *adj.* equal; equivalent.

6 Active Reading
Clarify

Possible responses It implies that his wife is important as an individual. It is daring for the husband to treat his wife as an equal.

7 Active Reading
Clarify

To reinforce the customary Muslim belief that the men in a family handle all the worldly actions and the women in a family are "invisible."

8 Reader's Response
Challenging the Text

Discuss the author's emphasis on the power of language to shape an individual's perception of reality.

- Ask second-language students if learning a new language has affected their world view.
- Ask students if using a title like "Mr." or calling a person by his or her first name makes a difference in the way they feel about the person.

Check Test

1. What is the narrator's father's profession? *(He is a teacher.)*
2. With whom did the mother begin to speak French? *(with the wives of men who taught with her husband)*
3. According to tradition, what words should the mother use to refer to her husband in conversation? *(pronouns like* he *or* him*)*
4. What words does the mother begin to use when referring to her husband? *("my husband," Tahar)*
5. To which family member do the other women think the postcard should have been sent? *(to the son)*

Unit 5 Resource Book
Alternate Check Test, p. 93

BUILDING ENGLISH PROFICIENCY

Expanding Vocabulary Through Prefixes

Draw attention to the prefixes *im-* and *in-*, which appear often in this story.

1. Explain that *im-* and *in-* often mean "not," as in these words from pages 646–647:
   - impartially (not taking one part or side)
   - incongruous (not consistent, not in agreement)
   - imperceptible (not able to be seen or perceived)
   - incredible (not believable)
2. Explain that other story words show that *im-* and *in-*sometimes mean "in" or "on":
   - innovation ("bringing in" new things)
   - intuition (from "looking in" to something)
3. Have groups of students use dictionaries to find other words with the prefixes *im-* and *in-*; encourage students to add some of the words to their vocabulary notebooks.

After Reading

MAKING CONNECTIONS

1. Possible responses: loving, progressive, adaptable

2. Possible responses: Both the mother and the father break with tradition; however, because the women are less powerful, the mother is perhaps risking more.

3. Possible response: She learned that education can empower one to oppose cultural repression.

4. Possible response: Because the setting is a small conservative village in an Islamic country, the postcard presents a public and religious issue, not just a private one.

5. Possible responses: the mother and father's external conflict with Muslim tradition; the mother's internal conflict between preserving her modesty and adopting Western ways; the harem's conflict between friendship for the mother and disapproval of her radical behavior

6. Possible responses: She wasn't hypocritical because she explored new freedoms for herself, but didn't try to change society as a whole.

7. Possible responses: "the power of love to free us" because without their strong love, the couple they might not have risked the change

8. In Head's story, the American challenges authority in the African village, displaying her liberated spirit. In "Rain Music," Linh works in the competitive, male-dominated world of medicine; her constraints seem to be her personal loyalty to her heritage, not sexism. The mother in Djebar's piece skillfully combines liberating choices with obedience to tradition.

9. Possible response: Encourage students to focus on roles connected with career, caring for children and the elderly, chores, and others.

After Reading

Making Connections

Shaping Your Response

1. In your notebook, write three words to describe the father and mother's relationship.
2. Whose actions in this selection do you think are the more daring—those of the mother or the father? Explain.
3. Judging from her biography on page 643, what lasting effects might this episode described in her autobiographical sketch have had on the young narrator?

Analyzing the Autobiography

4. How does the **setting** help to explain the significance of the letter?
5. What **conflicts** does this selection exhibit? Are they internal, external, or both?
6. In referring to her husband in the traditional way when she visited her older relatives, do you think the mother was being hypocritical or thoughtful? Explain.
7. Choose the phrase that best summarizes a **theme** of this selection—or state a theme of your own:

   a. the advantage of knowing two languages

   b. the power of love to free us

   c. the tyranny of tradition

Extending the Ideas

8. The selections by Djebar, Nguyen, and Head deal with women's **interactions** and reactions to cultural traditions. Which characters do you consider "liberated" from sexist cultural restraints? Explain.
9. What one behavior currently expected of American females or males would you most like to change? Why?

Literary Focus: Characterization

Characters can be static (unchanged) or active (changed) by people and events surrounding them. Review the chart you made in your notebook about static and active characters. All evidence in Djebar's narrative points to the fact that her mother is an active character. Write a paragraph comparing Djebar's mother to another active character from your chart.

LITERARY FOCUS: CHARACTER

You might suggest that students use a graphic organizer, such as a Venn diagram, to help them write their comparison. A sample is given.

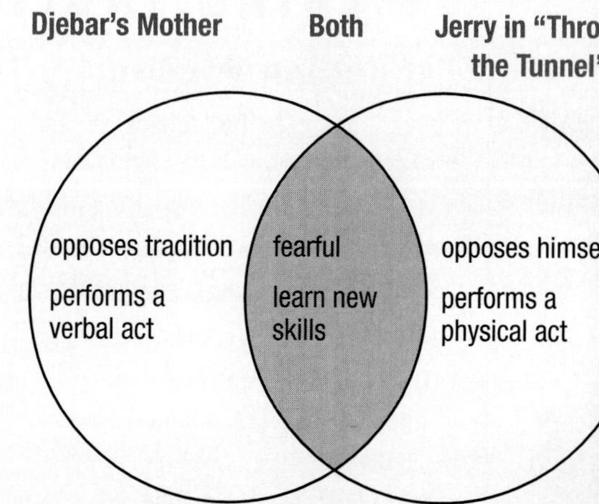

Vocabulary Study

On your paper, match the numbered word with the letter of its synonym.

betoken
brazenly
euphemism
imperceptible
irrefutable
portent
proviso
tantamount
taciturn
unequivocally

1. brazenly
2. tantamount
3. portent
4. euphemism
5. taciturn
6. unequivocally
7. betoken
8. irrefutable
9. proviso
10. imperceptible

a. stipulation
b. silent
c. equivalent
d. indicate
e. clearly
f. undeniable
g. mild saying
h. gradual
i. boldly
j. sign

Expressing Your Ideas

Writing Choices

Writer's Notebook Update Look at the quickwrite you did before reading this selection. How do you think people in a Muslim country would respond to your ideas? In another quickwrite, describe this response.

As the Roles Turn TV programs reveal a great deal about husband-wife roles in the United States. Watch several weekly programs and record your observations about couples. Write up your observations in a **media report.**

Heart-to-Heart The mother's friends are deeply concerned about her behavior. Write a **dialogue** in which they try to persuade her to return to the old ways.

A Male Perspective As he wrote and addressed the postcard, the father must have thought about the traditions he was breaking and the feelings he had for his wife. Capture his thoughts in an **interior monologue**, expressing ideas in the jumbled, unpunctuated way that thoughts tend to bounce into the mind.

Other Options

From Behind the Veil Muslim women, along with women throughout the world, spoke out for equality in the 1990s. With a group, do research on literature, conferences, and protests in the past decade in which women have sought equality. Find also copies of the laws that they were protesting and legislation they have promoted. Report your findings to the class as a **TV documentary**.

Love, Sweet Love Talk to a couple who has been married since before you were born. Find out how they met, what they initially thought about each other, how they solved any problems that occurred, and how their relationship has changed over the years. Record the **interview** and play it in class.

VOCABULARY STUDY

1. i
2. c
3. j
4. g
5. b
6. e
7. d
8. f
9. a
10. h

Unit 5 Resource Book
Vocabulary, p. 91
Vocabulary Test, p. 94

WRITING CHOICES

Writer's Notebook Update

Explain that even in Muslim countries, people disagree over the interpretation of the Koran's sayings. Use this opportunity for a cultural interaction. Invite Muslim students or adults to share information about their customs and beliefs.

As the Roles Turn

Suggest that students critically examine the dramatized relationships, asking themselves how the media representation reflects the cultural traditions of its audience.

A Male Perspective

For an example of stream-of-consciousness writing, see "A Dip in the Pool," page 292.

Selection Test

Unit 5 Resource Book
pp. 95–96

OTHER OPTIONS

From Behind the Veil

Suggest that students gain ideas from documentaries such as *The Death of a Princess*, an English television docudrama about Princess Misha'il bint Fahd bin Mohammed, a Saudi Arabian princess who was executed by her family in 1977 for committing adultery.

Love, Sweet Love

Encourage students to interview couples with multicultural backgrounds that can help them to further explore the theme Culture Crossroads.

Before Reading

Building Background

Possible responses

Reasons to emigrate	Emigrants
War	Vietnamese
Religious intolerance	Puritan English, Jewish Europeans
Racial injustice	Migration from southern U.S. to northern U.S.
Famine	Irish farmers
Political oppression	Haitians
Inadequate education	Africans
Business opportunities	Mexican and Central Americans

Literary Focus

Explain that an **allusion** can be a reference to any historical, cultural, mythical, or literary event or any other aspect of ancient or modern culture.

Question Why is allusion an especially useful tool for a poet? *(An allusion offers many ideas in a few words. It also triggers the reader's associations.)*

Writer's Notebook

Encourage students to think of metaphors and similes to describe how they felt.

Before Reading

Legal Alien by Pat Mora USA

I Am Not with Those by Anna Akhmatova Russia

For the White Poets Who Would Be Indian by Wendy Rose USA

Jerusalem by Yehuda Amichai Israel

Dos Patrias/Two Countries by José Martí Cuba

Building Background

Pulling Up Stakes Throughout history, people have been on the move—leaving family, friends, and the countries of their birth. What prompted them to do so? Examine the following chart, adding categories if necessary. Cite examples of people or groups who fit each category. If possible, determine which category fits your own family.

Reasons to Emigrate	Emigrants
War	
Religious intolerance	
Racial injustice	
Famine	
Political oppression	
Inadequate education	
Lack of economic opportunities	

Literary Focus

Allusion An **allusion** is a reference to a person, event, or place, real or fictitious, or to a work of art. For example, you might refer to someone with a mysterious smile as a Mona Lisa or someone with a bad attitude as a Scrooge. In literature, allusions serve to enhance meaning, beauty, or mood.

Writer's Notebook

Out of the Loop It doesn't take a move to a new country to make someone feel like an outsider. In your notebook, describe a time when you felt alienated or alone and explain what, if anything, you did to overcome the feeling.

SUPPORT MATERIALS OVERVIEW

Unit 5 Resource Book
- Graphic Organizer, p. 97
- Study Guide, p. 98
- Vocabulary, p. 99
- Grammar, p. 100
- Alternate Check Test, p. 101
- Vocabulary Test, p. 102
- Selection Test, pp. 103–104

Building English Proficiency
- Literature Summaries
- Activities, p. 218

Reading, Writing & Grammar SkillBook
- Vocabulary, pp. 15–19
- Writing, pp. 123–125
- Grammar, Usage, and Mechanics, pp. 150–151

Technology
- Audiotapes 17, Side B, and 18, Sides A, B
- Personal Journal Software
- Custom Literature Database: For another view of cultural interchanges see "Experiences of a Chinese Immigrant" from *The Independent* on the database.
- Test Generator Software

Pat Mora
born 1942

Pat Mora says, "I write, in part, because Hispanic perspectives need to be part of our literary heritage." Active in efforts to conserve Mexican American culture, Mora has published several books for children as well as a collection of essays and several volumes of poetry.

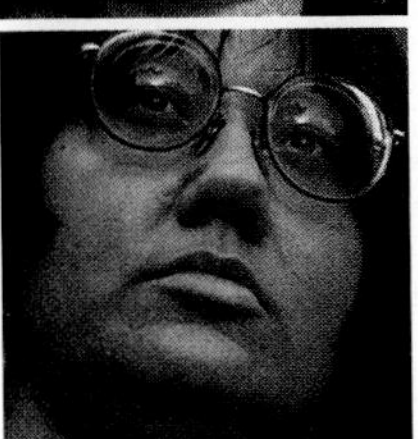

Wendy Rose
born 1948

Wendy Rose grew up in Oakland, California, the daughter of a Hopi father and an Anglo-Miwok mother. An artist, editor, and anthropologist, as well as a poet, Rose says, "For everything in this universe, there is a song to accompany its existence; writing is another way of singing these songs."

Anna Akhmatova
1889–1966

Anna Gorenko, who adopted the pen name Akhmatova (uk mät′ə və, äk′mə tō′və), suffered greatly at the hands of Soviet authorities: for years she was forbidden to publish, her husband was executed for his opposition to the government, and her son was sent to the labor camps. Nevertheless, she remained in the Soviet Union, leaving an impressive legacy as a poet and a human being.

Yehuda Amichai
born 1924

During World War II, Yehuda Amichai (yə hü′də ä′mi kī) served in the British army's Jewish Brigade in Egypt. In the Arab-Israeli war of 1948, he joined the Israeli defense forces. Afterwards, he completed his education and began writing short stories, radio plays, novels, and poetry. Amichai's poetry, written in Hebrew, is characterized by clarity and everyday language.

José Martí
1853–1895

José Martí (hō sā′ mär tē′) was a leader in the revolution against Spanish rule in 1895. Exiled from Cuba for his political activities, he lived from 1881 to 1895 in New York City, writing works that made him famous throughout Latin America. Martí's death in a skirmish with Spanish forces right after returning to Cuba in 1895 made him a national hero.

More About the Poets

Pat Mora

The picture books Mora writes reflect the values and customs of Hispanic culture, making it accessible to children of all backgrounds. Another work by the author is *Listen to the Desert,* (1994).

Wendy Rose

Rose's poems not only explore the Native American experience, they often tackle ecological, archaeological, and feminist issues as well. She also wrote *Going to War with All My Relations,* (1993).

Anna Akhmatova

During the years of the Stalinist purges, Akhmatova once spent 17 months waiting in line in front of a prison in order to find out what had happened to her son. *A Poem Without a Hero,* (1973), is another of her works.

Yehuda Amichai

Born in Germany in 1924, Yehuda Amichai moved to Israel with his family when he was 12 years old. Another work by the author is *Great Tranquillity: Questions and Answers,* (1983).

José Martí

Exiled from Cuba at the age of 17, José Martí continued his studies in Spain, where he was influenced by the revolts of 1868.

During Reading

Selection Objectives

- to explore poetic responses to the cultural crossroads created by political conflict
- to identify and understand the use of allusion
- to understand the connection between prefixes, suffixes, and parts of speech

Unit 5 Resource Book
Graphic Organizer, p. 97
Study Guide, p. 98

Theme Link

The theme of cultural crossroads is developed in five poems that convey the anguish and pride of those who struggle to establish their unique identity in spite of overt or subtle oppression.

Vocabulary Preview

bilingual, able to speak another language as well or almost as well as one's own
bicultural, having distinct cultures existing side by side
bilaterally, on two sides
primal, fundamental
heed, careful attention
deflect, bend or turn aside

Students can add the words and definitions to their Writer's Notebooks.

1 Reading/Thinking Skills
Analyze

Question Who are the insiders and outsiders in the poems? Consider the speakers and those whom they address. *(Possible response: In "Legal Alien," the speaker is outside of both the American and Mexican cultures she represents; in Rose's poem, the speaker is inside the Native American culture and says that whites are on the outside.)*

1

Legal Alien

Pat Mora

Bi-lingual,[1] Bi-cultural,[2]
able to slip from "How's life?"
to *"Me'stan volviendo loca,"*[3]
able to sit in a paneled office
drafting memos in smooth English,
able to order in fluent Spanish
at a Mexican restaurant,
American but hyphenated,
viewed by Anglos as perhaps exotic,
perhaps inferior, definitely different,
viewed by Mexicans as alien,
(their eyes say, "You may speak
Spanish but you're not like me")
an American to Mexicans
a Mexican to Americans
a handy token
sliding back and forth
between the fringes of both worlds
by smiling
by masking the discomfort
of being pre-judged
Bi-laterally.[4]

1. bi-lingual (bī ling′gwəl), *adj.* able to speak another language as well or almost as well as one's own. (Note that *bilingual, bicultural,* and *bilaterally* are usually written with no hyphen.)
2. bi-cultural (bī kul′chər əl), *adj.* having distinct cultures existing side by side.
3. ***Me'stan volviendo loca.*** They're driving me crazy. *[Spanish]*
4. bi-laterally (bī lat′ər əl ē), *adv.* on two sides.

For the White Poets Who Would Be Indian

Wendy Rose

just once
just long enough
to snap up the words
fish-hooked
from our tongues.
You think of us now
when you kneel
on the earth,
turn holy
in a temporary tourism
of our souls.
With words
you paint your faces.
chew your doeskin,
touch breast to tree
as if sharing a mother
were all it takes,
could bring
instant and primal[1]
of knowledge.
You think of us only
when your voice
wants for roots,
when you have sat back
on your heels
and become primitive.
You finish your poem
and go back.

1. primal (prī′məl), *adj.* fundamental.

SELECTION SUMMARY
Poems

Legal Alien The Mexican American narrator laments her alienation from both elements of her heritage.

For the White Poets Who Would Be Indian The speaker criticizes white poets who appropriate the rituals and symbols of Native Americans.

I Am Not with Those The speaker describes the different paths her fellow Russians have had to follow as civil unrest tears their native land asunder.

Jerusalem The narrator describes his limited yet intimate view of the lives of his neighbors—who live on the other side of the wall in old Jerusalem.

Dos Patrias, Two Countries The speaker compares Cuba to a widow holding a bloodstained carnation and seeks the darkness of night to hasten his death.

For summaries in other languages, see the ***Building English Proficiency*** *book.*

I AM NOT WITH THOSE

Anna Akhmatova

In *Portrait of Anna Akhmatova,* Nathan Altman uses triangular shapes, including the subject's knees and V-shaped neckline, to create a three-dimensional pattern. What effect do the icy blue cubes in the background have on your impression of the subject?

I am not with those who left their land
For enemies to tear apart.
No heed[1] I pay to their gross flattery,
My songs I will not give to them.

But I feel pity for the exiled, **2**
As for prisoners or the sick.
Obscure is your road, O wanderer,
Bitter the taste of alien corn.

But here, in the dense fumes of the fire
Destroying what's left of one's youth,
Not a single solitary blow
Did we try to deflect[2] from ourselves.

And we know that in the final count **3**
Each hour will have its reckoning . . .
But the world knows no people more tearless,
More proud, more simple than we.

1. **heed** (hēd), *n.* attention.
2. **deflect** (di flekt′), *v.* bend or turn aside.

Art Study

Responses to Caption Question
Students may say they suggest a cold impenetrability, or that they suggest a multi-faceted brilliance.

Visual Literacy Background: During the period of this portrait, Akhmatova was a key member of a literary movement called acmeism, which denounced symbolist mysticism in favor of concrete, real-life images. You might discuss whether Altman's painting reflects the principles of this avant-garde movement.

2 Reading/Thinking Skills
Evaluate

You might refer to facts about Akhmatova's life on page 651, and have students judge why she pities those who emigrated. Point out that by not emigrating she had to witness many human tragedies resulting from the Bolshevik Revolution and the Stalinist purges.

3 Literary Focus
Allusion

Question What biblical allusion is Akhmatova making in lines 13 and 14? *(The Book of Revelations predicts an hour of final judgment, when everyone will be judged on the record of his or her deeds.)*

BUILDING ENGLISH PROFICIENCY

Making Personal Connections

Invite students to talk about who the speakers in the poem felt they were and were not. Help them extend their comments to reflect their own experiences.

1. Give each student 5–7 index cards.
2. On one side of each card, have students complete this statement so that it reflects a way in which they think about themselves: "I am [grown-up]." Responses may or may not reflect students' ethnic or cultural backgrounds.
3. On the reverse of each card, have students complete this statement: "I am not [too old to learn]." If possible, these statements should connect with their first statement.
4. After students arrange the cards in an order that pleases them, have them write or dictate the statements.
5. Work with students to create a format for sharing the "found poems" that result.

Building English Proficiency
Activities, p. 218

4 Reading/Thinking Skills
Analyze

Discuss with students who the implied enemies are—the Arabs in the Old City and the Jews in West Jerusalem. Elicit from students what images the poet chooses in depicting the enemy: a hard-working man, a child with a kite, a woman hanging the wash.

5 Reading/Thinking Skills
Infer

Questions Do you think that the speaker really considers these people his enemies? Why or why not? *(Possible response: No, because he seems sympathetic to their simple, human concerns.)*

6 Literary Focus
Allusion

Questions

- Within the sphere of the poem, what are the "flags" and what do they represent? *(The white sheet symbolizes surrender, the sweaty towel represents toil, and the kite represents innocence.)*
- What situation beyond the poem do "flags" allude to? *(Possible response: the nationalistic flags that are used by each side to identify themselves and to claim their territory within the divided city)*

Jerusalem

Yehuda Amichai

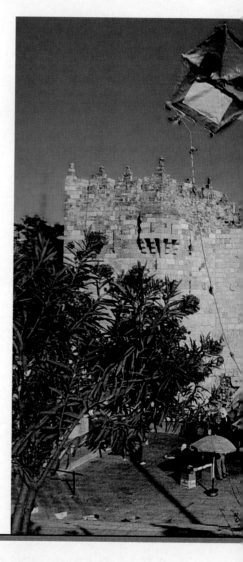

On a roof in the Old City
laundry hanging in the late afternoon sunlight:
4 the white sheet of a woman who is my enemy,
the towel of a man who is my enemy,
5 to wipe off the sweat of his brow.

In the sky of the Old City
a kite.
At the other end of the string,
a child
I can't see
because of the wall.

We have put up many flags,
6 they have put up many flags.
To make us think that they're happy.
To make them think that we're happy.

7

This photograph was taken near the Damascus Gate in East Jerusalem. Here an Arab boy flies a kite that resembles the Palestinian flag. Has the photographer chiefly captured an emotion? depicted an event? made a political statement? something else? ➤

MINI-LESSON: GRAMMAR
Using Prefixes and Suffixes

Teach Point out that the phrase "Legal Alien" is ironic because the prefix *il-* has been removed from the normal term *illegal alien.* Explain that prefixes and suffixes can change a word's meaning as well as its part of speech.

Questions

- Form a noun and an adverb by adding a suffix and/or a prefix to the adjective *legal. (Possible response: legalization, legally)*
- Form an adjective and a verb by adding a suffix and/or a prefix to the noun *alien. (Possible responses: inalienable, alienate)*

Activity Idea Have students search the poems for words that allow them to change the part of speech by adding or removing a suffix or a prefix. *(Possible responses: hyphenated—hyphen, tourism—detour, flattery—unflattering)*

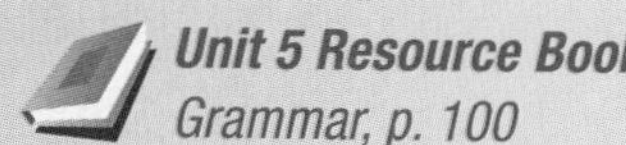

Unit 5 Resource Book
Grammar, p. 100

7 Historical Note
Old City and New City

After the creation of the State of Israel in 1948, Jerusalem was divided by walls that separated Arab East Jerusalem, the Old City, from Israeli West Jerusalem, which was guarded by military checkpoints. After Israel won the Six-Day War in 1967, the physical barriers were abolished. Political barriers, however, continue to divide the city.

Response to Caption Question
Possible responses: By focusing on the Arab flag flying over the Damascus Gate, the photographer makes the political statement that different views can co-exist, or that the kite, or flag, over the Damascus Gate symbolizes the constant tension and threat of hostility.

Visual Literacy In the 1980s, the Israeli authorities passed a Law for the Prevention of Terrorism that banned the display of Palestinian patriotic symbols. This law prohibited the display of the Palestinian flag and any materials that combined the colors of the flag: black, white, red, and green.

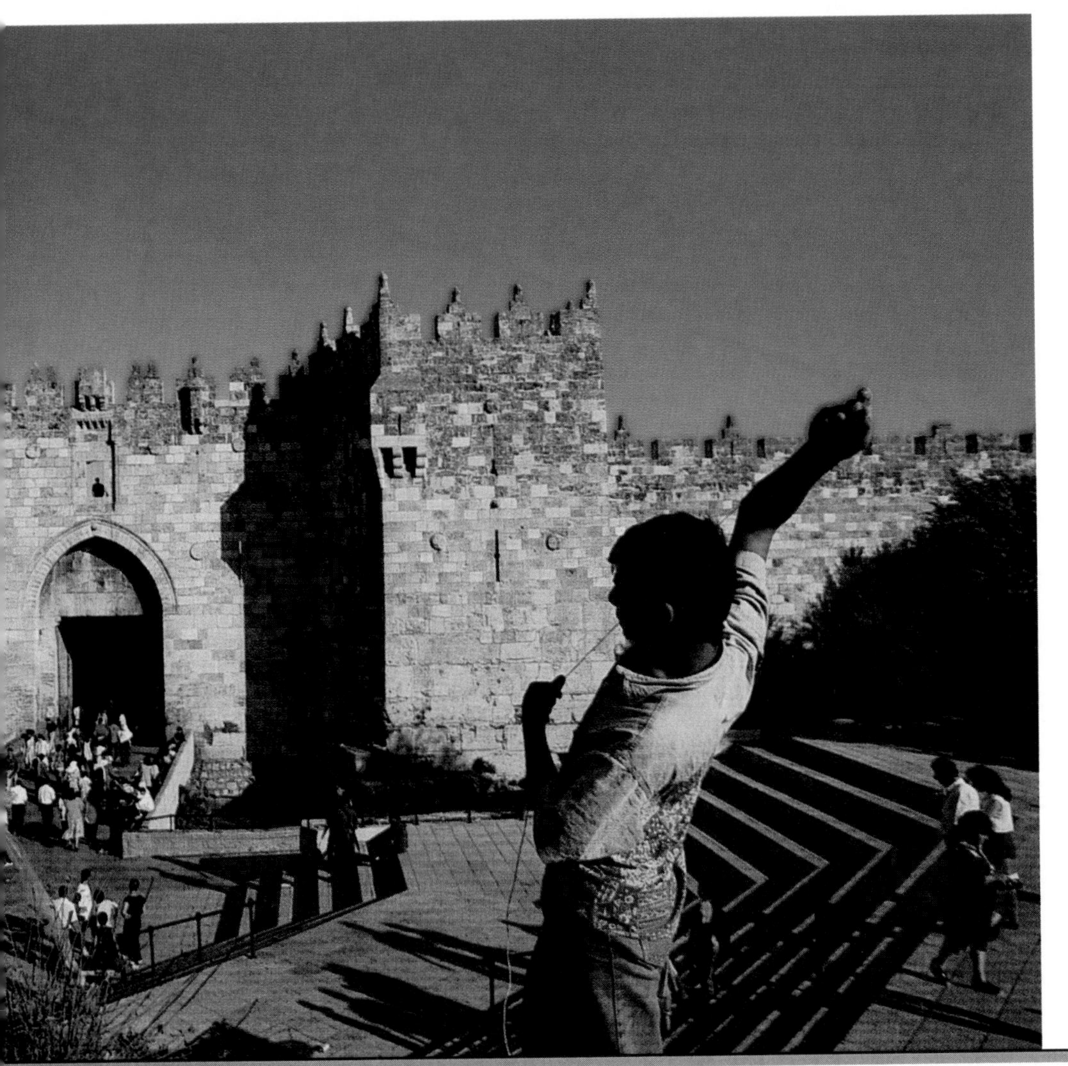

BUILDING ENGLISH PROFICIENCY

Exploring Symbolism

The following activities can help students grasp some of the symbols in "Jerusalem."

Activity Ideas

1. Have students close their eyes and imagine doing laundry. Ask them to name sights, sounds, textures, and smells that they associate with drying clothes. Discuss how doing laundry could have more meanings and ask students to identify them. *(Possible response: It is an everyday activity, done around the world so it could symbolize how people are the same in spite of political differences.)*

2. This time have students imagine flying a kite. Discuss what a kite symbolizes. *(Possible response: freedom)* Then let them visualize a kite flown by a child and decide what it might symbolize. *(Possible response: innocence, hope for the future)*

3. Have students draw flags, standards, or banners that relate to their own backgrounds or interests and explain what they mean.

8 Literary Element
Metaphor

Question Why does the speaker say that "Night" is his country? *(Possible response: because "Night" represents the dark place that he feels that Cuba has become)*

9 Literary Element
Symbolism

Ask students to identify the universal symbols in this poem: the night, the red carnation, the heart, and the candle.

Question How do these symbols add power to the poem? *(Possible response: by drawing on the universal human emotional response to death and darkness, bloodshed, love, and hope)*

Check Test

1. In "Legal Alien," how do Anglos view the speaker? *(as exotic, inferior, different)*
2. What words suggest time in "The White Poets Who Would Be Indian"? *(just long enough, now, temporary, instant)*
3. In "I Am Not with Those," who flatters whom? *(The people who left flatter the speaker, who stayed.)*
4. Why can't the speaker in "Jerusalem" see the child who is flying the kite? *(because there is a wall between them)*
5. What are the speaker's "Two Countries"? *(Cuba and the night)*

Unit 5 Resource Book
Alternate Check Test, p. 101

Dos Patrias

José Martí

Dos patrias tengo yo: Cuba y la noche.
¿O son una las dos? No bien retira
su majestad el Sol, con largos velos
y un clavel en la mano, silenciosa
Cuba cual viuda triste me aparece.
¡Yo sé cuál es ese clavel sangriento
que en la mano le tiembla! Está vacío
mi pecho, destrozado está y vacío
en donde estaba el corazón. Ya es hora
de empezar a morir. La noche es buena
para decir adiós. La luz estorba
y la palabra humana. El universo
habla mejor que el hombre.
Cual bandera
que invita a batallar, la llama roja
de la vela flamea. Las ventanas
abro, ya estrecho en mí. Muda, rompiendo
las hojas del clavel, como una nube
que enturbia el cielo, Cuba, viuda, pasa. . . .

Two Countries

translated by Cheli Durán

8 I have two countries: Cuba and the ni
Or are both one? No sooner does the
Withdraw its majesty, than Cuba,
With long veils and holding a carnatio
Appears as a sad and silent widow.
I know about that bloodstained carna
That trembles in her hand! My breast
Is empty, destroyed and empty
Where the heart lay. Now is the time
9 To commence dying. Night is a good
To say farewell. Light is a hindrance
As is the human word. The universe
Talks better than man.
Like a flag
That calls to battle, the candle's
Red flame flutters. I feel a closeness
And open windows. Crushing the carnation's
Petals silently, widowed Cuba passes by
Like a cloud that dims the heavens. . .

MINI-LESSON: VOCABULARY
Structural Analysis

Teach Explain that structural analysis can help students figure out the meaning of an unfamiliar word. For example, divide the word *bilingual* into its root and its affixes: *bi-lingu-al*.

Note: Mention that Mora spells *bi-lingual* with a hyphen, but that the word is commonly spelled without a hyphen.

Questions

- Think of a word with a similar sounding root to bilingual. *(Possible response: language)*
- Think of other words that begin with the prefix *bi-*. What is the meaning of the prefix? *(Possible responses: bicycle, bifocal, biplane; two)*
- What does the suffix *-al* mean? *(pertaining to)*

Discuss how the above clues would help students to figure out that *bilingual* means "speaking two languages equally well."

Activity Idea Have students repeat the above exercise with the words *bicultural* and *bilateral.*

After Reading

Making Connections

Shaping Your Response

1. What do you think of when you hear the term "Culture Crossroads"? Does the term have positive or negative associations for you?
2. If you could invite one of these poets to speak to your class, whom would you choose and what topics would you most want to hear about?

Analyzing the Poems

3. What do you think Mora means by "American but hyphenated"?
4. Explain both the **denotation** and the **connotation** of the word *token* in line 16 of Mora's poem.
5. What do you think the **figurative** phrase "temporary tourism of our souls" means in Rose's poem?
6. How does Akhmatova feel toward each of these three groups: those who left their land; the exiled; those who stayed?
7. In Amichai's poem, how might both the wall and the flags be **symbolic**?
8. In what ways does Martí **personify**, or give human characteristics to, Cuba?

Extending the Ideas

9. Identify the conflicting cultures and **interractions** in each of these five poems.

Literary Focus: Allusion

In order to understand the biblical **allusion** in lines 7 and 8 of Akhmatova's poem, you may need some background. In the Bible, Ruth was a young Moabite widow who wanted to follow her mother-in-law Naomi to Bethlehem. Naomi begged her to remain with her own people, but Ruth insisted on leaving, saying, ". . . whither thou goest, I will go. . . ." In Judah, Ruth worked in the fields gathering grain.

- How does this allusion to Ruth help express Akhmatova's pity for exiled people?
- How does the description of the *alien* (strange, disagreeable) corn reinforce the poet's attitude?

After Reading

MAKING CONNECTIONS

1. Possible response: negative, as colonization or military invasion occurs; positive, when new ways of acting and thinking are learned, as in "My Father Writes to My Mother."

2. Possible responses: for political topics—Martí, Amichai, Akhmatova; for dealing with cultural interactions—Mora; for preserving one's cultural identity—Rose

3. Possible response: Terms referring to minorities often are spelled with hyphens, such as African-American and Mexican-American. Mora says she isn't a "regular" American citizen.

4. Possible response: denotation—a mark or sign; connotation—someone who is accepted only to make it seem as if all are considered equal.

5. Possible response: White poets learn about ideas of Indian spirituality superficially just as tourists visit a monument and go on.

6. Possible response: She disrespects those who left their land, pities those who were exiled, and admires the courage of those who stayed.

7. The wall symbolizes the conflict of separation, the flag symbolizes nationalism.

8. He describes Cuba as a grieving widow holding a red carnation.

9. Responses

- "Legal Alien": A Mexican immigrant is working and living in America.
- "White Poets": Whites talk about Native American religion from a superficial viewpoint.
- "I Am Not with Those": Russian citizens remain to interact with a culture forced upon them while others flee to new cultures.
- "Jerusalem": Palestinian and Israeli neighbors struggle to survive in a divided city.
- "Two Countries": Cuba fights to shed another culture's dominance.

LITERARY FOCUS: ALLUSION

- Possible response: It draws on emotional associations of respect and sympathy for Ruth, who demonstrates the love, loyalty, and courage of an exile.
- Possible response: The speaker suggests that exiles will never feel at home in other lands.

VOCABULARY STUDY

1. bilaterally
2. primal
3. heed
4. bilingual
5. deflect

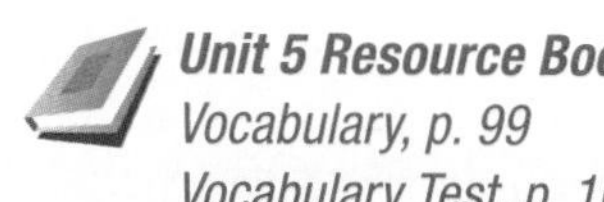

Unit 5 Resource Book
Vocabulary, p. 99
Vocabulary Test, p. 102

WRITING CHOICES

Writer's Notebook Update

Suggest that students write a short poem using the figures of speech and the impressions that they have gathered about the perspectives of insiders and outsiders.

Strangers in a Strange Land

Have students brainstorm club activities that will offer opportunities for cultural interaction, such as CD-listening parties, Flag Day, and comparative poetry readings.

Selection Test

Unit 5 Resource Book
pp. 103–104

Transparency Collection
Fine Art Writing Prompt 12

Vocabulary Study

On your paper, write the word that best completes each sentence next to its number. You will not use all the words.

bicultural
bilaterally
bilingual
deflect
heed
primal

1. A treaty signed ____ between Cuba and Spain might have satisfied José Martí's desire for Cuban independence.
2. Wendy Rose confirms that ____ knowledge is too fundamental to be quickly acquired.
3. Anna Akhmatova asks her country to pay more ____ to its suffering people.
4. Pat Mora says that ____ people are not always widely accepted just because they speak two languages.
5. How might Yehuda Amichai ____ the criticism that writing in Hebrew limits the audience for his work?

Expressing Your Ideas

Writing Choices

Writer's Notebook Update Review your description of being an outsider. Find or add words that express your feelings. Then list words or phrases that might describe the feelings of those who, in the same situation, were insiders.

Strangers in a Strange Land You are president of International Club, a school organization that brings together people of different cultures. In this capacity, write a **proposal** to your school administration suggesting ways to make people aware of the cultural diversity of the student body and the positive aspects of such diversity.

Bilingual Insights Students who speak Spanish can read "Dos Patrias" aloud and indicate on the board word pairs in both languages *(la noche/night; silenciosa/silent; morir/dying)* to help convey the different sounds and shades of meaning words have in different languages.

Other Options

American Mosaic As a class project, make a poster-sized **Culture Crossroads Chart** that represents the members of your class. In each quadrant, labeled National Origins, Languages, Religions, and one other category of your choosing, indicate the contributions of your classmates to the cultural mix that is the United States.

Pieces of America Using words and phrases from these poems and other poems in this book, make a **verbal collage** representing many facets of the United States and its people. Illustrate your verbal collage with pictures.

In Memoriam Washington, D.C., is a city of monuments: older ones like those honoring George Washington, as well as recent memorials such as the Holocaust Museum and the Vietnam Veterans Memorial. Design a **sketch** or **blueprint** for a monument or memorial that celebrates the multiplicity of peoples who have created the United States.

OTHER OPTIONS

American Mosaic

You might discuss stereotypes, myths, and common misinterpretations of cultural traditions as students research and complete the chart.

Pieces of America

Suggest that students decide upon a title to narrow the focus of their collage, for example, "Conflict of Cultures" or "A New Start."

In Memoriam

Ask students who have lived in or visited other countries to discuss foreign memorials and monuments.

Culture Crossroads

Culture Quilt

Multicultural Connection
A walk down almost any street serves as a reminder that ours is a society of cultural mixes. Whether these cultures blend or clash depends on the amount of respect and understanding each group has for the other.

Early in 1990, several African American groups began a boycott of a grocery store owned by Korean immigrants in the Flatbush section of Brooklyn. The African Americans charged that an incident in which a Haitian woman had allegedly been mistreated by one of the store's owners reflected the general lack of respect with which the Koreans treated their black customers. Later in 1990, African Americans began another boycott of a Korean-owned grocery. The second protest soon ended, but the original dispute was still unsettled when the following editorial, by K. Connie Kang, an Asian American journalist, appeared in The New York Times *on September 8, 1990. The "Confucian culture" mentioned by Kang is the code of social conduct based on the writings of the Chinese philosopher Confucius (551–479 B.C.). Emphasizing familial duty and respect for tradition, Confucianism has had an enormous impact on Asian civilization.*

IT'S HARD TO SMILE

K. CONNIE KANG

A crowd gathers on a Brooklyn street, listening to an African American speak out on the boycott of Korean businesses.

One of the two black-led boycotts of Korean grocers in Brooklyn ended last week, but the original, eight-month boycott continues. It is no longer a community affair, but a national concern.

As an Asian American, I was jolted at the beginning of the boycott, which allegedly began with an assault on a customer by a store employee, by a comment from a black resident: "The Koreans are a very rude people. They don't understand you have to smile."

Would she have reacted differently had she known smiling at strangers just isn't part of the Korean culture? Would it have made a difference had she known Koreans are just as "unfriendly" to their own because they equate being solicitous to being insincere? The Korean demeanor is the

Interdisciplinary Study

Theme Link

Cultural conflict can be a bitter and violent experience, but it can also lead people to reexamine themselves and to find ways to live in peace.

Curricular Connection: Multicultural

As students think about interactions with other cultures, provide them with this definition: **culture**, a complex integrated system of belief and behavior that may be both rational and nonrational.

Art Study

Question What is the mood suggested by the expressions on the faces in the crowd? *(Possible response: pent-up anger and frustration)*

Historical Note

The term *boycott*, meaning "a group effort to coerce change by refusing to buy from or deal with a disfavored party," takes its name from Charles Boycott, an English landowner whose Irish tenants refused to harvest his crops. One famous boycott is the Boston Tea Party of 1773.

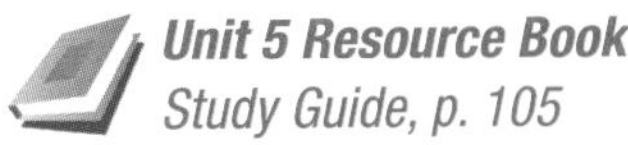

Unit 5 Resource Book
Study Guide, p. 105

BUILDING ENGLISH PROFICIENCY

ESL LEP ELD SAE LD

Dramatizing Key Concepts

"The Korean demeanor is the absence of a demeanor," says Kang, who gives the characteristic a name: *mu-pyo-jung.* Make sure students understand that *mu-pyo-jung* means "masking emotion," not "feeling no emotion." Open a discussion of what is of polite behavior in their cultures or families. Encourage them to mention hugging, smiling, shaking hands, kissing, and other outward signs of relationships. Also ask when it is proper to mask emotion. Then use role-playing to help students bring this concept to life.

1. Have volunteers improvise scenarios in which characters display *mu-pyo-jung* for various reasons. Offer these examples:

- A tourist stops a person and asks for directions. The person displays *mu-pyo-jung* while pointing the way.
- The guest of honor at a surprise birthday party displays *mu-pyo-jung.*

2. After each scenario, have students explain which behavior felt comfortable or uncomfortable to them. Discuss which emotions might be masked and how the "absence of a demeanor" might affect the other people involved.

Geographical Note

Korea, "the land of the morning calm," is a mountainous peninsula that extends from the northeastern coast of China into the Korea Strait, across which lies the island country of Japan. Korea's geographic location has made it vulnerable to invasion by both powerful neighbors. Following World War II, Korea was invaded by yet another bordering country, the Soviet Union. Conflict between the United States and the Soviet Union over the political structure of Korea led to the Korean War, which ended in 1953, leaving Korea a split and ravaged country. However, both North and South Korea have recovered economically and become viable international trading entities.

absence of a demeanor. Koreans have a name for it: *mu-pyo-jung*. It means "lack of expression."

Koreans who travel or live abroad are often concerned that this trait causes misunderstanding. Before the 1988 Seoul Olympics, South Korean officials launched a television and radio campaign urging citizens to greet visitors with a friendly smile. Some tried but found it difficult. As one housewife told me: "It's hard to smile at strangers when you're not used to it. It seems so phony."

Though it may be difficult for most Americans to tell Koreans apart from Japanese and Chinese, who have been in this country much longer, the contrast between Koreans and their Asian neighbors is striking. Having suffered invasions and a long period of colonization by Japan in this century, Koreans have had to fight for their lives to retain their language and culture. Koreans are feisty. They certainly don't fit the subservient or docile Asian stereotype.

And Koreans live by *cheong*—a concept that has no Western translation. *Cheong* is love, respect, affinity and loyalty rolled into one. *Cheong* comes only with time, and only betrayal can end it. For a people who live by this ethos [the characteristic attitudes of a group], a mechanical smile is hard to produce.

In America's inner cities, newcomers from Korea do business where no one else will, and where frustration levels are high. . . . Culturally and socially, the newcomers are ill equipped to run businesses in America's inner cities. But because they, like other Asian immigrants, are denied mainstream jobs, they pool their resources and start mom-and-pop stores.

Inner-city African Americans wonder how these newcomers, who can hardly speak English, have the money to run their own businesses when they themselves can't even get a small loan from a bank. They have little hope of escaping the poverty cycle,

yet they see new arrivals living in better neighborhoods and driving better cars.

What they don't see are the 16-hour days and the deep sacrifices made for their children. They don't see the contributions of family and friends, and the informal money-lending system called *kye* that Koreans use instead of banks.

All immigrants go through an "American passage" that requires cultural insight on both sides. Koreans, like other Asians who live in the U.S., mustn't forget that they are indebted to blacks for the social gains won by their civil rights struggle.

Asian Americans must also remember that while the Confucian culture has taught us how to be good parents, sons and daughters and how to behave with people we know, it has not prepared us for living in a democracy. The Confucian ethos lacks the social conscience that makes democracy work. It isn't enough that we educate our children; we need to think of other people's children too.

One of the boycotted grocers told me this had been a painful but valuable experience: "We Koreans must learn to participate in this society," he said. "When this is over, I'm going to reach out. I want to give part-time work to black youths."

By working together, maybe we can do privately what institutions can't. With Asian American drive and African American political experience, we can make it work not only in New York but in Los Angeles, San Francisco, Oakland and Chicago.

MINI-LESSON: SPEAKING SKILLS

Inflammatory Speeches

Teach Direct students' attention to the speaker in the photograph on page 659. Explain that a political speech, especially when delivered in an explosive setting, has a very specific tone, volume, pitch, and style.

Activity Ideas

- Have students analyze the style of the speaker's body language on page 659 and then describe how it would change if he were standing before a group of Korean grocers.
- Students can write a brief speech that they would deliver if they were the man in the photograph. Encourage volunteers to share their speeches with the class, focusing on the style of delivery.

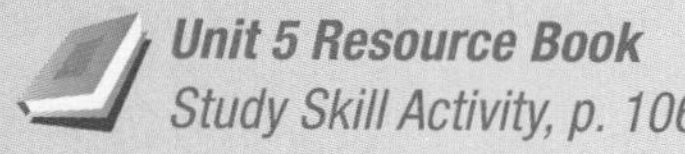

Unit 5 Resource Book
Study Skill Activity, p. 106

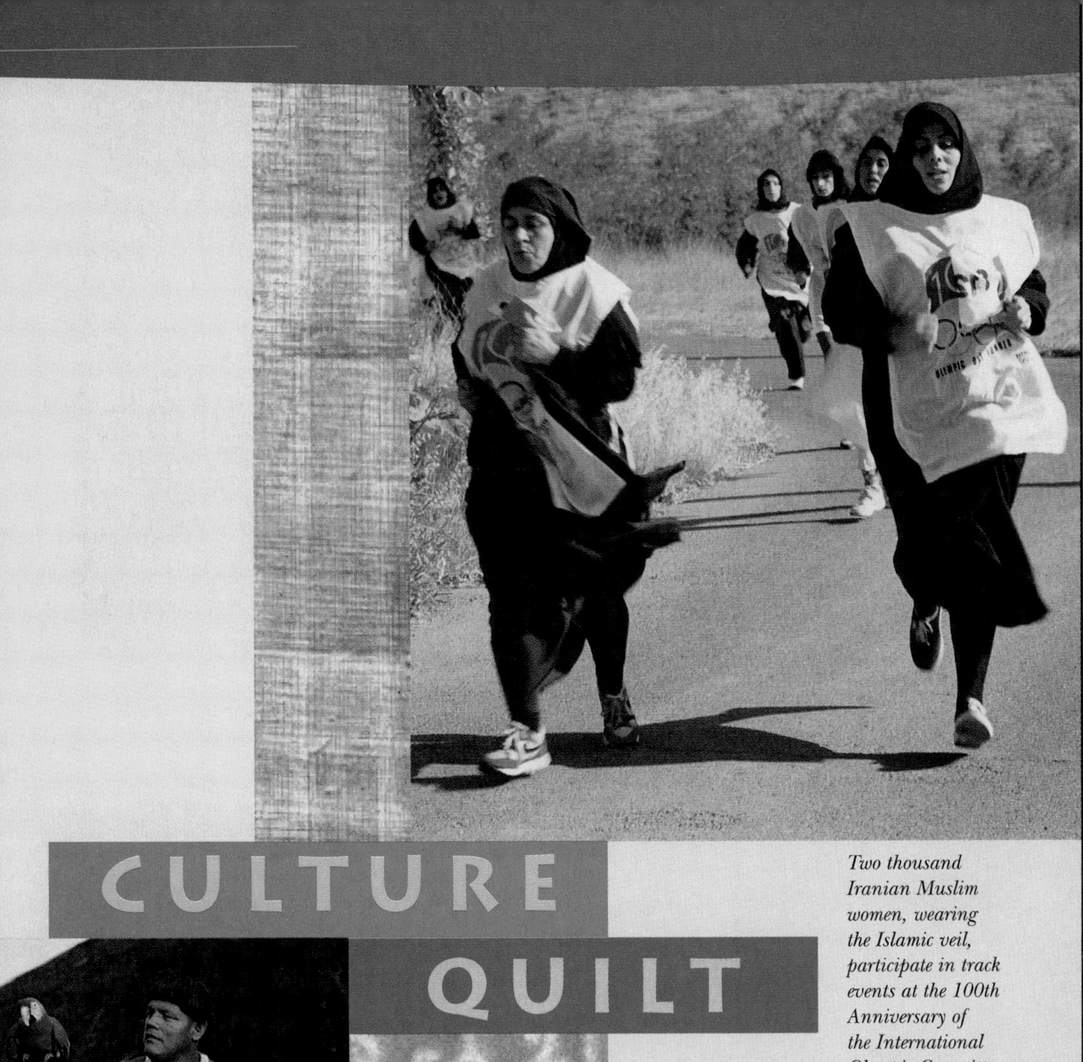

CULTURE QUILT

Two thousand Iranian Muslim women, wearing the Islamic veil, participate in track events at the 100th Anniversary of the International Olympic Committee in 1994.

An Amazonian Indian poses with his motorcycle.

Terms to Know

Muslim, person who believes in and follows the teachings of Mohammed; of the religion of Islam. Also, **Moslem**

Amazonian, of the Amazon River, which is the largest river in the world, flowing from the Andes Mountains of South America into the Atlantic

Mennonite (men′ə nīt), member of a Christian church opposed to taking oaths, holding public office, and military service. Mennonites often wear plain clothes and live simply.

Mongolia (mong gō′lē ə), vast region in Asia, south of Siberia. Mongolia includes part of Northern China and the Mongolian People's Republic

Additional Backround

The Olympic Games have been the scene of some international boycotts.

- 1956—Egypt, Iran, and Iraq boycott to protest England and France's control of the Suez Canal. Spain, Switzerland, and the Netherlands boycott to protest the Soviet Union's invasion of Hungary.
- 1976—Thirty-three African countries boycott to protest South African apartheid policies.
- 1980—The United States and other nations boycott to protest the Soviet Union's invasion of Afghanistan.
- 1984—The Soviet Union boycotts in retaliation.

BUILDING ENGLISH PROFICIENCY

ESL LEP ELD SAE LD

Responding to Visual Cues

Encourage a lively discussion as students react to the pictures and captions in "Culture Quilt," pages 661–662.

1. Have each student choose a photograph from pages 659–662 and imagine that it is a post card. Suggest that they use it to write two postcard messages—one as themselves, and another as the person or people in the photograph. First have them talk to one another about what they will say in their messages.

2. Discuss the "quilt" concept in the feature's title. Ask students to compare a quilt to a blend of cultures. *(A quilt combines pieces of cloth, often from other clothing, to create a single, beautiful product.)* Discuss what they find to be familiar and distinctive about the pictures.

3. As students complete Responding 3 on page 662, ask them to explain why their "eyewitness" choices of cultural blends would be good additions to this pictorial.

Responding

1. Possible Response She seems objective. To be more objective, we'd have to read a similar essay written from the African American viewpoint.

2. Possible Response Confucian culture teaches duty, loyalty, and respect within a family or a community. Democracy stresses individuality within a group of equal citizens of a country. Newcomers must adapt to democracy, but over time their values may affect the way the democracy evolves.

3. Students can use the photographs in the book to spark their memory.

Research Topics

- Racial incidents in Brooklyn, New York
- Confucianism in the '90s
- History of Korean immigration to the U.S.

Interdisciplinary Activity Idea

Students can expand a matrix like the one shown to analyze the cultural interactions suggested by the pictures on pages 661–662. Then let them draw conclusions and discuss them.

	Muslim	Amazonian	Mennonite	Mickey Mouse
gender	x		x	
geography				x
technology		x		
religion	x			

CULTURE QUILT

Two Mennonite women and a cross-country skater get acquainted.

Mickey Mouse and a friend offer tourists opportunities for souvenir photographs in Mongolia.

Responding

1. Do you think that K. Connie Kang presents both sides fairly? Explain.

2. According to this article, what values are emphasized by Confucian culture versus democracy? Do you think these values can be reconciled?

3. Illustrate, photograph, or describe a culture blend you have observed in your area, in a magazine, or in the media.

MINI-LESSON: TECHNOLOGY

Newspapers on Film

Teach Point out to students that if they wanted to find the copy of *The New York Times* in which K. Connie Lang's article first appeared, they would probably have to use a microfiche apparatus.

Apply Explain that a microfiche is a card or sheet of microfilm that holds a considerable number of pages of printed text in a reduced format. A magnifying lens enlarges the text, which is then projected onto a screen. The machine allows the reader to scroll easily through pages of newsprint that would otherwise be unwieldy and take up a lot of space. Microfiche also allows libraries to preserve newspapers and newsprint magazines that would otherwise disintegrate over time.

Writing Workshop

Cultured Questions

Assignment You have read about different cultures. Now research a topic about culture that intrigues you.

WRITER'S BLUEPRINT

Product	A personalized research report
Purpose	To explore intriguing questions you have about culture
Audience	You, your teacher, classmates, and friends
Specs	As the writer of a successful report, you should:

- ❑ Select an intriguing question you have about culture for the topic of your report.
- ❑ Begin your report by telling the reader why this topic intrigues you, what you already know—or think you know—about it, and what you would like to find out. Use the first-person ("I") point of view.
- ❑ Next, test your knowledge by researching your topic. Investigate any useful resources you can think of: books, magazines, online sources, videotapes, museums. Try to get at an interview with at least one firsthand source.
- ❑ Continue your report by narrating the story of your research. Tell what you discovered and where and how you discovered it. Mention any problems you encountered along the way and how you went about solving them.
- ❑ End your report by comparing and contrasting what you knew—or thought you knew—before your research with what you discovered later on. Draw conclusions from what you learned. Did your research provide a definitive answer to the original question, or did it raise new questions?
- ❑ Follow the rules of grammar for correct usage, spelling, and mechanics. Make sure that the facts you present are based on reliable sources that you have documented in a Works Cited list.

WRITER'S BLUEPRINT

Specs

The Specs in the Writer's Blueprint address these writing and thinking skills:

- using prior knowledge
- using first-person point of view
- researching
- interviewing
- solving problems
- comparing and contrasting
- drawing conclusions
- citing sources

These Specs serve as your lesson objectives, and they form the basis for the **Assessment Criteria Specs** for a superior paper, which appear on the final TE page for this lesson. You might want to read through the Assessment Criteria Specs with students when you begin the lesson.

Linking Literature to Writing

Have students brainstorm a list of definitions and connotations for the word *culture.* What makes up a culture? How is culture determined? How do students think our culture is defined? What are some characteristics of our culture? Are these characteristics the same for all cultures?

WRITING WORKSHOP OVERVIEW

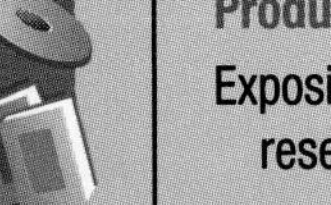

Product

Expository writing: A personalized research report

Prewriting

Review the literature—Add to your list—Try a quickwrite—Chart your knowledge—Research your topic—Plan your report

Unit 5 Resource Book

Prewriting Worksheets pp. 107–108

Drafting

Before you draft—As you draft—Compile a Works Cited list

Transparency Collection

Student Models for Writing Workshop 23, 24

Revising

Ask a partner—Strategy: Writing an Intriguing Opening

Unit 5 Resource Book

Revising Worksheet p. 109

Editing

Ask a partner—Strategy: Works Cited Form

Unit 5 Resource Book

Grammar Worksheet p. 110

Grammar Check Test p. 111

Presenting

Oral Presentation

Map or Time Line

Looking Back

Self-evaluate—Reflect—For Your Working Portfolio

Unit 5 Resource Book

Assessment Worksheet p. 112

Transparency Collection

Fine Art Transparency 12

STEP 1 PREWRITING

Review the literature

Encourage students to think about characteristics that are common to all cultures as well as those that are unique. For additional support, see the worksheet referenced below.

Unit 5 Resource Book
Prewriting Worksheet, p. 107

Add to your list

Students should take care to choose a question they can be reasonably sure they'll find information on. You might advise students to look through a library card catalogue before they settle on a topic.

Try a quickwrite

One goal of the quickwrite should be to refine broad questions into specific queries that can be more easily researched.

Chart your knowledge

New questions may emerge through the writing of this chart. Encourage students to add new questions and eliminate others until they develop a topic that interests them. For additional support, see the mini-lesson below.

STEP 1 PREWRITING

LITERARY SOURCE

"... no local man, poor or rich, ever referred to his wife and children in any other way than by the vague periphrasis: 'the household.' "
from "My Father Writes to My Mother" by Assia Djebar

Review the literature and list questions that come to mind. Here are a few examples:

- What is it like to be an outcast in another culture? What makes you an outcast? What injustices do you suffer?
- How do dating and courting customs differ from one culture to another?
- Why would men refer to their wives and family only as "the household"? Don't the wives and children have names?

Add to your list of questions about culture and choose the one that will serve as the topic of your report. Work with a small group, brainstorming ideas. The questions don't have to be from the literature. Perhaps you have a question about your own cultural heritage, or about the heritage of a classmate. Since you'll be spending a lot of time on this paper, make sure the question you choose is genuinely meaningful to you.

OR . . .
Discuss your question with the group and ask for comments.

Try a quickwrite. Write for five minutes. Explain what your question is, why you want to know about it, and how you plan to gather information. Share your quickwrite with your group. Perhaps they can help you refine your question or give you more ideas about gathering information.

Chart your knowledge. Write down what you already know, what you assume, and what you imagine about the topic, using a chart like the one shown. Also, note what you would like to find out. Remember to write in the first-person ("I") point of view.

How are women's roles changing in the Middle East?

What I Know	What I Assume	What I Imagine	What I Would Like to Find Out
I know that women must wear veils and long robes any time they leave the house.	I assume the women's lives are still controlled by men and that they have no rights.	I imagine that women and girls stay at home and don't have an opportunity to shop, go to school, or get jobs.	Have there been any changes lately in women's lives in the Middle East?

MINI-LESSON: PREWRITING

Defining Your Topic

Teach If a topic is too broad it will be difficult to research and will result in a paper full of generalities that will provide little new or interesting information.

Activity Idea Have students narrow the following topics as in the example given.

Example:
What are women's roles?
. . . in other countries?
. . . in the context of religion and state?
. . . in the Middle East?
. . . in comparison with generations past?

What is marriage?
What role do sports play in culture?
Are jokes and humor important to culture?
How is divorce viewed?

Apply Have students reconsider their topics to make sure they're not too broad.

Research your topic. Visit the library, museums, and other community institutions to find sources of useful information. Try to get an interview with at least one firsthand source: an expert who knows something about your topic.

For each source, make a **source card** that lists the information you'll need for your Works Cited list. Give each source card a separate number. Record relevant information on **note cards.** Include the source name and number and the appropriate page numbers. See the examples that follow.

Source Card

1

Schwartz, Melvin, and John R. O'Connor.

Exploring a Changing World.

Englewood Cliffs:

Globe Book Company, 1988.

Note Card

Exploring a Changing World 1

Saudi Arabian women follow rules laid down by the government; rules are part of the Islamic faith; Islamic faith allows women to own property and money separate from their husbands.

p. 424

STUDENT MODEL

Plan your report. Organize the information from your notes into a plan like this one:

Your topic
Why it intrigues you
What you already know about it
What you assume or imagine about it
What you would like to find out

Your research experience
The steps you took
Problems and how you handled them
What you discovered

What you already knew compared/contrasted with what you discovered
Similarities
Differences
Conclusions

OR . . .
Use a tape recorder to record your research experience first. Then, take notes from the tape and put them into the plan.

Research your topic

Show students how to conduct an Internet search in the library or media lab. Spend some time in class reviewing source cards and note cards. Remind students that source cards and note cards will help them organize their research and make planning their reports easier. For additional support, see the worksheet referenced below.

Unit 5 Resource Book
Prewriting Worksheet, p. 108

Plan your report

Encourage students to arrange and rearrange their note cards as they work on their writing plans. Remind students that a good plan will make writing a draft easier because the information will have already been arranged in a logical order.

Connections to **Writer's Notebook**

For selection-related prompts, refer to Writer's Notebook.

Connections to **Writer's Resource**

For additional writing prompts, refer to Writer's Resource.

BUILDING ENGLISH PROFICIENCY

Documenting Research

Have students keep a log to record their research journeys.

1. Ask students to begin by outlining a research plan.
2. Whenever students visit or contact a source, have them record the date, the sources of information they consult, and their difficulties and successes.
3. Advise them to jot down information such as phone numbers, hours that sources are open, and lists of bibliographic information to back up their source cards.
4. Suggest that students record their responses and update their plans as they go along.

STEP 2 DRAFTING

Before you draft

Tell students to gather their prewriting materials so they will have them close at hand as they begin to draft.

As you draft

Discuss with students the differences between writing a traditional expository essay and one that is framed as a journey or trip. The drafting tips will give students a jumping off point.

The Student Models

The **transparencies** referenced below are authentic student models. Review them with the students before they draft. These questions will help:

1. Tell how the writer of model 23 narrated the story of the research. Do you think the writer did an effective job on this part of the paper?

2. Discuss the opening of model 24. Make suggestions to improve it.

3. Put the sources from model 23 into a Works Cited list. Make sure the entries are formatted correctly.

Transparency Collection
Student Models for Writing Workshop 23, 24

Compile a Works Cited list

Remind students to check their drafted list against their source cards.

STEP 3 REVISING

Ask a partner (Peer assessment)

Have students begin by commenting only on the opening before moving on to the rest of the essay. Then have students read the narration of the research and comment on it.

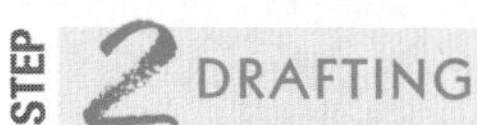

STEP 2 DRAFTING

Before you draft, look over your notes and writing plan and reread the Writer's Blueprint.

As you draft, concentrate on putting the ideas from your report plan on paper. Try these drafting tips to help you get started.

- Begin your report with an intriguing question, fact, anecdote, or other attention-getting device. See the Revising Strategy in Step 3.
- Narrate the story of your research experience as if you were taking a journey. Use words like *embark, destination, stops,* and *side trips*.
- For the third section, include personal insights that you discovered about the research process as well as about the topic itself.

Notice how this student includes personal insights about the research experience.

STUDENT MODEL

> The people I talked to felt that over time, society has become more tolerant of diversity. However, current events reported in the newspaper and magazines told a different story. Why would this discrepancy exist? Maybe individual people are ready to accept differences in others but this isn't always reflected in the news.

Compile a Works Cited list. Use your source cards. See the Editing Strategy in Step 4 of this lesson.

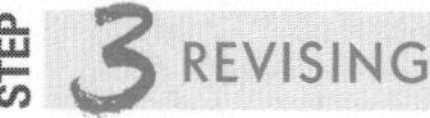

STEP 3 REVISING

Ask a partner to comment on your draft before you revise it. Use this checklist as a guide.

✔ Did I narrate my information search in a way that will not just inform but engage my reader?

✔ Did I compare and contrast what I knew and what I discovered later on?

✔ Did I begin the paper with an intriguing opening?

MINI-LESSON: WRITING STYLE

Writing an Intriguing Opening

Teach Have students imagine they are flipping through a magazine looking for material to read. Ask them how many seconds they estimate they give an article to catch their attention before flipping to the next page. What usually catches their attention? How can they incorporate these techniques into their own writing?

Activity Idea Have students rewrite the following opening paragraph to make it more enticing to a fickle reader.

El Día de los Muertos (The Day of the Dead) is a Mexican holiday that is similar to the American Halloween, but at the same time very different. Through these two holidays we can see differences in the two cultures. Death is celebrated in Mexico with costumed parades, trips to the cemetery to visit dead relatives, and sugary candy in the form of skeletons.

Apply Have students read the openings to thei[r] own essays aloud and have the class respond as [if] they were flipping through a magazine looking fo[r] articles. Are they hooked by the openings, or not?

Revising Strategy

Writing an Intriguing Opening

Since this is about a topic that intrigues you, you should open your paper in a way that intrigues the reader. When you revise, experiment with different types of openings to get the reader as involved as you are. Try one of these opening ideas:

- Pose a provocative question: "Why can't people accept each other's differences?"
- Relate an anecdote—an incident that you were involved in—that shows how you became interested in your topic: "The first time I realized there was such a thing as prejudice was the morning I. . . ."
- Write a short, lively question-answer dialogue about what you would like to discover about your topic, as if you were talking with yourself.

Notice how the writer in the student model revised her opening to turn it into a question-answer dialogue.

STUDENT MODEL

Why can't people accept each other's differences?
~~People have a hard time accepting each other's differences.~~ Throughout history there have been cultural differences between people and it seems there has also been prejudice. But people are born without prejudices. *Where do these biases come from?* ~~These biases must come from somewhere.~~ The people you grow up around influence the way you think and do things, so you think that's the only right way.

STEP 4 EDITING

Ask a partner to review your revised draft before you edit. When you edit, look for errors in grammar, usage, spelling, and mechanics. Make sure the research sources are cited correctly in the Works Cited list.

Revising Strategy: Writing an Intriguing Opening

Encourage students to try a variety of openers before settling on the best one. Discuss different ways to open the paper and have students provide examples from their own papers or from other sources they have read. For additional support, see the mini-lesson at the bottom of page 666 and the worksheet referenced below.

Unit 5 Resource Book
Revising Worksheet, p. 109

Connections to **Writer's Resource**

Refer to the Grammar, Usage, and Mechanics Handbook on Writer's Resource.

STEP 4 EDITING

Ask a partner (Peer assessment)

Remind students to proofread the Works Cited list as well as the text.

MINI-LESSON: GRAMMAR

Works Cited Form

Have students edit the following citations.

Jonathan Silvers. "Child labor in Pakistan" The Atlantic Monthly. Volume 27, February 1996. 79–88.

Mike Rose. Lives on the Boundary. Penguin Books, New York, 1989.

Telephone interview with Majorie Kelly, UCLA, March 28, 1986.

Unit 5 Resource Book
Grammar Worksheet, p. 110
Grammar Check Test, p. 111

Editing Strategy: Works Cited Form

For additional support, see the mini-lesson at the bottom of page 667 and the worksheets referenced below.

Unit 5 Resource Book
Grammar Worksheet, p. 110
Grammar Check Test, p. 111

Connections to
Writer's Resource

Refer to the Grammar, Usage, and Mechanics Handbook on Writer's Resource.

STEP 5 PRESENTING

Oral Presentation

Allow time for students to practice their presentations with a partner before speaking before the whole class.

Map or Time Line

For students who are more visually oriented, you might allow extra credit for elaborate and detailed visuals.

STEP 6 LOOKING BACK

Self-evaluate

The *Assessment Criteria Specs* at the bottom of this page are for a superior paper. You might want to post these in the classroom. Students can then evaluate themselves based on these criteria.
For a complete scoring rubric, use the *Assessment Worksheet* referenced below.

Unit 5 Resource Book
Assessment Worksheet, p. 112

Reflect

Discuss with students any difficulties they had with this writing assignment.

To further explore the theme, use the Fine Art Transparency referenced below.

Transparency Collection
Fine Art Writing Prompt 12

Editing Strategy

COMPUTER TIP
Create a working reference list on the computer and add to it as you find sources. You can easily keep the list in alphabetical order and use a printout as the first draft of your Works Cited list.

Works Cited Form

The Works Cited list is the last page of your report. All the sources you cited in your report are listed on this page. Here are examples of how to cite three different kinds of sources.

For a book with more than one author:
Schwartz, Melvin, and John R. O'Connor. *Exploring a Changing World.* Englewood Cliffs: Globe Book Company, 1988.
For a periodical:
Clarke, John I. "Islamic Populations: Limited Demographic Transitions." *Geography*, vol. 70 (1985), 118–128.
For a general reference book:
"Saudi Arabia." *The New Encyclopedia Britannica*. 1979 ed.

Your teacher might ask you to use **footnotes** to acknowledge sources of information within the text of your report. Find out which style of footnotes your teacher prefers. Then, be consistent.

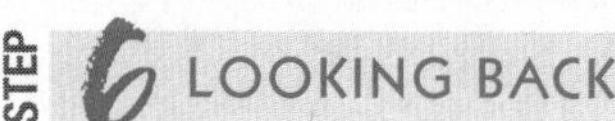

STEP 5 PRESENTING

COMPUTER TIP
Use a drawing program to create a map, flowchart, or time line of your research journey.

- Condense your paper into a five- or ten-minute oral presentation and share your questions and discoveries with the class.
- Include a map or time line to go along with the second part of your report. See the Computer Tip.

STEP 6 LOOKING BACK

Self-evaluate. Look back at the Writer's Blueprint and give your paper a score for each item, from 6 (superior) to 1 (inadequate).

Reflect. How was writing a personalized research report different from writing a standard research report?

For Your Working Portfolio Add your report and reflection responses to your working portfolio.

ASSESSMENT CRITERIA SPECS

6 Superior The writer of a 6 paper impressively meets these criteria:

- Demonstrates that the research has been a genuine learning experience for the writer.
- Provides special insight into the topic being discussed, using information gathered from a variety of sources.
- Is written in first-person point of view.
- Begins in an intriguing way to involve the reader.
- Supports the main points of the paper with strong details and examples, including accura[te] quotations and paraphrases.
- Documents the search portion in detail, includ[ing] problems encountered along the way.
- Draws insightful conclusions from the researc[h].
- Includes an accurate Works Cited list.
- Has few, if any, errors in grammar, usage, mechanics, or spelling.

Unit 5 Resource Book
Assessment Worksheet, p. 112

Beyond Print

Computer Terms

CD-ROM, Compact Disc Read Only Memory. This disc, which looks similar to an audio CD, is readable only with a computer that has a CD-ROM player and is used to store information such as text, sound, pictures, and movies.

Database, an organized collection of information, especially one in electronic form that can be accessed by computer software.

Internet, a series of computer servers connected together around the world.

Network, two or more computers connected together by cables, allowing them to communicate with each other.

Server, a computer that operates a network.

Electronic Research

As you prepare for any research project, review what electronic tools are available and how to make the best use of these tools. With modern technology at your fingertips, you can spend less research time tracking down materials and more time analyzing and sorting information. In your school, local library, or home, you may find these resources:

- A *magazine or newspaper index* stored on a CD-ROM. Many of these databases contain summaries or the full text of material in periodicals.
- *Reference materials* such as dictionaries, atlases, and almanacs on CD-ROM. Entire encyclopedias can be written onto a single CD-ROM!
- *Online services* connect you with other computers, giving you access to encyclopedias, magazines, reviews, interviews, and subject-specific databases. Using online services, librarians can search other libraries for books, articles, or other material necessary for your research. An important online database is the Internet, which can be accessed through government or educational institutions, as well as by individuals who buy membership in a consumer online service. With so much information at your fingertips, the biggest challenge is narrowing your search. Keep these things in mind:
- **Enter information accurately.** The computer can't read your mind, and it is extremely literal! If you are searching for an author, for example, be sure to spell the author's name correctly.
- **If you are searching by subject, try several different key words.** Don't quit if the first word you try doesn't turn up much. If you are researching apartheid in South Africa, the information you want may be filed under South Africa, Johannesburg, apartheid, Nelson Mandela, or any number of other key words. Keep trying!

Activity Options

1. Ask your librarian for a tour of the library's electronic research resources.
2. Work with a partner to create a list of key words on a particular subject, and use these words to collect information.

Beyond Print

Teaching Objectives

- to identify and understand terms related to electronic research tools
- to explore the application of these electronic research tools
- to practice efficient methods of electronic research

Curricular Connection: Technology Skills

Use this article to give students an overview of the research options available through computer technology.

Introduce

Ask students who have used electronic resources to give examples of the types of information they found, explain whether or not they found the material helpful, and tell whether they used the information for academic or other purposes.

Activity Options

Activity 1 Have students identify one resource that is unfamiliar to them and experiment with it.

Activity 2 Encourage students to research a topic from one of the selections: for example, Muslim women in the '90s or the political history of Botswana.

ANOTHER APPROACH

Electronic Research

Remind students that patience is a crucial element to the successful use of electronic resources. Most computer programs offer a "Help" icon on the menu bar at all times. Encourage students to use this function if they are in doubt about a step. Computers can perform incredible feats, but these processes take time. Prepare students for the inevitable moments of inaction that accompany all computer research tools: the Internet, CD-ROM, networking, even word processing. You might use this analogy: consider the time that it takes you to remember a detail or think of an answer to a difficult question. This mental process is similar to the number-crunching, string-searching, and line-connecting that we expect computers to execute in seconds flat.

Unit Wrap-Up

MULTICULTURAL CONNECTION

Invite students to suggest a theme for the unit. Ask them to base it on a poem that had a powerful impact on them.

Communication

Poets use their gift of language to put the forces of human emotion into memorable words and concrete images.

Possible responses

- In "A New Dress," the daughter doesn't share her feelings because she is afraid her mother won't understand.
- In "Those Winter Sundays," a child never thanks his father because he is too young to understand the concept of loving sacrifice.
- In "The Stone," the mourning lover is unable to speak because she is overwhelmed by sorrow.

Choice

- Despite technology and modern conveniences, humans are still subject to the whims and cycles of nature.
- The balance of order and chaos in nature, from the planets' rotation to the reproduction of a cell, is a model for human life.

Possible response Although people have a great deal of personal choice, these choices are subject to the natural cycles of life.

Interactions

Interactions are often made peaceful by a willingness to learn and an ability to recognize and accept the inevitability of change.

Possible responses

- Positive: "Woman From America," "My Father Writes to My Mother"
- Negative: "Rain Music," "Legal Alien," "For the White Poets Who Would Be Indian," "I Am Not with Those," "Jerusalem," "Two Countries"

Multicultural Connections

Communication

Part One: Connections Both culture and individual personalities determine the way we communicate. This group of poems reflects on the ways we reach out to communicate and connect—with family, with lovers, and with ourselves. Some poems provide poignant reminders of the pain of miscommunication and loss.

■ Choose three poems that deal with a lack of communication. Explain what is preventing communication in each case.

Choice

Part Two: Reflections Choice is often influenced by the cultural values of the society in which we live. But despite the different ceremonies, values, and directions we choose, there is a common life cycle that encompasses and reconciles various choices, as we are reminded in Ecclesiastes.

■ Do you think the message in Ecclesiastes suggests that people have a great deal of choice, or little choice, in determining their lives? Explain.

Interactions

Part Three: Culture Crossroads The cross-cultural interactions represented in this group of selections show that cultural mixes can have both positive and negative results.

■ Which selections in this group illustrate the positive effects of cross-cultural interactions? Which, the negative effects?

Activities

1. Examine your neighborhood, the Yellow Pages, or your school to find examples of cultures interacting. You might focus on bilingual signs and conversations, or music, foods, or clothing styles that reflect cultural combinations. Prepare a video, a poster, or an oral report to share with the class.
2. Ask a student who has immigrated to the U.S. to explain some of the main problems he or she has had with communication. Try to provide some solutions for preventing future problems.

Activities

Activity 1 Suggest that students organize their reports under the ideas of communication, choice, and interactions.

Activity 2 Suggest that students turn the interview around and try to answer their own questions. How do communication problems persist even for English-speaking students?

Independent and Group Projects

Media

Literary Quest You and your group are writers for a TV quiz show titled *A Place in the World*. It is your job to devise twenty questions for the category, Literature and Authors from Around the World, based on the biographies and works of authors represented in this unit. Have a group member act as host, and invite class members to be contestants.

Art

Multicultural Mixes Find photographs, articles, and quotations that show the influence of one culture on another (for example, elderly people attending rap or rock concerts). Use this material to make your own Interdisciplinary Study, like the one that begins on page 659. Write several questions to elicit student response to your words and images.

Oral Presentation

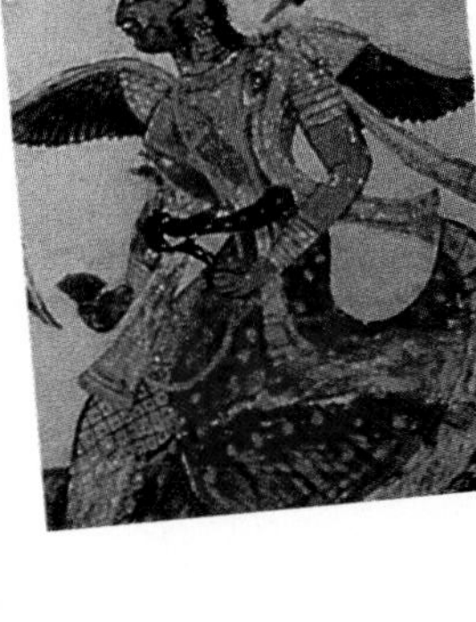

Book Talk You are a librarian who hosts a weekly program called *Book Talk* on cable TV. Prepare a two-minute sampler of the works in this unit and present the talk to the class. Remember, your job is to attract readers.

Translations

Many Tongues Several of the poems in this unit appear in their original language and in their English translations. Class members who are native speakers or students of a language other than English can provide translations of other poems in this unit. Studying the same word or phrase in various languages can spark a discussion about the skill and artistry required of a translator, as well as the complexities of a language.

Research

Take Off The Ministry of Tourism in one of the countries represented by selections in this unit has asked your ad agency to write copy and provide pictures for a travel brochure. In a group, decide what to include and how to present it. Display your brochure for the class.

UNIT 5 OPTIONS

Media

Remind students that the more thoroughly they research their topics, the more likely is the possibility that they will stump their classmates.

Connections to **AuthorWorks**

Data for competing this project can be found in the AuthorWorks CD-ROM series.

Art

Suggest that students work in groups to compile their interdisciplinary study pages into an Interdisciplinary Collection. Students with computer access might want to experiment with desktop publishing techniques. You might suggest that students research simple bookbinding techniques.

Oral Presentation

You might remind students that since television is a multimedia showcase, they might want to take advantage of the visual realm by using props, posters, and photographs.

Translations

Encourage students to read their translations aloud to the class. Suggest that students research the original versions of other translations and read them aloud as well. Have students who can read the translations fluently teach lines of verse to others.

esearch

dents might request brochures from travel agen-s or consulates of foreign countries and use them guides for their layouts and designs. Suggest that dents use multimedia resources such as CD-ROM ases and encyclopedias, as well as travel agencies the Internet, to broaden their research base.

Unit Test

Unit 5 Resource Book
New Selection, pp. 113–120
Test 1, pp. 121–122
Test 2, pp. 123–128

The Cost of Winning

Planning Unit 6: Power Plays

Literature	Integrated Language Arts			
	Literary	Writing/Grammar, Usage and Mechanics	Reading, Thinking, Listening, Speaking	Vocabulary/Spelling
Julius Caesar *by William Shakespeare* Play *(challenging)* **Act 1** p. 679	Plot, meter Allusion, diction Figurative language Characterization Style	Character summary Popularity tips Blank verse Development of the English language Use powerful verbs Homonyms	Draw conclusions Clarify, connect Summarize, analyze Infer, evaluate Question, predict Recognize propaganda	Expanding vocabulary using structural analysis Read uncommon low-frequency words
Act 2 p. 698	Theme Imagery Alliteration Metaphor Irony	Archaic adverbs Recognize the function of all parts of speech Blank verse Homonyms and homophones	Predict Make judgments Summarize Draw conclusions Connect, evaluate Question, clarify	
Act 3 p. 714	Suspense, irony Figurative language Structure, protagonists Characterization, pun Foreshadowing	Caesar's obituary Eyewitness letter Short dialogue The superlative form	Clarify, draw conclusions Connect, summarize Question, evaluate Recognize the use of persuasion Compare and contrast Predict, analyze Make judgments	Synonym or antonym
Act 4 p. 736	Characterization Figurative language Extended metaphor Foreshadowing	Stage bill Homonyms and homophones Noun and pronoun forms—relative pronouns Recognize sentence fragments	Summarize Draw conclusions Compare and contrast Predict, connect, infer Evaluate, question, clarify Make judgments	
Act 5 p. 750	Plot, figurative language Sound devices, symbolism Irony, characterization Final speech	Essay Write a translation Explanation Words commonly confused	Evaluate, compare and contrast Clarify, draw conclusions Summarize, predict Connection, question, infer	
The Balek Scales *by Heinrich Boll* Short Story *(average)* p. 766	Theme, plot Repetition, foreshadow Archetype, character, allusion	Write story opening Create an ad Dialogue, verbal phrases	Clarify, analyze Draw conclusions Summarize	Word relationship Finding synonyms in dictionaries
How Much Land Does a Man Need? *by Leo Tolstoy* Short Story *(average)* p. 775	Parable, allusion Figurative language Plot, stereotype Irony, repetition Characterization	Brief essay Essay Write a folktale Autobiographical sketch Paragraph indentation	Cause and effect Predict, make judgments Problem-solving Connect, clarify Visualize, draw conclusions	Understand content area vocabulary Connotation and denotation

Meeting Individual Needs

Multi-modal Activities	Mini-Lessons
Oral interpretation Exploring main ideas Linking past and present Exploring character Using gloss notes Exploring dramatic tension Exploring mood Analyzing persuasion Checking comprehension	Development of the English language Expanding vocabulary using structural analysis Read uncommon low-frequency words Using powerful verbs Homonyms
Supporting an opinion Relating to characters Keeping track of details Adjust reading rate Making real-life connections Analyzing character Exploring key statements	Archaic adverbs Recognizing the function of all parts of speech Blank verse Homonyms and homophones
Analyzing Shakespeare's language Dramatizing key events Analyzing a climax Exploring character relationships Contrasting speeches Analyzing persuasion Evaluating dramatic presentation Analyzing key events	Reading Shakespearean drama Recognizing puns Analyzing figurative language The superlative form Rhetorical devices Protagonist
Visualizing the stage Exploring motivation Contrasting series of events Keeping track of the story details Examining connotations Analyzing character	Homonyms and homophones Finding information Relative pronouns Recognizing sentence fragments
Analyzing loaded words Analyzing metaphor Examining literary criticism Relate literature to human concerns	Plot, make judgments Words commonly confused Build a time line
Exploring exposition Understanding sequence Responding to theme	Verbal phrases Finding synonyms in dictionaries
Debate Collector's guide Understanding sequence Making personal connections Speaking and listening Enacting a climax	Paragraph indentation Connotation and denotation Identify alternatives Reference sources

Interdisciplinary Studies
The Image Makers

Format	Content Area	Highlights	Skill
Article: **The Teflon President**	Media	This excerpt discusses Ronald Reagan's persona and presidency.	Monitor audience reactions
Article: **Creating an Image**	Career	This article describes how a candidate's image is created.	

Writing Workshop

Mode	Writing Format	Writing Focus	Proofreading Skills
Persuasive writing	A persuasive essay and speech	Using persuasive devices	Comparative and superlative forms of modifiers

Program Support Materials

For Every Selection	For Every Writing Workshop
Unit Resource Book Graphic Organizer Study Guide Vocabulary Worksheet Grammar Worksheet Spelling, Speaking and Listening, or Literary Language Worksheet Alternate Check Test Vocabulary Test Selection Test	**Unit Resource Book** Prewriting Worksheet Revising Strategy Worksheet Editing Strategy Worksheet Presentation Worksheet Writing Rubric **Transparency Collection** Fine Art Transparency Student Writing Model Transparencies

For Every Interdisciplinary Study	Assessment
Unit Resource Book Study Guide Mini-Lesson Skill Worksheet	**Unit Resource Book** TE Check Tests Alternate Check Test (blackline master) Vocabulary Test (blackline master) Selection Test (blackline master) **Test Generator Software** **Assessment Handbook**

Unit 6 Supplemental Resources

Media and Technology

Julius Caesar

Audiotape Anthony Quayle and others perform in *Julius Caesar,* 2 hours 30 minutes, Harper, 1989.

Videotape Students will enjoy *Shakespeare: The Man and His Times*, 38 minutes, Educational Audio Visual, 1989. *Julius Caesar*, 2 hours, 41 minutes, Ambrose, 1979, is a video production of the play. Also consider the classic film version starring Marlon Brando, *Julius Caesar*, 122 minutes, Library Video Company, 1953.

Computer Software *The Time, Life and Works of Shakespeare*, CD-ROM for IBM, Macintosh, and Windows, is available from Clearvue, 1995. Consider *Much Ado About Shakespeare*, CD-ROM for Windows, from the Bureau of Electronic Publishing.

Community Resources Students interested in acting might like to read about the Booth or Barrymore families of actors; members of both families appeared in Shakespearean roles. Other students might like to research the new Globe Theater, recently completed in London and based on what is known about the Globe of Shakespeare's time. A local library should have information on all these subjects.

The Balek Scales

Home Connection Who are the most powerful people in the world? in the United States? How does one achieve power?

Connections to
Custom Literature Database

For Part One "The Cost of Winning" Selections with Lessons

- "The Golden Fleece" by Thomas Bulfinch
- "War" by Jack London

Additional theme-based selections can be accessed on the ScottForesman database.

Classic Portrayal of Mark Anthony

Marlon Brando stars as Marc Antony in the classic film version of *Julius Caesar.*

influential friends? education? hard work? by seizing power through force? Is having power a desire of most people or only a few? Students might like to poll family and friends, asking these and similar questions about the nature of power.

How Much Land Does a Man Need?

Audiotape Students might enjoy Irene Worth's reading of Tolstoy's *Anna Karenina*, Caedmon/Harper Audio.

Community Resources The title of the Tolstoy story is a good starting point for a discussion about land ownership and use. Students might use library resources to find out more about views on owning land (Native Americans were amazed that America's first settlers thought that land could be acquired) and on who has the right (or power) to dictate what can be done on private land. Students might be interested in investigating the disputes between land owners and environmentalists and in discussing various philosophies about land ownership.

Connections to
BBC Shakespeare on CD-ROM Series

The BBC Shakespeare on CD-ROM series: *Julius Caesar* offers a rich variety of unique materials for teaching the play.

Connections to
AuthorWorks

Information about the life and times of Leo Tolstoy is available on ScottForesman's AuthorWorks CD-ROM.

Unit 6

Power Plays

Art Study

The Death of Caesar was painted in 1859 by Jean-Léon Gérôme, a French painter who lived from 1824–1904. This oil painting recreates one of the most famous scenes in history and theater. You may wish to avoid naming the picture so that the plot of the play is not revealed to students too early.

Questions

- What happened just before the scene that is shown? *(The man whose body lies in the right foreground of the painting was killed with the swords and knives that are being wielded by the crowd.)*
- Why are the characters grouped the way they are? *(Possible Response: They are celebrating the accomplishment of killing the man who is dead.)*
- What do you predict will happen next? *(Responses will vary. Students' responses should follow logically from the details depicted in the illustration.)*

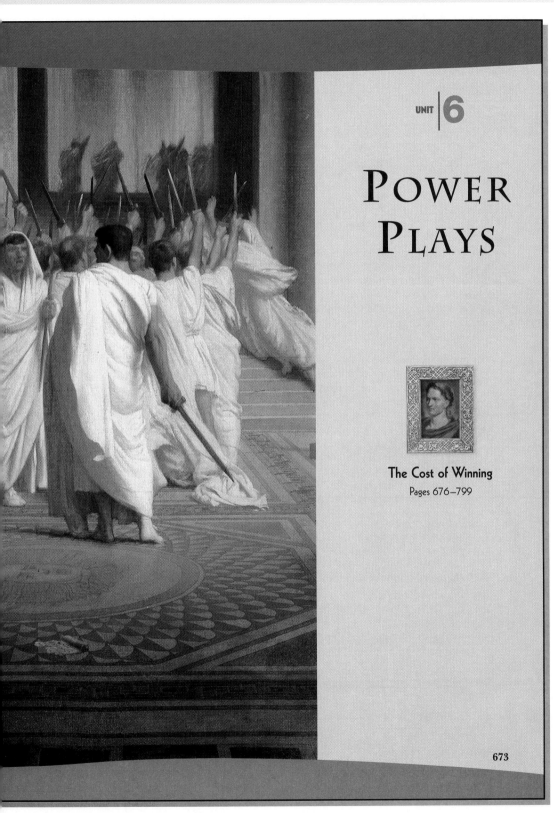

UNIT 6

POWER PLAYS

The Cost of Winning

THEMATIC CONNECTIONS

When individuals make power plays to attain more land, money, or political clout, they are taking serious risks. One may also risk everything by simply telling the truth. Sometimes, the cost of winning just isn't worth it.

The Cost of Winning

Ideas to Explore

- What risks are involved in seeking power?
- What price might people have to pay for gaining enormous political power? owning more and more land? telling the truth about those in power?

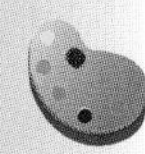

Art Study

Julius Caesar, Emperor is a painting by Peter Paul Rubens, a Flemish painter who lived from 1577–1640. Rubens is considered the predominant figure in Baroque art in northern Europe.

Genre Overview: Shakespearean Play

EXPLORING CONCEPTS

- Scene summaries at the head of each scene present the highlights of the action.
- Reading each scene twice can help—once for a general impression, and a second close reading to pick up the details missed the first time around.
- Marginal notes help with establishing precise meaning.
- Analysis of the major characters can help establish their role in the plot.
- Rearranging word order sometimes makes sentences easier to understand.
- Words which, if included, would repeat words already said, are sometimes omitted.
- Analyze figurative language to find the intended meaning.
- The poetic element of meter is varied according to need.
- Reading aloud is likely to increase comprehension.

Research Activity Encourage small groups of students to explore blank verse.

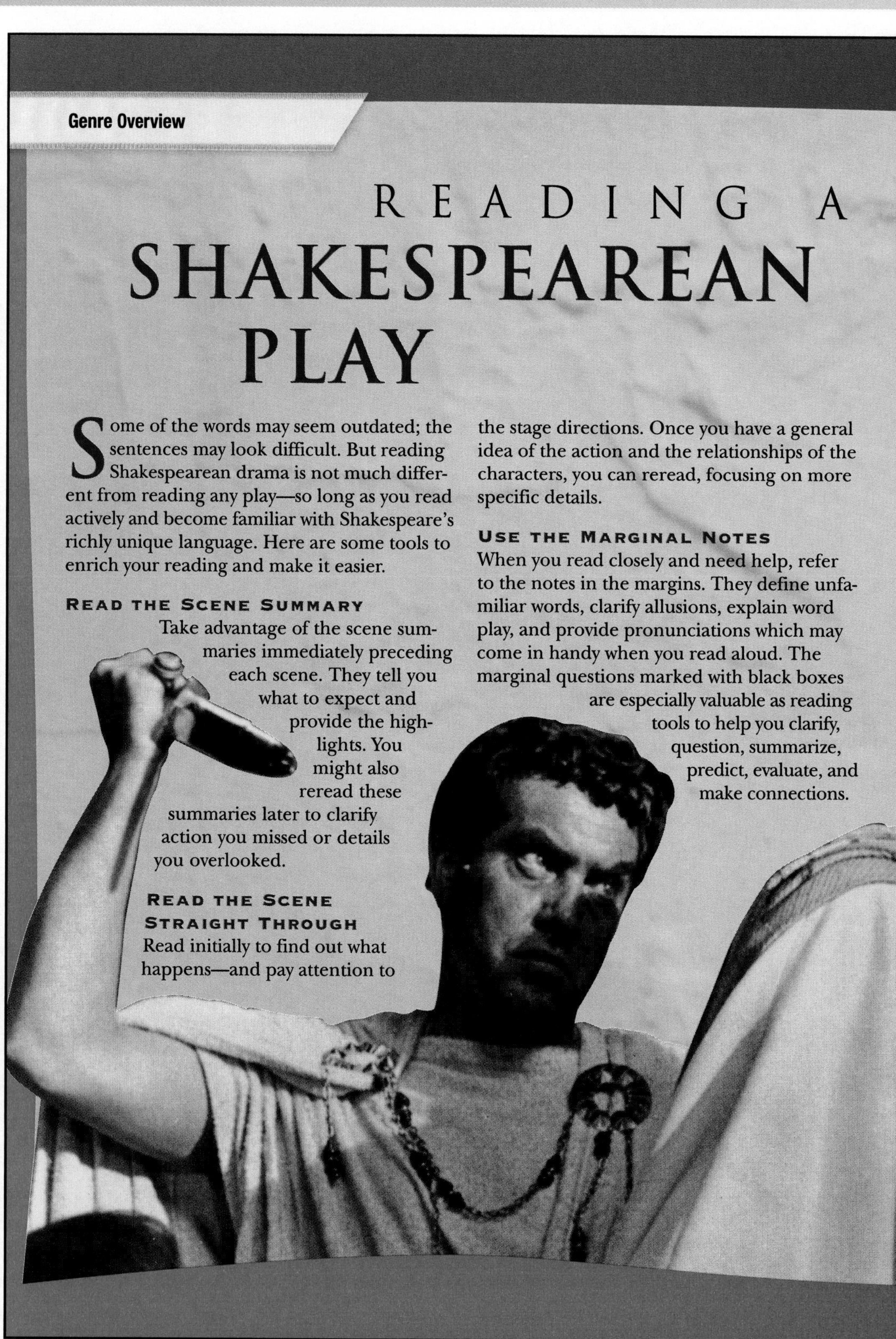

Genre Overview

READING A SHAKESPEAREAN PLAY

Some of the words may seem outdated; the sentences may look difficult. But reading Shakespearean drama is not much different from reading any play—so long as you read actively and become familiar with Shakespeare's richly unique language. Here are some tools to enrich your reading and make it easier.

READ THE SCENE SUMMARY
Take advantage of the scene summaries immediately preceding each scene. They tell you what to expect and provide the highlights. You might also reread these summaries later to clarify action you missed or details you overlooked.

READ THE SCENE STRAIGHT THROUGH
Read initially to find out what happens—and pay attention to the stage directions. Once you have a general idea of the action and the relationships of the characters, you can reread, focusing on more specific details.

USE THE MARGINAL NOTES
When you read closely and need help, refer to the notes in the margins. They define unfamiliar words, clarify allusions, explain word play, and provide pronunciations which may come in handy when you read aloud. The marginal questions marked with black boxes are especially valuable as reading tools to help you clarify, question, summarize, predict, evaluate, and make connections.

Think About the Characters

Focus on the major characters. What do these characters reveal in their conversations? What do others say about them? What conflicts or alliances do they have with others? What motivates and troubles them? What makes them "ring true"? Think also about why minor characters appear. To add humor? To introduce tension? To clarify situations or provide background?

Rearrange Inverted Sentences

English sentences typically begin with a subject followed by a verb. Shakespeare often changes that order. For example, in the first scene of *Julius Caesar,* Flavius says to Marullus, "Go you down that way towards the Capitol." Rearranged, this sentence would read: "You go down that way. . . ."

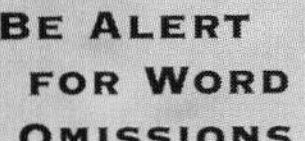

Be Alert for Word Omissions

In the preceding example, the line continues with these words: "This way will I." Modernized, this would read "I will go this way."

Interpret Figurative Language

Shakespeare often uses figurative language to convey important ideas. Ask yourself what the comparison is and what it suggests. For example, Cassius says about Caesar, "He were no lion, were not Romans hinds." Since a hind is a female deer, Cassius implies that Caesar's strength is due to the Roman citizens' cowardice (that is, "If the Romans weren't cowards, Caesar wouldn't be in power").

Recognize Blank Verse

Most of the characters in *Julius Caesar* speak in blank verse (also called iambic pentameter), a form of unrhymed poetry in which each line has ten syllables—five unstressed alternating with five stressed. This rhythm pattern can be shown like this, with ´ indicating stressed words and syllables and ˘ indicating those that are unstressed.

> And why/should Cae/sar be/a ty/rant then?

As you read, notice that a line of blank verse can be divided among two or more characters. Note also that, depending on his purpose, Shakespeare may vary the rhythm in this form, or abandon it altogether for prose.

Read Passages Aloud

Plays were meant to be *said,* not *read.* Read aloud to yourself or with a friend. Read for sense, using punctuation as clues. Once you determine the character's attitude and purpose in speaking, you should find just the right tone of voice.

These are some tools. But the best way to understand and enjoy a Shakespearean play is to see it in action. So rent a film (the 1953 production of *Julius Caesar* starring Marlon Brando, from which some of the photographs in this book are taken, would be a good place to begin); see a play; or put on your own classroom production. You'll be surprised to learn how modern the situations, themes, and even the language can seem!

"SPEAK, HANDS, FOR ME!"

MATERIALS OF INTEREST

Books

- *The Civil War* by Julius Caesar (Penguin, 1976)
- *The Twelve Caesars* by Suetonius (Penguin, 1957)
- *Lives of the Noble Grecians and Romans* by Plutarch (Random House, 1992)

Multimedia

The BBC Shakespeare on CD-ROM series: *Julius Caesar* offers a rich variety of unique materials for teaching the play.

Preview

The Cost of Winning

FOR ALL STUDENTS

- When is it worth suffering to reach a goal?
- How can we judge if someone has the right amount of power, land, and wealth, or if they have too much?

To further explore the theme, use the Fine Art Transparency referred to below.

Transparency Collection
Fine Art Writing Prompt 13

For At-Risk Students

Ask students to

- think about a time when winning didn't bring them the rewards they expected and tell what happened.
- talk about times when it's better to lose than to win.

For Students Who Need a Challenge

Have students analyze another play, such as *Romeo and Juliet,* using the idea of "The Cost of Winning." Who seemed to win and what was the cost of winning?

For Kinesthetic Students

Encourage students to pay attention to how the characters move together and apart during each scene.

MULTICULTURAL CONNECTION

Change can result in development and progress or in regression and destruction. Help students examine the concept by mentioning these change agents and pointing to the results of change.

- natural disasters
- political elections
- war
- volunteer work

The Cost of Winning

Power, land, wealth—all have their appeal. But is winning always worth it? The characters in these selections give up a great deal of what is human in their pursuits of power. And the cost? Respect, reputation, maybe life itself.

Multicultural Connection **Change** can be good for a society, but it can also devastate a social order. Read about people who try to make drastic changes in their lives or the lives of others.

IDEAS THAT WORK

Motivating with Comparison and Contrast

The idea of being overwhelmed by a force, an idea, or a personality remains a recurring theme in literature. The disproportionate nature of Caesar's sense of self-importance is rich fodder to explore. I like to have my students analyze the role of ego in leadership. How much is too much.? What other personality traits contribute to one's effectiveness as a leader? We explore these questions by comparing the personality of Julius Caesar to that of twentieth century leaders such as Adolf Hitler and Franklin Roosevelt.

Edison W. Barbe
Bourbonnais, Illinoi

Before Reading

Julius Caesar

by William Shakespeare   Great Britain

William Shakespeare
1564–1616

William Shakespeare grew up in a middle-class family in Stratford-upon-Avon, a small town north of London. He attended grammar school until he was fourteen, and by age eighteen he was married to Anne Hathaway. Their first child was born in 1583, followed two years later by twins. At school, Shakespeare may first have read Plutarch's *Lives of the Noble Greeks and Romans,* his chief source for *Julius Caesar.* No one knows why or when Shakespeare left Stratford for London, but by 1592 he was an actor; by 1602, he was a prolific dramatist and part owner of the Globe Theater. In 1611, he retired to Stratford, respected and wealthy. He died on April 16, 1616, the anniversary of his baptism.

Building Background

Power Struggle For many years Julius Caesar struggled with Pompey (pom′pē), once his ally, for control of Rome and its territories. Eventually war broke out between them and in 48 B.C. Caesar, a superb military leader, defeated Pompey, who fled to Egypt for safety and was murdered there. When Pompey's two sons took up the war, Caesar defeated them too. Returning to Rome, Caesar was named dictator, a title that gave him absolute authority for life. Many Romans became suspicious of Caesar's power, fearing that his desire to become king would put an end to their republic. Still other Romans were angry that Caesar celebrated a public triumph over Pompey's sons, who were not foreigners but Romans like themselves. The action of Shakespeare's *Julius Caesar* begins on the day Caesar has selected to celebrate his triumphant return to the city.

Literary Focus

Plot A series of related events that present and resolve a conflict is called **plot**. Watch for ways in which Shakespeare advances plot through action and dialogue. Reproduce the plot diagram in your notebook that appears on page 65, and add plot elements to the diagram as you read. The beginning of the play, or the **exposition**, introduces the viewers or readers to the background, characters, and setting. The first incident begins the **conflict**.

Writer's Notebook

Caesar As you read this play, fill out a chart like the one below, listing and illustrating Caesar's character traits, based both on what he says and does and on how others speak of him.

Character Trait	Illustration
suspicious	"Cassius . . . thinks too much."

Before Reading

Building Background

The following movies, available from Films for the Humanities & Sciences (800-247-5126) can be used to orient students to Shakespearean drama:

- *Shakespearean Tragedy* (This program explores Shakespeare's concept of action, character, and tragedy. 40 mins. color)
- *Shakespeare and the Globe* (Visual resources retrace Shakespeare's life and works. 31 mins. color)

Share the following information:

- Display a historical map of Caesar's massive holdings: all of Italy, Gaul, Spain, Macedonia, Greece, Palestine, Egypt, and virtually all of the Mediterranean islands.
- Caesar introduced many reforms: he reduced debts, revised the tax structure, extended Roman citizenship to non-Italians, and implemented the Julian calendar.
- Caesar was a skilled orator and writer. His two surviving works, *On the Gallic War* and *On the Civil War,* established the genre of personal war commentary.
- The ambitious Caesar was not only a superb military strategist and brilliant politician, but he was also intelligent, witty, and charismatic. Although he engendered loyalty and admiration among his contemporaries, his disdain for republican traditions drove his opponents to destroy him.

SUPPORT MATERIALS OVERVIEW

Unit 6 Resource Book
- Graphic Organizers, pp. 1, 9, 17, 25, 33
- Study Guides, pp. 2, 10, 18, 26, 34
- Vocabulary, pp. 3, 11, 19, 27, 35
- Grammar, pp. 4, 12, 20, 28, 36
- Alternate Check Tests, pp. 5, 13, 21, 29, 37
- Vocabulary Tests, pp. 6, 14, 22, 30, 38
- Selection Tests, pp. 7–9, 15–16, 23–24, 31–32, 39–40

Building English Proficiency
- Literature Summaries
- Activities, pp. 219–223

Reading, Writing & Grammar SkillBook
- Reading, pp. 22–23, 36–37, 45–46, 51–58, 61–62, 65–68, 79–86, 87–88, 93–94, 97–98
- Vocabulary, pp. 9–10, 18–19
- Writing, pp. 121–122
- Grammar, Usage, and Mechanics, pp. 181–182, 228–229, 234–235

The World of Work

Civil Servant, p. 25
Make a Chart, p. 26

Technology
- Personal Journal Software
- Custom Literature Database: Additional selections by Shakespeare, including some of his sonnets and *Midsummer Night's Dream,* can be found on the database.
- Test Generator Software

Literary Focus

Suggest that students make a **plot** Exposition Chart to keep track of background information.

Exposition Chart
Caesar returns victorious over Pompey's sons.

Writer's Notebook

Traits to illustrate include arrogance, impatience, and shrewdness.

Connections to **AuthorWorks**

The BBC Shakespeare on CD-ROM series: *Julius Caesar* offers a rich variety of unique materials for teaching the play. Also available on the BBC Shakespeare on CD-ROM series is *Midsummer Night's Dream.*

More About Shakespeare

Shakespeare's other tragedies include:

- *Romeo and Juliet* (Young lovers meet with a tragic end.)
- *Hamlet* (A prince seeks revenge on his uncle for murdering his father.)
- *Othello* (A husband is led by a villainous companion to kill his wife.)
- *King Lear* (A king divides his kingdom and brings about war and death.)
- *Macbeth* (A man murders the current king and takes his place.)

Source

Shakespeare drew on Plutarch's *Lives of the Noble Greeks and Romans*, translated from Latin by Sir Thomas North, for most of the material in the play. "The Life of Caesar" gave him much of the basic plot; "The Life of Brutus" provided characterization, especially of Brutus and Cassius; and "The Life of Mark Antony" gave him information about Antony, as well as the idea for another tragedy, *Antony and Cleopatra*, written in 1606.

Major Characters

Julius Caesar (100 B.C.–44 B.C.) was a great conqueror and politician. He gained territory for Rome and frequently sent money back to the city to be used for public works or to help the common people. Although he was given the honor of ruling Rome as long as he lived, many suspected that he wanted to set up a monarchy so that power would pass to his heirs. Caesar was married to Calpurnia, but thus far she had borne no children.

Marcus Brutus (85 B.C.–44 B.C.) was a descendant of Lucius Junius Brutus, who had driven out the Tarquin kings and made Rome a republic. Marcus Brutus was a quiet idealist who enjoyed reading and study. At one time, he had supported Pompey, one of Caesar's chief rivals for power, and had fought with him against Caesar. After Pompey's defeat Caesar pardoned Brutus, and the two resumed their friendship. Though Brutus liked Caesar, he feared Caesar's ambition. Brutus was married to Portia, whose father had killed himself rather than submit to Caesar's rule.

Caius Cassius (? B.C.–42 B.C.) was a thin, quick-tempered, practical man with a grudge against Caesar. Like Brutus, he had supported Pompey in the war against Caesar. After Brutus was pardoned, Caesar also pardoned Cassius, who was Brutus's brother-in-law.

Mark Antony (83 B.C.–30 B.C.) was a young man notorious for his wild living. He had fought under Caesar and supported Caesar's ambitious schemes. A holder of various public offices, including that of tribune, Antony understood the instability of the commoners and how a speaker could sway their emotions.

WILLIAM SHAKESPEARE

CHARACTERS

1 JULIUS CAESAR
CALPURNIA, *Caesar's wife*
2 MARK ANTONY, OCTAVIUS CAESAR, LEPIDUS — *triumvirs*[1] *after Caesar's death*
MARCUS BRUTUS
PORTIA, *Brutus's wife*
CAIUS CASSIUS, CASCA, DECIUS BRUTUS, CINNA, METELLUS CIMBER, TREBONIUS, CAIUS LIGARIUS — *conspirators with Brutus*
CICERO, PUBLIUS, POPILIUS LENA — *senators*
FLAVIUS, MARULLUS — *tribunes*[2] *of the people*
SOOTHSAYER
ARTEMIDORUS, *a teacher of rhetoric*
CINNA, *a poet*
Another POET
LUCILIUS, TITINIUS, MESSALA, YOUNG CATO, VOLUMNIUS, VARRO — *officers and soldiers in the army of Brutus and Cassius*
CLAUDIUS, CLITUS, DARDANIUS, LABEO, FLAVIUS — *officers and soldiers in the army of Brutus and Cassius*
PINDARUS, *Cassius's servant*
LUCIUS, STRATO — *Brutus's servants*
Caesar's SERVANT
Antony's SERVANT
Octavius's SERVANT
CARPENTER
COBBLER
Five PLEBEIANS
Three SOLDIERS *in Brutus's army*
Two SOLDIERS *in Antony's army*
MESSENGER
GHOST *of Caesar*
Senators, Plebians, Officers, Soldiers , and Attendants

1. **triumvirs** (trī um′vərz), three officials who jointly ruled Rome, from the Latin *trium virorum,* "of three men."
2. **tribunes,** elected officials who served as spokesmen for the commoners and protected them from the government if necessary.

During Reading

Selection Objectives

- to analyze the pursuit of power and its consequences
- to examine elements of plot
- to identify examples of homonyms and homophones

Unit 6 Resource Book
Graphic Organizer, p. 1
Study Guide, p. 2

Theme Link

Julius Caesar illustrates that the "Cost of Winning" is great to those who pursue power and who seek revenge.

Vocabulary Preview

meet, fitting; appropriate
mettle, spirit; courage
perilous, dangerous
prodigious, very great or huge
servile, like that of a slave

Students can add the words and definitions to their Writer's Notebooks.

1 Historical Note
Caesar's Honors

Caesar became a pontiff in the year 73 B.C., and then governor of Further Spain. Through bribery, he became Pontifex Maximus (high priest) and then was named a praetor. In 60 B.C., with Crassus and Pompey, he formed the First Triumvirate. After defeating Pompey and his sons, he was appointed dictator. His likeness appeared on coins, and a temple was erected to his clemency.

2 Historical Note
Octavius Caesar

Born Gaius Octavius, Julius Caesar's great nephew, who was to become the first Roman emperor, was adopted by Caesar in his will and became Gaius Julius Caesar. The power of the name allowed him to rally Caesar's forces on his own behalf.

SELECTION SUMMARY

Julius Caesar, Act 1

Scene 1: Commoners gather in celebration of Caesar's return from his victory over Pompey's sons. The tribunes, angered by the fickleness of the mob that had only recently cheered Pompey, rail at the crowd and attempt to disperse them.

Scene 2: Caesar, approaching the Capitol, is stopped by a Soothsayer who warns him of the ides of March. Brutus, disturbed by Caesar's behavior and ambition, withdraws from the procession and is joined by Cassius, who attempts to win Brutus to the conspiracy against Caesar. They learn that Caesar has refused a proffered crown. After the two part company, Cassius plans to plant anonymous notes where Brutus will find them, telling how freedom-loving citizens look to him for their salvation from Caesar's tyranny.

Scene 3: On the stormy eve of the ides of March, Cassius encounters Casca, reveals the plan to crown Caesar, and enlists Casca's aid.

For summaries in other languages, see the ***Building English Proficiency*** *book.*

3 Multicultural Note
The Lupercalia

The Lupercalia was a fertility festival celebrated in Rome until the fifth century A.D. The Lupercal cave, which is at the base of the Palatine Hill, was believed to be the place where Romulus and Remus, the twins who founded Rome, were suckled by a she-wolf.

4 Reading/Thinking Skills
Draw Conclusions

Question Describe the relations between the tribunes and the commoners. *(Possible response: The tribunes condescend to and bully the commoners, whom they know are easily swayed by rhetoric. It might be said that they treat them with contempt. The commoners tease the tribunes but maintain a show of respect.)*

ACT ONE

SCENE 1

Summary *When the tribunes Flavius and Marullus encounter a crowd of commoners gathered to celebrate Caesar's victory over Pompey's sons, Marullus angrily scolds them for forgetting their former allegiance to Pompey. The two men disperse the crowd, then exit, vowing to remove any decorations on Caesar's public statues.*

3 *A street in Rome. The* COMMONERS, *dressed in holiday garments for the Feast of Lupercalia and talking excitedly, look to the right, the direction from which* CAESAR'S *procession will appear. Offstage shouts and cheers send* COMMONERS *scurrying for vantage points.* FLAVIUS *and* MARULLUS *enter.*

FLAVIUS. Hence! Home, you idle creatures, get you home!
Is this a holiday? What, know you not,
Being mechanical, you ought not walk
Upon a laboring without the sign
Of your profession? Speak, what trade art thou?

CARPENTER. Why, sir, a carpenter.

MARULLUS. Where is thy leather apron and thy rule?
What dost thou with thy best apparel on?
You, sir, what trade are you?

COBBLER. Truly, sir, in respect of a fine workman, I am but, as you would say, a cobbler.

MARULLUS. But what trade art thou? Answer me directly.

COBBLER. A trade, sir, that I hope I may use with a safe conscience, which is indeed, sir, a mender of bad soles.

FLAVIUS. What trade, thou knave? Thou naughty knave, what trade?

COBBLER. Nay, I beseech you, sir, be not out with me. Yet if you be out, sir, I can mend you.

4 **FLAVIUS.** What mean'st thou by that? Mend me, thou saucy fellow?

COBBLER. Why, sir, cobble you.

FLAVIUS. Thou art a cobbler, art thou?

COBBLER. Truly, sir, all that I live by is with the awl. I meddle with no tradesman's matters nor women's matters, but withal I am indeed, sir, a surgeon to old shoes. When they are in great danger, I recover them. As proper men as ever trod upon neat's leather have gone upon my handiwork.

FLAVIUS. But wherefore art not in thy shop today? Why dost thou lead these men about the streets?

COBBLER. Truly, sir, to wear out their shoes, to get myself into more work. But indeed, sir, we make holiday to see Caesar and to rejoice in his triumph.

3 **mechanical,** workingmen.

3–5 **you ought not . . . profession,** a reference to a law of Shakespeare's time requiring workers to wear their laboring clothes and carry the tools of their profession.

11 **cobbler.** In Shakespeare's time this word meant not only a shoe mender but also a clumsy worker. This explains Marullus's question.

16 **be not . . . me,** a pun. To be out meant both "out of temper" as well as "having worn-out soles."

22 **withal,** yet. Another pun, on both "all" and "with awl" (a shoemaker's tool).

24 **neat's leather,** cowhide.

MINI-LESSON: GRAMMAR
Development of the English Language

Read Marullus's lines 6–8 aloud.

Where is *thy* leather apron and *thy* rule?
What *dost thou* with *thy* best apparel on?
You, sir, what trade are *you?*

- Point out that *thou* is an archaic form of the informal subject pronoun *you* and *thy* is an archaic form of the possessive pronoun *your.* Because *thou* is appropriate to be used only for an intimate associate or an inferior, it alerts the audience to the relationship between the tribunes and the commoners.
- Explain that *dost* is an archaic form of *do,* and that similar verb forms appear throughout the play (for example, *hast* and *art).*

Archaic Word	Meaning
thou	you
dost	do

Activity Idea Have students continue the chart of archaic forms in the play. For each form, they should use a dictionary, if necessary, to discover its meaning.

Art Study

Possible responses The viewer's eye is drawn to the sword that the customer is holding and examining. The armorer is probably pointing out some detail or feature of the sword, or negotiating price.

Visual Literacy A variety of techniques are used to focus attention in a painting.

- Proportion: The sword bisects the picture exactly in half and is pointed toward the central figure's throat.
- Color: Since the colors are predominantly dark, costumes that are white and cream attract attention.
- Lines and shapes: The extended hand and the sword's point, along with the shawl over the head of the tallest figure, direct the eyes to the central focal point.

The Armorer's Shop was painted in 1866 by Sir Lawrence Alma-Tadema, known for his attention to historical and archaeological detail. To what point is your eye immediately directed? What do you think the armorer is saying?

BUILDING ENGLISH PROFICIENCY

Exploring Main Ideas

In working to understand Shakespeare's English, students may miss the points that (1) Caesar is a very popular war hero and that (2) one political faction doesn't trust or admire Caesar. Help students to an awareness of these main ideas with questions such as the following:

- Which lines tell you how the commoners feel about Caesar? *(lines 29–30)*
- What is the point of Marullus's questions? *(He wants to chide them for forgetting their allegiance to Pompey.)*
- What possible courses of action—positive and negative—are open to the followers of a defeated leader? Which do you think Marullus and Flavius will follow? Why?

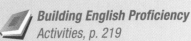

Building English Proficiency
Activities, p. 219

5 Historical Note
Anachronisms

Students who read the margin notes will already be aware that Shakespeare has superimposed some aspects of Elizabethan life onto his Roman play. Have students look for other anachronisms that are not mentioned in the side notes. (Examples: act 1, scene 2, line 228: *marry*, an oath that refers to the Virgin Mary; act 2, scene 1, line 73: The hats are Elizabethan wide-brimmed hats.)

6 Literary Focus
Plot

Question What does the conflict between the tribunes and commoners reveal about the central plot issues in this play? *(Possible responses: It will focus on Caesar's role and power. It will have to do with persuasion. It will have to do with a class struggle.)*

7 Reading/Thinking Skills
Clarify

Possible response The commoners submit to the tribunes' orders.

8 Reading/Thinking Skills
Draw Conclusions

Question What do the tribunes fear? *(Caesar's enormous power and ability to repress them)*

MARULLUS. Wherefore rejoice? What conquest brings he home?
What tributaries follow him to Rome
To grace in captive bonds his chariot wheels?
You blocks, you stones, you worse than senseless things!
O you hard hearts, you cruel men of Rome,
Knew you not Pompey? Many a time and oft
Have you climbed up to walls and battlements,
To towers and windows, yea, to chimney tops,
Your infants in your arms, and there have sat
The livelong day, with patient expectation,
To see great Pompey pass the streets of Rome.
And when you saw his chariot but appear,
Have you not made an universal shout,
That Tiber trembled underneath her banks
To hear the replication of your sounds
Made in her concave shores?
And do you now put on your best attire?
And do you now cull out a holiday?
And do you now strew flowers in his way
That comes in triumph over Pompey's blood?
Begone!
Run to your houses, fall upon your knees,
Pray to the gods to intermit the plague
That needs must light on this ingratitude.

FLAVIUS. Go, go, good countrymen, and for this fault
Assemble all the poor men of your sort;
Draw them to Tiber banks, and weep your tears
Into the channel, till the lowest stream
Do kiss the most exalted shores of all.
(All the COMMONERS *exit.)*
See whe'er their basest mettle be not moved.
They vanish tongue-tied in their guiltiness.
Go you down that way towards the Capitol;
This way will I. Disrobe the images
If you do find them decked with ceremonies.

MARULLUS. May we do so?
You know it is the Feast of Lupercal.

FLAVIUS. It is no matter. Let no images
Be hung with Caesar's trophies. I'll about
And drive away the vulgar from the streets;
So do you too, where you perceive them thick.
These growing feathers plucked from Caesar's wing
Will make him fly an ordinary pitch,
Who else would soar above the view of men
And keep us all in servile fearfulness. *(The* TRIBUNES *exit.)*

---

32 tributaries, captives who must pay tribute (ransom) to Rome for their freedom.

36 Knew . . . Pompey? The fickle mob had once cheered Pompey as they now cheer his enemy, Caesar.

37–38 battlements . . . chimney tops. Ancient Rome had neither battlements nor chimney tops. Such an error, deliberate or otherwise, is called an *anachronism* (ə-nak′rə niz′əm). Look for others as you read.

44 Tiber, the river that runs through Rome.

45 replication, echo.

50 Pompey's blood, Pompey's sons.

53 intermit, withhold.

55 Characters from upper social levels, like Marullus and Flavius, speak in *blank verse* (see page 675); commoners speak prose. What other indication is there that the tribunes outrank the commoners?

57–59 weep your tears . . . of all, weep enough tears to bring the lowest water line up to the highest.

63 Disrobe the images . . . ceremonies. Take down any decorations adorning Caesar's statues.

66 Feast of Lupercal, celebrated on February 15 in honor of Lupercus, god of fertility.

71 These growing feathers, Caesar's new followers.

74 servile (sėr′vəl), *adj.* like that of a slave.

SCENE 2

9

Summary *When Caesar and his entourage enter, a soothsayer warns him of the ides* (īdz), *the 15th, of March. Caesar dismisses the warning and moves on, and Cassius and Brutus remain. Cassius attempts to enlist Brutus in the conspiracy against Caesar. Later, Casca reports that Antony offered Caesar a crown three times, and when Caesar refused it, the crowd cheered. Cassius and Brutus agree to meet the next day.*

A public place in Rome. The COMMONERS *crowd in to await* CAESAR*'s arrival.* SOLDIERS *march on to control the crowd. After a trumpet flourish,* CAESAR *enters, accompanied by* ANTONY, CALPURNIA, PORTIA, DECIUS, CICERO, BRUTUS, CASSIUS, *and* CASCA; FLAVIUS *and* MARULLUS *enter. As the* COMMONERS *cheer and bow to* CAESAR, *a* SOOTHSAYER *edges toward* CAESAR.

soothsayer, person who claims to foretell events.

CAESAR. Calpurnia!
CASCA. Peace, ho! Caesar speaks.
CAESAR. Calpurnia!
CALPURNIA. Here, my lord.
CAESAR. Stand you directly in Antonio's way
When he doth run his course. Antonio!
ANTONY. Caesar, my lord?
CAESAR. Forget not, in your speed, Antonio,
To touch Calpurnia; for our elders say
The barren, touched in this holy chase,
Shake off their sterile curse.
ANTONY. I shall remember.
When Caesar says "Do this," it is performed.
CAESAR. Set on, and leave no ceremony out. *(Sound of trumpets.)*
SOOTHSAYER. Caesar!
CAESAR. Ha? Who calls?
CASCA. Bid every noise be still. Peace yet again!
(The music ceases.)
CAESAR. Who is it in the press that calls on me?
I hear a tongue shriller than all the music
Cry "Caesar!" Speak. Caesar is turned to hear.
SOOTHSAYER. Beware the ides of March.
CAESAR. What man is that?
BRUTUS. A soothsayer bids you beware the ides of March.
CAESAR. Set him before me. Let me see his face.
CASSIUS. Fellow, come from the throng. *(The* SOOTHSAYER *comes forward.)* Look upon Caesar.
CAESAR. What sayst thou to me now? Speak once again.
SOOTHSAYER. Beware the ides of March.

10

4 when he doth run his course. During the Lupercalia, groups watched priest-celebrants who ran a specified course, striking people in their way with goatskin thongs. Women desiring children purposely sought to be struck as a cure for infertility. Antony, as one of the priests, will be one of the young nobles making the run through the streets.

11

■ What traits does Caesar have in common with other leaders you have known or observed?

15 press, throng, crowd.

18 the ides of March. It fell one month after the feast of Lupercal.

9 Multicultural Note
The Ides of March

The ides refers to the 15th day of March, May, July, and October, as well as the 13th day of the other months in the ancient Roman calendar.

10 Reader's Response
Making Personal Connections

Questions

- What conclusions can you draw about Caesar, Antony, and Casca from lines 9–14? *(Possible responses: Caesar is arrogant, imperious, and enjoys the pomp and ceremony of his office. He has chosen to surround himself with people who will do his bidding. Antony is obliging, subservient, and flattering. Casca is servile and eager to carry out Caesar's orders.)*
- Are any of these qualities you would like in a friend? *(Possible response: No, I prefer honesty and equality in a friendship.)*

11 Reading/Thinking Skills
Connect

Response Students may mention his arrogance, desire to wield absolute power, tendency to surround himself with flatterers, and enjoyment of ceremonies of office.

BUILDING ENGLISH PROFICIENCY

Linking Past and Present

Help students understand Caesar's popularity by relating him to present-day military leaders.

1. Ask students for qualities that they think make a military leader popular. Encourage students to name military leaders that are honored in their native countries.

2. Suggest that students work in pairs or small groups to research recent American war heroes such as Norman Schwarzkopf of the Persian Gulf War or Colin Powell, former Joint Chief of Staff. Ask: What did they do to become heroes? Why could they have run for public office? Why did they refuse? How do these situations remind you of what is going on in *Julius Caesar?*

3. Follow up by discussing whether or not a good military leader also can be a good political leader.

12 Literary Element
Meter

Point out to students the accent on the second *e* in *Vexèd.* Explain that it means that this one-syllable word is pronounced with an extra syllable *vex-ed* instead of *vext.* Tell students that this is a technique Shakespeare used to make the meter work. You may also wish to discuss the technique of combining words to drop a syllable. (See page 685, line 86, where *the other* is written *th' other* and pronounced as two syllables.)

13 Reading/Thinking Skills
Summarize

Response Cassius says that Brutus is withdrawn and strange. Brutus replies that this is a personal problem, not one between him and Cassius.

14 Literary Focus
Plot

Question Is Brutus undergoing internal or external conflict here? *(internal)*

15 Reading/Thinking Skills
Analyze

Question Why isn't Cassius more straightforward in this speech? *(He is being subtle and trying to determine Brutus's feelings and allegiances.)*

CAESAR. He is a dreamer. Let us leave him. Pass.
(*All exit except* BRUTUS *and* CASSIUS.)
CASSIUS. Will you go see the order of the course?
BRUTUS. Not I.
CASSIUS. I pray you, do.
BRUTUS. I am not gamesome. I do lack some part
Of that quick spirit that is in Antony.
Let me not hinder, Cassius, your desires;
I'll leave you.
CASSIUS. Brutus, I do observe you now of late.
I have not from your eyes that gentleness
And show of love as I was wont to have.
You bear too stubborn and too strange a hand
Over your friend that loves you.
BRUTUS. Cassius,
Be not deceived. If I have veiled my look,
12 I turn the trouble of my countenance
Merely upon myself. Vexèd I am
Of late with passions of some difference,
Conceptions only proper to myself,
Which give some soil, perhaps, to my behaviors.
But let not therefore my good friends be grieved—
Among which number, Cassius, be you one—
14 Nor construe any further my neglect
Than that poor Brutus, with himself at war,
Forgets the shows of love to other men.
CASSIUS. Then, Brutus, I have much mistook your passion,
By means whereof this breast of mine hath buried
Thoughts of great value, worthy cogitations.
Tell me, good Brutus, can you see your face?
BRUTUS. No, Cassius, for the eye sees not itself
But by reflection, by some other things.
(*He moves downstage;* CASSIUS *follows.*)
CASSIUS. 'Tis just.
And it is very much lamented, Brutus,
That you have no such mirrors as will turn
Your hidden worthiness into your eye,
15 That you might see your shadow. I have heard
Where many of the best respect in Rome,
Except immortal Caesar, speaking of Brutus
And groaning underneath this age's yoke,
Have wished that noble Brutus had his eyes.
BRUTUS. Into what dangers would you lead me, Cassius,
That you would have me seek into myself
For that which is not in me?

28 gamesome, fond of sports, merry.
29 quick spirit, liveliness, responsiveness.

34 as I was wont to have, that I customarily had.
35 stubborn, rough.

38 countenance (koun′tə-nəns), expression of the face.
38–39 I turn the trouble . . . upon myself. Brutus's facial expression masks troubled thoughts, not any change of attitude toward Cassius.
42 soil, blemish.
13 ■ How does Cassius describe Brutus's unusual behavior, and what is Brutus's response?
48–50 Then . . . worthy cogitations. Here Cassius hints at the thoughts (cogitations) locked in his own breast and begins sounding out Brutus to see whether he has the same thoughts and, thus, will join with the conspirators.

58 shadow, image, reflection.
59 best respect, highest repute and station (class).

MINI-LESSON: VOCABULARY
Expand Vocabulary Using Structural Analysis

Teach Read Brutus's line:

I am not *gamesome.*

Tell students that many of the words with the suffix *-some* that we still use were coined around Shakespeare's time to form adjectives from adjectives and nouns. The suffix means "characterized by the quality, condition, or action mentioned in the root word."

Activity Ideas

- Have students brainstorm a list of words that have this suffix and then use a dictionary to determine or confirm meanings. (Possible words include *burdensome, frolicsome, gladsome, cumbersome, loathsome, wholesome, awesome, quarrelsome, adventuresome, bothersome, lonesome.*)
- Have students working in groups consult *The Oxford English Dictionary* to determine when these words were coined and if their meanings have changed over the centuries.

CASSIUS. Therefore, good Brutus, be prepared to hear;
And since you know you cannot see yourself
So well as by reflection, I, your glass,
Will modestly discover to yourself
That of yourself which you yet know not of.
And be not jealous on me, gentle Brutus.
Were I a common laughter, or did use
To stale with ordinary oaths my love
To every new protester; if you know
That I do fawn on men and hug them hard
And after scandal them, or if you know
That I profess myself in banqueting
To all the rout, then hold me dangerous.
(Sound of trumpets and a shout.)
BRUTUS. What means this shouting? I do fear the people
Choose Caesar for their king.
CASSIUS. Ay, do you fear it?
Then must I think you would not have it so.
BRUTUS. I would not, Cassius, yet I love him well.
But wherefore do you hold me here so long?
What is it that you would impart to me?
If it be aught toward the general good,
Set honor in one eye and death i' th' other
And I will look on both indifferently;
For let the gods so speed me as I love
The name of honor more than I fear death.
CASSIUS. I know that virtue to be in you, Brutus,
As well as I do know your outward favor.
Well, honor is the subject of my story.
I cannot tell what you and other men
Think of this life; but, for my single self,
I had as lief not be as live to be
In awe of such a thing as I myself.
I was born free as Caesar, so were you;
We both have fed as well, and we can both
Endure the winter's cold as well as he.
For once, upon a raw and gusty day,
The troubled Tiber chafing with her shores,
Caesar said to me, "Dar'st thou, Cassius, now
Leap in with me into this angry flood
And swim to yonder point?" Upon the word,
Accoutred as I was, I plungèd in
And bade him follow; so indeed he did.
The torrent roared, and we did buffet it
With lusty sinews, throwing it aside

71 jealous on, suspicious of.

72–74 common laughter . . . protester, a laughing-stock or one who cheapens his friendship with oaths to everyone who declares (protests) friendship.

78 the rout, the mob; worthless people.

17

■ Cassius pounces on Brutus's use of the word *fear.* What might this suggest about Cassius's feelings toward Caesar?

84 impart, communicate; tell.

85–87 If it be . . . indifferently. If what Cassius has in mind is for the public welfare and is honorable, Brutus will do it, even if it means death.

91 favor, appearance.

95 lief, willingly.

105 accoutred (ə kü′tərd), **as I was.** The statement implies that Cassius was fully dressed.

16 Historical Note
Roman Kings

Romulus, the founder of Rome, was the first of the seven kings who ruled from 753 to 510 B.C. When the son of the last king raped Lucretia, a married woman of Rome, his father, Tarquinius Superbus, was expelled and the Senate issued a decree stating that there should be no more kings in Rome. Remind students that Brutus was held to be a descendant of the man who helped drive out the Tarquin kings.

17 Reading/Thinking Skills
Clarify

Response It suggests that he also fears Caesar.

18 Reading/Thinking Skills
Draw Conclusions

Question What does Brutus value most highly? *(honor and the public good)*

19 Reading/Thinking Skills
Infer

Question What does Cassius mean in lines 90–99? *(Possible response: He would rather kill himself than see a man who was his equal come to attain the power that Caesar now holds and have to acknowledge that power.)*

BUILDING ENGLISH PROFICIENCY

ESL LEP ELD SAE LD

Exploring Character

The conversation on pages 684–685 introduces Cassius and Brutus, who become the two leaders of the conspiracy against Caesar. Help students focus on Brutus by beginning a chart. Work with them to list terms that Brutus uses to describe himself as well as terms that Cassius uses to describe Brutus. As students read on, encourage them to comment on which descriptions seem most accurate.

Brutus

Self-description	Cassius's description
vexed	good
poor	gentle
	noble

20 Literary Element
Allusion

Question Why does Cassius refer to Aeneas? *(Possible response: He wants to make Caesar seem frail and he himself appear a savior.)*

21 Literary Element
Diction

Question What are the effects of Cassius's use of the word *god* twice in reference to Caesar? *(Possible response: It is an ironic reference to Caesar's weakness.)*

22 Reading/Thinking Skills
Clarify

Response These lines suggest that Caesar is not a worthy ruler.

23 Reading/Thinking Skills
Draw Conclusions

Question What does this mean? *(They are not controlled by the stars but exercise free will and are responsible for their current situation.)*

24 Reader's Response
Draw Conclusions

Response Students may think Brutus will heed him.

And stemming it with hearts of controversy.
But ere we could arrive the point proposed,
Caesar cried, "Help me, Cassius, or I sink!"
20 Ay, as Aeneas, our great ancestor,
Did from the flames of Troy upon his shoulder
The old Anchises bear, so from the waves of Tiber
Did I the tirèd Caesar. And this man
Is now become a god, and Cassius is
A wretched creature and must bend his body
21 If Caesar carelessly but nod on him.
He had a fever when he was in Spain,
And when the fit was on him I did mark
How he did shake. 'Tis true, this god did shake.
His coward lips did from their color fly,
And that same eye whose bend doth awe the world
Did lose his luster. I did hear him groan.
Ay, and that tongue of his that bade the Romans
Mark him and write his speeches in their books,
Alas, it cried, "Give me some drink, Titinius,"
As a sick girl. Ye gods, it doth amaze me
A man of such a feeble temper should
So get the start of the majestic world
And bear the palm alone.
(Shouts and the sound of trumpets.)
BRUTUS *(turning his head upstage).* Another general shout?
I do believe that these applauses are
For some new honors that are heaped on Caesar.
CASSIUS. Why, man, he doth bestride the narrow world
Like a Colossus, and we petty men
Walk under his huge legs and peep about
To find ourselves dishonorable graves.
Men at some time are masters of their fates.
23 The fault, dear Brutus, is not in our stars,
But in ourselves, that we are underlings.
"Brutus" and "Caesar." What should be in that "Caesar"?
Why should that name be sounded more than yours?
Write them together, yours is as fair a name;
Sound them, it doth become the mouth as well;
Weigh them, it is as heavy; conjure with 'em,
"Brutus" will start a spirit as soon as "Caesar."
Now, in the names of all the gods at once,
Upon what meat doth this our Caesar feed
That he is grown so great? Age, thou art shamed!
Rome, thou has lost the breed of noble bloods!
When went there by an age since the great flood

112–114 as Aeneas (i nē′əs) **. . . Anchises** (an kī′sēz) **bear.** Aeneas carried his aged father Anchises out of Troy as it was falling to the Greeks. After wandering for years, he settled near the banks of the Tiber River and his descendants founded Rome.

22 ■ *Lines 100–131.* Why do you think Cassius draws Brutus's attention to Caesar's physical weaknesses?

122 His coward lips . . . fly. His lips became white.

123 bend, glance.

124 his, its, in modern usage.

129 a man . . . feeble temper, weak constitution. The Romans worshiped strength; here Cassius paints Caesar as a weakling.

131 the palm, the victor's prize, a palm leaf.

136 like a Colossus (kə-los′əs). The Colossus, a 100-foot-high bronze statue of Helios, the sun god, stood astride the entrance to the harbor at the island of Rhodes. According to legend, it was so enormous that ships could pass between its legs.

147 start a spirit, call forth a ghost from the spirit world

24 ■ *Lines 135–161.* What impact do you think these arguments of Cassius will have on Brutus?

But it was famed with more than with one man?
25 When could they say, till now, that talked of Rome,
That her wide walks encompassed but one man?
Now is it Rome indeed, and room enough,
When there is in it but one only man.
O, you and I have heard our fathers say
There was a Brutus once that would have brooked
Th' eternal devil to keep his state in Rome
As easily as a king.
26 **BRUTUS.** That you do love me, I am nothing jealous.
What you would work me to, I have some aim.

156 Rome . . . room, a pun, since in Shakespeare's time the two words were pronounced alike. Shakespeare's audience delighted in such word play.

A film of *Julius Caesar* was produced in 1953 by John Houseman and directed by Joseph Mankiewicz. The cast included the following: *Mark Antony* (Marlon Brando), *Brutus* (James Mason), *Cassius* (John Gielgud), *Julius Caesar* (Louis Calhern), *Casca* (Edmond O'Brien), *Calpurnia* (Greer Garson), and *Portia* (Deborah Kerr).

25 Literary Element
Figurative Language

Point out that Cassius does not literally mean that there is only room for one man in Rome. He is exaggerating Caesar's physical presence (using hyperbole) to make a rhetorical point, as well as punning (see sidenote).

26 Reading/Thinking Skills
Draw Conclusions

Question What does Brutus mean? *(Possible response: He is aware that Cassius is trying to sway him, and he is open to Cassius's persuasion because he has similar desires.)*

This picture shows Cassius (left) and Brutus (right). You may wish to discuss their expressions (they seem suspicious and guarded) and what they are looking at (Caesar, perhaps).

BUILDING ENGLISH PROFICIENCY

Using Gloss Notes

Have students focus on the marginal notes on these pages. Explain that these marginal notes, called *glosses,* help them better understand the play.

Activity Ideas

- Have students use pages 686–687 to find one example of each kind of gloss:
  vocabulary help
  paraphrase of a difficult line
  background information
  question directed to readers
- Allow students to write in their notebooks other items that require clarification.
- Help students use the glosses to recognize Cassius's envy of Caesar's fame and bitterness that he himself hasn't been so fortunate.

27 Historical Note
Cicero

Marcus Tullius Cicero (106-43 B.C.) was a skilled orator and supporter of Pompey. After he became consul, he faced exile. Caesar offered Cicero protection in return for his support of the First Triumvirate but was refused. Recalled in 57, Cicero joined Pompey in the war against Caesar. When Pompey was defeated, Cicero returned to Italy and Caesar pardoned him. He was not involved in Caesar's assassination, but he sided with Octavius against Mark Antony. When the Second Triumvirate of Antony, Octavius, and Lepidus was formed, Antony insisted on Cicero's death. He was killed on December 7, 43 B.C.

28 Historical Note
Familiar Quotations

Point out to students that many Shakespearean turns of phrase have become popular sayings. "Lean and hungry" is one example. "It was (It's) Greek to me" (page 690, line 274) is another.

29 Reader's Response
Making Personal Connections

Response Some students may think that it's not fair to judge people on physical appearance; others may think a dissatisfied expression may indicate a problem. Students may refer to the photograph on page 687.

How I have thought of this and of these times
I shall recount hereafter. For this present,
I would not, so with love I might entreat you,
Be any further moved. What you have said
I will consider; what you have to say
I will with patience hear, and find a time
Both meet to hear and answer such high things.
Till then, my noble friend, chew upon this.
Brutus had rather be a villager
Than to repute himself a son of Rome
Under these hard conditions as this time
Is like to lay upon us.

CASSIUS. I am glad that my weak words
Have struck but this much show of fire from Brutus.

(CAESAR *and his followers reenter at left and start across the stage,* ANTONY *on* CAESAR*'s left,* CASCA *following at rear.*)

BRUTUS. The games are done, and Caesar is returning.

CASSIUS. As they pass by, pluck Casca by the sleeve,
And he will, after his sour fashion, tell you
What hath proceeded worthy note today.

BRUTUS. I will do so. But look you, Cassius,
The angry spot doth glow on Caesar's brow,
And all the rest look like a chidden train.
27 Calpurnia's cheek is pale, and Cicero
Looks with such ferret and such fiery eyes
As we have seen him in the Capitol,
Being crossed in conference by some senators.

CASSIUS. Casca will tell us what the matter is.

(CAESAR *stops before he reaches center stage and looks speculatively at* CASSIUS.)

CAESAR. Antonio!

ANTONY. Caesar?

CAESAR. Let me have men about me that are fat,
28 Sleek-headed men, and such as sleep o' nights.
Yond Cassius has a lean and hungry look. 29
He thinks too much. Such men are dangerous.

ANTONY. Fear him not, Caesar, he's not dangerous.
He is a noble Roman, and well given.

CAESAR. Would he were fatter! But I fear him not.
Yet if my name were liable to fear,
I do not know the man I should avoid
So soon as that spare Cassius. He reads much,
He is a great observer, and he looks
Quite through the deeds of men. He loves no plays,
As thou dost, Antony; he hears no music.

184 like a chidden train, like followers who were harshly scolded (chided or chidden).

186 such ferret . . . eyes, red and angry-looking eyes, like a weasel's.

■ Do you agree with Caesar's reasons for calling Cassius dangerous?

197 given, disposed; having a favorable nature.

204 hears no music. In Shakespeare's time, this was regarded as a sign of a treacherous nature.

MINI-LESSON: VOCABULARY
Read Uncommon Low-Frequency Words

Teach Read Casca's words (lines 228–229):

> Ay, *marry,* was't, and he put it by thrice, every time gentler than other. . . .

Tell students that oaths are one kind of exclamation used by Shakespeare. Have students read the margin note, and point out that this oath is anachronistic—Christianity did not exist until the beginning of Jesus' ministry in A.D. 30.

Tell students that swearing by God's mother, or by parts of Jesus' body was a common practice in Renaissance times. *Swounds* or *Zounds* ("by God's wounds") became a popular oath in the seventeenth century. People also swore by God's teeth and nails.

Activity Idea Have students identify other exclamations that are no longer used (such as *Ay!* and *Ho!)* and try to pin down their usage and meaning from context.

Seldom he smiles, and smiles in such a sort
As if he mocked himself and scorned his spirit
That could be moved to smile at anything.
30 Such men as he be never at heart's ease
Whiles they behold a greater than themselves,
And therefore are they very dangerous.
I rather tell thee what is to be feared
Than what I fear, for always I am Caesar.
Come on my right hand, for this ear is deaf,
And tell me truly what thou think'st of him.

(ANTONY *steps to* CAESAR*'s right. The trumpets sound and the procession, with* CASCA *still at rear, moves slowly out at right. When* CASCA *reaches center stage, he is detained by* BRUTUS *and* CASSIUS.)

CASCA. You pulled me by the cloak. Would you speak with me?
BRUTUS. Ay, Casca. Tell us what hath chanced today,
That Caesar looks so sad.
CASCA. Why, you were with him, were you not?
BRUTUS. I should not then ask Casca what had chanced.

CASCA. Why, there was a crown offered him; and, being offered him, he put it by with the back of his hand, thus, and then the people fell a-shouting.

BRUTUS. What was the second noise for?
CASCA. Why, for that too.
CASSIUS. They shouted thrice. What was the last cry for?
CASCA. Why, for that too.
BRUTUS. Was the crown offered him thrice?

CASCA. Ay, marry, was't, and he put it by thrice, every time gentler than other, and at every putting-by mine honest neighbors shouted.

CASSIUS. Who offered him the crown?
CASCA. Why, Antony.
BRUTUS. Tell us the manner of it, gentle Casca.

CASCA. I can as well be hanged as tell the manner of it. It was mere foolery; I did not mark it. I saw Mark Antony offer him a crown yet 'twas not a crown neither 'twas one of these coronets—and, as I told you, he put it by once; but for all that, to my thinking, he would fain have had it. Then he offered it to him again; then he put it by again; but to my thinking he was very loath to lay his fingers off it. And then he offered it the third time. He put it the third time by, and still as he refused it the rabblement hooted and clapped their chapped hands, and threw up their sweaty nightcaps, and uttered such a deal of stinking breath because Caesar refused the crown that it had almost choked Caesar, for he swooned and fell down at it. And for mine own part I durst not laugh for fear of opening my lips and receiving the bad air.

CASSIUS. But soft, I pray you. What, did Caesar swoon?

31 ■ What insight into Caesar's character does this speech give?

217 sad, serious.

228 marry, a mild exclamation or oath. Originally, "by the Virgin Mary."

242 nightcaps, a scornful allusion to the felt cap worn by the commoners on festival days.

244 durst, dared.

32 ■ Based on Casca's description, how do you think the commoners felt about Caesar's being offered a crown?

30 Reader's Response
Making Personal Connections

Question Do you think this is a just criticism of Cassius? *(Some students may think that Cassius's hatred of Caesar could be fueled by envy. Others may believe that Cassius's complaints are legitimate and this is Caesar's self-serving interpretation.)*

31 Reading/Thinking Skills
Clarify

Possible responses This speech reveals Caesar to be arrogant, extremely self-conscious, cautious, and a shrewd observer of other men. Alternatively, he is vulnerable (he admits his deafness) and desirous to know Antony's real opinion of Cassius.

32 Reading/Thinking Skills
Evaluate

Possible response Casca relates that the crowd cheered Caesar's refusal of the crown. The phrase "I durst not laugh" implies that Casca feels Caesar's actions are calculated to manipulate the crowd.

BUILDING ENGLISH PROFICIENCY

Exploring Dramatic Tension

Remind students that *Julius Caesar,* like all plays, was meant to be read aloud.

Activity Idea Have students work in pairs to prepare as readers' theater the exchanges between Caesar and Antony, and Casca and Brutus on these pages.

- Lead them to note details that indicate a buildup of tension.
- Encourage them to add facial expressions, movements and gestures, whispered comments, and other things they feel will enhance the drama.
- Help establish the rhythms of speeches by reminding them that these lines are generally blank verse, with the exception of Casca's lines, which are in prose.

33 Reading/Thinking Skills
Question

Response Some students might wish to ask why Casca is so contemptuous of the common people.

34 Literary Element
Characterization

Question How does Cassius characterize Casca in this speech? *(He suggests that Casca plays the fool in order to win others over to his outspoken views.)*

The World of Work
Civil Servant

For the real-life experiences of a civil servant, use —

The World of Work
pp. 25–26

CASCA. He fell down in the marketplace, and foamed at mouth, and was speechless.

BRUTUS. 'Tis very like. He hath the falling sickness.

CASSIUS. No, Caesar hath it not, but you and I,
And honest Casca, we have the falling sickness.

CASCA. I know not what you mean by that, but I am sure Caesar fell down. If the tag-rag people did not clap him and hiss him, according as he pleased and displeased them, as they use to do the players in the theater, I am no true man.

BRUTUS. What said he when he came unto himself?

CASCA. Marry, before he fell down, when he perceived the common herd was glad he refused the crown, he plucked me ope his doublet and offered them his throat to cut. An I had been a man of any occupation, if I would not have taken him at a word, I would I might go to hell among the rogues. And so he fell. When he came to himself again, he said if he had done or said anything amiss, he desired their worships to think it was his infirmity. Three or four wenches where I stood cried, "Alas, good soul!" and forgave him with all their hearts. But there's no heed to be taken of them; if Caesar had stabbed their mothers they would have done no less.

BRUTUS. And after that, he came thus sad away?

CASCA. Ay.

CASSIUS. Did Cicero say anything?

CASCA. Ay, he spoke Greek.

CASSIUS. To what effect?

CASCA. Nay, an I tell you that, I'll ne'er look you i' the face again. But those that understood him smiled at one another and shook their heads; but, for mine own part, it was Greek to me. I could tell you more news too. Marullus and Flavius, for pulling scarves off Caesar's images, are put to silence. Fare you well. There was more foolery yet, if I could remember it.

CASSIUS. Will you sup with me tonight, Casca?

CASCA. No, I am promised forth.

CASSIUS. Will you dine with me tomorrow?

CASCA. Ay, if I be alive, and your mind hold, and your dinner worth the eating.

CASSIUS. Good. I will expect you.

CASCA. Do so. Farewell both. (CASCA *exits.*)

BRUTUS. What a blunt fellow is this grown to be!
He was quick mettle when he went to school.

CASSIUS. So is he now in execution
Of any bold or noble enterprise,
However he puts on this tardy form.
This rudeness is a sauce to his good wit,
Which gives men stomach to digest his words

249 falling sickness, epilepsy. Note how Cassius, in the next few lines, uses the words figuratively, suggesting a similarity between "falling" and failing to take action.

258–259 doublet, a man's close-fitting jacket. Doublets were not worn until about the 1400s; hence, another anachronism.

259 an, if.

■ What question would you ask Casca about his account of the events?

274 . . . it was Greek to me, a saying popular even today when a person is unable to understand something.

276 put to silence, deprived of their rank as tribunes, a position that permitted them to speak for the people.

286 mettle (met′l), *n.* spirit; courage. *Quick mettle* means "of a lively and spirited temperament."

289 tardy form, appearance of sluggishness.

290 wit, intellect.

MINI-LESSON: WRITING STYLE
Using Powerful Verbs

Teach Shakespeare was a master of precise, active verbs. He had to be. Working with a relatively bare stage and few props, he relied on words to waken the imagination of his audience, to help them "see" the action through words. Direct students' attention to Casca's speech on page 691. Point out the powerful description of the ocean in line 7, created by the verbs *swell, rage,* and *foam.*

Activity Ideas

- Have students copy in their notebooks other powerful verbs that appear in Casca's speeches on page 691. *(fell, foamed, clap, hiss, plucked, stabbed)*
- Write a note to Caesar warning him what might happen if Cassius gains support against him. Use powerful verbs.

With better appetite.
BRUTUS. And so it is. For this time I will leave you.
Tomorrow, if you please to speak with me,
I will come home to you; or, if you will,
Come home to me, and I will wait for you.
CASSIUS. I will do so. Till then, think of the world.
(BRUTUS *exits.*)
Well, Brutus, thou art noble. Yet I see
Thy honorable mettle may be wrought
From that it is disposed. Therefore it is meet
That noble minds keep ever with their likes;
For who so firm that cannot be seduced?
Caesar doth bear me hard, but he loves Brutus.
If I were Brutus now, and he were Cassius,
He should not humor me. I will this night
In several hands in at his windows throw,
As if they came from several citizens,
Writings, all tending to the great opinion
That Rome holds of his name, wherein obscurely
Caesar's ambition shall be glancèd at.
And after this let Caesar seat him sure,
For we will shake him, or worse days endure. (CASSIUS *exits.*)

299–300 Thy honorable . . . disposed, your spirit can be turned from its natural inclination.

300 meet (mēt), *adj.* fitting; appropriate.

303 Caesar . . . hard, Caesar bears me a grudge.

305 humor me, win me over to his opinions.

306 in several hands, in different handwritings.

35

310 glancèd at, hinted at.

■ Explain in your own words what Cassius is saying in this, the play's first soliloquy.

SCENE 3

Summary *Cassius persuades a frightened Casca to join the conspiracy, then instructs Cinna, another conspirator, to place letters condemning Caesar where Brutus will find them. Cassius and Casca plan a visit to Brutus later that evening.*

A street in Rome. A stormy night. Eve of the ides of March. Thunder and lightning. CICERO *enters at left;* CASCA, *his sword drawn, enters at right.*

CICERO. Good even, Casca. Brought you Caesar home?
Why are you breathless? And why stare you so?
CASCA. Are not you moved, when all the sway of earth
Shakes like a thing unfirm? O Cicero,
I have seen tempests when the scolding winds
Have rived the knotty oaks, and I have seen
Th' ambitious ocean swell and rage and foam
To be exalted with the threatening clouds;
But never till tonight, never till now,
Did I go through a tempest dropping fire.
(More thunder, then a scream; CASCA *darts behind a pillar.)*
Either there is a civil strife in heaven,
Or else the world, too saucy with the gods,

1 even, evening.

3 sway, established order.

8 exalted with, raised to the level of.

12 saucy, showing lack of respect; rude.

35 Reading/Thinking Skills
Summarize

Response Cassius recognizes that the support of Brutus in this conspiracy is crucial. Cassius still believes in Brutus's nobility, but now has discovered that Brutus can be swayed to his purposes. Cassius claims that were their situations reversed, Brutus would be unable to sway him. He then declares his intention of sending Brutus anonymous letters that flatter him and attack Caesar. When the letters have taken their effect, Caesar had better beware, for Cassius and company will dispose of him.

BUILDING ENGLISH PROFICIENCY

ESL LEP ELD SAE LD

Exploring Mood

With the opening of scene 3, Shakespeare heightens the atmosphere of tension and foreboding. Encourage students to examine the ways in which he accomplishes this.

1. Divide students into groups and have them reread lines 1–32.

2. Ask some groups to identify words and phrases that describe the unsettled atmosphere.

3. Ask other groups to name the unusual sights that Casca says have frightened him this night.

4. Allow groups time to work on an impromptu reading or performance of lines 1–32. Urge students to think of sound effects and voice intonations that will convey the feelings of terror and foreboding that Casca introduces.

36 Reading/Thinking Skills
Summarize

Response Students should mention sights named in lines 10 and 15–28. Lead them to see the commonality of these bizarre sights (things are acting against the laws of nature).

37 Literary Focus
Plot

Question What do you think these bizarre sights foretell? *(Possible response: They seem to be foreshadowing future plot events that reflect chaos: civil war and especially Caesar's death.)*

38 Reader's Response
Making Personal Connections

Response Remind students that in the films they mention, weather should be a dominating force that shapes events and themes, not an incidental backdrop. They may mention current mysteries, in which weather casts a pervasive gloom over the narration, or disaster movies, in which acts of nature determine events. *(Other possible responses: The Wizard of Oz, King Lear, Back to the Future)*

Incenses them to send destruction.
CICERO. Why, saw you anything more wonderful?
CASCA. A common slave—you know him well by sight—
Held up his left hand, which did flame and burn
Like twenty torches joined, and yet his hand,
Not sensible of fire, remained unscorched.
Besides—I ha' not since put up my sword—
Against the Capitol I met a lion,
Who glazed upon me and went surly by
Without annoying me. And there were drawn
Upon a heap a hundred ghastly women,
Transformèd with their fear, who swore they saw
Men all in fire walk up and down the streets.
And yesterday the bird of night did sit
Even at noonday upon the marketplace,
Hooting and shrieking. When these prodigies
Do so conjointly meet, let not men say,
"These are their reasons, they are natural,"
For I believe they are portentous things
Unto the climate that they point upon.
CICERO. Indeed, it is a strange-disposèd time.
But men may construe things after their fashion,
Clean from the purpose of the things themselves.
Comes Caesar to the Capitol tomorrow?
CASCA. He doth; for he did bid Antonio
Send word to you he would be there tomorrow.
CICERO. Good night then, Casca. This disturbèd sky
Is not to walk in.
CASCA. Farewell, Cicero.
(CICERO *exits at right. There is another flash of lightning and* CASCA *retreats further upstage, taking shelter under a balcony.* CASSIUS *enters at left.*)
CASSIUS. Who's there?
CASCA. A Roman.
CASSIUS. Casca, by your voice.
CASCA. Your ear is good. Cassius, what night is this!
CASSIUS. A very pleasing night to honest men.
CASCA. Who ever knew the heavens menace so?
CASSIUS. Those that have known the earth so full of faults.
For my part, I have walked about the streets,
Submitting me unto the perilous night,
And thus unbracèd, Casca, as you see,
Have bared my bosom to the thunder-stone;
And when the cross blue lightning seemed to open
The breast of heaven, I did present myself
Even in the aim and very flash of it.

18 not sensible of fire, not feeling the fire.

20 against, opposite; nearby.
21 glazed, peered, stared.

■ What unusual sights has Casca seen?

28–32 When these prodigies . . . upon. Though some may try to explain these marvels (prodigies) as natural, Casca regards them as omens (portentous things) foretelling disaster for Rome.

43 what night, what a night!

47 perilous (per′ə ləs), *adj.* dangerous.
48 thus unbracèd. Cassius unlaces (unbraces) his garment at the neck, exposing his chest to the thunderbolts (thunder-stones).
50 cross, forked, jagged.
■ What films have you seen in which weather reinforces mood?

CASCA. But wherefore did you so much tempt the heavens?
It is the part of men to fear and tremble
When the most mighty gods by tokens send
Such dreadful heralds to astonish us.
CASSIUS. You are dull, Casca, and those sparks of life
That should be in a Roman you do want,
Or else you use not. You look pale, and gaze,
And put on fear, and cast yourself in wonder,
To see the strange impatience of the heavens.
But if you would consider the true cause
Why all these fires, why all these gliding ghosts,
Why birds and beasts from quality and kind,
Why old men, fools, and children calculate,
Why all these things change from their ordinance,
Their natures, and preformèd faculties,
To monstrous quality—why, you shall find
That heaven hath infused them with these spirits
To make them instruments of fear and warning
Unto some monstrous state.
Now could I, Casca, name to thee a man
Most like this dreadful night,
That thunders, lightens, opens graves, and roars
As doth the lion in the Capitol—
A man no mightier than thyself or me
In personal action, yet prodigious grown
And fearful, as these strange eruptions are.
CASCA. 'Tis Caesar that you mean, is it not, Cassius?
CASSIUS. Let it be who it is. For Romans now
Have thews and limbs like to their ancestors;
But, woe the while, our fathers' minds are dead,
And we are governed with our mothers' spirits.
Our yoke and sufferance show us womanish.
CASCA. Indeed, they say the senators tomorrow
Mean to establish Caesar as a king,
And he shall wear his crown by sea and land
In every place save here in Italy.
CASSIUS. I know where I will wear this dagger then;
Cassius from bondage will deliver Cassius.
Therein, ye gods, you make the weak most strong;
Therein, ye gods, you tyrants do defeat.
Nor stony tower, nor walls of beaten brass,
Nor airless dungeon, nor strong links of iron,
Can be retentive to the strength of spirit;
But life, being weary of these worldly bars,
Never lacks power to dismiss itself.

65 calculate, prophesy.
66 ordinance, established nature; accustomed ways.
67 preformèd faculties, innate or inborn mental powers or capabilities.

39

■ How does Cassius use emotional appeal to influence Casca?

40

77 prodigious (prə dij′əs), *adj.* very great or huge; ominous.

82 woe the while, alas for the age.

41

92 therein, in the ability to commit suicide.

39 Reading/Thinking Skills
Clarify

Response Possible responses: He connects Casca's fear of the night with his fear of Caesar. He plays up his fear and dullness as not worthy of a Roman.

40 Multicultural Note
Gender Roles

The Romans had definite views on gender roles, as shown in this play (see Portia's speeches later). Ask students what Cassius may have meant by *womanish.* Encourage students to speculate on how a military society of that time might influence gender roles.

41 Literary Element
Style

Point out the following stylistic elements in this speech:

- Repetition (*therein, nor, Cassius)*
- Use of third-person rather than *I*
- Apostrophe *(Therein, ye gods)*
- Imagery (*walls of beaten brass, links of iron)*

BUILDING ENGLISH PROFICIENCY

Analyzing Persuasion

In the conversation with Casca on this page, Cassius reveals his keen persuasive abilities. Ask questions such as the following to help students understand how clever Cassius is at manipulating Casca.

- How does Cassius turn a personal atttack on Casca into a political attack in lines 57–60? *(He says Casca's dullness and fear are not fitting in a Roman.)*
- How does Cassius attack Caesar in lines 72–78? *(He compares him to the "dreadful night," which causes fear, and he reminds Casca that Caesar is no mightier than either of them.)*
- According to Cassius, how has Casca misinterpreted the stormy weather? *(It is a warning that Caesar must be stopped.)*
- What dramatic threat does Cassius make in lines 89–97? *(He threatens to kill himself, if necessary, to free himself from Caesar's tyranny.)*

42 Reading/Thinking Skills
Recognize Propaganda

Questions

- What loaded words appear in lines 101–103? *(bondman, power, captivity, tyrant)*
- How do these words serve as a call to action? *(They justify the conspiracy by casting Caesar as a tyrant.)*

43 Literary Element
Figurative Language

Questions

- How does Cassius use animals to make his point? *(He compares Romans who refuse to reject Caesar to hinds and sheep; only with such weak, submissive animals does Caesar appear as a wolf or lion.)*
- What other figures of speech appear in Cassius's speech? *(Rome and Romans are compared to weak straws and trash by which Caesar will ignite a mighty fire—establish a destructive rule.)*

44 Reader's Response
Making Personal Connections

Response Some students may wonder if Casca really knows that he has joined a plot to murder Caesar. Some may think that he has made a serious mistake, while others will applaud his taking a stand.

If I know this, know all the world besides,
That part of tyranny that I do bear
I can shake off at pleasure.
(Thunder still.)
CASCA. So can I.
[42] So every bondman in his own hand bears
The power to cancel his captivity.
[43] CASSIUS. And why should Caesar be a tyrant then?
Poor man, I know he would not be a wolf
But that he sees the Romans are but sheep;
He were no lion, were not Romans hinds.
Those that with haste will make a mighty fire
Begin it with weak straws. What trash is Rome,
What rubbish and what offal, when it serves
For the base matter to illuminate
So vile a thing as Caesar! But, O grief,
Where hast thou led me? I perhaps speak this
Before a willing bondman; then I know
My answer must be made. But I am armed,
And dangers are to me indifferent.
CASCA. You speak to Casca, and to such a man
That is no fleering telltale. Hold. My hand.
Be factious for redress of all these griefs,
And I will set this foot of mine as far
As who goes farthest. *(They shake hands.)*
CASSIUS. There's a bargain made.
Now know you, Casca, I have moved already
Some certain of the noblest-minded Romans
To undergo with me an enterprise
Of honorable-dangerous consequence;
And I do know by this they stay for me
In Pompey's porch. For now, this fearful night,
There is no stir or walking in the streets,
And the complexion of the element
In favor's like the work we have in hand,
Most bloody, fiery, and most terrible.
(CINNA *enters.*)
CASCA. Stand close awhile, for here comes one in haste.
CASSIUS. 'Tis Cinna; I do know him by his gait.
He is a friend. Cinna, where haste you so?
CINNA. To find out you. Who's that? Metellus Cimber?
CASSIUS. No, it is Casca, one incorporate
To our attempts. Am I not stayed for, Cinna?
CINNA. I am glad on 't. What a fearful night is this!
There's two or three of us have seen strange sights.

106 he were . . . hinds. He would be no lion if Romans were not submissive like deer. (A hind is a female deer.)

117 fleering, deceitful, fawning.

118 Be factious . . . griefs, be ready to join the faction (group) to right the grievances Romans have suffered at Caesar's hands.

[44] ■ Do you think Casca has made the right decision in joining the conspiracy?

125–126 stay . . . porch, wait for me on the porch of Pompey's theater.

128–129 the element . . . favor's, the sky is in appearance.

131 close, concealed.

135–136 one incorporate . . . attempts, one who knows our plans and is in sympathy with them.

MINI-LESSON: GRAMMAR
Homonyms and Homophones

Teach Read lines 107–108:

Those that with haste will make a mighty fire
Begin it with *weak* straws.

Write the words *weak* and *week* on the board or overhead projector. Review for students that these words, which sound alike but have different spellings and meanings, are called *homonyms.* Then write the word *there* and elicit two homonyms (*their, they're*). Review the meaning and appropriate use for each homonym and challenge students to devise a sentence using all three homonyms.

Activity Idea Have students look for other homonyms on page 694 and start a list. Make sure they know the meanings and spellings of words in each homonym group. They can add to the list as they finish the act. *(Homonyms on page 694 include* bears, sees, led, made, here, gait, two, sights.)

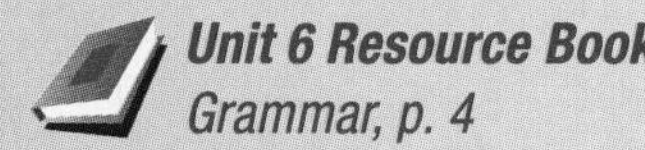

Unit 6 Resource Book
Grammar, p. 4

CASSIUS. Am I not stayed for? Tell me.
CINNA. Yes, you are. O Cassius, if you could
But win the noble Brutus to our party—
CASSIUS. Be you content. Good Cinna, take this paper,
(Giving papers.)
And look you lay it in the praetor's chair,
Where Brutus may but find it. And throw this
In at his window. Set this up with wax
Upon old Brutus's statue. All this done,
Repair to Pompey's porch, where you shall find us.
Is Decius Brutus and Trebonius there?
CINNA. All but Metellus Cimber, and he's gone
To seek you at your house. Well, I will hie,
And so bestow these papers as you bade me.
(CINNA *exits.*)
CASSIUS. That done, repair to Pompey's theater.
Come Casca, you and I will yet ere day
See Brutus at his house. Three parts of him
Is ours already, and the man entire
Upon the next encounter yields him ours.
CASCA. O, he sits high in all the people's hearts;
And that which would appear offense in us,
His countenance, like richest alchemy,
Will change to virtue and to worthiness.
CASSIUS. Him and his worth, and our great need of him,
You have right well conceited. Let us go,
For it is after midnight, and ere day
We will awake him and be sure of him.
(They exit.)

143 in the praetor's chair. Brutus at this time was a praetor (prē′tər), a Roman judge or magistrate.

146 old Brutus's, Lucius Junius Brutus's. Brutus was reputed to be his descendent.

150 hie, go quickly.

154–155 Three parts . . . ours. Brutus is three-quarters persuaded to join the conspirators; when they next meet with him, they undoubtedly will win him over completely.

162 conceited, grasped.

46

■ Whom do you think Brutus will support—Caesar or the conspirators?

45 Reader's Response
Challenging the Text

Questions

Have students analyze and respond to the conspiracy by asking the following:

- Would you have joined the conspiracy? Why or why not? *(Possible responses: Yes, I think freedom and equality are very important. No, I think Cassius is self-serving and using the others, and I don't think they'll succeed.)*
- What do you think of the methods Cassius has used to recruit people? *(Possible responses: All of the methods are manipulative. He should use reason, not rhetoric and phony anonymous letters. When you're up against a tyrant who's been declared dictator for life, you have to use the methods available to you. Cassius is doing a good job of that.)*

46 Reading/Thinking Skills
Predict

Possible response I think Brutus will join the conspirators.

Check Test

1. Who has Caesar recently defeated in battle? *(Pompey's sons)*

2. Why does Caesar ask Antony to touch Calpurnia during his running of the course? *(to cure her sterility)*

3. Who does Caesar accuse of having "a lean and hungry look"? *(Cassius)*

4. What does Cassius plant so that Brutus will find them? *(notes saying that citizens want Brutus to free them from Caesar's tyranny)*

5. What does Caesar refuse three times? *(a crown)*

Unit 6 Resource Book
Alternate Check Test, p. 5

BUILDING ENGLISH PROFICIENCY

ESL LEP ELD SAE LD

Checking Comprehension

Review with students what has happened in act 1, having them reread the summaries that begin each scene, if necessary. Have a recorder list major events on the board in order.

Activity Ideas

- Invite students to envision this as the first of a five-part TV miniseries. Have them prepare an ad that recaps high points thus far and lures the audience to view future episodes.
- Ask students to name TV programs or movies about political intrigue. Ask: Has Shakespeare presented his story in the most interesting way possible? What techniques or special effects might a modern TV director use to entice viewers?

After Reading

MAKING CONNECTIONS

1. Many students may think Caesar is too arrogant to make a good ruler.

2. Some students may suspect that Caesar would not heed anyone's advice. Some might advise him to give power to senators and tribunes.

3. Possible response: Caesar—Robert de Niro, Antony—Brad Pitt, Cassius—Jeremy Irons, Brutus—Martin Sheen, Casca—Danny de Vito

4. He's arrogant, self-assured, self-conscious, imperious.

5. Students may point out the disparity between the desire for a monarchy and the desire for a republic as the key change.

6. Cassius shows Caesar's weakness to support his argument that Caesar is not a god, nor better than he and Brutus.

7. Possible response: No—although Caesar seems to play up to the public image of being unmoved by the things that touch ordinary mortals, he takes the same approach when he is speaking privately with Mark Antony.

8. Possible responses: the struggles to make Brutus ruler; to dethrone Caesar; or to restore republican government to Rome

9. Possible response: He will join Cassius because he is already leaning that way.

10. Possible response: civil unrest or the death of Caesar

11. Students may mention the effects of contemporary charismatic speakers on modern crowds.

12. Students may mention the shift in responsibility for decisions, the increased governmental control over the individual, or the lack of freedom and equality.

Act 1

After Reading

Making Connections

Shaping Your Response

1. Do you think Caesar has the qualities of an effective politician? Why or why not?
2. What advice would you give him?
3. For a television production, what actor would you choose to play Caesar? Antony? Cassius? Brutus? Casca? Explain your casting choices.

Analyzing the Play

4. **Characterize** Caesar as he appears in the opening lines of scene 2.
5. How do the contrasting opinions that characters express about Caesar in this act reflect social **change** at this point in Roman history?
6. What can you **infer** is the reason for the mention of such things as his deafness and his "falling sickness"?
7. Do you think the presence of the crowd influences Caesar's response to the Soothsayer's warning? Explain.
8. What can you **infer** will be the main **conflict** in the play?
9. Which side do you think Brutus will join? Why?
10. What do you think the strange events seen by Cassius and Casca **foreshadow**?

Extending the Ideas

11. Do you think that a modern crowd would be as emotional and as swayed by speeches as the Roman commoners seem to be? Explain, citing specific examples.
12. Before Caesar was declared dictator for life, Romans had enjoyed a republican government for over four centuries. What kinds of drastic **changes** do you think a dictatorship would cause in *your* country?

Literary Focus: Plot

Look at the plot diagram you copied in your notebook. Under the diagram, briefly describe the background and the situation as the play opens. Then jot down a few sentences describing the incidents that have set the plot in motion in act 1.

LITERARY FOCUS: PLOT

In describing the background, students should include:

- the place at which the action is set
- a description of the current government
- plans of the conspiracy thus far
- a brief analysis of the relationships of the characters

Vocabulary Study

On your paper, write the word that best fits each numbered description.

meet
mettle
perilous
prodigious
servile

1. ____ describes a person who acts like a slave.
2. ____ describes something dangerous.
3. ____ denotes something large or vast.
4. ____ refers to something that is appropriate.
5. ____ denotes courage and spirit.

Expressing Your Ideas

Writing Choices

Writer's Notebook Update Look over the entries you made about Caesar in your chart. Compare the traits you listed with those listed by other members of your class. Are you in agreement? Try to sum up his character in a sentence or two.

Roman Holiday Caesar has hired a public relations expert to spruce up his image. Submit five **tips** for upgrading Caesar's popularity rating. Use a few vocabulary words to enliven your writing.

Ancient Chronicle Imagine that you are a reporter in ancient Rome. Your assignment is to write an **article** about Caesar's rejection of the crown. Decide whether your article will be objective—a straight news story—or a human interest feature that includes imaginative details such as Calpurnia's reaction, Casca's opinions, and so forth.

Blank Check Jot down your impressions of one of the characters appearing in this act. Then recast your impressions in **blank verse**—the verse form Shakespeare usually employs. Refer to the description of blank verse on page 675 if you need to review its features.

Other Options

In the Spotlight Choose a speech from act 1 to deliver in a dramatic reading. After rehearsing it, give an **oral interpretation** before the class, complete with costume or props, if you wish.

Times Roman Do some research about life in ancient Rome—the clothes, customs, living quarters, entertainment, and so on. Make drawings or photocopy pictures, provide captions, and present your information and **visual display** to classmates.

Caesar Song Select a musical piece that you consider fit for a king whose rule is in jeopardy. Make arrangements to play this music for the class and explain why you think this piece is appropriate.

VOCABULARY STUDY

1. servile
2. perilous
3. prodigious
4. meet
5. mettle

Unit 6 Resource Book
Vocabulary, p. 3
Vocabulary Test, p. 6

WRITING CHOICES

Ancient Chronicle

Students might get ideas from news paper articles or by reviewing tabloid features that employ farfetched images and loaded words.

Selection Test

Unit 6 Resource Book
pp. 7–8

OTHER OPTIONS

Times Roman

You may want to specify the time period—the forties B.C. Groups of students may want to expand the project into a diorama, or to present a reenactment of an appropriate scene or event.

During Reading

1 Reading/Thinking Skills
Predict

Response Students should realize that there are several answers to this question: the thunder, lightning and other signs and portents of the evening and his deepening concerns about Caesar's tyrannical rule.

2 Literary Focus
Plot

Brutus's lack of personal animosity and his high-minded motives are an essential plot element. Alert students to look for motives that the other conspirators have for killing Caesar.

3 Reading/Thinking Skills
Make Judgments

As students read act 2, remind them of this comment by Brutus, and ask them to decide whether Brutus's characterization is accurate. *(Possible response: Caesar makes the point that he is the least likely creature in the universe to be moved by feelings to change his judgment.)*

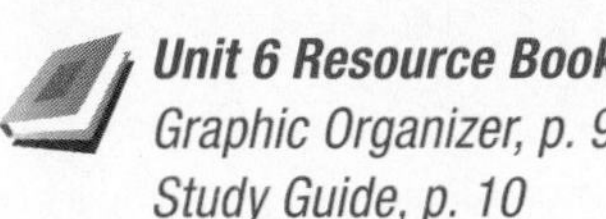

Unit 6 Resource Book
Graphic Organizer, p. 9
Study Guide, p. 10

ACT TWO

Scene 1

Summary *Alone, Brutus weighs the arguments for joining the conspiracy. His servant Lucius brings him one of Cassius's "letters." Cassius and five other conspirators enter. Brutus becomes a conspirator but opposes three ideas: swearing an oath, including Cicero in the conspiracy, and killing Mark Antony. Portia, Brutus's wife, begs her husband to reveal why he is troubled. Brutus refuses and, accompanied by Caius Ligarius, leaves for the Capitol.*

BRUTUS*'s orchard, between midnight and 3:00* A.M.*, the ides of March.* BRUTUS*, who has been awake most of the night, is seated on a small bench. As the scene develops, he alternates between sitting and walking back and forth.*

1

BRUTUS. What, Lucius, ho!
I cannot by the progress of the stars
Give guess how near to day. Lucius, I say!
I would it were my fault to sleep so soundly.
When, Lucius, when? Awake, I say! What, Lucius!
(LUCIUS *appears, rubbing his eyes.*)
LUCIUS. Called you, my lord?
BRUTUS. Get me a taper in my study, Lucius.
When it is lighted, come and call me here.
LUCIUS. I will, my lord.
(As LUCIUS *withdraws,* BRUTUS *resumes his restless pacing.)*
BRUTUS. It must be by his death. And for my part
I know no personal cause to spurn at him,
But for the general. He would be crowned.
How that might change his nature, there's the question.
It is the bright day that brings forth the adder,
And that craves wary walking. Crown him that,
And then I grant we put a sting in him
That at his will he may do danger with.
2 Th' abuse of greatness is when it disjoins
Remorse from power. And to speak truth of Caesar, **3**
I have not known when his affections swayed
More than his reason. But 'tis a common proof
That lowliness is young ambition's ladder,
Whereto the climber-upward turns his face;
But when he once attains the upmost round
He then unto the ladder turns his back,
Looks in the clouds, scorning the base degrees
By which he did ascend. So Caesar may.

■ Why do you think Brutus is so wakeful?

7 taper, candle.

10 his, Caesar's.

11–12 I know no personal . . . general. Though Brutus has no personal reason for striking at (spurning) Caesar, he nevertheless feels he should do so for the public (general) good.

15 craves, requires.

20 affections, passions (as opposed to reason).

SELECTION SUMMARY

Julius Caesar, Act 2

Scene 1: Brutus joins the conspiracy, announcing his decision to Cassius and the others before dawn on the ides of March. The conspirators lay their plans for the attack of Caesar in the Senate. Brutus overrides Cassius in a discussion about killing Antony as well, thus taking from Cassius the leadership of the group. After the conspirators depart, Portia extracts from Brutus a promise that he will tell her what has been on his mind.

Scene 2: Calpurnia has a dream that foreshadows Caesar's death and begs him not to go to the Capitol. The conspirator Decius, however, reinterprets Calpurnia's dream in a favorable manner, and Caesar leaves for the Senate.

Scenes 3 and 4: Artemidorus has learned of the conspiracy and plans to hand Caesar a warning note as Caesar enters the Capitol. Portia, having learned of the plot, is anxious and sends the servant Lucius to the Capitol for a report.

*For summaries in other languages, see the **Building English Proficiency** book*

Then, lest he may, prevent. And since the quarrel
Will bear no color for the thing he is,
Fashion it thus: that what he is, augmented,
Would run to these and these extremities.
And therefore think him as a serpent's egg
Which, hatched, would, as his kind, grow mischievous;
And kill him in the shell.

(LUCIUS, *yawning, enters carrying a letter—a small scroll.*)

LUCIUS. The taper burneth in your closet, sir.
Searching the window for a flint, I found
This paper, thus sealed up, and I am sure
It did not lie there when I went to bed.

(Gives him the letter.)

BRUTUS. Get you to bed again. It is not day.
Is not tomorrow, boy, the ides of March?

LUCIUS. I know not, sir.

BRUTUS. Look in the calendar and bring me word.

LUCIUS. I will, sir. (LUCIUS *exits.*)

BRUTUS. The exhalations whizzing in the air
Give so much light that I may read by them.

(Opens the letter and reads.)

"Brutus, thou sleep'st. Awake, and see thyself!
Shall Rome, et cetera? Speak, strike, redress!"
"Brutus, thou sleep'st. Awake!"
Such instigations have been often dropped
Where I have took them up.
"Shall Rome et cetera?" Thus must I piece it out.
Shall Rome stand under one man's awe? What, Rome?
My ancestors did from the streets of Rome
The Tarquin drive, when he was called a king.
"Speak, strike, redress!" Am I entreated
To speak and strike? O Rome, I make thee promise,
If the redress will follow, thou receivest
Thy full petition at the hand of Brutus.

(LUCIUS *enters.*)

LUCIUS. Sir, March is wasted fifteen days.

(Knock within.)

BRUTUS. 'Tis good. Go to the gate; somebody knocks.

(LUCIUS *exits.*)

Since Cassius first did whet me against Caesar,
I have not slept.
Between the acting of a dreadful thing
And the first motion, all the interim is
Like a phantasma or a hideous dream.
The genius and the mortal instruments

28 prevent, he must be prevented.

30 augmented, increased.

33 as his kind, according to his nature.

■ What reasons does Brutus consider for assassinating Caesar?

35 closet, private chamber, room.

44 exhalations, meteors, which were thought to be caused by vapors exhaled into the atmosphere.

49 instigations, urgings on; stirrings up.

54 The Tarquin, Tarquinius Superbus (sü pėrb′əs), the last Roman king.

61 whet, make keen or eager; stimulate.

64 motion, proposal.

66 the genius . . . instruments, the soul and the body.

4 Reading/Thinking Skills
Summarize

Possible responses Brutus feels that gaining the crown and additional power would change Caesar's nature and make him more dangerous; Caesar does not temper justice with mercy; Caesar is ambitious; it is better to kill him before he grows greater and begins to wreak havoc.

5 Historical Note
Et Cetera

The reason that the words *et cetera* appear in the text is that the actor had an actual letter to read and therefore the letter's content did not need to be included in the manuscript of the play.

6 Reader's Response
Making Personal Connections

Questions

- Why do you think Brutus hasn't slept? *(Possible response: It may be because of a troubled conscience or just because of the difficulty of committing to the dreadful act.)*
- Do you think the reaction of Brutus is typical for someone in his place? *(Possible response: Yes, anyone making a decision like this would necessarily be distressed, conscious-stricken, and wakeful.)*

BUILDING ENGLISH PROFICIENCY

ESL LEP ELD SAE LD

Supporting an Opinion

Brutus believes that once Caesar is crowned absolute monarch of Rome his personality will change for the worse. Ask students to agree or disagree with Brutus and to support their opinions with examples.

1. Ask a volunteer to read aloud the statements by Brutus on page 698 (lines 10–27).

2. Have students paraphrase what Brutus thinks power does to a person. Ask: Do you think that a person can become powerful without forgetting his or her "roots"?

3. Invite students to agree or disagree with Brutus's beliefs. Encourage them to give examples of powerful people—contemporary or historic—that support their opinions.

Building English Proficiency
Activities, p. 220

7 Reading/Thinking Skills
Analyze

Question Why might Shakespeare have chosen this moment to introduce the fact that Cassius and Brutus are brothers-in-law? *(Possible responses: It would explain why Brutus would welcome Cassius in the middle of the night; if we had known it first, we might have assumed that Brutus would be persuaded—not knowing allowed us to doubt and made the play more interesting; perhaps it was common knowledge in Shakespeare's time and the word* brother *was inserted here for metrical reasons.)*

8 Reading/Thinking Skills
Draw Conclusions

Question Why should conspirators smile, according to Brutus? *(Response: to disguise their intentions and plotting)*

9 Reading/Thinking Skills
Predict

Possible response He will join—if he were not going to, he would not be planning how the conspiracy could conceal its dark purpose.

Are then in council; and the state of man,
Like to a little kingdom, suffers then
The nature of an insurrection.
(LUCIUS *enters.*)
[7] **LUCIUS.** Sir, 'tis your brother Cassius at the door,
Who doth desire to see you.
BRUTUS. Is he alone?
LUCIUS. No, sir. There are more with him.
BRUTUS. Do you know them?
LUCIUS. No sir. Their hats are plucked about their ears,
And half their faces buried in their cloaks,
That by no means I may discover them
By any mark of favor.
BRUTUS. Let 'em enter.
(LUCIUS *exits.*)
They are the faction. O conspiracy,
Sham'st thou to show thy dangerous brow by night,
When evils are most free? O, then by day
Where wilt thou find a cavern dark enough
[8] To mask thy monstrous visage? Seek none, conspiracy!
Hide it in smiles and affability;
For if thou put thy native semblance on,
Not Erebus itself were dim enough
To hide thee from prevention.
(LUCIUS *ushers in the* CONSPIRATORS—CASSIUS, CASCA, DECIUS, CINNA, METELLUS CIMBER *and* TREBONIUS—*and then exits.*)
CASSIUS. I think we are too bold upon your rest.
Good morrow, Brutus. Do we trouble you?
BRUTUS. I have been up this hour, awake all night.
Know I these men that come along with you?
CASSIUS. Yes, every man of them, and no man here
But honors you; and every one doth wish
You had but that opinion of yourself
Which every noble Roman bears of you.
This is Trebonius.
BRUTUS. He is welcome hither.
CASSIUS. This, Decius Brutus.
BRUTUS. He is welcome too.
CASSIUS. This, Casca; this, Cinna; and this, Metellus Cimber.
BRUTUS. They are all welcome.
What watchful cares do interpose themselves
Betwixt your eyes and night?
CASSIUS. Shall I entreat a word?
(BRUTUS *and* CASSIUS *whisper.*)

70 brother, actually brother-in-law; Cassius was married to Brutus's sister.

76 any mark of favor, any features by which they can be recognized.

83–85 for if thou . . . prevention. If the conspirators walk about wearing their natural appearance, not even Erebus (er′ə bəs) would be dark enough to keep them from detection. In Greek mythology, Erebus was a dark, gloomy place through which the dead passed en route to Hades.

[9] ■ Given his statements in lines 77–85, do you think Brutus will join the conspiracy? Explain.

98 interpose, come or be between other things.

MINI-LESSON: GRAMMAR
Archaic Adverbs

Teach Read these lines from pages 700 and 701:

He is welcome *hither.*

And every man *hence* to his idle bed.

Explain that Shakespeare used adverbs of place that are no longer commonly used. Then show students this chart.

Word	Meaning
hence	from this place
thence	from that place
whence	from what place?
hither	to or toward this place
thither	to or toward that place
whither	to what place?

Point out that each of these adverbs packs a lot of words into one or two syllables, which could be useful to a poet.

Activity Idea Find lines in which Shakespeare uses these adverbs. Rephrase them in modern English.

DECIUS. Here lies the east. Doth not the day break here?
CASCA. No.
CINNA. O, pardon, sir, it doth; and yon gray lines
That fret the clouds are messengers of day.
CASCA. You shall confess that you are both deceived.
Here, as I point my sword, the sun arises,
Which is a great way growing on the south,
Weighing the youthful season of the year.
Some two months hence, up higher toward the north
He first presents his fire; and the high east
Stands, as the Capitol, directly here.
BRUTUS *(coming forward)*. Give me your hands all over, one by one.
CASSIUS. And let us swear our resolution.
BRUTUS. No, not an oath. If not the face of men,
The sufferance of our souls, the time's abuse—
If these be motives weak, break off betimes,
And every man hence to his idle bed;
So let high-sighted tyranny range on
Till each man drop by lottery. But if these,
As I am sure they do, bear fire enough
To kindle cowards and to steel with valor
The melting spirits of women, then, countrymen,
What need we any spur but our own cause
To prick us to redress? What other bond
Than secret Romans that have spoke the word
And will not palter? And what other oath
Than honesty to honesty engaged
That this shall be or we will fall for it?
Swear priests and cowards and men cautelous,
Old feeble carrions, and such suffering souls
That welcome wrongs; unto bad causes swear
Such creatures as men doubt. But do not stain
The even virtue of our enterprise,
Nor th' insuppressive mettle of our spirits,
To think that or our cause or our performance
Did need an oath, when every drop of blood
That every Roman bears—and nobly bears—
Is guilty of a several bastardy
If he do break the smallest particle
Of any promise that hath passed from him.
CASSIUS. But what of Cicero? Shall we sound him?
I think he will stand very strong with us.
CASCA. Let us not leave him out.
CINNA. No, by no means.
METELLUS. O, let us have him, for his silver hairs

114–119 If not the face . . . by lottery. If the wrongs the conspirators see about them are not sufficient to bind them to firm purpose, then let each man go his own way, become a weakling, and die when it suits a tyrant's whims.
119 these, that is, these injustices just cited.
126 palter, use trickery.
129 cautelous, deceitful.
135 or . . . or, either . . . or. To maintain a ten-syllable line, Shakespeare often uses "or . . . or" or "nor . . . nor."

This Roman coin, showing a liberty cap and two daggers, commemorates the assassination of Caesar. The inscription reads "The Ides of March." What does such an artifact suggest about Roman attitudes toward political violence?

Art Study

Response to Caption Question
Some students may see the coin as more indicative of the Romans' hatred of kingship than of a general attitude towards political violence. Some students may say that the coin reflects the sentiments of the government that minted it, not necessarily of the Roman populace. Some students may think it shows a general acceptance of violence as a means to a justified political end.

10 Reader's Response
Challenging the Text

Questions
- Do you agree with Brutus's characterization of their enterprise? Why or why not? *(Possible responses: Some students may think Brutus is simply glorifying murder. Others may think that the end justifies the means. Students should support their opinions with reasons.)*
- At this point, do you think the conspiracy will succeed? Why or why not? *(Possible responses: Students may express concern about leaks, about the warning Caesar has received, etc.)*

11 Reading/Thinking Skills
Connect

Question What does it mean to Brutus to be a Roman? *(to be honorable, have certain rights and a republican government)*

BUILDING ENGLISH PROFICIENCY

Relating to Characters

Now that the students have been introduced to the conspirators, ask them to infer how these characters would look and act. (This activity can be expanded, with students taking the roles of all the major characters in this play.)

- Have a group of students choose a character to "be" throughout their reading of the play, acting out the role when that character appears in a scene. Alternatively, write the names of the characters on slips of paper and let students draw one from a hat.
- Have students keep track of their character by making inferences and noting personality traits in their notebooks.
- Tell your student characters that at any point during the play others may ask them questions about their feelings or actions. They can use hints from the play, along with their own imaginations, to answer.
- At the end of each act, have students write a journal entry from their character's perspective.

12 Reading/Thinking Skills
Evaluate

Response Students will probably say no unless they either (1) know Roman history or the outcome of the play or (2) are considering Brutus as the hero in a tragedy and expecting something to go desperately wrong.

13 Reader's Response
Making Personal Connections

Question Do you think what Brutus is suggesting—a respectful murder—is humanly possible? Why or why not? *(Possible responses: Many students may say that since murder is a violation against humanity it is necessarily wrathful. The term* purgers *makes the conspirators no less murderers. Other students may think that the conspirators may conduct Caesar's execution in a discreet and "considerate" manner.)*

Will purchase us a good opinion
And buy men's voices to commend our deeds.
It shall be said his judgment ruled our hands;
Our youths and wildness shall no whit appear,
But all be buried in his gravity.
BRUTUS. O, name him not. Let us not break with him,
For he will never follow anything
That other men begin.
CASSIUS. Then leave him out.
CASCA. Indeed he is not fit.
DECIUS. Shall no man else be touched but only Caesar?
CASSIUS. Decius, well urged. I think it is not meet
Mark Antony, so well beloved of Caesar,
Should outlive Caesar. We shall find of him
A shrewd contriver; and you know his means,
If he improve them, may well stretch so far
As to annoy us all. Which to prevent,
Let Antony and Caesar fall together.
BRUTUS. Our course will seem too bloody, Caius Cassius, [12]
To cut the head off and then hack the limbs,
Like wrath in death and envy afterwards;
For Antony is but a limb of Caesar.
Let's be sacrificers, but not butchers, Caius.
We all stand up against the spirit of Caesar,
And in the spirit of men there is no blood
O, that we then could come by Caesar's spirit
And not dismember Caesar! But, alas,
[13] Caesar must bleed for it. And, gentle friends,
Let's kill him boldly, but not wrathfully;
Let's carve him as a dish fit for the gods,
Not hew him as a carcass fit for hounds.
And let our hearts, as subtle masters do,
Stir up their servants to an act of rage
And after seem to chide 'em. This shall make
Our purpose necessary, and not envious;
Which so appearing to the common eyes,
We shall be called purgers, not murderers.
And for Mark Antony, think not of him;
For he can do no more than Caesar's arm
When Caesar's head is off.
CASSIUS. Yet I fear him,
For in the engrafted love he bears to Caesar—
BRUTUS. Alas, good Cassius, do not think of him.
If he love Caesar, all that he can do
Is to himself—take thought and die for Caesar.

150 break with, confide in.

160 improve, exploit; make good use of.
161 annoy, injure.

■ Do you think Brutus has erred in opposing the killing of Antony?

172 gentle, noble.

177 their servants, that is, our hands.

188–189 take thought . . . should, despair and die for Caesar, and that would be too much for him to do; hence, it is unlikely.

And that were much he should, for he is given
To sports, to wildness, and much company.
TREBONIUS. There is no fear in him. Let him not die,
For he will live, and laugh at this hereafter.
(Clock strikes.)
BRUTUS. Peace! Count the clock.
CASSIUS. The clock hath stricken three.
TREBONIUS. 'Tis time to part.
CASSIUS. But it is doubtful yet
Whether Caesar will come forth today or no;
For he is superstitious grown of late,
Quite from the main opinion he held once
Of fantasy, of dreams, and ceremonies.
It may be these apparent prodigies,
The unaccustomed terror of this night,
And the persuasion of his augurers
May hold him from the Capitol today.
DECIUS. Never fear that. If he be so resolved,
I can o'ersway him; for he loves to hear
That unicorns may be betrayed with trees,
And bears with glasses, elephants with holes,
Lions with toils, and men with flatterers;
But when I tell him he hates flatterers,
He says he does, being then most flattered.
Let me work;
For I can give his humor the true bent,
And I will bring him to the Capitol.
CASSIUS. Nay, we will all of us be there to fetch him.
BRUTUS. By the eighth hour. Is that the uttermost?
CINNA. Be that the uttermost, and fail not then.
METELLUS. Caius Ligarius doth bear Caesar hard,
Who rated him for speaking well of Pompey.
I wonder none of you have thought of him.
BRUTUS. Now, good Metellus, go along by him.
He loves me well, and I have given him reasons;
Send him but hither, and I'll fashion him.
CASSIUS. The morning comes upon 's. We'll leave you, Brutus.
And, friends, disperse yourselves; but all remember
What you have said, and show yourselves true Romans.
BRUTUS. Good gentlemen, look fresh and merrily;
Let not our looks put on our purposes,
But bear it as our Roman actors do,
With untired spirits and formal constancy.
And so good morrow to you every one.
(The CONSPIRATORS exit.)

191 There is no fear in him. There is no reason to fear Antony.

193 Count the clock, one of the most famous anachronisms in the play; yet Shakespeare needed some way of conveying to his audience what time it was.

197 quite from the main opinion, contrary to the strong opinion.

201 augurers, priests who predicted the future by reading signs. Sometimes spelled *augurs*.

15

■ In Cassius's view (lines 194–202), what might prevent Caesar from going to the Capitol?

205–207 That unicorns . . . toils, methods thought effective for capturing animals. When the hunter stepped behind a tree, a charging unicorn would trap himself by driving his horn into the tree. A bear, given a mirror, would be so fascinated by its image that it became easy prey. Elephants were captured in pits; lions were sometimes rendered helpless by nets (toils).

216–217 bear Caesar hard. . . rated him. Caius bears a grudge toward Caesar who had angrily scolded (berated) him.

226 put on, wear in open view; that is, betray.

14 Literary Focus
Plot

Question How does this uncertainty affect the rising action? *(Possible response: It provides suspense about whether or not the scheme can be carried out as planned.)*

15 Reading/Thinking Skills
Summarize

Possible response Caesar's superstitions, combined with the unusual night and the opinion of his augurers, could prevent him from going to the Capitol.

16 Literary Element
Theme

Question How is persuasion becoming an important theme in the work? *(Possible response: The creation of the conspiracy has depended on Cassius's persuasion of Brutus and Casca; Caesar's appearance tomorrow may depend on the persuasion of his augurers as opposed to the persuasion Decius can bring to bear.)*

BUILDING ENGLISH PROFICIENCY

Keeping Track of Details

On pages 702–703, the conspirators discuss the details of the assassination, making decisions that will shape the rest of the play. Work with students to chart the questions and problems raised, the solutions decided upon, and the reasons for the decisions.

Question or Problem	Should Cicero join?
Answer or Solution	No
Reason	He never obeys orders.

17 Reading/Thinking Skills
Evaluate

Possible response Portia's description of Brutus indicates that he is temperamental and so disturbed that he cannot eat, sleep, or talk to her.

18 Reading/Thinking Skills
Predict

Question Do you think Brutus will tell Portia his plans? Why or why not? *(Possible responses: Yes, the couple seem to have an open, honest relationship. No, he would not betray the secrecy of the conspiracy; he would probably want to protect Portia from involvement.)*

Boy! Lucius! Fast asleep? It is no matter.
Enjoy the honey-heavy dew of slumber.
Thou hast no figures nor no fantasies
Which busy care draws in the brains of men;
Therefore thou sleep'st so sound.
(PORTIA *enters.*)
PORTIA. Brutus, my lord!
BRUTUS. Portia, what mean you? Wherefore rise you now?
It is not for your health thus to commit
Your weak condition to the raw cold morning.
PORTIA. Nor for yours neither. You've ungently, Brutus,
Stole from my bed. And yesternight, at supper,
You suddenly arose, and walked about
Musing and sighing, with your arms across,
And when I asked you what the matter was,
You stared upon me with ungentle looks.
I urged you further; then you scratched your head
And too impatiently stamped with your foot.
Yet I insisted, yet you answered not,
But with an angry wafture of your hand
Gave sign for me to leave you. So I did,
Fearing to strengthen that impatience
Which seemed too much enkindled, and withal
Hoping it was but an effect of humor,
Which sometimes hath his hour with every man.
It will not let you eat, nor talk, nor sleep,
And could it work so much upon your shape
As it hath much prevailed on your condition,
I should not know you Brutus. Dear my lord,
18 Make me acquainted with your cause of grief.
BRUTUS. I am not well in health, and that is all.
PORTIA. Brutus is wise, and were he not in health
He would embrace the means to come by it.
BRUTUS. Why, so I do. Good Portia, go to bed.
PORTIA. Is Brutus sick? And is it physical
To walk unbracèd and suck up the humors
Of the dank morning? What, is Brutus sick,
And will he steal out of his wholesome bed
To dare the vile contagion of the night,
And tempt the rheumy and unpurgèd air
To add unto his sickness? No, my Brutus,
You have some sick offense within your mind,
Which by the right and virtue of my place
I ought to know of. *(She kneels.)* And upon my knees
I charm you, by my once-commended beauty,

232 figures, imaginings.

241 across, folded.

17 ■ What does Portia's thumbnail description of Brutus indicate about his state of mind?

262 physical, healthful.
263 humors, damps, mists.

267 the rheumy . . . air, air that causes colds because it has not yet been purified (purged) by the sun.

272 charm, conjure.

MINI-LESSON: GRAMMAR

Recognize the Function of All Parts of Speech

Teach Read these lines from Portia's first long speech on page 704:

Nor for yours ***neither.*** You've ***un***gently, Brutus,
Stole from my bed. . . .
Yet I insisted, yet you answered ***not.***

Point out that there are a number of ways in English to present a negative. In these examples, Shakespeare uses a negative prefix (*un-*), the negative adverb *not,* and the negative conjunctions *neither* and *nor.*

Activity Idea Have students work in small groups to search Portia's long speeches on pages 704–705 for examples of negative ideas and make a list of them. Discuss the effect of so many negative ideas in her speeches.

By all your vows of love, and that great vow
Which did incorporate and make us one,
That you unfold to me, your self, your half,
Why you are heavy, and what men tonight
Have had resort to you; for here have been
Some six or seven, who did hide their faces
Even from darkness.

BRUTUS. Kneel not, gentle Portia.
(He raises her.)

PORTIA. I should not need if you were gentle Brutus.
Within the bond of marriage, tell me, Brutus,
Is it excepted I should know no secrets
That appertain to you? Am I your self
But as it were in sort or limitation,
To keep with you at meals, comfort your bed,
And talk to you sometimes? Dwell I but in the suburbs
Of your good pleasure? If it be no more,
Portia is Brutus's harlot, not his wife.

BRUTUS. You are my true and honorable wife,
As dear to me as are the ruddy drops
That visit my sad heart.

PORTIA. If this were true, then should I know this secret.
I grant I am a woman, but withal
A woman that Lord Brutus took to wife.
I grant I am a woman, but withal
A woman well reputed, Cato's daughter.
Think you I am no stronger than my sex,
Being so fathered and so husbanded?
Tell me your counsels, I will not disclose 'em.
I have made strong proof of my constancy,
Giving myself a voluntary wound
Here, in the thigh. Can I bear that with patience,
And not my husband's secrets?

BRUTUS. O ye gods,
Render me worthy of this noble wife!
(Knock within.)
Hark, hark, one knocks. Portia, go in awhile,
And by and by thy bosom shall partake
The secrets of my heart.
All my engagements I will construe to thee,
All the charactery of my sad brows.
Leave me with haste. (PORTIA *exits.*) Lucius, who's that knocks?
(LUCIUS *and* CAUIS LIGARIUS, *who is wearing a kerchief, enter.*)

LUCIUS. Here is a sick man that would speak with you.

282-283 Is it excepted . . . you? Portia asked if an exception was made in the marriage vows so that she would have no legal right to inquire into affairs pertaining to Brutus.

286 suburbs, periphery, outskirts.

298 being so fathered. Portia's father, Cato, had killed himself rather than submit to Caesar's tyranny. He was Brutus's uncle as well as his father-in-law.

■ What question do you think the actress playing Portia in this scene might ask of her director?

309 charactery, handwriting; i.e., lines of worry on his face.

19 Multicultural Note
Marriage Vows

In many cultures, the act of marriage is formalized by vows between husband and wife. Portia refers to those solemn promises in her speech.

20 Reading/Thinking Skills
Question

Possible responses How assertive should I be? What tone should I adopt? How can I keep from seeming servile? I have trouble with the sentiments expressed in lines 293–301—how can you help me identify with what Portia says and does?

BUILDING ENGLISH PROFICIENCY

ESL LEP ELD SAE LD

Adjust Reading Rate

Remind students that this play was performed by actors who interpreted the lines as they recited. Their own readings can also speed up for emotion or slow down for clarity. Encourage them to slow down when they encounter any of the following situations:

- the meaning of a word needs to be checked in the marginal annotations
- the syntax of a sentence makes it difficult to identify clearly the subject, verb, or direct or indirect objects
- figurative language is not immediately clear

Activity Idea For practice, have each student choose a passage of from five to ten lines. Have them read the passage aloud at three different speeds. Then ask them to tell what is gained or lost (clarity, meaning, rhythm, humor, naturalness) with each different reading.

21 Reading/Thinking Skills
Clarify

Possible responses It seems that Caius Ligarius is not really ill. He has put on a kerchief and feigned illness because he is going to join the conspiracy and does not want to be identified. But in the moments that Brutus thinks that Caius is ill, it seems that Caius will not be able to participate and students may wonder what effect that will have on the conspiracy's success.

22 Reading/Thinking Skills
Draw Conclusions

Question What do lines 328–329 mean? *(Response: Brutus means that killing Caesar will restore the rights and privileges of Roman citizens, making them "healthy" again. Ligarius means that the aim of the conspiracy is to murder Caesar.)*

BRUTUS. Caius Ligarius, that Metellus spake of.
Boy, stand aside. (LUCIUS *exits.*)
Caius Ligarius, how?
LIGARIUS. Vouchsafe good morrow from a feeble tongue.
BRUTUS. O, what a time have you chose out, brave Caius,
To wear a kerchief! Would you were not sick!
LIGARIUS. I am not sick, if Brutus have in hand
Any exploit worthy the name of honor.
BRUTUS. Such an exploit have I in hand, Ligarius,
Had you a healthful ear to hear of it.
LIGARIUS. By all the gods that Romans bow before,
I here discard my sickness! Soul of Rome!
(He throws off his kerchief.)
Brave son, derived from honorable loins!
Thou like an exorcist hast conjured up
My mortifièd spirit. Now bid me run,
And I will strive with things impossible,
Yea, get the better of them. What's to do?
BRUTUS. A piece of work that will make sick men whole.
LIGARIUS. But are not some whole that we must make sick?
BRUTUS. That must we also. What it is, my Caius,
I shall unfold to thee as we are going
To whom it must be done.
LIGARIUS. Set on your foot,
And with a heart new-fired I follow you
To do I know not what; but it sufficeth
That Brutus leads me on. *(Thunder.)*
BRUTUS. Follow me, then. *(They exit.)*

313 how? how are you?
314 vouchsafe, agree or deign (to accept).

21 ■ What dramatic effect might Shakespeare have been trying to achieve by establishing Caius Ligarius's illness?

324–325 conjured . . . spirit, brought to life my deadened spirit.

Scene 2

Summary *Calpurnia, Caesar's wife, begs Caesar not to go to the Capitol. At first he laughs at her fears but eventually agrees to remain at home. Decius enters, flatters Caesar, and succeeds in changing Caesar's mind. The conspirators enter, then Mark Antony, and all set off for the Capitol.*

Caesar's House. Wearing a dressing-gown, CAESAR *enters at right. Speaking to himself, he crosses left where his street robe is draped across a chair.*

CAESAR. Nor heaven nor earth have been at peace tonight.
Thrice hath Calpurnia in her sleep cried out,
"Help, ho, they murder Caesar!" *(Calling.)* Who's within? (*He claps.*)
(A SERVANT *enters.)*
SERVANT. My lord?
CAESAR. Go bid the priests do present sacrifice
And bring me their opinions of success.
SERVANT. I will, my lord.
(He exits through a rear door as CALPURNIA, *in night clothes, enters at right.)*
CALPURNIA. What mean you, Caesar? Think you to walk forth?
You shall not stir out of your house today.
CAESAR. Caesar shall forth. The things that threatened me
Ne'er looked but on my back. When they shall see
The face of Caesar, they are vanishèd.
CALPURNIA. Caesar, I never stood on ceremonies, 24
Yet now they fright me. There is one within,
Besides the things that we have heard and seen,
Recounts most horrid sights seen by the watch.
A lioness hath whelpèd in the streets,
And graves have yawned and yielded up their dead.
Fierce fiery warriors fight upon the clouds
In ranks and squadrons and right form of war, 25
Which drizzled blood upon the Capitol.
The noise of battle hurtled in the air;
Horses did neigh, and dying men did groan,
And ghosts did shriek and squeal about the streets. 26
O Caesar, these things are beyond all use,
And I do fear them.
CAESAR. What can be avoided
Whose end is purposed by the mighty gods?
Yet Caesar shall go forth; for these predictions
Are to the world in general as to Caesar.
CALPURNIA. When beggars die there are no comets seen;
The heavens themselves blaze forth the death of princes.
CAESAR. Cowards die many times before their deaths;

1 Nor . . . nor, neither . . . nor.

5–6 Go bid the priests . . . success. By killing a bird and examining its entrails, the priest-augurers predicted the future. Caesar commands the augurers to sacrifice a bird and to report the result (opinions of success). 23

14 one within, probably a servant.

20 right form, regular formations.

25 use, normal experience; that is, supernatural.
26–27 What can be . . . gods? Note Caesar's fatalism, a belief that fate controls everything that happens.

23 Historical Note
Augurers

Augurers were so important in ancient Rome that the state ran a college to train them.

24 Historical Note
Stand on Ceremony

Calpurnia means that she never paid attention to omens. Today people use the phrase to mean people who expect or demand to be treated with elaborate courtesy or formality.

25 Literary Element
Imagery

Draw attention to the imagery in Calpurnia's account. Ask students to visualize the scene. If they were staging this scene, how might they suggest these bizarre images? *(perhaps on an overhead projector, through sound effects, with symbolic gestures such as clanking swords for warriors or a bloody hand for violence)*

26 Literary Element
Alliteration

Explain to students that alliteration is the repetition of sounds at the beginning of words or in stressed syllables that appear close together. Point out the *y*'s in line 18, the *f*'s in line 19, and the *s*'s in line 24.

BUILDING ENGLISH PROFICIENCY

Making Real-Life Connections

Help students relate to Calpurnia's observation about the "death of princes" (line 31).

1. Ask students to share what they know about the deaths of any world leaders—political, military, and/or religious.

2. Ask students if and/or how a country's situation is affected when a leader dies by assassination.

3. Have students review Calpurnia's statement in the light of this discussion.

4. Consider showing news documentaries of events following the assassinations of Dr. Martin Luther King, Jr. (1968), John F. Kennedy (1963), or Yitzhak Rabin (1995). Students might predict what will happen when Caesar is assassinated.

5. Provide a variety of American and world history textbooks. Have pairs or small groups of students skim to find instances of assassinations and their aftermaths. Let groups share their findings and then generalize about the causes and effects of assassination.

27 Reader's Response

Making Personal Connections

Questions

- Compare and contrast Caesar's comments on bravery with your own ideas. *(Students may agree with his philosophy that we should not fear death because it is inevitable.)*
- What does he mean by "The valiant never taste of death but once"? In answering, refer to line 32 on the preceding page. *(Possible response: Those who are truly valiant and brave face the challenges of life without being afraid; they recognize the difference between these daily challenges and the ultimate challenge of death, over which they have no control.)*

28 Literary Focus

Plot

Question How might Caesar's decision to stay at home affect the conspirators' plans? *(Possible response: It may ruin their plot; the longer they have to wait before carrying out their plans, the greater likelihood that they will be exposed.)*

The valiant never taste of death but once.
Of all the wonders that I yet have heard,
27 It seems to me most strange that men should fear,
Seeing that death, a necessary end,
Will come when it will come.
(A SERVANT *enters.)*
What say the augurers?
SERVANT. They would not have you to stir forth today.
Plucking the entrails of an offering forth,
They could not find a heart within the beast.
CAESAR. The gods do this in shame of cowardice.
Caesar should be a beast without a heart
If he should stay at home today for fear.
No, Caesar shall not. Danger knows full well
That Caesar is more dangerous than he.
We are two lions littered in one day,
And I the elder and more terrible;
And Caesar shall go forth.
CALPURNIA. Alas, my lord,
Your wisdom is consumed in confidence.
Do not go forth today! Call it my fear
That keeps you in the house, and not your own.
We'll send Mark Antony to the Senate House,
And he shall say you are not well today.
Let me, upon my knee, prevail in this. *(She kneels.)*
28 **CAESAR.** Mark Antony shall say I am not well,
And for thy humor I will stay at home. *(He raises her.)*
(DECIUS *enters.)*
Here's Decius Brutus. He shall tell them so.
DECIUS. Caesar, all hail! Good morrow, worthy Caesar.
I come to fetch you to the Senate House.
CAESAR. And you are come in very happy time
To bear my greeting to the senators
And tell them that I will not come today.
Cannot is false, and that I dare not, falser;
I will not come today. Tell them so, Decius.
CALPURNIA. Say he is sick.
CAESAR. Shall Caesar send a lie?
Have I in conquest stretched mine arm so far
To be afeared to tell graybeards the truth?
Decius, go tell them Caesar will not come.
DECIUS. Most mighty Caesar, let me know some cause,
Lest I be laughed at when I tell them so.
CAESAR. The cause is in my will. I will not come.

46 we, Caesar and danger.

56 humor, whim.

60 happy, opportune.

MINI-LESSON: LITERARY ELEMENT

Blank Verse

Read aloud Caesar's speech that begins, "The gods do this. . . (lines 41–48). Point out that although these lines appear to be ordinary prose speech, they are actually blank verse.

Teach Blank verse is poetry that does not rhyme but that has a regular rhythm. Each line follows a pattern called iambic pentameter, consisting of five unstressed words or syllables alternating with five stressed ones. The beat of a blank-verse line can be indicated as follows: ta DUM ta DUM ta DUM ta DUM ta DUM.

Some words are condensed or stretched to keep the rhythm; for example, on page 707 *ne'er* in line 11 has one syllable (shortened from *never); vanishèd* in line 12 has three syllables. Sometimes a blank verse line is split between two speakers (line 48).

Activity Idea Have students read a blank verse speech from act 2 aloud, noting the rhythm. Have them note any words Shakespeare has manipulated to make the verse regular, as well as any departures from the ten-syllable rhythm in a line.

29

That is enough to satisfy the Senate.
But for your private satisfaction,
Because I love you, I will let you know.
Calpurnia here, my wife, stays me at home.
She dreamt tonight she saw my statue,
30 Which like a fountain with an hundred spouts
Did run pure blood; and many lusty Romans
Came smiling and did bathe their hands in it.
And these does she apply for warnings and portents
Of evils imminent, and on her knee
Hath begged that I will stay at home today.

DECIUS. This dream is all amiss interpreted;
It was a vision fair and fortunate.
Your statue spouting blood in many pipes,
In which so many smiling Romans bathed,
Signifies that from you great Rome shall suck
Reviving blood, and that great men shall press
For tinctures, stains, relics, and cognizance.
This by Calpurnia's dream is signified.

76–79 She dreamt . . . hands in it. These lines foreshadow future events. Keep them in mind as you read further.

80 apply for, interpret as.

89 cognizance (kog′nə-zəns), heraldic emblems worn by a nobleman's followers.

29 Historical Note
Acting Companies

Under Queen Elizabeth I, the acting profession in England was just becoming respectable. Since laws still existed for the imprisonment of "rogues, vagabonds, and strolling players," acting companies were protected by lords, who issued warrants permitting them to travel throughout England. Shakespeare's own company, first known as the Lord Chamberlain's Men, was taken under the royal protection of James I and became the King's Men. King's *Men* was an apt title, since all roles—including that of Calpurnia, played by Greer Garson as shown in this film still—were played by males.

30 Literary Element
Metaphor

This passage affords an opportunity to discuss metaphor. The spouting fountain is interpreted variously as representing the massacred Caesar spouting blood or the life-source for renewed Rome.

BUILDING ENGLISH PROFICIENCY

Analyzing Character

Scene 2 presents Caesar at some length. Help students recognize what a complex, three-dimensional, and contradictory character he is, based on this scene alone. Have them consider his qualities by constructing a character trait web such as the one shown. They should provide an example for each character trait mentioned.

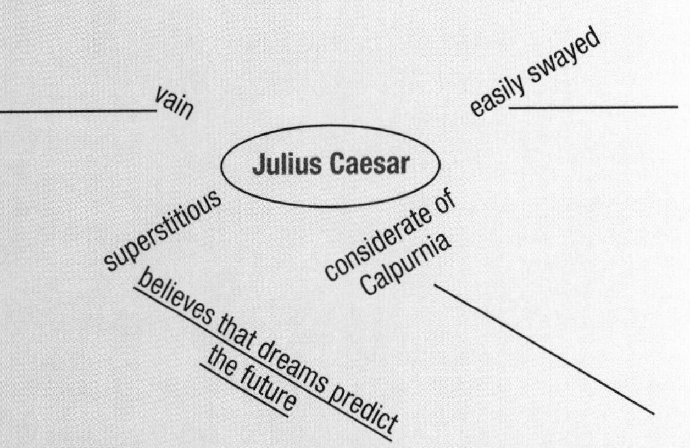

31 Literary Focus
Plot

Question How does news of the imminent coronation affect the plot? *(Possible response: If Caesar possesses the additional powers of a monarch, he may be even more formidable; they must act quickly to carry out their plot.)*

32 Reading/Thinking Skills
Summarize

Possible response Decius equates Caesar's blood with the lifeblood—the leadership—Rome needs. He entices Caesar with the promise of a crown and implies that others may think Caesar is afraid if he stays at home.

33 Literary Element
Irony

Explain that verbal irony occurs when a character says something that, although true, is sure to be misinterpreted by the hearer. Thus, the word *near,* though reassuring to Caesar, carries Trebonius's threat to kill him. Alert students to the stage direction *Aside,* which indicates something intended for the audience but not for another character.

CAESAR. And this way have you well expounded it.
DECIUS. I have, when you have heard what I can say;
31 And know it now. The Senate have concluded
To give this day a crown to mighty Caesar.
If you shall send them word you will not come,
Their minds may change. Besides, it were a mock
Apt to be rendered for someone to say
"Break up the Senate till another time
When Caesar's wife shall meet with better dreams."
If Caesar hide himself, shall they not whisper
"Lo, Caesar is afraid"?
Pardon me, Caesar, for my dear dear love
To you proceeding bids me tell you this,
And reason to my love is liable.
CAESAR. How foolish do your fears seem now, Calpurnia!
I am ashamèd I did yield to them.
Give me my robe, for I will go.
(BRUTUS, LIGARIUS, METELLUS, CASCA, TREBONIUS, CINNA, *and* PUBLIUS *enter.*)
And look where Publius is come to fetch me.
PUBLIUS. Good morrow, Caesar.
CAESAR. Welcome, Publius.
What, Brutus, are you stirred so early too?
Good morrow, Casca. Caius Ligarius,
Caesar was ne'er so much your enemy
As that same ague which hath made you lean.
What is 't o'clock?
BRUTUS. Caesar, 'tis strucken eight.
CAESAR. I thank you for your pains and courtesy.
(ANTONY *enters.*)
See, Antony, that revels long o' nights,
Is notwithstanding up. Good morrow, Antony.
ANTONY. So to most noble Caesar.
CAESAR (*to a* SERVANT). Bid them prepare within.
(SERVANT *exits.*)
I am to blame to be thus waited for.
Now, Cinna. Now, Metellus. What, Trebonius,
I have an hour's talk in store for you;
Remember that you call on me today.
Be near me, that I may remember you.
33 **TREBONIUS.** Caesar, I will. *(Aside.)* And so near will I be
That your best friends shall wish I had been further.
CAESAR. Good friends, go in and taste some wine with me,
And we, like friends, will straightway go together.
BRUTUS *(aside).* That every like is not the same, O Caesar,

96–97 a mock . . . rendered, witty remark that someone would be apt to make.

102–104 my dear dear love . . . liable, love bids me speak frankly and prudence (reason) must bow to my affection for you.

32 ■ In reinterpreting Calpurnia's dream, what incentives does Decius give Caesar to go to the Capitol?

113 ague (ā′gyū), *n.* fever.

119 prepare within, set out refreshments in another room.

The heart of Brutus earns to think upon!
(CAESAR, *followed by the others, exits; a worried* CALPURNIA *waits a moment, then exits.*)

129–130 that every . . . think upon. Brutus's heart grieves that everyone who appears to be a friend is not a friend.

SCENE 3

34 **Summary** *Artemidorus, a teacher of rhetoric, reads a paper which he intends to present to Caesar.*

A street near the Capitol. Morning of the ides of March. ARTEMIDORUS *enters at left, reading from a paper.*

ARTEMIDORUS. "Caesar, beware of Brutus; take heed of Cassius; come not near Casca; have an eye to Cinna; trust not Trebonius; mark well Metellus Cimber; Decius Brutus loves thee not; thou has wronged Caius Ligarius. There is but one mind in all these men, and it is bent against Caesar. If thou beest not immortal, look about you. Security gives way to conspiracy. The mighty gods defend thee! Thy lover,
Artemidorus."
Here will I stand till Caesar pass along,
And as a suitor will I give him this.
My heart laments that virtue cannot live
Out of the teeth of emulation. 35
If thou read this, O Caesar, thou mayest live;
If not, the Fates with traitors do contrive. *(He exits.)*

6 Security . . . conspiracy, overconfidence eases the way for conspirators.
7 lover, often used by Shakespeare to mean "friend."
10 suitor, petitioner.
12 emulation, copying or imitating in order to equal or excel the achievements or qualities of an admired person.
14 contrive, conspire.
■ If you were Artemidorus, would you reveal what you know about the conspiracy? Why or why not?

SCENE 4

Summary *An anxious Portia sends her servant Lucius to the Capitol for news, then talks briefly to the Soothsayer, who intends to warn Caesar a second time.*

A street outside the house of BRUTUS. *The ides of March.* PORTIA *enters followed by* LUCIUS.

PORTIA. I prithee, boy, run to the Senate House.
Stay not to answer me, but get thee gone.
Why dost thou stay?
LUCIUS. To know my errand, madam.
PORTIA. I would have had thee there and here again
Ere I can tell thee what thou shouldst do there.
(Aside.) O constancy, be strong upon my side;
Set a huge mountain 'tween my heart and tongue!
I have a man's mind, but a woman's might.
How hard it is for women to keep counsel!

1 prithee, pray thee; request of you.

6 constancy, self-control.

9 to keep counsel, to keep a secret.

34 Literary Element
Theme

Artemidorus, a rhetorician, will try to use his skill to save Caesar. Alert students to watch and see how his rhetoric (the art of using words effectively) works.

35 Reader's Response
Making Personal Connections

Possible responses Yes, if I either hoped for advancement from a grateful Caesar or I were one of Caesar's supporters. No, if I feared for my life. *(Students might try to devise another speech that they think could influence Caesar.)*

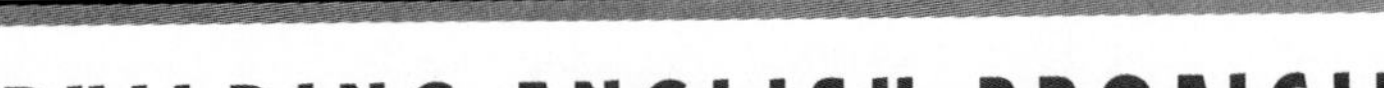

Exploring Key Scenes

Although scene 3 is very short, it presents critical information. Help students see how it adds to the play as a whole.

1. Read aloud, or have a volunteer read aloud, the monologue by Artemidorus.

2. Ask students whether Artemidorus supports Caesar or the conspirators; encourage explanations.

3. Invite students to speculate about how Artemidorus might have found out about the assassination plot. (You may want to point out that rumors are an integral part of most political intrigues.)

4. Remind students that Artemidorus is likely not the only Roman who supports Caesar. Ask students to suggest what a "pro-Caesar" group might do after Caesar is killed.

36 Reading/Thinking Skills
Clarify

Response Portia is nervous and distraught because she knows of the conspiracy and fears for Brutus's safety. (Brutus said he would tell her before Caius Ligarius came.)

37 Reading/Thinking Skills
Draw Conclusions

Question Why do you think Portia asks this question? *(Possible response: She wonders if the conspirators' plan has been leaked.)*

38 Reading/Thinking Skills
Predict

Possible responses The conspirators could be thwarted if Caesar doesn't go to the Capitol; if the Soothsayer or Artemidorus is successful in warning Caesar; if there is a leak; if Brutus begins to question the morality of his decision.

Check Test

1. What act does Portia commit to show Brutus that she is worthy of his trust? *(She inflicts a wound in her thigh.)*

2. How does Decius convince Caesar to go to the Capitol? *(He reinterprets Calpurnia's dream and promises Caesar the crown.)*

3. Who requests that the conspirators act mercifully, killing Caesar as "purgers, not murderers"? *(Brutus)*

4. Which two characters plan to warn Caesar? *(Artemidorus and the Soothsayer)*

5. Where is Caesar headed at the end of the act? *(to the Capitol)*

Unit 6 Resource Book
Alternate Check Test, p. 13

Art thou here yet?
LUCIUS. Madam, what should I do?
Run to the Capitol, and nothing else?
And so return to you, and nothing else?
PORTIA. Yes, bring me word, boy, if thy lord look well,
For he went sickly forth; and take good note
What Caesar doth, what suitors press to him.
Hark, boy, what noise is that?
LUCIUS. I hear none, madam.
PORTIA. Prithee, listen well.
I heard a bustling rumor, like a fray,
And the wind bring it from the Capitol.
LUCIUS. Sooth, madam, I hear nothing.
(The SOOTHSAYER *enters.)*
PORTIA. Come hither, fellow. Which way hast thou been?
SOOTHSAYER. At mine own house, good lady.
PORTIA. What is 't o'clock?
SOOTHSAYER. About the ninth hour, lady.
PORTIA. Is Caesar yet gone to the Capitol?
SOOTHSAYER. Madam, not yet. I go to take my stand,
To see him pass on to the Capitol.
PORTIA. Thou has some suit to Caesar, hast thou not?
SOOTHSAYER. That I have, lady, if it will please Caesar
To be so good to Caesar as to hear me:
I shall beseech him to befriend himself.
37 **PORTIA.** Why, know'st thou any harms intended towards him?
SOOTHSAYER. None that I know will be, much that I fear may chance.
Good morrow to you. Here the street is narrow.
The throng that follows Caesar at the heels,
Of senators, of praetors, common suitors,
Will crowd a feeble man almost to death.
I'll get me to a place more void, and there
Speak to great Caesar as he comes along. *(He exits.)*
PORTIA. I must go in. Ay me, how weak a thing
The heart of woman is! O Brutus,
The heavens speed thee in thine enterprise!
Sure, the boy heard me. Brutus hath a suit
That Caesar will not grant. O, I grow faint.
Run, Lucius, and commend me to my lord;
Say I am merry. Come to me again
And bring me word what he doth say to thee.
(LUCIUS *runs off at right;* PORTIA *exits into house.)*

36 ■ What might account for Portia's state of mind?

19 bustling rumor, like a fray, confused sound, like fighting.

21 Sooth, truly.

38 void, empty; less crowded.

38 ■ What could prevent the conspirators from accomplishing their goal?

MINI-LESSON: VOCABULARY
Multiple Meaning Words

Write the word *press* on the board. Ask students to quickwrite associations they have for this word. Then invite them to discuss these associations. Explain that *press* has many dictionary meanings, including the following.

1. act on by force or pushing

2. printing press

Point out that words such as *press,* meaning "printing press," and *press,* meaning "act on by force," are spelled the same but come from different roots and have different meanings. Make sure students see the difference between words with related meanings ("squeeze" and "push" for *press)* and those with different meanings and different roots.

Activity Idea Give students the following words from page 712: *well, fray, mine, may, will.* Have them work in small groups using dictionaries to find different meanings for each word.

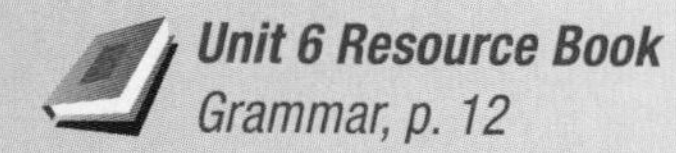
Unit 6 Resource Book
Grammar, p. 12

Act 2

After Reading

Making Connections

Shaping Your Response

1. Do you think that Cassius has been unwise in giving in to Brutus's demand to spare Antony? Explain.
2. Given these qualities—loyalty, honor, insight, independence—who, in your opinion, is the bettter wife, Portia or Calpurnia? Explain.
3. In your notebook, write three adjectives you think best describe Brutus's character.

Analyzing the Play

4. Given his personality, do you think it is easy or difficult for Brutus to endure this period of political and cultural **change?** Explain.
5. In line 14 of scene 1, Brutus introduces the **image** of an adder. With what other words or phrases in this soliloquy does Shakespeare develop this **metaphor**? What point is Brutus making?
6. On the basis of Brutus's short **soliloquies**, what do you think most motivates him to join the conspiracy to assassinate Caesar?
7. In scene 1, what is the difference in **connotation** between the words in each pair: "sacrificers, but not butchers" (line 167) and "purgers, not murderers" (line 181)?
8. Describe the relationship between Brutus and Portia as revealed in their **dialogue.**
9. How does Decius demonstrate his understanding of Caesar's **character**?
10. How do scenes 1 and 2 advance the action of the **plot**?
11. Mention some elements that contribute to the **suspense** of the play.
12. Speculate on why Artemidorus's lines in scene 3 are not written in **blank verse.**
13. What details lead you to **infer** that Portia has learned Brutus's secret?

Extending the Ideas

14. Do you think *Julius Caesar* has the components of a bestselling modern thriller? Why or why not?

After Reading

MAKING CONNECTIONS

1. Possible responses: Yes, the destruction of Mark Antony might weaken the opposition; No, Mark Antony will be a valuable conspirator.

2. Portia seems to have more of these qualities. Students might differ on what role independence plays in a good marriage partner.

3. Possible responses: *noble, honorable, painstaking, idealistic*

4. Brutus, described in the introduction on page 678 as "a quiet idealist," seems more cautious and less eager for a dramatic change than other conspirators.

5. "wary walking" (l. 15), a "sting" (l. 16), "serpent's egg" (l. 32), "hatched" (l. 33), "kill him in the shell" (l. 34).

6. Possible responses: He fears Caesar's power as king, promotes the general good, and is anxious to live up to the deeds of his ancestors.

7. Both *sacrificers* and *purgers* have more positive connotations than *butchers* and *murderers*. In fact, *sacrificers* has a religious aura.

8. They seem to have a close, frank relationship based on mutual respect.

9. He plays on Caesar's vanity and fears to get him to go to the Capitol.

10. They show the final stages of conspiracy plans and the crucial decision of Caesar to go to the Capitol.

11. Caesar's warnings, doubts about going to the Capitol; the concern over the character of Antony

12. Possible response: The choppy prose lends urgency to his letter.

13. She is agitated, talks about how hard it is to "keep counsel," and refers to Brutus's "enterprise."

14. Some students may consider the violence and intrigue very modern.

Selection Test

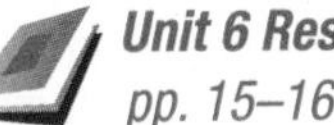

Unit 6 Resource Book
pp. 15–16

During Reading

Vocabulary Preview

bequeath, give or leave by a will
bootless, in vain
censure, express disapproval of; blame
discourse, talk, converse
grievous, causing great pain or suffering
inter, bury
legacy, something handed down in a will
puissant, powerful
rent, tear; torn place
unassailable, not able to be attacked

Students can add the words and definitions to their Writer's Notebooks.

1 Literary Element
Suspense

Question Why might Shakespeare have opened the scene with this exchange between Caesar and the Soothsayer? *(perhaps to create suspense about what will happen)*

2 Reading/Thinking Skills
Clarify

Possible response Cassius, as a member of the conspiracy, is trying to prevent anyone from warning Caesar. They are appalled at Artemidorus's lack of civility.

3 Reading/Thinking Skills
Draw Conclusions

Question What is worrying Cassius? *(He is worried that Popilius is revealing the plot to Caesar.)*

ACT THREE

SCENE 1

Summary *With the conspirators, Caesar goes to the Capitol. He encounters but ignores the Soothsayer and Artemidorus. The conspirators stab Caesar and Mark Antony flees. Brutus then promises to explain to the people the reasons for Caesar's death, after which Antony will be allowed to deliver Caesar's funeral oration. Antony returns, pretending friendship. Later, alone, Antony vows vengeance with the help of Octavius, who is camped near Rome.*

Rome. Before the Capitol. ARTEMIDORUS *and the* SOOTHSAYER *enter at left among a crowd of well-wishers.* CAESAR *enters at right, followed by* ANTONY, BRUTUS, CASSIUS, CASCA, DECIUS, METELLUS CIMBER, TREBONIUS, CINNA, LEPIDUS, POPILIUS, PUBLIUS, *and others.* CAESAR *approaches the* SOOTHSAYER *and speaks defiantly.*

1 **CAESAR** *(to the* SOOTHSAYER*).* The ides of March are come.
SOOTHSAYER. Ay, Caesar, but not gone.
(ARTEMIDORUS *approaches and presents his paper to* CAESAR.)
ARTEMIDORUS. Hail, Caesar! Read this schedule.
DECIUS. Trebonius doth desire you to o'erread,
At your best leisure, this his humble suit.
ARTEMIDORUS. O Caesar, read mine first, for mine's a suit
That touches Caesar nearer. Read it, great Caesar.
CAESAR. What touches us ourself shall be last served.
ARTEMIDORUS. Delay not, Caesar, read it instantly.
CAESAR. What, is the fellow mad?
PUBLIUS. Sirrah, give place.
CASSIUS. What, urge you your petitions in the street?
Come to the Capitol. 2
(All but the SOOTHSAYER *and* ARTEMIDORUS *enter the Senate-house where, downstage and to the left, a prominent statue of Pompey stands.)*
POPILIUS. *(to* CASSIUS*).* I wish your enterprise today may thrive.
CASSIUS. What enterprise, Popilius?
POPILIUS *(to* CASSIUS*).* Fare you well. *(He advances to* CAESAR.*)*
BRUTUS. What said Popilius Lena?
CASSIUS. He wished today our enterprise might thrive.
I fear our purpose is discovered.
3 **BRUTUS.** Look how he makes to Caesar. Mark him.
(POPILIUS *speaks apart to* CAESAR.)
CASSIUS. Casca, be sudden, for we fear prevention.
Brutus, what shall be done? If this be known,
Cassius or Caesar never shall turn back,
For I will slay myself.

3 **schedule**, document.

10 **sirrah** (sir′ə), a form of address used for servants or inferiors.
■ Why do you think both Cassius and Decius force Artemidorus aside?

19 **makes to Caesar**, advances toward Caesar.

SELECTION SUMMARY

Julius Caesar, Act 3

Scene 1: Approaching the Capitol, Caesar spurns the warning note of Artemidorus and enters to hear Metellus Cimber's pleas for the return of his exiled brother. When Caesar refuses the request, the conspirators stab him; seeing that Brutus is among them, Caesar gives up and dies. Against Cassius's advice, Brutus allows Antony to speak at Caesar's funeral. After Brutus leaves, Antony addresses Caesar's corpse, expressing his desire for revenge.

Scenes 2 and 3: Brutus speaks to the assembled crowd, justifying the assassination. Then he yields the pulpit to Antony and leaves. Antony delivers an impassioned oration, displaying Caesar's mutilated body and reading his will. Antony plans to meet with Octavius Caesar, Julius Caesar's grandnephew. The commoners go on a rampage, attacking Cinna the poet because he has the same name as a conspirator.

*For summaries in other languages, see the **Building English Proficiency** book.*

BRUTUS. Cassius, be constant.
Popilius Lena speaks not of our purposes;
For look, he smiles, and Caesar doth not change.
(ANTONY *and* TREBONIUS *move away from* CAESAR *and the others.*) **4**
CASSIUS. Trebonius knows his time, for look you, Brutus,
He draws Mark Antony out of the way.
DECIUS. Where is Metellus Cimber? Let him go
And presently prefer his suit to Caesar.
BRUTUS. He is addressed. Press near and second him.
CINNA. Casca, you are the first that rears your hand.
(BRUTUS, CASSIUS, CASCA, DECIUS, *and* CINNA *move toward* CAESAR.)
CAESAR. Are we all ready? What is now amiss
That Caesar and his Senate must redress?
METELLUS *(kneeling).* Most high, most mighty, and most puissant Caesar,
Metellus Cimber throws before thy seat
An humble heart—
CAESAR. I must prevent thee, Cimber. **5**
These couchings and these lowly courtesies
Might fire the blood of ordinary men,
And turn preordinance and first decree
Into the law of children. Be not fond
To think that Caesar bears such rebel blood
That will be thawed from the true quality
With that which melteth fools—I mean, sweet words,
Low-crookèd curtsies, and base spaniel fawning.
Thy brother by decree is banishèd.
If thou dost bend and pray and fawn for him,
I spurn thee like a cur out of my way.
Know, Caesar doth not wrong, nor without cause
Will he be satisfied.
METELLUS. Is there no voice more worthy than my own
To sound more sweetly in great Caesar's ear
For the repealing of my banished brother?
BRUTUS *(kneeling).* I kiss thy hand, but not in flattery, Caesar,
Desiring thee that Publius Cimber may
Have an immediate freedom of repeal.
CAESAR. What, Brutus?
CASSIUS *(kneeling).* Pardon, Caesar! Caesar, pardon!
As low as to thy foot doth Cassius fall,
To beg enfranchisement for Publius Cimber.
CAESAR. I could be well moved, if I were as you; **6**
If I could pray to move, prayers would move me. **7**
But I am constant as the northern star,
Of whose true-fixed and resting quality

■ Why does Trebonius draw Antony aside?

29 presently prefer his suit, immediately present his petition (suit).
30 addressed, ready.

34 puissant (pyü′ə sənt), *adj.* powerful.

37 couchings, kneelings.

39–40 and turn . . . children, and turn matters already firmly decided into laws to be changed just as children change rules in their games.

45 Thy brother, Publius Cimber, who had earlier incurred Caesar's wrath.

52 repealing, recall, return.

58 enfranchisement (en-fran′chīz mənt), liberation; that is, he asks that Publius Cimber be allowed to return to Rome as a citizen with full rights (franchises).

4 Reading/Thinking Skills
Clarify

Possible Response If he were present, he would try to prevent the assassination.

5 Literary Element
Irony

Question Why is this speech ironic? *(because Caesar is present in the Capitol as a result of Decius's ability to sway him with flattery, to which he here claims to be totally immune)*

6 Literary Criticism
Caesar's Self-Image

Caesar places himself far above others when he insists he does not succumb to fawning as do "ordinary men," when he likens himself to the constant North Star and others to meandering stars, and when he compares himself to the mountain of the gods. Shakespeare might have wanted to lessen our sympathy for Caesar and strengthen the cause of the conspirators by exposing the conceit of Caesar.

7 Literary Element
Figurative Language

Point out that this metaphor is extended throughout Caesar's speech, with Caesar as the North Star and others as "unnumbered sparks."

BUILDING ENGLISH PROFICIENCY

Analyzing Shakespeare's Language

Students should be becoming more familiar with Shakespeare's language by the third act. You can monitor their comprehension with the following activities.

Activity Ideas

- Divide the class into small groups and read aloud Caesar's speech that begins on page 715 (lines 59–74).
- Have each group work together to rewrite these lines in modern English. If necessary, help them understand the dominant image of Caesar as a fixed star.
- Have group representatives share the rewrites with the class. Invite the class, as a whole, to help if the group had trouble with particular lines.

8 Literary Element
Irony

Have students note the irony of Caesar's self-description as "unassailable" and "unshaked of motion," given his present situation.

9 Reading/Thinking Skills
Clarify

Possible responses Students may note the arrogance of Caesar's claim to be unyielding as the North Star. He says that he ranks foremost above men in his constancy, and then goes even further by equating himself to a god on Mt. Olympus.

10 Literary Focus
Plot

This is commonly considered the climax of the play—the moment of highest dramatic tension and interest.

11 Reading/Thinking Skills
Connect

Possible responses Yitzhak Rabin, Abraham Lincoln, Martin Luther King, Jr., Gandhi.

There is no fellow in the firmament.
The skies are painted with unnumbered sparks;
They are all fire and every one doth shine;
But there's but one in all doth hold his place.
So in the world: 'tis furnished well with men,
And men are flesh and blood, and apprehensive;
Yet in the number I do know but one
That unassailable holds on his rank, 8
Unshaked of motion. And that I am he,
Let me a little show it even in this—
That I was constant Cimber should be banished,
And constant do remain to keep him so.

9 CINNA *(kneeling).* O Caesar—
CAESAR. Hence! Wilt thou lift up Olympus?
DECIUS *(kneeling).* Great Caesar—
CAESAR. Doth not Brutus bootless kneel?
CASCA. Speak, hands, for me!

(The other CONSPIRATORS, *daggers in hand, surge forward, and all but* BRUTUS *stab* CAESAR. CAESAR *tries to ward off the blows until he sees* BRUTUS*'s uplifted dagger, then covers his face with his cloak and submits.)*

10 CAESAR *(as* BRUTUS *stabs him).* Et tu, Brutè? Then fall, Caesar! *(Dies.)*
CINNA. Liberty! Freedom! Tyranny is dead!
Run hence, proclaim, cry it about the streets.
CASSIUS. Some to the common pulpits, and cry out
"Liberty, freedom and enfranchisement!"

(As the CONSPIRATORS *move down left and stand together, the crowd, including* ARTEMIDORUS *and the* SOOTHSAYER, *momentarily stands stunned, then flees in panic.)*

BRUTUS. People and senators, be not affrighted.
Fly not; stand still. Ambition's debt is paid.
CASCA. Go to the pulpit, Brutus.
DECIUS. And Cassius too.
BRUTUS. Where's Publius?
CINNA. Here, quite confounded with this mutiny.
METELLUS. Stand fast together, lest some friend of Caesar's
Should chance—
BRUTUS. Talk not of standing. Publius, good cheer.
There is no harm intended to your person,
Nor to no Roman else. So tell them, Publius.
CASSIUS. And leave us, Publius, lest that the people,
Rushing on us, should do your age some mischief.
BRUTUS. Do so, and let no man abide this deed
But we the doers. *(Everyone exits but the* CONSPIRATORS.*)*
(TREBONIUS *enters.)*
CASSIUS. Where is Antony?

63 fellow, equal.

68 apprehensive, capable of reason.

70 unassailable (un ə sāl′ə bəl), *adj.* not able to be attacked (with violent blows, hostile words, arguments, or abuse).

■ How does this allusion to Olympus (a mountain in Greece and the home of the gods), as well as the content of his speeches in lines 36–49 and 59–74, show Caesar's egotism?

77 bootless (büt′lis), *adv.* in vain.

78 ***Et tu, Brutè*** (brü′tā) "And you, Brutus!" *[Latin].* The betrayal overwhelms Caesar.

81 common pulpits, elevated areas where public debates were held.

■ What other famous political leaders can you name who have been assassinated because of principle rather than madness or private vengeance? 11

86 Publius, an elderly senator too astounded to flee.

95 abide this deed, answer for this deed.

MINI-LESSON: READING STRATEGIES

Reading Shakespearean Drama

Teach Our way of speaking and writing has changed considerably since Shakespeare wrote *Julius Caesar* nearly four hundred years ago. Knowing this, students sometimes assume that they won't understand the words in a Shakespearean play. Share the following strategies to make reading easier:

Keep Reading Shakespeare's audience could both listen to the words and see the action. Like students, that audience probably didn't "get" every word, but it got the gist of scenes. Remind students to keep on reading—through a speech or an entire page.

Use the Notes In this book, the play is printed with notes in the margin that provide pronunciations, definitions of difficult words, or background information. The number next to a definition indicates the line in the play. In addition, there are questions, indicated with a black square, to check on comprehension at intervals.

TREBONIUS. Fled to his house amazed.
Men, wives, and children stare, cry out, and run
As it were doomsday.

12

BRUTUS. Fates, we will know your pleasures.
That we shall die, we know; 'tis but the time,
And drawing days out, that men stand upon.
CASCA. Why, he that cuts off twenty years of life
Cuts off so many years of fearing death.
BRUTUS. Grant that, and then is death a benefit.
So are we Caesar's friends, that have abridged
His time of fearing death. Stoop, Romans, stoop,
And let us bathe our hands in Caesar's blood

99 Fates, the three goddesses who were thought to control human destinies.
101 stand upon, attach importance to.

Art Study

Questions

- What clues can you use to figure out who the two men shown in the picture are? (*Response: Caesar can be recognized as the bloody man on the left, with the large signet ring. He may be recognized from the illustration on page 709. Students may recognize Brutus on the right from the earlier photograph on page 686.)*
- With what line number does the picture fit? (*Because Caesar's arm is around Brutus, students may infer that this photo goes with line 78.)*

12 Literary Focus
Plot

Question Predict what will happen to the conspirators. *(Possible responses: Brutus will become Consul. The people will make Brutus king. Antony will fight Brutus and kill him for revenge.)*

BUILDING ENGLISH PROFICIENCY

Dramatizing Key Events

To experience the unexpectedness and swiftness with which the assassination occurs, have students reenact the scene (without props).

1. Assign or let students volunteer for various characters.

2. Urge students to practice the movements of their assigned characters to make the actions of kneeling seem natural. Remind them that "Caesar" mustn't suspect anything from the movements and that the actions of Brutus are more delayed than those of the others.

3. Invite students to discuss how the conspiracy might have been different if any character had been omitted.

13 Reading/Thinking Skills
Summarize

Possible responses They shout that "Tyranny is dead" and proclaim liberty and freedom; they move together, work to calm the spectators, and decide their next course of action (speaking to the people). They smear themselves with Caesar's blood and begin to follow Brutus out of the Capitol. It has been foreshadowed in Calpurnia's dream in act 2, scene 2.

14 Literary Element
Structure

Explain that it is usually a goal of playwrights to have their audience suspend their disbelief and live in the world of the play while it is being acted. Point out this reference to the re-enactment of Caesar's death can break the audience's suspension of disbelief because it reminds them they are viewing or reading a play. Students may wish to speculate on why Shakespeare included these lines. *(Perhaps as a way of showing how sure Cassius and Brutus were that they had done a noble deed for the general good)*

15 Reading/Thinking Skills
Question

Possible responses Do you still think you did the right thing? Why are you so willing to take everyone at face value?

Up to the elbows and besmear our swords. **13**
Then walk we forth even to the marketplace,
And, waving our red weapons o'er our heads,
Let's all cry "Peace, freedom, and liberty!"

CASSIUS. Stoop, then, and wash. *(They bathe their hands and weapons.)*
How many ages hence
Shall this our lofty scene be acted over
In states unborn and accents yet unknown!

14 **BRUTUS.** How many times shall Caesar bleed in sport,
That now on Pompey's basis lies along
No worthier than the dust!

CASSIUS. So oft as that shall be,
So often shall the knot of us be called
The men that gave their country liberty.

DECIUS. What, shall we forth?

CASSIUS. Ay, every man away.
Brutus shall lead, and we will grace his heels
With the most boldest and best hearts of Rome.

(SERVANT *enters.*)

BRUTUS. Soft, who comes here? A friend of Antony's.

SERVANT *(kneeling).* Thus, Brutus, did my master bid me kneel;
Thus did Mark Antony bid me fall down,
And, being prostrate, thus he bade me say:
"Brutus is noble, wise, valiant, and honest;
Caesar was mighty, bold, royal, and loving.
Say I love Brutus and I honor him;
Say I feared Caesar, honored him, and loved him.
If Brutus will vouchsafe that Antony
May safely come to him and be resolved
How Caesar hath deserved to lie in death,
Mark Antony shall not love Caesar dead
So well as Brutus living, but will follow
The fortunes and affairs of noble Brutus
Thorough the hazards of this untrod state
With all true faith." So says my master Antony.

BRUTUS. Thy master is a wise and valiant Roman;
I never thought him worse.
Tell him, so please him come unto this place, **15**
He shall be satisfied and, by my honor,
Depart untouched.

SERVANT. I'll fetch him presently.

(SERVANT *exits.*)

BRUTUS. I know that we shall have him well to friend.

CASSIUS. I wish we may. But yet have I a mind
That fears him much, and my misgiving still

■ What actions do the conspirators take immediately following the stabbing of Caesar and prior to the entrance of Antony's servant? Where has this been foreshadowed?

116 on Pompey's . . . along, at the foot of Pompey's statue Caesar lies prostrate.

122 grace his heels, do honor to (by following closely).

133 be resolved, receive an explanation of.

138 untrod state, new and unfamiliar state of affairs; the image can be compared to a field unmarked by footsteps (untrod).

■ What question would you ask Brutus at this point in the play?

Falls shrewdly to the purpose.
(ANTONY *enters.*)
BRUTUS. But here comes Antony. Welcome, Mark Antony.
ANTONY. O mighty Caesar! Dost thou lie so low?
Are all thy conquests, glories, triumphs, spoils,
Shrunk to this little measure? Fare thee well.
I know not, gentlemen, what you intend,
Who else must be let blood, who else is rank;
If I myself, there is no hour so fit
As Caesar's death's hour, nor no instrument
Of half that worth as those your swords, made rich
With the most noble blood of all this world.
I do beseech ye, if you bear me hard,
Now, whilst your purpled hands do reek and smoke,
Fulfill your pleasure. Live a thousand years,
16 I shall not find myself so apt to die;
No place will please me so, no mean of death,
As here by Caesar, and by you cut off,
The choice and master spirits of this age.
BRUTUS. O Antony! Beg not your death of us.
Though now we must appear bloody and cruel,
As by our hands and this our present act
You see we do, yet see you but our hands
And this the bleeding business they have done.
Our hearts you see not. They are pitiful;
17 And pity to the general wrong of Rome—
As fire drives out fire, so pity pity—
Hath done this deed on Caesar. For your part,
To you our swords have leaden points, Mark Antony.
Our arms in strength of malice, and our hearts
Of brothers' temper, do receive you in
With all kind love, good thoughts, and reverence.
CASSIUS. Your voice shall be as strong as any man's
In the disposing of new dignities.
BRUTUS. Only be patient till we have appeased
The multitude, beside themselves with fear,
And then we will deliver you the cause
Why I, that did love Caesar when I struck him,
Have thus proceeded.
ANTONY. I doubt not of your wisdom.
Let each man render me his bloody hand.
(*He shakes hands with the* CONSPIRATORS.)
19 First, Marcus Brutus, will I shake with you;
Next, Caius Cassius, do I take your hand;
Now, Decius Brutus, yours; now yours, Metellus;

154 who else . . . rank, who else must be killed.

161–162 Live . . . die. [If I should] live a thousand years, I would not find myself so ready (apt) to die.
163 mean, means or method.

173 so pity pity, so pity for the wrongs Rome has endured from Caesar overshadows pity for his death.

180 dignities, new government positions.
18 ■ What is the difference between what Cassius offers Antony and what Brutus has offered him?

16 Reading/Thinking Skills
Recognize the Use of Persuasion

Question Why does Antony offer to let the conspirators kill him? *(Possible response: It is a rhetorically charged move to show them that he is not a threat to them.)*

17 Literary Element
Protagonist

Point out to students that this boundless idealism is Brutus's tragic flaw.

18 Reading/Thinking Skills
Clarify

Possible responses Brutus's offer of love and honor is far less practical than Cassius's offer of a role in the new government. Brutus wants to be sure of Antony's love; Cassius wants to be sure that Antony won't betray them.

19 Reading/Thinking Skills
Recognize the Use of Persuasion

Question Why does Antony shake every conspirator's hand? *(Possible responses: He is stressing the responsibility of each man in this collective act. He is committing to memory the conspirators' names. He may also be silently vowing revenge on each conspirator.)*

BUILDING ENGLISH PROFICIENCY

ESL LEP ELD SAE LD

Analyzing a Climax

Students may be surprised that such a high point of action has occurred in the middle of the play. Explain that the murder of Caesar is actually the beginning of a chain of events, rather than the end. Have students chart the cause-and-effect relationships that are set in motion in scene 1 by the assassination of Caesar.

Cause →	Effect →	Effect →	Effect
Caesar is assassinated.	The conspirators promise an explanation.	Antony vows revenge to the corpse.	Antony sends word to Octavius.

20 Reading/Thinking Skills
Recognize the Use of Persuasion

Explain to students that it is a common rhetorical technique to accuse one's self first to undercut the power of the accusation that would come from someone else. Antony uses this technique here.

21 Reading/Thinking Skills
Compare and Contrast

Question How is Antony's address to Caesar unique? *(Possible response: He is the only person to address him by his given name, Julius.)*

22 Reading/Thinking Skills
Draw Conclusions

Question What does Antony mean in lines 214–215? *(Even Caesar's enemies would praise him as I have done, so you should not think that I, who was his friend, am showing excessive emotion about his death.)*

Yours, Cinna; and, my valiant Casca, yours;
Though last, not least in love, yours, good Trebonius.
Gentlemen all—alas, what shall I say?
20 My credit now stands on such slippery ground
That one of two bad ways you must conceit me,
Either a coward or a flatterer.
That I did love thee, Caesar, O, 'tis true!
If then thy spirit look upon us now,
Shall it not grieve thee dearer than thy death
To see thy Antony making his peace,
Shaking the bloody fingers of thy foes—
Most noble!—in the presence of thy corpse?
Had I as many eyes as thou has wounds,
Weeping as fast as they stream forth thy blood,
It would become me better than to close
21 In terms of friendship with thine enemies.
Pardon me, Julius! Here wast thou bayed, brave hart,
Here didst thou fall, and here thy hunters stand,
Signed in thy spoil and crimsoned in thy lethe.
O world, thou wast the forest to this hart,
And this indeed, O world, the heart of thee!
How like a deer, strucken by many princes,
Dost thou here lie!

CASSIUS. Mark Antony—

22 **ANTONY.** Pardon me, Caius Cassius.
The enemies of Caesar shall say this;
Then in a friend it is cold modesty.

CASSIUS. I blame you not for praising Caesar so,
But what compact mean you to have with us?
Will you be pricked in number of our friends,
Or shall we on and not depend on you?

ANTONY. Therefore I took your hands, but was indeed
Swayed from the point by looking down on Caesar.
Friends am I with you all, and love you all,
Upon this hope, that you shall give me reasons
Why and wherein Caesar was dangerous.

BRUTUS. Or else were this a savage spectacle.
Our reasons are so full of good regard
That were you, Antony, the son of Caesar,
You should be satisfied.

ANTONY. That's all I seek,
And am moreover suitor that I may
Produce his body to the marketplace,
And in the pulpit, as becomes a friend,
Speak in the order of his funeral.

194 conceit, think, judge.

204 close, come to an agreement.

206 hart. Here and in lines 209–210, Antony puns on *hart* ("stag," as in deer) and *heart.*

208 lethe (lē′thē), death.

196–212 That I did love . . . lie. In this, as in his preceding speech, Antony cleverly alternates between placating the conspirators and revealing his feelings about Caesar's death.

215 modesty, moderation.

218 pricked in number, marked off on a list.

226 good regard, merit.

232 order, ceremony.

MINI-LESSON: LITERARY ELEMENT

Recognizing Puns

Teach In lines 206–212 Shakespeare puns on the words *hart* (deer) and *heart,* comparing the vicious murder of Caesar to the killing of an animal by a group of hunters, and Caesar himself to the heart of the world. Recognizing Shakespeares *puns,* or plays on words, enriches readers' understanding of his plays.

Activity Ideas

- Invite students to find puns in the opening scene of the play, page 680. (soles/souls; recover. See also sidenotes on page 680.)
- Challenge students to find other puns in *Julius Caesar.* Note, for example, the frequent play on the word fall (falling sickness, fall from power, fail to act, stumble).

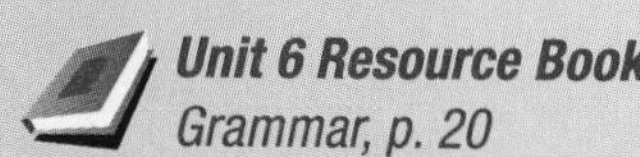
Unit 6 Resource Book
Grammar, p. 20

BRUTUS. You shall, Mark Antony.
CASSIUS. Brutus, a word with you.
(aside to BRUTUS). You know not what you do. Do not consent
23 That Antony speak in his funeral.
Know you how much the people may be moved
By that which he will utter?
BRUTUS (*aside to* CASSIUS). By your pardon:
I will myself into the pulpit first
And show the reason of our Caesar's death.
What Antony shall speak, I will protest
He speaks by leave and by permission,
And that we are contented Caesar shall
Have all true rites and lawful ceremonies.
It shall advantage more than do us wrong.
CASSIUS (*aside to* BRUTUS). I know not what may fall. I like it not.
BRUTUS. Mark Antony, here, take you Caesar's body.
You shall not in your funeral speech blame us,
But speak all good you can devise of Caesar,
And say you do 't by our permission.
Else shall you not have any hand at all
About his funeral. And you shall speak
In the same pulpit whereto I am going,
After my speech is ended.
ANTONY. Be it so.
I do desire no more.
BRUTUS. Prepare the body then, and follow us.
(All exit except ANTONY.)
ANTONY. O, pardon me, thou bleeding piece of earth,
That I am meek and gentle with these butchers!
Thou art the ruins of the noblest man
That ever livèd in the tide of times.
Woe to the hand that shed this costly blood!
Over thy wounds now do I prophesy—
Which, like dumb mouths, do ope their ruby lips
To beg the voice and utterance of my tongue—
A curse shall light upon the limbs of men;
Domestic fury and fierce civil strife
Shall cumber all the parts of Italy;
Blood and destruction shall be so in use
And dreadful objects so familiar
That mothers shall but smile when they behold
Their infants quartered with the hands of war,
All pity choked with custom of fell deeds;
And Caesar's spirit, ranging for revenge,
With Ate by his side come hot from hell,

240 protest, announce.

24 ■ *Lines 225–253.* In what respect has Brutus made another error in judgment? Keep these lines in mind as you read scene 2, to see whether Antony obeys Brutus's directions when speaking to the commoners.

259 tide of times, course of all history.

268 objects, sights.
271 with custom of fell deeds, with the familiarity of cruel (fell) deeds.
273 Ate (ā′tē), Greek goddess of discord and moral chaos.

23 Literary Focus
Plot

When students have finished the act, you may wish to return to the speeches on this page and point out that they indicate the turning point of the play—the moment at which the fate of the protagonist's aims is decided. Brutus's misjudgment of Antony and his agreement to Antony's speech marks the change in Brutus's fortunes.

24 Reading/Thinking Skills
Evaluate

Possible responses Brutus either does not recognize Antony's gifts as a rhetorician and persuader or does not have the insight to foresee his possible effect on a crowd. In addition, he appears unaware that Antony's feelings and beliefs are not consistent with his own.

Exploring Character Relationships

Scene 1 focuses on the character of Mark Antony, the man who will dominate the remainder of the play. Have students work together to begin a character chart to describe him. Alert students to character clues provided by the following:

1. Antony refers to the conspirator's hands that "reek and smoke." (line 160)

2. Antony invites them to kill him as well. (lines 161–164)

3. He addresses Caesar by his first name. (line 206)

4. He praises Caesar in front of the conspirators, calling him brave and noble. (lines 201, 206)

Art Study

Encourage students to analyze Antony's expression as he kneels next to Caesar's body. *(Possible responses: He looks tortured, unbelieving, accusatory.)*

Question What is ironic about Caesar dying at the base of Pompey's statue? *(Caesar dies at the feet of the man he defeated. In a sense, Pompey has achieved the final victory.)*

MINI-LESSON: LITERARY ELEMENT

Analyzing Figurative Language

Teach Explain that Shakespeare often uses a dominant metaphor throughout a work. In his tragedies, he frequently compares political and social corruption to disease, sickness, and death. In lines 275–277, the words *foul, smell,* and *carrion* (rotten, decaying flesh) convey such comparisons.

Activity Ideas

- Invite students to search for other images of sickness, death, and decay in *Julius Caesar.*
- Students can find other metaphors that are developed throughout a passage, such as a fountain, the North Star, various animals, and disorder in the physical world.

Shall in these confines with a monarch's voice
Cry havoc and let slip the dogs of war,
That this foul deed shall smell above the earth
With carrion men, groaning for burial.
(OCTAVIUS'S SERVANT *enters.*)
You serve Octavius Caesar, do you not?
SERVANT. I do, Mark Antony.
ANTONY. Caesar did write for him to come to Rome.
SERVANT. He did receive his letters, and is coming,
And bid me say to you by word of mouth—
O Caesar! *(Seeing the body.)*
ANTONY. Thy heart is big. Get thee apart and weep.
Passion, I see, is catching, for mine eyes,
Seeing those beads of sorrow stand in thine,
Began to water. Is thy master coming?
SERVANT. He lies tonight within seven leagues of Rome.
ANTONY. Post back with speed and tell him what hath chanced.
Here is a mourning Rome, a dangerous Rome,
No Rome of safety for Octavius yet;
Hie hence and tell him so. Yet stay awhile;
Thou shalt not back till I have borne this corpse
26 Into the marketplace. There shall I try,
In my oration, how the people take
The cruel issue of these bloody men,
According to the which thou shalt discourse
To young Octavius of the state of things.
Lend me your hand.
(ANTONY *and the* SERVANT *carry off Caesar's body.)*

275 cry havoc . . . let slip the dogs of war, give a command to sack, pillage, and slaughter (which could be given only by a king) and unleash fire, sword, and famine.
25 ■ What does Antony promise in this soliloquy (lines 256–277)?

288 He lies . . . Rome. With the news that Caesar's grandnephew Octavius is within seven leagues (twenty miles) of Rome, Antony's side is strengthened. As Caesar's adopted son and heir, Octavius would attract Caesar's supporters.
294 try, test.
296 issue, deed.
297 discourse (dis kôrs′), *v.* talk, converse.
27 ■ Do you think that Antony will be effective in his speech before the citizens? Why or why not?

SCENE 2

Summary *After Brutus explains why Caesar had to be killed, the mob cheers him. Antony's oration arouses in the mob both gratitude toward Caesar, who has left them a generous bequest, and anger against the conspirators. A servant announces that Octavius has ridden into the city, and Brutus and Cassius have fled.*

Rome. The Forum. BRUTUS *and* CASSIUS *enter at left. Indignant* CITIZENS *clamor for an explanation of* CAESAR*'s assassination.*

28 **PLEBEIANS.** We will be satisfied! Let us be satisfied!
BRUTUS. Then follow me, and give me audience, friends.
Cassius, go you into the other street
And part the numbers.
Those that will hear me speak, let 'em stay here;
Those that will follow Cassius, go with him;

1 We . . . satisfied. Note how throughout this scene the commoners are easily swayed to support first one side, then the other.
4 part the numbers, divide the crowd.

25 Reading/Thinking Skills
Summarize

Possible response vengeance and civil war

26 Historical Note
Octavius Caesar

Remind students that Octavius was only adopted and given the name Caesar in Julius Caesar's will. This suggests that Mark Antony has the will and has read it.

27 Reading/Thinking Skills
Predict

Possible responses Yes, if he can gull Brutus, he can certainly persuade the commoners. Yes, he has passion and anger at what has been done; he has, to his mind, a just cause; his speeches so far suggest that he has the rhetorical ability to sway the multitudes.

28 Historical Note
Plebeians

Plebeians was another name for the commoners of ancient Rome.

BUILDING ENGLISH PROFICIENCY

ESL LEP ELD SAE LD

Making Cultural Connections

Scene 1 ends with Antony planning Caesar's funeral. Use one or both of the following activities to focus on the universality of this experience.

Activity Ideas

- Invite students to share what they know of funeral traditions in various cultures. Ask: How long a period of mourning is required? Who should attend the funeral? Why is it common to display the body? How "public" should a public funeral be?
- Have students name famous people, now dead, who have had elaborate funerals. Ask why heads of state, for example, have elaborate funerals.

29 Reading/Thinking Skills
Clarify

Possible response "I place the welfare of Rome above my love for Caesar." You might direct students' attention to the similarity of this sentiment with that expressed in Richard Lovelace's poem, "To Lucasta, on Going to the Wars":

I could not love thee, dear, so much,
Loved I not honor more.

30 Reading/Thinking Skills
Connect

Question Now Brutus offers to die, just as Antony has. What do you think is the connection? *(Some students may think that it is a cultural connection—that's what you do if you are a Roman in a position of power and others find fault with you. Some students may think that Brutus is imitating Antony's effective rhetorical ploy, knowing full well that his offer will be refused.)*

And public reasons shall be renderèd
Of Caesar's death.

(BRUTUS *ascends a speaker's platform.*)

FIRST PLEBEIAN. I will hear Brutus speak.

SECOND PLEBEIAN. I will hear Cassius, and compare their reasons
When severally we hear them renderèd.

(CASSIUS *moves off at right, accompanied by various* CITIZENS.)

THIRD PLEBEIAN. The noble Brutus is ascended. Silence!

BRUTUS. Be patient till the last.

Romans, countrymen, and lovers, hear me for my cause, and be silent that you may hear. Believe me for mine honor, and have respect to mine honor, that you may believe. Censure me in your wisdom, and awake your senses, that you may the better judge. If there be any in this assembly, any dear friend of Caesar's, to him I say that Brutus's love to Caesar was no less than his. If then that friend demand why Brutus rose against Caesar, this is my answer: not that I loved Caesar less, but that I loved Rome more. Had you rather Caesar were living and die all slaves, than that Caesar were dead, to live all free men? As Caesar loved me, I weep for him; as he was fortunate, I rejoice at it; as he was valiant, I honor him; but, as he was ambitious, I slew him. There is tears for his love; joy for his fortune; honor for his valor; and death for his ambition. Who is here so base that would be a bondman? If any, speak, for him have I offended. Who is here so rude that would not be a Roman? If any, speak, for him have I offended. Who is here so vile that will not love his country? If any, speak, for him have I offended. I pause for a reply.

ALL. None, Brutus, none!

BRUTUS. Then none have I offended. I have done no more to Caesar than you shall do to Brutus. The question of his death is enrolled in the Capitol, his glory not extenuated wherein he was worthy, nor his offenses enforced for which he suffered death.

(MARK ANTONY *and others enter with* CAESAR*'s body.*)

Here comes his body, mourned by Mark Antony, who, though he had no hand in his death, shall receive the benefit of his dying, a place in the commonwealth, as which of you shall not? With this I depart, that, as I slew my best lover for the good of Rome, I have the same dagger for myself when it shall please my country to need my death. 30

ALL. Live, Brutus, live, live! (BRUTUS *comes down.*)

FIRST PLEBEIAN. Bring him with triumph home unto his house.

SECOND PLEBEIAN. Give him a statue with his ancestors.

THIRD PLEBEIAN. Let him be Caesar.

FOURTH PLEBEIAN. Caesar's better parts

10 severally, separately.

13 lovers, friends.

15 censure, (sen′shər), *v.* express disapproval of; blame.

16 senses, intellectual powers.

■ What does Brutus mean by "not that I loved Caesar less, but that I loved Rome more"? 29

27 rude, barbarous.

33–35 The question . . . enforced. The reason for Caesar's death is recorded; his fame is not minimized, nor his crime exaggerated.

31

Shall be crowned in Brutus.
FIRST PLEBEIAN. We'll bring him to his house with shouts and clamors.
BRUTUS. My countrymen—
SECOND PLEBEIAN. Peace, silence! Brutus speaks.
FIRST PLEBEIAN. Peace, ho!
BRUTUS. Good countrymen, let me depart alone,
And, for my sake, stay here with Antony.
Do grace to Caesar's corpse, and grace his speech

32

Tending to Caesar's glories, which Mark Antony,
By our permission, is allowed to make.
I do entreat you, not a man depart,
Save I alone, till Antony have spoke. *(Exits.)*
FIRST PLEBEIAN. Stay, ho, and let us hear Mark Antony.
THIRD PLEBEIAN. Let him go up into the public chair.
We'll hear him. Noble Antony, go up.
ANTONY. For Brutus's sake I am beholding to you.
(ANTONY *ascends the platform. His* ATTENDANTS *place* CAESAR*'s body below him and near the crowd.*)
FOURTH PLEBEIAN. What does he say of Brutus?
THIRD PLEBEIAN. He says, for Brutus's sake
He finds himself beholding to us all.
FOURTH PLEBEIAN. 'Twere best he speak no harm of Brutus here.
FIRST PLEBEIAN. This Caesar was a tyrant.
THIRD PLEBEIAN. Nay, that's certain.
We are blest that Rome is rid of him.
SECOND PLEBEIAN. Peace! Let us hear what Antony can say.
ANTONY. You gentle Romans—

33

ALL. Peace, ho! Let us hear him.
ANTONY. Friends, Romans, countrymen, lend me your ears.
I come to bury Caesar, not to praise him.
The evil that men do lives after them;
The good is oft interrèd with their bones.
So let it be with Caesar. The noble Brutus
Hath told you Caesar was ambitious.
If it were so, it was a grievous fault,
And grievously hath Caesar answered it.
Here, under leave of Brutus and the rest—
For Brutus is an honorable man,
So are they all, all honorable men—
Come I to speak in Caesar's funeral.
He was my friend, faithful and just to me;
But Brutus says he was ambitious,
And Brutus is an honorable man.
He hath brought many captives home to Rome,

52 Do grace . . . speech, show respect to Caesar's corpse, and listen courteously to Antony's speech.

■ How do you think Antony's oration will differ from Brutus's oration?

72 inter (in tėr′), *v.* bury.

75 grievous (grē′vəs), *adj.* causing great pain or suffering.

78 Brutus is an honorable man. The crowd's anger at words against Brutus makes Antony quick to express his admiration for the man—and for the other conspirators.

84 He, Caesar.

31 Reading/Thinking Skills
Analyze

Question What do the plebeians' reactions in lines 42–46 indicate about them? *(Possible response: They do not understand that the purpose of killing Caesar was to restore the republic and destroy the monarchy. Now they want to make Brutus king.)*

32 Reading/Thinking Skills
Make Judgments

Question Is Brutus's decision wise? Why does he make it? *(Possible responses: No, Antony is an effective speaker and will sway the mob against the conspirators. Yes, he is showing Antony he trusts him.)*

33 Reading/Thinking Skills
Predict

Possible responses Brutus's speech was logical and the commoners didn't understand it; Antony's speech will be emotional and will capture them.

BUILDING ENGLISH PROFICIENCY

Contrasting Speeches

Both Brutus and Antony realize the necessity of gaining the support of the Roman people. Help students better understand each speech—and discover more about each character.

1. As students consider Brutus's speech, alert them to:
- the introductory remarks made by the plebians
- the appeal to patriotism
- Brutus's justification for his act
- the importance of the concept of honor and how Brutus uses it to move the crowd

2. As they consider Antony's address, help students:
- determine what tone he would use. Remind them that this speech (and tone) must incite the crowd, yet not antagonize the conspirators. Have volunteers try out a tone aloud.
- analyze how Antony uses the concept of honor to work against Brutus and the conspirators

3. Students might discuss whether or not a present-day crowd could be as easily swayed as this one appears to be.

34 Literary Element
Characterization

Question What virtues does Antony find in Caesar? *(Possible responses: generosity, compassion, self-control. He provided support for the city and citizens of Rome; he loved the poor and suffered when they did; he refused the crown.)*

Discuss with students the elements in the picture that show Antony's effectiveness as a speaker. *(All eyes are on him; there are no signs of inattention—everyone looks still and enthralled. He appears in control and is using effective gestures.)*

35 Reader's Response
Making Personal Connections

Questons

- When Antony pauses, do you think he is acting naturally, or merely for dramatic effect? *(Possible response: He must realize the dramatic effect he achieves, but his emotion seems genuine.)*
- Do you consider silence an effective dramatic tool? *(Possible response: Yes, sometimes silence can be more powerful than words.)*

Whose ransoms did the general coffers fill.
Did this in Caesar seem ambitious?
When that the poor have cried, Caesar hath wept;
Ambition should be made of sterner stuff.
Yet Brutus says he was ambitious,
And Brutus is an honorable man.
You all did see that on the Lupercal
34 I thrice presented him a kingly crown,
Which he did thrice refuse. Was this ambition?
Yet Brutus says he was ambitious
And sure he is an honorable man.
I speak not to disprove what Brutus spoke,
But here I am to speak what I do know.
You all did love him once, not without cause.
What cause withholds you then to mourn for him?
O judgment! Thou art fled to brutish beasts,
And men have lost their reason. Bear with me;
My heart is in the coffin there with Caesar,
And I must pause till it come back to me.
35 **FIRST PLEBEIAN.** Methinks there is much reason in his sayings.
SECOND PLEBEIAN. If thou consider rightly of the matter,

85 the general coffers fill, Caesar gave the ransom money to the city; he hadn't kept it for himself.

91–93 Lupercal . . . ambition. Compare this explanation of Caesar's reaction with Casca's view in act one, scene 2.

MINI-LESSON: THINKING SKILLS
Recognize Rhetorical Devices

Teach Antony uses rhetorical devices to great effect in his "Friends, Romans, countrymen" speech. Review with students the following rhetorical techniques.

1. repetition ("Brutus is an honorable man.")
2. rhetorical questions ("Did this in Caesar seem ambitious?")
3. balance/contrast ("The evil that men do lives after them; The good is oft interrèd with their bones.")
4. apostrophe ("O judgment!")
5. hyperbole or exaggeration ("My heart is in the coffin there with Caesar.")

Activity Ideas

- Encourage students to memorize this speech and to present it to the class.
- Find examples of these rhetorical devices in Antony's speech on page 727.
- Have students note these devices in their Writer's Notebooks and use them in their own speeches and writing.

Caesar has had great wrong.
THIRD PLEBEIAN. Has he, masters?
I fear there will a worse come in his place.
FOURTH PLEBEIAN. Marked ye his words? He would not take the crown,
Therefore 'tis certain he was not ambitious.
FIRST PLEBEIAN. If it be found so, some will dear abide it.
SECOND PLEBEIAN. Poor soul, his eyes are red as fire with weeping.
THIRD PLEBEIAN. There's not a nobler man in Rome than Antony.
FOURTH PLEBEIAN. Now mark him. He begins again to speak.
ANTONY. But yesterday the word of Caesar might
Have stood against the world. Now lies he there,
And none so poor to do him reverence.
O masters! If I were disposed to stir
Your hearts and minds to mutiny and rage,
I should do Brutus wrong, and Cassius wrong,
Who, you all know, are honorable men.
I will not do them wrong; I rather choose
To wrong the dead, to wrong myself and you,
Than I will wrong such honorable men.
But here's a parchment with the seal of Caesar.
I found it in his closet; 'tis his will. *(He shows the will.)*
Let but the commons hear this testament—
Which, pardon me, I do not mean to read—
And they would go and kiss dead Caesar's wounds
And dip their napkins in his sacred blood,
Yea, beg a hair of him for memory,
And dying, mention it within their wills,
Bequeathing it as a rich legacy
Unto their issue.
FOURTH PLEBEIAN. We'll hear the will! Read it, Mark Antony.
ALL. The will, the will! We will hear Caesar's will.
ANTONY. Have patience, gentle friends: I must not read it.
It is not meet you know how Caesar loved you.
You are not wood, you are not stones, but men;
And being men, hearing the will of Caesar,
It will inflame you, it will make you mad.
'Tis good you know not that you are his heirs,
For if you should, O, what would come of it?
FOURTH PLEBEIAN. Read the will! We'll hear it, Antony.
You shall read us the will, Caesar's will.
ANTONY. Will you be patient? Will you stay awhile?
I have o'ershot myself to tell you of it.
I fear I wrong the honorable men
Whose daggers have stabbed Caesar; I do fear it.

110 dear abide it, pay a heavy penalty for.
■ Do you think that Antony's tears are genuine? Are they effective? **36**

116 and none . . . reverence, not even the lowliest Roman is poorer (lower in estate) than Caesar now.

125 closet, study; private chamber.

129 napkins, handkerchiefs.

132 bequeath (bi kwēᴛʜ′), *v.* give or leave (money or property) by a will; **legacy** (leg′ə sē), *n.* something handed down in a will.
■ What might be behind Antony's refusal to read the will? **38**

146 I have o'ershot myself, I have said more than I intended—or so Antony pretends.

36 Reader's Response
Making Personal Connections

Response Lines 284–287 on page 723 may suggest to some students that they are genuine. Students' knowledge of Antony's persuasive abilities may lead them to believe that the tears were manufactured to convince the populace of his finer feelings.

37 Reading/Thinking Skills
Recognize the Use of Persuasion

Point out to students:

- Antony addresses the commoners as "masters"—a flattering form of address.
- By the end of the speech the term "honorable men" has become ironic and has assumed the meaning "dishonorable men."
- Antony "teases" the commoners by begging their pardon for not reading the will.

38 Reading/Thinking Skills
Clarify

Possible responses He may want to bait the crowd, to make them wonder what is in the will so they will demand to hear it and it will be their choice, not his. He is creating tension and audience involvement.

BUILDING ENGLISH PROFICIENCY

Analyzing Persuasion

Antony is a persuasive speaker—and a master at manipulation.

1. Assign four groups of students—one to study each of Antony's four long speeches (page 725, lines 74–103; page 727, lines 114–133; page 728, lines 164–192; page 729, lines 205–225).
2. Have a representative of the group read the speech aloud, while group members listen for words and techniques designed to manipulate the crowd.
3. Group members should make a chart like the one here to show how Antony uses persuasive devices.

How Antony manipulates the crowd
Says opposite of what he means
Recalls Caesar's virtues
Draws attention to Caesar's wounds
Ironically refers to conspirators as "honorable"
Mentions Caesar's will as a "rich legacy"
Speaks of mutiny

39 Literary Element
Irony

Point out that the quotation marks in line 149 indicate that the words within are spoken ironically—that is, they mean the opposite of what they literally mean. Although Antony's frequent use of the word *honorable* is also ironic, this is the first time the word is used with open disdain.

40 Reading/Thinking Skills
Evaluate

Possible responses He wants to keep fresh in the crowd's mind who the chief conspirators were to give the crowd's anger an object on which to focus. He wants to dramatize the killing to create more sentiment about it. He wants to dramatize that Brutus, most beloved of Caesar, delivered the fatal blow. (Again, Antony displays his superb rhetorical skills.)

41 Literary Elements
Pun, Foreshadowing

Question Compare these lines to those in act 1, scene 2, lines 247–253 (page 690). *(Possible response: These lines extend the multiple meanings of the word* fall*—fall from power, physical ailment, stumble, die, failure to take action. Students may now understand the earlier lines as foreshadowing.)*

39

FOURTH PLEBEIAN. They were traitors. "Honorable men"!
ALL. The will! The testament!
SECOND PLEBEIAN. They were villains, murderers. The will! Read the will!
ANTONY. You will compel me then to read the will?
Then make a ring about the corpse of Caesar
And let me show you him that made the will.
Shall I descend? And will you give me leave?
ALL. Come down.
SECOND PLEBEIAN. Descend.
THIRD PLEBEIAN. You shall have leave.
(ANTONY *comes down. They gather around* CAESAR.)
FOURTH PLEBEIAN. A ring; stand round.
FIRST PLEBEIAN. Stand from the hearse. Stand from the body.
SECOND PLEBEIAN. Room for Antony, most noble Antony!
ANTONY. Nay, press not so upon me. Stand far off.
ALL. Stand back! Room! Bear back!
ANTONY. If you have tears, prepare to shed them now.
You all do know this mantle. I remember
The first time ever Caesar put it on;
'Twas on a summer's evening in his tent,
That day he overcame the Nervii.
Look, in this place ran Cassius' dagger through.
See what a rent the envious Casca made.
Through this the well-belovèd Brutus stabbed,
And as he plucked his cursèd steel away,
Mark how the blood of Caesar followed it,
As rushing out of doors to be resolved
If Brutus so unkindly knocked or no;
For Brutus, as you know, was Caesar's angel.
Judge, O you gods, how dearly Caesar loved him!
This was the most unkindest cut of all;
For when the noble Caesar saw him stab,
Ingratitude, more strong than traitors' arms,
Quite vanquished him. Then burst his mighty heart,
And in his mantle muffling up his face,
Even at the base of Pompey's statue,
Which all the while ran blood, great Caesar fell.
41
O, what a fall was there, my countrymen!
Then I, and you, and all of us fell down,
Whilst bloody treason flourished over us.
O, now you weep, and I perceive you feel
The dint of pity. These are gracious drops.
Kind souls, what weep you when you but behold
Our Caesar's vesture wounded? Look you here,

160 hearse, bier (coffin stand).

168 Nervii (nėr′vē ī), a Celtic tribe whom Caesar defeated.

170 rent (rent), *n.* tear; torn place.

40 ■ Since Antony could not have known which conspirator was responsible for which wound, why do you think he associates various cuts in Caesar's cloak with individual conspirators?

189 dint, effect.

191 Caesar's vesture wounded, Caesar's clothing (vesture) cut.

MINI-LESSON: GRAMMAR
The Superlative Form

Read the following line from page 728:

This was the *most unkindest* cut of all.

Teach Explain that in modern English, we usually form the comparative of adjectives by using *more* or adding the suffix *-er* to the positive form; we usually form the superlative by using *most* or adding the suffix *-est* to the positive form. Often *-er* and *-est* are used with words of one syllable, while *more* and *most* are used with longer words. But we never use both *more* or *most* and a suffix, as was commonly done in Elizabethan English.

Activity Idea Ask students to form the comparative and superlative forms of the following words: *difficult, wonderful, sad, lazy, loud, excited.* They can check their work in a dictionary.

Here is himself, marred as you see with traitors.
(He lifts CAESAR'*s mantle.)*
FIRST PLEBEIAN. O piteous spectacle!
SECOND PLEBEIAN. O noble Caesar!
THIRD PLEBEIAN. O woeful day!
FOURTH PLEBEIAN. O traitors, villains!
FIRST PLEBEIAN. O most bloody sight!
SECOND PLEBEIAN. We will be revenged.
ALL. Revenge! About! Seek! Burn! Fire! Kill! Slay! Let not a traitor live!
ANTONY. Stay, countrymen.
FIRST PLEBEIAN. Peace there! Hear the noble Antony.
SECOND PLEBEIAN. We'll hear him, we'll follow him, we'll die with him!
ANTONY. Good friends, sweet friends, let me not stir you up
To such a sudden flood of mutiny.
They that have done this deed are honorable.
What private griefs they have, alas, I know not,
That made them do it. They are wise and honorable,
And will no doubt with reasons answer you.
I come not, friends, to steal away your hearts.
I am no orator, as Brutus is,
But, as you know me all, a plain blunt man
That love my friend, and that they know full well
That gave me public leave to speak of him.
For I have neither wit, nor words, nor worth,
Action, nor utterance, nor the power of speech
To stir men's blood. I only speak right on.
I tell you that which you yourselves do know,
Show you sweet Caesar's wounds, poor poor dumb mouths,
And bid them speak for me. But were I Brutus,
And Brutus Antony, there were an Antony
Would ruffle up your spirits and put a tongue
In every wound of Caesar that should move
The stones of Rome to rise and mutiny.
ALL. We'll mutiny!
FIRST PLEBEIAN. We'll burn the house of Brutus!
THIRD PLEBEIAN. Away, then! Come, seek the conspirators.
ANTONY. Yet hear me, countrymen. Yet hear me speak.
ALL. Peace, ho! Hear Antony, most noble Antony!
ANTONY. Why, friends, you go to do you know not what.
Wherein hath Caesar thus deserved your loves?
Alas, you know not. I must tell you then:
You have forgot the will I told you of.
ALL. Most true. The will! Let's stay and hear the will.

42 ■ What is Antony's purpose in showing the body?

208 private griefs, personal reasons.

44 ■ *Lines 205–225.* How does this speech relate to Antony's soliloquy near the end of scene 1 (lines 256–277)?

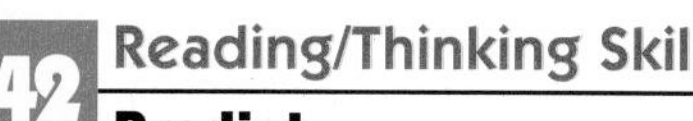

42 Reading/Thinking Skills
Predict

Possible response He wants to impress the crowd with the horror of Caesar's murder and with the many vicious stab wounds.

43 Reading/Thinking Skills
Recognize the Use of Persuasion

Point out that whereas Brutus's main defense has been all along that he was acting for the public good and had no private quarrel with Caesar, Antony has made it seem as if the motives for the assassination must have been private, undercutting the conspirators' chief defense.

44 Reading/Thinking Skills
Connect

Possible response There, he promised civil war; here, he overtly encourages it by the use of the phrase "rise and mutiny."

45 Reading/Thinking Skills
Recognize the Use of Persuasion

Here Antony uses powerful rhetorical tricks—affecting artlessness and posing as a "plain, blunt man," while he uses loaded words and powerful images to manipulate his audience and incite them to mutiny.

BUILDING ENGLISH PROFICIENCY

ESL
LEP
ELD
SAE
LD

Evaluating Dramatic Presentation

To better understand Antony's mesmerizing effect on the crowd, play a recording of the four long speeches appearing on pages 725–729. Then have students present their own renditions of the speeches.

1. Divide students into four groups.

2. Ask each group to read a speech together. Have them decide upon intonations and other various dramatic techniques that they feel would make the speech powerful and moving.

3. Have each group choose one or more students to present this speech. Allow time for the groups to rehearse.

4. Invite each "Antony" to present the group's interpretation of the speech.

5. Ask students to compare and discuss presentations. Encourage them to note the best and/or most appropriate intonations and gestures from each interpretation.

46 Literary Focus
Plot

Students may recognize that the falling action is occurring already. You may wish to point out that this play shows an unusually quick turnaround in the protagonist's fortunes. Remind them to note relevant details on their plot charts.

47 Reading/Thinking Skills
Question

Possible responses Will Octavius be able to help Antony? How can Antony get away with such open defiance of the conspirators? Will Antony be killed before he can implement his plans? Will Antony become as ambitious as Caesar was?

ANTONY. Here is the will, and under Caesar's seal.
To every Roman citizen he gives,
To every several man, seventy-five drachmas.
SECOND PLEBEIAN. Most noble Caesar! We'll revenge his death.
THIRD PLEBEIAN. O royal Caesar!
ANTONY. Hear me with patience.
ALL. Peace, ho!
ANTONY. Moreover, he hath left you all his walks,
His private arbors, and new-planted orchards,
On this side Tiber; he hath left them you,
And to your heirs forever—common pleasures,
To walk abroad and recreate yourselves.
Here was a Caesar! When comes such another?
FIRST PLEBEIAN. Never, never! Come, away, away!
We'll burn his body in the holy place
And with the brands fire the traitors' houses.
Take up the body.
SECOND PLEBEIAN. Go fetch fire!
THIRD PLEBEIAN. Pluck down benches!
FOURTH PLEBEIAN. Pluck down forms, windows,
anything! (PLEBIANS *exit with the body.*)
46 **ANTONY.** Now let it work. Mischief, thou art afoot.
Take thou what course thou wilt.
(OCTAVIUS*'s servant enters.*) How now, fellow?
SERVANT. Sir, Octavius is already come to Rome.
ANTONY. Where is he?
SERVANT. He and Lepidus are at Caesar's house.
ANTONY. And thither will I straight to visit him.
He comes upon a wish. Fortune is merry,
And in this mood will give us anything.
SERVANT. I heard him say Brutus and Cassius
Are rid like madmen through the gates of Rome. 47
ANTONY. Belike they had some notice of the people,
How I had moved them. Bring me to Octavius.
(ANTONY *leads his* ATTENDANTS *and the* SERVANT *out at left.*)

238 seventy-five drachmas (drak′mə), Although experts estimate this amount as being worth anywhere from $10 to $100, it represented a substantial bequest.

245 on this side Tiber, on this side of the Tiber, Rome's river. Shakespeare shortened the phrase to maintain the rhythm of this speech.

254 forms, public benches.

265 are rid, have ridden.
■ In your notebook write any questions you have about the events of the play to this point.

Scene 3

Summary *Mistaken for Cinna the conspirator, Cinna the poet is attacked by the mob. The mob then moves off to find the conspirators or to burn their houses.*

Rome. A street near the Forum. CINNA *enters followed by a group of angry and suspicious* CITIZENS.

MINI-LESSON: LITERARY ELEMENT
Protagonist

Teach According to Aristotle, a tragic hero is a person of high rank who possesses a tragic flaw that leads to that person's downfall.

Activity Idea After reading act 3, students should have opinions on who—Caesar or Brutus—best fits this definition. Lead them to consider elements such as the following and make a chart to arrive at which character is protagonist. They can add to the chart after reading acts 4 and 5.

Caesar as Protagonist
The play is named after him.
Tragic flaw: arrogance, ambition
Has higher rank than Brutus

Brutus as Protagonist
Brutus delivers important soliloquies. Caesar has none.
Brutus is a more complex character.
Tragic flaw: idealistic, impractical nature

CINNA. I dreamt tonight that I did feast with Caesar,
And things unluckily charge my fantasy.
I have no will to wander forth of doors,
Yet something leads me forth.
FIRST PLEBEIAN. What is your name?
SECOND PLEBEIAN. Whither are you going?
THIRD PLEBEIAN. Where do you dwell?
FOURTH PLEBEIAN. Are you a married man or a bachelor?
SECOND PLEBEIAN. Answer every man directly.
FIRST PLEBEIAN. Ay, and briefly.
FOURTH PLEBEIAN. Ay, and wisely.
THIRD PLEBEIAN. Ay, and truly, you were best.
CINNA. What is my name? Whither am I going? Where do I dwell? Am I a married man or a bachelor? Then to answer every man directly and briefly, wisely and truly: wisely I say, I am a bachelor.
SECOND PLEBEIAN. That's as much as to say they are fools that marry. You'll bear me a bang for that, I fear. Proceed directly.
CINNA. Directly, I am going to Caesar's funeral.
FIRST PLEBEIAN. As a friend or an enemy?
CINNA. As a friend.
SECOND PLEBEIAN. That matter is answered directly.
FOURTH PLEBEIAN. For your dwelling—briefly.
CINNA. Briefly, I dwell by the Capitol.
THIRD PLEBEIAN. Your name, sir, truly.
CINNA. Truly, my name is Cinna.
FIRST PLEBEIAN. Tear him to pieces! He's a conspirator!
CINNA. I am Cinna the poet, I am Cinna the poet!
FOURTH PLEBEIAN. Tear him for his bad verses, tear him for his bad verses!
CINNA. I am not Cinna the conspirator.
FOURTH PLEBEIAN. It is no matter, his name's Cinna.
Pluck but his name out of his heart, and turn him going.
THIRD PLEBEIAN. Tear him, tear him! Come, brands, ho, firebrands! To Brutus's, to Cassius's; burn all! Some to Decius's house, and some to Casca's; some to Ligarius's. Away go!
(*All the* PLEBEIANS *exit, dragging off* CINNA.)

1 **tonight**, last night.

17 **bear me a bang**, get a beating.

■ What does this scene show about the nature of the commoners?

48 Reading/Thinking Skills
Summarize

Possible responses They are highly emotional, easily swayed, not very perceptive, not politically astute, and easily roused to mischief and violence.

49 Reading/Thinking Skills
Draw Conclusions

Question What will the commoners do with Cinna? *(Possible response: probably kill him)*

Check Test

1. Why doesn't Artemidorus's warning work? *(Caesar won't read the letter.)*

2. What do the conspirators do to their hands and swords immediately after they kill Caesar? *(bathe them in his blood)*

3. What does Antony request the conspirators allow him to do? *(to show Caesar's body in the marketplace and speak at his funeral)*

4. What adjective does Antony repeatedly apply to Brutus in his "Friends, Romans, countrymen" speech? *(honorable)*

5. Why is Cinna the poet attacked? *(His name is the same as one of the conspirators.)*

Unit 6 Resource Book
Alternate Check Test, p. 21

BUILDING ENGLISH PROFICIENCY

Analyzing Key Events

Point out to students that the crowd becomes a mob at the end of act 3.

Activity Idea Have students discuss times they have seen or heard about the actions of a mob. Use questions such as the following to direct discussion:

- What is the difference between a crowd and a mob?
- At what point does a crowd become a mob? When did this Roman crowd become a mob?
- What is a "mob" mentality? What are ways to manipulate a mob?
- What do you think this mob will do?

After Reading

MAKING CONNECTIONS

1. Possible responses: I would prefer to serve under Cassius: he is brave, practical, and insightful about others. Brutus is honorable, but does not read his opponents well and Antony is too manipulative to make a good leader, although he would be highly charismatic.

I would prefer Antony, as long as I supported his cause. Cassius is too jealous and lacks the personality to lead; Brutus is too hesitant.

2. Crowd noises and trumpets as Caesar enters; paper rustling from Artemidorus's scroll; groans from Caesar; murmurs of the crowd

3. Possible response: On-stage for maximum effect on the audience

4. Possible response: lines 202–212; 220–224; 229–232

5. He presumes that others are as honorable as he is.

6. Possible response: It's appropriate. A hart, a powerful deer, is hunted and violently killed by packs of hounds. A pun on the word *heart* enriches the metaphor.

7. It expresses Antony's repulsion at the act and serves as a call to arms.

8. Any words praising the conspirators, and especially the word *honorable* would be spoken ironically.

9. Possible response: It is both humorous and necessary. The humor points up the horror that Antony has unleashed in revenge—a mindless mob, set on violence.

10. Students who have lived under a dictatorship may have stronger and better-informed views than others.

11. Answers will depend on students' biographical knowledge of the examples and on their own opinions. Students may say that evil exposed after a celebrity's death sometimes enhances that person's image.

Act 3

After Reading

Making Connections

Shaping Your Response

1. If you were a soldier, would you prefer to serve under Brutus, Antony, or Cassius? Why?
2. For a radio presentation of *Julius Caesar,* what sound effects would you need for scene 1?
3. If you were directing this play for television or stage, would you have the murder take place on or off camera or stage? Explain.

Analyzing the Play

4. From which of Antony's lines in scene 1 should the conspirators **infer** that he is not to be trusted?
5. What trait in Brutus's **character** leads him to misjudge Antony so consistently?
6. Explain what is being compared in the hart **metaphor** (scene 1, lines 206–212), and whether you think the metaphor is appropriate for Caesar.
7. A **soliloquy** is a speech made by an actor to himself or herself when alone on the stage. It reveals the character's thoughts and feelings to the audience, but not to other characters in the play. What do you think is the purpose of Antony's soliloquy in scene 1, lines 256-277?
8. Which lines in Antony's funeral oration do you think an actor would express in an **ironic** tone? Why?
9. One purpose of scene 3 is to provide comic relief. Yet it shows a murderous mob setting upon an innocent victim. In your judgment, is this scene really humorous? necessary? Explain.

Extending the Ideas

10. Caesar considered himself a defender of the common people. Do you think that a dictator can have the interests of the group at heart? Why or why not?
11. In the opening of his funeral oration, Antony observes that "The evil that men do lives after them; / The good is oft interrèd with their bones." Using such modern examples as John F. Kennedy, Christa McAuliffe, Elvis Presley, Malcolm X, or others, discuss whether you agree or disagree with this observation.

Literary Focus: Plot

On the plot chart in your notebook under **rising action**, list the events that point toward Caesar's assassination. The **climax** occurs when the central problem of the plot must be resolved. It also signals a change in the fortune of the main character. Write what you think the climax is.

LITERARY FOCUS: PLOT

Most students will consider Caesar's assassination the climax of the play, since it establishes the fate of the title character and pits Antony and his followers against the conspirators. You might ask students to speculate on how the conflict might be resolved.

Vocabulary Study

Tell whether the following word pairs are synonyms, antonyms, or neither by writing *S, A,* or *N* on your paper.

bequeath
bootless
censure
discourse
grievous
inter
legacy
puissant
rent
unassailable

1. grievous: causing pain
2. discourse: talk
3. bequeath: inherit
4. unassailable: ambitious
5. censure: praise
6. puissant: weak
7. bootless: poor
8. rent: torn place
9. inter: dig up
10. legacy: dagger

Expressing Your Ideas

Writing Choices

Writer's Notebook Update Write an obituary for Caesar that mentions some of the traits you included in your chart.

Eyewitness Assume that you are Lucius and write a **letter** to a friend telling what you have witnessed, overheard, and participated in from midnight to mid-morning of the ides of March.

Et Tu Write a short **dialogue** that ends "Et tu, Brutè!" Alternatively, you might draw an original cartoon based on these words.

"Et tu, Baxter?"

Other Options

Home Sweet Home Assume that you are the set designer for a stage production of *Julius Caesar.* Research the kind of house and garden that Brutus, a wealthy Roman, would have had. Then draw or construct a **model** of your set.

I, Antony Analyze the lines in Mark Antony's oration for clues to tone and gestures. Then memorize lines from the speech, or the entire speech. Enhance your delivery with stage props or costumes, if you wish, and **act out** the oration for the class.

VOCABULARY STUDY

1. S
2. S
3. A
4. N
5. A
6. A
7. N
8. S
9. A
10. N

Unit 6 Resource Book
Vocabulary, pp. 11, 19
Vocabulary Test, pp. 14, 22

WRITING CHOICES

Writer's Notebook Update

You may wish to encourage students to assume the persona of one of the characters in the play. Encourage students to think of a creative way that a Roman could have published an honest obituary of Caesar without being killed.

Selection Test

Unit 6 Resource Book,
pp. 23–24

)THER OPTIONS

, Antony

ɔu may wish to have some students prepare rutus's speech and have students present the oraons in pairs, first Brutus and then Antony, for their lassmates to compare. When students are done with ɪeir presentations, you may wish to play or replay a ecording of the play for them, so they can hear proɛssional actors deliver the two speeches.

THE GLOBE THEATER

Teaching Objectives

- to visualize the action of a play staged in Shakespeare's time
- to use graphic aids

Introduce

Ask students to read the article on the Globe Theater. Remind them to keep the stages of the Globe Theater in mind as they read and visualize the action in *Julius Caesar*.

Follow Up

Point out that Shakespeare wrote *Julius Caesar* in 1599 and that it was one of the first plays to be acted at the new Globe Theater. Nearly all parts of the Globe's performing area were used in the production. Most outdoor scenes took place on the platform and most indoor scenes on the inner stage or balcony. In some scenes the platform and inner stage were used simultaneously. Allow students time to refer to this diagram as they begin each scene.

The Globe Theater

London Bridge teems with pedestrians and men on horseback; boats large and small move along the Thames River carrying eager spectators toward a dock on the south bank. Their destination? The octagonal, three-story Globe Theater, where a flag flies atop the building to indicate that a performance will take place this afternoon.

As the spectators enter through the double wooden doors, they begin to separate according to class. The groundlings (apprentices and the lower class) crowd into the round Yard, or pit area, where they will stand during the performance. Middle class folks move to the bench areas in the roofed galleries. Nobles take their places in special boxes. Vendors hawk both food and drink. The mood of the nearly 3,000 spectators is festive—and in the pit, even rowdy. As the audience begins to settle down in anticipation of the play, what do they see?

From a few surviving maps, carpenters' contracts, and written descriptions, we can put together the following picture of the Globe. The main acting area, the Platform, extended well into the Yard so that the spectators almost surrounded the actors. At the back was the Study, a curtained room used for interior scenes. At either side were large Permanent Doors, similar to the street doors of Elizabethan townhouses. These were the main stage entrances. In the floor of the Platform were several trap doors. Imagine smoke and fog rising and falling to announce the appearance of Caesar's ghost.

On the second level was another curtained room, the Chamber, typically used for domestic scenes. In front of this was a narrow balcony called the Tarras (ter′is). Often the Tarras and the Platform would be used together, with the Tarras representing a hill, the wall of a town, or a gallery from which observers watched the action below. On the third level, was a narrow musicians' gallery. Above it was a canopied roof supported by two large stage posts that rose from the Platform. Above the canopy were the Huts that housed a pulley system for lowering objects supposed to appear from midair. Sound effects such as thunder or battle alarums (sounds of fighting) also came from the Huts. This entire three-story structure was known as the Tiring House. It was the Globe's permanent set.

Shakespeare quiets his audience by beginning *Julius Caesar* with the noise and bustle of excited crowds. There is little scenery. In later scenes, a bed, a table, a bench, or a chair suggests the setting. Often, a trumpet or a line or two of dialogue is enough to alert the audience to a change of scene.

The first Globe Theater, completed in 1599, burned to the ground in 1613. The second Globe, which was built immediately afterward, stood until 1644. Today, many Shakespearean-style theaters have been built—in Chichester, England; in Stratford, Canada; and in Minneapolis, Minnesota. A full-scale replica of the Globe has been recently completed as part of a Shakespearean complex in London, close to the site of the original Globe Theater.

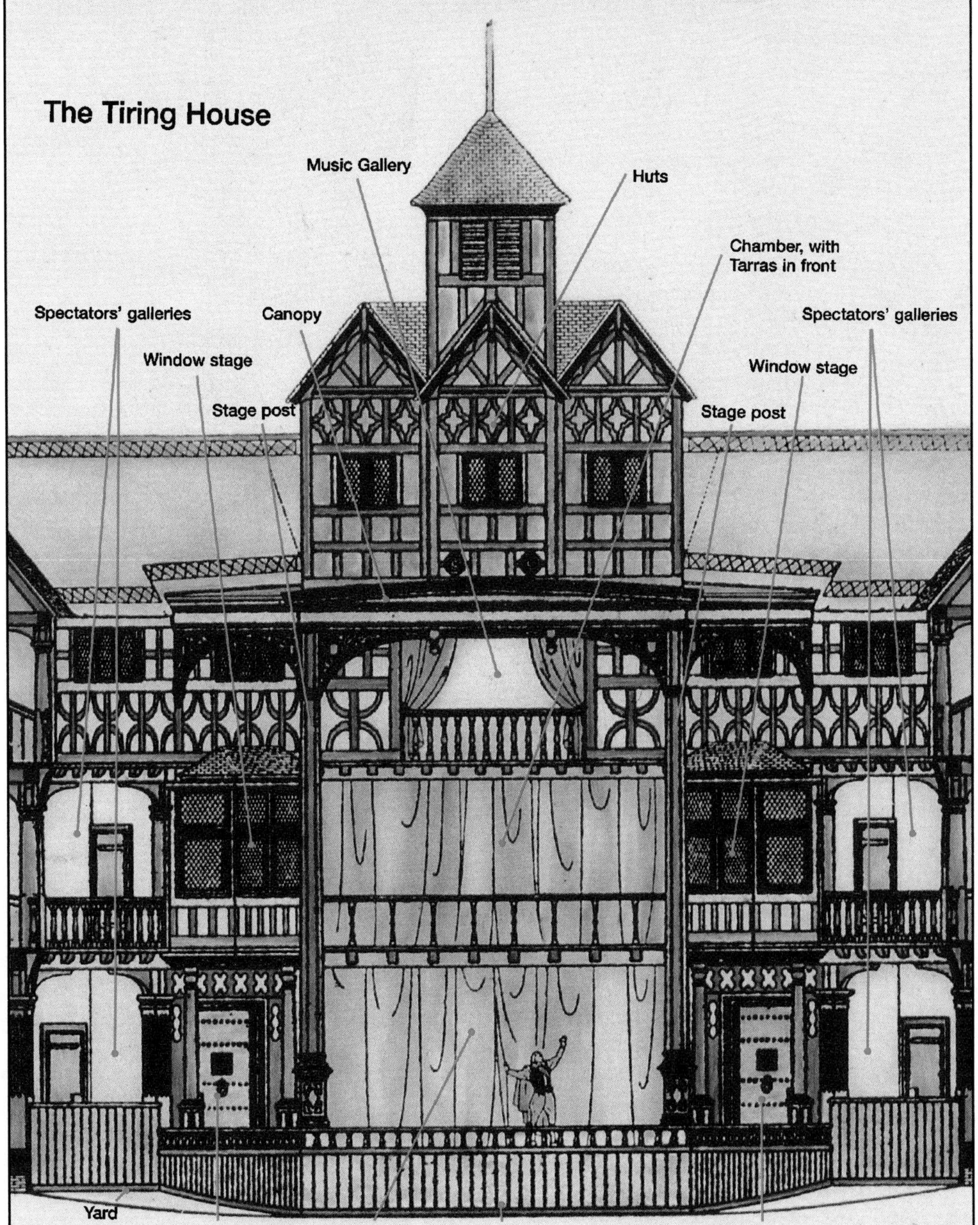

The Tiring House

Music Gallery
Huts
Chamber, with Tarras in front
Spectators' galleries
Canopy
Spectators' galleries
Window stage
Window stage
Stage post
Stage post
Yard (for spectators)
Permanent door
Study
Platform
Permanent door

Activity Options

Activity 1 Select scenes from *Julius Caesar*. Have some scenes performed with the audience seated in front of the actors. Have other scenes performed with the audience arranged in a horseshoe shape around the actors, as in the Globe Theater. After presenting the scenes, discuss differences in the two stagings.

Activity 2 Students can take advantage of the vast research done on sixteenth-century theaters, especially the Globe, and make a model theater.

Activity 3 Some students may want to design a theater of the future that incorporates technology and interactive opportunities for the audience.

BUILDING ENGLISH PROFICIENCY

Visualizing the Stage

Explain that the versatile Globe Theater provided a setting for exciting stage presentations. Have students examine the diagram to appreciate the many possibilities for staging.

Activity Ideas

- Have students identify performing areas of the theater where different scenes would be staged. For example:

  The Study: The interior scenes between Caesar and Calpurnia and between Brutus and Portia

  The trap doors of the Platform: The appearance of Caesar's ghost

  The Tarras or third level: Parts of the battle scenes

- Students interested in filming techniques and special effects can speculate on or research how sound effects (the bustle of a crowd, battle noise, thunder), staging tricks (the "killing" of Caesar, suggestions of the "portentous" things described by Calpurnia on page 707), and battle scenes that involve multiple stages were achieved in Elizabethan drama. Then have them suggest what modern filming techniques could be used to achieve these effects.

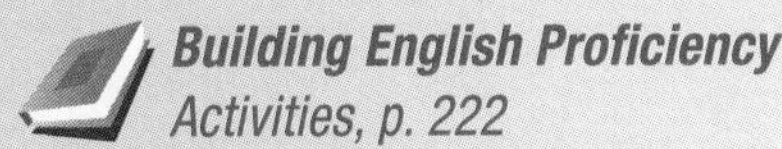

During Reading

1 Historical Note
Marcus Aemilius Lepidus

Lepidus was consul with Julius Caesar in 46 B.C. He was a member of the Second Triumvirate along with Antony and Octavius, and after Brutus and Cassius were defeated at Philippi in 42 B.C., Lepidus governed Africa. In 36 B.C., he tried to claim Sicily, but Octavius forestalled him.

2 Historical Note
Cicero

In Plutarch's account, Antony demanded that Cicero die. Cicero had supported the young Octavius, yet Octavius acceded to the orator's murder. Shakespeare chose to omit this detail.

3 Reading/Thinking Skills
Summarize

Response Antony has planned executions, including that of his nephew; he is going to try to change Caesar's will; and he is trying to remove Lepidus from power. Earlier he pretended to make peace with Brutus and the others, then knowingly and skillfully turned the crowd against them.

4 Reading/Thinking Skills
Draw Conclusions

Question What point is Octavius making? *(Possible response: Antony is a hypocrite and has exercised bad judgment.)*

Unit 6 Resource Book
Graphic Organizer, p. 25
Study Guide, p. 26

ACT FOUR

Scene 1

Summary *Brutus and Cassius have fled to Greece and Asia Minor. After his civil war against Octavius, Antony has joined forces with Octavius and Lepidus. This triumvirate meets to condemn those Romans who might be opposed to them. After Antony sends Lepidus to get a copy of Caesar's will, he and Octavius agree that war against Brutus and Cassius is imminent.*

A house in Rome. One year after Caesar's assassination. Seated around a table, ANTONY, OCTAVIUS, *and* LEPIDUS *are closely examining a wax tablet and making plans to crush their opposition.*

ANTONY. These many, then shall die. Their names are pricked.
1 **OCTAVIUS.** Your brother too must die. Consent you, Lepidus?
LEPIDUS. I do consent—
OCTAVIUS. Prick him down, Antony.
LEPIDUS. Upon condition Publius shall not live,
2 Who is your sister's son, Mark Antony.
ANTONY *(picking up the stylus).* He shall not live. Look, with a spot I damn him.
But Lepidus, go you to Caesar's house.
Fetch the will hither, and we shall determine
How to cut off some charge in legacies.
LEPIDUS. What, shall I find you here?
OCTAVIUS. Or here or at the Capitol. (LEPIDUS *leaves by a rear door.*)
ANTONY. This is a slight, unmeritable man,
Meet to be sent on errands. Is it fit, 3
The threefold world divided, he should stand
One of the three to share it?
4 **OCTAVIUS.** So you thought him,
And took his voice who should be pricked to die
In our black sentence and proscription.
ANTONY. Octavius, I have seen more days than you;
And though we lay these honors on this man
To ease ourselves of divers slanderous loads,
He shall but bear them as the ass bears gold,
To groan and sweat under the business,
Either led or driven as we point the way;
And having brought our treasure where we will,
Then take we down his load, and turn him off,
Like to the empty ass, to shake his ears
And graze in commons.
OCTAVIUS. You may do your will;
But he's a tried and valiant soldier.

1 These many . . . pricked, many Roman citizens are marked for death.

6 stylus, a pointed instrument for writing.
6 with a spot I damn him, with my mark (with the stylus) I condemn him to death.
8–9 we shall determine . . . legacies. Antony wishes to find a way to reduce the amount Caesar has bequeathed each Roman.
■ In the first fifteen lines of this scene, what three questionable activities has Antony been involved in? What, if anything, in earlier acts has foreshadowed Antony's behavior?
16–17 took his voice . . . proscription, accepted his statements about who should be marked for death or banishment (proscription).
20 divers (dī′vərz) **slanderous loads,** various false charges.

27 commons, public pastures.

SELECTION SUMMARY
Julius Caesar, Act 4

Scene 1: The Second Triumvirate—Antony, Octavius, and Lepidus—decide which of their political opponents to put to death. After Lepidus leaves, Antony expresses his low opinion of the man, and he and Octavius discuss pursuing the armies of Brutus and Cassius.

Scene 2: Cassius comes to Brutus's war camp to discuss disagreements they are having. When Cassius arrives in a defensive mood, Brutus invites him inside his tent for a private talk.

Scene 3: The two men quarrel bitterly, the idealistic Brutus disagreeing with Cassius's more practical methods of maintaining an army. Brutus admits being upset over Portia's suicide, and they make plans to march to Philippi to engage Antony's and Octavius's forces. Caesar's ghost appears to Brutus and warns that Brutus will see him at Philippi. Disturbed, Brutus sends Cassius word that the attack should be begun quickly.

*For summaries in other languages, see the **Building English Proficiency** Book.*

ANTONY. So is my horse, Octavius, and for that
I do appoint him store of provender.
It is a creature that I teach to fight,
To wind, to stop, to run directly on,
His corporal motion governed by my spirit.
And in some taste is Lepidus but so.
He must be taught, and trained, and bid go forth—
A barren-spirited fellow, one that feeds
On objects, arts, and imitations,
Which, out of use and staled by other men,
Begin his fashion. Do not talk of him
6 But as a property. And now, Octavius,
Listen great things. Brutus and Cassius
7 Are levying powers. We must straight make head.

30 appoint . . . provender, provide him with food.
33 corporal, of the body; bodily.
37 objects, arts, and imitations, wonders and things that are artificial and fashionable.
5 ■ What do you predict will ultimately happen to Lepidus?
41–42 Brutus and Cassius . . . head. Brutus and Cassius have been gathering forces (powers); so must Antony and his associates.

5 Reading/Thinking Skills
Predict

Possible response Lepidus could be dropped from the triumvirate and possibly killed.

6 Literary Element
Characterization

Question How has Antony's character changed from act 3? *(Antony, who seemed horrified by the conspirators' murder of Caesar, is now plotting many murders for less lofty motives, including the murder of a member of his own family in a kind of tit-for-tat deal with Lepidus.)*

7 Reading/Thinking Skills
Compare and Contrast

Question Compare and contrast Octavius and Antony. *(Antony is power-hungry, greedy, unscrupulous and back-biting. Octavius is power-hungry, but is disturbed by Antony's remarks behind Lepidus's back.)*

Discuss the clues in this picture about the relationships among the triumvirate. *(Students may note how young Lepidus appears. Attention is focused on Antony, who looks like he is arguing with Lepidus. All the men appear tense.)*

BUILDING ENGLISH PROFICIENCY

Exploring Motivation

Write the word *power* on the board. Invite students to quickwrite names of things they associate with power. Invite discussion. Then use the following activities to help students understand how the desire for power affects Antony, as shown in act 4.

Activity Ideas

- Bring to class several newspapers and magazines. Ask pairs or small groups of students to look for examples of powerful people—people who are seeking power or who already seem to have power. Have students identify how these people achieved power and how they use their power.
- Invite students to discuss how attaining power can change a person and what a person might lose in his or her search for power. You may wish to introduce and establish the meaning of the saying "Absolute power corrupts absolutely."

8 Reader's Response
Making Personal Connections

Bear-baiting was an Elizabethan "sport" in which a bear (or bull) was tied to a stake while fierce English mastiff dogs attacked it.

Question Do you consider bear-baiting more violent than modern sports? Explain. *(Possible responses: Some sports today, such as bullfighting, can be brutal. Students might want to discuss other sports in the light of violence.)*

9 Reading/Thinking Skills
Connect

Questions

- What does Octavius mean? *(Some people who appear friendly to their cause are plotting against them.)*
- What earlier lines does this connect with? *(Brutus's suggestion that the conspirators can hide their plans by smiling and appearing affable, act 2, scene 1, lines 79–85)*

10 Literary Focus
Plot

During the falling action, the fate of the protagonist works toward a final conclusion. Here, we witness the deterioration in the relationship between Brutus and Cassius.

Therefore let our alliance be combined,
Our best friends made, our means stretched;
And let us presently go sit in council
How covert matters may be best disclosed
And open perils surest answerèd.
8 **OCTAVIUS.** Let us do so, for we are at the stake
And bayed about with many enemies;
9 And some that smile have in their hearts, I fear,
Millions of mischiefs.
(ANTONY *and* OCTAVIUS *exit.*)

45 sit in council, discuss.
46–47 how covert . . . answerèd, how hidden (covert) dangers may be discovered, and dangers already known be met most securely.
48–49 we are at the stake . . . enemies, we are tied to a stake (like a bear in the sport of bear baiting), while enemies bark (bay) like dogs about to attack us.

Scene 2

Summary *Lucilius, one of Brutus's officers, alerts Brutus that Cassius is near. He also verifies Brutus's suspicion that Cassius has changed. Preceded by his servant Pindarus, Cassius enters to find an angry Brutus.*

BRUTUS*'s tent at Sardis, a city in Asia Minor. Several months later.* LUCIUS, BRUTUS*'s servant, enters from the left, followed by* BRUTUS *and several* SOLDIERS. LUCILIUS *and* TITINIUS, *friends of* BRUTUS, *enter at the right, accompanied by* CASSIUS*'s servant* PINDARUS.

BRUTUS. Stand, ho!
LUCILIUS. Give the word, ho, and stand!
BRUTUS. What now, Lucilius, is Cassius near?
LUCILIUS. He is at hand, and Pindarus is come
To do you salutation from his master.
10 **BRUTUS.** He greets me well. Your master, Pindarus,
In his own change, or by ill officers,
Hath given me some worthy cause to wish
Things done undone; but if he be at hand
I shall be satisfied.
PINDARUS. I do not doubt
But that my noble master will appear
Such as he is, full of regard and honor.
BRUTUS. He is not doubted. A word, Lucilius.
(BRUTUS *and* LUCILIUS *speak apart.*)
How he received you let me be resolved.
LUCILIUS. With courtesy and with respect enough,
But not with such familiar instances
Nor with such free and friendly conference
As he hath used of old.
BRUTUS. Thou hast described
A hot friend cooling. Ever note, Lucilius:
When love begins to sicken and decay

1–2 Stand . . . stand! Halt! Pass the word (to Cassius's soldiers) to halt.

5 to do you salutation, to bring you greeting.

7 in his own . . . officers, by his own change of heart or by bad advice from troublemakers.

10 be satisfied, have things explained to my satisfaction.

13–14 A word . . . resolved. Not content with Pindarus's assurance of Cassius's loyalty, Brutus asks Lucilius, his own man, for a further report.

MINI-LESSON: GRAMMAR
Homonyms and Homophones

Teach Write the following on the board.

And let us presently go sit in *council*

. . . Let us do so, for we are at the *stake*. . . .

Make sure that students understand the meanings of *council* (group assembled to discuss or give advice) and *stake* (stick or post pointed at one end for driving into the ground). Have a volunteer provide homonyms for these words *(counsel, steak)*, along with their meanings.

Activity Idea Have students find homonyms for the following words that appear in scene 2: *plane* (line 22), *mettle* (line 24), and *horse* (line 29).

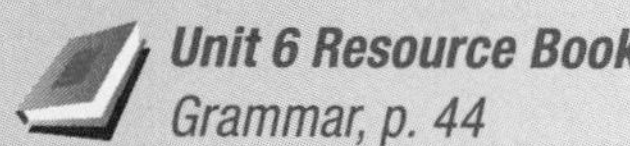

Unit 6 Resource Book
Grammar, p. 44

It useth an enforcèd ceremony.
There are no tricks in plain and simple faith.
But hollow men, like horses hot at hand,
Make gallant show and promise of their mettle;
(Martial music within.)
But when they should endure the bloody spur,
They fall their crests and like deceitful jades
Sink in the trial. Comes his army on?
LUCILIUS. They mean this night in Sardis to be quartered.
The greater part, the horse in general,
Are come with Cassius.
(CASSIUS *enters with some of his soldiers.*)
BRUTUS. Hark, he is arrived.
March gently on to meet him.
CASSIUS. Stand, ho!
BRUTUS. Stand, ho! Speak the word along.
FIRST SOLDIER. Stand!
SECOND SOLDIER. Stand!
THIRD SOLDIER. Stand!
CASSIUS. Most noble brother, you have done me wrong.
BRUTUS. Judge me, you gods! Wrong I mine enemies?
And if not so, how should I wrong a brother?
CASSIUS. Brutus, this sober form of yours hides wrongs;
And when you do them—
BRUTUS. Cassius, be content;
Speak your griefs softly. I do know you well.
Before the eyes of both our armies here,
Which should perceive nothing but love from us,
Let us not wrangle. Bid them move away.
Then in my tent, Cassius, enlarge your griefs,
And I will give you audience.
CASSIUS. Pindarus,
Bid our commanders lead their charges off
A little from this ground.
BRUTUS. Lucius, do you the like, and let no man
Come to our tent till we have done our conference.
Let Lucilius and Titinius guard our door.
(BRUTUS *watches as his* SOLDIERS *follow* LUCILIUS *off at left.*)

21 enforcèd ceremony, forced politeness.
23 hollow, insincere.

11

26 jades, worthless horses.
■ How has the relationship between Brutus and Cassius changed?
28 the horse in general, all the cavalry.

40 sober form, dignified manner.

13

■ Is Brutus wise in insisting that he and Cassius meet in private? Why?

11 Reading/Thinking Skills
Clarify

Possible response They are no longer in each other's confidence; they are mistrustful.

12 Reading/Thinking Skills
Infer

Question What is Brutus thinking? *(Possible response: Perhaps he fears that Cassius is going to attack him; Brutus may fear that Cassius will not support him in battle.)*

13 Reading/Thinking Skills
Evaluate

Response There will be differences of opinion on whether or not the private meeting is wise. Yes, because a public argument would have a bad effect on morale in their armies. Yes, because if Cassius is planning something treacherous, it will be a good plan to separate him from his officers.

BUILDING ENGLISH PROFICIENCY

Contrasting Series of Events

The contrast in the relationships and fortunes of the two pairs of leaders becomes evident in scenes 1 and 2. From this point, Antony and Octavius will fare well, but Brutus and Cassius will suffer. Help students begin a graphic such as the one shown here to contrast the rise of one pair of leaders with the downfall of the other.

Antony/Octavius	Brutus/Cassius
Discuss their differences	Argue about petty problems
Agree on a plan of action	Disagree on a plan of action

14 **Literary Element**

Figurative Language

Have students speculate on the meaning of the expression "itching palm" and how the expression might have come about. *(This signifies greed. An extended palm, eager for money, might appear to be itching.)*

15 **Reading/Thinking Skills**

Question

Possible response Brutus and Cassius don't seem to agree on what has happened, so I would need a clear account that they both agreed was true. I would also like to know if they are arguing because they are edgy about battle or if there is a real basis for their argument.

16 **Reading/Thinking Skills**

Summarize

Question Summarize Brutus's point in this speech. *(Possible response: After taking justice into their own hands to punish Caesar, one of whose chief faults was protecting dishonest public figures, it is particularly horrible if we commit the same faults for which he died.)*

Scene 3

Summary *Brutus reprimands Cassius for defending an officer who took bribes and for being too greedy. Their argument heats up when Brutus accuses Cassius of dishonoring their cause. Distressed, Cassius offers Brutus his life. Brutus then reveals that Portia has killed herself. Titinius and Messala, another officer, enter. The men discuss strategy for the upcoming battle against Antony and Octavius's forces on the plains of Philippi. As Brutus prepares for bed, he is visited by the sudden appearance of the ghost of Caesar who promises that he will see Brutus again at Philippi.*

Within BRUTUS*'s tent. Immediately following.* LUCIUS *and* TITINIUS *guard the entrance to* BRUTUS*'s tent.* BRUTUS *and* CASSIUS *stand facing each other.* CASSIUS *is very angry.*

CASSIUS. That you have wronged me doth appear in this.
You have condemned and noted Lucius Pella
For taking bribes here of the Sardians,
Wherein my letters, praying on his side,
Because I knew the man, was slighted off.
BRUTUS. You wronged yourself to write in such a case.
CASSIUS. In such a time as this it is not meet
That every nice offense should bear his comment.
BRUTUS. Let me tell you, Cassius, you yourself
Are much condemned to have an itching palm,
To sell and mart your offices for gold
To undeservers.
14
CASSIUS. I an itching palm?
You know that you are Brutus that speaks this,
Or, by the gods, this speech were else your last.
BRUTUS. The name of Cassius honors this corruption,
And chastisement doth therefore hide his head.
CASSIUS. Chastisement?
BRUTUS. Remember March, the ides of March remember.
Did not great Julius bleed for justice' sake?
What villain touched his body that did stab
And not for justice? What, shall one of us,
That struck the foremost man of all this world
16
But for supporting robbers, shall we now
Contaminate our fingers with base bribes,
And sell the mighty space of our large honors
For so much trash as may be graspèd thus?
I had rather be a dog and bay the moon
Than such a Roman.
CASSIUS. Brutus, bait not me.
I'll not endure it. You forget yourself

2 noted, publicly disgraced.

3 for taking . . . Sardians. Brutus had publicly accused Lucius Pella of embezzling public money and, finding him guilty, had condemned him.

8 that every . . . comment, that every trivial (nice) offense should be criticized.

10 condemned to have an itching palm, accused of being greedy for money.

11 mart, traffic in.

15 ■ What do you still need to know to understand why Brutus and Cassius are so angry with one another?

15–16 The name of Cassius . . . head. Because Cassius, a man of influence, approves of these dishonest practices, legal authority is afraid to act.

22–23 that struck . . . robbers, who killed Caesar for protecting dishonest public figures.

MINI-LESSON: STUDY SKILLS

Finding Information

Students may notice the place names Asia Minor, Sardis, and Philippi in this act. Tell them that there are a variety of resources that can help them find out more about these places. Electronic encyclopedias, like *Groliers,* can give them historical background. Historical atlases can show the location. For very brief entries, even a dictionary will help.

Activity Ideas

- Divide the class into small groups. Have each group locate four different sources (including at least one multimedia/electronic source if possible) and compare the kinds of information they find in each one on the topics of Asia Minor, Sardis, and Philippi.
- On a suitable map that includes the Mediterranean area, point out regions mentioned in this act and their geographic relationships to each other. (scene 2: Rome; scenes 2 and 3: Sardis—roughly present-day Turkey.) The clash foreshadowed in this act will take place at Philippi in Macedonia, midway between Rome and Sardis.

To hedge me in. I am a soldier, I,
Older in practice, abler than yourself
To make conditions.
BRUTUS. Go to! You are not, Cassius.
CASSIUS. I am.
BRUTUS. I say you are not.
17
CASSIUS. Urge me no more; I shall forget myself.
Have mind upon your health. Tempt me no farther.
BRUTUS. Away, slight man!
CASSIUS. Is't possible?
BRUTUS. Hear me, for I will speak.
Must I give way and room to your rash choler?
Shall I be frighted when a madman stares?
CASSIUS. O ye gods, ye gods! Must I endure all this?
BRUTUS. All this? Ay, more. Fret till your proud heart break.
Go show your slaves how choleric you are
And make your bondmen tremble. Must I budge?
Must I observe you? Must I stand and crouch
Under your testy humor? By the gods,
You shall digest the venom of your spleen
Though it do split you; for, from this day forth,
I'll use you for my mirth, yea, for my laughter,
When you are waspish.
CASSIUS. Is it come to this?
BRUTUS. You say you are a better soldier.
Let it appear so; make your vaunting true,
And it shall please me well. For mine own part,
I shall be glad to learn of noble men.
CASSIUS. You wrong me every way! You wrong me, Brutus.
I said an elder soldier, not a better.
Did I say "better"?
BRUTUS. If you did, I care not.
CASSIUS. When Caesar lived he durst not thus have moved me.
18
BRUTUS. Peace, peace! You durst not so have tempted him.
CASSIUS. I durst not?
BRUTUS. No.
CASSIUS. What, durst not tempt him?
BRUTUS. For your life you durst not.
CASSIUS. Do not presume too much upon my love,
I may do that I shall be sorry for.
BRUTUS. You have done that you should be sorry for.
There is no terror, Cassius, in your threats,
For I am armed so strong in honesty
That they pass by me as the idle wind,
Which I respect not. I did send to you

30 hedge me in, interfere with me.

32 to make conditions, manage affairs; that is, about the behavior of such men as Pella and for the appointment of officers.

■ In lines 33–58 Brutus and Cassius resort to childish argument and name-calling. How should the actors playing their parts deliver the lines?

40 rash choler (kol′ər), wrathful temperament.

47 testy, easily irritated; impatient.

59 moved, angered.

70 respect not, pay no attention to.

17 Reading/Thinking Skills
Clarify

Possible response If available, play an audio rendition of this scene to let students hear appropriate tones of mistrust and hurt pride. The lines should be delivered with control, although they must convey intense anger so as not to appear silly. Listening to a recording will also serve as a reminder that a rhetorical tone, such as that used with Shakespeare, differs from the delivery students are accustomed to hearing on TV and in movies.

18 Reading/Thinking Skills
Make Judgments

Question Who has the upper hand in this argument? *(Possible responses: Brutus, despite the fact that he is not always in the right, is able to maintain the momentum and disturb Cassius, who considers himself wronged. The question is irrelevant—the point is that they are bickering and their persuasion is ineffective. This suggests that their cause is doomed because there is no mutual trust or ability to compromise.)*

BUILDING ENGLISH PROFICIENCY

ESL LEP ELD SAE LD

Keeping Track of Story Details

Scene 3 reveals that the conspirators' relationship has not fared well since Caesar's assassination. Help students become aware of how far the relationship has deteriorated.

1. Have students jot down the details of the argument between Brutus and Cassius, using a graphic organizer such as the one shown.

2. Point out that a deteriorating relationship often is marked by petty bickering. You may wish to have students use completed charts to discuss how well Shakespeare understood his characters in this regard.

Deteriorating Relationship
Brutus thinks some of Cassius's actions should be "undone."
Cassius thinks Brutus is wronging him behind his back.

19 Reading/Thinking Skills
Summarize

Possible response Brutus mentions his own honesty, his inability to raise money to pay his army, and his resentment at Cassius's refusal to send him the money he needed.

20 Reader's Response
Making Personal Connections

Questions Cassius says, "A friend should bear his friend's infirmities."

- What does he mean? *(A true friend will put up with another friend's weaknesses. Cassius implies that Brutus not only fails to do this, but makes them "greater than they are.")*
- How do you expect your friends to react to your weaknesses? How do you react to their weaknesses? *(Students will probably mention tolerance and patience. They may also suggest working together to correct weaknesses.)*

For certain sums of gold, which you denied me;
For I can raise no money by vile means.
By heaven, I had rather coin my heart
And drop my blood for drachmas than to wring
From the hard hands of peasants their vile trash
By any indirection. I did send
To you for gold to pay my legions,
Which you denied me. Was that done like Cassius?
Should I have answered Caius Cassius so?
When Marcus Brutus grows so covetous
To lock such rascal counters from his friends,
Be ready, gods, with all your thunderbolts;
Dash him to pieces!

CASSIUS. I denied you not.

BRUTUS. You did.

CASSIUS. I did not. He was but a fool
20 That brought my answer back. Brutus hath rived my heart.
A friend should bear his friend's infirmities,
But Brutus makes mine greater than they are.

BRUTUS. I do not, till you practice them on me.

CASSIUS. You love me not.

BRUTUS. I do not like your faults.

CASSIUS. A friendly eye could never see such faults.

BRUTUS. A flatterer's would not, though they do appear
As huge as high Olympus.

CASSIUS. Come, Antony, and young Octavius, come,
Revenge yourselves alone on Cassius;
For Cassius is aweary of the world,
Hated by one he loves, braved by his brother,
Checked like a bondman, all his faults observed,
Set in a notebook, learned and conned by rote
To cast into my teeth. O, I could weep
My spirit from mine eyes! There is my dagger,
(offering his unsheathed dagger)
And here my naked breast; within, a heart
Dearer than Pluto's mine, richer than gold.
If that thou be'st a Roman, take it forth.
I, that denied thee gold, will give my heart.
Strike, as thou didst at Caesar; for I know,
When thou didst hate him worst, thou loved'st him better
Than ever thou loved'st Cassius.

BRUTUS. Sheathe your dagger.
Be angry when you will, it shall have scope;
Do what you will, dishonor shall be humor.
O Cassius, you are yokèd with a lamb

76 indirection, devious or unjust means.

80 covetous, desiring things that belong to others.

81 rascal counters, worthless coins.

19 ■ What subjects does Brutus touch on in lines 66–83?

85 rived, split; broken.

97 checked, rebuked.

98 conned by rote, memorized until letter-perfect.

102 Pluto's mine. Pluto, the god of the underworld, is here confused with Plutus, the Greek god of riches.

109 dishonor shall be humor, that is, I'll regard your corruption as something to be humored.

MINI-LESSON: GRAMMAR
Noun and Pronoun Forms—Relative Pronouns

Teach Read these lines:

- I did send to you for gold to pay my legions,
  Which you denied me.
- I, *that* denied thee gold, will give my heart.

Point out that the words *which* and *that* are relative pronouns. A relative pronoun introduces an adjective clause and relates it to the word or words that the clause modifies. The relative pronouns are *that, which, who, whom,* and *whose.* Explain that in modern English we do not commonly use the relative pronoun *that* to refer to a person, as Shakespeare does in the second example. Instead, we would say, "I, *who* denied thee gold, will give my heart."

Make sure students can distinguish between a relative pronoun and a demonstrative pronoun. The first *that* in the following sentence is a demonstrative pronoun; the second *that* is a relative pronoun: *That* is the man *that* I described.

Activity Idea Have students find the relative pronouns in Brutus's speech, lines 110–113. *(that, who)*

That carries anger as the flint bears fire,
Who, much enforcèd, shows a hasty spark
And straight is cold again.
CASSIUS. Hath Cassius lived
To be but mirth and laughter to his Brutus
When grief and blood ill-tempered vexeth him?
BRUTUS. When I spoke that, I was ill-tempered too.
CASSIUS. Do you confess so much? Give me your hand.
BRUTUS. And my heart too. *(They embrace.)*
CASSIUS. O Brutus!
BRUTUS. What's the matter?
CASSIUS. Have not you love enough to bear with me,
When that rash humor which my mother gave me
Makes me forgetful?
BRUTUS. Yes, Cassius, and from henceforth,
When you are overearnest with your Brutus,
He'll think your mother chides, and leave you so.
(A POET *enters, followed by* LUCIUS, TITINIUS, *and* LUCILIUS.)
POET. Let me go in to see the generals!
There is some grudge between 'em; 'tis not meet
They be alone.
LUCILIUS. You shall not come to them.
POET. Nothing but death shall stay me.
CASSIUS. How now? What's the matter?
POET. For shame, you generals! What do you mean?
Love and be friends, as two such men should be;
For I have seen more years, I'm sure, than ye.
CASSIUS. Ha, ha, how vilely doth this cynic rhyme!
BRUTUS. Get you hence, sirrah. Saucy fellow, hence!
CASSIUS. Bear with him, Brutus. 'Tis his fashion.
BRUTUS. I'll know his humor when he knows his time.
What should the wars do with these jigging fools?
Companion, hence!
CASSIUS. Away, away, begone!
(POET *exits.*)
BRUTUS. Lucilius and Titinius, bid the commanders
Prepare to lodge their companies tonight.
CASSIUS. And come yourselves, and bring Messala with you
Immediately to us. (LUCILIUS *and* TITINIUS *exit.*)
BRUTUS *(to* LUCIUS *within).* Lucius, a bowl of wine.
CASSIUS. I did not think you could have been so angry.
BRUTUS. O Cassius, I am sick of many griefs.
CASSIUS. Of your philosophy you make no use
If you give place to accidental evils.
BRUTUS. No man bears sorrow better. Portia is dead.

21 ■ How does Cassius manage to sidestep responsibility for his behavior?

123 leave you so, let it go at that.

135 I'll know his humor . . . time. I'll indulge his eccentric behavior when he knows the proper time for it.

22 ■ What question would you like to ask Shakespeare about this short episode with the poet?

24 **144 Of your philosophy . . . use.** Brutus was a Stoic (stō′ik). Believers in this philosophy thought that people should rise above emotional upsets and be unmoved by any of life's happenings.

21 Reading/Thinking Skills
Clarify

Response He claims that his ill temper is due to his inherited nature.

22 Reading/Thinking Skills
Question

Response Possible questions: Why did you include this episode? Is this scene supposed to provide comic relief? Does this fight require a mediator?

23 Literary Criticism
Why the Poet?

Some critics find no reason for the scene with the poet. Others find that it provides comic relief, or at least a respite from the emotional intensity of the argument and Brutus's forthcoming announcement of Portia's death.

24 Historical Note
Cynics/Stoics

The Cynics were ancient Greek philosophers who considered virtue the sole good and self-control the means to achieve virtue. Stoicism was a Greek school of philosophy founded by Zeno around 308 B.C. Stoics believed that people should free themselves from passion and accept all occurrences calmly as the result of divine will or the natural order.

BUILDING ENGLISH PROFICIENCY

Making Personal Connections

Although the argument portrayed on pages 741–743 occurs between two political powers on a battlefield, students should be able to relate it to disagreements they have had with friends. Point out that the elements in this argument—accusations, misunderstandings, self-pity, denial, threats, excuses, declarations, reconciliation—are common to most arguments.

1. Invite students to think about arguments that they have had that share some of the elements of the disagreement between Brutus and Cassius.

2. Ask students if they think an unbiased third party can be effective in settling a dispute between two people, or if those two people themselves must settle their own dispute.

3. Have volunteers enact lines 66–123. Encourage them to demonstrate the different tones of voice that the characters may have used and to explain how Brutus and Cassius eventually reconcile.

25 Reading/Thinking Skills
Connect

Response Lines 300–302, in which Portia describes the wound she inflicted in her thigh to prove her constancy to Brutus.

26 Literary Element
Characterization

Questions

- How do the reactions of Cassius and Brutus differ? *(Brutus is trying to suppress his feelings in accordance with his philosophy and doesn't want Cassius to further agitate him, but Cassius is deeply moved.)*
- Consider Cassius's behavior in this scene. Does he seem to fit Caesar's appraisal as someone who is cold, jealous, mistrustful, and potentially dangerous? Explain. *(He seems very attached to Brutus and Portia, kind and forgiving with the poet and with Brutus, and more concerned with personal relationships than with politics. He shows none of the signs of jealousy, ambition, or pettiness of which Caesar accused him.)*

CASSIUS. Ha? Portia?
BRUTUS. She is dead.
CASSIUS. How scaped I killing when I crossed you so?
O insupportable and touching loss!
Upon what sickness?
BRUTUS. Impatient of my absence,
And grief that young Octavius with Mark Antony
Have made themselves so strong—for with her death
That tidings came—with this she fell distract
And, her attendants absent, swallowed fire.
CASSIUS. And died so?
BRUTUS. Even so.
CASSIUS. O ye immortal gods!
(LUCIUS *pours a bowl of wine for* CASSIUS. *As he does,* BRUTUS *greets* TITINIUS, *who has reentered at left.* TITINIUS *is accompanied by* MESSALA, *a friend of* BRUTUS.)
BRUTUS. Speak no more of her. Give me a bowl of wine.
In this I bury all unkindness, Cassius. *(Drinks.)*
CASSIUS. My heart is thirsty for that noble pledge.
Fill, Lucius, till the wine o'erswell the cup;
I cannot drink too much of Brutus's love.
(He drinks. LUCIUS *exits.)*
(TITINIUS *and* MESALA *enter.)*
BRUTUS. Come in, Titinius. Welcome, good Messala.
Now sit we close about this taper here
And call in question our necessities. *(They sit.)*
26 CASSIUS. Portia, art thou gone?
BRUTUS. No more, I pray you.
Messala, I have here receivèd letters
That young Octavius and Mark Antony
Come down upon us with a mighty power,
Bending their expedition toward Philippi.
(He shows letters.)
MESSALA. Myself have letters of the selfsame tenor.
BRUTUS. With what addition?
MESSALA. That by proscription and bills of outlawry
Octavius, Antony, and Lepidus
Have put to death an hundred senators.
BRUTUS. Therein our letters do not well agree;
Mine speak of seventy senators that died
By their proscriptions, Cicero being one.
CASSIUS. Cicero one?
MESSALA. Cicero is dead,
And by that order of proscription.
Had you your letters from your wife, my lord?

150 insupportable, unbearable; intolerable.

155 swallowed fire. According to Plutarch, Portia "took hot burning coals and cast them in her mouth, and kept her mouth so close that she choked herself."
■ Which of her lines in act two, scene 1 foreshadow Portia's ability to bring about such a painful death?

164 call in question our necessities, discuss our problems.

169 Philippi (fə lip′ī), a city in ancient Macedonia, now part of Greece.
170 of the selfsame tenor, bearing the same tidings.
172 bills of outlawry, public notices declaring certain persons no longer protected by Roman law. As enemies of the state they could be killed.

BRUTUS. No, Messala.
MESSALA. Nor nothing in your letters writ of her?
BRUTUS. Nothing, Messala.
MESSALA. That, methinks, is strange.
BRUTUS. Why ask you? Hear you aught of her in yours?
MESSALA. No, my lord.
BRUTUS. Now, as you are a Roman, tell me true.
MESSALA. Then like a Roman bear the truth I tell,
For certain she is dead, and by strange manner.
BRUTUS. Why, farewell, Portia. We must die, Messala.
With meditating that she must die once,
I have the patience to endure it now.
MESSALA. Even so great men great losses should endure.
CASSIUS. I have as much of this in art as you,
But yet my nature could not bear it so.
BRUTUS. Well, to our work alive. What do you think
Of marching to Philippi presently?
CASSIUS. I do not think it good.
BRUTUS. Your reason?
CASSIUS. This it is:
'Tis better that the enemy seek us.
So shall he waste his means, weary his soldiers,
Doing himself offense, whilst we, lying still,
Are full of rest, defense, and nimbleness.
BRUTUS. Good reasons must of force give place to better.
The people twixt Philippi and this ground
Do stand but in a forced affection,
For they have grudged us contribution.
The enemy, marching along by them,
By them shall make a fuller number up,
Come on refreshed, new-added, and encouraged;
From which advantage shall we cut him off
If at Philippi we do face him there,
These people at our back.
CASSIUS. Hear me, good brother—
BRUTUS. Under your pardon. You must note besides
That we have tried the utmost of our friends;
Our legions are brim full, our cause is ripe.
The enemy increaseth every day;
We, at the height, are ready to decline.
29 There is a tide in the affairs of men
Which, taken at the flood, leads on to fortune;
Omitted, all the voyage of their life
Is bound in shallows and in miseries.
On such a full sea are we now afloat,

27 ■ Some scholars think this retelling of the news of Portia's death was the episode Shakespeare actually wanted to use in the play, but that he forgot to take out the earlier episode dealing with it. Others argue that the earlier episode provides a perfect reason for Brutus's uncharacteristic emotional tirade and that he shows his stoicism as he listens to Messala bring up the subject again.

193 art, that is, the acquired wisdom of stoical fortitude.

196 presently, immediately.

208 new-added, reinforced.

28 ■ In lines 202–223. Brutus persuades the others to go to Philippi. What do you predict will happen to his and Cassius's forces? Why?

27 Reader's Response
Challenging the Text

Question How would you handle the discrepancy between these two accounts if you were the director of a production? *(Possible responses: Students may choose to cut one or the other discussion of Portia's death; they may also think that the two scenes show Brutus's private and public reaction and choose to keep them both.)*

28 Reading/Thinking Skills
Predict

Response If there is consistency in Brutus's judgments, things will go badly, as have all situations in which he has overruled Cassius.

29 Literary Element
Extended Metaphor

This is one of many extended metaphors in this play.

Question What is being compared? *(Life is compared to a voyage. Brutus and Cassius must act now, taking advantage of their power—high tide—striking when their army is at its peak. Immediate action will let them "take the current" to their advantage.*

BUILDING ENGLISH PROFICIENCY

ESL LEP ELD SAE LD

Examining Connotations

Write the word *Roman* on the board. Point out that when Messala tells Brutus of Portia's death, he says to bear it "like a Roman." Ask: What does he mean? Help students see that in the dozens of references to Romans throughout the play, the label acquires many positive connotations. Review that connotations are personal associations people have for a word, as opposed to its *denotations,* or dictionary meanings.

Activity Ideas

- Have students examine the uses of the word *Roman* in this play. (Previously, Cassius says that Casca lacks the "sparks of life" that should be in a Roman and bids the conspirators to show themselves "true Romans." Brutus speaks of valiant Romans, and Antony calls the dead Brutus at the end of the play, "the noblest Roman of them all.")
- Invite students to make a connotations web for *Roman.*

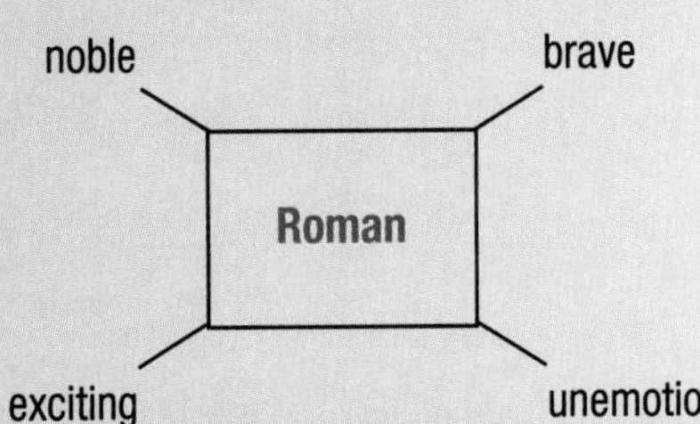

30 Reading/Thinking Skills
Draw Conclusions

Question Every time Cassius and Brutus have seen things differently, Cassius has been right. Yet, Cassius does not oppose Brutus's judgment here. Why? *(Possible responses: Their recent misunderstanding is too fresh in his mind; he is disturbed by Portia's death, and not up to arguing; he does not want to fight Brutus for the leadership of the armies; he thinks dissension would be bad for morale.)*

31 Historical Note
Anachronism

You may wish to point out that this is an anachronistic detail: Brutus would have had a papyrus scroll, not a book.

And we must take the current when it serves
Or lose our ventures.
30 **CASSIUS.** Then, with your will, go on.
We'll along ourselves and meet them at Philippi.
BRUTUS. The deep of night is crept upon our talk,
And nature must obey necessity,
Which we will niggard with a little rest.
There is no more to say.
CASSIUS. No more. Good night.
Early tomorrow will we rise and hence.
BRUTUS. Lucius! (LUCIUS *enters.*) My gown. (LUCIUS *exits.*)
Farewell, good Messala.
Good night, Titinius. Noble, noble Cassius,
Good night and good repose.
CASSIUS. Oh my dear brother!
This was an ill beginning of the night.
Never come such division 'tween our souls!
Let it not, Brutus.
(LUCIUS *enters with the gown.*)
BRUTUS. Everything is well.
CASSIUS. Good night, my lord.
BRUTUS. Good night, good brother.
TITINIUS, MESSALA. Good night, Lord Brutus.
BRUTUS. Farewell, everyone.
(CASSIUS, TITINIUS *and* MESSALA *exit right.* LUCIUS *unfolds his master's night robe.*)
Give me the gown. Where is thy instrument?
LUCIUS. Here in the tent.
BRUTUS. What, thou speak'st drowsily?
Poor knave, I blame thee not; thou art o'erwatched.
Call Claudius and some other of my men;
I'll have them sleep on cushions in my tent.
LUCIUS. Varro and Claudius!
(VARRO *and* CLAUDIUS *enter at left and cross toward* BRUTUS.)
VARRO. Calls my lord?
BRUTUS. I pray you, sirs, lie in my tent and sleep.
It may be I shall raise you by and by
On business to my brother Cassius.
VARRO. So please you, we will stand and watch your pleasure.
BRUTUS. I will not have it so. Lie down, good sirs.
It may be I shall otherwise bethink me.
(VARRO *and* CLAUDIUS *lie down.*)
31 Look, Lucius, here's the book I sought for so;
I put it in the pocket of my gown.
LUCIUS. I was sure your lordship did not give it me.

227 we will niggard, we will satisfy somewhat.

241 thy instrument, your lute.

243 Poor knave . . . o'erwatched, Poor lad, I don't blame you; you are exhausted.

MINI-LESSON: GRAMMAR
Sentence Fragments

Teach Read the following line from page 746:

Lucius! My gown.

Point out that both of these utterances are sentence fragments. Explain that often in literary works, we expect the formal rules of grammar to be followed. But since this work is meant to be performed, Shakespeare wrote colloquially, rather than in literary style. It is clear that Brutus meant: "Come here, Lucius. Fetch me my gown." But Brutus was noted for his "clipped style" and would likely have used as few words as possible.

Activity Idea Have students search for other instances of sentence fragments that add to the sense of colloquial speech. Invite them to fill in the missing parts to make them complete sentences.

Flemish artist Peter Paul Rubens (1577–1640) painted this bust of Julius Caesar wearing a crown of olive leaves. Does this representation show a Caesar with the weaknesses Cassius describes or the Caesar who conquered Gaul?

BRUTUS. Bear with me, good boy, I am much forgetful.
Canst thou hold up thy heavy eyes awhile
And touch thy instrument a strain or two?
LUCIUS. Ay, my lord, an 't please you.
BRUTUS. It does, my boy.
I trouble thee too much, but thou art willing.
LUCIUS. It is my duty, sir.
BRUTUS. I should not urge thy duty past thy might;
I know young bloods look for a time of rest.
LUCIUS. I have slept, my lord, already.
33 **BRUTUS.** It was well done, and thou shalt sleep again;
I will not hold thee long. If I do live,
I will be good to thee.
(*Music, and a song.* LUCIUS *falls asleep.*)
This is a sleepy tune. O murderous slumber,
Layest thou thy leaden mace upon my boy,
That plays thee music? Gentle knave, good night;
I will not do thee so much wrong to wake thee.
If thou dost nod, thou break'st thy instrument;

32 **260 an 't,** if it.
■ Do you think a modern general would calm himself before a battle by reading or listening to music?

270 thy leaden mace. Morpheus (môr′phē əs), the Greek god of dreams, carried a leaden club, or mace, with which he cast the spell of slumber.

Responses to Caption Question
Possible responses: Some viewers will say it shows a man who is keen-eyed, strong-willed, decisive, and very much in control—the man who conquered Gaul. Other viewers might think this picture suggests a man who is arrogant, cruel, and ambitious, thus justifying Cassius's appraisal.

32 Reader's Response
Making Personal Connections

Response It would depend. General Patton, for example, did keep a book by his bedside. Some modern military leaders would be more inclined to pursue less intellectual diversions.

33 Literary Element
Foreshadowing

Brutus acknowledges in this speech that the end may be near.

BUILDING ENGLISH PROFICIENCY

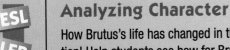

Analyzing Character

How Brutus's life has changed in the year since Caesar's assassination! Help students see how far Brutus's fortunes have fallen by constructing a t-chart that contrasts Brutus's life before the murder at this point. (You may wish students to reread earlier scenes in which Brutus appears.)

Brutus then	Brutus now
one of Rome's most respected citizens	conspirator on the run
good home	wife is dead
loving wife	

34 Reading/Thinking Skills
Evaluate

Possible responses I'd think he'd be more frightened; yes, his stoicism has helped him stay in control.

35 Geographical Note
Philippi

Philippi, a city in ancient Macedonia, is now part of Greece. Show on an ancient map the route the army is taking.

36 Reader's Response
Making Personal Connections

Question Ghosts in literature are sometimes understood to be hallucinations, sometimes actual beings. How do you interpret this ghost? Why? *(Students should base opinions on their knowledge of other Shakespearean plays, or on the context in this play. Some students may feel the revenge motif is stronger if the ghost is a physical being.)*

37 Multicultural Note
Ghosts

Explain that Shakespeare's audience believed that ghosts were visible only to those by whom they wished to be seen.

Check Test

1. Who ruled Rome with Antony and Octavius? *(Lepidus)*
2. How does Portia die? *(She commits suicide by swallowing fire.)*
3. What did Brutus request for his legions that Cassius refused? *(gold)*
4. Who appears to Brutus through a trap door? *(Caesar's ghost)*
5. Where are the armies of Brutus and Cassius headed at the end of the act? *(Philippi)*

Unit 6 Resource Book
Alternate Check Test, p. 29

I'll take it from thee. And, good boy, good night.
(He removes LUCIUS*'s instrument, and begins to read.)*
Let me see, let me see; is not the leaf turned down
Where I left reading? Here it is, I think.
(The GHOST OF CAESAR *slowly ascends through an upstage trap door.)*
How ill this taper burns! Ha! Who comes here?
I think it is the weakness of mine eyes
That shapes this monstrous apparition.
It comes upon me. Art thou any thing?
Art thou some god, some angel, or some devil,
That mak'st my blood cold and my hair to stare?
Speak to me what thou art.
GHOST. Thy evil spirit, Brutus.
BRUTUS. Why com'st thou?
35 **GHOST.** To tell thee thou shalt see me at Philippi.
BRUTUS. Well; then I shall see thee again?
36 **GHOST.** Ay, at Philippi.
BRUTUS. Why, I will see thee at Philippi, then. (GHOST *exits.*)
Now I have taken heart, thou vanishest.
Ill spirit, I would hold more talk with thee.
Boy, Lucius! Varro! Claudius! Sirs, awake!
Claudius!
LUCIUS. The strings, my lord, are false.
BRUTUS. He thinks he still is at his instrument.
Lucius, awake!
LUCIUS. My lord?
BRUTUS. Didst thou dream, Lucius, that thou so criedst out?
LUCIUS. My lord, I do not know that I did cry.
BRUTUS. Yes, that thou didst. Didst thou see anything?
LUCIUS. Nothing, my lord.
BRUTUS. Sleep again, Lucius. Sirrah Claudius!
(*To* VARRO.) Fellow thou, awake!
VARRO. My lord?
(They get up.)
CLAUDIUS. My lord?
BRUTUS. Why did you so cry out, sirs, in your sleep?
VARRO, CLAUDIUS. Did we, my lord?
37 **BRUTUS.** Ay. Saw you anything?
VARRO. No, my lord, I saw nothing.
CLAUDIUS. Nor I, my lord.
BRUTUS. Go and commend me to my brother Cassius.
Bid him set on his powers betimes before,
And we will follow.
VARRO, CLAUDIUS. It shall be done, my lord.
(VARRO *and* CLAUDIUS *exit at right, leaving* BRUTUS *and* LUCIUS *on stage.*)

275 the leaf turned down, an anachronism. Roman books were in the form of scrolls; there were no pages to turn down.

34 ■ Do you think Brutus has responded appropriately to the ghost? Why or why not?

292 false, out of tune.

306 set on . . . before, advance his troops early in the morning, before me.

MINI-LESSON: GRAMMAR
Homonyms and Homophones

Teach Write this sentence on the board:

Art thou some god . . . That mak'st my blood cold and my hair to stare?

Question What are homonyms for each of the last three words in the preceding sentence? *(hare, too, two, stair)*

Activity Ideas

- Have small groups list as many homonyms as they can find on page 747. *(bear, two, you, too, not, past, know, done, do, night)* When their lists are complete, have them compare lists with other groups and explain the homonyms.
- Invite students to compose original sentences that contain at least three homonyms.

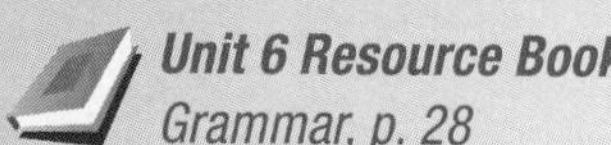

Act 4

After Reading

Making Connections

Shaping Your Response

1. Do you find Antony ruthless? Why or why not?
2. Why do you think Shakespeare includes the report of Portia's death?
3. Given their actions so far, where would you place Mark Antony, Brutus, and Cassius on the following scale of morality?

immoral —————————— **moral**

Analyzing the Play

4. When Cassius first arrives outside Brutus's tent, is the conduct of each man consistent with what you have learned of his **character**? Explain.
5. What do the events in scenes 1 and 2 **foreshadow** about the future of the triumvirate? of Brutus and Cassius?
6. In scene 3, lines 43–51, what is **ironic** about Brutus's accusation that Cassius is bad-tempered?
7. What undesirable traits does Brutus reveal during his argument with Cassius?
8. What do you think the appearance of Caesar's ghost might **foreshadow**?

Extending the Ideas

9. *Julius Caesar* is very much a play about politics. Do you think world political leaders today are motivated mostly by a desire for power, a desire to make government better, or something else? Explain.
10. If Brutus, Antony, Cassius, Caesar, Cicero, Portia, and Calpurnia were in the United States government today, what posts would each seem best suited for? (Consider positions in all three branches of government.)

Expressing Your Ideas

Writing Choice

Spirits on Stage This is only one of several plays in which Shakespeare included ghosts. Explain why you think he included this supernatural element. Then describe what special effects a director could use to make the ghost's appearance a dramatic feature of the play. Write several paragraphs that could appear in a **stage bill.**

After Reading

MAKING CONNECTIONS

1. Most students will think Antony is ruthless, based on the first scene.

2. Possible responses: It explains Brutus's behavior; demonstrates his stoicism, and adds to the falling action.

3. Possible responses: Mark Antony will do anything to gain his end—he's completely immoral; Cassius is true to Brutus but seems greedy, so he goes in the middle. Brutus is consistently moral and should be at the far right.

4. Cassuis's acquiescence and unease confirm his love of Brutus. Brutus displays characteristic calm.

5. Scene 1: the expulsion from the triumvirate of Lepidus and a power struggle between Octavius and Antony. Scene 2: the demise of the republicans' cause.

6. Brutus is himself bad-tempered.

7. Possible responses: childishness, self-righteousness, quick temper, inappropriate behavior, lack of forethought

8. Possible response: his revenge

9. Students may refer to current scandals in world and national politics as indications of the continuing desire for and abuse of power. Conversely, they may cite the humanitarian efforts of leaders such as former U.S. President Jimmy Carter.

10. Possible answers: Brutus as a Supreme Court justice; Antony as Secretary of State; Caesar as President (Calpurnia as First Lady); Cassius as National Security Adviser; Cicero as Press Secretary; Portia as Secretary of Health

Unit 6 Resource Book
Vocabulary, p. 27
Vocabulary Test, p. 30

WRITING CHOICE

Spirits on Stage

Remind students to first think of some special effects—an entrance through a trap door or from above on invisible cables, billowing smoke, eerie sounds projected throughout the theater, and so on. Then have them cast descriptions of these special effects the way a stage bill might. For example, "The technical brilliance of the production. . . ." or "This is no ordinary ghost, as viewers will learn when they see. . . ."

Selection Test

Unit 6 Resource Book
pp. 31–32

During Reading

Theme Link

By the end of the play, the cost of winning is clear. The price can be loved ones, reputation, even life itself.

Vocabulary Preview

consort, accompany
demeanor, behavior; manner
disconsolate, without hope; unhappy
fawn, try to get favor or notice by slavish acts
misconstrue, misunderstand; misinterpret
presage, predict

Students can add the words and definitions to their Writer's Notebooks.

Have students discuss under what circumstances Antony might have made this gesture. *(Possible response: in giving the command to his troops to attack the enemy)*

Question Do you think this victorious stance foretells the outcome of the play? *(If students know the outcome of the play, they will say, yes. Otherwise, there is no definitive information provided at this point to assure his victory, although students might want to speculate about the outcome.)*

Unit 6 Resource Book
Graphic Organizer, p. 33
Study Guide, p. 34

SELECTION SUMMARY

Julius Caesar, Act 5

Scene 1: Octavius and Antony argue with Brutus and Cassius. Brutus and Cassius discuss suicide, and bid farewell, lest they not meet again.

Scene 2: Brutus plans to attack Octavius's army, and Cassius is to attack Antony's.

Scene 3: Brutus's army attacks but does not support Cassius's troops. Cassius sends Titinius to investigate oncoming horsemen, who are actually Brutus's troops. But due to a miscommunication, Cassius despairs and orders Pindarus to kill him. Titinius returns and kills himself.

Scene 4: Lucilius is captured, pretending he is Brutus to gain his leader more time.

Scene 5: Brutus realizes defeat is inevitable. At the approach of Antony's and Octavius's forces, Brutus asks his slave Strato to hold his sword so he can run on it. His last thoughts are that Caesar is avenged. Antony praises Brutus as the "noblest Roman of them all."

*For summaries in other languages, see the **Building English Proficiency** book.*

ACT FIVE

SCENE 1

Summary *The opposing generals meet and exchange taunts and insults. Antony and Octavius return to their armies. To Messala, Cassius reveals that this is his birthday, and that he is concerned about some bad omens. Cassius and Brutus bid farewell to one another. Cassius vows suicide rather than be captured. Brutus seems to reject the idea of suicide.*

The plains of Philippi. Early morning, the day of the battle. Offstage battle sounds. OCTAVIUS *enters, followed by* ANTONY *and a few* OFFICERS.

OCTAVIUS. Now, Antony, our hopes are answerèd.
You said the enemy would not come down,
But keep the hills and upper regions.
It proves not so. Their battles are at hand;
They mean to warn us at Philippi here,
Answering before we do demand of them.
ANTONY. Tut, I am in their bosoms, and I know
Wherefore they do it. They could be content
To visit other places, and come down
With fearful bravery, thinking by this face
1 To fasten in our thoughts that they have courage;
But 'tis not so.
(A MESSENGER *enters.)*
MESSENGER. Prepare you, generals.
The enemy comes on in gallant show.
Their bloody sign of battle is hung out,
And something to be done immediately.
ANTONY. Octavius, lead your battle softly on
Upon the left hand of the even field.
OCTAVIUS. Upon the right hand, I. Keep thou the left.
ANTONY. Why do you cross me in this exigent?
OCTAVIUS. I do not cross you, but I will do so.
(Drum. BRUTUS, CASSIUS, *and their army enter;* LUCILIUS, TITINIUS, MESSALA, *and others enter.)*
BRUTUS. They stand and would have parley.
CASSIUS. Stand fast, Titinius. We must out and talk.
OCTAVIUS. Mark Antony, shall we give sign of battle?
ANTONY. No, Caesar, we will answer on their charge.
Make forth. The generals would have some words.
OCTAVIUS *(to his officers).* Stir not until the signal.
(The two sides advance toward one another.)
BRUTUS. Words before blows. Is it so, countrymen?
OCTAVIUS. Not that we love words better, as you do.

4 battles, armies.
5 warn, challenge.
7 bosoms, secret councils.
8-9 They could . . . places, they would prefer to be elsewhere.
14 bloody sign, red flag.
19 exigent (ek′sə jənt), *n.* critical moment.
2 ■ How has the relationship between Antony and Octavius changed since act 4, scene 1?
24 answer . . . charge, respond when they attack us. Notice that Antony is addressing Octavius by the title Caesar.
25 Make forth, march forward.

1 Reading/Thinking Skills
Evaluate

Possible response The balance of power has shifted to Octavius: In the first instance Antony spoke and said that Octavius was wrong about how to deal with Lepidus, and Octavius gave in to him. Octavius speaks first and says that Antony was wrong in his prediction about how the enemy would behave, and rather than follow Antony's suggestion for the battle array, he insists on the opposite arrangement and warns Antony that he will cross him in the future.

2 Reading/Thinking Skills
Compare and Contrast

Question In act 4, Brutus and Cassius had a disagreement. In act 5, Antony and Octavius argue. Compare and contrast how the two pairs of men handle their differences. *(Possible responses: Cassius and Brutus argue in public and in private. Their argument is extended and childish, filled with bad-tempered one-upsmanship. Octavius and Antony argue about military strategy rather than personal differences and stop as soon as other people arrive, presenting a united front to their enemies. Their words to each other are mature and to the point.)*

BUILDING ENGLISH PROFICIENCY

Analyzing Loaded Words

The meeting of Brutus and Cassius with Antony and Octavius in scene 1 turns into a name-calling contest. Review the concept of loaded words—words with strong emotional appeal.

Activity Ideas

- Challenge students to make a list of loaded words and phrases that appear on page 752 and explain their connotations. Their list might include some of the following: *villains, vile daggers, hacked, fawned, damnèd, cur, flatterers, conspirators, avenged, slaughter, traitors, noblest, honorable, worthless, honor, masker, reveler.*
- Have volunteers deliver the speeches on page 752, using appropriate intonation for the loaded words.

3 Literary Element
Figurative Language

Point out that Shakespeare often uses figures of speech comparing humans to insects and animals.

Question What are the similarities he implies between people and bees? apes? dogs? *(Possible responses: Those who speak sweetly while doing harm are like bees, who produce honey, yet sting; hypocrites grin like apes and grovel like dogs, as they do damage.)*

4 Reading/Thinking Skills
Clarify

Response If the conspirators had killed Antony along with Caesar, as Cassius had wanted, Antony would not now be insulting them.

5 Reading/Thinking Skills
Draw Conclusions

Question What does Brutus mean? *(His men are not traitors, as Octavius has suggested. He still believes in the rightness of killing Caesar.)*

6 Literary Element
Sound Devices

Point out the repeated sounds in this line: *w*, *b*, and *sw*. Help students understand how these sounds suggest wind and a violent storm.

BRUTUS. Good words are better than bad strokes, Octavius.
ANTONY. In your bad strokes, Brutus, you give good words.
Witness the hole you made in Caesar's heart,
Crying "Long live! Hail, Caesar!"
CASSIUS. Antony,
The posture of your blows are yet unknown;
But for your words, they rob the Hybla bees,
And leave them honeyless.
ANTONY. Not stingless too?
BRUTUS. O, yes, and soundless too.
For you have stolen their buzzing, Antony,
And very wisely threat before you sting.
ANTONY. Villains! You did not so when your vile daggers
Hacked one another in the sides of Caesar.
You showed your teeth like apes, and fawned like hounds,
And bowed like bondmen, kissing Caesar's feet,
Whilst damnèd Casca, like a cur, behind,
Struck Caesar on the neck. O you flatterers!
CASSIUS. Flatterers? Now, Brutus, thank yourself!
This tongue had not offended so today
If Cassius might have ruled.
OCTAVIUS. Come, come, the cause. If arguing make us sweat,
The proof of it will turn to redder drops.
Look, *(He draws.)*
I draw a sword against conspirators.
When think you that the sword goes up again?
Never, till Caesar's three-and-thirty wounds
Be well avenged, or till another Caesar
Have added slaughter to the sword of traitors.
BRUTUS. Caesar, thou canst not die by traitors' hands,
Unless thou bring'st them with thee.
OCTAVIUS. So I hope.
I was not born to die on Brutus's sword.
BRUTUS. O, if thou wert the noblest of thy strain,
Young man, thou couldst not die more honorable.
CASSIUS. A peevish schoolboy, worthless of such honor,
Joined with a masker and a reveler!
ANTONY. Old Cassius still.
OCTAVIUS. Come, Antony, away!
Defiance, traitors, hurl we in your teeth.
If you dare fight today, come to the field;
If not, when you have stomachs.
(OCTAVIUS, ANTONY, *and army exits.)*
CASSIUS. Why, now, blow wind, swell billow and swim bark!
The storm is up, and all is on the hazard.

34 Hybla (hī′blə) **bees**, bees from Hybla, an area in ancient Sicily famous for its honey.

40 You did not so, you did not give warning.

42 fawn (fôn), *v.* try to get favor or notice by slavish acts.

■ What is Cassius referring to in lines 46-48?

60 strain, lineage.

62 schoolboy . . . reveler. Octavius was nineteen at the time of Caesar's assassination; Antony was known as a playboy.

BRUTUS. Ho, Lucilius! Hark, a word with you.
LUCILIUS *(stands forth).* My lord?
(BRUTUS *and* LUCILIUS *converse apart.*)
CASSIUS. Messala!
MESSALA *(stands forth).* What says my general?
CASSIUS. Messala,
This is my birthday; as this very day
Was Cassius born. Give me thy hand, Messala.
Be thou my witness that against my will,
As Pompey was, am I compelled to set
Upon one battle all our liberties.
7 You know that I held Epicurus strong
And his opinion. Now I change my mind
And partly credit things that do presage.
8 Coming from Sardis, on our former ensign
Two mighty eagles fell, and there they perched,
Goring and feeding from our soldiers' hands,
Who to Philippi here consorted us.
This morning are they fled away and gone,
And in their steads do ravens, crows, and kites
Fly o'er our heads and downward look on us
As we were sickly prey. Their shadows seem
A canopy most fatal, under which
Our army lies, ready to give up the ghost.
MESSALA. Believe not so.
CASSIUS. I but believe it partly,
For I am fresh of spirit and resolved
To meet all perils very constantly.
BRUTUS. Even so, Lucilius. *(He rejoins* CASSIUS.*)*
CASSIUS. Now, most noble Brutus,
The gods today stand friendly, that we may,
Lovers in peace, lead on our days to age!
But since the affairs of men rest still incertain,
Let's reason with the worst that may befall.
If we do lose this battle, then is this
The very last time we shall speak together.
What are you then determinèd to do?
BRUTUS. Even by the rule of that philosophy
By which I did blame Cato for the death
Which he did give himself—I know not how,
But I do find it cowardly and vile,
For fear of what might fall, so to prevent
The time of life—arming myself with patience
To stay the providence of some high powers
That govern us below.

80 Epicurus (ep′ə kyůr′əs), Greek philosopher who did not believe in omens or superstitions.
82 presage (pri sāj′), *v.* predict.
83–84 on our former ensign . . . fell, on the foremost or forwardmost standard two eagles swooped down.
86 consort (kən sôrt′), *v.* accompany.

9 ■ What reasons does Cassius give for being pessimistic about the outcome of the battle?

96–98 Now . . . days to age! Cassius hopes that the gods will be on their side so the two will end their days as friends in peaceful times.

104–106 Even by . . . give himself. Stoicism, the philosophy Brutus follows, does not favor suicide; thus Brutus blames his father-in-law Cato for killing himself.
108–109 prevent the time of life, cut short one's own life by suicide.
110–111 to stay . . . below, to await (stay) a normal death to be sent when the gods so decree.

7 Historical Note
Epicurus

Epicurus (341–270 B.C.) was a Greek philosopher and the founder of Epicureanism. He taught that people should seek pleasure and avoid pain, and did not believe in the immortality of the soul or life after death.

8 Literary Element
Symbolism

Point out that traditionally an eagle represents power, while ravens, crows, and kites, which feed on dead flesh, indicate death and corruption.

9 Reading/Thinking Skills
Summarize

Possible response Cassius is uneasy about staking everything on one battle and about an omen—the departure of two eagles and the arrival of birds that are portents of disaster. Students may note the contrast with Cassius's attitude about the portents in act 1, scene 3, lines 45–52 and 57–78, and the sentiments expressed in lines 83–92 of this scene.

BUILDING ENGLISH PROFICIENCY

Analyzing Metaphor

In lines 34–39, Cassius and Brutus compare Antony to the Hybla bees through a metaphor. Extend the gloss note to help students grasp what is being compared in this figurative language (People can speak pleasant words [make honey] before committing deadly acts [sting].)

Activity Ideas

1. Review that a metaphor compares two unlike things without using words such as *like* or *as.* Offer an example such as "He's a bear until he's had coffee." Have students translate. (He's grouchy.)

2. Invite students to make up their own metaphors, using a comparison between an animal and a human with similar qualities.

10 Reading/Thinking Skills
Clarify

Possible response They have put their disagreement aside and courageously face danger, even death.

11 Reader's Response
Making Personal Connections

Questions

- What does Brutus assure Cassius in lines 114–116? *(that he will not be taken prisoner)*
- If you were going into battle and might not return, what would you say to a close friend? *(Students may want to answer in their notebooks.)*

12 Reading/Thinking Skills
Clarify

Possible response Brutus sees signs of faltering (cold demeanor) in Octavius's men and thinks one strong attack will overcome them. Therefore his message is probably that Cassius's forces should not attack Antony's and Brutus's will charge Octavius's troops.)

13 Historical Note
Sound Effects

This scene is played on the platform and the balcony. Heard throughout are drums, trumpets, the clash of arms, and shouts.

CASSIUS. Then, if we lose this battle,
You are contented to be led in triumph
Thorough the streets of Rome?
11 BRUTUS. No, Cassius, no. Think not, thou noble Roman,
That ever Brutus will go bound to Rome;
He bears too great a mind. But this same day
Must end that work the ides of March begun.
And whether we shall meet again I know not;
Therefore our everlasting farewell take.
Forever and forever farewell, Cassius!
If we do meet again, why, we shall smile;
If not, why then this parting was well made.
CASSIUS. Forever and forever farewell, Brutus!
If we do meet again, we'll smile indeed;
If not, 'tis true this parting was well made.
BRUTUS. Why, then, lead on. O, that a man might know
The end of this day's business ere it come!
But it sufficeth that the day will end,
And then the end is known. Come, ho, away!
(They exit.)

10 ■ Lines 94–125 show that Brutus and Cassius have set aside their earlier quarrel. What do the lines reveal about their characters in the face of danger?

SCENE 2

Summary *Brutus sends Messala with orders for Cassius.*

The field of battle. Mid-morning. Brutus and Messala enter at left.

BRUTUS. Ride, ride, Messala, ride, and give these bills
Unto the legions on the other side.
(He hands him written orders. Loud trumpets and drum beats.)
Let them set on at once; for I perceive
But cold demeanor in Octavio's wing,
And sudden push gives them the overthrow.
Ride, ride, Messala! Let them all come down.
(They exit separately.)

1 bills, orders.
2 side, wing; that is, Cassius's wing.
4 demeanor (di mē′nər), *n.* behavior; manner. Brutus sees signs of faltering in Octavius's men.
6 come down, come down from the hills where they have been awaiting the battle.

12 ■ What do you think is Brutus's message to Cassius?

SCENE 3

13 **Summary** *Cassius sends Titinius to find out whose troops he sees. When Pindarus mistakenly reports that Titinius has been captured, Cassius orders Pindarus to kill him. Titinius returns wearing a crown of victory. Finding Cassius dead, Titinius kills himself.*

A hill in another part of the battlefield. Mid-afternoon. Several SOLDIERS,

MINI-LESSON: LITERARY FOCUS
Plot

Teach Read aloud the first 46 lines of scene 3. Remind students that this scene contributes to the falling action in the following ways.

- It conveys Brutus's haste in attacking Octavius and his enabling Antony to encircle them. *(You may need to explain that by attacking Octavius and then plundering his camp, Brutus's soldiers left Cassius's troops unguarded, thus allowing them to be encircled by Antony's troops.)*
- It shows the misunderstanding that prompts Cassius's suicide.
- It gives a sense of the conspirators' desperate situation.

Activity Idea Have students search acts 4 and 5 for ways that Shakespeare indicates the falling action—both in plot development and in characterization.

weary from the fighting, enter at right and fall exhausted. As offstage trumpets sound, CASSIUS *and* TITINIUS *enter at right and climb to the top of the shorter of two hills.* CASSIUS, *carrying a broken standard, speaks angrily.*

14 **CASSIUS.** O, look, Titinius, look, the villains fly!
Myself have to mine own turned enemy.
This ensign here of mine was turning back;
I slew the coward and did take it from him.
TITINIUS. O Cassius, Brutus gave the word too early,
Who, having some advantage on Octavius,
Took it too eagerly. His soldiers fell to spoil,
Whilst we by Antony are all enclosed. (PINDARUS *enters.*) 15
PINDARUS. Fly further off, my lord, fly further off!
Mark Antony is in your tents, my lord.
Fly therefore, noble Cassius, fly far off.
CASSIUS. This hill is far enough. Look, look, Titinius.
Are those my tents where I perceive the fire?
TITINIUS. They are, my lord.
CASSIUS. Titinius, if thou lovest me,
Mount thou my horse, and hide thy spurs in him
Till he have brought thee up to yonder troops
And here again, that I may rest assured
Whether yond troops are friend or enemy.
TITINIUS. I will be here again even with a thought. (*Exits.*)
CASSIUS. Go, Pindarus, get higher on that hill.
My sight was ever thick. Regard Titinius,
And tell me what thou not'st about the field.
(Pointing to the higher hill.)
(PINDARUS *ascends the hill.)*
This day I breathèd first. Time is come round,
And where I did begin, there shall I end.
My life is run his compass. Sirrah, what news?
PINDARUS *(above).* O my lord!
CASSIUS. What news?
PINDARUS *(above).* Titinius is enclosed round about
With horsemen, that make to him on the spur,
Yet he spurs on. Now they are almost on him.
Now, Titinius! Now some light. O, he
16 Lights too. He's ta'en *(Shout.)* And hark! They shout for joy.
CASSIUS. Come down, behold no more.
O coward that I am, to live so long
To see my best friend ta'en before my face. (PINDARUS *descends and rejoins* CASSIUS.)
Come hither, sirrah.
In Parthia did I take thee prisoner,

1 the villains fly. Cassius's own troops are fleeing.
2–4 Myself . . . from him. Cassius killed one of his own men, a cowardly ensign, and took the standard (flag) he now holds.
7 fell to spoil, began looting Octavius's camp.
■ Is it Cassius's or Brutus's fault that Cassius's men have been encircled by Antony's forces? Explain.

17–18 that I may . . . enemy. Cassius wonders if the approaching horsemen belong to his or Brutus's army, or to Antony's.
19 even . . . thought, as quick as thought.
21 My sight . . . thick, my eyesight is imperfect, dim.
23–24 This day . . . end, I shall die on the same day I was born.

31 light, alight; dismount.

37 Parthia, an ancient country, now Iran.

14 Reading/Thinking Skills
Clarify

Question Explain the meaning of line 2. *(Possible response: It is as if I am the enemy to my own men who have turned tail and fled.)*

15 Reading/Thinking Skills
Evaluate

Response Brutus's fault—He was attacking Octavius, and as his soldiers looted, Cassius's troops were left unprotected.

16 Reading/Thinking Skills
Predict

Question What do you think has happened? *(Most students may say that Titinius has been captured by the enemy. Some may suggest that he is surrounded by friendly troops, which is what is actually happening.)*

BUILDING ENGLISH PROFICIENCY

Exploring Key Events

To help students understand the mistake that causes Cassius to commit suicide, suggest that they enact scene 3, lines 1–46.

1. Assign or let volunteers take the roles of Cassius, Titinius, and Pindarus.

2. Have students paraphrase lines 1–8 and consult the sidenotes to be sure that they understand what has happened so far in the battle.

3. Suggest that students diagram the setting, as described in lines 9–25. Below is one interpretation.

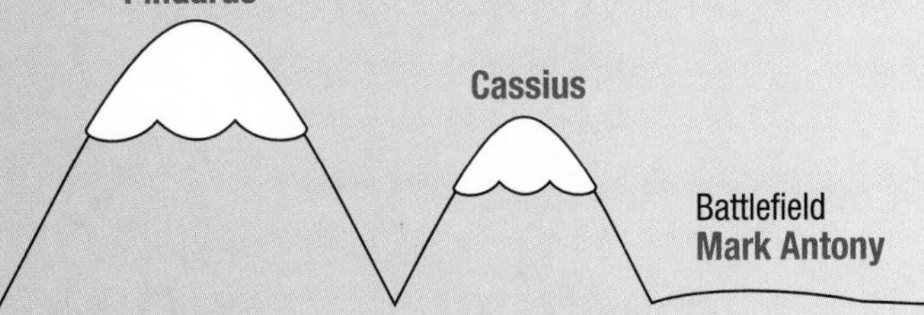

17 Literary Element
Irony

Question Explain the irony of this statement. *(Pindarus becomes free by carrying out an order to hold the sword for Cassius—an act that he is not free to refuse.)*

18 Literary Focus
Plot

Question In what way(s) is Caesar avenged? *(Possible responses: The man who was the force behind the conspiracy is dead, having killed himself on the sword with which he killed Caesar; the conspirators' goals have not been realized—there has not been a return to republican government—and now another Caesar, appointed by the first, is coming into power.)*

Art Study

Response to Caption Question
Perhaps they valued the individual spirit and felt obliged to preserve things for posterity.

19 Reading/Thinking Skills
Predict

Possible responses No, he is a Stoic, and he said he wouldn't. Yes, he vowed not to be taken prisoner.

And then I swore thee, saving of thy life,
That whatsoever I did bid thee do
17 Thou shouldst attempt it. Come now, keep thine oath;
Now be a freeman, and with this good sword,
That ran through Caesar's bowels, search this bosom.
Stand not to answer. Here, take thou the hilts,
And when my face is covered, as 'tis now,
Guide thou the sword. *(Pindarus does so.)* Caesar, thou
art revenged,
18 Even with the sword that killed thee.
(He dies.)
PINDARUS. So, I am free, yet would not so have been,
Durst I have done my will. O Cassius!
Far from this country Pindarus shall run,
Where never Roman shall take note of him.
(PINDARUS, leaving CASSIUS's sword behind, hastens left and exits. TITINIUS, with MESSALA, reenters at right. On his head TITINIUS wears a victory garland.)
MESSALA. It is but change, Titinius; for Octavius
Is overthrown by noble Brutus's power,
As Cassius's legions are by Antony.
TITINIUS. These tidings will well comfort Cassius.
MESSALA. Where did you leave him?
TITINIUS. All disconsolate,
With Pindarus his bondman, on this hill.
MESSALA. Is not that he that lies upon the ground?
TITINIUS. He lies not like the living. O my heart!
MESSALA. Is not that he?
TITINIUS. No, this was he, Messala,
But Cassius is no more. O setting sun,
As in thy red rays thou dost sink to night,
So in his red blood Cassius's day is set.
The sun of Rome is set. Our day is gone;
Clouds, dews, and dangers come; our deeds are done.
Mistrust of my success hath done this deed.
MESSALA. Mistrust of good success hath done this deed.
O hateful Error, Melancholy's child,
Why dost thou show to the apt thoughts of men
The things that are not? O Error, soon conceived,
Thou never com'st unto a happy birth,
But kill'st the mother that engendered thee.
TITINIUS. What, Pindarus! Where art thou, Pindarus?
MESSALA. Seek him, Titinius, whilst I go to meet
The noble Brutus, thrusting this report

Portrait sculptures, such as this marble head of Mark Antony, were very popular in ancient Rome and provide a good idea of how the Romans looked. What does their concern about preserving such accurate likenesses suggest about the cultural values of the ancient Romans?

41–42 now be . . . bosom. Cassius will give Pindarus his freedom if Pindarus will kill Cassius. It was a custom in ancient warfare to avoid the shame of captivity at all costs, even death, to preserve military honor.
19 ■ Do you think that Brutus will commit suicide, too? Why or why not?
51 but change, an exchange of advantage.
55 disconsolate (dis kon′sə lit), *adj.* without hope, unhappy.
63 sun of Rome. (Note pun on son.)
68–69 Why dost thou . . . not? Why do people so readily accept things as true when they are really not?

Into his ears. I may say "thrusting" it,
For piercing steel and darts envenomèd
Shall be as welcome to the ears of Brutus
As tidings of this sight.

TITINIUS. Hie you, Messala,
And I will seek for Pindarus the while.
(MESSALA *exits.*)
Why didst thou send me forth, brave Cassius?
Did I not meet thy friends? And did not they
Put on my brows this wreath of victory
And bid me give it thee? Didst thou not hear their shouts?
Alas, thou hast misconstrued everything.
But, hold thee, take this garland on thy brow.
(He places the garland on CASSIUS*'s brow.)*
Thy Brutus bid me give it thee, and I
Will do his bidding. Brutus, come apace
And see how I regarded Caius Cassius.
By your leave, gods! This is a Roman's part.
Come, Cassius's sword, and find Titinius's heart.
(He stabs himself and dies.)
(Trumpets. BRUTUS, MESSALA, YOUNG CATO, STRATO, VOLUMNIUS, LUCILIUS, LABEO, *and* FLAVIUS *enter.)* 20

BRUTUS. Where, where, Messala, doth his body lie?

MESSALA. Lo, yonder, and Titinius mourning it.

BRUTUS. Titinius's face is upward.

CATO. He is slain.

BRUTUS. O Julius Caesar, thou art mighty yet!
Thy spirit walks abroad and turns our swords
In our own proper entrails. *(Low drumbeats.)*

CATO. Brave Titinius!
Look whe'er he have not crowned dead Cassius.

BRUTUS. Are yet two Romans living such as these?
The last of all the Romans, fare thee well!
It is impossible that ever Rome
Should breed thy fellow. Friends, I owe more tears
To this dead man than you shall see me pay.
I shall find time, Cassius, I shall find time.
Come, therefore, and to Thasos send his body.
His funerals shall not be in our camp,
Lest it discomfort us. Lucilius, come,
And come, young Cato, let us to the field. 22
Labeo and Flavius, set our battles on.
'Tis three o'clock, and, Romans, yet ere night
We shall try fortune in a second fight. *(They exit with the bodies.)*

81 thy friends, Brutus's man Messala and his army.

84 misconstrue (mis′kən-strü′), *v.* misunderstand; misinterpret.

89 This is a Roman's part. The Romans prided themselves on being freemen. To avoid capture, Titinius also commits suicide.
■ How has Shakespeare emphasized the power of Caesar, even beyond the grave?

104 Thasos (thā′sôs), an island in the Aegean Sea, near Philippi.

20 Reading/Thinking Skills
Connect

Possible response Shakespeare emphasizes the power of Caesar by including the ghost to remind characters and audience of Caesar's influence and by characters' references to Caesar's influence on their actions (act 5, scene 3, lines 45–46; 94–96).

21 Literary Focus
Plot

Point out that falling action marks the fifth act of a Shakespearean drama. Brutus's fortune are soon to fade at word of Cassius's death.

22 Historical Note
Cato

Cato is Portia's brother; therefore, Brutus's brother-in-law.

23 Reading/Thinking Skills
Evaluate

Question Brutus doesn't have much time to eulogize Cassius and Titinius. Does he do a good job? Why or why not? *(Students should note that Brutus praises them as the last true Romans, meaning Romans who hold republican ideals, live honorably, and die nobly. His last words to Cassius put friendship above his Stoic philosophy and are touching. Many students will think he did well.)*

BUILDING ENGLISH PROFICIENCY

Analyzing Characters

Creating an "open mind" drawing will help students analyze Brutus's feelings at this point. Use his speech (lines 94–96 and 98–110) to provide clues to his feelings.

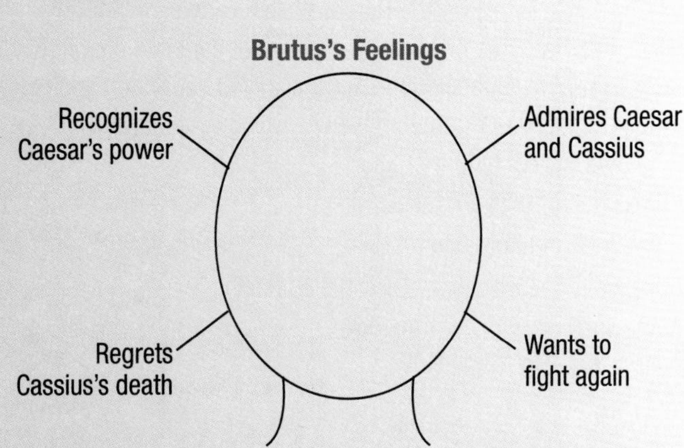

24 Reading/Thinking Skills
Clarify

Response Lucilius is posing as Brutus to deter Antony's soldiers and give Brutus a chance to escape.

25 Literary Element
Characterization

Question In act 4, scene 1, Antony was particularly ruthless in planning to kill enemies. Here he takes the opposite approach, trying to convert his enemies to friendship. How do you explain this? *(Possible response: Antony seems to do whatever is most advantageous at the moment. Perhaps killing senators was most advantageous then, and keeping good soldiers alive—perhaps to use as hostages—is most advantageous now. Maybe he thinks mercy will impress Octavius.)*

SCENE 4

Summary *The tides of war swing back to Antony and Octavius. A captured Lucilius pretends to be Brutus and tells Antony that Brutus will not be taken alive.*

Another part of the battlefield. Late afternoon. BRUTUS, *exhausted, runs on from right, sword in hand, followed by* MESSALA, YOUNG CATO, LUCILIUS, *and* FLAVIUS.

BRUTUS. Yet, countrymen, O, yet hold up your heads!
(*He exits, followed by* MESSALA *and* FLAVIUS.)
CATO. What bastard doth not? Who will go with me?
I will proclaim my name about the field:
I am the son of Marcus Cato, ho!
A foe to tyrants, and my country's friend.
I am the son of Marcus Cato, ho!
(SOLDIERS *enter and fight.*)
LUCILIUS. And I am Brutus, Marcus Brutus I!
Brutus, my country's friend! Know me for Brutus!
(YOUNG CATO *is slain by* ANTONY*'s men.*)
O young and noble Cato, art thou down?
Why, now thou diest as bravely as Titinius,
And mayst be honored, being Cato's son.
FIRST SOLDIER (*capturing* LUCILIUS). Yield, or thou diest.
LUCILIUS (*offering money*). Only I yield to die.
There is so much that thou wilt kill me straight;
Kill Brutus, and be honored in his death.
FIRST SOLDIER. We must not. A noble prisoner!
SECOND SOLDIER. Room, ho! Tell Antony, Brutus is ta'en.
(ANTONY *enters.*)
FIRST SOLDIER. I'll tell the news. Here comes the General.
Brutus is ta'en, Brutus is ta'en, my lord.
ANTONY. Where is he?
LUCILIUS. Safe, Antony, Brutus is safe enough.
I dare assure thee that no enemy
Shall ever take alive the noble Brutus.
The gods defend him from so great a shame!
When you do find him, or alive or dead,
He will be found like Brutus, like himself.
ANTONY (*to* FIRST SOLDIER). This is not Brutus, friend, but, I assure you,
A prize no less in worth. Keep this man safe;
Give him all kindness. I had rather have
Such men my friends than enemies. Go on,
And see whe'er Brutus be alive or dead;

2 what . . . doth not? Who is so base or low-born that he would not (hold up his head)?

24 ■ Why might Lucilius be claiming to be Brutus?

13 only I . . . die, I surrender only to die immediately.

25

MINI-LESSON: READING AND THINKING
Make Judgments

Teach In order to determine whether or not the main characters in *Julius Caesar* have made sound decisions, you might first analyze what characterizes good judgment. Review with students the factors that go into making a good judgment:

- Knowledge of relevant facts
- Awareness of alternatives
- Absence of prejudices and preconceptions
- Application of objective standards
- Application of personal values
- Consideration of consequences

Activity Ideas

- Have students apply these criteria to the major decisions made by one of the following: Caesar, Brutus, Antony, Cassius.
- Have groups choose a decision about a person, place, object, or idea that is either appealing or disturbing. They can apply the six factors to the subject, make a judgment, and share it with the class.

And bring us word unto Octavius's tent
How everything is chanced.
(SOLDIERS *lead* LUCILIUS *off left;* ANTONY *exits right).*

26

■ What questions about the events of this act do you still have?

SCENE 5

Summary *With Strato's help, Brutus kills himself. The victorious Antony and Octavius promise that all soldiers will receive the proper burial rites.*

Another part of the battlefield. Early evening. VOLUMNIUS, *carrying a lighted torch, enters at left, followed by* BRUTUS, CLITUS, DARDANIUS, *and* STRATO. *Overcome with fatigue and a sense of defeat, they sit, leaning against a large rock placed downstage center.*

BRUTUS. Come, poor remains of friends, rest on this rock.
(He sits.)
CLITUS. Statilius showed the torchlight, but, my lord,
He came not back. He is or ta'en or slain.
BRUTUS. Sit thee down, Clitus. Slaying is the word.
It is a deed in fashion. Hark thee, Clitus. *(He whispers.)*
CLITUS. What, I, my lord? No, not for all the world.
BRUTUS. Peace then. No words.
CLITUS. I'll rather kill myself.
BRUTUS. Hark thee, Dardanius. *(He whispers.)*
DARDANIUS. Shall I do such a deed?
(DARDANIUS *and* CLITUS *move away from* BRUTUS.)
CLITUS. O Dardanius!
DARDANIUS. O Clitus!
CLITUS. What ill request did Brutus make to thee?
DARDANIUS. To kill him, Clitus. Look, he meditates.
CLITUS. Now is that noble vessel full of grief,
That it runs over even at his eyes.
BRUTUS. Come hither, good Volumnius. List a word.
VOLUMNIUS. What says my lord?
BRUTUS. Why, this, Volumnius.
The ghost of Caesar hath appeared to me
Two several times by night—at Sardis once,

And this last night here in Philippi fields.
I know my hour is come.
VOLUMNIUS. Not so, my lord.
BRUTUS. Nay, I am sure it is, Volumnius.
Thou seest the world, Volumnius, how it goes;
Our enemies have beat us to the pit. *(Low trumpets and drums.)*
It is more worthy to leap in ourselves
Than tarry till they push us. Good Volumnius,
Thou know'st that we two went to school together.

2–3 Statilius (stə til′ē əs) . . . **slain.** A scout named Statilius has gone to see if Cassius's camp is still occupied; he signals back but is captured and slain.

23 beat us . . . pit, driven us to a trap (for wild animals; also a grave).

26 Reading/Thinking Skills
Question

Possible responses Why did Antony let Lucilius live? What role is Caesar's ghost really playing in the development of events?

27 Literary Focus
Plot

Question In what ways has Julius Caesar won? In what ways has Brutus won? *(Caesar has the backing of the plebeian class; his heir is gaining political power and is winning this battle; many of his opponents, both conspirators and those who weren't, are dead. Brutus has gained nothing except the satisfaction of knowing he did what he thought was right.)*

BUILDING ENGLISH PROFICIENCY

Examining Literary Criticism

Write the following comments on the board, or dictate while students write them in their notebooks. Explain that they may agree or disagree with these interpretations of the play.

1. There are no winners in this play.
2. Caesar, Cassius, and Brutus are all worthy of our praise despite their faults. But it is Brutus—idealistic and stubborn—whom we admire most.
3. Antony, who appears honorable at first, becomes too ruthless and dishonest to deserve our sympathy.
4. This is a play about power and its corrupting effects.

Activity Idea Divide the class into four groups and assign one of the quotations to each group. Have students work together to provide commentary on their quote—in the form of a speech, illustration, skit, rap, essay, or poem.

28 Reading/Thinking Skills
Summarize

Possible response Both life and death should be faced with resignation and dignity. Brutus has no regrets for his actions and feels he was right to join the conspiracy. He believes that death is the end of life.

29 Literary Element
Final Speech

Question In what respect do Brutus's last words resemble those of Cassius? *(Possible response: Both refer to Caesar, their murder of him, and the fact that he is now avenged.)*

30 Reading/Thinking Skills
Draw Conclusions

Question What two meanings could lines 53–54 have? *(Brutus is not a prisoner like Messala; Brutus is no longer a "prisoner of life" like Messala.)*

31 Reading/Thinking Skills
Infer

Question Why might Octavius want Brutus's soldiers in his service? *(Possible responses: He admires Brutus and believes that anyone who served Brutus would have the same high ideals; he thinks people will think well of him if he is merciful; he doesn't want unnecessary killing.)*

Even for that, our love of old, I prithee,
Hold thou my sword hilts whilst I run on it.
VOLUMNIUS. That's not an office for a friend, my lord.
(Drums still.)
CLITUS. Fly, fly, my lord! There is no tarrying here.
BRUTUS. Farewell to you, and you, and you, Volumnius.
Strato, thou hast been all this while asleep;
Farewell to thee too, Strato. Countrymen,
My heart doth joy that yet in all my life
I found no man but he was true to me.
I shall have glory by this losing day
More than Octavius and Mark Antony
By this vile conquest shall attain unto.
So fare you well at once, for Brutus's tongue
Hath almost ended his life's history.
Night hangs upon my eyes; my bones would rest,
That have but labored to attain this hour.
(*Trumpets. Cry within,* "Fly, fly, fly!")
CLITUS. Fly, my lord, fly!
BRUTUS. Hence, I will follow.
(CLITUS, DARDANIUS, *and* VOLUMNIUS *exit.*)
I prithee, Strato, stay thou by thy lord.
Thou art a fellow of a good respect;
Thy life hath had some smatch of honor in it.
Hold then my sword, and turn away thy face,
While I do run upon it. Wilt thou, Strato?
STRATO. Give me your hand first. Fare you well, my lord.
BRUTUS. Farewell, good Strato. *(He runs on his sword.)*
Caesar, now be still.
29 I killed not thee with half so good a will. *(Dies.)*
(Trumpets sound retreat within. ANTONY, OCTAVIUS *and the army enter with* MESSALA *and* LUCILIUS *as prisoners.)*
OCTAVIUS. What man is that?
30 **MESSALA.** My master's man. Strato, where is thy master?
STRATO. Free from the bondage you are in, Messala.
The conquerors can but make a fire of him,
For Brutus only overcame himself,
And no man else hath honor by his death.
LUCILIUS. So Brutus should be found. I thank thee, Brutus,
31 That thou hast proved Lucilius's saying true.
OCTAVIUS. All that served Brutus, I will entertain them.
Fellow, wilt thou bestow thy time with me?
STRATO. Ay, if Messala will prefer me to you.
OCTAVIUS. Do so, good Messala.
MESSALA. How died my master, Strato?

28 ■ Explain Brutus's attitude toward his life and death in this speech.

46 smatch, taste; touch.

55 The conquerors . . . him, a reference to the Roman custom of burning the dead.
57 no man . . . death, no one can claim the honor of defeating him in combat.
59 Lucilius's . . . true. Lucilius had said that Brutus's enemies would never take him alive.
60 I will . . . them. I will take all of Brutus's servants and soldiers and make them my own.
62 prefer, recommend.

MINI-LESSON: USAGE
Words Commonly Confused

Teach Explain that certain word pairs cause problems both with spelling and usage. Write the following commentary on the board:

By the end of act 5, the *principle/principal* characters in the play have died, *accept/except* Antony. Antony and Octavius have *ceased/seized* power and *emerge/immerge* victors. One theme in *Julius Caesar* is the *affect/effect* of power on people.

Apply Have volunteers underline the correct word in each pair and explain their choices.

Activity Idea Have pairs of students write some general observations about the play, using the correct form of these words: *Capitol/capital, cease/siege, through/though, advice/advise, breathe/breath.*

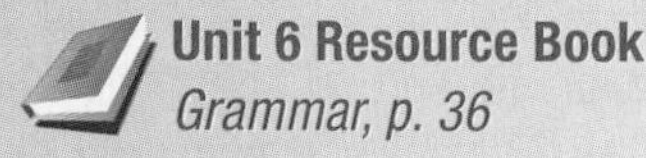

Unit 6 Resource Book
Grammar, p. 36

Art Study

Ask students to discuss what they think Antony is thinking as he looks on the dead Brutus. *(Possible responses: He is, for once, facing the truth—that a better man than he is has died. He can't quite take it in that his chief enemy is dead.)*

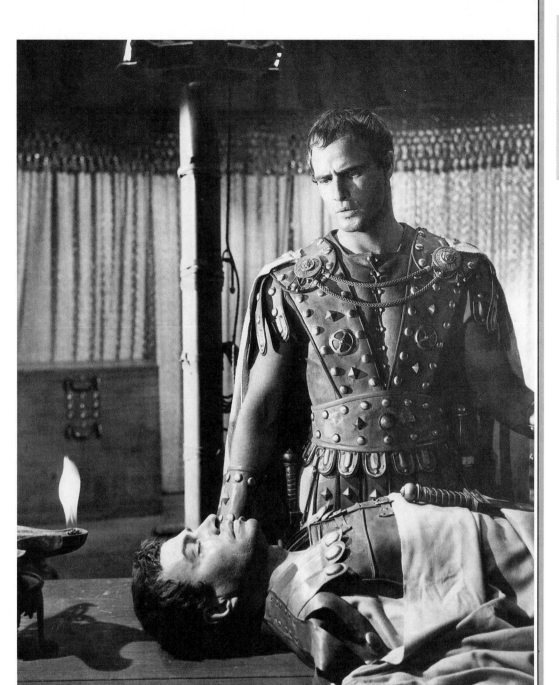

BUILDING ENGLISH PROFICIENCY

ESL LEP ELD SAE LD

Relate Literature to Human Concerns

Use the following information to get students thinking about the universal themes in *Julius Caesar.*

In 1937, as the dictators Hitler and Mussolini were gaining power, American director Orson Welles staged *Julius Caesar* in modern dress. (Caesar wore a military uniform; the conspirators wore overcoats and felt hats.) The setting was a modern city, the murder weapons were gangsters' daggers. The stage was bare, with brick walls painted red. Two dominant effects were the frequent noise of the mobs and enveloping shadows.

Have groups work on the following activities.

Activity Ideas

- Identify some universal themes in this play. (the abuse of power, uncontrolled ambition, the cost of winning)
- If you were staging this play around the year 2000, what person or movement would be your "Caesar," representing an abuse of power? What would be the victorious forces, if any?

32 Reader's Response
Making Personal Connections

Questions

- What is Antony's assessment of Brutus? *(He was noble, honest, public-spirited, and admirable.)*
- Are these qualities you would want in a friend? *(Students might list 5–10 qualities they look for in a friend and then check which ones Brutus possesses.)*

33 Reading/Thinking Skills
Question

Possible response Is this what you honestly think, or is this just more rhetoric for Octavius's benefit? Did you admire Brutus all along?

34 Literary Focus
Plot

Question How is the plot resolved? *(Possible responses: The war is over; Antony and Octavius are in accord for the moment; Octavius has made peace with and forgiven Brutus's followers; Brutus has finally received his due from his enemies in their eulogies.)*

Check Test

1. Why does Lucilius tell the enemy he is Brutus? *(to gain time for Brutus)*

2. What misunderstanding about Titinius and the enemy troops causes Cassus to despair? *(Titinius is reportedly captured, but is really being received by Brutus's victorious troops.)*

3. The sword that kills Cassius has also killed whom? *(Caesar)*

4. How does Brutus die? *(He runs on his sword.)*

5. Who calls Brutus "the noblest Roman of them all"? *(Antony)*

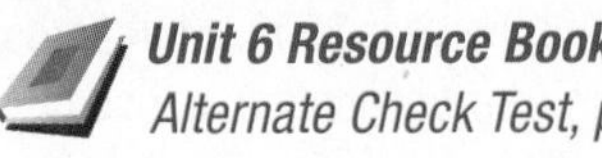

Unit 6 Resource Book
Alternate Check Test, p. 37

STRATO. I held the sword, and he did run on it.
MESSALA. Octavius, then take him to follow thee,
That did the latest service to my master.
ANTONY. This was the noblest Roman of them all. 32
All the conspirators save only he
Did that they did in envy of great Caesar;
He only in a general honest thought
And common good to all made one of them.
His life was gentle, and the elements
So mixed in him that Nature might stand up
And say to all the world, "This was a man!"
OCTAVIUS. According to his virtue let us use him,
With all respect and rites of burial.
Within my tent his bones tonight shall lie,
Most like a soldier, ordered honorably.
So call the field to rest, and let's away
To part the glories of this happy day. 34
(All exit with BRUTUS*'s body.)*

72 made one of them, joined them.
73 elements. The ancients believed that people were made of four basic elements—earth, air, fire, and water. Antony says they were mixed in Brutus in ideal proportions.

33 ■ What question would you ask Antony about his assessment (lines 68–75) of Brutus?
81 part the glories, share the honors.

MINI-LESSON: STUDY SKILLS
Build a Time Line

Students can review story events and see how they build to a climax and a resolution by creating a time line. You might supply them with the following skeleton and have them work in small groups to supply eight intervening events they consider major in the plot.

Major events in *Julius Caesar*

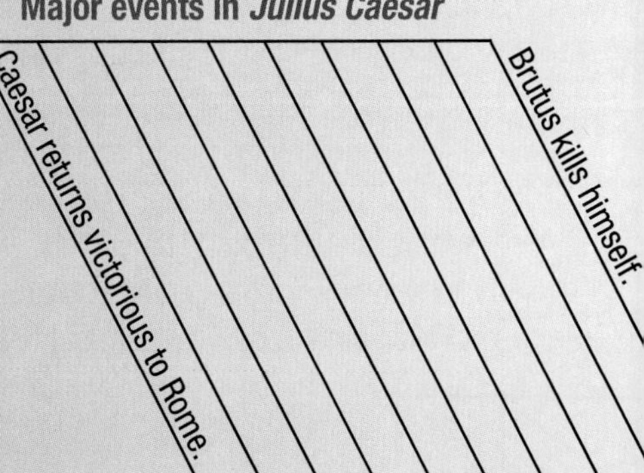

Act 5

After Reading

Making Connections

Shaping Your Response

1. How did you feel about Cassius's death? Did you have the same feeling about the death of Brutus? Explain.
2. Some scholars say Caesar's tragic flaw is ambition. What might Brutus's flaw be?

Analyzing the Play

3. In literature, characters are frequently used as **foils**; that is, the traits of one point up by contrast the traits of another. How is Antony a foil for Octavius? for Brutus?
4. In scene 1, lines 40–45, what attitude is conveyed in the **similes** Antony uses?
5. In terms of **plot**, what dramatic purposes does the short scene 2 serve?
6. How is Cassius's manner of death in keeping with his **character**?
7. What qualities do his soldiers show in their refusal to kill Brutus?
8. In bidding his friends farewell, Brutus says, "I found no man but he was true to me." Do you find Brutus's remark **ironic**? Why or why not?
9. Do you find Brutus's suicide in keeping with his character, or is his act dictated by his culture? Explain.
10. Do you think Antony's remarks over Brutus's body are sincere? Explain.
11. Who would you say are the real winners in this play? Who are the losers?

Extending the Ideas

12. Although ambition is sometimes considered a positive quality, it can become a negative one. In your opinion, when does ambition cross the line and become destructive?

Literary Focus: Plot

The fifth act of a Shakespearean drama always contains the **falling action** and the **resolution.** On your plot diagram, list at least one example of how Brutus's fortune changes. Then write a description of how Shakespeare resolves the plot.

After Reading

MAKING CONNECTIONS

1. Possible responses: Many students will feel more sympathy for Brutus, although some may have felt uncomfortable as he asked four different people to help him kill himself.

2. Possible responses: pride, self-righteousness, stubbornness, idealism, poor judgment

3. Possible responses: Antony is subtle and devious, while Octavius is plain-spoken and direct. Brutus is honorable and idealistic, while Antony is immoral and practical.

4. Possible response: contempt

5. Possible responses: It shows a change in fortune, suggests battle action; and indicates time passing.

6. Possible response: He is a man of action, emotional and proud, so it is not surprising that he prefers death by suicide to the humiliation of capture.

7. Possible responses: loyalty, love

8. Possible response: It is ironic because Brutus wasn't true to Caesar.

9. Students may find evidence in the play to support both interpretations. Some may cite Brutus's statement that suicide was not for him, and his Stoic philosophy suggests that it was not in keeping with his character. But he died what was considered an honorable death for a Roman.

10. Some students may think that, for once, Antony is speaking the truth; others may think these remarks are self-serving attempts to impress Octavius.

11. Octavius and Antony win in that they are in power; Caesar wins in that his will is still dominant; Brutus wins in that he has a clear conscience. Some readers would insist that nobody has really won.

12. Possible responses: Ambition is destructive when it is an obsession, hurts others, or is self-serving.

LITERARY FOCUS: PLOT

Remind students that the falling action begins right after the turning point in act 3 and continues up until the resolution in act 5.

VOCABULARY STUDY

Students' answers will vary, depending on their choice of topic. They are unlikely to use the word *presage* in the second two.

Vocabulary words, as used in context, should reflect correct meanings and connotations.

Unit 6 Resource Book
Vocabulary, pp. 27, 35
Vocabulary Test, pp. 30, 38

WRITING CHOICES

War Hero

If students do not get the joke on their own, give them a broader hint, or read the poem aloud with emphasis and pauses to establish meaning, so they do not spend too much time trying to figure out the "Latin" and become frustrated. They might enjoy writing a "Latin" poem of their own.

Heroic Status

You may want to give students the option of writing about Brutus.

Selection Test

Unit 6 Resource Book
pp. 39–40

Vocabulary Study

consort
demeanor
disconsolate
fawn
misconstrue
presage

Using five of the listed words, write one of the following.

- a plot summary of *Julius Caesar*
- a commercial using propaganda to endorse a product that has "snob appeal"
- a news item about a crime or scandal

Expressing Your Ideas

Writing Choices

Writer's Notebook Update In act 2, scene 2, Brutus dismisses Antony as "but a limb of Caesar." After Caesar's death, however, Antony, along with Octavius, surprises the conspirators. In your notebook, give reasons to explain why Caesar or Antony is the better leader.

War Hero Caesar's fame grew out of his military victories over tribes in the Roman province of Gaul—which included what are today France, Belgium, and Switzerland, as well as parts of Holland and Germany. Read the following poem aloud to make sense of the "words." Then write a **translation** of the poem. (Hint: Vercingetorix was a leader defeated by Caesar.)

Caesar cari dona militari orgi versus Belgae,
Helvetii, Germani, Venetii, Britanni—iunemit.
"Romis glorius," sed Caesar, "Nomen me impunit!"
Meni tridit—Vercingetorix, forin stans—
Caesar noctim sili fors ticinis nec aut.
Ab ludi, nervi felo, Caius Julius, iubet.

from *Inklings* by Maurice Sagoff

Heroic Status A tragic hero is a noble character who, through some flaw in character, causes his or her own downfall. Write an **explanation** of whether or not Caesar measures up to this description of a tragic hero.

Other Options

Breaking the Pattern In Shakespeare's day, it was believed that a monarch had a God-given right to rule. Anything that disrupted a stable and orderly reign caused chaos, which affected the entire social order. Given this cultural view of power, do you think assassination and the drastic political **changes** that result from this act were more devastating, or less so, than in our society? Hold a **debate** on the subject.

A Banner Day Design a **standard** to be carried by the armies of either the conspirators or the triumvirate. Be prepared to explain your choice of design.

Making Fun-nies Of A comic book publisher has hired you to draw colored illustrations for *Julius Caesar.* Do a **plot strip** for one of the scenes, complete with dialogue captions and any background information you think is necessary.

Caesar Sampler Work with a group to create a **performance** for another class, a sampler of the best of *Julius Caesar*— soliloquies, short scenes, action sequences, anything that will give an audience a taste of the play. Provide background information whenever necessary.

OTHER OPTIONS

Breaking the Pattern

You may also wish to have students consider how this cultural view would have led Shakespeare and his contemporaries to view this play: would they have seen Brutus, who killed the reigning monarch, and brought about the destruction of the existing social order, as a hero? Their thoughts could lead to a debate on the topic or to a research paper on the interpretation of Brutus's role in *Julius Caesar* in Shakespeare's time and in ours.

Before Reading

The Balek Scales

by Heinrich Böll Germany

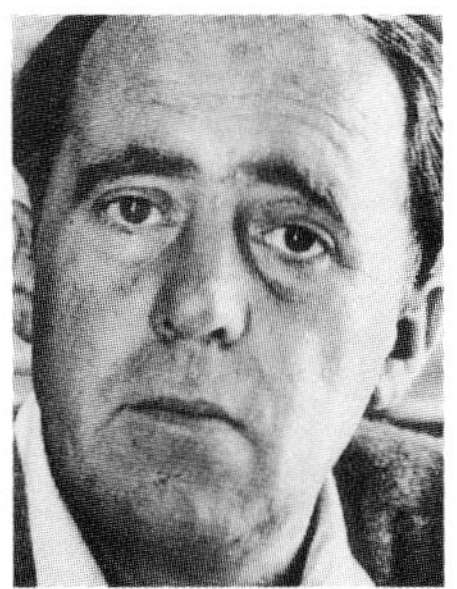

Heinrich Böll
1917–1985

A reluctant soldier, Heinrich Böll (hin′riH bōl) served with the German army from 1939 to 1945 and spent the last part of World War II in an American prison camp. After the war, he worked in his brother's cabinet shop while attending Cologne University. By 1951, he had published two novels about his war experiences. In 1972, for his perceptive and ironic short stories and novels, Böll won the Nobel Prize for literature. An active defender of freedom, he donated part of his prize money to aid writers imprisoned for their beliefs.

Building Background

Seeking Justice Although "The Balek Scales" is fiction, the situation it depicts is based on history. In the 1800s, much of eastern Europe was made up of many small states, mostly controlled by wealthy landowners who dominated every aspect of village and peasant life. Many of the impoverished peasants, who were totally dependent on these aristocrats for their livelihood, eventually fled Europe for America. In this story, Böll portrays the wealthy Balek family and the results of a peasant boy's attempt to obtain justice.

Literary Focus

Theme An underlying meaning of a work is called its **theme.** You have already learned that a theme is not always directly stated but must often be inferred. One technique for discovering theme in a short story is to note one or two words, ideas, or motifs that recur within the narrative. You will notice that throughout "The Balek Scales," especially in the final three paragraphs, an important word appears repeatedly. Look for it, and use it as a key to identify the theme of the story.

Writer's Notebook

It's Your World Böll's story takes place in another country and another century—a setting he skillfully re-creates through descriptions of food, the countryside, work, and other aspects of that society. Assume that someone one hundred years from now will read about your world. Make a list of details that you think are most revealing of your life, culture, surroundings, and society. You might use a chart like the one below.

Food	Entertainment	Clothing	Transportation	Other

Before Reading

Building Background

Have students imagine that they live in a remote area where one person owns all the key businesses, such as the bank, gas station, grocery store, radio station, and air transportation. Involve the class in a discussion of the power the owner would have over the residents.

Literary Focus

Remind students that different readers may state a story's **theme** in slightly different ways. Each reader's theme statement will reflect his or her own prior knowledge and personal understanding.

Writer's Notebook

Encourage students to create other categories that they think will be revealing, for example, family members, neighborhood description, housing, cost of goods, and so on.

More About Heinrich Böll

In English, an ö may be transliterated as *oe*, so much information about Heinrich Böll in English will be found by looking for Heinrich Boell. His other given name, Theodor, is also sometimes included. Böll is the author of *Absent Without Leave, and Other Stories*, (1967).

SUPPORT MATERIALS OVERVIEW

Unit 5 Resource Book
- Graphic Organizer, p. 41
- Study Guide, p. 42
- Vocabulary, p. 43
- Grammar, p. 44
- Alternate Check Test, p. 45
- Vocabulary Test, p. 46
- Selection Test, pp. 47–48

Building English Proficiency
- Literature Summaries
- Activities, p. 224

Reading, Writing & Grammar SkillBook
- Vocabulary, pp. 1–2
- Reading, pp. 79–80
- Writing, pp. 115–116
- Grammar, Usage, and Mechanics, pp. 140–141

Technology
- Audiotape 19, Sides A, B
- Personal Journal Software
- Custom Literature Database: For more stories about justice, see a variety of adventures of Robin Hood by Howard Pyle; for a story related to giants, see stories about Thor by Padraic Colum—all on the database.
- Test Generator Software

During Reading

Selection Objectives

- to understand the theme of the cost of winning
- to identify themes in a short story
- to explore the use of syntax

Unit 6 Resource Book
Graphic Organizer, p. 41
Study Guide, p. 42

Theme Link

When a young villager fights for the simple justice of having his mushrooms weighed with accurate scales, he incurs a heavy cost.

Vocabulary Preview

chateau, a large country house
dispel, drive away
meager, scanty
mute, silent
theology, study of religion and religious beliefs

Students can add the words and definitions to their Writer's Notebooks.

1 Reading/Thinking Skills
Clarify

Question Why do the adults check the potato peels? *(to make sure that no edible parts of the potato are wasted)*

2 Reader's Response
Making Personal Connections

Question Do these people's habits and attitudes remind you of anyone you know? What about them seems familiar? *(Students may mention people who are frugal and always busy; strict parents; a family where everyone pitches in.)*

The Balek Scales

Heinrich Böll

Where my grandfather came from, most of the people lived by working in the flax sheds. For five generations they had been breathing in the dust which rose from the crushed flax[1] stalks, letting themselves be killed off by slow degrees, a race of long-suffering, cheerful people who ate goat cheese, potatoes, and now and then a rabbit; in the evening they would sit at home spinning and knitting; they sang, drank mint tea, and were happy. During the day they would carry the flax stalks to the antiquated machines, with no protection from the dust and at the mercy of the heat which came pouring out of the drying kilns.[2] Each cottage contained only one bed, standing against the wall like a closet and reserved for the parents, while the children slept all round the room on benches. In the morning the room would be filled with the odor of thin soup; on Sundays there was stew, and on feast days the children's faces would light up with pleasure as they watched the black acorn coffee turning paler and paler from the milk their smiling mother poured into their coffee mugs.

The parents went off early to the flax sheds, the housework was left to the children: they would sweep the room, tidy up, wash the dishes, and peel the potatoes, precious pale-yellow fruit, whose thin peel had to be produced afterwards to dispel[3] any suspicion of extravagance or carelessness. 1

As soon as the children were out of school they had to go off into the woods and, depending on the season, gather mushrooms and 2

1. **flax** (flaks), *n.* a plant that can be crushed, dried, and spun into thread for weaving into linen.
2. **kiln** (kil, kiln), *n.* furnace or oven for burning, baking, or drying.
3. **dispel** (dis pel′), *v.* drive away.

SELECTION SUMMARY

The Balek Scales

The narrator's grandfather, Franz Brücher, is a boy living in a village where the only scales for weighing all goods are owned by the wealthy Balek family. By chance, Franz discovers that the scales' weight is 55 grams too heavy. He is overwhelmed with this injustice, for he realizes that the hard-working people have been cheated for generations. Soon all the villagers know. At the New Year's Mass, Franz confronts the Balek family and the congregation bursts into a hymn about justice. Meanwhile, a poacher steals the scales and the record book, so the villagers meet at the Brücher cottage to calculate what they are owed. The gendarmes disperse them, killing Franz's little sister. Exiled from the village, the remaining Brücher family wanders about, telling their story of injustice. Few people are interested.

*For summaries in other languages, see the **Building English Proficiency** book.*

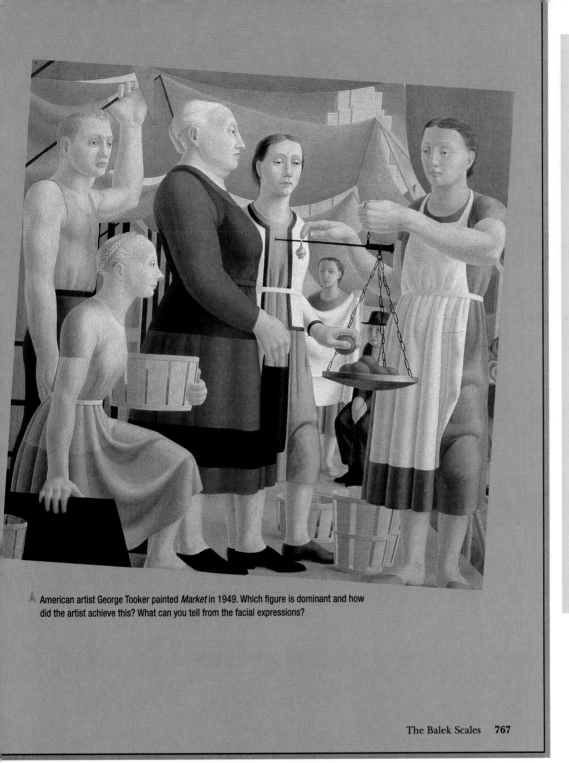

American artist George Tooker painted *Market* in 1949. Which figure is dominant and how did the artist achieve this? What can you tell from the facial expressions?

Art Study

Response to Caption Questions
The older woman dominates through use of color—she wears dark red and black while the other women wear light colors—and through position—she is the central figure. Her strong bearing and large size also distinguish her.

The older woman seems to be waiting, like a queen, while the other figures look serious as they perform or watch the transaction.

Visual Literacy Background or foreground images provide interesting contrasts.

Question Compare the work people do in a skyscraper, like the one in the background, with work people do in the marketplace. *(Possible response: In the skyscraper, people do mental work and produce or sell services, while in the marketplace people do physical work and produce or sell goods.)*

Question What effect do you think the skyscraper has on the picture? *(Possible response: It suggests that the atmosphere of the marketplace, with its simple scale, is as intense as the board room of "big business.")*

BUILDING ENGLISH PROFICIENCY

ESL
LEP
ELD
SAE
LD

Exploring Exposition

Use one or both of the following activities to help students grasp the title and the opening paragraphs and their importance to the story.

Activity Ideas

- Have students read the title and look at the picture on page 767. Explain that Balek is a family name, and that the scales work in the same way as those shown in *Market.* Lead a discussion on what scales do, when people use them, and how they work.
- Ask students if they are familiar with the image of the scales of justice. Draw a simple image of scales on the board. Brainstorm words connected with scales and justice, such as *decide, measure, compare, balance, fairness, lawful, fair dealing.* Ask students to suggest examples of injustice.

Building English Proficiency
Activities, p. 224

3 Literary Element
Plot

Point out that theme and plot are related, and that the reader should pay attention to details the author emphasizes in the plot.

Questions

- How much do the apothecaries make for each pfennig the children make? *(For hayflowers, they make 20 pfennigs for each pfennig the children make; for mushrooms, they make 6 pfennigs for each pfennig the children make.)*
- Why was the line redrawn yearly? *(Possible responses: to make sure that the measurements were fair; to give the appearance that the measurements were fair)*
- What was an important law of the Baleks? *(No one but the Baleks could own a scale.)*

4 Literary Element
Repetition

Explain to students that repetition creates emphasis and may signal a thematic meaning.

Question What words or ideas have been repeated so far? *("the old-fashioned, bronze-gilt Balek scales"; the idea of generations of children picking the mushrooms and flowers; words about measuring and counting)*

herbs: woodruff and thyme, caraway, mint, and foxglove, and in summer, when they had brought in the hay from their meager[4] fields, they gathered hayflowers. A kilo[5] of hayflowers was worth one pfennig,[6] and they were sold by the apothecaries[7] in town for twenty pfennigs a kilo to highly strung ladies. The mushrooms were highly prized: they fetched twenty pfennigs a kilo and were sold in the shops in town for one mark twenty. The children would crawl deep into the green darkness of the forest during the autumn when dampness drove the mushrooms out of the soil, and almost every family had its own places where it gathered mushrooms, places which were handed down in whispers from generation to generation.

The woods belonged to the Baleks, as well as the flax sheds, and in my grandfather's village the Baleks had a chateau,[8] and the wife of the head of the family had a little room next to the dairy, where mushrooms, herbs, and hayflowers were weighed and paid for. There on the table stood the great Balek scales, an old-fashioned, ornate, bronze-gilt contraption, which my grandfather's grandparents had already faced when they were children, their grubby hands holding their little baskets of mushrooms, their paper bags of hayflowers, breathlessly watching the number of weights Frau Balek had to throw on the scale before the swinging pointer came to rest exactly over the black line, that thin line of justice which had to be redrawn every year. Then Frau Balek would take the big book covered in brown leather, write down the weight, and pay out the money, pfennigs or ten-pfennig pieces and, very, very occasionally, a mark. And when my grandfather was a child, there was a big glass jar of lemon drops standing there, the kind that cost one mark a kilo, and when Frau Balek—whichever one happened to be presiding over the little room—was in a good mood, she would put her hand into this jar and give each child a lemon drop, and the children's faces would light up with pleasure, the way they used to when on feast days their mother poured milk into their coffee mugs, milk that made the coffee turn paler and paler until it was as pale as the flaxen pigtails of the little girls.

3 One of the laws imposed by the Baleks on the village was: no one was permitted to have any scales in the house. The law was so ancient that nobody gave a thought as to when and how it had arisen, and it had to be obeyed, for anyone who broke it was dismissed from the flax sheds, he could not sell his mushrooms or his thyme or his hayflowers, and the power of the Baleks was so far-reaching that no one in the neighboring villages would give him work either, or buy his forest herbs. But since the days when my grandfather's parents had gone out as small children to gather mushrooms and sell them in order that they might season the meat of the rich people of Prague[9] or be baked into game pies, it had never occurred to anyone to break this law: flour could be measured in cups, eggs could be counted, what they had spun could be measured by the yard, and besides, the old-fashioned, bronze-gilt, ornate Balek scales 4 did not look as if there was anything wrong with them, and five generations had entrusted the swinging black pointer with what they had gone out as eager children to gather from the woods.

True, there were some among these quiet people who flouted the law, poachers bent on making more money in one night than they could earn in a whole month in the flax sheds, but even these people apparently never thought of buying scales or making their own. My grandfather was the first person bold enough to test

4. meager (mē′gər), *adj.* scanty.
5. **kilo** (kē′lō, kil′ō), *n.* one thousand grams; the equivalent of 2.2 lbs.
6. **pfennig** (pfen′ig), *n.* Just as a penny is worth 1/100th of a dollar, a pfennig was worth 1/100th of a mark.
7. **apothecary** (ə poth′ə ker′ē), *n.* druggist.
8. chateau (sha tō′), *n.* a large country house.
9. **Prague** (präg), the capital and largest city of Czechoslovakia, now the Czech Republic. At the time of the story, it was located in the Austro-Hungarian Empire.

MINI-LESSON: GRAMMAR
Verbal Phrases

Teach Tell students that an *-ing* word, or verbal, by itself can never act as the verb of a sentence. Let them read the passage below and note that the phrase containing the verbal can't stand alone.

There on the table stood the great Balek scales which my grandfather's grandparents had already faced when they were children, their grubby hands holding their little baskets of mushrooms.

Point out that when people write sentence fragments, they often are mistaking verbals for verbs.

Activity Idea Have students write full sentences that incorporate the following sentence fragments derived from verbals or verbal phrases, or identify them as complete sentences.

1. Breathlessly watching the number of weights Frau Balek threw on the scale.
2. Never realizing that the pound weight was heavier than a pound.
3. Heat came pouring out of the drying kilns.

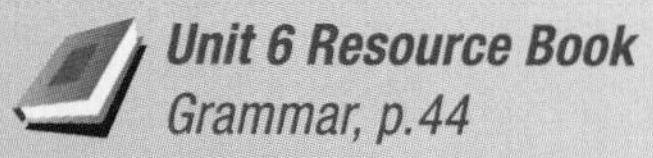
Unit 6 Resource Book
Grammar, p.44

the justice of the Baleks, the family who lived in the chateau and drove two carriages, who always maintained one boy from the village while he studied theology[10] at the seminary in Prague,
5 the family with whom the priest played tarok[11] every Wednesday, on whom the local reeve,[12] in his carriage emblazoned with the imperial coat of arms, made an annual New Year's Day call, and on whom the emperor conferred a title on the first day of the year 1900.

My grandfather was hard-working and smart: he crawled farther into the woods than the children of his clan had crawled before him, he
6 penetrated as far as the thicket where, according to legend, Bilgan the Giant was supposed to dwell, guarding a treasure. But my grandfather was not afraid of Bilgan: he worked his way deep into the thicket, even when he was quite little, and brought out great quantities of mushrooms; he even found truffles,[13] for which Frau Balek paid thirty pfennigs a pound. Everything my grandfather took to the Baleks he entered on the back of a torn-off calendar page: every pound of mushrooms, every gram of thyme, and on the right-hand side, in his childish handwriting, he entered the amount he received for each item; he scrawled in every pfennig, from the age of seven to the age of twelve, and by the time he was twelve, the year 1900 had arrived, and because the Baleks had been raised to the aristocracy by the emperor, they gave every family in the village a quarter of a pound of real coffee, the Brazilian kind; there was also free beer and tobacco for the men, and at the chateau there was a great banquet; many carriages stood in the avenue of poplars leading from the entrance gates to the chateau.

But the day before the banquet the coffee was distributed in the little room which had housed the Balek scales for almost a hundred years, and the Balek family was now called Balek von Bilgan because, according to legend,
7 Bilgan the Giant used to have a great castle on the site of the present Balek estate.

My grandfather often used to tell me how he went there after school to fetch the coffee for four families: the Cechs, the Weidlers, the Vohlas, and his own, the Brüchers. It was the afternoon of New Year's Eve: there were the front rooms to be decorated, the baking to be done, and the families did not want to spare four boys and have each of them go all the way to the chateau to bring back a quarter of a pound of coffee.

And so my grandfather sat on the narrow, wooden bench in the little room while Gertrud the maid counted out the wrapped four-ounce packages of coffee, four of them, and he looked at the scales and saw that the pound weight was still lying on the left-hand scale; Frau Balek von Bilgan was busy with preparations for the banquet. And when Gertrud was about to put her hand into the jar with the lemon drops to give my grandfather one, she discovered it was empty: it was refilled once a year, and held one kilo of the kind that cost a mark.

Gertrud laughed and said: "Wait here while I get the new lot," and my grandfather waited with the four four-ounce packages which had been wrapped and sealed in the factory, facing the scales on which someone had left the pound 8
weight, and my grandfather took the four packages of coffee, put them on the empty scale, and his heart thudded as he watched the black finger of justice come to rest on the left of the black line: the scale with the pound weight stayed down, and the pound of coffee remained up in the air; his heart thudded more than if he had been lying behind a bush in the forest waiting for Bilgan the Giant, and he felt in his pocket for the pebbles he always carried with him so he could use his catapult to shoot the

10. theology (thē ol′ə jē), *n.* study of religion and religious beliefs.
11. **tarok** (tar′ək), a card game played in central Europe.
12. **reeve** (rēv), *n.* the chief official of a town or district.
13. **truffle** (truf′əl), *n.* an edible fungus that resembles a mushroom and is considered a delicacy.

5 Reading/Thinking Skills
Analyze

Question What do these activities and commendations make you think about the Baleks? *(Possible response: that they are religious, holy, good, fine people)*

6 Literary Element
Foreshadow

Discuss who Bilgan the Giant might represent.

Question What does Franz's lack of fear of the giant foreshadow? *(a conflict with the Baleks)*

7 Literary Element
Archetype

Here the giant and the Balek family come to be associated. Point out to students that as a literary archetype, giants are known for their stupidity, their ruthlessness, and their abuse of the power that comes from their size. Help students see that by association, these traits are being attributed to the Baleks as well.

8 Reading/Thinking Skills
Draw Conclusions

Question Why is it important that the coffee was sealed in the factory? *(The reader can believe that the weight is accurate.)*

BUILDING ENGLISH PROFICIENCY

Understanding Sequence

Some students may lose track of the sequence of events in "The Balek Scales."

Activity Idea Students can complete these cloze sentences to understand important events in the story. Also, they can use their own ideas to expand the sentences. You may wish to provide multiple choice answers and add sentences as needed.

1. The narrator is telling a story about his ____ who is a ____ between the ages of seven and twelve. *(grandfather, boy)*
2. The children in the village ____ hayflowers and mushrooms and ____ them to the Baleks. *(gather, pick; bring, sell)*
3. After the Baleks ____ the hayflowers and other things on the scale, they ____ the children. *(weigh, pay)*
4. No one is ____ to have any scales except the _____. *(allowed, permitted; Baleks)*
5. Some people _____ Bilgan lives in the _____, but Franz isn't _____ to go there and look for mushrooms. *(believe, woods, afraid)*
6. On New Year's Eve, Franz goes to the Baleks' to get free ____. Each ____ weighs exactly four ounces. *(coffee, package)*
7. Franz puts ____ packages of coffee on the scale and finds that the pound weight is ____ than the coffee. *(four, heavier)*

9 Literary Element
Character

A character's thoughts, actions, or speech may indicate the theme.

Question What are the boy's reactions when he finds out that the scales are wrong, and which of his characteristics does he show? *(He analytically computes the amount of the scale's error and is furious. He indignantly refuses to accept the Balek's gift, and bravely demands to see Frau Balek.)*

10 Reading/Thinking Skills
Draw Conclusions

Question Why did Gertrud laugh? *(The idea that a village boy should demand to see a Balek von Bilgan was absurd to her.)*

11 Literary Focus
Theme

Here the main character makes a thematic statement.

Question The story is told by a narrator who creates an omniscient viewpoint. Would the narrator agree with the statement that the boy makes here? How can you tell? *(Yes, the narrator refers to justice in the same way: "that thin line of justice that had to be redrawn every year" (page 768), "to test the justice of the Baleks" (pages 768–769.))*

sparrows which pecked away at his mother's cabbage plants—he had to put three, four, five pebbles beside the packages of coffee before the scale with the pound weight rose and the pointer at last came to rest over the black line. My grandfather took the coffee from the scale, wrapped the five pebbles in his kerchief, and when Gertrud came back with the big kilo bag of
9 lemon drops, which had to last for another whole year in order to make the children's faces light up with pleasure, when Gertrud let the lemon drops rattle into the glass jar, the pale little fellow was still standing there, and nothing seemed to have changed. My grandfather only took three of the packages, then Gertrud looked in startled surprise at the white-faced child, who threw the lemon drop onto the floor, ground it under his heel, and said: "I want to see Frau Balek."

"Balek von Bilgan, if you please," said Gertrud.

10 "All right, Frau Balek von Bilgan," but Gertrud only laughed at him, and he walked back to the village in the dark, took the Cechs, the Weidlers, and the Vohlas their coffee, and said he had to go and see the priest.

Instead he went out into the dark night with his five pebbles in his kerchief. He had to walk a long way before he found someone who had scales, who was permitted to have them; no one in the villages of Blaugau and Bernau had any, he knew that, and he went straight through them till, after two hours' walking, he reached the little town of Dielheim, where Honig the apothecary lived. From Honig's house came the smell of fresh pancakes, and Honig's breath, when he opened the door to the half-frozen boy, already smelled of punch, there was a moist cigar between his narrow lips, and he clasped the boy's cold hands firmly for a moment, saying: "What's the matter, has your father's lung got worse?"

"No, I haven't come for medicine, I wanted—" My grandfather undid his kerchief, took out the five pebbles, held them out to Honig, and said: "I wanted to have these weighed." He glanced anxiously into Honig's face, but when Honig said nothing and did not get angry, or even ask him anything, my grandfather said: "It is the amount that is short of justice," and now, as he went into the warm room, 11
my grandfather realized how wet his feet were. The snow had soaked through his cheap shoes, and in the forest the branches had showered him with snow, which was now melting, and he was tired and hungry and suddenly began to cry because he thought of the quantities of mushrooms, the herbs, the flowers, which had been weighed on the scales which were short five pebbles' worth of justice. And when Honig, shaking his head and holding the five pebbles, called his wife, my grandfather thought of the generations of his parents, his grandparents, who had all had to have their mushrooms, their flowers, weighed on the scales, and he was overwhelmed by a great wave of injustice, and began to sob louder than ever, and, without waiting to be asked, he sat down on a chair, ignoring the pancakes, the cup of hot coffee which nice, plump Frau Honig put in front of him, and did not stop crying till Honig himself came out from the shop at the back and, rattling the pebbles in his hand, said in a low voice to his wife: "Fifty-five grams, exactly."

My grandfather walked the two hours home through the forest, got a beating at home, said nothing, not a single word, when he was asked about the coffee, spent the whole evening doing sums on the piece of paper on which he had written down everything he had sold to Frau Balek, and when midnight struck, and the cannon could be heard from the chateau, and the whole village rang with shouting and laughter and the noise of rattles, when the family kissed and embraced all round, he said into the New Year's silence: "The Baleks owe me eighteen marks and thirty-two pfennigs." And again he thought of all the children there were in the village, of his brother Fritz who had gathered so many mushrooms, of his sister Ludmilla; he thought of the many hundreds of children who had all gathered mush-

MINI-LESSON: VOCABULARY
Finding Synonyms in Dictionaries

Teach Use the word *confer* as an example of how to find synonyms in a dictionary and consider which synonym to use in their writing. First have students note the sentence beginning at the bottom of page 768, and the use of *conferred.*

"My grandfather was the first person bold enough to test the justice of the Baleks . . . on whom the emperor <u>conferred</u> a title on the first day of the year 1900."

Activity Idea Students can look up *confer* and find the definitions. *(consult together; give, award)* Then they can:

1. Identify the definition of *confer* as used in the sentence above. *(give, award)*
2. Look up *give* to find the synonym study. *(give, present, confer)*
3. Analyze whether the choice of the synonym was appropriate. *(Yes, conferred, meaning "to present graciously," fits well with the idea of an emperor giving a title.)*
4. Repeat the exercise using these words from the story: *dispel* (page 766), *distributed* (page 769), *hostile* (page 771).

rooms for the Baleks, and herbs and flowers, and this time he did not cry but told his parents and brothers and sisters of his discovery.

When the Baleks von Bilgan went to High Mass on New Year's Day, their new coat of arms—a giant crouching under a fir tree—already emblazoned in blue and gold on their carriage, they saw the hard, pale faces of the people all staring at them. They had expected garlands in the village, a song in their honor, cheers, and hurrahs, but the village was completely deserted as they drove through it, and in church the pale faces of the people were turned toward them, mute[14] and hostile, and when the priest mounted the pulpit to deliver his New Year's sermon, he sensed the chill in those otherwise quiet and peaceful faces, and he stumbled painfully through his sermon and went back to the altar drenched in sweat. And as the Baleks von Bilgan left the church after Mass, they walked through a lane of mute, pale faces. But young Frau Balek von Bilgan stopped in front of the children's pews, sought out my grandfather's face, pale little Franz Brücher, and asked him, right there in the church: "Why didn't you take the coffee for your mother?" And my grandfather stood up and said: "Because you owe me as much money as five kilos of coffee would cost." And he pulled the five pebbles from his pocket, held them out to the young woman, and said: "This much, fifty-five grams, is short in every pound of your justice"; and before the woman could say anything, the men and women in the church lifted up their
12 voices and sang: "The justice of this earth, O Lord, hath put Thee to death. . . ."

While the Baleks were at church, Wilhelm Vohla, the poacher, had broken into the little room, stolen the scales and the big, fat, leather-bound book in which had been entered every kilo of mushrooms, every kilo of hayflowers, everything bought by the Baleks in the village, and all afternoon of that New Year's Day the men of the village sat in my great-grandparents' front room and calculated, calculated one tenth of everything that had been bought—but when they had calculated many thousands of talers and had still not come to an end, the reeve's gendarmes arrived, made their way into my great-grandfather's front room, shooting and stabbing as they came, and removed the scales and the book by force. My grandfather's little sister Ludmilla lost her life, a few men were wounded, and one of the gendarmes was stabbed to death by Wilhelm Vohla the poacher.

Our village was not the only one to rebel: Blaugau and Bernau did, too, and for almost a week no work was done in the flax sheds. But a great many gendarmes appeared, and the men and women were threatened with prison, and the Baleks forced the priest to display the scales publicly in the school and demonstrate that the finger of justice swung to and fro accurately. And the men and women went back to the flax sheds—but no one went to the school to watch the priest: he
stood there all alone, helpless and forlorn with his 13
weights, scales, and packages of coffee.

And the children went back to gathering mushrooms, to gathering thyme, flowers, and foxglove, but every Sunday, as soon as the Baleks entered the church, the hymn was struck up: "The justice of this earth, O Lord, hath put Thee to death," until the reeve ordered it proclaimed in every village that the singing of this hymn was forbidden.

My grandfather's parents had to leave the village and the new grave of their little daughter; they became basket weavers, but did not stay long anywhere because it pained them to see how everywhere the finger of justice swung falsely. They walked along behind their cart, which crept slowly over the country roads, taking their thin goat with them, and passers-by could sometimes hear a voice from the cart singing: "The justice of this earth, O Lord, hath put Thee to death." And those who wanted to listen could hear the tale of
the Baleks von Bilgan, whose justice lacked a 14
tenth part. But there were few who listened.

14. mute (myüt), *adj.* silent.

Literary Element
Allusion

This hymn refers to the "justice" of the earthly court that ordered Jesus put to death. It suggests that only God is just—that there is no true justice among people.

13 Reading/Thinking Skills
Summarize

Question What is the result of the villagers' attempt to have justice? *(Possible responses: Their demands are met with violence and they continue to live under repression. The boy and his family are exiled from their community.)*

14 Reader's Response
Making Personal Connections

Involve students in a discussion of whether or not justice can lack "a tenth part." Prompt them to discuss whether a little injustice means no justice.

Check Test

1. Where did the people in Franz's village work? *(flax sheds)*

2. What two jobs did children have? *(housework and gathering)*

3. What was the most prized food the children could find? *(truffles)*

4. Where did Franz find a scale to check the weight of the pebbles? *(at Honig, the apothecary's house, a two-hour walk from his village)*

5. Who died in the fighting? *(Franz's little sister, Ludmilla, and a gendarme)*

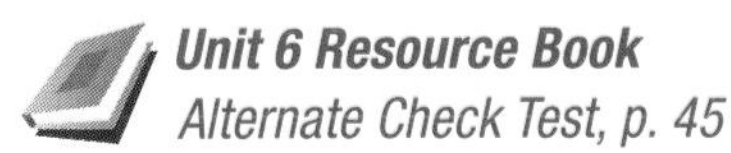

Unit 6 Resource Book
Alternate Check Test, p. 45

BUILDING ENGLISH PROFICIENCY

ESL LEP ELD SAE LD

Responding to a Theme

Encourage students to use the theme of injustice to relate this story to other situations that they know about.

1. Display or draw a simple scale. Have students "weigh" the power of the villagers against the power of the Baleks by "loading" the sides of the scale with facts, as shown.

2. Students can use the same visual to analyze a historical or personal injustice that they consider important.

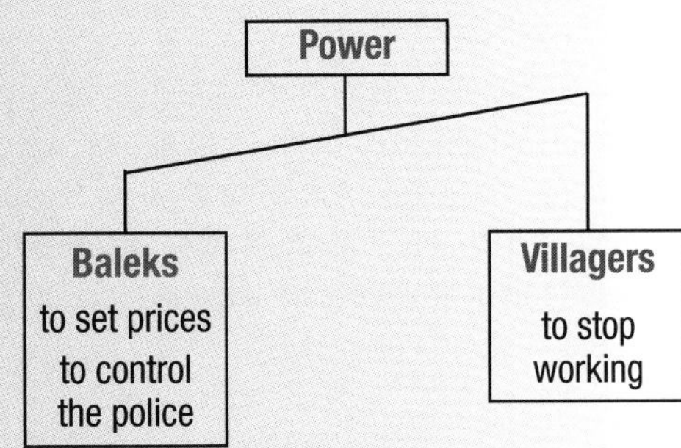

After Reading

MAKING CONNECTIONS

1. Possible response: The reader realizes how valuable justice is by seeing the consequences of injustice.

2. Possible responses: brave, just, proud, smart

3. Possible responses: children sleeping on benches, crawling around to find mushrooms, Frau Balek handing out lemon drops, a carriage with an imperial coat of arms

4. Possible response: when the boy stands up in church and announces that the scales are wrong and the people sing "The justice. . . . "

5. Possible response: The Baleks didn't have to admit anything because they had the power to crush any opposition; they fear giving the people any power.

6. Students may say that the hymn is one way of stating the theme.

7. Possible response: It is better not to know about what you can't change; it is always better to know the truth.

8. Guide students to identify

- elite groups, such as extremely wealthy persons and corporations
- types of injustice, such as lack of access to jobs and education
- methods used in the Baleks' time and today, such as token benevolence, threatening jobs, violence

9. Possible responses: wealth, education, family history; students who have lived in other cultures may have observed that different groups have more prestige in other countries than in the U.S.

10. Students may refer to incidents of popular rebellion, Marxism, the role of the bishops in getting King John to sign the Magna Charta and the rebellion of the American colonies.

After Reading

Making Connections

Shaping Your Response

1. Do you think this would have been a better story if justice had been obtained at the end? Explain.
2. What three words would you choose to describe Franz Brücher, the **narrator**'s grandfather?

Analyzing the Story

3. Böll's story is filled with **local color,** details that convey the feeling of rural Middle Europe a good many years ago. What specific details produce that feeling?
4. Where does the **climax** appear in this story?
5. Why do you think the Baleks did not admit their guilt?
6. How does the hymn relate to the **theme** of the story?
7. Do you feel the villagers would have been better off not knowing about the false scales? Why or why not?

Extending the Ideas

8. As representatives of a socially, politically, and economically elite class, the Balek family gets away with a terrible injustice. Does this happen today in the United States? Explain.
9. What marks the difference between social classes today? education? wealth? luck? talent? race? Explain.
10. What do you think it takes to **change** a class system like the one described in the story?

Literary Focus: Theme

Explain whether or not each of the following statements is an appropriate expression of a **theme** of "The Balek Scales."

- "Might makes right."
- "A little child shall lead them."
- "A penny saved is a penny earned."
- "Justice delayed is justice denied."
- "No use crying over spilt milk."

LITERARY FOCUS: THEME

"Justice delayed is justice denied" is the most appropriate theme.

Students should support their statements by pointing to ideas emphasized by the characters' words and actions, the setting, the point of view, repetition, and the title. Remind students that sometimes a direct statement of the theme may be found in the story itself.

Vocabulary Study

Determine the relationship between the first pair of capitalized words. Then write the letter of the pair of words with a similar relationship to complete the analogy.

chateau
dispel
meager
mute
theology

1. MEAGER : AMPLE :: **a.** hungry : starving **b.** humid : warm **c.** timid : courageous **d.** precise : accurate
2. CHATEAU : COTTAGE :: **a.** yacht : canoe **b.** tree : oak **c.** shoe: sock **d.** tailor: thread
3. THEOLOGY: RELIGION :: **a.** church : synagogue **b.** dollar : dime **c.** botany : plants **d.** kitten: purr
4. MUTE : SILENT :: **a.** sharp : blunt **b.** loyal : dog **c.** clumsy : agile **d.** plain : simple
5. DISPEL : DRIVE AWAY :: **a.** permit : forbid **b.** scatter : leaves **c.** combine : mix **d.** distribute : gather

Expressing Your Ideas

Writing Choices

Writer's Notebook Update Review your list of details that reveal your life, surroundings, and society. Use this information to write the opening of a story. Start your story the way Böll starts his: "Where ____ [insert your name] came from, most of the people. . . ."

Read All About It! People or organizations often buy space in a newspaper to air their grievances. As Franz, combine words with pictures to create an **ad** that tells the world what the Balek family has done.

Family Discussion The young Frau Balek has discovered that the weights used to balance the family scales are inaccurate. Write a **dialogue** in which she tries to persuade her mother-in-law to exchange them for accurate ones.

Other Options

Family Symbol The Balek's coat of arms is described as a "giant crouching under a fir tree." Draw either what you think it actually looked like, or draw the coat of arms that you think the Baleks should have had.

Knock and Mock Political cartoons are visual as well as verbal satires. Create a **political cartoon** that focuses on the major event of "The Balek Scales" and reveals its injustice. Add a caption.

Where Upon a Time From hints in the narrative, the events in this story take place during the time of the Austro-Hungarian empire. Find or draw a **map** of the boundaries of that empire, locating and labeling its capital. Then decide where the villages mentioned in the story are located and show what events in the story happen in each.

VOCABULARY STUDY

1. c
2. a
3. c
4. d
5. c

Unit 6 Resource Book
Vocabulary, p. 43
Vocabulary Test, p. 46

WRITING CHOICES

Writer's Notebook Update

Remind students that since they are writing about people and an environment that they know well, they can begin by freewriting continuously for at least ten minutes before stopping to review what they wrote.

Family Discussion

Before writing the dialogue, students should assign some characteristics to young Frau Balek, such as timidity, rebelliousness, or curiosity. Her personality should be evident in the dialogue.

Selection Test

Unit 6 Resource Book
pp. 47–48

OTHER OPTIONS

Family Symbol

tudents may be interested to learn that heraldry is n ancient visual language used to identify warriors. n armored man wore these identifications first on is shield, and then on a coat worn over the armor. became known as his "coat of arms." Among the aditional components of a coat of arms are a otto and supporters, such as lions on either side f a shield.

Where Upon a Time

Encourage students to use an atlas, an historical atlas, or a geographical dictionary to locate Blaugau, Bernau, and Dielheim so that they can place them accurately on their map.

Before Reading

Building Background

Ask students to suggest a modern analogy for "hunger for land." Discuss what people are eager to acquire today, and how getting these things affects other groups.

Literary Focus

Explain that the word **parable** is from a Greek word meaning "juxtaposition" or "comparison."

Writer's Notebook

Tell students that understanding the antagonist and the antagonist's behavior will also help them follow the plot. For example, another significant event in section 1 is the Devil's decision to tempt Pahom.

More About Leo Tolstoy

Tolstoy's ideas influenced many leaders and thinkers from many countries, including George Bernard Shaw, Mohandas Ghandi, and William Dean Howells.

Connections to **AuthorWorks**

Leo Tolstoy is a featured author in the AuthorWorks CD-ROM series.

Before Reading

How Much Land Does a Man Need?

by Leo Tolstoy Russia

Leo Tolstoy
1828–1910

One night, at the age of 82, Leo Tolstoy, a wealthy Russian count and world-famous writer, dressed in peasant clothes, fled his estate, and set out on a religious pilgrimage. He died while on the journey, in search of a peace that had eluded him throughout his long life. Despite the advantages of his birth and the great successes in his life, Tolstoy was tormented by a sense of failure. At different times he sought escape in idealistic schemes of reform on his estate, in sprees of compulsive gambling, in military service, in family life, and in creative efforts. But at the end of his life, he was still searching.

Building Background

A Hunger for Land Because of poor soil, frequent drought, and a short growing season, farming was difficult in much of Russia. Throughout most of the country's history, mainly because of the distribution of rainfall, Russia had one bad harvest out of every three. To make matters worse, Russian peasants were inefficient farmers who exhausted the fertility of the soil and then sought more land. This hunger for land drove Russia to expand east and south, seizing the grazing lands of the nomadic peoples of Central Asia, such as those of the Bashkirs mentioned in Tolstoy's story.

Literary Focus

Parable A **parable** is a brief narrative that illustrates a moral or philosophical teaching. The New Testament uses parables such as the Prodigal Son or the Good Samaritan to stress the value of forgiveness and compassion; the Greek philosopher Plato used his Parable of the Cave to express his view that our senses reveal only a shadowy glimpse of reality to us.

Writer's Notebook

Pahom's Progress? In each of the nine sections of this story, events occur that have an important effect on the protagonist and the development of his character. After you read each section, jot down notes for the following chart. The first one is done for you.

Section	Significant Event	Effect on Pahom
1	Visit of sister-in-law from town	Dissatisfaction with land he owns
2		
3		

SUPPORT MATERIALS OVERVIEW

Unit 5 Resource Book
- Graphic Organizer, p. 49
- Study Guide, p. 50
- Vocabulary, p. 51
- Grammar, p. 52
- Alternate Check Test, p. 53
- Vocabulary Test, p. 54
- Selection Test, pp. 55–56

Building English Proficiency
- Literature Summaries
- Activities, p. 225

Reading, Writing & Grammar SkillBook
- Reading, pp. 24–27
- Writing, pp. 128–129
- Grammar, Usage, and Mechanics, pp. 236–239

Technology
- Audiotape 20, Sides A and B
- Personal Journal Software
- Custom Literature Database: See "Christmas Every Day" by William Dean Howells and a variety of tales by Aesop, Sa'di, Edward Thomas, and others on the database.
- Test Generator Software

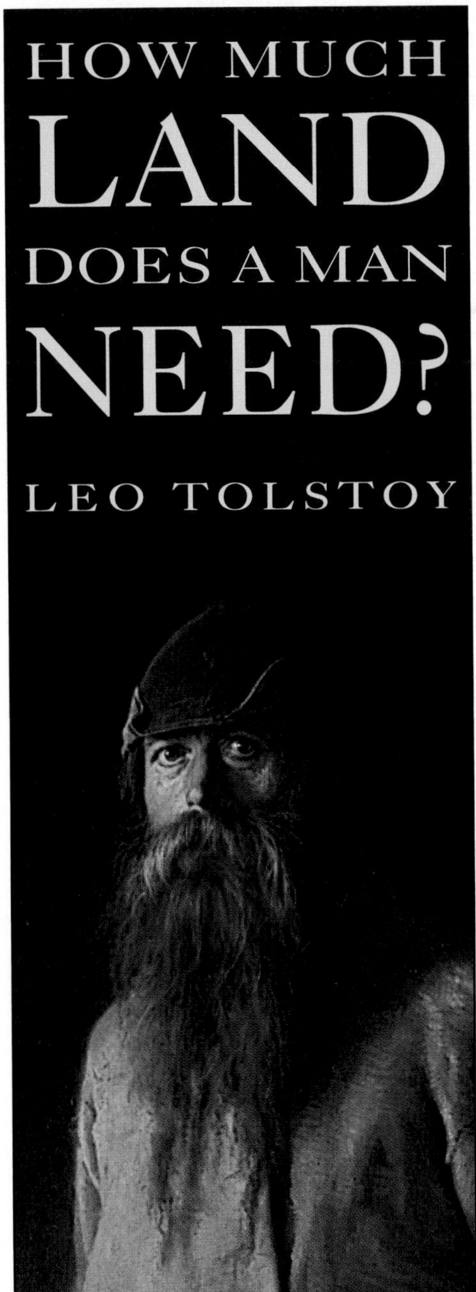

HOW MUCH LAND DOES A MAN NEED?

LEO TOLSTOY

1

An elder sister came to visit her younger sister in the country. The elder was married to a shopkeeper in town, the younger to a peasant in the village. As the sisters sat over their tea talking, the elder began to boast of the advantages of town life, saying how comfortably they lived there, how well they dressed, what fine clothes her children wore, what good things they ate and drank, and how she went to the theater, promenades, and entertainments.

The younger sister was piqued, and in turn disparaged[1] the life of a shopkeeper, and stood up for that of a peasant. 1

"I wouldn't change my way of life for yours," said she. "We may live roughly, but at least we're free from worry. You live in better style than we do, but though you often earn more than you need, you're very likely to lose all you have. You know the proverb, 'Loss and gain are brothers twain.' It often happens that people who're wealthy one day are begging their bread the next. Our way is safer. Though a peasant's life is not a rich one, it's long. We'll never grow rich, but we'll always have enough to eat."

The elder sister said sneeringly:

"Enough? Yes, if you like to share with the pigs and the calves! What do you know of elegance or manners! However much your good man may slave, you'll die as you live—in a dung heap—and your children the same."

"Well, what of that?" replied the younger sister. "Of course our work is rough and hard. But on the other hand, it's sure,

1. disparage (dis par′ij), *v.* belittle; discredit.

Forester by Russian artist Ivan N. Kramskoi (1837–1887) was painted in 1874. All successful portraits reveal something of the inner person. What can you tell about this man?

During Reading

Selection Objectives

- to explore the theme of the cost of winning
- to understand the genre of parable
- to understand the use of paragraphing

Unit 6 Resource Book
Graphic Organizer, p. 49
Study Guide, p. 50

Theme Link

In winning a race for land, Pahom loses his judgment and pays the highest cost — his life.

Vocabulary Preview

arable, suitable for producing crops
communal, owned jointly by all
discord, disagreement
disparage, belittle; discredit
disperse, go off in different directions

Students can add the words and definitions to their Writer's Notebooks.

Art Study

Response to Caption Question
His fearful eyes dominate the image and suggest suffering. The beard is like a mask that hides his individuality, as if the artist were trying to make him a symbol of poverty and perhaps injustice.

1 Literary Element
Allusion

Question What other tales does this argument remind you of? *(Possible responses: "The City Mouse and the Country Mouse"; students familiar with other cultures may offer other titles.)*

SELECTION SUMMARY

How Much Land Does a Man Need?

A peasant named Pahom claims that if he had enough land, he wouldn't worry again, and that he wouldn't even fear the Devil. The Devil decides to entrap him. Pahom first buys forty acres. Though he is prosperous, he is unhappy. Then he buys a farm of 125 acres and even rents more, but remains discontented. Finally, he goes to the rich land of the Bashkirs, where huge tracts of land can be bought "almost for nothing." For a thousand rubles, the Baskhir nomads agree to give Pahom all the land he can encircle by walking for a day. Eagerly he sets out, but he tries to take in too much land and time runs out. Running frantically, Pahom reaches the starting point and dies just as the sun sets. They bury him there in a six-foot plot.

*For summaries in other languages, see the **Building English Proficiency** book.*

2 Literary Element
Figurative Language

Questions

- Explain the literal and figurative meanings of this statement. *(It literally means that Pahom thinks that owning land will keep him safe from damnation. Figuratively, it means that Pahom wouldn't worry about ever being poor or unable to provide for his family.)*
- What are some examples of similar wishes that people make today? *(If I could [win the lottery, pass a test, have a car, live with my dad], everything would be perfect.)*

3 Literary Focus
Parable

Point out to students that many parables, like those of Jesus, have a supernatural element.

4 Literary Element
Plot

Question What basic plot conflict is initiated here? *(The Devil is going to try to win Pahom's soul through the temptation of land ownership.)*

5 Active Reading
Connect

Response Students may find similarities in *Faust*, "The Devil and Daniel Webster," "The Monkey's Paw," and other stories.

and we need not bow to anyone. But you, in your towns, are surrounded by temptations; today all may be right, but tomorrow the Evil One may tempt your husband with cards, wine, or women, and all will go to ruin. Don't such things happen often enough?"

Pahom, the master of the house, was lying on the top of the stove[2] and he listened to the women's chatter.

"It is perfectly true," thought he. "Busy as we are from childhood tilling mother earth, we peasants have no time to let any nonsense settle in our heads. Our only trouble is that we haven't
2 land enough. If I had plenty of land I shouldn't fear the Devil himself!"

The women finished their tea, chatted a while about dress, and then cleared away the tea things and lay down to sleep.

3 But the Devil had been sitting behind the stove and had heard all that had been said. He was pleased that the peasant's wife had led her husband into boasting and that he had said that if he had plenty of land he would not fear the Devil himself.

"All right," thought the Devil. "We'll have a
4 tussle. I'll give you land enough; and by means of the land I'll get you into my power."

5 **CONNECT: What other stories do you recall in which power or money is acquired through an arrangement with the Devil?**

2

Close to the village there lived a lady, a small landowner who had an estate of about three hundred acres. She had always lived on good terms with the peasants until she engaged as her manager an old soldier, who took to burdening the people with fines. However careful Pahom tried to be, it happened again and again that now a horse of his got among the lady's oats, now a cow strayed into her garden, now his calves found their way into her meadows—and he always had to pay a fine.

Pahom paid up, but grumbled, and, going home in a temper, was rough with his family. All through that summer Pahom had much trouble because of this manager, and he was actually glad when winter came and the cattle had to be stabled. Though he grudged the fodder when they could no longer graze on the pasture land, at least he was free from anxiety about them.

In the winter the news got about that the lady was going to sell her land and that the keeper of the inn on the high road was bargaining for it. When the peasants heard this they were very much alarmed.

"Well," thought they, "if the innkeeper gets the land, he'll worry us with fines worse than the lady's manager. We all depend on that estate."

So the peasants went on behalf of their village council and asked the lady not to sell the land to the innkeeper, offering her a better price for it themselves. The lady agreed to let them have it. Then the peasants tried to arrange for the village council to buy the whole estate, so that it might be held by them all in common. They met twice to discuss it, but could not settle the matter; the Evil One sowed discord[3] among them and they could not agree. So they decided to buy the land individually, each according to his means; and the lady agreed to this plan as she had to the other.

Presently Pahom heard that a neighbor of his was buying fifty acres, and that the lady had consented to accept one half in cash and to wait a year for the other half. Pahom felt envious.

"Look at that," thought he, "the land is all being sold, and I'll get none of it." So he spoke to his wife.

"Other people are buying," said he, "and we must also buy twenty acres or so. Life is becom-

2. **lying . . . stove.** In Russian cottages, flat-topped stoves were large enough for people to lie on.
3. **discord** (dis′kôrd), *n.* disagreement.

MINI-LESSON: GRAMMAR
Paragraph Indentation

Teach Refer students to the last three paragraphs on page 776. Point out that the paragraphs have different purposes.

- The first is a description by the narrator.
- The second reveals Pahom's thoughts.
- The third quotes Pahom's words to his wife.

Remind students that in general these three items—description or narration, thoughts, and direct quotations—are placed in separate paragraphs for clarity.

Activity Idea Have students use the places above and those listed below to divide passages into separate paragraphs when peer editing.

- shifts in time signaled by *first, then, afterwards*
- shifts in place signaled by *over there, on the other side*
- shifts in direction signaled by *on the other hand, nevertheless, however*
- shifts in emphasis signaled by new emphases or new aspects of the topic sentence

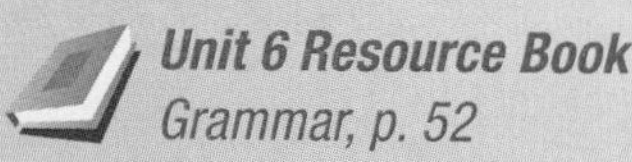

Unit 6 Resource Book
Grammar, p. 52

ing impossible. That manager is simply crushing us with his fines."

So they put their heads together and considered how they could manage to buy it. They had one hundred rubles laid by. They sold a colt and one half of their bees, hired out one of their sons as a farm hand and took his wages in advance, borrowed the rest from a brother-in-law, and so scraped together half the purchase money.

Having done this, Pahom chose a farm of forty acres, some of it wooded, and went to the lady to bargain for it. They came to an agreement, and he shook hands with her upon it and paid her a deposit in advance. Then they went to town and signed the deeds, he paying half the price down, and undertaking to pay the remainder within two years.

6 So now Pahom had land of his own. He borrowed seed and sowed it on the land he had bought. The harvest was a good one, and within a year he had managed to pay off his debts both to the lady and to his brother-in-law. So he became a landowner, plowing and sowing his own land, making hay on his own land, cutting his own trees, and feeding his cattle on his own pasture. When he went out to plow his fields, or to look at his growing corn, or at his grass meadows, his heart would fill with joy. The grass that grew and the flowers that bloomed there seemed to him unlike any that grew elsewhere. Formerly, when he had passed by that land, it had appeared the same as any other land, but now it seemed quite different.

3

7 So Pahom was well contented, and everything would have been right if the neighboring peasants would only not have trespassed on his wheatfields and meadows. He appealed to them most civilly, but they still went on: now the herdsmen would let the village cows stray into his meadows, then horses from the night pasture would get among his corn. Pahom turned them out again and again, and forgave their owners, and for a long time he forbore to prosecute anyone. But at last he lost patience and complained to the District Court. He knew it was the peasants' want of land, and no evil intent on their part, that caused the trouble, but he thought:

"I can't go on overlooking it, or they'll destroy all I have. They must be taught a lesson."

So he had them up, gave them one lesson, and then another, and two or three of the peasants were fined. After a time Pahom's neighbors began to bear him a grudge for this, and would now and then let their cattle on to his land on purpose. One peasant even got into Pahom's wood at night and cut down five young lime trees for their bark. Pahom, passing through the wood one day, noticed something white. He came nearer and saw the stripped trunks lying on the ground, and close by stood the stumps where the trees had been. Pahom was furious.

"If he'd only cut one here and there it would have been bad enough," thought Pahom, "but the rascal has actually cut down a whole clump. If I could only find out who did this, I'd get even with him."

He racked his brains as to who it could be. Finally he decided: "It must be Simon—no one else could have done it." So he went to Simon's homestead to have a look around, but he found nothing and only had an angry scene. However, he now felt more certain than ever that Simon had done it, and he lodged a complaint. Simon was summoned. The case was tried, and retried, and at the end of it all Simon was acquitted, there being no evidence against him. Pahom felt still more aggrieved, and let his anger loose upon the Elders and the Judges.

"You let thieves grease your palms," said he. "If you were honest folk yourselves you wouldn't let a thief go free."

So Pahom quarreled with the judges and with his neighbors. Threats to burn his hut began to be uttered. So though Pahom had more land, his place in the community was much worse than before. 8

6 Literary Focus
Parable

Question What might be the moral of the parable if it ended with this paragraph? *(Possible response: Ownership makes a person happy and secure.)*

7 Reading/Thinking Skills
Cause and Effect

Question What events cause Pahom to change from "well-contented" to "much worse than before"? *(Possible response: neighbors trespassing, other peasants' cows grazing on his land, others' horses eating his corn, Pahom fining the neighbors, the neighbors' holding a grudge and retaliating by cutting down Pahom's trees, the trial, Pahom's quarrels with the judges)*

8 Literary Element
Stereotype

Discuss whether students think Pahom is a stereotype. Remind them that a stereotype is a conventional character, plot, or setting that possesses little or no individuality or complexity. Ask students what other conventional characters they know of who are continually thwarted by their own faults or circumstances. *(Possible responses: cartoon characters such as Charlie Brown, secondary characters in many TV shows.)*

BUILDING ENGLISH PROFICIENCY

Understanding Sequence

Use these paraphrased statements made by Pahom as cloze sentences to help students understanding the plot and Pahom's motivation.

1. "Our only trouble is that we haven't enough ____." *(land)* page 776

2. "I can't let the ____ cows eat my ____. I will ____ them a lesson." *(neighbors', peasants; corn; teach)* page 777

3. "I am too ____ to be comfortable here; I will ____ my land and with the ____ I will buy more." *(cramped, crowded; sell; money)* page 778

Students can work in pairs to create more cloze sentences that continue the plot.

9 Active Reading
Evaluate

Response Pahom begins as someone who is discontented and worried about his situation. When he first gets the land it gives him great joy, but then he again becomes discontented and worried. This seems to be a pattern showing that Pahom may be greedy and power-hungry at heart.

10 Literary Focus
Parable

Archetypal characters are often present in a parable. Here, the Devil appears with characteristics that are typically assigned to him: he is a stranger and has no name.

11 Reader's Response
Challenge the Text

Open a discussion of whether Pahom is just being a smart businessperson or a greedy, discontented man in his quest for land. Students should consider what Pahom's reasons for acquiring land have been since the beginning of the parable.

9 **EVALUATE: How has Pahom's character changed since the beginning of the story?**

About this time a rumor got about that many people were moving to new parts.

"There's no need for me to leave my land," thought Pahom. "But some of the others may leave our village and then there'd be more room for us. I'd take over their land myself and make my estates somewhat bigger. I could then live more at ease. As it is, I'm still too cramped to be comfortable."

One day Pahom was sitting at home when a peasant, passing through the village, happened to drop in. He was allowed to stay the night, and supper was given him. Pahom had a talk with this peasant and asked him where he came
10 from. The stranger answered that he came from beyond the Volga,[4] where he had been working. One word led to another, and the man went on to say that many people were settling in those parts. He told how some people from his village had settled there. They had joined the community there and had had twenty-five acres per man granted them. The land was so good, he said, that the rye sown on it grew as high as a horse, and so thick that five cuts of a sickle made a sheaf. One peasant, he said, had brought nothing with him but his bare hands, and now he had six horses and two cows of his own.

Pahom's heart kindled with desire.

"Why should I suffer in this narrow hole if one can live so well elsewhere?" he thought. "I'll sell my land and my homestead here, and with the money I'll start afresh over there and get everything new. In this crowded place one is always having trouble. But I must first go and find out all about it myself."

Toward summer he got ready and started out. He went down the Volga on a steamer to Samara, then walked another three hundred miles on foot, and at last reached the place. It was just as the stranger had said. The peasants had plenty of land: every man had twenty-five acres of communal[5] land given him for his use and anyone who had money could buy, besides, at a ruble and a half an acre, as much good freehold land[6] as he wanted.

Having found out all he wished to know, Pahom returned home as autumn came on, and began selling off his belongings. He sold his land at a profit, sold his homestead and all his cattle, and withdrew from membership in the village. He only waited till the spring, and then started with his family for the new settlement.

4

As soon as Pahom and his family reached their new abode, he applied for admission into the council of a large village. He stood treat to the Elders and obtained the necessary documents. Five shares of communal land were given him for his own and his sons' use: that is to say—125 acres (not all together, but in different fields) besides the use of the communal pasture. Pahom put up the buildings he needed and bought cattle. Of the communal land alone he had three times as much as at his former home, and the land was good wheat land. He was ten times better off than he had been. He had plenty of arable[7] land and pasturage, and could keep as many head of cattle as he liked.

At first, in the bustle of building and settling 11
down, Pahom was pleased with it all, but when he got used to it he began to think that even here he hadn't enough land. The first year he sowed wheat on his share of the communal land and had a good crop. He wanted to go on sowing wheat, but had not enough communal land for the purpose, and what he had already used was not available, for in those parts wheat is sown only

4. **Volga**, river in western Russia.
5. **communal** (kə myü′nl), *adj.* owned jointly by all.
6. **freehold land.** In legal terms, freehold land is land held or owned free and clear. In many countries a person can own a house, but the land that it sits on is merely leased for a period of time—usually 100 years. Such a house would be called a leasehold.
7. **arable** (ar′ə bəl), *adj.* suitable for producing crops.

MINI-LESSON: VOCABULARY
Understanding Content Area Vocabulary

Teach Read the following words from page 778 to students. Challenge them to use context clues to identify their meanings. Elicit from them that the words are related to agriculture. Clarify the definition when necessary.

homestead, the place where a family makes its home—their house and outbuildings and the land it rests on

pasturage, the same as *pasture*—land that is suitable for grazing

virgin soil, land that has never been used for agriculture

fallow, land that is plowed but not seeded so that it can rest

Activity Idea Have students use the words listed above as well as other agriculture words from the selection, such as *freehold land, sickle, sheaf,* and others, to write a brief tale or poem with an agricultural theme or setting.

on virgin soil or on fallow land. It is sown for one or two years, and then the land lies fallow till it is again overgrown with steppe[8] grass. There were many who wanted such land, and there was not enough for all, so that people quarreled about it. Those who were better off wanted it for growing wheat, and those who were poor wanted it to let to dealers, so that they might raise money to pay their taxes. Pahom wanted to sow more wheat, so he rented land from a dealer for a year. He sowed much wheat and had a fine crop, but the land was too far from the village—the wheat had to be carted more than ten miles. After a time Pahom noticed that some peasant dealers were living on separate farms and were growing wealthy, and he thought:

"If I were to buy some freehold land and have a homestead on it, it would be a different thing altogether. Then it would all be fine and close together."

The question of buying freehold land recurred to him again and again.

He went on in the same way for three years, renting land and sowing wheat. The seasons turned out well and the crops were good, so that he began to lay by money. He might have gone on living contentedly, but he grew tired of having to rent other people's land every year and having to scramble for it. Wherever there was good land to be had, the peasants would rush for it and it was taken up at once, so that unless you were sharp about it, you got none. It happened in the third year that he and a dealer together rented a piece of pasture land from some peasants, and they had already plowed it up, when there was some dispute and the peasants went to law about it, and things fell out so that the labor was all lost.

"If it were my own land," thought Pahom, "I
12 should be independent, and there wouldn't be all this unpleasantness."

So Pahom began looking out for land which he could buy, and he came across a peasant who had bought thirteen hundred acres, but having got into difficulties was willing to sell again cheap. Pahom bargained and haggled with him, and at 13
last they settled the price at fifteen hundred rubles, part in cash and part to be paid later. They had all but clinched the matter when a passing dealer happened to stop at Pahom's one day to get feed for his horses. He drank tea with Pahom, and they had a talk. The dealer said that he was just returning from the land of the Bashkirs,[9] far away, where he had bought thirteen thousand acres of land, all for a thousand rubles. Pahom questioned him further, and the dealer said:

"All one has to do is to make friends with the chiefs. I gave away about one hundred rubles' worth of silk robes and carpets, besides a case of tea, and I gave wine to those who would drink it; and I got the land for less than three kopecks an acre." And he showed Pahom the title deed, saying:

"The land lies near a river, and the whole steppe is virgin soil."

Pahom plied him with questions, and the dealer said:

"There's more land there than you could cover if you walked a year, and it all belongs to 14
the Bashkirs. They're as simple as sheep, and land can be got almost for nothing."

"There, now," thought Pahom, "with my one thousand rubles, why should I get only thirteen hundred acres, and saddle myself with a debt besides? If I take it out there, I can get more than ten times as much for my money.

5

Pahom inquired how to get to the place, and as soon as the grain dealer had left him, he prepared to go there himself. He left his wife to look after the homestead, and started on his journey, taking his hired man with him. They stopped at a town on their way and bought a case of tea, some wine, and other presents, as the grain dealer had advised.

---

8. **steppe,** vast, treeless plains.
9. **Bashkirs,** nomadic people living in central Asia.

12 Reading/Thinking Skills
Predict

Questions

- What advantages does Pahom see in owning his own land? *(Possible response: He can be free of all kinds of troublesome dealings with other human beings.)*
- Do you believe this or something else will satisfy him? *(Possible response: No, he will always be tempted when someone else seems to have an advantage.)*

13 Literary Element
Irony

After students understand that both strangers are the Devil in disguise, you may wish to have them return to this paragraph and note the narrator's comment "happened to stop." Help them see that the "dealer's" passing was completely planned and that the narrator's comment is ironic.

14 Reading/Thinking Skills
Make Judgments

Question If you were an experienced landowner and farmer, how would you react to this news? *(Possible responses: believe the dealer and hurry to buy Bashkir land; doubt that land could be gotten so easily; believe that the Bashkirs are really foolish and do not recognize the value of land)*

BUILDING ENGLISH PROFICIENCY

ESL LEP ELD SAE LD

Making Personal Connections

Discuss with students what Pahom's bases his happiness on. Lead them to express their ideas about the fact that he always seems to feel that he will be happy if he has more land. Then let them develop a personal t-chart like the following in which they list and explain a few possessions that they think would improve their lives. Challenge students to consider whether or not they would pursue these items with Pahom's zeal. They do not have to share their list.

If I had	Then I could
a car	have more fun with my friends do errands have a job

Art Study

Response to Caption Question
Students may say the mood is one of contentment and joy suggested by the warm light, fullness of the harvest, the bird in flight in the background, and the endless grain.

Visual Literacy A basic rule of perspective is that objects appear to get smaller the further away they are.

Question How does Myasoyedov apply this rule? *(He paints the separate stalks of grain in the foreground as large and detailed, and the people a little further back as smaller and smaller. Eventually vertical objects disappear, and only horizontal lines of color are left.)*

Question What effect does this produce? *(an illusion of depth, the idea that the land goes on forever)*

15 Literary Element
Stereotype

Questions What stereotype does this description bring to mind? *(Possible response: the noble savage, the pure-hearted person who is in tune with nature and is not corrupted by material things)*

The Mowers (1887) was painted by Grigori G. Myasoyedov. Explain whether you would describe the mood of the picture as gloomy, sentimental, happy, or something else.

On and on they went until they had gone more than three hundred miles, and on the seventh day they came to a place where the Bashkirs had pitched their round tents. It was all just as the dealer had said. The people lived on the steppe, by a river, in felt-covered tents. They neither tilled the ground nor ate bread. Their cattle and horses grazed in herds on the steppe. The colts were tethered behind the tents, and the mares were driven to them twice a day. The mares were milked, and from the milk kumiss[10] was made. It was the women who prepared the kumiss, and they also made cheese. As far as the men were concerned, drinking kumiss and tea, eating mutton, and playing on their pipes was all they cared about.
15 They were all stout and merry, and all the summer long they never thought of doing any work. They were quite ignorant, and knew no Russian, but were good-natured enough.

As soon as they saw Pahom, they came out of their tents and gathered around the visitor. An interpreter was found, and Pahom told them he had come about some land. The Bashkirs seemed very glad; they took Pahom and led him into one of the best tents, where they made him sit on some down cushions placed on a carpet, while they sat around him. They gave him some tea and kumiss, and had a sheep killed, and gave him mutton to eat. Pahom took presents out of his cart and distributed them among the Bashkirs, and divided the tea amongst them. The Bashkirs were delighted. They talked a great deal among themselves and then told the interpreter what to say.

"They wish to tell you," said the interpreter, "that they like you and that it's our custom to do all we can to please a guest and to repay him for his gifts. You have given us presents, now tell us which of the things we possess please you best, that we may present them to you."

"What pleases me best here," answered Pahom, "is your land. Our land is crowded and

10. **kumiss,** fermented mare's or camel's milk.

MINI-LESSON: STUDY SKILLS

Locate, Use, and Evaluate Reference Sources

Teach Point out that on page 780, some references are made to Bashkir culture. Tell students that they will understand the story better if they make the effort to find out more about the culture. Explain that they can find different kinds of information from different sources. For example, a dictionary may reveal that the Bashkir are a Turkic Moslem people and where they live.

Activity Idea Let students develop a question about the peoples of the Russian steppes, research the answer, and write a summary of their findings. Questions may relate to food, resources, modern pressures on their culture and way of life, and other reactions to statements in the story. Encourage students to use an atlas, encyclopedia, geographic dictionary, books about eastern Russia, and online catalogs and encyclopedias.

the soil is worn out, but you have plenty of land, and it is good land. I never saw the likes of it."

The interpreter told the Bashkirs what Pahom had said. They talked among themselves for a while. Pahom could not understand what they were saying, but saw that they were much amused and heard them shout and laugh. Then they were silent and looked at Pahom while the interpreter said:

16 "They wish me to tell you that in return for your presents they will gladly give you as much land as you want. You have only to point it out with your hand and it is yours."

The Bashkirs talked again for a while and began to dispute. Pahom asked what they were disputing about, and the interpreter told him that some of them thought they ought to ask their chief about the land and not act in his absence, while others thought there was no need to wait for his return.

6

While the Bashkirs were disputing, a man in
17 a large fox-fur cap appeared on the scene. They all became silent and rose to their feet. The interpreter said: "This is our chief himself."

Pahom immediately fetched the best dressing gown and five pounds of tea, and offered these to the chief. The chief accepted them and seated himself in the place of honor. The Bashkirs at once began telling him something. The chief listened for a while, then made a sign with his head for them to be silent, and addressing himself to Pahom, said in Russian:

"Well, so be it. Choose whatever piece of land you like; we have plenty of it."

"How can I take as much as I like?" thought Pahom. "I must get a deed to make it secure, or else they may say: 'It is yours,' and afterward may take it away again."

"Thank you for your kind words," he said aloud. "You have much land, and I only want a little. But I should like to be sure which portion is mine. Could it not be measured and made over to me? Life and death are in God's hands. You good people give it to me, but your children might wish to take it back again."

"You are quite right," said the chief. "We will make it over to you."

"I heard that a dealer had been here," continued Pahom, "and that you gave him a little land, too, and signed title deeds to that effect. I should like to have it done in the same way."

The chief understood.

"Yes," replied he, "that can be done quite easily. We have a scribe, and we will go to town with you and have the deed properly sealed."

"And what will be the price?" asked Pahom.

"Our price is always the same: one thousand rubles a day."

Pahom did not understand.

"A day? What measure is that? How many acres would that be?"

"We do not know how to reckon it out," said the chief. "We sell it by the day. As much as you can go around on your feet in a day is yours, and the price is one thousand rubles a day."

Pahom was surprised.

"But in a day you can get around a large tract of land," he said.

The chief laughed.

"It will all be yours!" said he. "But there is one condition: If you don't return on the same
day to the spot whence you started, your money 18
is lost."

PREDICT: Why do you think the Bashkirs are so generous with land? 19

"But how am I to mark the way that I have gone?"

"Why, we shall go to any spot you like and stay there. You must start from that spot and make your round, taking a spade with you. Wherever you think necessary, make a mark. At every turning, dig a hole and pile up the turf; then afterward we will go around with a plow from hole to hole. You may make as large a circuit as you please, but before the sun sets you

16 Reading/Thinking Skills
Problem-Solving

Question What problem does this deal present for Pahom? *(Possible response: He has to put a limit on how much he wants, and he is never satisfied.)*

17 Literary Focus
Parable

You may wish to point out that many parables use symbols, such as the pearl of great price in one of Jesus' parables.

Question What might the fox-fur cap symbolize? *(Possible response: that the chieftain is wily, wild, tricky)*

18 Literary Focus
Parable

Point out that in a parable or tale the main character often must meet a clearly stated goal or limit, such as a time limit. Invite students to recall conditions of bargains in other tales, such as the fairy godmother telling Cinderella to return from the ball by midnight.

19 Active Reading
Predict

Response It may be a trick. Their lifestyle is not based on land ownership.

BUILDING ENGLISH PROFICIENCY

Speaking and Listening

Help students grasp the importance of the Bashkirs' "one condition" for selling their land to Pahom.

Activity Ideas

- Invite several volunteers to form a tableau consisting of Pahom, the Bashkir chief, the interpreter, and various other Bashkirs. Have them enact the bargain; then ask them to speak to the class, one by one, expressing the thoughts that they are thinking but not saying to each other. Display the word list to help students as they speak.
- Have students imagine that they can step into the story at this point (perhaps as the character of Pahom's servant). Ask: Would you encourage Pahom or warn him—and why? What would you say to the Bashkirs?

rubles	circuit
price	sunset
condition	deed
turf	

20 **Reading/Thinking Skills**
Connect

You might wish to compare Tecumsah's speech "Sell a Country! Why Not Sell the Air?" and his view of land ownership with the attitudes of the Bashkir people. The brief speech is available on the Custom Literature Database.

21 **Reading/Thinking Skills**
Clarify

Question What did Pahom's dream clarify for you about the story? *(Possible response: that the Devil was transforming himself in order to trick Pahom)*

22 **Reader's Response**
Problem-Solving

Question If you were Pahom, how would you plan your circuit in order to get the best land? *(Possible responses: including land with certain features, like flat land for pasture, wooded land for fuel, and land with running water for power)*

20 must return to the place you started from. All the land you cover will be yours."

Pahom was delighted. It was decided to start early next morning. They talked a while, and after drinking some more kumiss and eating some more mutton, they had tea again, and then the night came on. They gave Pahom a feather bed to sleep on, and the Bashkirs dispersed[11] for the night, promising to assemble the next morning at daybreak and ride out before sunrise to the appointed spot.

7

Pahom lay on the feather bed, but could not sleep. He kept thinking about the land.

"What a large tract I'll mark off!" thought he, "I can easily do thirty-five miles in a day. The days are long now, and within a circuit of thirty-five miles what a lot of land there will be! I'll sell the poorer land or let it to peasants, but I'll pick out the best and farm it myself. I'll buy two ox teams and hire two more laborers. About a hundred and fifty acres shall be plowland, and I'll pasture cattle on the rest."

Pahom lay awake all night and dozed off only just before dawn. Hardly were his eyes closed when he had a dream. He thought he was lying in that same tent and heard somebody chuckling outside. He wondered who it could be, and rose and went out, and he saw the Bashkir chief sitting in front of the tent holding his sides and rolling about with laughter. Going nearer to the chief, Pahom asked, "What are you laughing at?" But he saw that it was no longer the chief but the grain dealer who had recently stopped at his house and had told him about the land. Just as Pahom was going to ask: "Have you been here long?" he saw that it was not the dealer, but the peasant who had come up from the Volga long ago to Pahom's old home. Then he saw that it was not the peasant either, but the Devil himself with hoofs and horns, sitting there and chuckling, and before him lay a man, prostrate on the ground, barefooted, with only trousers and a shirt on. And Pahom dreamed that he looked more attentively to see what sort of man it was lying there, and he saw that the man was dead, and that it was himself. Horror-struck, he awoke. 21

"What things one dreams about!" thought he.

Looking around he saw through the open door that the dawn was breaking.

"It's time to wake them up," thought he. "We ought to be starting."

He got up, roused his man (who was sleeping in his cart), bade him harness, and went to call the Bashkirs.

"It's time to go to the steppe to measure the land," he said.

The Bashkirs rose and assembled, and the chief came, too. Then they began drinking kumiss again, and offered Pahom some tea, but he would not wait.

"If we are to go, let's go. It's high time," said he.

8

The Bashkirs got ready and they all started: some mounted on horses and some in carts. Pahom drove in his own small cart with his servant and took a spade with him. When they reached the steppe, the red dawn was beginning to kindle. They ascended a hillock (called by the Bashkirs a *shikhan)* and, dismounting from their carts and their horses, gathered in one spot. The chief came to Pahom and, stretching out his arm toward the plain:

"See," said he, "all this, as far as your eye can reach, is ours. You may have any part of it you like."

Pahom's eyes glistened; it was all virgin soil, as flat as the palm of your hand, as black as the seed of a poppy, and in the hollows different kinds of grasses grew breast-high.

The chief took off his fox-fur cap, placed it on the ground, and said:

"This will be the mark. Start from here, and return here again. All the land you go around 22
shall be yours."

11. **disperse** (dis pėrs′), *v.* go off in different directions.

MINI-LESSON: READING/THINKING SKILLS
Identify Alternatives

Teach Prompt students to identify many problems that Pahom faces as he works to improve his life. List them on the board. *(Possible responses: He is poor; he needs more land; he worries about his calves going on to the wealthy lady's property; he objects to people who let their animals eat his corn; he always wants more land.)*

Activity Idea Ask students to

1. classify the problems as financial, personal, interpersonal, and so on
2. create solutions for the problems
3. pick up the story at the point of some problem and retell it using the suggested solutions, allowing Pahom to live at the end.

Pahom took out his money and put it on the cap. Then he took off his outer coat, remaining in his sleeveless undercoat. He unfastened his girdle[12] and tied it tight below his stomach, put a little bag of bread into the breast of his coat, and, tying a flask of water to his girdle, he drew up the tops of his boots, took the spade from his man, and stood ready to start. He considered for some moments which way he had better go—it was tempting everywhere.

"No matter," he concluded, "I'll go toward the rising sun."

He turned his face to the east, stretched himself, and waited for the sun to appear above the rim.

"I must lose no time," he thought, "and it's easier walking while it's still cool."

The sun's rays had hardly flashed above the horizon when Pahom, carrying the spade over his shoulder, went down into the steppe.

Pahom started walking neither slowly nor quickly. After having gone a thousand yards he stopped, dug a hole, and placed pieces of turf one on another to make it more visible. Then he went on; and now that he had walked off his stiffness he quickened his pace. After a while he dug another hole.

Pahom looked back. The hillock could be distinctly seen in the sunlight, with the people on it, and the glittering iron rims of the cart-wheels. At a rough guess Pahom concluded that he had walked three miles. It was growing warmer; he took off his undercoat, slung it across his shoulder, and went on again. It had grown quite warm now; he looked at the sun—it was time to think of breakfast.

"The first shift is done, but there are four in a day, and it's too soon yet to turn. But I'll just take off my boots," said he to himself.

He sat down, took off his boots, stuck them into his girdle, and went on. It was easy walking now.

"I'll go on for another three miles," thought he, "and then turn to the left. This spot is so fine
that it would be a pity to lose it. The further one 23
goes, the better the land seems."

He went straight on for a while, and when he looked around, the hillock was scarcely visible and the people on it looked like black ants, and he could just see something glistening there in the sun.

"Ah," thought Pahom, "I have gone far enough in this direction; it's time to turn. Besides, I'm in a regular sweat, and very thirsty."

He stopped, dug a large hole, and heaped up pieces of turf. Next he untied his flask, had a drink, and then turned sharply to the left. He went on and on; the grass was high, and it was very hot.

Pahom began to grow tired; he looked at the sun and saw that it was noon.

"Well," he thought, "I must have a rest."

He sat down, and ate some bread and drank some water; but he did not lie down, thinking that if he did he might fall asleep. After sitting a little while, he went on again. At first he walked easily, the food had strengthened him; but it had become terribly hot and he felt sleepy. Still
he went on, thinking: "An hour to suffer, a life- 24
time to live."

He went a long way in this direction also, and was about to turn to the left again, when he perceived a damp hollow; "It would be a pity to leave that out," he thought. "Flax would do well there." So he went on past the hollow and dug a hole on the other side of it before he made a sharp turn. Pahom looked toward the hillock. The heat made the air hazy; it seemed to be quivering, and through the haze the people on the hillock could scarcely be seen.

"Ah," thought Pahom, "I have made the 25
sides too long; I must make this one shorter." And he went along the third side, stepping faster. He looked at the sun: it was nearly halfway to the horizon, and he had not yet done two miles of the third side of the square. He was still ten miles from the goal.

---

12. **girdle** (gėr′dl), *n.* belt worn around the waist.

23 Literary Element
Repetition

Point out that this is another example of temptation, an idea that has been repeated often and is an important element of the parable.

24 Literary Element
Irony

When students have finished the story, have them return to this sentence and discover the irony of Pahom's use of this particular saying.

25 Reading/Thinking Skills
Visualize

Let students draw Pahom's path approximately to scale, showing the hillock as the starting point and the holes he digs. They should also mark the time of day along the path.

BUILDING ENGLISH PROFICIENCY

Enacting a Climax

Kinesthetic students, in particular, will appreciate the extra comprehension that comes from enacting Sections 8 and 9.

1. Ask students to read these two sections and comment upon them in small groups.

2. Have students set up a circular path in the classroom to suggest the land that Pahom walks around. A volunteer can also draw on the board the circuit that Pahom walks. Some students can serve as spots where Pahom stops.

3. Invite a volunteer to play the part of Pahom. Have him or her move about the classroom, from one stopping point to the next. At each stop, discuss Pahom's thoughts at that point.

26 Literary Element
Characterization

Question What were Pahom's motivations to continue running? *(greed and dislike of being thought a fool)*

27 Reading/Thinking Skills
Draw Conclusions

Question Why is the chief laughing? *(Possible responses: because he knows he has succeeded in tricking Pahom; because he is the Devil and is laughing victoriously now that Pahom is in his power)*

28 Literary Focus
Parable

Question What is the answer to the question posed by the title? *(Possible responses: enough for a grave; enough to bring health and a good life)*

Check Test

1. What do Pahom's wife and sister-in-law argue about? *(whether town life is better than peasant life)*

2. How does the Devil plan to trick Pahom? *(through Pahom's desire for land)*

3. How much does the dealer say 13,000 acres of the Bashkir's land costs? *(1,000 rubles and about 100 rubles' worth of gifts)*

4. What is used to mark the beginning of Pahom's circuit? *(the Bashkir chief's fox-fur hat)*

5. Why does Pahom keep running even though it is dark? *(It is still light at the top of the hillock.)*

Unit 6 Resource Book
Alternate Check Test, p. 53

"No," he thought, "though it will make my land lopsided, I must hurry back in a straight line now. I might go too far, and as it is I have a great deal of land."

So Pahom hurriedly dug a hole and turned straight toward the hillock.

9

Pahom went straight toward the hillock, but he now walked with difficulty. He was exhausted from the heat, his bare feet were cut and bruised, and his legs began to fail. He longed to rest, but it was impossible if he meant to get back before sunset. The sun waits for no man, and it was sinking lower and lower.

"Oh, Lord," he thought, "If only I have not blundered trying for too much! What if I am too late?"

He looked toward the hillock and at the sun. He was still far from his goal, and the sun was already near the rim of the sky.

Pahom walked on and on; it was very hard walking but he went quicker and quicker. He pressed on, but was still far from the place. He began running, threw away his coat, his boots, his flask, and his cap, and kept only the spade which he used as a support.

"What am I to do?" he thought again. "I've grasped too much and ruined the whole affair. I can't get there before the sun sets."

And this fear made him still more breathless. Pahom kept on running; his soaking shirt and trousers stuck to him, and his mouth was parched. His breast was working like a blacksmith's bellows, his heart was beating like a hammer, and his legs were giving way as if they did not belong to him. Pahom was seized with terror lest he should die of the strain.

Though afraid of death, he could not stop.

"After having run all that way they will call me a fool if I stop now," thought he.

26 And he ran on and on, and drew near and heard the Bashkirs yelling and shouting to him, and their cries inflamed his heart still more. He gathered his last strength and ran on.

The sun was close to the rim of the sky and, cloaked in mist, looked large, and red as blood. Now, yes, now, it was about to set! The sun was quite low, but he was also quite near his goal. Pahom could already see the people on the hillock waving their arms to make him hurry. He could see the fox-fur cap on the ground and the money in it, and the chief sitting on the ground holding his sides. And Pahom remem- 27
bered his dream.

"There's plenty of land," thought he, "but will God let me live on it? I have lost my life, I have lost my life! Never will I reach that spot!"

Pahom looked at the sun, which had reached the earth: one side of it had already disappeared. With all his remaining strength he rushed on, bending his body forward so that his legs could hardly follow fast enough to keep him from falling. Just as he reached the hillock it suddenly grew dark. He looked up—the sun had already set!

He gave a cry: "All my labor has been in vain," thought he, and was about to stop, but he heard the Bashkirs still shouting and remembered that though to him, from below, the sun seemed to have set, they on the hillock could still see it. He took a long breath and ran up the hillock. It was still light there. He reached the top and saw the cap. Before it sat the chief, laughing and holding his sides. Again Pahom remembered his dream, and he uttered a cry: his legs gave way beneath him, he fell forward and reached the cap with his hands.

"Ah, that's a fine fellow!" exclaimed the chief. "He has gained much land!"

Pahom's servant came running up and tried to raise him, but he saw that blood was flowing from his mouth. Pahom was dead.

The Bashkirs clicked their tongues to show their pity.

His servant picked up the spade and dug a 28
grave long enough for Pahom to lie in, and buried him in it.

Six feet from his head to his heels was all he needed.

MINI-LESSON: VOCABULARY

Connotation and Denotation

Teach Read the following sentence from page 784:

"The sun was close to the rim of the sky and, cloaked in mist, looked large, and red as blood."

Point out to students that in this sentence the word *blood* has a denotation, a literal meaning, and a connotation, other meanings associated with it.

denotation—bright red color

connotation—death, horror

Tolstoy could have chosen other items that are red and compared them with the sun, such as, beets, tomatoes, and lips. His choice of the word *blood* tells the reader that the sun was red in hue and foreshadows Pahom's death.

Activity Idea Have students reread this story looking for other instances in which a word's connotation is important. Some are *stout, ignorant* (page 780), *glistened* (page 782).

After Reading

Making Connections

Shaping Your Response

1. Three lifestyles are described in this story—that of the town-dweller, the peasant, and the steppe nomad. Explain which seems the most desirable to you.
2. Do you think this parable, or lesson, is relevant to life today in the U.S.? Explain.

Analyzing the Story

3. Tolstoy introduces the Devil into a largely realistic narrative. Do you think the story would be better without this supernatural element? Why or why not?
4. In section 3, what is **ironic** about Pahom's treatment of his neighbors?
5. What is **symbolic** about Pahom's journey from one place to another? about the fox fur hat the Bashkir chief wears?
6. What does Pahom's insistence on a title deed from the Bashkirs contribute to his **characterization**?
7. List the events in the story that **foreshadow** the ending.
8. How does the wife's **proverb,** "Loss and gain are brothers twain," illustrate a **theme** of this story?

Extending the Ideas

9. In the last two centuries many nomadic groups, such as the peoples of Central Asia and the Plains Indians of the American West, have been forced to face enormous cultural **change.** Discuss some of the social problems these groups have experienced in adjusting to change.

Literary Focus: Parable

A **parable** is a brief narrative that concretely illustrates an abstract moral or philosophical teaching.

- How would you sum up the lesson of this story?
- How do the **title** and final sentence use **irony** to illustrate this lesson?

LITERARY FOCUS: FABLE

As students think about the answers to the two questions, remind them that most stories do not have a single lesson that can be stated in a single way. Possible responses:

- If gaining more possessions causes harm to others or yourself, you probably shouldn't have them.
- Giving in to temptation ruins a lifetime of hard work.
- When you become greedy, you become blind to danger.

Encourage students to express what they see in the story. Some students, for example, may interpret the story as being about greed, while others see it as reflecting individual interests versus community interests.

After Reading

MAKING CONNECTIONS

1. Possible responses: Students should use story details to justify their choices and imagine what kind of temptations would be faced.

2. Possible responses: Private ownership is responsible for many of the ills in today's society; temptation exists because material things are valued greatly; people often harm their health for careers or fame.

3. Possible responses: The Devil is used in other works with realistic settings, such as "The Devil and Daniel Webster" and works well here; the presence of the Devil makes the parable too preachy.

4. It is ironic that Pahom's treatment of his neighbors resembles the treatment of Pahom by the lady's manager.

5. Possible responses: Owning land often symbolizes permanence, but Pahom's continual moving symbolizes his discontent, as if he has no real home. The fox is wily and tricky like the Devil.

6. Possible response: He shows he lacks insight into people by thinking that the Bashkirs would honor any titles or deeds to land.

7. Possible responses include the dream, Pahom's prediction that he will die, and the sun the color of blood.

8. Possible response: Pahom gains his heart's desire and loses his life—all within a few moments; a high price must always be paid for what is important.

9. Typical problems may include loss of identity, language, cultural values; migration to the cities, poor living conditions in urban areas; susceptibility to certain diseases such as smallpox and alcoholism.

VOCABULARY STUDY

1. discord
2. disparage
3. communal
4. arable
5. disperse

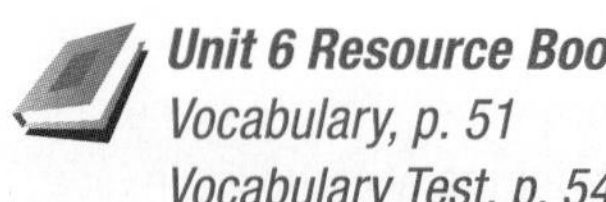

Unit 6 Resource Book
Vocabulary, p. 51
Vocabulary Test, p. 54

WRITING CHOICES

Grin and Bear It

Encourage students to brainstorm a list of other sayings that represent a similar point of view such as:

"Grin and bear it."

"No pain, no gain."

"The cross before the crown."

Let them choose any of the sayings brainstormed to use in their sketches.

Selection Test

Unit 6 Resource Book
pp. 55–56

Transparency Collection
Fine Art Writing Prompt 13

Vocabulary Study

On your paper write the listed vocabulary word that best completes each sentence below.

arable
communal
discord
disparage
disperse

1. Wherever he went, Pahom stirred up ____.
2. Pahom's sister-in-law tried to ____ the life of her country sister.
3. Pahom became dissatisfied with ____ land because he longed to have his own homestead.
4. Pahom was delighted to find that the land of the Bashkirs was so rich and ____.
5. The Bashkirs promised Pahom all the land he could cover by sunset; then they decided to ____ for the night.

Expressing Your Ideas

Writing Choices

Writer's Notebook Update Review the notes you kept for the chart. In your notebook, respond to the following statement: Pahom's reasons for wanting more and more land changed as he grew older.

A Victim of Circumstances? Do human beings have free will? Are the things that happen to people the result of their own actions or of outside forces? Is Pahom a victim of circumstances? Write an **essay** in which you discuss these issues, citing as evidence details from the story.

Listen My Children Bashkir parents now tell the story of Pahom as a warning to their children. Write a **folk tale** about Pahom from the Bashkir point of view. End with a brief statement of the moral.

Grin and Bear It Pahom says to himself, "An hour to suffer, a lifetime to live." Write an **autobiographical sketch** that illustrates the truth of that idea as it applies to some event in your own life. Incorporate the saying into your sketch.

Other Options

In Common By 1886, when he wrote this story, Tolstoy had concluded that the ownership of private property was evil. What arguments might support or refute Tolstoy's view? Present a **debate** on the following premise: It is evil to own property.

Show-and-Tell Acquiring land is only one example of the human desire to collect and own. People collect coins, plates, dolls, hubcaps, whatever. Bring to class an example of something that you collect. Present a **collector's guide** showing your objects and explaining how your collection came about.

Home Is Where the Hearth Is A Russian peasant's home typically consisted of one room. One side of the room included a large stove, with fireplace and ovens below and a flat, tiled surface above for sleeping. One corner contained the family's religious icons. The family, sitting on benches, ate at a plank table. They stored their clothes in large wooden trunks. Draw a **picture** or make a **three-dimensional model** of the interior of a typical Russian cottage.

OTHER OPTIONS

In Common

Have students prepare for the debate by reviewing the story, especially what Tolstoy thought about property ownership, and his attitude toward communal ownership and efforts. Then they can incorporate this information in the debate.

Home Is Where the Hearth Is

Share with students some pictures of Russian religious icons, and explain that they are the Russian Orthodox Church's way of depicting Jesus and saints. Point out the use of gold and ornate design and explain that these icons would contrast markedly with the overall simplicity of a peasant's home. Encourage students to depict an icon in their pictures or models.

Media Connection

The selections in this unit deal with power, the people who have it, and the impressions they make on others. The following pages examine how favorable impressions are created and maintained by image makers.

A trained actor, President Reagan was extraordinarily successful in the role of a kind of "super-salesman" of the policies of his administration. But although one of Reagan's nicknames – "the Great Communicator" – suggested a positive view of the phenomenon of his continuing popularity, another one – "the Teflon President" – expressed a more critical attitude.

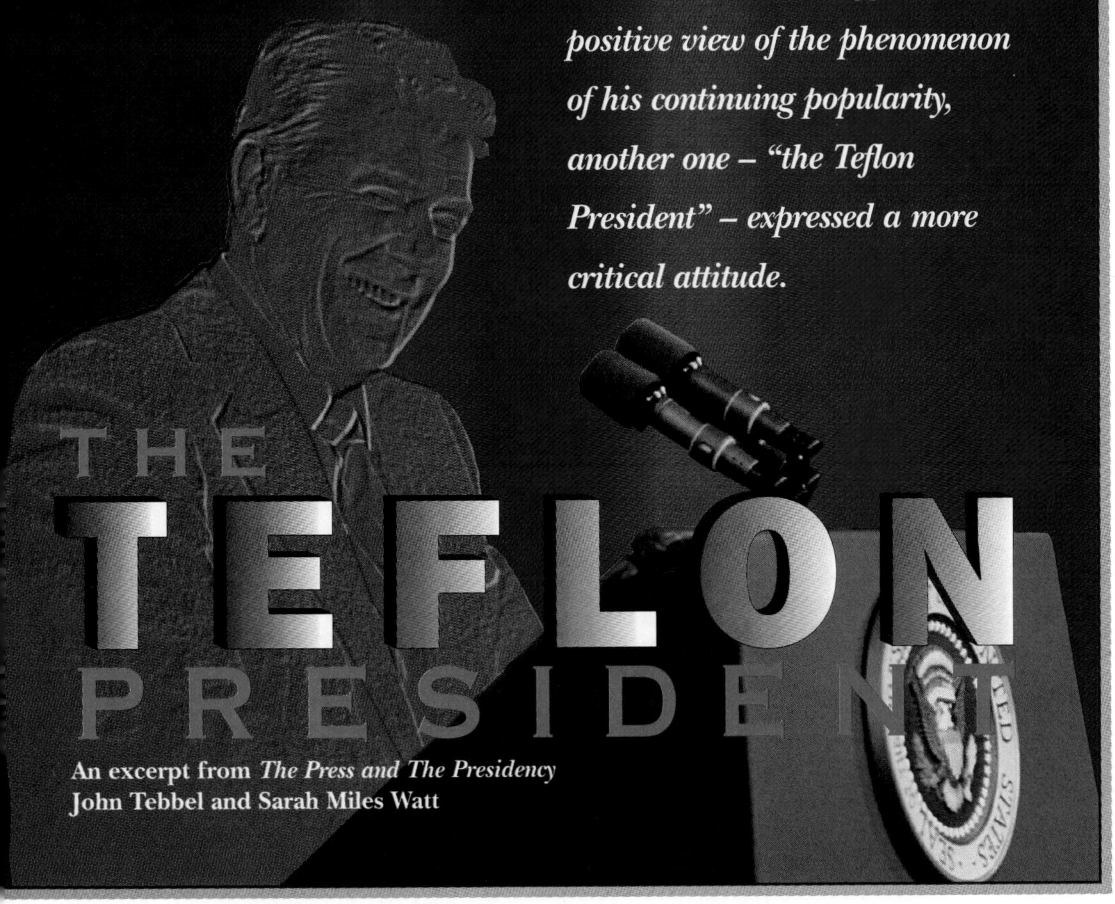

THE TEFLON PRESIDENT

An excerpt from *The Press and The Presidency*

John Tebbel and Sarah Miles Watt

Interdisciplinary Study

Theme Link

Politicians can sometimes minimize the cost of winning by projecting an image that makes them popular.

Curricular Connection: Media

You can use the information in this Interdisciplinary Study to explore with students the role of the media in designing and/or controlling how a political leader appears to the public.

Additional Background

Discuss the role of dress in image-making. How does Reagan's suit help establish an image? *(Possible response: People will expect him to be dignified, traditional, and nonthreatening, like his suit.)*

Teflon is the trademark of polytetrafluoroethylene, which is used to coat cooking utensils so that food doesn't stick to them. Here it is used figuratively to express a negative attribute. Encourage students to guess its figurative meaning.

Unit 6 Resource Book
Study Guide, p.57

BUILDING ENGLISH PROFICIENCY

ESL LEP ELD SAE LD

Responding to Headnotes

Help set the stage for the articles on pages 788 and 789 by discussing the headnote with students.

1. Students may not recall the Reagan administration. Review his years in office (possibly team-teaching with a social studies teacher) and the significant events of his two terms. (Examples include the invasion of Grenada; changing relations with the Soviet Union, Reaganomics, and the Iran-Contra Scandal.)

2. Discuss whether power makes both positive and negative impressions on people; invite explanations. (For example, some people find powerful people attractive; others automatically resent or fear the powerful.)

3. Ask: If you wanted to create a favorable image, what would that image be? What might you do to get people to think of you in that way?

Terms to Know

formidable, hard to defeat

suspend disbelief, pay attention without engaging in critical judgment, evaluation, or analysis

panoply (pan′ə plē), ceremonial attire and accessories

epic, of heroic stature

amiable, friendly

introspective, self-examination

albeit, although

eminent, distinguished

Responding

1. Possible Responses Idealistic students are likely to choose intelligence as the most important feature and may suggest good character as another essential property. Pragmatic students may choose other qualities.

2. Possible Responses You may wish to have some students direct their attention to national polls (for example, the Harris poll), while others focus on how polls are conducted locally by campaign organizations within your state.

3. Possible Responses Encourage students to think of short slogans.

THE TEFLON PRESIDENT

As the first actor ever to occupy the White House, he found himself in command of a formidable propaganda machine that had been building steadily since the Kennedy administration, and with each advance in technology, had become a still more powerful instrument in the hands of a President who knew how to use it. To it Reagan brought the fundamental skills peculiar to the actor's craft, particularly the ability to suspend disbelief, as in the theater, and make illusion seem like reality. Since the vast panoply of the White House had been designed to do just that, the joining of the two was an epic conjunction – an actor working in a studio dwarfing in power if not in size the sound stages of Hollywood, and whose audience was an entire nation.

To manipulate this machine and make it work effectively, Reagan possessed an ideal combination of qualities. He was highly popular, as both the Roosevelts and Eisenhower had been, and he had the acquired ability, which no previous President had enjoyed, to create a character the whole country could enjoy–amiable, wisecracking, pointedly nonintellectual, embodying the virtues Carter talked about without agonizing over them. Nor did he have the negative qualities that had destroyed other presidents. He was not a tortured, introspective, complicated sufferer, as Johnson, Nixon, and Carter had been, but, as he sincerely believed, a plain, simple, eternally optimistic man of the people (albeit rich himself and living in the world of the rich and privileged) of a sort the Democrats had always talked about being. Such a man had never before emerged as a Republican.

Until recently, the White House had taken the public pulse by carefully scanning and analyzing what was printed and broadcast by the media. Reagan, however, now made use of the sophisticated new polling techniques available to him. Using funds from the Republican National Committee, he hired a firm called Decision Making Information, directed by an eminent plotter named Richard Wirthlin, to carry out the most comprehensive (and expensive) poll taking on a continous basis ever done for a President. What Wirthlin's figures showed became an important part of White House political strategy and sometimes influenced the President's decisions.

[White House aide David] Gergen was valuable in these operations because he, too, had been a successful poll taker, founder and editor of *Public Opinion,* a periodical devoted to that arcane art.

There were those who believed that some of this was wasted motion. [White House correspondent for *Time,* Laurence] I. Barrett, for example, considered it a myth that Wirthlin's figures gave Reagan an extraordinary power to shape public perceptions. If that were true, he pointed out, Reagan should have been relatively free from criticism, which was far from the case, and the process should also have insulated him from the political effects of bad news, which was also not the case. What helped the President more was not statistics but his amazing popularity. No matter how bad the news might be, none of it stuck to the presidential image – "the Teflon President," as his critics called him. The public simply refused to associate Reagan with the results of his policies, unless those results were good.

Responding

1. How important do you think the following are in a presidential candidate: acting skills, good looks, intelligence, money, youth? Work with a group to create a description of the ideal presidential candidate.

2. With a partner, research polling techniques used in presidential campaigns. Report on these techniques and their value.

3. Think of a slogan that could have enhanced Caesar's image.

MINI-LESSON: SPEAKING AND LISTENING

Monitor Audience Reactions

Teach Point out that in the illustration, President Reagan shows the qualities of poise, relaxation, and humor that characterize practiced public speakers. Despite this, Reagan received diametrically opposed reviews of his speeches, as the text on page 788 explains. Just as important as speech presentation, is monitoring the audience's reaction, to make sure they are with you, and taking steps if you see that you've lost them. Approaches that help with a hostile audience include

- inviting audience questions and answering them thoroughly and honestly
- including documentation for your ideas
- citing authoritative sources

Activity Idea Give students the opportunity to watch a debate staged for television, for instance an episode of "Crossfire," and analyze whether and how the speakers monitor and respond to their audience.

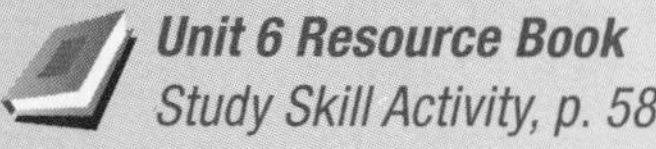

Unit 6 Resource Book
Study Skill Activity, p. 58

INTERDISCIPLINARY STUDY

Career Connection
Image maker Diego Muñoz paints a "portrait" of a political candidate. But before the paint dries, he may touch up or play down features, in order to create the most effective image for his client.

CREATING AN IMAGE

in Three Easy Steps

Image maker Diego Muñoz studied political science in college and works as a political consultant in the state of New York for both candidates and issues. He considers a political image a portrait rather than a mask and works to present that portrait to the public.

For Muñoz, the creation of an image is easy as one, two, three:

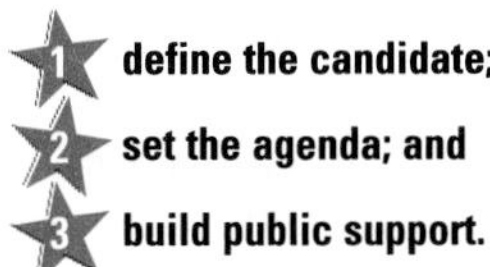

1. **define the candidate;**
2. **set the agenda; and**
3. **build public support.**

He goes on to explain. "To define the candidate, I develop a detailed portrait of what that person believes in and stands for. The more detailed the list of principles is, the better it will be later in the campaign when negatives crop up–and they always do. Prioritize the list. Have a clear idea of what the candidate wants to accomplish.

"The second step–setting the agenda–involves deciding on a time frame for the campaign and then developing your strategy. First, evaluate your resources. How much money does the campaign have to spend? How many volunteers? What media exposure can you get? Do you have the telephones, computers, and supplies that you'll need? Are there lawyers who will help the candidate follow the campaign and election laws and defend against possible election law suits? Form alliances with organizations that would like to see your candidate elected. Once you've identified and contacted your resources, work out a time line for the use of those resources. "Use that time line to build public support, the third step. Educate the public on the issues and the candidate. Identify the audience that you are trying to reach. What people are likely to vote for your candidate if they know what he or she stands for? Where do they live? Go to them. Pass out leaflets. Send faxes. Drive around in cars with bullhorns. Use the media and community meetings.

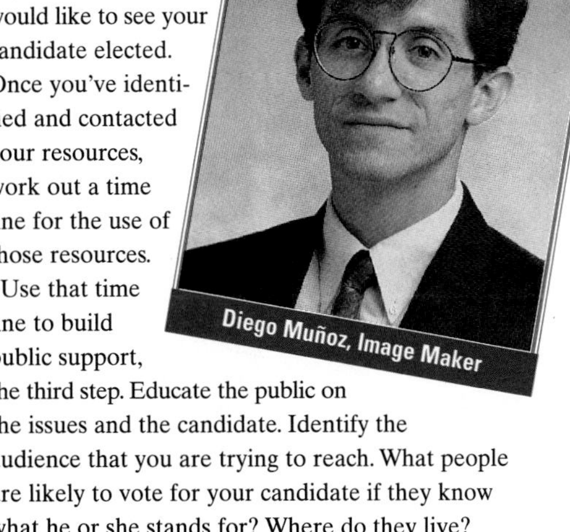

Diego Muñoz, Image Maker

"The campaign is underway, but your problems aren't over yet! Negative information that can hurt your candidate's image may be made public. You can address the criticism by adjusting, downplaying, or highlighting aspects of the candidate's portrait. You might even turn a negative into a positive. Another way to counter a negative is with a negative, but I don't like to run a "smear campaign." I prefer to work with the people who have raised negative issues and to develop a collaboration that is beneficial to us all.

"And there, in three steps, you have the foundation of any campaign. Now jump on the roller coaster and ride it out to election day."

Responding
If you were campaign manager for a friend running for class office, how would you use or adapt the steps that Diego Muñoz mentions? How would you build support?

Interdisciplinary Study

Theme Link

Whether a political image is a mask or reality impacts how a campaign will be run and at what price.

Curricular Connection: Career

You can use the information in this Interdisciplinary Study to explore with students the role of political consultants in shaping public opinion.

Terms to Know

prioritize, place in order of importance
alliance, form close associations
collaboration, cooperative effort

Responding

Students may suggest leaving out the considerations of money, elections, telephones, and computers, and rescaling other areas to fit the arena of action.

Interdisciplinary Activity Idea

Ask students to research the image of a public figure (sports, entertainment, political, etc.). Then have them write a short paragraph that sums up the figure's public "portrait."

BUILDING ENGLISH PROFICIENCY

Looking at a Newspaper

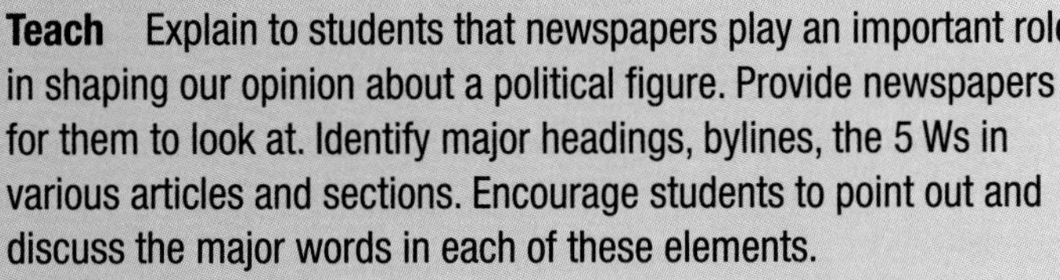

Teach Explain to students that newspapers play an important role in shaping our opinion about a political figure. Provide newspapers for them to look at. Identify major headings, bylines, the 5 Ws in various articles and sections. Encourage students to point out and discuss the major words in each of these elements.

Activity Idea If possible, provide for students copies of a speech by Reagan or another political figure. As students read the speech, ask them to write words that they feel are important. Afterwards, have students compare lists and discuss the meanings of any unfamiliar words. Ask students if any of the words noted help them form an opinion of the politician.

Reading Mini-Lesson

Teaching Objectives

- to recognize propaganda
- to improve reading and thinking skills
- to distinguish fact and opinion

Introduce

Show students a blatant example of propaganda in a newspaper or television advertisement. Talk about the use of language to influence feelings as well as thoughts. Encourage students to mention times when they felt that their feelings were being "worked on." Then have them read the lesson.

Follow Up

Have students use the lesson criteria to look for and analyze propaganda in the text of a speech by a political figure.

Activity Option

Have volunteers share their thoughts on which mailing had the most persuasive appeal and which had the least persuasive appeal.

Reading Mini-Lesson

Propaganda

Wherever you look in books, TV, radio, music, magazines, or newspapers, you can find propaganda—attempts to persuade you to adopt someone's opinions or beliefs. Propaganda isn't always bad. Any persuasive appeals to use seat belts or to exercise more, for example, are worthwhile. But propaganda can be used to manipulate you into doing or thinking something unawares. Use the following criteria to evaluate information, ads, articles, speeches, and comments.

Is information relevant? "Vote for Bob Billings for President—family man, pillar of the community, decorated war veteran, and founder of Micro-Chips, the leading exporter of minicomputers." Although these attributes suggest basic decency, stability, bravery, and initiative—important qualities—they do not qualify this man as a national leader. Nevertheless, such qualities often affect the way people vote. Information about Billings's job experience and political views bear more directly on his suitability for public office.

What is fact? What is opinion? Watch out for words and phrases like *clearly*, *everybody knows,* and *without question.* Examine the rest of the statement. Is it a fact that expansion of an airport will improve a community or that building a low-income high-rise will ruin the area?

Beware of oversimplification. Simplifying complicated issues is a common propaganda device. Slogans, bumper stickers, and use of stereotypes are all simplifications. "More jobs with Jacobs" makes a promise that may be hard to deliver.

Watch out for loaded words. Be on the lookout for words designed to appeal to your emotions. In "The Teflon President" (page 788), Ronald Reagan is spoken of as a "trained actor," a "super-salesman" and "pointedly nonintellectual." These three attributes contributed to Reagan's popularity, according to the article. But these phrases are also designed to affect your feelings about Reagan and his sincerity. What effect do you think they are intended to have?

Activity Options

Collect all unsolicited mail that your family receives asking for money for one week and analyze the persuasive appeals and propaganda.

CONTENT AREA READING

Evaluating Texts

People are most aware of propaganda when it is used to present views that they do not share or when it is in publications in which they expect to find propaganda. People are less likely to notice propaganda used to present views they support, or hidden in texts which they assume to be objective, like textbooks.

Alert students to beware of propaganda in all political arguments and discussions of social issues, no matter who is expressing the views.

Encourage students to read critically and, if necessary, skeptically, for objectivity in any text that claims to present factual information, such as in social studies textbooks.

Writing Workshop

Making Caesar Over

Assignment Things might have turned out differently for Julius Caesar if, like some modern politicians, he'd hired a public relations specialist to reshape his public image. Imagine that he's hired you to do the job.

WRITER'S BLUEPRINT

Product	A persuasive essay and speech
Purpose	To improve Caesar's public image and refute criticism
Audience	The people of Rome
Specs	To create a successful persuasive essay and speech, you should:

- ❑ Imagine that you are Caesar's public relations specialist and write an essay that characterizes the emperor as a strong, wise, considerate, capable leader. To accomplish this, turn things upside down by recasting Caesar's negative points as positive points, as well as emphasizing his strong points.
- ❑ Begin your essay in a dramatic way. Establish a bond with your audience. Strike a tone of authority by using persuasive techniques.
- ❑ Neutralize the opposition by acknowledging and then disposing of potential criticisms.
- ❑ Finish with an emotional conclusion that appeals to the patriotism and nationalistic pride of your audience.
- ❑ Make note cards from your essay and use them to deliver a persuasive speech.
- ❑ Follow the rules of grammar, usage, spelling, and mechanics. Pay special attention to comparative and superlative forms of adjectives and adverbs.

Writing Workshop

WRITER'S BLUEPRINT

Specs

The Specs in the Writer's Blueprint address these writing and thinking skills:

- analyzing character
- hooking the reader
- using an authoritative tone
- justifying a position
- using persuasive devices
- anticipating objections
- giving a speech
- using the comparative and superlative forms of modifiers

These Specs serve as your lesson objectives, and they form the basis for the **Assessment Criteria Specs** for a superior paper, which appear on the final TE page for this lesson. You might want to read through the Assessment Criteria Specs with students when you begin the lesson.

Linking Literature to Writing

Discuss with students their perceptions of the similarities and differences between politics today and the politics of Caesar's time.

WRITING WORKSHOP OVERVIEW

Product
Persuasive writing: A persuasive essay and speech

Prewriting
Chart Caesar's character—Recast Caesar's character—Address potential criticisms—Quickwrite an emotional appeal—Examine the funeral speeches—Plan your essay
Unit 6 Resource Book
Prewriting Worksheets, pp. 59-60

Drafting
Before you draft—As you draft
Transparency Collection
Student Models for Writing Workshop 25, 26

Revising
Ask a partner—Strategy: Using Persuasive Devices
Unit 6 Resource Book
Revising Worksheet p. 61

Editing
Ask a partner—Strategy: Comparative and Superlative Forms of Modifiers
Unit 6 Resource Book
Grammar Worksheet p. 62
Grammar Check Test p. 63

Presenting
Prepare your speech—Practice your speech

Looking Back
Self-evaluate—Reflect—For Your Working Portfolio
Unit 6 Resource Book
Assessment Worksheet p. 64
Transparency Collection
Fine Art Transparency 13

STEP 1 PREWRITING

Chart Caesar's character

Groups might want to divide up the work according to acts and scenes.

Recast Caesar's character

Discuss with students ways in which modern political campaigns attempt to present their candidates. For additional support, see the worksheet referenced below.

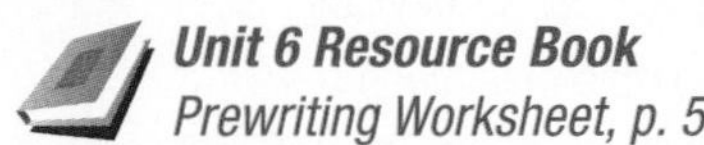

Unit 6 Resource Book
Prewriting Worksheet, p. 59

Address potential criticisms

Encourage students to come up with several arguments refuting each criticism.

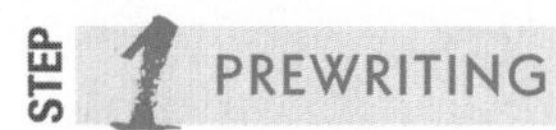

STEP 1 PREWRITING

Chart Caesar's character. In a group, review the play and create a chart, like the one shown, of Caesar's words and actions that reveal his positive and negative character traits.

Caesar's Comments or Actions	Quote from the Play	What Caesar Is Trying to Do	What This Reveals About Him: Positive	What This Reveals About Him: Negative
Tells Antony that Cassius is a dangerous man but that he, Caesar, is above such fear.	"I rather tell thee what is to be feared/ Than what I fear, for always I am Caesar." act 1, scene 2	To make his enemy, Cassius, look dangerous and make himself look powerful	—Self-confident, believes in himself	—manipulative —arrogant, too sure of himself

Recast Caesar's character. On a note card, jot down each negative point from your chart along with ideas about how you might recast it as a positive point.

STUDENT MODEL

Negative point:
manipulative—tries to make his enemy, Cassius, look dangerous
Recast as positive point:
helpful—looking out for Antony's welfare, just as he always looks out for the people's welfare

Address potential criticisms. On the flip side of each note card, jot down potential criticisms of this recasting and a positive response for each criticism.

STUDENT MODEL

Potential Criticism:
But Caesar is being dishonest in trying to make Cassius look dangerous
Positive Response:
Caesar is not being dishonest; he's being cautious and fatherly, as a leader who is looking out for the welfare of his people must be.

MINI-LESSON: PREWRITING

Quickwrite an Emotional Appeal

Model for students how to extract the best ideas from their quickwrites. Show students how these ideas can be used and extended in their drafts. Ask for volunteers and photocopy their quick-writes onto an overhead transparency. Then, as a class, read through the work, highlighting the most memorable words and phrases. Discuss ways in which these pieces of prose can be used to build an essay.

Quickwrite an emotional appeal to the citizens of Rome, based on the arguments on your note cards. Use both reasonable-sounding arguments ("Caesar must deal firmly with his enemies, for his enemies are our enemies") and emotional appeals ("Caesar is our father and we are his children!").

OR . . .
Get together with a partner or small group and together, discuss how you could reshape Caesar's public image.

Examine the funeral speeches delivered by Brutus and Mark Antony. Look for how Shakespeare uses persuasive devices, such as rhetorical questions and repetition of key words. (See the Revising Strategy in Step 3 of this lesson.) Then examine the Interdisciplinary Study on image makers on pages 787–789 for more examples of how to reshape someone's public image.

Plan your essay. Use your note cards as a guide. Organize your notes into a plan similar to the one shown here. The examples in parentheses might give you some ideas.

Introduction

- Dramatic opening ("Are we all gathered here at the Coliseum to bite the hand of Caesar, the mighty hand that feeds us?")
- Establish bond with audience ("No, we've all of us gathered here for a far more sensible reason than that. . . .")

Body

- Build on Caesar's personal strengths ("Here is a man who is intimately acquainted with our deepest fears and desires.")
- Recast negative points in a positive light ("Here is a man who is not harsh and vindictive but firm and realistic.")
- Neutralize potential criticisms ("To all those who would say that Caesar is out for revenge, I would say. . . .")

Conclusion

- Emotional appeal to patriotism ("Is our nation to be less than the mightiest nation on earth? Then, I ask you, how can Rome be led by any but the mightiest of leaders?")

Before you draft, review your writing plan and reread the Writer's Blueprint.

As you draft, concentrate on getting the ideas down on paper. See the drafting tips on the next page.

BUILDING ENGLISH PROFICIENCY

Speaking Versus Writing

Remind students that when they give their speeches, they will not be reading their essays but speaking from notes taken from their essays. When they practice their speeches, remind them to do the following:

1. Beware of sentences that are too long. You will run out of breath.

2. Try to vary sentence length and variety as you speak to hold your listeners' attention.

3. Practice your speech in a mirror so that you can evaluate your gestures and facial expressions.

4. Tape your speech to find out if you are speaking clearly and at an appropriate speed.

Quickwrite an emotional appeal

After students quickwrite, have them make distinctions between their rational and emotional appeals. For additional support see the mini-lesson at the bottom of page 792.

Examine the funeral speeches

After students complete this activity individually, have the class create a chart together outlining all of the devices Shakespeare has his characters use. For additional support, see the worksheet referenced below.

Unit 6 Resource Book
Prewriting Worksheet, p. 60

Plan your essay

Have students consider where they want their strongest arguments to be—at the beginning to hook the audience, or at the closing to leave them with a lasting impression.

For selection-related prompts, refer to Writer's Notebook.

For additional writing prompts, refer to Writer's Resource.

STEP 2 DRAFTING

Before you draft

Review the points in the Writer's Blueprint with students to make sure they understand everything that should be included in their essays.

As you draft

Students may want to look over the Revising Strategy before they begin drafting.

The Student Models

The **transparencies** referenced below are authentic student models. Review them with the students before they draft. These questions will help:

1. Read the conclusions of both models. Which do you think is more effective and why?

2. How could the writers have improved their papers through the use of repetition and rhetorical questions? Give examples.

3. Read the opening of model 26. Did the writer begin in a dramatic way? Make suggestions to improve the opening.

Transparency Collection
Student Models for Writing Workshop 25, 26

STEP 3 REVISING

Ask a Partner (Peer Assessment)

Students may want to write down the general impressions of Caesar they get from their partner's essay.

Revising Strategy: Using Persuasive Devices

Have students mark the areas in their peers' papers that they feel are the most persuasive and note the persuasive device used. For additional support, see the mini-lesson at the bottom of this page and the worksheet referenced below.

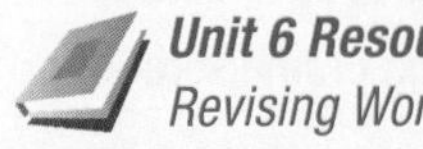

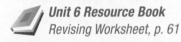

Unit 6 Resource Book
Revising Worksheet, p. 61

Connections to **Writer's Resource**

Refer to the Grammar, Usage, and Mechanics Handbook on Writer's Resource.

- Use persuasive devices, such as rhetorical questions and repetition of key words, to get your points across. See the Revising Strategy in Step 3 of this lesson. See also the lesson on Propaganda on page 790.
- Spend more time addressing Caesar's strengths than defending his weaknesses, since his strengths are what you want the audience to remember.
- As you discredit Caesar's enemies, write as if you respected them ("But these fine, goodhearted people do not know what they do").

Ask a partner to comment on your draft before you revise it. Use this checklist as a guide.

✔ Did I show Caesar as a strong, capable, considerate leader?

✔ Did I refute possible criticisms of him?

✔ Did I use persuasive devices, such as rhetorical questions and the repetition of key words?

Revising Strategy

LITERARY SOURCE
". . . Who is here so base that would be a bondman? . . . Who is here so rude that would not be a Roman? . . . Who is here so vile that will not love his country?"
from *Julius Caesar* by William Shakespeare

Using Persuasive Devices

Rhetorical questions are asked to emphasize a point and push readers in the direction the writer wants them to go. No real answers are expected to rhetorical questions, such as those in the Literary Source, except the obvious "Yes" the writer assumes.

Repetition of a word or phrase is used to create a sense of rhythm and emphasis, as in the repetition of "Who is here" in the Literary Source.

In their funeral speeches, Brutus and Mark Antony use both rhetorical questions and repetition as persuasive devices. As you revise your essay, look back at these speeches for ideas on using these persuasive devices.

MINI-LESSON: WRITING STYLE

Using Persuasive Devices

Teach Go over with students the funeral speeches of Brutus and Mark Antony to identify the persuasive devices. Discuss how these per-suasive devices create a sense of rhythm and emphasis. (The activity on page 60 of the Unit Six Resource Book addresses this task.)

Activity Idea Provide examples of other famous speeches. Divide students into groups and have each group deliver a speech—once without the persuasive devices and once with them so they can tell the difference in the impact of the two deliveries.

Apply Have students prepare a list of questior that their essays answer for readers. They could then use some of these to create rhetorical ques tions as they revise their essays.

STEP 4 EDITING

Ask a partner to review your revised draft before you edit. When you edit, look for errors in grammar, usage, spelling, and mechanics. Look over each sentence to make sure you have used modifiers correctly.

Editing Strategy

Comparative and Superlative Forms of Modifiers

Take care to form the comparative and superlative forms of adjectives and adverbs correctly. Most of the time, use *-er* or *-est:*
prettier, stronger, greenest, soonest

For some longer words, use *more* or *most* instead:
more corrupt, most carelessly

Never use *more* and *-er* or *most* and *-est* together:

Don't write:	**more dangerouser**
Write:	**more dangerous**
Don't write:	**most latest**
Write:	**latest**

FOR REFERENCE
See the Language and Grammar Handbook in the back of this text for more information on comparative and superlative forms of modifiers.

When you edit, check to see that you formed comparative and superlative forms of adjectives and adverbs correctly. Notice how this student model has been corrected for the use of comparative and superlative forms.

Caesar is also the most generousest of all his peers. He goes out of his way to thank Brutus and Cassius for their pain and courtesy and blames himself for keeping others waiting. He also invited his friends to share his wine. Caesar is more modester than other rulers and doesn't care for flattery. He only wishes to serve his people to the best of his ability.

STEP 4 EDITING

Ask a partner (Peer Assessment)

Encourage students to discuss their recommended revisions with their peers.

Editing Strategy: Comparative and Superlative Forms of Modifiers

Discuss with students the differences in using the positive, comparative, and superlative degrees of adjectives and adverbs. For additional support, see the mini-lesson at the bottom of this page and the worksheets referenced below.

Unit 6 Resource Book
Grammar Worksheet, p. 62
Grammar Check Test, p. 63

Connections to **Writer's Resource**

Refer to the Grammar, Usage, and Mechanics Handbook on Writer's Resource.

MINI-LESSON: GRAMMAR

Comparative and Superlative Forms of Modifiers

Have students edit the following sentences to correct the superlative and comparative forms. Suggestions have been given in parentheses.

1. Sometimes the most civilized oppressor is the dangerest (most dangerous).

2. Please give me the most latest (don't use *most*) information.

3. This beach is more sandier (don't use *more*) than the other one.

4. Writing a speech to promote Caesar is most (more) challenging than writing a speech that criticizes him.

5. Marc Antony's speech was more better (don't use *more*) than Brutus's speech.

Unit 6 Resource Book
Grammar Worksheet, p. 62
Grammar Check Test, p. 63

STEP 5 PRESENTING

Prepare your speech

Discuss with students how to prepare their note cards for delivering a speech. Suggest highlighting the main points and putting only one idea on a card.

Practice your speech

Go over the Beyond Print article with students. You might videotape students delivering their speeches so they, as well as their peers, can critique their presentations.

STEP 6 LOOKING BACK

Self-evaluate

The *Assessment Criteria Specs* at the bottom of this page are for a superior paper. You might want to post these in the classroom. Students can then evaluate themselves based on these criteria. For a complete scoring rubric, use the *Assessment Worksheet* referenced below.

Unit 6 Resource Book
Assessment Worksheet, p. 64

Reflect

Discuss with students any difficulties they had with this assignment. Ask students what they felt was the most valuable lesson learned from this assignment.

To further explore the theme, use the Fine Art Transparency referenced below.

Transparency Collection
Fine Art Writing Prompt 13

STEP 5 PRESENTING

Prepare your speech. Make new note cards to capture the main points of your essay, paragraph by paragraph. Jot down key words and phrases from your essay to remind you of what you'll want to say.

Practice your speech. Look at the Beyond Print article on page 797 for tips on delivering a speech. Then ask a small group to listen and comment as you practice your speech. Use this checklist as a guide.

✔ Did I use persuasive techniques?

✔ Did I include rational and emotional appeals?

✔ Did I present a convincing case for Caesar?

✔ Was my delivery effective?

Consider these ideas for presenting your speech to an audience.

- Create a campaign poster about Caesar to use as a visual aid when you give your speech.
- Present your speech as part of a mock political rally in your classroom.

STEP 6 LOOKING BACK

Self-evaluate. What grade would you give your essay and speech? Look back at the Writer's Blueprint and give yourself a score for each item, from 6 (superior) to 1 (inadequate).

Reflect. Think about what you have learned in organizing and presenting this speech as you write answers to these questions.

✔ How difficult was it for you to create a convincing picture of someone by contradicting the facts? Why?

✔ Do you feel your real strength lies in writing or speaking? Why?

For Your Working Portfolio Add your persuasive essay, note cards, and reflection responses to your working portfolio.

ASSESSMENT CRITERIA SPECS

Here are the criteria for a superior paper. A full six-level rubric for this paper appears on the *Assessment Worksheet* referenced below.

6 Superior The writer of a 6 essay and speech impressively meets these criteria:

- Hooks the reader with a dramatic introduction which sets a persuasive, authoritative tone that is maintained throughout the essay.
- Uses persuasive devices, such as rhetorical questions and repetition, to present a convincing picture of Caesar as a benevolent, fatherly ruler.
- Effectively counters potential objections to this position.
- Concludes with a powerful emotional appeal.
- Follows the conventions of standard written English, including using the correct comparative forms of adjectives and adverbs.
- Delivers a speech in the same persuasive, authoritative tone as the essay on which it is based.

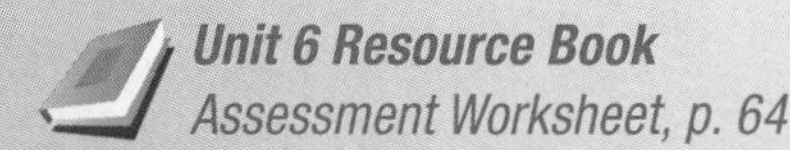

Unit 6 Resource Book
Assessment Worksheet, p. 64

Beyond Print

Speaking Up

A successful speech requires preparation and practice. Effective speeches don't just happen. And even the smoothest speakers must work to make their speeches sound lively and effortless. Though you may experience some nervousness (nearly everyone does), there are ways to reduce your anxiety. Here are some pointers on how to make your audience pay attention to what you have to say.

Rehearse. If you're well prepared, you'll be more self-assured. Rehearse your speech aloud several times, perhaps recording it, and try out different gestures, pauses, or tones of voice. This helps you become familiar with your material. If you're using visuals, rehearse with them.

Get organized. If you spend the first minute or so in front of an audience shuffling your notes or locating your materials, you might lose their attention before you begin. Get everything in order before you stand up to deliver your speech.

Try to relax. Take several deep breaths as you wait for your audience to become quiet and ready to listen. Deep breathing will help calm you.

Maintain good posture. Good posture will help you project your voice. Stand straight and on both feet, keeping your shoulders back and your head up. If you are behind a desk, don't lean on it.

Look at your audience. Talk *to* your listeners, not *at* them. If you are speaking from notes, look at them only briefly, making your points as you look at different members of the audience.

Speak up. Speak in a normal voice, but try to project it to the back of the room. Remember to speak slowly, enunciate clearly, and pronounce words correctly. (For example, say *have to,* not *hafta; going to,* not *gonna.)* Rehearse in front of a family member, or videotape yourself.

Activity Option

Prepare a three-minute speech on some aspect of winning or power. Use persuasive techniques to sway your audience.

Beyond Print

Teaching Objectives

- to prepare effectively for a speech
- to use speaking behavior that will not distract the audience

Curricular Connection: Speaking/Listening Skills

You can use the materials in this article to give students practice in becoming more comfortable with public speaking.

Introduce

Ask students how they prepare to present a speech in class, and make a list of their practices and strategies on the board. Then have students read the article. Afterwards, have a volunteer add recommended practices and strategies to the list as class members name them.

Activity Option

In order to have a topic that requires persuasive techniques, students will need to choose a topic that is at least mildly controversial. Encourage students to choose a topic that is familiar to them and concentrate their time on developing the persuasive approach to that topic.

ANOTHER APPROACH

Students who use sign language to communicate may benefit from these additional tips:

- Practice in front of a mirror.
- Be sure that each sign has the correct handshape, palm orientation, location, and movement, and that non-manual behaviors are properly coordinated with manual behaviors.
- Stand still as you speak.
- Look at the audience and interpreter to check for signs of comprehension.
- Sign slowly and clearly.

Unit Wrap-Up

MULTICULTURAL CONNECTION

Students have certainly experienced changes in their own lives. The following ideas may facilitate discussion on changes that affect large groups of people.

Change

- Reaction to change may vary by culture, gender, age, and personal religious and political beliefs.
- Large scale change—even change designed to make things easier—makes life complicated by requiring a large group of people to adjust to a new way of doing things.
- Changes that seem to be individual may impact a whole society.

Possible Response The villagers may have been able to become wealthier and eventually have a voice in governing their town.

Possible Response Caesar hosted many parties and festivals for the common people.

Possible Response If Pahom owned most of the land, he would have to bow to no one, and the other peasants would be forced to work for him and bow to his wishes. This would change the social structure to a dictatorship.

Activities

Activity 1 Students who stick to the criterion given may include religious leaders as well as infamous villains.

Activity 2 Students may point out that some change is not drastic, but a development or addition to tradition.

Activity 3 Students may use reference works on clothing, articles about clothing fads, interviews with older people, and students' own observations.

Multicultural Connections

Change

The Cost of Winning Change creates challenges by introducing new dimensions to cultural situations. People respond both by clinging to existing cultural patterns and by changing traditions to fit new situations. In this way, new cultures are created, by deliberate acts of people and by the simple fact that change is bound to occur.

■ Kinds of change may include political, social, and economic—or a combination of the three. Discuss the long-range changes that would have occurred if the Baleks had acknowledged the injustice they had committed over the years, fixed their scales, and made restitution.

■ An abrupt change of government, such as Caesar's dictatorship after centuries of a republic, was bound to cause social turmoil. Why, then, was Caesar nevertheless popular with many of the common people?

■ Consider how owning a large tract of land could change the life of a peasant like Pahom. In what ways would he become more independent? How could this threaten the existing social system?

Activities

Work in small groups on the following activities.

1. Brainstorm a list of ten people you feel have had a leading role in changing the world. Rank these change-makers from 1 to 10, with 1 being the person you feel has effected the greatest changes. Prepare a picture gallery of change-makers with an illustration and caption for each person. Present your gallery to the class and explain your choices and rankings.
2. Think of a tradition in your circle of friends, family, school, or community that has changed, or is threatening to change. What is causing the change? Who favors it? Who opposes it? What, if anything, will this change mean to you?
3. Make a time line indicating major changes in clothing fashions during the past five decades in the U.S. Explain how different social and cultural influences affected these changes.

Independent and Group Projects

Poem

Power Poem Using a variety of computer fonts or display type, reproduce words, phrases, and lines from each of the selections in this unit that say something about power. Arrange the lines to create a "found poem" about power.

Game

Are You Game? Getting ideas from *Julius Caesar* and the two stories from this unit, think of a computer game that could be titled *Power Plays.* Identify the first and last levels of the game. Write a description of this game and draw an illustration that could appear on the game's box.

Discussion

The Cost of Winning In a group of five, plan a TV talk show, with one student playing the host and the others playing Julius Caesar, Mark Antony, a representative of the Balek family, and Pahom. The topic of the show is power—its advantages and disadvantages. Devise three questions to use as the basis for this group discussion. Put on your talk show for the class.

Media

Power Surge Work with a partner to analyze current TV programs, magazines, and movies, including the ads, noting their portrayal of power. Consider questions such as these: With what is power equated? Is power used or misused? Is power generally equated with a particular sex, social class, or personal quality? Analyze your information, make some generalizations about power as represented in the media, and give a report to the class.

UNIT 6 OPTIONS

Poem

Tell students that some passages of prose have poetic qualities, such as images and figurative language, and can be arranged in a poetic structure. Have students complete the following steps:

- Skim the selections, searching for passages that deal with "power."
- Record sentences or phrases that deal with power and are evocative and poetic.
- Try organizing the selected material ways, using the following techniques.
  - Use one strong image per line.
  - Put important words at the ends of lines.
  - Use single word lines for emphasis.
  - Use the lines to create a picture on the page.

Game

This project requires familiarity with multi-level computer games or games from Sega™ or Nintendo™, and so on.

Discussion

Students should all participate in forming the questions. Individuals may develop a script, or ad-lib responses.

Media

Students who do not have access to a television or whose TV and movie viewing is restricted, may be able to use a talk radio station as a source.

Unit Test

Unit 6 Resource Book
New Selection, pp. 65–72
Test 1, pp. 73–74
Test 2, pp. 75–80

Glossaries, Handbooks, and Indexes

Glossary of Vocabulary Words

a hat	o hot	ü rule				
ā age	ō open	ch child	ə	a in about		
ä far	ô order, all	ng long		e in taken		
e let	oi oil	sh she		i in pencil		
ē equal	ou out	th thin		o in lemon		
ė term	u cup	ᴛʜ then		u in circus		
i it	u̇ put	zh measure				
ī ice						

A

abscess (ab′ses), *n.* pus resulting from infected tissues of the body.

abyss (ə bis′), *n.* bottomless or very great depth.

acquittal (ə kwit′l), *n.* discharge; release.

adlib (ad lib′), *v.* make up words or music as one goes along; improvise.

advertent (əd vėrt′nt), *adj.* alert.

advocate (ad′və kāt), *v.* support.

albeit (ôl bē′it), *conj.* even though; although.

aloft (ə lôft′), *adj.* in the air.

aloof (ə lüf′), *adj.* unsympathetic; reserved.

amulet (am′yə lit), *n.* a small object worn as a magic charm against evil, disease, or bad luck.

anguish (ang′gwish) *n.* severe physical pain or mental suffering.

antimacassar (an′ti mə kas′ər), *n.* a small covering to protect the back or arms of a chair, sofa, etc., against soiling.

aperture (ap′ər chər), *n.* an opening; hole.

aphorism (af′ə riz′əm), *n.* brief statement expressing a truth.

aplomb (ə plom′), *n.* assurance; poise.

appalled (ə pôld′), *adj.* shocked; dismayed.

apprehension (ap′ri hen′shən), *n.* fear.

arable (ar′ə bəl), *adj.* suitable for producing crops which require plowing and tillage.

arpeggio (är pej′ē ō), *n.* the sounding of the individual notes of a chord.

assail (ə sāl′), *v.* bother; trouble.

atrophy (at′rə fē), *v.* waste away.

attribute (ə trib′yüt), *v.* think of as caused by.

audaciously (ô dā′shəs lē), *adv.* courageously taking risks; daringly.

audible (ô′də bəl), *adj.* that can be heard; loud enough to be heard.

austere (ô stir′), *adj.* stern in manner or appearance.

avaricious (av′ə rish′əs), *adj.* greedy for wealth.

B

balefully (bāl′fə lē), *adv.* destructively or threateningly.

barbaric (bär bar′ik), *adj.* not civilized; coarse.

belligerent (bə lij′ər ənt), *adj.* fond of fights.

bequeath (bi kwēᴛʜ′), *v.* give or leave (money or property) by a will.

bereaved (bi rēvd′), *adj.* deprived ruthlessly; robbed.

beseeching (bē sēch′ing), *adj.* asking earnestly; begging.

bestow (bi stō′), *v.* give (something) as a gift.

betoken (bi tō′kən), *v.* indicate.

bickering (bik′ər ing), *n.* petty, noisy quarreling.

bicultural (bī kul′chər əl), *adj.* having distinct cultures existing side by side.

bifocals (bī fō′kəlz), *n.* pair of glasses having two focuses.

bigot (big′ət), *n.* intolerant person.

bilaterally (bī lat′ər əl ē), *adv.* on two sides.

bilingual (bī ling′gwəl), *adj.* able to speak another language as well or almost as well as one's own.

blandly (bland′lē), *adv.* in a smoothly agreeable, polite manner.

blasphemy (blas′fə mē), *n.* abuse or contempt for God or sacred things.

blight (blīt), *n.* disease, or anything that causes destruction or ruin.

bootless (büt′lis), *adj.* in vain; useless.

brazenly (brā′zn lē), *adv.* boldly.

brooding (brü′ding), *adj.* worried.

C

calabash (kal′ə bash), *n.* a gourdlike fruit whose dried shell is used to make bottles, bowls, drums, pipes, and rattles.

candid (kan′did), *adj.* frank and sincere.

capricious (kə prish′əs), *adj.* changeable.

carnage (kär′nij), *n.* slaughter of a great number of people.

cascade (ka skād′), *v.* fall or pour.

castellated (kas′tl ā′tid), *adj.* built like a castle with turrets and battlements.

cataclysm (kat′ə kliz′əm), *n.* any violent change or upheaval.

censure, (sen′shər), *v.* express disapproval of; blame.

chateau or **château** (sha tō′), *n.* a large country house.

chauvinist (shō′və nist), *n.* person excessively enthusiastic about his or her sex, race, or group.

chronic (kron′ik), *adj.* never stopping.

commodious (kə mō′dē əs), *adj.* having plenty of room.

communal (kə myü′nl), *adj.* owned jointly by all.

compact (kom′pakt), *n.* 1 agreement or contract. 2 a small case containing face powder or rouge.

compensation (kom′pən sā′shən), *n.* something given to make up for a loss or injury.

complacent (kəm plā′snt), *adj.* self-satisfied.

composure (kəm pō′zhər), *n.* calmness; quietness.

comprehensible (kom′pri hen′sə bəl), *adj.* able to be understood.

confiscated (kon′fə skāt əd), *adj.* seized; taken.

conjecture (kən jek′chər), *v.* guess; admit without sufficient evidence.

conniving (kə nī′ving), *adj.* giving aid to wrongdoing by not telling of it or by helping it secretly.

consort (kən sôrt′), *v.* accompany.

contagious (kən tā′jəs), *adj.* spreading by direct or indirect contact; catching.

contemplate (kon′təm plāt). *v.* gaze at; think about.

contort (kən tôrt′), *v.* twist or bend out of shape.

contrition (kən trish′ən), *n.* guilt.

convivial (kən viv′ē əl), *adj.* sociable.

countenance (koun′tə nəns), *n.* face.

crag (krag), *n.* steep, rugged rock or cliff rising above others.

cropped (kropt), *adj.* cut short; clipped.

crucial (krü′shəl), *adj.* very important or decisive;

cubicle (kyü′bə kəl), *n.* a very small room or compartment.

D

daunt (dônt), *v.* overcome with fear; frighten.

dauntless (dônt′lis), *adj.* brave.

dawdle (dô′dl), *v.* waste time; loiter.

debauchery (di bô′chər ē), *n.* corruption.

decorum (di kôr′əm), *n.* proper behavior; good taste in conduct, speech, or dress.

defilement (di fīl′mənt), *n.* destruction of the purity or cleannesss of (anything sacred); desecration.

deflect (di flekt′), *v.* bend or turn aside.

degrading (di grā′ding), *adj.* dishonorable.

dejectedly (di jek′tid lē), *adv.* sadly.

demeanor (di mē′nər), *n.* behavior; manner.

denizen (den′ə zən), *n.* inhabitant or occupant of a place or region.

deploy (di ploi′), *v.* spread out in a planned or strategic position.

despise (di spīz′), *v.* feel hatred or scorn for.

despot (des′pət), *n.* ruler having unlimited power.

devastate (dev′ə stāt′), *v.* make desolate; destroy.

devastation (dev′ə stā′shən), *n.* waste; destruction.

device (di vīs′), *n.* plan, scheme, or trick.

diagram (dī′ə gram), *n.* sketch showing an outline or general scheme of something with its various parts.

dilemma (də lem′ə), *n.* difficult choice.

disconsolate (dis kon′sə lit), *adj.* without hope; unhappy.

discord (dis′kôrd), *n.* disagreement of opinions and aims; dissension.

discordant (dis kôrd′nt), *adj.* not in harmony.

discourse (dis kôrs′), *v.* talk, converse.

disdain (dis dān′), *n.* scorn.

disparage (dis par′ij), *v.* belittle; discredit.

dispel (dis pel′), *v.* drive away.

disperse (dis pėrs′), *v.* go off in different directions.

dissembled (di sem′bəld), *adj.* hidden; disguised.

distortion (dis tôr′shən), *n.* twisting out of shape.

distraction (dis trak′shən), *n.* disturbance of thought.

diverge (də vėrj′), *v.* move or lie in different directions from the same point.

doggedly (dô′gid lē), *adv.* not giving up; stubbornly.

dolefully (dōl′fəl lē), *adv.* mournfully.

droll (drōl), *adj.* odd and amusing.

dubious (dü′bē əs), *adj.* filled with or being in doubt; uncertain.

duly (dü′lē), *adv.* rightly; suitably.

E

ecstatic (ek stat′ik), *adj.* feeling great joy.

edict (ē′dikt), *n.* degree or law proclaimed by a king or other ruler on his sole authority.

elapse (i laps′), *v.* slip away; pass.

elixir (i lik′sər), *n.* medicine with special curing powers.

emanate (em′ə nāt′), *v.* come forth; spread out.

embark (em bärk′), *v.* set out.

embellishment (em bel′ish mənt), *n.* decoration; adornment.

ember (em′bər), *n.* ashes in which there is still some fire.

en masse (en mas′), in a group; all together. *[French]*

enhance (en hans′), *v.* add to; heighten.

ensue (en sü′), *v.* follow.

entice (en tīs′), *v.* tempt; lure.

entranced (en transd′), *adj.* delighted; charmed.

entreatingly (en trēt′ing lē), *adv.* in a begging or praying manner.

eradicable (i rad′ə kə bəl), *adj.* that can be gotten rid of or destroyed.

essence (es′ns), *n.* that which makes a thing what it is; important feature or features.

euphemism (yü′fə miz′əm), *n.* use of a mild or indirect expression instead of a harsh, direct one.

expiation (ek′spē ā′shən), *n.* atonement.

exploitation (ek′sploi tā′shən), *n.* selfish or unfair use.

F

falsetto (fôl set′ō), *n.* an artifically high-pitched voice, especially in a man.

fawn (fôn), *v.* try to get favor or notice by slavish acts.

fiasco (fē as′kō), *n.* a complete or ridiculous failure; humiliating breakdown.

flagrant (flā′grənt), *adj.* glaringly offensive; outrageous.

flout (flout), *v.* treat with contempt or scorn.

fluently (flü′ənt lē), *adv.* speaking or writing easily and rapidly.

forcefully (fôrs′fəl lē), *adv.* powerfully.

frenzied (fren′zēd), *adj.* greatly excited; frantic.

friction (frik′shən), *n.* a rubbing of one object against another; a clash.

frigid (frij′id), *adj.* cold in feeling or manner.

funereal (fyü nir′ē əl), *adj.* gloomy.

furtive (fėr′tiv), *adj.* done quickly and with stealth to avoid being noticed; sly.

futile (fyü′tl), *adj.* not successful; useless.

G

galvanized (gal′və nīzd), *adj.* covered with a thin coating of zinc to prevent rust.

garrulity (gə rü′lə tē), *n.* wordiness.

glaze (glāz), *v.* become smooth, glassy, or glossy.

gratifying (grat′ə fī ing), *adj.* satisfying; pleasing.

grievance (grē′vəns), *n.* a cause for complaint.

grievous (grē′vəs), *adj.* causing great pain or suffering.

grimace (grə mās′, grim′is), *n.* a twisting of the face; ugly or funny smile.

guile (gīl), *n.* sly trick; cunning.

H

haphazard (hap′haz′ərd), *adj.* not planned; random.

hapless (hap′lis), *adj.* unlucky; unfortunate.

heed (hēd), *n.* careful attention.

homage (hom′ij), *n.* dutiful respect.

husbanded (huz′bənd əd), *adj.* managed carefully; saved.

hypocrisy (hi pok′rə sē), *n.* pretense.

I

ignoble (ig nō′bəl), *adj.* not of noble birth or position; without honor; humble.

imminent (im′ə nənt), *adj.* about to occur.

impale (im pāl′), *v.* pierce through with something pointed.

impel (im pel′), *v.* cause to move forward.

imperceptible (im′pər sep′tə bəl), *adj.* gradual.

imperiously (im pir′ē əs lē), *adv.* haughtily or arrogantly.

impersonate (im pėr′sə nāt), *v.* pretend to be.

imperturbably (im′pər tėr′bə blē), *adv.* calmly.

impiety (im pī′ə tē), *n.* lack of respect.

implicit (im plis′it), *adj.* meant, but not clearly expressed or distinctly stated; implied.

impotence (im′pə təns), *n.* helplessness.

impotent (im′pə tənt), *adj.* powerless; helpless.

improvise (im′prə vīz), *v.* make up on the spur of the moment.

impunity (im pyü′nə tē), *n.* freedom from injury, punishment, or other bad consequences.

incandescent (in′kən des′nt), *adj.* shining brightly; brilliant.

incredulous (in krej′ə ləs), *adj.* doubting; skeptical.

incur (in kər′), *v.* bring on oneself.

indifferently, (in dif′ər ənt lē), *adv.* in a manner that shows little interest.

indiscreet (in′dis krēt′), *adj.* not wise; foolish.

inexorable (in ek′sər ə bəl), *adj.* relentless, unyielding.

infamy (in′fə mē), *n.* a very bad reputation; public disgrace.

inimical (in im′ə kəl), *adj.* unfavorable.

initiative (i nish′ē ə tiv), *n.* active part in taking the first steps in any undertaking; lead.

insatiable (in sā′shə bəl), *adj.* that cannot be satisfied; greedy.

inscrutable (in skrü′tə bəl), *adj.* so mysterious or obscure that one cannot make out its meaning.

insidious (in sid′ē əs), *adj.* working secretly or subtly.

insignificant (in′sig nif′ə kənt), *adj.* unimportant; trivial.

insurrection (in′sə rek′shən), *n.* a rising against established authority; revolt.

inter (in tėr′), *v.* bury.

interminable (in tėr′mə nə bəl), *adj.* seemingly endless.

intimidate (in tim′ə dāt), *v.* 1 frighten. 2 influence or force by fear.

intolerant (in tol′ər ənt), *adj.* unwilling to let others do or believe as they want.

irrefutable (i ref′yə tə bəl), *adj.* undeniable.

irreproachable (ir′i prō′chə bəl), *adj.* free from blame; faultless.

J

jauntily (jôn′tē lē), *adv.* in an easy and lively way.

jeopardy (jep′ər dē), *n.* risk; danger.

jest (jest), *n.* something said to cause laughter; joke.

K

kittled (kit′ld), *adj.* born.

L

labyrinth (lab′ə rinth′), *n.* a confusing, complicated passage or arrangement.

legacy (leg′ə sē), *n.* something handed down in a will.

lethargy (leth′ər jē), *n.* lack of energy; inactivity.

liaison (lē′ā zon′), *n.* connection between military units, branches of a service, etc., to secure proper cooperation.

lineage (lin′ē ij), *n.* descent in a direct line from a common ancestor.

listlessly (list′lis lē), *adv.* seemingly too tired to care about anything.

loathsome (lōᴛʜ′səm), *adj.* disgusting.

loiter (loi′tər), *v.* linger idly or aimlessly.

lull (lul), *n.* period of less noise or violence; brief calm.

luminous (lü′mə nəs) *adj.* full of light; shining.

lustrous (lus′trəs), *adj.* shining; glossy.

M

malicious (mə lish′əs), *adj.* showing ill will; spiteful.

maligned (mä līnd′), *adj.* spoken against; slandered.

marrow (mar′ō), *n.* the inmost or essential part.

meager (mē′gər), *adj.* scanty.

meet (mēt), *adj.* fitting; appropriate.

mêlée (mā′lā), *n.* confused fight.

menace (men′is), *n.* threat.

mesmerizing (mez′mə rī′zing), *adj.* hypnotic.

meticulous (mə tik′yə ləs), *adj.* extremely or excessively careful about small details.

mettle (met′l), *n.* spirit, courage.

millet (mil′it), *n.* a cereal grass cultivated as a food grain.

mimic (mim′ik), *v.* make fun of by imitating.

minutely (mī nüt′lē), *adv.* in a small way or detailed manner.

misconstrue (mis′kən strü′), *v.* misunderstand; misinterpret.

monopoly (mə nop′ə lē), *n.* the exclusive possession or control of something.

motif (mō tēf′), *n.* a distinctive figure or pattern in a design, painting, etc.

muse (myüz), *v.* say thoughtfully.

muster (mus′tər), *v.* gather together.

mute (myüt), *adj.* silent.

mutilated (myü′tl āt′əd), *adj.* cut, torn, or broken off a limb or other important part of; maimed.

myriad (mir′ē əd), *n.* a great number.

N

naïve (nä ēv′), *adj.* simple in nature; like a child.

naught (nôt), *n.* nothing.

nonentity (non en′tə tē), *n.* a person or thing of little or no importance.

O

odious (ō′dē əs), *adj.* hateful; offensive.

officious (ə fish′əs), *adj.* too ready to offer services.

onslaught (ôn′slôt′), *n.* a vigorous attack.

oppressive (ə pres′iv), *adj.* hard to bear.

P

pandemonium (pan′də mō′nē əm), *n.* wild disorder.

passé (pa sā′), *adj.* old, stale. *[French]*

peevishness (pē′vish nəs), *n.* irritability; crossness.

perfunctorily (pər fungk′tər ə lē), *adv.* mechanically; indifferently.

peril (per′əl), *n.* danger.

perilous (per′ə ləs), *adj.* dangerous.

permeated (pėr′mē āt əd), *adj.* spread throughout; filled with.

peruse (pə rüz′), *v.* read, especially thoroughly and carefully.

perversity (pər vėr′sə tē), *n.* quality of being contrary and willful.

pigment (pig′mənt), *n.* natural substance that colors skin tissue.

piqued (pēkd), *adj.* aroused; stirred up.

plausible (plô′zə bəl), *adj.* appearing true, reasonable, or fair.

plight (plīt), *n.* 1 condition or situation, usually bad. 2 a solemn promise or pledge.

pluck (pluk), *v.* pull or tug.

poached (pōchd), *adj.* cooked by simmering in a liquid.

poppy (pop′ē), *n.* a bright red.

portent (pôr′tent), *n.* sign.

precarious (pri ker′ē əs), *adj.* not safe or secure; uncertain.

precedence (pres′ə dəns), *n.* higher position or rank; great importance.

preoccupation (prē ok′yə pā′shən), *n.* thing that absorbs or engrosses.

prerogative (pri rog′ə tiv), *n.* right or privilege that nobody else has.

presage (pri sāj′), *v.* predict.

pressurized (presh′ə rīzd′), *adj.* having the atmospheric pressure inside (the cabin of an aircraft) kept at a normal level in spite of the altitude.

presumptuous (pri zump′chü əs), *adj.* acting without permission or right; bold.

pretext (prē′tekst), *n.* a false reason concealing the real reason; misleading excuse.

primal (prī′məl), *adj.* fundamental.

prodigious (prə dij′əs), *adj.* very great; huge.

prodigy (prod′ə jē), *n.* person endowed with amazing brilliance or talent, especially a remarkably talented child.

profoundly (prə found′lē), *adv.* going more deeply than what is easily understood.

proletarian (prō′lə ter′ē ən), *n.* someone belonging to the proletariat, the lowest class in economic and social status, including all unskilled laborers.

promontory (prom′ən tôr′ē), *n.* high point of land extending from the coast.

propriety (prə prī′ə tē), *n.* proper behavior.

prosaic (prō zā′ik), *adj.* ordinary; not exciting.

prostrate (pros′trāt), *adj.* lying flat with face downward.

proverbial (prə vėr′bē əl), *adj.* relating to proverbs; commonly spoken of.

proviso (prə vī′zō), *n.* any provision or stipulation.

prowess (prou′is), *n.* bravery; skill.

puissant (pyü′ə sənt), *adj.* powerful.

pungent (pun′jənt), *adj.* sharply affecting the organs of taste and smell.

Q

quagmire (kwag′mīr′), *n.* soft, muddy ground.

quarry (kwôr′ē), *n.* 1 animal chased in a hunt; prey. 2 place where stone, slate, etc., is dug, cut, or blasted out for use in building.

R

rampant (ram′pənt), *adj.* growing without any limits.

rapport (ra pôr′, ra pôrt′), *n.* agreement; connection.

rebuke (ri byük′), *v.* express disapproval of.

recount (ri kount′), *v.* tell in detail.

redundant (ri dun′dənt), *adj.* not needed; extra.

refracted (ri frak′təd), *adj.* bent (a ray of light, waves, etc.) from a straight course.

rejuvenate (ri jü′və nāt), *v.* make young or vigorous again; renew.

rent (rent), *n.* tear; torn place.

reprimand (rep′rə mand), *v.* criticize.

reproach (ri prōch′), *n.* blame or disapproval.

resplendent (ri splen′dənt), *adj.* very bright; splendid.

retaliation (ri tal′ē ā′shən), *n.* paying back wrong.

reticence (ret′ə sens), *n.* tendency to be silent or say little.

revelry (rev′əl rē), *n.* boisterous merrymaking or festivity.

reverberate (ri vėr′bər āt′), *v.* echo back.

reverie (rev′ər ē), *n.* dreamy thoughts, especially of pleasant things.

ribald (rib′əld), *adj.* offensive in speech; obscene.

rite (rīt), *n.* solemn ceremony.

ritualist (rich′ü ə list), *n.* person who practices or advocates observance of the form or system of rites, or ceremonies.

rock crystal, a colorless, transparent variety of quartz, often used for jewelry, ornaments, etc.

rook (ru̇k), *n.* a bird that resembles the crow.

rout (rout), *n.* a complete defeat.

rubicund (rü′bə kund), *adj.* reddish; ruddy.

rudiment (rü′də mənt), *n.* part to be learned first; beginning.

rummage (rum′ij), *v.* search in a disorderly way.

rune (rün), *n.* inscription or letter.

ruse (rüz), *n.* scheme or device to mislead others; trick.

S

sacrilege (sak′rə lij), *n.* an intentional injury or disrespectful treatment of anyone or anything sacred.

sadist (sā′dist, sad′ist), *n.* person displaying cruel tendencies.

sagacious (sə gā′shəs), *adj.* wise in a keen, practical way; shrewd.

scribe (skrīb), *n.* writer; author.

scrutinize (skrüt′n īz), *v.* examine closely.

serenity (sə ren′ə tē), *n.* quiet; calmness.

servile (sėr′vəl), *adj.* like that of a slave.

sexton (sek′stən), *n.* person who takes care of a church building.

shard (shärd), *n.* broken piece.

sheepishly (shē′pish lē), *adv.* awkwardly bashful or embarrassed.

sheer (shir), *adj.* unmixed with anything else; complete.

shillelagh (shə lā′lē), *n.* a club used in fights.

shoal (shōl), *n.* a large number.

shrewd (shrüd), *adj.* clever; keen.

shrine (shrīn), *n.* place of worship.

simulated (sim′yə lāt əd), *adj.* fake; pretend.

skeptical (skep′tə kəl), *adj.* doubtful.

sordid (sôr′did), *adj.* filthy, contemptible.

soulful (sōl′fəl), *adj.* full of feeling; deeply emotional or passionate.

sovereignty (sov′rən tē), *n.* supreme power or authority.

spinster (spin′stər), *n.* an unmarried woman, especially an older woman.

sporadic (spə rad′ik), *adj.* appearing or happening at intervals in time; occasional.

spur (spėr), *n.* 1 ridge sticking out from or smaller than the main body of a mountain or mountain range. 2 a spiked instrument worn on a rider's heel for urging a horse on.

staidness (stād′nes), *n.* the condition of having a settled, quiet character.

statistic (stə tis′tik), *n.* a numerical fact about people, the weather, business conditions, etc., in order to show their significance.

steward (stü′ərd), *n.* a person employed on a ship to look after passangers.

stifle (stī′fəl), *v.* keep back; stop.

subdued (səb düd′), *adj.* suppressed; toned down.

subside (səb sīd′), *v.* die down.

subversive (səb vėr′siv), *adj.* tending to overthrow; causing ruin.

superficial (sü′pər fish′əl), *adj.* concerned with or understanding only what is on the surface; shallow.

supplication (sup′lə kā′shən), *n.* a humble and earnest prayer.

surplice (sėr′plis), *n.* a broad-sleeved, white gown or vestment worn by members of the clergy and choir singers.

surreptitiously (sėr′əp tish′əs lē), *adv.* secretly, deceptively.

T

taciturn (tas′ə tėrn′), *adj.* silent.

taint (tānt), *n.* a stain or spot.

talisman (tal′is mən, tal′iz mən), *n.* stone, ring, etc., engraved with figures or characters supposed to have magic power; charm.

tantamount (tan′tə mount), *adj.* equal; equivalent.

tempered (tem′pərd), *adj.* softened or moderated.

tenaciously (ti nā′shəs lē), *adv.* stubbornly.

tentative (ten′tə tiv), *adj.* hesitating.

tepid (tep′id), *adj.* lukewarm.

theology (thē ol′ə jē), *n.* study of religion and religious beliefs.

throng (thrông), *n.* a crowd; multitude.

translucent (tran slü′snt), *adj.* letting light through without being transparent.

traumatized (trô′mə tīzd), *adj.* undergoing great shock.

tribulation (trib′yə lā′shən), *n.* great trouble; severe trial.

tumultuous (tü mul′chü əs), *adj.* very noisy or disorderly.

turbot (tėr′bət, tėr′bō), *n.* a European fish, much valued as food.

turbulent (tėr′byə lənt), *adj.* filled with commotion; violent.

U

ulterior (ul tir′ē ər), *adj.* beyond what is seen or expressed; hidden.

unassailable (un ə sāl′ə bəl), *adj.* not able to be attacked (with violent blows, hostile words, arguments, or abuse).

uncanny (un kan′ē), *adj.* something that is strange and mysterious.

unequivocally (un′i kwiv′ə kəl ē), *adv.* clearly.

unfledged (un flejd′), *adj.* inexperienced.

unmolested (un mə lest′əd), *adj.* undisturbed.

unscathed (un skāᴛʜd′), *adj.* not harmed.

unshakable (un shā′kə bl), *adj.* undisturbed; not able to be upset.

usurp (yü zėrp′), *v.* seize by force.

usury (yü′zhər ē), *n.* the lending of money at an unusually high or unlawful rate of interest.

V

virile (vir′əl), *adj.* vigorous; forceful.

visceral (vis′ər əl), *adj.* arising from instinct or strong feelings; not intellectual or rational.

viscous (vis′kəs), *adj.* thick like heavy syrup; sticky.

vixen (vik′sən), *n.* a female fox.

vociferousness (vō sif′ər əs nəs), *n.* noisiness; shouting.

W

waft (waft), *n.* breath or puff of air, wind, scent, etc.

waveringly (wā′vər ing lē), *adv.* unsteadily.

wily (wī′lē), *adj.* crafty; sly.

wisteria (wi ster′ē ə), *n.* a climbing shrub of the pea family with large drooping clusters of purple, blue, or white flowers.

wistful (wist′fəl), *adj.* longing; yearning.

wizened (wiz′nd), *adj.* dried up; withered.

wont (wunt), *adj.* accustomed.

wrath (rath), *n.* very great anger; rage.

Z

zeal (zēl), *n.* eager desire or effort; earnest enthusiasm.

Glossary of Literary Terms

Words in small capital letters within entries refer to other entries in the Glossary of Literary Terms.

A

alliteration (ə lit′ə rā′shən), the REPETITION of consonant sounds at the beginnings of words or within words, particularly in accented syllables. It can be used to reinforce meaning, unify thought, or create a musical effect. "The setting sun silhouettes a sailboat" is an example of alliteration.

allusion (ə lü′zhən), a brief reference to a person, event, or place, real or fictitious, or to a work of art. A writer who describes a shortage or something that is missing with the words "The cupboard is bare" is alluding to the nursery rhyme "Old Mother Hubbard."

analogy (ə nal′ə jē), a literal comparison made between two items, situations, or ideas that are somewhat alike but unlike in most respects. Frequently an unfamiliar or complex object or idea will be compared to a familiar or simpler one in order to explain the first.

antagonist (an tag′ə nist), a character in a story or play who opposes the chief character, or PROTAGONIST.

assonance (as′n əns), the REPETITION of similar vowel sounds followed by different consonant sounds in stressed syllables or words. It is sometimes used instead of RHYME. *Made* and *played* are examples of rhyme; *made* and *pale* are examples of assonance.

autobiography, story of all or part of a person's life written by the person who lived it. *Kaffir Boy* (page 456) is an autobiography.

B

ballad, a NARRATIVE passed on in the oral tradition. It often makes use of REPETITION and DIALOGUE.

biography, an account of a person's life written by someone else.

blank verse, unrhymed verse written in IAMBIC PENTAMETER—that is, ten-syllable lines with five unstressed syllables alternating with five stressed syllables. The following blank-verse lines are spoken by Julius Caesar. Note that the stressed syllables are marked ′ and the unstressed syllables are marked ˘.

> Have I in conquest stretched mine arm so far,
> To be afeard to tell graybeards the truth?

See also page 675.

C

characterization, the methods authors use to acquaint a reader with their characters. We may learn about characters through their DIALOGUE and actions, or through what others say about them.

climax, the decisive point in a story or play when the central problem of the PLOT must be resolved in one way or another. Not every story or play has a dramatic climax. Sometimes a character may simply resolve a problem in his or her mind. At times there is no resolution of the plot; the climax then comes when a character realizes that a resolution is impossible.

comedy, a play written primarily to amuse the audience. In addition to arousing laughter, comic writing often appeals to the intellect.

conflict, struggle between two opposing forces. The four basic kinds of conflict are: (1) a person against another person; (2) a person against nature; (3) a person against society; and (4) two elements within a person struggling for mastery. More than one kind of conflict can be present in a work. In *Red Azalea,* page 145, Anchee Min experiences several kinds of conflict: struggling within herself, with Secretary Chain, and with the principles of the Cultural Revolution.

connotation, the emotional associations surrounding a word or phrase, as opposed to its literal meaning or DENOTATION. Some connotations are fairly universal, others quite personal.

See also page 492.

consonance (kon′sə nəns), the repetition of similar or identical consonant sounds that are preceded by different vowel sounds. The *m* sound is repeated in the following lines.

The moan of doves in immemorial elms,
And murmuring of innumerable bees.
Alfred, Lord Tennyson

couplet, a pair of rhyming lines with the same METER.

D

denotation, the strict, literal meaning of a word.

See also CONNOTATION.

dialect, a form of speech that is characteristic of a particular region or class, differing from the standard language in pronunciation, vocabulary, and grammatical form. The mother in "Two Kinds" (page 19) speaks in dialect.

dialogue, conversation between two or more people in a literary work. Dialogue can help develop the CHARACTERIZATION of those speaking and those spoken about, create MOOD, advance PLOT, and develop THEME.

diction, writers' choices of words, determined by their subject, audience, and desired effect. Diction may be casual or formal, simple or complex, old-fashioned or modern.

dimeter (dim′ə tər), line of VERSE having two metrical feet.

drama, a literary genre in verse or prose, written to be acted, that tells a story through the speech and actions of the characters; a play. *Julius Caesar* (page 679) is an example of drama.

See also pages 184–185.

E

end rhyme, the rhyming of words at the ends of lines of POETRY.

See also INTERNAL RHYME *and* RHYME.

essay, a brief prose composition that presents a personal viewpoint. "Woman from America" (page 632) is an essay that expresses the views of Bessie Head.

exposition, the beginning of a work of FICTION, particularly a play, in which the author sets the atmosphere and TONE, explains the SETTING, introduces the characters, and provides the reader with any other information needed to understand the PLOT.

extended metaphor, a figure of speech that compares two things throughout an entire work or a great part of it. It is more common in poetry than in prose.

See also METAPHOR.

F

fable, a brief TALE, in which the characters often are animals, told to point out a MORAL truth. "The Fox and the Woodcutter" (page 287) is one of many fables by Aesop.

falling action, the RESOLUTION of a dramatic PLOT, which takes place after the CLIMAX.

fantasy/science fiction. Both fantasy and science fiction are literary works set wholly or partly in an unreal world. Often, at least one character is unlike a human being. Frequently the PLOT concerns events that cannot be explained by current science. For example, Poe's classic story, "The Masque of the Red Death (page 95)," is a fantasy.

farce, comedy that involves improbable situations, exaggerated characters, and slapstick action. Farce relies on fast pacing, exaggeration, and physical action, and often includes mistaken identity and deception. *The Flying Doctor* by Molière (page 270) is a farce.

fiction, a type of literature drawn from the imagination of the author, that tells about imaginary people and events. NOVELS, SHORT STORIES, and many plays are fiction.

figurative language, language used in a nonliteral way to express a suitable relationship between essentially unlike things. SIMILE and METAPHOR are both examples of figurative language.

flashback, interruption of a NARRATIVE to show events that happened before that particular point in time.

folk literature, a type of literature that has been passed orally from generation to generation and written down only after centuries. The authors of folk literature, such as epics, LEGENDS, and the like, are unknown.

foot, in VERSE, a group of syllables usually consisting of one accented syllable and all unaccented syllables associated with it, as in the following lines by Robert Herrick. (Note that each foot is shown within slanted lines.)

Then be/not coy,/but use/your time,/
And, while/ye may,/go marry;/

foreshadowing, a hint given to the reader of what is to come.

free verse, a type of POETRY that differs from conventional VERSE in being free from a fixed pattern of METER and RHYME, but that uses RHYTHM and other devices.

G

genre (zhän rə), a form or type of literary work. For example, the NOVEL, SHORT STORY, DRAMA, and poem are all genres.

H

haiku (hī′kü), a brief poem of three lines that often consist of five syllables, seven syllables, and five syllables, respectively. Haiku often describe scenes in nature. Haiku poems appear on page 616.

hero, the central character in a NOVEL, SHORT STORY, DRAMA, or other work of FICTION. When the central character is a female, she is often called a heroine. The term *hero,* however, can be used to refer to both males and females.

historical fiction, fiction set in a time other than that in which it is written. The excerpt from *The Once and Future King* (page 365) is historical fiction based on Arthurian LEGEND.

hyperbole (hī pėr′bə lē), a figure of speech involving great exaggeration. The effect may be satiric or comic.

I

iambic pentameter, a line consisting of five two-syllable metrical feet—that is, five unstressed syllables alternating with five stressed syllables.

See also BLANK VERSE.

idiom, an expression whose meaning cannot be understood from the ordinary meaning of the words in it. For example, to "hold your tongue" or to "be all ears" are idioms.

imagery, sensory details that provide vividness in a literary work and tend to arouse emotions or feelings in a reader.

inference, a reasonable conclusion about the behavior of a character or the meaning of an event drawn from the limited information presented by the author.

internal rhyme, rhyming words or accented syllables within a line which may or may not have a rhyme at the end of the line as well.

inversion, reversal of the usual order of the parts of a sentence, primarily for emphasis or to achieve a certain RHYTHM or RHYME. Inversion is sometimes called *anastrophe* (ə nas′trə fē). The following line from *Julius Caesar* illustrates inversion:

Go you down that way towards the Capitol.

irony, the term used to describe a contrast between what is expected, or what appears to be, and what really is. In *verbal irony,* the actual meaning of a statement is different from (often the opposite of) what the statement literally says. *Irony of situation* refers to an occurrence that is contrary to what is expected. *Dramatic irony* refers to a situation in which events or facts not known to a character on stage or in a fictional work are known to the audience or reader.

L

legend, a story handed down from the past, often associated with some period in the history of a people. A legend differs from a MYTH in having some historical truth and often less of the supernatural. Malory's *Le Morte d'Arthur* and other Arthurian TALES are based on legends of King Arthur and the Knights of the Round Table.

See also page 337.

light verse, short poems written chiefly to amuse or entertain. "One Perfect Rose" (page 503) is an example of light verse.

lyric, a poem, usually short, that expresses some basic emotion or state of mind. A lyric usually creates a single impression and is highly personal. It may be rhymed or unrhymed. "If You'll Only Go to Sleep" (page 562) is a lyric.

M

metaphor (met′ə fôr), a figure of speech that involves an implied comparison between two different things. "His eyes are dark pools" is a metaphor.

meter, the pattern of stressed and unstressed syllables in POETRY.

mood, the overall atmosphere or prevailing feeling within a work of art. Words such as *peaceful, gloomy, mysterious,* and *expectant* can be used to describe mood.

moral, the lesson or teaching in a FABLE or story.

motivation, the process of presenting a convincing cause for the actions of a character in a dramatic or fictional work in order to justify those actions. Motivation usually involves a combination of external events and the character's personality traits. The mother's actions in "Tuesday Siesta" (page 510) are motivated by her love for her son and her desire to see him properly buried.

mystery, a work of fiction that contains a puzzling problem or an event not explained until the end, so as to keep the reader in suspense.

myth, a traditional story connected with the religion or beliefs of a people, usually attempting to account for something in nature. In ancient Greek myths, for example, lightning was depicted as thunderbolts cast down from Mount Olympus by the god Zeus. A myth has less historical background than a LEGEND.

N

narrative, a story or an account of an event or a series of events. A narrative may be true or fictional.

narrator, the teller of a story. The narrator may be a character in the story or someone outside the story.

See also POINT OF VIEW.

nonfiction, literature about real people and events, rather than imaginary ones. Nonfiction includes history, AUTOBIOGRAPHY, BIOGRAPHY, ESSAY, and article.

See also pages 452–453.

novel, a long work of NARRATIVE prose FICTION dealing with characters, situations, and settings that imitate those of real life. A novelette is a short novel. A similar type of work, the novella, is longer than a short story but not as long as a novel.

O

onomatopoeia (on′ə mä′tə pē′ə), a word or words used in such a way that the sound imitates the sound of the thing described. Words such as *crack, gurgle,* and *swoosh* are onomatopoetic. The following lines from "Willliam and Helen" by Sir Walter Scott illustrate onomatopoeia:

> Tramp! tramp! along the land they rode,
> Splash! Splash! along the sea.

P

parable, a brief fictional work that concretely illustrates an abstract idea or teaches some lesson or truth. It differs from a FABLE in that the characters in it are generally people rather than animals. "How Much Land Does a Man Need?" (page 775) can be considered a parable.

paradox, a statement, person, or situation that seems at first to be self-contradictory but that has a valid meaning. In *Antigone,* Teiresias, the blind seer, is a paradox.

pentameter (pen tam′ə tər), a metrical line of five feet.

See also IAMBIC PENTAMETER.

persona (pėr sō′nə), the mask or voice of the author or the author's creation in a particular work.

See also NARRATOR *and* POINT OF VIEW.

personification (pėr son′ə fə kā′shən), the representation of abstractions, ideas, or inanimate objects as living things or as human beings by endowing them with human qualities. In "Sunday Morning" (page 598) , the sun is described as "naked" and the sea as a "green monster." Personification is one kind of FIGURATIVE LANGUAGE.

play *See* DRAMA.

plot, a series of happenings in a literary work. The word is used to refer to the action as it is organized around a CONFLICT and builds through complication to a CLIMAX followed by the RESOLUTION. A plot diagram appears on page 65.

poetry, a literary GENRE that creates an emotional response by the imaginative use of words patterned to produce a desired effect through RHYTHM, sound, and meaning. Poetry may be rhymed or unrhymed. Among the many forms of poetry are the LYRIC, SONNET, and BALLAD. Most of the selections in Unit 5 are poems.

point of view, the relation between the teller of the story and the characters in it. The teller, or NARRATOR, may be a character in the story, in which case it is told from the *first-person* point of view. A writer who describes, in the *third person,* the thoughts and actions of any or all of the characters as the need arises is said to use the *omniscient* (om nish′ənt) point of view. A writer who, in the third person, follows along with one character and tends to view events from that character's perspective is said to use a *limited omniscient* point of view. An author who describes only what can be seen, like a newspaper reporter, is said to use the *dramatic* point of view.

See also NARRATOR *and* PERSONA.

prologue, section that precedes the main body of a work and serves as an introduction.

protagonist (prō tag′ə nist), the leading character in a literary work.

proverb, a brief, traditional saying that contains popular wisdom. An Ashanti proverb states, "No one tests the depth of a river with both feet."

psalm, (säm, sälm), a song or poem in praise of God. The term is most often applied to the hymns in the Book of Psalms of the Bible.

pun, a play on words; a humorous use of a word where it can have different meanings, or of two or more words with the same or nearly the same sound but different meanings. In the opening scene of *Julius Caesar,* a cobbler puns on words such as *sole* and *soul.*

Q

quatrain (kwôt′rān), verse STANZA of four lines. This stanza may take many forms, according to line lengths and rhyme patterns.

R

realism, a way of representing life that emphasizes ordinary people in everyday experiences.

repetition, a poetic device in which a sound, word, or phrase is repeated for emphasis or effect.

resolution (rez′ə lü′shən), the part of a PLOT following the CLIMAX in which the complications of the plot are resolved or settled.

rhyme, exact repetition of sounds in at least the final accented syllables of two or more words. For example, William Blake wrote in "A Poison Tree" (page 288):

> I was angry with my *friend;*/I told my wrath, my wrath did *end.*

rhyme scheme, any pattern of rhyme in a STANZA.

rhythm (riᴛʜ′əm), the arrangement of stressed and unstressed sounds in speech and writing. Rhythm in poetry may be regular or irregular.

rising action, the part of a dramatic plot that leads up to the CLIMAX. In rising action, the complication caused by the CONFLICT of opposing forces is developed.

romance, a long NARRATIVE in poetry or prose that originated in the medieval period. Its main elements are adventure, love, and magic. There are elements of the romance in the LEGENDS of Arthur.

romanticism, a way of representing life that, unlike REALISM, tends to portray the uncommon. The material selected often deals with extraordinary people in unusual SETTINGS having unusual experiences. In romantic literature there often is a stress on past times and an emphasis on nature.

S

satire, a technique in writing that employs wit to ridicule a subject, usually some social institution or human weakness, with the purpose of pointing out problems in society or inspiring reform. In "The Censors" (page 30), Luisa Valenzuela satirizes both government censorship and people who succumb to it.

scansion (skan′shən), the marking off of lines of poetry into feet.
See also RHYTHM.

science fiction *See* FANTASY.

setting, the time (both time of day or season and period in history) and place in which the action of a NARRATIVE occurs. The setting may be suggested through DIALOGUE and action, or it may be described by the narrator or one of the other characters. Setting contributes strongly to the MOOD or atmosphere and plausibility of a work. For example, the heat and poverty of the setting of "Tuesday Siesta" (page 510) contribute to a mood of oppressiveness and futility.

short story, a prose NARRATIVE that is shorter than a novel and that generally describes just one event or a tightly constructed series of events. Although brief, a short story must have a beginning, a middle, and an end.
See also pages 2–3.

simile (sim′ə lē), a figure of speech involving a comparison using a word such as *like* or *as:* "Her hair looked like spun gold."

slant rhyme, rhyme in which the vowel sounds are not quite identical, as in these lines: Gather friends and gather *foods*. Count your blessings, share your *goods*.

soliloquy (sə lil′ə kwē), a dramatic convention that allows a CHARACTER alone on stage to speak his or her thoughts aloud. If someone else is on stage but cannot hear the character's words, the speech becomes an *aside.*

sonnet, a LYRIC poem with a traditional form of fourteen IAMBIC PENTAMETER lines and one of a variety of RHYME SCHEMES.

sound devices, the choice and arrangement of words to please the ear and suit meaning. RHYME, RHYTHM, ASSONANCE, ONOMATOPOEIA, and ALLITERATION are examples of sound devices.

speaker, the imaginary voice a poet chooses to "tell" a poem. This "I," who presents information in the first person, is not necessarily the poet.

speech, a literary composition written to be given as a public talk. A speech may be formal or informal in style, and the topic usually depends on the intended audience. The Nobel speeches of Albert Camus and Elie Wiesel appear on pages 525–529.

stage directions, directions given by the author of a play to indicate the action, costumes, SETTING, arrangement of the stage, and other instructions to the actors and director of the DRAMA. Stage directions are usually written in italics. For example, in *Twelve Angry Men* (page 228), we are introduced to the jury room, which is *a large, bare, unpleasant-looking room* full of men *who are ill at ease.*

stanza, a group of lines that are set off and form a division in a poem.

stereotype (ster′ē ə tīp′), a conventional character, PLOT, or SETTING that possesses little or no individuality or complexity. Inspector Moronoff in "The Chameleon" (page 283) is a stereotype of a politician who acts according to his own best interests.

style, the distinctive handling of language by an author. It is part of an author's special way of choosing words, shaping sentences, and expressing thoughts.

suspense, the methods an author uses to maintain readers' interest, and the resulting MOOD of anxious uncertainty in many interesting stories. In her excerpt from *An American Childhood* (page 475), Annie Dillard builds suspense as she describes a chase.

symbol, a person, place, event, or object that has meaning in itself but also suggests other meanings as well. The flag, for example, is a symbol for patriotism.

T

tale, a spoken or written NARRATIVE, usually less complicated than a SHORT STORY.

theme, an underlying meaning of a literary work. A single work may have several themes. A theme may be directly stated but more often is implied.

tone, an author's attitude toward the subject of his or her literary work and toward the reader.

tragedy, dramatic or narrative writing in which the main character suffers disaster after a serious and significant struggle but faces his or her downfall in such a way as to attain heroic stature. The play *Julius Caesar* is considered a tragedy because of the fate that befalls the overly ambitious Caesar.

trimeter (trim′ə tər), line of VERSE having three metrical feet.

V

verse, in its most general sense, a synonym for poetry. Verse also may be used to refer to poetry carefully composed as to RHYTHM and RHYME SCHEME, but of inferior literary value.

Language and Grammar Handbook

Skill-building worksheets can be found in the *Reading, Writing and Grammar SkillBook,* referenced in the blue tabs throughout this handbook.

Are you sometimes confused when your teacher returns papers with comments such as, "Incorrect subject-verb agreement," or "Unclear antecedent for your pronoun"? This Handbook will help you respond to such comments as you edit your writing and also provide answers to questions that arise about language during peer- and self-evaluation.

The Handbook is alphabetically arranged with each entry explaining a term or concept. For example, if you can't remember when to use *accept* and *except,* look up the entry **accept, except** and you'll find an explanation of the meaning of each word and a sentence (many from selections in this book) using each word.

accept, except The similarity in sound causes these words to be confused. *Accept* means "to take or receive; consent to receive; say yes to." It is always a verb. *Except* is most commonly used as a preposition meaning "but."

- It is with a profound sense of humility that I accept the honor you have chosen to bestow upon me.
  from "Nobel Acceptance Speech" by Elie Wiesel

- Everyone broke into a nervous laugh, except me.
  from *Kaffir Boy* by Mark Mathabane

p. 210

active and passive voice A verb is said to be in the active voice when its subject is the doer of the action, and in the passive voice when its subject is the receiver of the action. A passive verb is a form of the verb *be* plus the past participle of the verb: *is* written, *had been* written, *will be* written, and so on.

ACTIVE: The teacher prepared the class for the exam.
PASSIVE: The class was prepared for the exam by the teacher.

Active verbs are more natural, direct, and forceful than passive verbs. Passive verbs are useful and effective, however, when the doer of the action is unknown, unimportant, or obvious, or when special emphasis is wanted for the receiver of the action:

- My name was constantly mentioned by the school authority. . . .
  from *Red Azalea* by Anchee Min

- The power of his eyes was considerably enhanced by their position. . . .
  from "An Astrologer's Day" by R. K. Narayan

p. 224

adjective Adjectives are modifiers that describe nouns and pronouns and make their meaning more exact. Adjectives tell *what kind, which one,* or *how many.*

What kind:	*white* rose	*fast* car	*tall* building
Which one:	*this* book	*that* movie	*those* shirts
How many:	*three* days	*few* customers	*many* runners

See also **comparative forms of adjectives and adverbs.**

p. 226

adverb Adverbs modify verbs, adjectives, or other adverbs. They tell *how, when,* or *where* about verbs.

How:	carefully	rapidly	bravely
When:	later	now	yesterday
Where:	there	near	outside

See also **comparative forms of adjectives and adverbs.**

affect, effect *Affect* is a verb. It is most frequently used to mean "to influence." *Effect* is mainly used as a noun meaning "result" or "consequence."

- The weather always affects my allergies.
- Your dirty tricks will have no more effect on me!
  from *Red Azalea* by Anchee Min

In formal English, *effect* is also used as a verb meaning "to bring about or make happen."

- Sir Modred . . . laid siege to the Tower, but despite his large army, siege engines, and guns, was unable to effect a breach.
  from "The Death of King Arthur" by Sir Thomas Malory

agreement

p. 212
p. 218
p. 222

1. subject-verb agreement When the subject and verb of a sentence are both singular or both plural, they agree in number. This is called subject-verb agreement. Usually, singular verbs in the present tense end in *s.* Plural verbs do not have the *s* ending.

Michael drives. (singular subject; singular verb)
Kate and Michael drive. (plural subject; plural verb)

p. 191

Pronouns generally follow the same rule. However, *I* and *you* always take plural verbs.

	Singular	Plural
1st person	I drive	we drive
2nd person	you drive	you drive
3rd person	he/she/it drives	they drive

Changes also occur with the verb *to be* in both the present and past tense.

Present Tense		Past Tense	
I am	we are	I was	we were
you are	you are	you were	you were
he/she/it is	they are	he/she/it was	they were

p. 214

a. Most compound subjects joined by *and* or *both . . . and* are plural and are followed by plural verbs.

- A sofa and a chair were in front of the fireplace.

b. A compound subject joined by *or, either . . . or,* or *neither . . . nor* is followed by a verb that agrees in number with the closer subject.

- Neither Maria nor her relatives live there anymore.
- Neither her relatives nor Maria lives there anymore.

Problems arise when it isn't obvious what the subject is. The following rules should help you with some of the most troublesome situations.

c. Phrases or clauses coming between the subject and the verb do not affect the subject-verb agreement.

- A variety of trades and occupations was represented all along its way. . . .
  from "An Astrologer's Day" by R. K. Narayan

- . . . the freedom, maybe even the life, of both sender and receiver is in jeopardy.
  from "Nobel Acceptance Speech" by Albert Camus

d. Singular verbs are used with singular indefinite pronouns—*each, every, either, neither, anyone, anybody, one, everyone, everybody, someone, somebody, nobody, no one.*

- Neither of us was hungry.
  from "Rain Music" by Longhang Nguyen

e. Plural indefinite pronouns take plural verbs. They are *both, few, many,* and *several.*

s v
- Both of these authors write science fiction.

p. 220

f. The indefinite pronouns *all, any, most, none,* and *some* can be either singular or plural depending on their meaning in a sentence.

Singular	Plural
All of the journey *was* exciting.	*All* of the travelers *were* hungry.
Most of the voyage *was* calm.	*Most* of the inns *were* full.
None of the menu *was* in English.	*None* of the chairs *were* empty.

g. The verb agrees with the subject regardless of the number of the predicate complement (after a form of a linking verb).

s v
- The greatest problem was the mosquitoes.

s v
- Mosquitoes were the biggest problem.

h. Unusual word order does not affect agreement; the verb generally agrees with the subject, whether the subject follows or precedes it.

v s
- . . . and there flows a ruddier light through the blood-colored panes . . . .
  from "The Masque of the Red Death" by Edgar Allan Poe

In informal English, you may often hear sentences like "There's a book and some paper for you on my desk." *There's* is a contraction for "There is." Technically, since the subject is a *book and some paper,* the verb should be plural and the sentence should begin, "There are. . . ." Since this may sound strange, you may want to revise the sentence to something like "A book and some paper are on my desk." Be especially careful of sentences beginning with *There;* be sure the verb agrees with the subject.

v s
- There are no secrets in here!
  from *Twelve* Angry Men by Reginald Rose

v s
- There was a flutter of excitement, everybody reaching for plates. . . .
  from "Dip in the Pool" by Roald Dahl

2. Pronoun-antecedent agreement An *antecedent* is a word, clause, or phrase to which a pronoun refers. The pronoun agrees with its antecedent in person, number, and gender.

a p p
- The girl took off her shoes. Then she went to the washroom to put the bouquet of flowers in some water.
  from "Tuesday Siesta" by Gabriel García Márquez

a. Singular pronouns are generally used to refer to the indefinite pronouns *one, anyone, each, either, neither, everybody, everyone, somebody, someone, nobody,* and *no one.*

- Neither (a) of the women could practice her (p) tennis.
- Everybody (a) brought his (p) ticket to the gate.

The second sentence poses problems. It is clearly plural in meaning, and *everybody* may not refer to men only. To avoid the latter problem, you could write "Everybody brought his or her ticket to the gate." This solution is clumsy and wordy, though. Sometimes it is best to revise:

- The students brought their tickets to the gate.

This sentence is now clear and nonsexist.

among, between *Among* implies more than two persons, places, or things. *Between* usually refers to two, followed either by a plural or by two expressions joined by *and*—not by *or.*

- All these years . . . she thought she understood them. But now she discovered that she was a stranger among them.
  from "The Rain Came" by Grace Ogot
- Between semesters, James hiked fifty miles.
- Sam couldn't decide between the fish sandwich and the pasta.

See also **between you and me.**

apostrophe (') An apostrophe is used in possessive words, both singular and plural, and in contractions. It is also used to form the plurals of letters and numbers.

Jeffrey's jacket	A's and B's	won't
women's basketball	6's and 7's	wasn't

It may be used to indicate places in words in which certain sounds or letters are omitted.

- "Where are we going, Gran'ma?" I said. . . .
  from *Kaffir Boy* by Mark Mathabane

appositive An *appositive* is a word or word group that follows another word or word group and identifies or explains it more fully. It is usually set off by commas or dashes.

- The latest heartache for Dutchmen was an edict making it a crime to sing the "Wilhelmus," our national anthem.
  from "The Secret Room" by Corrie ten Boom
- The library staffed two assistants—Rachel and Ben.

If, however, the appositive is used to specify a particular person or thing, it is not set off.

◆ Moronoff recognizes the man as Grunkin the goldsmith.
from "The Chameleon" by Anton Chekhov

awkward writing A general term (abbreviated *awk*) sometimes used in theme correcting to indicate such faults as inappropriate word choice, unnecessary repetition, clumsy phrasing, confusing word order, or any other weakness or expression that makes reading difficult and obscures meaning.

Many writers have found that reading their first drafts aloud helps them detect clumsy or unclear phrasing in their work. Once identified, awkward construction can almost always be improved by rethinking and rewording.

B

bad, badly In formal English and in writing, *bad* (the adjective) is used to modify a noun or pronoun and is used after a linking verb. *Badly* (the adverb) modifies a verb.

◆ She felt bad about hurting his feelings. (Adjective used with linking verb *felt*)
◆ The game was played badly. (Adverb modifying a verb)

HINT: To check yourself, realize that you would never say "between we." You would say "between us," *us* being the objective form of the pronoun *we.*

between you and me After **prepositions** such as *between,* use the objective form of the personal pronouns: *between you and* ***me,*** *between you and* ***her,*** *between you and* ***him,*** *between you and* ***us,*** *between you and* ***them.***

◆ The misunderstanding is between you and her.
◆ Was the agreement between you and them?
◆ Here between us, the white light blazed and the blade shivered.
from *The Hollow Hills* by Mary Stewart

borrow, lend To *borrow* means to "get something from someone else with the understanding that it will be returned." To *lend* means to "let another have or use something temporarily."

◆ I borrowed a pen from Dad; he borrowed my calculator.
◆ Carlos offered to lend me his video.

Borrow is often followed by *from*—never by *off* or *off of.*

bring, take To *bring* means to "carry something toward." To *take* means to "carry something away."

◆ "Bring him back two weeks from today."
from *Kaffir Boy* by Mark Mathabane

◆ I rubbed the old silk against my skin, then wrapped them in tissue and decided to take them home with me.
from "Two Kinds" by Amy Tan

C

capitalization

p. 256

1. Capitalize all proper nouns and adjectives.

Proper Nouns	Proper Adjectives
Canada	Canadian
China	Chinese
Victoria	Victorian

p. 259

2. Capitalize people's names and titles.

General Powell	Bishop Clark
Justice Ginsburg	Dr. Fernandez
Ms. Sarah Stoner	Grandma
Uncle Jack	Senator Hanrahan

3. Capitalize the names of ethnic groups, languages, religions, revered persons, deities, religious bodies, buildings, and writings. Also capitalize any adjectives made from these names.

Indo-European	Buddha
German	Catholicism
Islam	Allah
Grace Lutheran Church	the Bible

NOTE: Do not capitalize directions of the compass or adjectives that indicate direction: Front Street runs north and south. The weather map showed showers in the northwest.

4. Capitalize geographical names (except for articles and prepositions) and any adjectives made from these names.

Australia	the Red Arrow Highway
Gila River	Danish pastry
Straits of Mackinac	Spanish rice
the Rockies	Southern accent
Arctic Circle	Gettysburg
Tampa Bay	Zion National Park

NOTE: Earth, sun, and moon are not capitalized unless used with the names of other planets: Is Venus closer to the Sun than Saturn? The earth revolves around the sun.

5. Capitalize the names of structures, organizations, and bodies in the universe.

the Capitol	the House of Representatives
Carnegie Hall	the United Way
the Eiffel Tower	Neptune
the Cubs	the Milky Way

6. Capitalize the names of historical events, times, and documents.

the Hundred Years' War	the Elizabethan Period
the Treaty of Versailles	the Emancipation Proclamation

NOTE: Do not capitalize the names of the seasons.

7. Capitalize the names of months, days, holidays, and time abbreviations.

February	Sunday
Thanksgiving	A.M. P.M.

NOTE: Some modern poets do not begin each line with a capital letter.

8. Capitalize the first letters in sentences, lines of poetry, and direct quotations.

◆ If thou shouldst never see my face again,
Pray for my soul. More things are wrought by prayer
Than this world dreams of.
from *Idylls of the King* by Alfred, Lord Tennyson

◆ The announcer said, "It will be cloudy and windy."

9. Capitalize certain parts of letters and outlines.

Dear Mrs. Moore, Sincerely yours,

I. Early types of automobiles
  A. Gasoline powered
    1. Haynes
    2. Ford
    3. Other makes
  B. Steam powered
  C. Electric cars

10. Capitalize the first, last, and all other important words in titles.
See also **italics.**

book	Dickens's *Great Expectations*
newspaper	story in the *Washington Post*
play and movie	starred in *Showboat*
television series	liked *Murphy Brown*
short story	read "The Monkey's Paw"
music (long)	saw *The Pirates of Penzance*
music (short)	sang "Swing Low, Sweet Chariot"
work of art	Winslow Homer's *Breezing Up*
magazine	*Seventeen* magazine

p. 148

clause A clause is a group of words that has a subject and a verb. A clause is independent when it can stand alone and make sense. A dependent clause has a subject and a verb, but when it stands alone it is incomplete, and the reader is left wondering about the meaning.

Independent Clause	Dependent Clause
Bailey (s) White wrote (v) *Mama Makes Up Her Mind*.	Since Bailey (s) White wrote (v) *Mama Makes Up Her Mind*.

p. 267 **colon (:)** A colon is often used to explain or clarify what has preceded it.

- That was one thing the occupation had done for Holland: churches were packed.
  from "The Secret Room" by Corrie ten Boom

A colon is also used after phrases that introduce a list or quotation.

- When he prepared for his hike, he packed the following items: a map, extra batteries, and a flashlight.
- One old man said: "Our son is a good man. . . ."
  from "The Voter" by Chinua Achebe

p. 261
p. 265 **comma (,)** Commas are used to show a pause or separation between words and word groups in sentences, to avoid confusion in sentences, to separate items in addresses, in dialogue, and in figures.

1. Use commas between items in a series. Words, phrases, and clauses in a series are separated by commas.

- He knows that they examine, sniff, feel, and read between the lines of each and every letter. . . .
  from "The Censors" by Luisa Valenzuela

NOTE: If the items in a series are all separated by a word like *and,* no comma is necessary: Rain and wind and sleet all hampered the rescue.

2. Use a comma after certain introductory words and groups of words such as clauses and prepositional phrases of five words or more.

- When my mother began dropping hints that I would soon be going to school, I vowed never to go. . . .
  from *Kaffir Boy* by Mark Mathabane

- During the absence of King Arthur from Britain, Sir Modred had decided to usurp the throne.
  from "The Death of King Arthur" by Sir Thomas Malory

3. Use a comma to set off nouns of direct address. The name or title by which persons (or animals) are addressed is called a noun of direct address.

- "Did you give him anything for it, Father?" inquired Mrs. White. . . .
  from "The Monkey's Paw" by W. W. Jacobs

- Sire, is it your will that Arthur shall succeed to the throne. . . ?
  from "The Coronation of Arthur" by Sir Thomas Malory

4. Use commas to set off interrupting elements and appositives. Any phrase or clause that interrupts the flow of a sentence is often set off by commas. Parenthetical expressions like *of course, after all, to be sure, on the other hand, I suppose,* and *as you know;* and words like *yes, no, oh,* and *well* are all set off by commas.

- The average woman of twenty, it has been estimated, could expect about twelve years of childbearing. . . .
  from "Youth and Chivalry" by Barbara Tuchman
- The reporter, on the other hand, was determined to snatch her from death.
  from "And of Clay Are We Created" by Isabel Allende

5. Use a comma before a coordinating conjunction *(and, but, for, or, nor, yet, so)* in a compound sentence.

- Both men spoke with the bitterness of possible defeat before them, for each knew that it might be long before his men would seek him out or find him. . . .
  from "The Interlopers" by Saki
- She was exhausted, but the path was still winding.
  from "The Rain Came" by Grace Ogot
- The girl was twelve years old, and it was the first time she'd ever been on a train.
  from "Tuesday Siesta" by Gabriel García Márquez

6. Use a comma after a dependent clause that begins a sentence. Do not use a comma before a dependent clause that follows the independent clause.

- Though night had scarcely come and the heat was great, we gathered at the fire to see each other's faces. . . .
  from "The Boar Hunt" by José Vasconcelos
- Occasionally we had to stop firing because the frequent shooting heated the barrels of our rifles.
  from "The Boar Hunt" by José Vasconcelos

7. Use a comma to separate items in an address. The number and street are considered one item. The state and Zip Code are also considered one item. Use a comma after the Zip Code if it is within a sentence.

Diane Wong	Todd's address is 721 N. Buckeye,
5341 Palm Dr.	Columbus, OH 73215, but don't
Messa, AZ 85210	have his phone number.

8. Use a comma to separate numerals greater than three digits.

900,321 4,500

9. Use commas in punctuating dialogue. *See* **dialogue.**

Comma splice *See* **run-on sentence.**

comparative forms of adjectives and adverbs To show a greater degree of the quality or characteristic named by an adjective or adverb, *-er* or *-est* is added to the word, or *more* or *most* is put before it.

Positive: Ron is quiet.

Comparative: Ron is quieter than Allen.

Superlative: Ron is the quietest person in the class.

More and *most* are generally used with longer adjectives and adverbs, and with all adverbs ending in *-ly.*

Positive: The movie was peculiar.

Comparative: The second movie was more peculiar than the first.

Superlative: The movie was the most peculiar one I have ever seen.

◆ Jan is more likely than Pat to enter the marathon.

The *comparative* forms are usually used in comparing two things or people, and the *superlative* in comparing more than two.

◆ Kim is the fastest runner on the team.
◆ Sarita is the taller of the two sisters.

Writers sometimes have trouble phrasing comparisons so that a reader can see immediately what things are being compared.

Faulty: The seats in the auditorium are better than the theater. [Seats are being compared to a theater.]

Corrected: The seats in the auditorium are better than those in the theater. *See also* **modifiers.**

conjunction A conjunction is a word that links one part of a sentence to another. It can join words, phrases, or entire sentences.

D

dash (—) A dash is used to indicate a sudden break or change of thought.

◆ By the time the last man had spoken it was possible—without great loss of dignity—to pick up the things from the floor.
from "The Voter" by Chinua Achebe

dialogue Dialogue is often used to enliven many types of writing. Notice the paragraphing and punctuation of the following passage.

◆ "Tell me," he said, coming straight to the point, "what did you think of the auction last night?"

"Auction?" she asked, frowning. "Auction? What auction?"
from "Dip in the Pool" by Roald Dahl

See also **quotation marks.**

direct address *See* **comma 3.**

E

ellipsis (. . .) An ellipsis is used to indicate that words (or sentences or paragraphs) have been omitted. An ellipsis consists of three dots, but if the omitted portion would have completed the sentence, a fourth dot is added for the period.

> Next, to establish peace and order in the counties near London. . . .
> from "The Coronation of Arthur" by Sir Thomas Malory

exclamation point (!) An exclamation mark is used at the end of an exclamatory sentence—one that shows excitement or strong emotion. Exclamation points can also be used with strong interjections.

F

fragment *See* **sentence fragment.**

G

gerund A verb form usually ending in *-ing* that is used as a noun. In the sentence following, *going* is the object of the preposition *by.*

p. 242

- It was unexplored underbrush into which we could enter only by going down the river in a canoe.
  from "The Boar Hunt" by José Vasconcelos

A gerund used as the object of a preposition should be related to the subject. Otherwise the phrase will dangle.

Dangling: After driving one block, the tire was flat.

Corrected: After driving one block, she noticed the tire was flat.

good, well *Good* is used as an adjective to modify a noun or pronoun. Do not use it to modify a verb. *Well* is usually used as an adverb to modify a verb.

- Her teacher commented that she had written a good paper.
- Kathleen behaved well when, some months later, her fiancé was reported missing, presumed killed.
  from "The Demon Lover" by Elizabeth Bowen

HINT: When you are referring to health, use *well* if the meaning is "not ill."

- "Dear Sister," she began, followed by a little time-buying cough and throat clearing. "We are all well here."
  from "The Need to Say It" by Patricia Hampl

If the meaning is "pleasant" or "in good spirits," use *good:*

◆ I feel really good today!

hopefully This is often used to mean "it is hoped," or "I hope," as in the sentence, "Hopefully she will be able to console herself." However, in formal writing, avoid this usage and write the sentence as follows:

◆ They hoped she would, in a year or two, console herself. . . .
from "The Demon Lover" by Elizabeth Bowen

however Words like *however, moreover, nevertheless,* and *consequently,* (known as conjunctive adverbs) require special punctuation. If the word comes within a clause, it is generally set off by commas.

◆ The man, however, was gazing in idle reverie at the city's skyline growing ever more beautiful. . . .
from "He—y, Come on Ou—t!" by Shinichi Hoshi

If the conjunctive adverb separates two independent clauses, a semicolon is used preceding the word.

◆ I like sports; however, I seldom have time to be on a team.

infinitive An infinitive is the simple form of the verb, usually preceded by *to.* Infinitives are used as nouns, adjectives, or adverbs. In the following passage, each infinitive acts as an adjective.

◆ A time to weep, and a time to laugh: a time to mourn, and a time to dance. . . .
from Ecclesiastes

p. 255

interjection An interjection is a word or phrase used to express strong emotion.

Ouch! Stay off my foot.

Yes! I was accepted.

Oh, no, the show is sold out!

NOTE: In handwritten or non-computer writing, use underlining to indicate italics.

italics Italic type is used to indicate titles of whole works such as books, magazines, newspapers, plays, films, and so on. It is also used to indicate foreign words and phrases.

◆ ". . . there's still a table by the bay window, if *madame* and *monsieur* would like to enjoy the view."
from "The Other Wife" by Colette

NOTE: In formal English, the correct way to respond to a question such as, "Who's there?" is "It is I." This sounds too formal in some situations, however. While it is not correct to say, "It's them," "It's him," "It's us," or "It's her," "It's me" is generally accepted as standard usage.

its, it's *Its* is the possessive form of the personal pronoun *it; it's* is the contraction meaning "it is."

◆ He brought the lamp close and tilted it at the money . . . to make sure he had not mistaken its value.
from "The Voter" by Chinua Achebe

◆ Juan knows there won't be a problem with the letter's contents, that it's irreproachable, harmless.
from "The Censors" by Luisa Valenzuela

lay, lie This verb pair presents problems because, in addition to the similarity between the words, the past tense of *lie* is *lay.* The verb *to lay,* means "to put or place something somewhere."

Present	Past	Past Participle
lay	laid	(has) laid

The principal parts of the verb to *lie,* which means "to rest," "to be at rest," or "in a reclining position," are the following.

Present	Past	Past Participle
lie	lay	(has) lain

Notice how the verbs are used in the following sentences.

◆ "Our cattle lie dying in the fields," they reported. "Soon it will be our children and then ourselves." (The cattle are in a reclining position.)
from "The Rain Came" by Grace Ogot

◆ "I will lay down my life, if necessary, and the life of my household, to save this tribe from the hands of the enemy." (I will put down my life.)
from "The Rain Came" by Grace Ogot

◆ America was where all my mother's hopes lay. (Where all my mother's hopes rested.)
from "Two Kinds" by Amy Tan

◆ But his sickness grew worse, and after he had lain speechless for three days and three nights Merlin summoned the nobles. . . . (He had been in a reclining position.)
from "The Coronation of Arthur" by Sir Thomas Malory

NOTE: *Lied* refers only to not telling the truth: Many people thought he *lied* on the witness stand.

lead, led The present tense of this verb rhymes with *seed;* the past tense (and past participle) is spelled *led* and rhymes with *red.*

◆ I forgot what I was supposed to do—to lead the crowd to shout the slogans—until Secretary Chain came to remind me of my duty.
from *Red Azalea* by Anchee Min

◆ I led my schoolmates in collecting pennies. We wanted to donate the pennies to the starving children in America.
from *Red Azalea* by Anchee Min

Hint: Remember that *lose* often means the opposite of *gain.* Each word has just four letters.

lose, loose *Lose* (to lose one's way, to lose a watch) is a verb; *loose* (to come loose, loose-fitting) is an adjective.

◆ As Oganda opened the gate a child, a young child, broke loose from the crowd and ran toward her.
from "The Rain Came" by Grace Ogot

◆ In marking the path to the landing, we were careful not to lose ourselves in the thicket.
from "The Boar Hunt" by José Vasconcelos

M

p. 232
p. 236

modifier A modifier is a word or group of words that restrict, limit, or make more exact the meaning of other words. The modifiers of nouns and pronouns are usually adjectives, participles, adjective phrases, and adjective clauses. The modifiers of verbs, adjectives, and adverbs are adverbs, adverb phrases, and adverb clauses. In the following examples, the italicized words modify the words that directly follow them in boldface type.

◆ The *seventh* ***apartment*** was *closely* ***shrouded*** in *black velvet* ***tapestries***. . . .
from "The Masque of the Red Death" by Edgar Allan Poe

HINT: When trying to decide which pronoun to use, remember that you would not say "Myself is going to the game." You would say *I*.

myself (and himself, herself, and so on) Be careful not to use *myself* and the other reflexive and intensive pronouns when you simply need to use the personal pronoun *I* or its objective form *me.*

Incorrect: John and myself are going to the game.
Correct: John and I are going to the game.
Incorrect: Chidi told Laura and myself a funny story.
Correct: Chidi told Laura and me a funny story.

N

none, no one When *none* tells how many, a plural verb is generally used, unless the idea of "not a single one" is to be emphasized, as in the following example.

◆ . . . Oganda fought desperately to find another exit. . . .
But there was none.
from "The Rain Came" by Grace Ogot

No one is singular and is often used for emphasis.

◆ For some time they had predicted that the heat of the eruption could detach the eternal ice from the slopes of the volcano, but no one heeded their warnings.
from "And of Clay Are We Created" by Isabel Allende

See also **agreement 1f.**

p. 169 p. 173

noun A noun is a word that names a person, place, thing, or idea. Most nouns are made plural by adding *-s* or *-es* to the singular. When you are unsure about a plural form, check a dictionary.

p. 165

parallel construction Items in a sentence that are of equal importance should be expressed in parallel (or similar) forms. These can take the form of noun phrases, verb phrases, infinitive phrases, and prepositional phrases.

◆ We sang at the top of our lungs, sang our oneness, our hope, our love for Queen and country.
from "The Secret Room" by Corrie ten Boom

◆ The boy would learn to ride, to fight, and to hawk . . . to play chess and backgammon, to sing and dance, play an instrument, and compose. . . .
from "Youth and Chivalry" by Barbara Tuchman

parentheses ( ) Parentheses are used to enclose words that interrupt or add explanation to a sentence. They are also used to enclose references to page numbers, chapters, or dates. Punctuation marks that belong to the sentence come after the parentheses, not before.

◆ I allowed myself a descriptive aria on the beauty of Minnesota winters (for the benefit of my California reader who might need some background material on the subject of ice hockey).
from "The Need to Say It" by Patricia Hampl

◆ Langston Hughes (1902–1967) was part of the Harlem Renaissance.

p. 240

participle A participle is a verb form used in forming various tenses of verbs. The present participle ends in *-ing:* growing. The past participle usually ends in *-ed, -t, -d, -en,* or *-n:* scared, kept, said, risen, blown.

I am thinking. We were running. Leaves have blown away.

Participles are also used as adjectives, modifying nouns and pronouns.

◆ The purser looked at the anxious frowning face of Mr. Botibol and he smiled. . . .
from "Dip in the Pool" by Roald Dahl

p. 175
p. 177

possessive case The possessive case is formed in various ways. For singular nouns and indefinite pronouns, add an apostrophe and *s.*

my sister's car someone's shoe everybody's grade

For plural nouns ending in an *s,* add only an apostrophe.

the doctors' offices the babies' pool the churches' members

However, if the plural is irregular and does not end in *s,* add an apostrophe and then an *s.*

NOTE: Apostrophes are not used with personal pronouns to show possession.

◆ . . . even when a suspicion of a smile flickered across the other women's faces . . . I thought that a rare distinction lit up my mother's face.

from "My Father Writes to My Mother" by Assia Djebar

p. 250

prepositions Prepositions are words such as *about, between, during, from, of, over, until,* and *with* that show the relationship between a noun or pronoun and some other word in a sentence.

p. 250

prepositional phrase Prepositional phrases are groups of words that begin with a preposition and end with a noun or pronoun. These phrases act as modifiers and create vivid pictures for the reader. Notice the three prepositional phrases in the following sentence.

◆ This woman from America married a man of our village and left her country to come and live with him here.

from "Woman from America" by Bessie Head

p. 179
p. 181
p. 193

pronoun Subject pronouns are used as subjects of sentences. Object pronouns can be used as direct objects, indirect objects, or objects of prepositions.

When a pronoun is used as the subject of a sentence, the pronoun is in the nominative case and is called a subject pronoun: *He* and *I* met at the movies.

p. 183

Subject Pronouns

Singular	I	you	he, she, it
Plural	we	you	they

HINT: When you are uncertain about whether to use a subject pronoun or an object pronoun in a sentence, take out the first pronoun to test the sentence. (You wouldn't say "The coach asked *he* to arrive early.")

When a pronoun is used as an object, the pronoun is in the objective case and is called an object pronoun: The coach asked *me* and *him* to arrive early.

Object Pronouns

Singular	me	you	him, her, it
Plural	us	you	them

See also **agreement 2** *for pronoun-antecedent agreement.*

Q

quotation marks (" ")

quotation marks (" ") Quotation marks enclose a speaker's exact words. They are also used to enclose some titles. When you use someone's exact words in your writing, use the following rules:

p. 269

1. Enclose all quoted words within quotation marks.

◆ Anchee Min wrote, "I stood up and felt dizzy."

2. The first word of a direct quotation begins with a capital letter. When a quotation is broken into two parts, use two sets of quotation marks. Use one capital letter if the quote is one sentence. Use two capital letters if it is two sentences.

◆ "You'd better close the window," the woman said. "Your hair will get full of soot."
from "Tuesday Siesta" by Gabriel García Márquez

3. Use a comma between the words that introduce the speaker and the words that are quoted. Place the end punctuation or the comma that ends the quotation inside the quotation marks. Put question marks and exclamation points inside the quotation marks only if they are a part of the quotation. Begin a new paragraph each time the speaker changes.

◆ "Come along," she said, frowning slightly. "What's your name, dear?"
"I don't know," I said finally.
from "By Any Other Name" by Santha Rama Rau

When a quoted passage is made up of more than one paragraph, opening quotation marks are put at the beginning of each paragraph, but closing marks are put only at the end of the last paragraph. *See also* **dialogue.**

R

raise, rise Use *raise* to mean "lift"; use *rise* to mean "get up."

Present	Past	Past Participle	Present Participle
raise	raised	had raised	is raising
rise	rose	had risen	is rising

◆ Then he sank trembling into a chair as the old woman, with burning eyes, walked to the window and raised the blind.
from "The Monkey's Paw" by W. W. Jacobs

◆ I rose obediently and started to walk toward my sister.
from "By Any Other Name" by Santha Rama Rau

reflexive pronouns Reflexive pronouns reflect the action of the verb back to the subject. An intensive pronoun adds emphasis to the noun or pronoun just named.

- That woman must be talking to herself. [reflexive]
- Merlin prophesied that they could be checked only by the presence of the king himself on the battlefield. . . . [intensive]
  from "The Coronation of Arthur" by Sir Thomas Malory

p. 142

run-on sentence A run-on sentence occurs when there is only a comma (known as a comma splice) or no punctuation between two independent clauses. Separate the clauses into two complete sentences, join them with a semicolon, or join them with a comma and a coordinating conjunction.

Run-on: The man bought his groceries then he went to the party.
Run-on: The man bought his groceries, then he went to the party.
Correct: The man bought his groceries. Then he went to the party.
Correct: The man bought his groceries; then he went to the party.
Correct: The man bought his groceries, and then he went to the party.

Sometimes, in narrative writing, authors choose to use run-ons for effect, such as in the following passage.

- She sat, she brooded, she stared out the window.
  from "The Need to Say It" by Patricia Hampl

See also **stringy sentences.**

p. 267

semicolon (;) Use this punctuation mark to separate the two parts of a compound sentence when they are not joined by a comma and a conjunction.

- In the day he made his speeches; at night his stalwarts conducted their whispering campaign.
  from "The Voter" by Chinua Achebe

sentence fragment A fragment often occurs when one sentence is finished, but another thought occurs to the writer. That thought is written and punctuated as a complete sentence, even though it may be missing a subject, verb, or both.

Fragment: I love reading mysteries. *Especially on cold evenings.*
Correct: I love reading mysteries, especially on cold evenings.

As with run-ons, fragments are sometimes used by writers for effect.

- ◆ I was never forgiven. Even after twenty-some years. After the Revolution was over.

  from *Red Azalea* by Anchee Min

sit, set Use *sit* to mean "to sit down"; use *set* to mean "to put something somewhere."

Present	Past	Past Participle	Present Participle
sit	sat	had sat	is sitting
set	set	had set	is setting

- ◆ Who is that sitting next to Diego?
- ◆ Laura set the sandwiches on the counter.

stringy sentences A stringy sentence is one in which several independent clauses are strung together with *and.* Since all the ideas seem to be treated equally, a reader may have difficulty seeing how they are related. Correct a stringy sentence by breaking it into individual sentences or changing some of the independent clauses into subordinate clauses or phrases.

Stringy sentence: I went to the library to find a book about Henry VIII for my research paper and then I met Martin and he wanted me to help him find a newspaper article on microfilm and when the library closed I still didn't have my book and my paper was overdue.

Corrected: When I went to the library to find a book about Henry VIII for my research paper, I met Martin. He wanted me to help him find a newspaper article on microfilm. Consequently, when the library closed, I still didn't have my book, and my paper was overdue.

Corrected: I met Martin when I went to the library to find a book about Henry VIII for my research paper. Since Martin wanted me to help him find a newspaper article on microfilm, the library closed before I could get my book. As a result, my paper was overdue.

T

their, there, they're *Their* is a possessive, *there* is an introductory word or adverb of place, and *they're* is the contraction for "they are."

HINT: Remember that *there* has the word *here* in it; these two words are related in that they can both be indicators of place.

- The blinding midday heat had forced the people into their huts.
  from "The Rain Came" by Grace Ogot
- There were sharp pains, and sudden dizziness, and then profuse bleeding. . . .
  from "The Masque of the Red Death" by Edgar Allan Poe
- Those cards have to be accounted for in a dozen ways. They're checked and double-checked.
  from "The Secret Room" by Corrie ten Boom

to, too, two *To* is a preposition that means "toward, in that direction" or is used in the infinitive form of the verb, as in "to follow" or "to run." *Too* means "also" or "more than enough." *Two* means "more than one."

- To take two tests in one day is too much.

V

p. 195
p. 199
p. 201
p. 203
p. 205

verb A verb is a word that tells about an action or a state of being. The form or tense of the verb tells whether the action occurred in the past, is occurring in the present, or will occur in the future.

verb shifts in tense Use the same tense to show two or more actions that occur at the same time.

Incorrect: Marla arrives *(present)* early and parked *(past)* her bike.
Correct: Marla arrived *(past)* early and parked *(past)* her bike.

When the verb in the main clause is in the present tense, the verb in the subordinate clause is in whatever tense expresses the meaning intended.

- Jeremy *thinks* that the popcorn *was* too salty.
- Anna *believes* that she *passed* the test.

W

p. 189

who, whom *Who* is used as a subject; *whom* is used as a direct object or the object of a preposition.

- Auntie Lindo's daughter, Waverly, who was about my age, was standing farther down the wall about five feet away.
  from "Two Kinds" by Amy Tan
- Danielle couldn't decide whom she would ask for a ride.
- Give the leftovers to whomever you wish.

who's, whose *Who's* is a contraction meaning "who is." *Whose* is a possessive.

◆ Who's the fellow in the straw hat?

◆ Whose gym bag is in my locker?

would of This expression is often used mistakenly because it sounds like *would've,* the contraction for *would have.* In formal writing, write out *would have,* and you won't be confused.

NOTE: In sentences beginning with the phrase "If (I) had" or when referring to a wish in the past, use the verb *had*—not *would have had.*

◆ I would have called, but Dad was on the phone.

Incorrect: If I would have had more time, I could make my paper better.

Correct: If I had more time, I could make my paper better.

Correct: If I had had more time, I could have made my paper better.

Y

your, you're *Your* is the possessive form of the personal pronoun *you; you're* is a contraction meaning "you are."

◆ The woman added, "We hear you and your friends laughing every Saturday night. . . ."
from "Living Well. Living Good." by Maya Angelou

◆ You're too small to have them.
from "By Any Other Name" by Santha Rama Rau

Index of Skills and Strategies

Literary Genres, Terms, and Techniques

Writing Forms, Modes, and Processes

Reading/Thinking Strategies

Vocabulary and Study Skills

Grammar, Usage, Mechanics, and Spelling

Speaking, Listening, and Viewing

Interdisciplinary Connections

Multicultural Awareness and Appreciation

Media and Technology

Index of Fine Art and Artists

Index of Authors and Titles

Acknowledgments

continued from iv

118 From *Innumeracy* by John Allen Paulos. Copyright © 1988 by John Allen Paulos. Reprinted by permission of Hill and Wang, a division of Farrar, Straus & Giroux, Inc.

136 "The Boar Hunt" by José Vasconcelos, trans. by Paul Waldorf from *The Muse in Mexico: A Mid-Century Miscellany,* Supplement to the Texas Quarterly, Vol. II. Reprinted by permission of University of Texas Press.

145 From *Red Azalea* by Anchee Min. Copyright © 1994 by Anchee Min. Reprinted by permission of Pantheon Books, a division of Random House, Inc.

156 "He—y, Come on Ou—t!" by Shinichi Hoshi, translated by Stanleigh H. Jones, Jr. Reprinted by permission of the author.

164 "Flash Cards" from *Grace Notes* by Rita Dove. Copyright © 1989 by Rita Dove. Reprinted by permission of W. W. Norton & Company, Inc.

165 "In Memory of Richi" from *Sonnets to Human Beings and Other Selected Works* by Carmen Tafolla. Copyright © 1992 by Carmen Tafolla. Reprinted by permission of the author.

166 "The Rabbit" by Edna St. Vincent Millay from *Collected Poems.* Copyright 1939, © 1967 by Edna St. Vincent Millay and Norma Millay Ellis. Reprinted by permission of Elizabeth Barnett, Literary Executor.

170 "The Elephant in the Dark House" from *Rumi, Poet and Mystic* translated by Reynold A. Nicholson. Reprinted by permission of George, Allen and Unwin, an imprint of HarperCollins Publishers Limited.

171 "Thought For a Sunshiny Morning" by Dorothy Parker from *The Portable Dorothy Parker* by Dorothy Parker. Introduction by Brendan Gill. Copyright 1928, renewed © 1956 by Dorothy Parker. Reprinted by permission of Viking Penguin, a division of Penguin Books USA Inc.

191 *Antigone* from *The Theban Plays* by Sophocles, translated by E. F. Watling. Copyright 1947 E. F. Watling. Reprinted by permission of Penguin Books Ltd.

228 *Twelve Angry Men* by Reginald Rose. Copyright © 1956, renewed 1984 Reginald Rose. Reprinted by permission of International Creative Management, Inc.

256 "We the Jurors" from "Do You Swear That You Will Well and Truly Try . . .?" by Barbara Holland, *Smithsonian,* March 1995, Vol. 25, #12. Reprinted by permission of the author.

270 Adapted from *The Flying Doctor* from *One-Act Comedies of Molière,* translated by Albert Bermel. Copyright © 1962, 1963, 1964, 1975 by Albert Bermel. Reprinted by permission of Applause Theatre Books, 211 W. 71st St., New York, NY 10023.

283 "The Chameleon" from *Chekhov: The Early Stories, 1883–1888* translated by Patrick Miles and Harvey Pitcher. Copyright © 1982 by Patrick Miles and Harvey Pitcher. Reprinted by permission of John Murray Publishers, Ltd.

287 "The Fox and the Woodcutter" from *Aesop's Fables,* trans. by Dennison B. Hull. Copyright © 1960 The University of Chicago Press. Reprinted by permission of The University of Chicago Press.

292 Adapted from "Dip in the Pool" by Roald Dahl from *Someone Like You* by Roald Dahl. Copyright 1948 by Roald Dahl. Reprinted by permission of the author and the Watkins/Loomis Agency.

305 From "The Need To Say It" by Patricia Hampl. Copyright © 1991 by Patricia Hampl. Originally published in *The Writer on Her Work* edited by Janet Sternberg. Published by W. W. Norton. Reprinted by permission of Rhoda Weyr Agency, NY.

310 This work originally appeared as *Crossroads* by Carlos Solórzano in *Selected Latin American One-Act Plays,* Francesca Colecchia and Julio Matas, eds. and trans. Published in 1973 by the University of Pittsburgh Press. Reprinted by permission of the Publisher.

317 "Two Bodies" from *Selected Poems* by Octavio Paz. Copyright © 1973 by Octavio Paz and Muriel Rukeyser. Reprinted by permission of New Directions Publishing Corp.

340, 371 From *Le Morte d'Arthur* by Sir Thomas Malory, translated by Keith Baines. Translation copyright © 1962 by Keith Baines, renewed © 1990 by Francesca Evans. Introduction © 1962 by Robert Graves, renewed © 1990 by Beryl Graves. Reprinted by permission of Dutton Signet, a division of Penguin Books USA Inc.

344 From *The Hollow Hills* by Mary Stewart. Copyright © 1977 by Mary Stewart. Reprinted by permission of William Morrow & Company, Inc. and Hodder & Stoughton Ltd.

350 "Youth and Chivalry" from *A Distant Mirror* by Barbara Tuchman. Copyright © 1978 by Barbara W. Tuchman. Reprinted by permission of Alfred A. Knopf, Inc.

358 From *Le Morte d'Arthur* by Sir Thomas Malory, translated by Keith Baines. Translation copyright © 1962 by Keith Baines, renewed © 1990 by Francesca Evans. Introduction © 1962 by Robert Graves, renewed © 1990 by Beryl Graves. Reprinted by permission of Dutton Signet, a division of Penguin Books USA Inc. Abridged.

365 From *The Once and Future King* by T. H. White. Reprinted by permission of David Higham Associates.

384–385 "Bus Chivalry" from *Miss Manners' Guide to Excruciatingly Correct Behavior* by Judith Martin. Copyright © 1979, 1980, 1981, 1982 by United Features Syndicates, Inc. Reprinted by permission of Scribner, a Division of Simon & Schuster Inc.

384 From *Math for Smarty Pants* by Marilyn Burns. Copyright © 1982 by Yolla Bolly Press. Reprinted by permission of Little, Brown and Company.

385 "The Knight" from *Collected Early Poems: 1950–1970* by Adrienne Rich. Copyright © 1993 by Adrienne Rich. Copyright © 1967, 1963, 1962, 1961, 1960, 1959, 1958, 1957, 1956, 1955, 1954, 1953, 1952, 1951 by Adrienne Rich. Copyright © 1984, 1975, 1971, 1969, 1966 by W. W. Norton & Company, Inc. Reprinted by permission of W. W. Norton & Company, Inc.

396 "And of Clay Are We Created" from *The Stories of Eva Luna* by Isabel Allende, translated from the Spanish by Margaret Sayers Peden. Copyright © 1989 by Isabel Allende. English translation copyright © 1991 by Macmillan Publishing Company. Reprinted by permission of Scribner, an imprint of Simon & Schuster, Inc.

409 "A Soldier of Urbina" from *Jorge Luis Borges Selected Poems* 1923–1967 by Jorge Luis Borges. Copyright © 1968, 1969, 1970, 1971, 1972 by Jorge Luis Borges, Emece Editores, S. A. and Normal Thomas Di Giovanni. Reprinted by permission of Delacorte Press/Seymour Lawrence, a division of Bantam Doubleday Dell Publishing Group, Inc.

411 "Lineage" from *This is My Century: New and Collected Poems* by Margaret Walker Alexander. Reprinted by permission of The University of Georgia Press.

411 "The Gift" from *Rose* by Li-Young Lee. Copyright © 1986 by Li-Young Lee. Reprinted by permission of BOA Editions, Ltd., 92 Park Ave., Brockport, NY 14420.

412 "Turning Pro" from *New and Collected Poems* by Ishmael Reed. Copyright © 1988 by Ishmael Reed. Reprinted by permission of Ellis J. Freedman.

417 "The Secret Room" from *The Hiding Place* by Corrie ten Boom with John and Elizabeth Sherrill. Copyright © 1971 by Corrie ten Boom and John and Elizabeth Sherrill. Reprinted by permission of Chosen Books.

429 "The Street of the Cañon" from *Mexican Village* by Josefina Niggli. Copyright 1945 by The University of North Carolina Press. Reprinted by permission of the publisher.

437 From "Heroic Possibilities" by Michael Dorris, *Teaching Tolerance,* Spring 1995, Vol. 4, No. 1, pp. 13–14. Copyright © 1995 Southern Poverty Law Center. Reprinted by permission of Teaching Tolerance.

456 Adapted from *Kaffir Boy* by Mark Mathabane. Copyright © 1986 by Mark Mathabane. Reprinted by permission of Simon & Schuster, Inc.

469 "Living Well. Living Good." from *Wouldn't Take Nothing For My Journey Now* by Maya Angelou. Copyright © 1993 by Maya Angelou. Reprinted by permission of Random House Inc.

475 Excerpt from *An American Childhood* by Annie Dillard. Copyright © 1987 by Annie Dillard. Reprinted with permission of HarperCollins Publishers, Inc.

481 "By Any Other Name" from *Gifts of Passage* by Santha Rama Rau. Originally appeared in *The New Yorker.* Copyright 1951 by Vasanthi Rama Rau Bowers. Copyright renewed. Reprinted by permission of HarperCollins Publishers, Inc.

488 "The Naming of Cats" from *Old Possum's Book of Practical Cats.* Copyright 1939 by T. S. Eliot and renewed © 1967 by Esme Valerie Eliot. Reprinted by permission of Harcourt Brace & Company and Faber and Faber Limited, London.

489 Illustration from *Old Possum's Book of Practical Cats* by T. S. Eliot. Illustration copyright © 1982 by Edward Gorey. Reprinted by permission of Harcourt Brace & Company.

503 "One Perfect Rose" by Dorothy Parker from *The Portable Dorothy Parker* by Dorothy Parker. Introduction by Brendan Gill. Copyright 1929 renewed © 1957 by Dorothy Parker. Reprinted by permission of Viking Penguin, a division of Penguin Books USA Inc.

504 "Daybreak in Alabama" from *Selected Poems* by Langston Hughes. Copyright 1948 by Alfred A. Knopf, Inc. and renewed © 1976 by the Executors of the Estate of Langston Hughes. Reprinted by permission of the publisher.

506 "The Flying Cat" from *Hugging the Jukebox* by Naomi Shihab Nye. Copyright © 1982 Naomi Shihab Nye. Reprinted by permission of the author.

510 "Tuesday Siesta" from *No One Writes to the Colonel* by Gabriel García Márquez. Copyright © 1968 in the English translation by Harper & Row, Publishers, Inc. Reprinted by permission of HarperCollins Publishers, Inc.

518 "A Preacher Ought to Be Good-Looking" from *The Pillow Book of Sei Shōnagon,* trans. by Ivan Morris. Copyright © 1967 by Columbia University Press. Reprinted with permission of the publisher.

518 "Elegant Things" from *The Pillow Book of Sei Shōnagon,* trans. by Ivan Morris. Copyright © 1967 by Columbia University Press. Reprinted with permission of the publisher.

518 "Things That Give A Good Feeling" from *The Pillow Book of Sei Shōnagon,* trans. by Ivan Morris. Copyright © 1967 by Columbia University Press. Reprinted with permission of the publisher.

518 "Things That Have Lost Their Power" from *The Pillow Book of Sei Shōnagon,* trans. by Ivan Morris. Copyright © 1967 by Columbia University Press. Reprinted with permission of the publisher.

520 "Porsche" from *Mama Makes up Her Mind: and Other Dangers of Southern Living* by Bailey White, pp. 19–21. Copyright © 1993 by Bailey White. Reprinted by permission of Addison-Wesley Publishing Company, Inc.

536 Lyrics from "Mercedes Benz" by Janis Joplin, Michael McClure and Bobby Neuwirth. Copyright © 1970 Strong Arm Music. Reprinted by permission. All Rights Reserved.

553 "A New Dress" by Ruth Dallas from *Collected Poems.* Copyright © 1987 by John McIndoe Publishers. Reprinted by permission of the University of Otago Press, New Zealand.

554 "Those Winter Sundays" from *Angle of Ascent: New and Selected Poems* by Robert Hayden. Copyright © 1966 by Robert Hayden. Reprinted by permission of Liveright Publishing Corporation.

556 "Tía Chucha" from *The Concrete River* by Luis Rodriguez. Copyright © 1991 by Luis J. Rodriguez. Reprinted by permission of Curbstone Press.

561 "Girls Can We Educate We Dads?" from *When I Dance.* Copyright © 1991, 1988 by James Berry. Reprinted by permission of Harcourt Brace & Company and Penguin Books Ltd.

562 "If You'll Only Go To Sleep" from *The Collected Poems of Gabriela Mistral* by Doris Dana. Copyright © 1961, 1964, 1970, 1971 by Doris Dana. Reprinted by arrangement with Doris Dana, c/o Joan Daves Agency as agent for the proprietor.

563 "Mi prima Agueda" from *Poesias Completas Y El Minutero* by Ramón López Velarde, edited by Antonio Castro Leal, 3/E, 1963. Reprinted by permission of Editorial Porrua S. A., Mexico.

564 From "My Cousin Agatha" (orig.: "Mi prima Agueda") by Ramón López Velarde from *The Yellow Canary Whose Eye Is So Black,* edited and translated by Cheli Durán. Copyright © 1977 by Cheli Durán Ryan. Reprinted by permission of Simon & Schuster Books for Young Readers, an imprint of Simon & Schuster Children's Publishing Division.

564 "My Cousin Agueda" by Ramón López Velarde from *Spanish-American Literature in Translation,* translated by Willis Knapp Jones. Copyright © 1963 by Frederick Ungar Publishing Company, Inc. Reprinted by permission of the publisher.

570 "First Frost" from *Antiworlds and the Fifth Ace: Poetry* by Andrei Voznesensky, edited by Patricia Blake and Max Hayward. Copyright © 1966, 1967 by Basic Books, Inc. Copyright © 1963 by Encounter Ltd. Copyright renewed. Reprinted by permission of Basic Books, a division of HarperCollins Publishers, Inc.

571 "For Anne Gregory" by W. B. Yeats from *The Poems of W. B. Yeats: A New Edition,* edited by Richard J. Finneran. Copyright 1933 by Macmillan Publishing Company, renewed © 1961 by Bertha Georgia Yeats. Reprinted by permission of Simon & Schuster, Inc.

571 "The Fist" from *Collected Poems 1948–1984* by Derek Walcott. Copyright © 1986 by Derek Walcott. Reprinted by permission of Farrar, Straus & Giroux, Inc.

572 "The Stone" from *Collected Poems* by W. W. Gibson. Reprinted by permission of Mr. Michael Gibson and Macmillan General Books, London.

579 "The Other" by Judith Ortiz Cofer from *Reaching for the Mainland* appearing in *Triple Crown,* 1987. Reprinted by permission of Bilingual Press/Editorial Bilingüe, Arizona State University, Tempe, AZ.

580 "To Julia de Burgos" by Julia de Burgos, translated by Maria Arrillaga, 1971. Reprinted by permission of Maria Consuelo Saez Burgos.

583 "We Are Many" from *Five Decades: Poems 1925–1970* by Pablo Neruda, translated by Ben Belitt. Copyright © 1961, 1969, 1972, 1974 by Ben Belitt. Reprinted by permission of Grove/Atlantic, Inc.

586 Abridgement of "Reading a Family Portrait" by Caroline Sloat. Copyright © 1982 by Caroline Sloat. Reprinted by permission of the author

598 "Sunday Morning" by Oscar Peñaranda. Copyright © 1969 by Oscar Peñaranda. Reprinted by permission of the author.

605 "Ceremony" by Leslie Marmon Silko. Copyright © 1981 by Leslie Marmon Silko. Reprinted by permission of Wylie, Aitken & Stone, Inc.

606 "A Story" from *The Collected Poems* 1931–1987 by Czeslaw Milosz. Translated by Renata Gorczynski and Robert Pinsky. Copyright © 1988 by Czeslaw Milosz Royalties, Inc. First published by The Ecco Press in 1988. Reprinted by permission of The Ecco Press.

607 "The Road Not Taken" by Robert Frost from *The Poetry of Robert Frost* edited by Edward Connery Lathem. Published in 1969 by Henry Holt and Co., Inc. Reprinted by permission of Henry Holt and Co., Inc.

608 *The Holy Bible.* Cleveland: The World Publishing Co.

614 "This is a Photograph of Me" from *The Circle Game* by Margaret Atwood, House of Anansi Press, Toronto, 1978. Reprinted with the permission of Stoddart Publishing Co., Limited, Don Mills, Ontario, Canada.

615 "Water Picture" from *The Complete Poems to Solve* by May Swenson. Copyright © 1966 by May Swenson. Copyright © 1993 by The Literary Estate of May Swenson. Originally appeared in *The New Yorker.* Reprinted by permission of Simon & Schuster Books for Young Readers, an imprint of Simon & Schuster Children's Publishing Division.

616 "On a Bare Branch," "Clouds Now and Then" and "Spring" by Matsuo Bashō from *The Penguin Book of Japanese Verse* translated by Geoffrey Bownas and Anthony Thwaite. Copyright © 1964 Geoffrey Bownas and Anthony Thwaite. Reprinted by permission of Penguin Books Ltd., England.

616 "Spring Rain," "Mosquito Buzz" and "Sudden Shower" by Yosa Buson from *The Penguin Book of Japanese Verse* translated by Geoffrey Bownas and Anthony Thwaite. Copyright © 1964 Geoffrey Bownas and Anthony Thwaite. Reprinted by permission of Penguin Books Ltd., England.

620 From "The Cerebral Snapshot" from *Sunrise with Seamonsters* by Paul Theroux. Copyright © 1985 by Cape Cod Scriveners. All rights reserved. Reprinted by permission of Houghton Mifflin Co.

632 "The Woman from America" by Bessie Head. Reprinted by permission of John Johnson Ltd.

637 Adapted from "Rain Music" by Longhang Nguyen. Copyright © 1992 by Longhang Nguyen. Reprinted by permission of the author.

644 "My Father Writes to My Mother" by Assia Djebar. Reprinted by permission of Quartet Books Ltd.

652 "For the White Poets Who Would Be Indian" from *Bone Dance: New and Selected Poems 1965–1993* by Wendy Rose. Copyright © 1994 by Wendy Rose. Reprinted by permission of Malki Museum Press.

652 "Legal Alien" by Pat Mora from *Chants,* 1985. Reprinted by permission of Arte Publico Press, University of Houston.

653 "I am not with those who left their land . . ." by Anna Akhmatova, translated by Peter Norman from *The Akhmatova Journals: Volume One 1938–1941* by Lydia Chukovskaya. Copyright © 1994 by Lydia Chukovskaya. Reprinted by permission of Farrar, Straus & Giroux, Inc.

654 "Jerusalem" from *The Selected Poetry of Yehuda Amichai* by Yehuda Amichai. Edited and translated by Chana Bloch and Stephen Mitchell. English translation copyright © 1986 by Chana Bloch and Stephen Mitchell. Reprinted by permission of HarperCollins Publishers, Inc.

656 "Dos Patrias" and "Two Countries" by José Martí from *José Martí: Major Poems.* Translated by Elinor Randall, edited by Philip S. Foner. Copyright © 1982 by Holmes & Meier Publishers, Inc. Reprinted by permission of the publisher, Holmes & Meier, New York.

659 "It's Hard to Smile" from "Koreans Have a Reason Not to Smile" by Connie Kang, *The New York Times,* September 8, 1990. Copyright © 1990 by The New York Times Company. Reprinted by permission.

764 "Caesar's Commentaries on the Gallic Wars" from *Shrinklits* by Maurice Sagoff. All rights reserved. Reprinted by permission of Workman Publishing Company, Inc.

766 "The Balek Scales" from *18 Stories* by Heinrich Böll, trans. by Leila Vennewitz. Copyright © 1966 by Heinrich Böll. Reprinted by arrangement with Verlag Kiepenheuer & Witsch, c/o Joan Daves Agency as agent for the proprietor and by permission of Leila Vennewitz.

775 "How Much Land Does a Man Need?" from *Twenty-three Tales* by Leo Tolstoy, translated by Louise and Aylmer Maude, 1906. Reprinted by permission of Oxford University Press, Oxford.

788 John Tebbel and Sarah Miles Watts, *The Press and the Presidency.* New York: Oxford University Press, 1985, pp. 535–36, 541.

Acknowledgments

Illustration

Unless otherwise acknowledged, all photographs are the property of Scott, Foresman and Company. Page abbreviations are as follows: (t)top, (c)center, (b)bottom, (l)left, (r)right, (INS)inset.

Cover (detail) and Frontispiece *The Afterglow in Egypt* by William Holman Hunt, 1834. Southampton City Art Gallery.

ix Scala/Art Resource

xi Bridgeman/Art Resource

xiii Tsing-Fang Chen, *Human Achievement,* Lucia Gallery, New York City/Superstock, Inc.

xvii Boris Kustodiev, *The Fair*, 1908/Scala/Art Resource

xviii Jean-Leon Gerome, *Death of Caesar*, 1859, The Walters Art Gallery, Baltimore

xxiv Photo Reunion des Musées Nationaux

xxxii–1 Antonio Ruiz, *The Bicycle Race*, 1938. Philadelphia Museum of Art; Purchased by Nebinger Fund.

1, 4, 50, 56, 62 (icon) Normand Cousineau/SIS

1, 64, 114, 119, 125 (icon) Husain Haqqash, *Akbar Hunting a Tiger Near Gwalior*, From the Akbar-Nama, By Courtesy of the Board of Trustees of the Victoria and Albert Museum, London/Bridgeman Art Library, London/Superstock, Inc.

1, 126, 170, 174, 179 (icon) Wheel of Fortune tarot card, The Pierpont Morgan Library/Art Resource

2 Private Collection. Photo: Jeffrey Ploskonka

3(t) From the collection of Nancy Berliner

3(b) Stuart Handler Family Collection, Evanston, Illinois/Photo: P.P.O.W.

5 Jill Krementz

10–11 Stuart Handler Family Collection, Evanston, Illinois/Photo: P.P.O.W.

17(l) Photo by Robert Foothorap

17(r) Sidney Harris

18–19 © Service photographique, Ville de Nice, © 1995 Succession H. Matisse, Paris/Artists Rights Society (ARS), New York

25 From the collection of Nancy Berliner

29(t) Layle Silbert

29(b) Drawing by Lorenz; ©1977 New Yorker Magazine, Inc.

31 Collection Nelly and Guido Di Tella, Buenos Aires/Museum of Modern Art, Oxford

35 Don Hamerman

37 Collection IWALEWA-Haus-INV.Nr. 14106

43 Corbis-Bettmann Archive

44 Tate Gallery, London/Art Resource

50(l) Scala/Art Resource

50(r) Cynthia Johnson/Time-Warner, Inc.

51(tl) Steve Schapiro/Gamma-Liaison

51(tr) Suolang Loubu/Xinhua/Gamma-Liaison

51(br) Copyright British Museum

53 Copyright British Museum

63 Everett Collection, Inc.

65 Granger Collection, New York

68 National Portrait Gallery, London/Superstock, Inc.

77 Culver Pictures Inc.

78 Aarhus Kunstmuseum

86 AP/Wide World

88 British Library, MS OR 5259 fols 56v-57r

93 Reprinted with permission of Four Winds Press, an imprint of Macmillan Publishing Company from *Calendar Art* written and illustrated by Leonard Everett Fisher. ©1987 Leonard Everett Fisher.

94 Poems, Manuscripts Dept/Lilly Library, Indiana University, Bloomington, IN.

96 Giraudon/Art Resource

105 Courtesy of Herbert Cole/Photo by unknown photographer

110 Private Collection. Photo: Jeffrey Ploskonka

114 Photofest

115(t) Superstock, Inc.

115(br) Superstock, Inc.

115(bl) UPI/Corbis-Bettmann

127 Viking Press

129 Bridgeman/Art Resource

135 AP/Wide World

138 Neg. No. 323730 Painting by George Catlin, Courtesy Department Library Services, American Museum of Natural History

143(l) Emily Da

143(r) UPI/Corbis-Bettmann

144 From *Prop Art: Over 1000 Contemporary Political Posters* by Gary Yanker. Darien House, New York, distributed by New York Graphic Society, 1972. Copyright ©1972 by Gary Yanker.

151 Huhsien County, People's Republic of China

155(t) Courtesy of Sinchosha Publishing Co., Tokyo

155(b) Doug Wright, "Editorial Cartoons," (1973)

157 Courtesy of David Em

163(t) Fred Viebahn/Vintage Books

163(b) Courtesy Carmen Tafolla

163(b) Courtesy, Vassar College

164 Jacob Lawrence, *In the North the Negro had better educational facilities. Panel 58 from THE MIGRATION SERIES.* (1940–41; text and title revised by the artist, 1993.) Tempera on gesso on composition board, 12 x 18 (30.5 x 45.7 cm). The Museum of Modern Art, New York. Gift of Mrs. David M. Levy. Photograph © The Museum of Modern Art, New York.

167 Collection of The New-York Historical Society

169 Private Collection/Bridgeman Art Collection, London/Superstock, Inc.

170 The Pierpont Morgan Library/Art Resource/M500f.13

170 (icon) The Pierpont Morgan Library/Art Resource

172 National Museum of African Art, Eliot Elisofon Photographic Archives, Smithsonian Institution

173 The Saint Louis Art Museum/Superstock, Inc.

180 Collection IWALEWA-Haus-INV.Nr. 14106

181(t) Private Collection. Photo: Jeffrey Ploskonka
181(c) From the collection of Nancy Berliner

181(b) Collection Nelly and Guido Di Tella, Buenos Aires/Museum of Modern Art, Oxford

182–183 Scala/Art Resource

183, 186, 256, 262, 267 (icon) Bob Daemmrich/Image Works

184 Jennifer Girard

185 Museum of Modern Art/Film Stills Archive

187(tl) Alinari/Art Resource

187(tr), (br) Copyright British Museum

187(bl) Staatliche Museen, Berlin, Antikensammlung

188 Superstock, Inc.

189 Corbis-Bettmann Archive

190–191 Copyright British Museum

196, 203, 208, 213, 217, 224 Jennifer Girard

196, 228, 232, 235, 239, 244, 247, 251 Museum of Modern Art, Film Stills Archive

201 Bulloz

210 Copyright British Museum

221 Staatliche Museen, Berlin, Antikensammlung

226 Georges Rouault, *The Old King*, (detail), 1916-36. The Carnegie Museum of Art, Pittsburgh; Patrons Art Fund, 40.1

227 AP/Wide World

256 Scala/Art Resource

256–257 Palazzo Della Ragione, Padua/Mauro Magliani/Superstock, Inc.

258 Copyright British Museum

259 Lester Sloan/Gamma-Liaison

260 Courtesy Tamara Camp

270–271 The Metropolitan Museum of Art, The Lesley and Emma Sheafer Collection, Bequest of Emma A. Sheafer, 1973 (1974.356.524-525)

273 Giraudon/Art Resource

278 The Metropolitan Museum of Art, The Lesley and Emma Sheafer Collection, Bequest of Emma A. Sheafer, 1973 (1974.356.524-525)

282(t) Corbis-Bettmann Archive

282(c) Corbis-Bettmann Archive

282(b) National Portrait Gallery, London

285 *Adskaya Pochta*, 1906, No. 3

288 Guy Billout/Stock Illustration Source, Inc.

293 Bob Scott/Koralik Associates

303 Rhett J. Arens

304 The Phillips Collection, Washington, D.C.

309 UPI/Corbis-Bettmann

310 Robert Gantt Steele

320(l) Erich Lessing/Art Resource

320(c) Erich Lessing/Art Resource

320(r) Alinari/Art Resource

320–321(b) Andrea Booner/Tony Stone Images

321(t) Alistair Spooner/Gamma-Liaison

321(bc) Vienna Society for the Friends of Music/E. T. Archive, London/Superstock, Inc.

321(br) Focus on Sports, Inc.

322 Musée du Louvre/Superstock, Inc.

323 ©1993 Time, Inc., Reprinted by permission.

331 National Portrait Gallery, Washington, D. C., Smithsonian Institution

332 Museum of Modern Art, Film Stills Archive

333 Jennifer Girard

334–335 Bridgeman/Art Resource

335, 338, 382, 386, 392 (icon) Pierpont Morgan Library/Art Resource

335, 394, 437, 442, 447 (icon) Kasimir Malevich, *The Mower*, Russian State Museum, St.Petersburg /A.Burkatousky/Superstock, Inc.

336 Bridgeman/Art Resource

337 Giraudon/Art Resource

339 Courtesy William Morrow, photo by Mark Gerson

340 Courtesy of Sotheby's

345 Giraudon/Art Resource

349 © Randi Hendrix

351 The Bodleian Library, Oxford

356 Y Swyddfa Gymreig/Welsh Office

357 AP/Wide World

361 Bridgeman/Art Resource

366–367 The Pierpont Morgan Library/Art Resource

370 National Portrait Gallery, London

373 Bridgeman/Art Resource

381 E. Hugo

382(tl) National Museum of African Art, Eliot Elisofon Photographic Archives, Smithsonian Institution (GHSA89(6335)

382(bl) Skinsness

382-383(c) Pete Dancs/Tony Stone Images

382(icon) Pierpont Morgan Library/Art Resource

383(t) Photofest

383(bl) Giraudon/Art Resource

383(br) Superstock, Inc.

384(t) K. Marine

384(b) K. Marine

385 K. Marine

393 Bridgeman/Art Resource

395 AP/Wide World

397 The Menil Collection, Houston, Gift of Philippa and Heiner Friedrich. Photo by Paul Hester, Houston

403 The Metropolitan Museum of Art, Hilson Fund, Inc. Gift, 1990 (1990.188)

407 Reprinted with special permission of North America Syndicate

408(t) Organization of American States

408(tc) University of Georgia Press

408(bc) B. O. A. Editions, Ltd., photo by Arthur Furst

408(b) ©1990 Jay Blakesberg

410 The Evans Tibbs Collection

413 Courtesy of Leo Jensen

416 Courtesy Archives of The Billy Graham Center, Wheaton, IL

419 Courtesy Archives of The Billy Graham Center, Wheaton, IL

422 Courtesy Archives of The Billy Graham Center, Wheaton, IL

428 Gary V. Fields

431 Private Collection. Courtesy of Sotheby's, New York

437(icon) Kasimir Malevich, *The Mower,* Russian State Museum, St.Petersburg/A.Burkatousky/ Superstock, Inc.

438(l) Granger Collection, New York

438(c) Hamburg Museum

438(r) Giraudon/Art Resource

438–439(background) British Library

439(l) Granger Collection, New York

439(c) Culver Pictures Inc.

439(r) Ancient Art & Architecture Collection/Ronald Sheridan Photo-Library

440 Courtesy Emilia Askari

448 Bridgeman/Art Resource

449 The Evans Tibbs Collection

450–451 Tsing-Fang Chen, *Human Achievement*, (detail) Lucia Gallery, New York City/Superstock, Inc.

452 From *An American Childhood* by Annie Dillard. Copyright ©1987 by Annie Dillard, All rights reserved. Harper & Row Publishers, Inc., New York

453 From *Kaffir Boy* by Mark Mathabane. Copyright ©1986 by Mark Mathabane. Macmillan Publishers, New York

455(l) Gail Mathabane

455(r) South Light/ Gamma Liaison

456 David Turnley/Black Star

463 David Turnley/Black Star

468(l) AP/Wide World Photos

468(r) United States Bureau of Labor Statistics

469 Howard University Gallery of Art, Washington, D.C.

474 Rollie McKenna

475 Corbis-Bettmann Archive

480(l) UPI/Corbis-Bettmann

480(r) British Library

483 Superstock, Inc.

489 From *Old Possum's Book of Practical Cats* by T. S. Eliot. Drawings by Edward Gorey, Harcourt Brace Jovanovich Publishers. Copyright 1939 by T. S. Eliot. Copyright renewed ©1967 by Esme Valerie Eliot. Illustrations copyright ©1982 by Edward Gorey.

502(t) Viking Press

502(c) UPI/Corbis-Bettmann

502(b) Michael Nye

505 Art and Artifacts Division, Schomberg Center for Research in Black Culture, The New York Public Library, Astor, Lenox and Tilden Foundations

506 Oleg Tselkov, *With Cat*, 1993, oil on canvas, 51" x 38", Courtesy of The Sloane Gallery/ Contemporary Russian Art, Denver, Colorado

509 AP/Wide World **510** El pequeño cementerio de Culebra, by María de Mater O'Neill. ©1990 María de Mater O'Neill. Oils crayons, oils on linen. 64" x 94". Photograph by John Betancourt. Collection of Iliana Fonts.

517 Spencer Jarnigan

518 Copyright British Museum

521 The Sculpture Park at Le Monciel, Jouy-en Josas, France

524(t) Ricki Rosen

524(b) Hulton Deutsch Collection Ltd.

527 Roger-Viollet

532-533(t) David LeBon/Tony Stone Images

532(b) Superstock, Inc.

533(t) Superstock, Inc.

533(c) Superstock, Inc.

533-534(b) Keith Bernstein/FSP/Gamma Liaison

534(t) Courtesy, General Motors Corporation

534-535 E. Hugo

535(b) Martyn Goddard/Tony Stone Images

536 John Turner/Tony Stone Images

544 David Turnley/Black Star

545 Tsing-Fang Chen, *Human Achievement*, (detail) Lucia Gallery, New York City/Superstock, Inc.

546-547 Boris Kustodiev, *The Fair*, (detail), 1908/Scala/Art Resource

547, 550, 586, 590, 593, 596, 619, 624, 628 (icon) Superstock, Inc.

548–549 AP/Wide World

551 Drawing by Stan Hunt; ©1987 The New Yorker Magazine, Inc.

552(t) Courtesy of University of Otago Press

554-555 Collection Leontine D. Scott

559 Drawing by Lorenz; ©1995 The New Yorker Magazine, Inc.

560(t) Courtesy Harcourt Brace & Company

560(c) Organization of American States

562 Galerie Garces Velasquez, Bogata

565 Jeanette Ortiz Osorio

569(t) AP/Wide World

569(tc) National Portrait Gallery, London

569(bc) Evan Richman/Reuters/Corbis-Bettmann

570 Burt Glinn/Magnum Photos

573 Franz Altschuler

577 Christie's, London/Superstock, Inc./©1995 Artists Rights Society(ARS), New York/SPADEM, Paris

578(t) Courtesy of Arte Publico Press

578(b) AP/Wide World

581 Reproduced by authorization of the Instituto Nacional de Bellas Artes y Literatura, Mexico City

582 Superstock, Inc.

587 Gift of Maxim Karolik for the M. and M. Karolik Collection of American Paintings, 1815–1865. Courtesy, Museum of Fine Arts, Boston

588(t) Kobal Collection

588(c) Everett Collection, Inc.

588(bl) Kobal Collection

588(br) Everett Collection, Inc.

589(tl) Photofest

589(tr) Everett Collection, Inc.

589(b) Photofest

597(t) Courtesy of Oscar Peñaranda

597(b) Trustees of Amherst College

599 Ansel Adams, *Silverton Colorado*, c. 1951. Photograph by Ansel Adams, Copyright ©1993 by the Trustees of the Ansel Adams Publishing Trust. All Rights Reserved.

603(c) UPI/Corbis-Bettmann

603(t) ©1981 Linda Fry Poverman

603(b) Dartmouth College

604 Jerry Jacka

609 Roloff Beny

613(t) Laurence Acland

613(tc) UPI/Corbis-Bettmann

613(bc) Collection Kimiko and John Powers. Photo: Fogg Art Museum, Harvard University

614-615 Robert Amft

616 Chishaku-in temple, Kyoto/I.S.E.I., Tokyo, Japan

619 Courtesy, Wade Patton

620-621 Mitch Reardon/Tony Stone Images

622(tl) Howard Sochurek/Stock Market

622(tr) The Harold E. Edgerton 1992 Trust, courtesy of Palm Press, Inc.

622(c) North American Philips corporation

629 André Kertész, American, 1894–1985, *Shadows of the Eiffel Tower* (view looking down from tower to people underneath), silver gelatin print, 1929. 16.5 x 21.9 cm, Julien Levy Collection, Special Photography Acquisition Fund, 1979.77, photograph ©1994 The Art Institute of Chicago. All Rights Reserved.

631 Courtesy Heineman Publishers, Oxford, England. Photo: Michael Uaha

633 Christine Kristen

636 Courtesy of Longhang Nguyen

639 Superstock, Inc.

643 Courtesy of Quartet Books Limited

644 Isabel Cutler/Gamma Liaison

651(t) Courtesy of Arte Público Press

651(tc) Pat Wolk

651(c) RIA-Novosti/Sovfoto

651(bc) Layle Silbert

651(b) Corbis-Bettmann Archive

653 Scala/Art Resource

654-655 Esais Baitel/Gamma Liaison

659(all) AP/Wide World

660(all) AP/Wide World

661(t) Farnood/Sipa Press

661(b) Ricardo Beliel/GLMR/Gamma Liaison

662(t) Michael Dwyer/Stock Boston

662(b) Leong Ka Tai/Material World

670(t) Reproduced by authorization of the Instituto Nacional de Bellas Artes y Literatura, Mexico City

670(b) Jeanette Ortiz Osorio

671 Roloff Beny

672–673 Jean-Leon Gerome, *Death of Caesar,* 1859 (detail), The Walters Art Gallery, Baltimore

673, 676, 787, 791, 797(icon) Christie's, London/Superstock, Inc.

674–675 Museum of Modern Art, Film Stills Archive

677 National Portrait Gallery, London

681 Courtesy of Sotheby's

687 Museum of Modern Art, Film Stills Archive

733 Drawing by Robert Mankoff; ©1987 The New Yorker Magazine, Inc.

734(t) Copyright British Museum

735 Scale drawing by Irwin Smith from *Shakespeare's Globe Playhouse: A Modern Reconstruction in Text and Scale Drawings* by Irwin Smith. Charles Scribner's Sons, New York, 1956. Hand colored by Cheryl Kucharzak

737 Photofest

747 Christie's, London/Superstock, Inc.

756 Ancient Art & Architecture Collection/Ronald Sheridan Photo-Library

765 McGraw Hill

767 Collection John P. Axelrod. Photo: Marisa del Ray Gallery

774 Granger Collection, New York

775 Tass/Sovfoto

780 Novosti/Sovfoto

787 Pete Souza/The White House

788 Pete Souza/The White House

789 Courtesy Diego Muñoz

Custom Literature Database

The *ScottForesman Custom Literature Database* is a collection of over 1400 literary selections. Over 200 titles in the database have lessons to support students as they read. Eight indices—Title, Author, Genre, Subject, Nationality, Literary Themes, Anthology Correlations, and Lessons for Selected Titles—help you navigate through the database, allowing you to search for, view, and print the exact selection you want. The Anthology Correlations index lets you identify titles in the database correlated to *ScottForesman Literature and Integrated Studies.*

Address to the Apostles from Bible, Matthew, 10:5–42*
African Proverbs
"Aladdin, or The Wonderful Lamp" from *A Thousand and One Nights*
"Ali Baba and the Forty Thieves" from *A Thousand and One Nights*
Anglo-Saxon Riddles
Apocalyptic Utterances from Bible, Matthew 24:4–25:46
Articles of Confederation
Babylonian Law from *The Hammurabi Code*
Battle of Brunanburh, The
"Battle of Otterbourne, The"
Bhagavad Gita
Bible, Acts of the Apostles
Bible, Corinthians 1:13
Bible, Genesis 1–3
Bible, John
Bible, Luke 10:25–37*
Bible, Mark
Bible, Psalm 1
Bible, Psalm 8
Bible, Psalm 23 in Six Translations
Bible, Psalm 24
Bible, Psalm 91
Bible, Psalm 100*
Bible, Psalm 137
Bible, Ruth*
"Birth of Hatshepsut, The"
Birth of Jesus, The from Bible, Matthew 1:18–4:17
"Bonnie George Campbell"
"Bonny Barbara Allan"
Book of Jonah, The from The Hebrew Bible
"Brahman, the Tiger and the Six Judges, The"*
Brown v. *Board of Education of Topeka**
"Caedmon's Hymn"
Chinese Exclusion Act*
Civil Rights Act of 1964*
"Clementine"
Code of Manu, The
Constitution of the Confederate States of America, The
Constitution of the United States
Death of Jesus, The from Bible, Matthew 26:14–28:20
"Deep River"
"Demon Lover, The"
"Descent of Ishtar into the Underworld, The"
Dred Scott v. *Sandford*
"Egyptian Love Song"
"Emergence Song"
"Enchanted Horse, The" from *A Thousand and One Nights*
Everyman
"Experiences of a Chinese Immigrant" from *The Independent**
"Follow the Drinking Gourd"*
"Get Up and Bar the Door"
Gibbons v. *Ogden*
"Go Down, Moses"*
Hammurabi Code, The
"How Thoutii Took the Town of Joppa"
"Joshua Fit de Battle ob Jericho"
Kingdom of Heaven Parables from Bible, Matthew 13:1–52
Laws, The from Bible, Exodus 19:1–23:33
"Little Old Sod Shanty on the Claim, The"
"Lord Randal"
Magna Carta
Marbury v. *Madison*
"May Colvin"*
Mayflower Compact, The
NAACP v. *Alabama*
"Old Chisholm Trail, The"
On Humility and Forgiveness from Bible, Matthew 18:1–35
Parables from Bible, Luke*
"Pat Works on the Railway"
"Peasant and the Workman, The"
Plessy v. *Ferguson*
Preamble to the Constitution of the Knights of Labor
Prince Shotuku's Constitution
Resolution of the Stamp Act Congress
"Scheherazade" from *A Thousand and One Nights*
"Seafarer, The"
Second Shepherd's Play, The
Seneca Falls Declaration of Sentiments and Resolutions, The
Sermon on the Mount from Bible, Matthew 5:1–7:27
"Seven Voyages of Sindbad the Sailor, The" from *A Thousand and One Nights**
"Shenandoah"
"Shipwrecked Sailor, The"
*Sir Gawain and the Green Knight**
"Sir Patrick Spens"*
Song of Creation
"Story of Rhampsinites, The"
"Story of the Fisherman, The" from *A Thousand and One Nights*
"Sumer is icumen in"
Sura LXXV—The Resurrection from *The Koran*
Sura LXXVI—Man from *The Koran*
"Swing Low, Sweet Chariot"
"Three Ravens, The"
Treaty of Peace with Great Britain
Trustees of Dartmouth College v. *Woodward*
"Twa Corbies, The"
Virginia Bill of Rights
Vishnu Purana
Volstead Act, The
"Wanderer, The"
"Western Wind"
"Wife of Usher's Well, The"

Adams, Henry
Education of Henry Adams, The, Chapter XXV, "The Dynamo and the Virgin"
"Prayer to the Virgin of Chartres"

Addison, Joseph
"Artifices in Tragedy" from *The Spectator*
"Party Patches" from *The Spectator*
"Sir Roger at Church" from *The Spectator*
"Westminster Abbey" from *The Spectator*
"Will Wimble" from *The Spectator**
"Wit: True, False, and Mixed"

Aelfric, Abbot
"Colloquy on the Occupations, A"

Aesop
"Crow and the Pitcher, The"
"Fox and the Crow, The"
"Fox and the Grapes, The"

---

*This selection includes background information, a study guide, and comprehension and critical thinking questions in a lesson on the disc.

Custom Literature Database

"Hound and the Hare, The"
"Mice and the Weasels, The"
"North Wind and the Sun, The"

Alcaeus
"Drinking Song"
"Summer"
"Winter"

Alcott, Louisa May
"Amy's Valley of Humiliation" from *Little Women**
Hospital Sketches
"Old-Fashioned Thanksgiving, An"*
"Onawandah, Fourth Spinning Wheel Story"

Alighieri, Dante
Divine Comedy, The, " The Inferno," Canto I
Divine Comedy, The, "The Inferno," Canto III
Divine Comedy, The, "The Inferno," Canto XXXIV

Alline, Henry
"The Conduct of Most Sailors"

Anacreon
"Beauty"
"Combat, The"
"Cup, The"
"Love"

Andersen, Hans Christian
"Emperor's New Clothes, The"*
"Little Mermaid, The"
"Red Shoes, The"
"Snow Queen, The"
"Steadfast Tin Soldier, The"
"Swineherd, The"
"Thumbelina"
"Tinder-Box, The"
"Ugly Duckling, The"*

Anderson, Sherwood
"Discovery of a Father"*
"Stolen Day"

Anonymous
Independent, The
"My mind to me a kingdom is"
"There is a Lady Sweet and Kind"

Anthony, Susan B.
On Woman's Right to Suffrage*
"Political Economy of Women"

Antin, Mary
"Immigrant Goes to School, An" from *The Promised Land**

Aristotle
Poetics, The

Arnold, Matthew
"Isolation, To Marguerite"
"Last Word, The"
"Requiescat"
"Scholar-Gipsy, The"
"Self-Dependence"
"Thyrsis"

Aspinwall, Alicia
"Upsidedownians, The"

Aulnoy, Comtesse d'
"White Cat, The"
"Yellow Dwarf, The"

Aupaumut, Hendrick
A Short Narration of My Last Journey to the Western Contry

Babur
*Babur-nama**

Bacon, Francis
"Of Studies"
"Of Truth"

Bambara, Toni Cade
"Blues Ain't No Mockin Bird"*
"Happy Birthday"*

Barbour, Ralph Henry
"Brewster's Debut"

Beach, Lewis
Clod, The*

Bede
Ecclesiastical History of the English People, The, Book II, Chapters 9–13*
Ecclesiastical History of the English People, The, Book IV, Chapter 24

Behn, Aphra
"Lady's Looking Glass, The"
"Love in Fantastic Triumph Sat from Abdelazar"
Oroonoko

Bellamy, Edward
*Looking Back**

Belloc, Hilaire
"Lion, The"
"Yak, The"

Benét, Stephen Vincent
"By the Waters of Babylon"

Benet, William Rose
"Skater of Ghost Lake, The"

Bennet, John
"Fritz the Master Fiddler"

Bierce, Ambrose
"Occurrence at Owl Creek Bridge, An"

Blackwell, Alice Stone
Indifference of Women, The*

Blake, William
"And did those feet" from *Milton*
"Chimney Sweeper, The" from *Songs of Experience*
"Chimney Sweeper, The," from *Songs of Innocence*
"Divine Image, The" from *Songs of Innocence*
"Holy Thursday" from *Songs of Experience*
"Holy Thursday" from *Songs of Innocence*
"Human Abstract, The" from *Songs of Experience*
"Infant Joy"
"Infant Sorrow"
Introduction ("Hear the voice of the Bard") from *Songs of Experience*
Introduction ("Piping down the valleys") from *Songs of Innocence*
"Lamb, The" from *Songs of Innocence*
"Nurse's Song" from *Songs of Experience*
"Poison Tree, A"
"Proverbs of Hell" from *The Marriage of Heaven and Hell*
"Sick Rose, The"
Song ("How sweet I roamed")
"Tyger, The" from *Songs of Experience*

Bleecker, Ann Eliza
"On the Immensity of Creation"

Boas, Franz
"Raven's Adventures"
"Sedna, Mistress of the Underworld"

Boswell, James
Life of Samuel Johnson, LL.D, The
London Journal, 1762–1763

Bradstreet, Anne
"Contemplations"
"Prologue, The"
"To My Dear and Loving Husband"
"Upon the Burning of Our House, July 10th, 1666"

Brontë, Emily
"No coward soul is mine"
"Remembrance"
Song ("The linnet in the rocky dells")

Brooke, Rupert
"Peace"*

Brooks, Gwendolyn
"Pete at the Zoo"

Brothers Grimm
"Bremen Town Musicians, The"*
"Elves and the Shoemaker, The"
"Fisherman and His Wife, The"
"Frog Prince, The"
"Gallant Tailor, The"
"Hansel and Grethel"
"Juniper Tree, The"
"Rapunzel"
"Rumpelstiltskin"*
"Sleeping Beauty, The"
"Snow-white"
"Twelve Dancing Princesses, The"

Brown, Dee
"Katlian and the Iron People"*

Brown, John
Last Speech

Browning, Elizabeth Barrett
Sonnet 1 ("I thought once how Theocritus had sung") from *Sonnets from the Portuguese*
Sonnet 14 ("If thou must love me, let it be for naught") from *Sonnets from the Portuguese*
Sonnet 26 ("I lived with visions for my company") from *Sonnets from the Portuguese*

---

*This selection includes background information, a study guide, and comprehension and critical thinking questions in a lesson on the disc.

Custom Literature Database

Chopin, Kate
"Pair of Silk Stockings, A"*

Christie, Agatha
"Third-Floor Flat, The"*

Churchill, Winston
Blood, Sweat, and Tears
Dunkirk
Iron Curtain Has Descended, An*
Their Finest Hour

Clay, Henry
On the Compromise of 1850

Clough, Arthur Hugh
"Epi-Strauss-um"
"Latest Decalogue, The"
"Say not the struggle nought availeth"

Cobb, Frank I. and Walter Lippmann
Interpretation of President Wilson's Fourteen Points

Coleridge, Samuel Taylor
Biographia Literaria
"Christabel"
"Eolian Harp, The"
"Frost at Midnight"
"Kubla Khan"
"Rime of the Ancient Mariner, The"
"This Lime-Tree Bower My Prison"

Colum, Padraic
"Aegir's Feast: How Thor Triumphed"
"Baldur's Doom"
"Building of the Wall, The"
"Children of Loki, The"
"Dwarf's Hoard, and the Curse That It Brought"
"How Brock Brought Judgement on Loki"
"How Freya Gained Her Necklace and How Her Loved One Was Lost to Her"
"How Thor and Loki Be-Fooled Thrym the Giant"
"Iduna and Her Apples: How Loki Put the Gods in Danger"
"Odin Goes to Mimir's Well; His Sacrifice for Wisdom"
"Sif's Golden Hair: How Loki Wrought Mischief in Asgard"
"Sigurd's Youth" from *The Children of Odin*
"Thor and Loki in the Giants' City"
"Twilight of the Gods, The"
"Valkyrie, The"

Conrad, Joseph
Secret Sharer, The
*Youth**

Crane, Stephen
"Bride Comes to Yellow Sky, The"
"Do not weep, maiden, for war is kind"
"Episode of War, An"
"I met a seer"
"Man saw a ball of gold in the sky, A"
"Mystery of Heroism, A"
"Open Boat, The"*
Red Badge of Courage, The
"Think as I Think"

Crevecoeur, Michel-Guillaume Jean de
Letters from an American Farmer

Curtin, Jeremiah, and Hewitt, J. N. B.
"Woman Who Fell from the Sky, The"

Curtis, Natalie
"Creation"
"Deathless One and the Wind, The"
"Morning Star and the Evening Star, The"
"Origin of Corn and Pemmican, The"
"Stories of Wak-Chung-Kaka, the Foolish One"
"Story of Gomoidema Pokoma-Kiaka, The"
"Story of the First Mother, The"
"Story of Wakiash and the First Totem-Pole, The"*
"Vision of the Earth-Maker, A"*

Davis, Jefferson
Inaugural Address of Jefferson Davis
Last Message to the People of the Confederacy
Message to Congress

Davis, Richard H.
"Midsummer Pirates"

de la Mare, Walter
"All But Blind"
"All That's Past"
"Cake and Sack"
"Dwelling Place, The"
"Flight, The"
"Listeners, The"*
"Nobody Knows"
"Silver"
"Song of the Mad Prince, The"
"Tartary"
"Up and Down"

De Quincey, Thomas
"On the Knocking at the Gate in *Macbeth*"
"Poetry of Pope, The"

Defoe, Daniel
Essay Upon Projects, An
Journal of the Plague Year, A

Dekker, Thomas
"Lullaby"

Delgado, Reverend Father Fray Carlos
Report Made By Reverend Father Fray Carlos Delgado

Dickens, Charles
David Copperfield
"Signalman, The"*

Dickinson, Emily
"Alter! When the Hills do"
"Apparently with no surprise"
"Because I could not stop for death"
"Bustle in a House, The"
" 'Faith' Is a fine invention"
" 'Hope' is the thing with feathers"
"I felt a Funeral, in my Brain"
"I heard a Fly buzz – when I died"
"I like to see it lap the Miles"
"I taste a liquor never brewed"
"I Years had been from Home"
"I'll tell you how the Sun rose"
"If you were coming in the Fall"
"Morns are meeker than they were, The"
"Much Madness is divinest Sense"
"Narrow Fellow in the grass, A"*
"Of all the Souls that stand create"
"Some keep the Sabbath going to Church"
"Success is counted sweetest"*
"Surgeons must be very careful"
"There's a certain Slant of light"
"This is my letter to the World"
"To make a prairie it takes a clover"
"Triumph – may be of several kinds"*

Dixon, Roland B.
"Creation, The"
"Theft of Fire, The"

Donne, John
"Bait, The"
"Ecstacy, The"
"Flea, The"
"Indifferent, The"
Meditation 17 from *Devotions*
"On His Mistress"
Song ("Go and catch a falling star")
Sonnet 4 ("At the round earth's imagined corners, blow") from *Holy Sonnets**
Sonnet 6 ("This is my play's last scene; here heavens appoint") from *Holy Sonnets*
Sonnet 10 ("Death, be not proud, though some have called thee") from *Holy Sonnets**
Sonnet 14 ("Batter my heart, three-personed God; for You") from *Holy Sonnets*
"Sun Rising, The"
"Valediction: Forbidding Mourning, A"
"Woman's Constancy"

Dorsey, George and Kroeber, Alfred L.
"Star Husband, The"

Douglass, Frederick
*Life and Times of Frederick Douglass, The**
Meaning of July Fourth for the Negro, The*
Narrative of the Life of Frederick Douglass, The
Oration in Memory of Abraham Lincoln

Dowson, Ernest
"Cynara"
"They are not long"

Doyle, Sir Arthur Conan
"Adventure of the Blue Carbuncle, The"*
*Hound of the Baskervilles, The**
"Man with the Twisted Lip, The"*
"Musgrave Ritual, The"
"Redheaded League, The"
"Silver Blaze"

Dryden, John
Absalom and Achitophel
Essay of Dramatic Poesy, An
"I Feed a Flame Within"
Mac Flecknoe
Preface to *Fables Ancient and Modern, The*
"Song for St. Cecilia's Day, A"
"Song Sung by Venus in Honor of Britannia"
"To the Memory of Mr. Oldham"

DuBois, W. E. B.
Behold the Land
Crisis, The
"Of the Meaning of Progress" from *The Souls of Black Folk*
"Of the Sorrow Songs" from *The Souls of Black Folk*

Dunbar, Paul Laurence
"Booker T. Washington"*
"Douglass"*
"Keep A-Pluggin' Away"*
"Life's Tragedy"*
"Love's Apotheosis"*
"We Wear the Mask"

Duncan, Sara Jeannette
Saunterings

Eastman, Charles
*From the Deep Woods to Civilization**

Edwards, Jonathan
Personal Narrative
"Sarah Pierrepont"
"Sinners in the Hands of an Angry God"

Eisenhower, Dwight
Atoms for Peace

Eliot, George
"Lifted Veil, The"*

Elizabeth I
"When I was fair and young"

Emerson, Ralph Waldo
"American Scholar, The"
"Brahma"
"Concord Hymn"
"Days"
"Each and All"
"Experience"
"Fable"
Journals
"Maxims"
"Nature"
"Rhodora, The"
"Self-Reliance"
"Snowstorm, The"

Emmett, Daniel
"Dixie"*

Euripides
*Medea**

Fitzgerald, Edward
Rubáiyát of Omar Khayyám, The

Forster, E. M.
"Celestial Omnibus, The"

Franklin, Benjamin
Autobiography of Benjamin Frankin, The, Franklin's Childhood
Autobiography of Benjamin Franklin, The, Seeking Moral Perfection
"Dialogue Between Franklin and the Gout"
"Edict by the King of Prussia, An"
"Ephemera, The"
Letter of November 21, 1783
"Receipt to Make a New England Funeral Elegy, A"
Speech at the Constitutional Convention
"Way to Wealth, The"
"Whistle, The"
"Witch Trial at Mount Holly, A"*

Freeman, Mary E. Wilkins
"New England Nun, A"*

Freneau, Philip
"Indian Burying-Ground, The"
"On the Memorable Victory"
"To a Caty-Did"
"Wild Honeysuckle, The"

Frost, Robert
"Death of the Hired Man, The"*
"It Bids Pretty Fair"
"Oven Bird, The"
"Pasture, The"
"Road Not Taken, The"
"Runaway, The"
"Time to Talk, A"
"Wood-Pile, The"

Fuller, Margaret
"Woman in the Nineteenth Century"

Garrison, William Lloyd
"Liberator, The"
On the Death of John Brown

Gascoigne, George
"Lullaby of a Lover"

Gilbert, W. S.
"Aesthete, The"
"Englishman, The" from *H. M. S. Pinafore*
"Let the Punishment Fit the Crime" from *The Mikado*
"Policeman's Lot, The"
"They'll None of 'Em Be Missed"

Gissing, George
"Scrupulous Father, The"*

Goddard, Pliny Earle
"Creation, The"

Goldsmith, Oliver
She Stoops to Conquer, Act One
She Stoops to Conquer, Act Two
She Stoops to Conquer, Act Three
She Stoops to Conquer, Act Four
She Stoops To Conquer, Act Five

Gray, Thomas
"Bard, The"
"Elegy Written in a Country Churchyard"*
"Ode on a Distant Prospect of Eton College"
"Sonnet on the Death of Richard West"

Gregory, Lady Augusta
"Boy Deeds of Cuchulain"
*Spreading the News**

Greville, Fulke, Lord Brooke
"Chorus Sacerdotum"
"Of His Cynthia"
"You Little Stars"

Haines, Alice Calhoun
"Tenderhearted Dragon, A"

Hale, Edward Everett
"Man Without a Country, The"*

Hale, Lucretia P.
"Mrs. Peterkin's Tea-party"
"Peterkins Celebrate the Fourth of July, The"

Hancock, H. Irving
"Rip Van WInkle Man-O'-War, The"

Hardy, Thomas
"Afterwards"
"Ah, are you digging on my grave?"
"Beeny Cliff"
"Channel Firing"
"Convergence of the Twain, The"
"Darkling Thrush, The"
"Epitaph on a Pessimist"
"Hap"*
"In Tenebris"
"In Time of 'The Breaking of Nations' "*
"Man He Killed, The"
"Neutral Tones"
*Our Exploits at West Poley**
"Three Strangers, The"
"Walk, The"
"When I Set Out for Lyonesse"
"Withered Arm, The"

Harper, Ellen Watkins
Colored People in America, The
On the Twenty-Fourth Anniversary of the American Anti-Slavery Society

Harris, Joel Chandler
"Creature with No Claws, The"
"Wonderful Tar-Baby Story, The"

---

*This selection includes background information, a study guide, and comprehension and critical thinking questions in a lesson on the disc.

Custom Literature Database

Harte, Bret
"Baby Sylvester"
"Brown of Calaveras"
"Iliad of Sandy Bar, The"
"Luck of Roaring Camp, The"
"Miggles"
"Outcasts of Poker Flat, The"*
"Plain Language from Truthful James"
"Tennessee's Partner"

Hawthorne, Nathaniel
"Birthmark, The"
"Dr. Heidegger's Experiment"
"Drowne's Wooden Image"
"Golden Touch, The"*
"Maypole of Merry Mount, The"
"Minister's Black Veil, The"*
"My Kinsman, Major Molineaux"
Notebooks, The
"Rappacinni's Daughter"
"Young Goodman Brown"*

Hayford, J. E. Casely
"As in a Glass Darkly" from *Ethiopia Unbound*
"Black Man's Burden, The" from *Ethiopia Unbound*
"Gold Coast Native Institutions"
"Saving the Wind" from *Ethiopia Unbound*

Hayne, Paul Hamilton
"Aspects of the Pines"

Hazlitt, William
"Macbeth"
My First Acquaintance with Poets
"On Going a Journey"

Heine, Heinrich
"Loreley, The"*

Henley, William Ernest
"Invictus"

Henry, Patrick
Speech in the Virginia Convention, March 23, 1775

Herbert, George
"Altar, The"
"Avarice"
"Bitter-Sweet"
"Collar, The"
"Easter Wings"*
"Love (III)"
"Man"
"Pulley, The"
"Redemption"
"Virtue"*

Heredia y Heredia, Jose Maria
"Ode to Niagara"

Herrick, Robert
"Argument of His Book, The" from *Hesperides*
"Corinna's Going A-Maying"
"Ode for Ben Jonson, An"
"To the Virgins, to Make Much of Time"
"Upon Julia's Clothes"

Hobbes, Thomas
Leviathan, Part I, Chapters 13–15

Holmes, Oliver Wendell
"Ballad of the Oysterman, The"
"Chambered Nautilus, The"
"Last Leaf, The"
"My Last Walk with the Schoolmistress"
"Old Ironsides"

Hoover, Herbert
Philosophy of Rugged Individualism, The

Hopkins, Gerard Manley
"Carrion Comfort"*
"Felix Randal"
"God's Grandeur"
"Habit of Perfection, The"
"No worst, there is none"*
"Pied Beauty"
"Spring and Fall"
"Thou Art Indeed Just, Lord"
"Windhover, The"

Horace
"Ad Leuconeon"
"Death of Cleopatra, The"
"Golden Mean, The"
"Ship of State, The"

Housman, A. E.
"Loveliest of trees, the cherry now"
"Night is freezing fast, The"
"Oh, when I was in love with you"
"On moonlit heath and lonesome bark"
"To an Athlete Dying Young"
"White in the moon the long road lies"

Howard, Henry, Earl of Surrey
"Alas, So All Things Now Do Hold Their Peace"
"Love, that doth reign and live within in my thought"
"Lover's Vow, A"

Howe, Julia Ward
"Battle Hymn of the Republic, The"*

Howells, William Dean
"Christmas Every Day"*
"Editha"

Hudson, W. H.
Idle Days in Patagonia, The, Chapter XII*

Hughes, Rupert
"Latest News About the Three Wishes, The"

Hunt, James Henry Leigh
"Abou Ben Adhem and the Angel"

Huxley, Thomas Henry
"Method of Scientific Investigation, The"

Irving, Washington
"Early Life in Manhattan" from *A History of New York*
"Legend of Sleepy Hollow, The"*
"Rip Van Winkle"
Tour on the Prairies, A

Jackson, Andrew
Second Inaugural Address

Jacobs, Harriet Ann
Incidents in the Life of a Slave Girl, Chapter I*

Jacobs, Joseph
"Dick Whittington and His Cat"*
"Jack and the Beanstalk"
"Jack the Giant-Killer"

Jacobs, W. W.
*Monkey's Paw, The**

James, Henry
"Four Meetings"
"Middle Years, The"
"Real Thing, The"

James, William
"On a Certain Blindness in Human Beings"

Jefferson, Thomas
Declaration of Independence, The
Jefferson's First Inaugural Address
Virginia Statute of Religious Liberty

Jewett, Sarah Orne
"Courting of Sister Wisby, The"
"Hiltons' Holiday, The"
"Miss Tempy's Watchers"
"Native of Winby, A"*
"White Heron, A"

Johnson, Andrew
Johnson's Proclamation of Amnesty

Johnson, James Weldon
Autobiography of an Ex-Colored Man, The, Chapters 1–2*
Autobiography of an Ex-Colored Man, The, Chapters 3–4*

Johnson, Lyndon
Speech at Johns Hopkins University

Johnson, Pauline
"Corn Husker, The"
"Silhouette"

Johnson, Samuel
Dictionary of the English Language
*Life of Milton, The**
London
"On Choosing Friends" from *the Rambler* No. 160
"On Fiction" from *the Rambler* No. 4
"On Forgiveness" from *the Rambler* No. 185
"On Self-Indulgence" from *the Rambler* No. 155
"On Spring" from *the Rambler* No. 5
"On the Death of Dr. Robert Levet"
"On the Tyranny of Parents" from *the Rambler* No. 148
Preface to Shakespeare, The

Jonson, Ben
"Elegy, An"
"Ode to Himself, An"
"On My First Daughter"
"On My First Son"
"Song: To Celia"
"Still to Be Neat"

*This selection includes background information, a study guide, and comprehension and critical thinking questions in a lesson on the disc.

Custom Literature Database

Major, Charles
"Big Bear, The"

Malory, Sir Thomas
"Arthur Marries Gwynevere"
Morte d'Arthur, Le, Book 21, Chapters 5–7

Marlowe, Christopher
"Passionate Shepherd to His Love, The"*
Tragical History of Doctor Faustus, The, Act One
Tragical History of Doctor Faustus, The, Act Two
Tragical History of Doctor Faustus, The, Act Three
Tragical History of Doctor Faustus, The, Act Four
Tragical History of Doctor Faustus, The, Act Five

Marshall, George C.
Marshal Plan, The

Marvell, Andrew
"Bermudas"
"Dialogue Between the Soul and Body, A"
"Garden, The"
"Picture of Little T. C. in a Prospect of Flowers, The"

Masefield, John
"Cargoes"*
"Sea-Fever"*

Masters, Edgar Lee
"Cooney Potter"
"Dow Kritt"
"Hortense Robbins"
"Mrs. Kessler"
"Samuel Gardner"

Mather, Cotton
*Wonders of the Invisible World, The**

Maupassant, Guy de
"Boule de Suif" (Ball of Fat)
"Devil, The"
"Diamond Necklace, The"
"Horla, The"
"Piece of String, The"*
"Two Friends"*

McCrae, John
"In Flanders Fields"*

McNeil, Everett
"King of the Golden Woods, The"

Melville, Herman
"Art"
"Bartleby the Scrivener"
"Maldive Shark, The"
"Portent, The"
"Shiloh"

Meredith, George
"Lucifer in Starlight"

Mill, John Stuart
Autobiography of John Stuart Mill, The
On Liberty
"Black Hero of the Ranges, The"*

Milton, John
"Il Penseroso"
"L'Allegro"
"Lycidas"
"On Shakespeare"
"On the Late Massacre in Piedmont"
Paradise Lost, Book VI
Paradise Lost, Book IX*
Paradise Lost, Book XII
"When I consider how my light is spent"

Monroe, James
Monroe Doctrine, The

Montagu, Lady Mary Wortley
"Answer to a Love-Letter in Verse, An"
"Lady's Resolve, The"
"On The Death of Mrs. Bowes"

Moore, Milcah Martha
"Female Patriots, The"

Moore, Thomas
"Harp that once through Tara's halls, The"
"Minstrel Boy, The"

More, Hannah
"Slavery, a Poem"

Morris, William
"Apology, An" from *The Earthly Paradise*
"Defence of Guenevere, The"*
"Haystack in the Floods, The"
"Love Is Enough"

Morton, Sarah Wentworth
"African Chief, The"

Nashe, Thomas
"Autumn"
"Litany in Time of Plague, A"

Nesbit, E.
"Beautiful As the Day"
"Jungle, The"
"Plush Usurper, The"*
"Pride of Perks, The" from *The Railway Children**

Newman, John Henry Cardinal
"Lead, Kindly Light"

Nightingale, Florence
Cassandra

Northup, Solomon
"Christmas on the Plantation" from *Twelve Years a Slave*
"Picking Cotton" from *Twelve Years a Slave*

O. Henry (William Sidney Porter)
"After Twenty Years"
"Cop and the Anthem, The"*
"Furnished Room, The"
"Hearts and Hands"*
"Man Higher Up, The"*
"Ransom of Red Chief, The"*
"Retrieved Reformation, A"*
"Unfinished Story, An"

Owen, Wilfred
"Anthem for Doomed Youth"*
"Strange Meeting"

Ozaki, Yei Theodora
"Momotaro, or the Story of the Son of a Peach"
"Story of Urashima Taro, the Fisher Lad, The"*
"Tongue-Cut Sparrow, The"

Paine, Thomas
American Crisis, The
Common Sense

Palou, Francisco
Life of Junípero Serra

Parris, Robert
"Refusal to Pay Taxes, A" from *The Liberator*

Peacock, Thomas Love
"War Song of Dinas Vawr, The"

Pepys, Samuel
Diary, The

Perrault, Charles
"Bluebeard"
"Cinderella"
"Little Red Ridinghood"
"Puss in Boots"

Plato
Apology
Crito
Phaedo

Po Chu-i
"After Passing the Examination"
"Chu Ch'en Village"*
"Escorting Candidates to the Examination Hall"
"Golden Bells"*
"In Early Summer Lodging in a Temple to Enjoy the Moonlight"
"Old Man with the Broken Arm, The"
"On Board Ship: Reading Yu Chen's Poems"
"Prisoner, The"
"Remembering Golden Bells"*
"Watching the Reapers"

Poe, Edgar Allan
"Annabel Lee"
"Bells, The"
"Cask of Amontillado, The"
"Eldorado"
"Fall of the House of Usher, The"*
"Hop-Frog"
"Israfel"
"Ligeia"
"Masque of the Red Death, The"
"Oval Portrait, The"
"Philosophy of Composition, The"
Poetic Principle, The
"Purloined Letter, The"*
"Tell-Tale Heart, The"
"To Helen"*
"Ulalume"
"William Wilson"

*This selection includes background information, a study guide, and comprehension and critical thinking questions in a lesson on the disc.

Much Ado About Nothing, Act Five
"O Mistress Mine" from *Twelfth Night*
Othello, the Moor of Venice, Act One
Othello, the Moor of Venice, Act Two
Othello, the Moor of Venice, Act Three
Othello, the Moor of Venice, Act Four
Othello, the Moor of Venice, Act Five
"Sigh No More" from *Much Ado About Nothing*
Sonnet 1 ("From fairest creatures we desire increase")
Sonnet 3 ("Look in thy glass, and tell the face thou viewest")
Sonnet 8 ("Music to hear, why hear'st thou music sadly?")
Sonnet 12 ("When I do count the clock that tells the time")
Sonnet 15 ("When I consider everything that grows")
Sonnet 18 ("Shall I compare thee to a summer's day?")
Sonnet 22 ("My glass shall not persuade me I am old")
Sonnet 23 ("As an unperfect actor on the stage")
Sonnet 27 ("Weary with toil, I haste me to my bed")
Sonnet 29 ("When, in disgrace with fortune and men's eyes")
Sonnet 30 ("When to the sessions of sweet silent thought")*
Sonnet 33 ("Full many a glorious morning have I seen")
Sonnet 46 ("Mine eye and heart are at mortal war")
Sonnet 47 ("Betwixt mine eye and heart a league is took")
Sonnet 49 ("Against that time, if ever that time come")
Sonnet 51 ("Thus can my love excuse the slow offense")
Sonnet 54 ("O, how much more doth beauty beauteous seem")
Sonnet 55 ("Not marble nor the gilded monuments")*
Sonnet 56 ("Sweet love, renew thy force!")
Sonnet 62 ("Sin of self-love possesseth all mine eye")
Sonnet 64 ("When I have seen by Time's fell hand defaced")
Sonnet 65 ("Since brass, nor stone, nor earth, nor boundless sea")
Sonnet 71 ("No longer mourn for me when I am dead")
Sonnet 73 ("That time of year though mayst in me behold")
Sonnet 76 ("Why is my verse so barren of new pride?")
Sonnet 80 ("O, how faint when I of you do write")
Sonnet 87 ("Farewell! Thou art too dear for my possessing")
Sonnet 92 ("But do thy worst to steal thyself away")
Sonnet 93 ("So shall I live, supposing thou art true")
Sonnet 94 ("They that have power to hurt and will do none")
Sonnet 97 ("How like a winter hath my absence been")
Sonnet 98 ("From you have I been absent in the spring")
Sonnet 104 ("To me, fair friend, you never can be old")
Sonnet 106 ("When in the chronicle of wasted time")
Sonnet 107 ("Not mine own fears nor the prophetic soul")
Sonnet 109 ("O, never say that I was false of heart")
Sonnet 110 ("Alas, 'tis true, I have gone here and there")
Sonnet 113 ("Since I left you, mine eye is in my mind")
Sonnet 115 ("Those lines that I before have writ do lie")
Sonnet 116 ("Let me not to the marriage of true minds")
Sonnet 120 ("That you were once unkind befriends me now")
Sonnet 128 ("How oft, when thou, my music, music play'st")
Sonnet 129 ("Th' expense of spirit in a waste of shame")
Sonnet 132 ("Thine eyes I love, and they, as pitying me")
Sonnet 138 ("When my love swears that she is made of truth")
Sonnet 140 ("Be wise as thou art cruel")
Sonnet 144 ("Two loves I have, of comfort and despair")
Sonnet 146 ("Poor soul, the center of my sinful earth")
Sonnet 147 ("My love is as a fever, longing still")
Taming of the Shrew, The, Act One
Taming of the Shrew, The, Act Two
Taming of the Shrew, The, Act Three
Taming of the Shrew, The, Act Four
Taming of the Shrew, The, Act Five
Tempest, The, Act One
Tempest, The, Act Two
Tempest, The, Act Three
Tempest, The, Act Four
Tempest, The, Act Five
"Under the Greenwood Tree" from *As You Like It*
"Who Is Silvia?" from *Two Gentlemen of Verona*
"Winter" from *Love's Labour's Lost*

Shaw, Bernard
Epilogue from *Pygmalion*

Shelley, Mary
Frankenstein

Shelley, Percy Bysshe
"Cloud, The"
Defence of Poetry, A
"Dirge, A"
"England in 1819"
"Hymn of Pan"
"Lines: 'When the lamp is shattered' "
"Song to the Men of England"
"To a Skylark"*
"To Jane: The Invitation"
"To—" ("Music, When Soft Voices Die")
"To Wordsworth"

Sheridan, Richard Brinsley
School for Scandal, The, Act One
School for Scandal, The, Act Two
School for Scandal, The, Act Three
School for Scandal, The, Act Four
School for Scandal, The, Act Five

Sidney, Sir Philip
"My true love hath my heart" from *The Arcadia*
"Oft Have I Mused"
Sonnet 31 ("With how sad steps, Oh Moon, thou climb'st the skies") from *Astrophel and Stella*
Sonnet 39 ("Come sleep! O sleep the certain knot of peace") from *Astrophel and Stella*
Sonnet 41 ("Having this day my horse, my hand, my lance") from *Astrophel and Stella*
"Thou Blind Man's Mark"

Skinner, Alanson, and Slaterlee, John V.
"Manabozho"

Smith, John
Description of New England, A
Generall Historie of Virginia, New England, and the Summer Isles, The

Sophocles
Antigone
Electra
Oedipus at Colonus
Oedipus the King

Southey, Robert
"Cataract of Lodore, The"
"Old Man's Comforts, The"*
" 'You are old, Father William' "*

Spenser, Edmund
"Epithalamion"
Faerie Queene, The, from Canto I
Sonnet 1 ("Happy ye leaves when as those lilly hands") from *Amoretti*
Sonnet 26 ("Sweet is the rose, but grows upon a briar") from *Amoretti*
Sonnet 30 ("My love is like to ice, and I to fire") from *Amoretti*
Sonnet 34 ("Like a ship, that through the ocean wide") from *Amoretti*
Sonnet 54 ("Of this worlds theatre in which we stay") from *Amoretti*
Sonnet 67 ("Lyke as a huntsman after weary chase") from *Amoretti*
Sonnet 75 ("One day I wrote her name upon the strand") from *Amoretti*
Sonnet 79 ("Men call you fayre, and you doe credit it") from *Amoretti*

Stansbury, Joseph
"Ode for the Year 1776"

*This selection includes background information, a study guide, and comprehension and critical thinking questions in a lesson on the disc.

Custom Literature Database

Wheatley, Phillis
Letter to Rev. Occum
"To His Excellency General Washington"
"To S. M., A Young African Painter on Seeing His Works"
"To the Right Honourable William, Earl of Dartmouth"

Whitman, Walt
"A Child's Amaze"
"As Toilsome I Wander'd Virginia's Woods"
"Beat! Beat! Drums!"*
"Beautiful Women"
"Bivouac on a Mountain Side"
"Cavalry Crossing a Ford"
"Crossing Brooklyn Ferry"*
"For You O Democracy"*
"I saw in Louisiana a live-oak growing"
"Joy, Shipmate, Joy!"
"Noiseless patient spider, A"
"On the Beach at Night"
"On the Beach at Night Alone"
"Passage to India"
"Sight in Camp in the Daybreak Gray and Dim, A"
"Song of Myself," 1,16,17,24
"Song of Myself," 3
"Sparkles from the Wheel"
"We Two Boys Together Clinging"
"When I heard the learn'd astronomer"
"When Lilacs Last in the Dooryard Bloomed"*

Whittier, John Greenleaf
"Barbara Frietchie"*
"Hampton Beach"
"Ichabod"
"Kansas Emigrants, The"
"Telling the Bees"

Wiesel, Elie
Acceptance Speech for the Nobel Peace Prize

Wilde, Oscar
"Ballad of Reading Gaol, The"*
"Birthday of the Infanta, The"
"Canterville Ghost, The"
"De Profundis"
"Few Maxims for the Instruction of the Over-Educated, A"
"Grave of Shelley, The"
"Happy Prince, The"
Importance of Being Earnest, The, Act One*
Importance of Being Earnest, The, Act Two
Importance of Being Earnest, The, Act Three
"Phrases and Philosophies for the Use of the Young"
"Prison Reform" from the *Daily Chronicle*
"Symphony in Yellow"

Wilson, Woodrow
First Inaugural Address
Peace Without Victory

Wordsworth, William
"Composed upon Westminster Bridge"*
"Elegiac Stanzas"
"Expostualtion and Reply"
"I travelled among unknown men"
"I Wandered Lonely as a Cloud"
"It is a beauteous evening, calm and free"*
"Lines Written in Early Spring"
"London, 1802"
"Lucy Gray"
"Michael"
"Nuns fret not at their convent's narrow room"
"Ode: Intimations of Immortality from Recollections of Early Childhood"*
Preface to *Lyrical Ballads*
Prelude, The, Book 1
"Resolution and Independence"
"She Dwelt Among the Untrodden Ways"
"slumber did my spirit seal, A"
"Solitary Reaper, The"
"Strange fits of passion have I known"
"Three Years She Grew"
"To a Skylark"

Wyatt, Sir Thomas
"Divers Doth Use"
"He is not dead that sometime hath a fall"
"My lute awake!"
"They Flee from Me"
"Varium et Mutabile"
"Whoso List to Hunt"

Zimmermann, Arthur
Zimmerman Note, The

---

*This selection includes background information, a study guide, and comprehension and critical thinking questions in a lesson on the disc.